Frommer's

KU-540-030

Seville, Granada & the Best of Andalusia

1st Edition

by Darwin Porter & Danforth Prince

WILEY

Wiley Publishing, Inc.

About the Authors

As a team of veteran travel writers, **Darwin Porter** and **Danforth Prince** have produced numerous titles for Frommers, including bestselling guides to Italy, France, the Caribbean, England, and Germany. Porter, a former bureau chief of *The Miami Herald,* is also a Hollywood biographer; his most recent releases are *Katharine the Great,* a close-up of the private life of the late Katharine Hepburn, and *Howard Hughes: Hell's Angel.* Prince was formerly employed by the Paris bureau of the *New York Times,* and today is president of Blood Moon Productions and other media-related firms.

Published by:

Wiley Publishing, Inc.

111 River St.
Hoboken, NJ 07030-5774

ISBN-13: 978-0-7645-7793-2
ISBN-10: 0-7645-7793-X

Editor: Margot Weiss
Production Editor: Suzanna R. Thompson
Cartographer: Nick Trotter
Photo Editor: Richard Fox
Production by Wiley Indianapolis Composition Services

Front cover photo: Arched window at the Alhambra
Back cover photo: Women in costume traveling by scooter to Seville's Feria de Abril

For information on our other products and services or to obtain technical support, please contact our Customer Care Department within the U.S. at 800/762-2974, outside the U.S. at 317/572-3993 or fax 317/572-4002.

Wiley also publishes its books in a variety of electronic formats. Some content that appears in print may not be available in electronic formats.

Manufactured in the United States of America

5 4 3 2 1

Contents

List of Maps

An Invitation to the Reader

In researching this book, we discovered many wonderful places—hotels, restaurants, shops, and more. We're sure you'll find others. Please tell us about them, so we can share the information with your fellow travelers in upcoming editions. If you were disappointed with a recommendation, we'd love to know that, too. Please write to:

Frommer's Seville, Granada & the Best of Andalusia, 1st Edition
Wiley Publishing, Inc. • 111 River St. • Hoboken, NJ 07030

An Additional Note

Please be advised that travel information is subject to change at any time—and this is especially true of prices. We therefore suggest that you write or call ahead for confirmation when making your travel plans. The authors, editors, and publisher cannot be held responsible for the experiences of readers while traveling. Your safety is important to us, however, so we encourage you to stay alert and be aware of your surroundings. Keep a close eye on cameras, purses, and wallets, all favorite targets of thieves and pickpockets.

Other Great Guides for Your Trip:

Frommer's Spain

Frommer's Barcelona, Madrid & Seville

Frommer's Spain's Best-Loved Driving Tours

Frommer's Europe

Frommer's Road Atlas Europe

Frommer's Star Ratings, Icons & Abbreviations

Every hotel, restaurant, and attraction listing in this guide has been ranked for quality, value, service, amenities, and special features using a **star-rating system.** In country, state, and regional guides, we also rate towns and regions to help you narrow down your choices and budget your time accordingly. Hotels and restaurants are rated on a scale of zero (recommended) to three stars (exceptional). Attractions, shopping, nightlife, towns, and regions are rated according to the following scale: zero stars (recommended), one star (highly recommended), two stars (very highly recommended), and three stars (must-see).

In addition to the star-rating system, we also use **seven feature icons** that point you to the great deals, in-the-know advice and unique experiences that separate travelers from tourists. Throughout the book, look for:

Finds	Special finds—those places only insiders know about
Fun Fact	Fun facts—details that make travelers more informed and their trips more fun
Kids	Best bets for kids, and advice for the whole family
Moments	Special moments—those experiences that memories are made of
Overrated	Places or experiences not worth your time or money
Tips	Insider tips—great ways to save time and money
Value	Great values—where to get the best deals

The following **abbreviations** are used for credit cards:

AE American Express	DISC Discover	V Visa
DC Diners Club	MC MasterCard	

Frommers.com

Now that you have the guidebook to a great trip, visit our website at **www.frommers.com** for travel information on more than 3,000 destinations. With features updated regularly, we give you instant access to the most current trip-planning information available. At Frommers.com, you'll also find the best prices on airfares, accommodations, and car rentals—and you can even book travel online through our travel booking partners. At Frommers.com, you'll also find the following:

- Online updates to our most popular guidebooks
- Vacation sweepstakes and contest giveaways
- Newsletter highlighting the hottest travel trends
- Online travel message boards with featured travel discussions

The Best of Seville, Granada & Andalusia

This once-great stronghold of Muslim Spain is rich in history and tradition, containing some of the country's most celebrated treasures: the world-famous Mezquita (mosque) in Córdoba, the Alhambra in Granada, and the great Gothic cathedral in Seville. It also has many smaller towns just waiting to be discovered—Ubeda, Jaén, gorge-split Ronda, Jerez de la Frontera, and the gleaming white port city of Cádiz. Give Andalusia at least a week and you'll still have only skimmed the surface.

This dry mountainous region also encompasses the Costa del Sol (Málaga, Marbella, and Torremolinos), a popular coastal strip. Go to the Costa del Sol for beach resorts, nightlife, and relaxation; visit Andalusia for its architectural wonders and beauty.

1 The Most Unforgettable Travel Experiences

- **Getting Lost in the Barrio de Santa Cruz:** In Seville, "famous for its oranges and women," according to Lord Byron, you can wander at leisure through this Arab-looking ghetto of narrow streets. The brilliantly whitewashed little houses festooned with flowering plants and graced Andalusian courtyards epitomize romantic Seville. While away a meal or a whole afternoon at one of the outdoor cafe tables tucked into a handkerchief-size, hidden square. Under the Moors, Jews flourished in this ghetto, but were chased out by the Christians at the time of the Inquisition. The great artist Murillo also called this barrio home. See chapter 5.
- **Drinking Sherry at the Bodegas of Jerez:** Spain's most distinctive fortified wine—"sherry" in English, *jerez* in Spanish—uses this charming little Andalusian town of Jerez de la Frontera as its main production center. Touring the sherry wineries, or bodegas, is one of the province's most evocative undertakings. You can see mixing tanks, fermentation rooms, and warehouses for aging, but nothing is more memorable than an actual tasting. You'll quickly determine your favorite, ranging from *fino* (extra dry) to *dulce* (sweet). It's best to arrive in early September for the annual wine harvest. See chapter 8.
- **Visiting the Great Alhambra:** People from all over the world flock to Granada to enjoy wandering the Alhambra, Andalusia's last remaining fortress-palace constructed by the Muslim caliphs, who staged their last stand here against the Catholic monarchs. Washington Irving, in his *Tales of the Alhambra* in 1832, virtually put it on the tourist map after decades of neglect. Inside its walls is a once royal city and a testament

to past Muslim glory. Expect fountained courtyards, fanciful halls (once filled with dancing girls from the sultan's harem), and miles of intricate plasterwork and precious mosaics. In all, the splendor of *Arabian Nights.* See chapter 7.

- **Experiencing a Bullfight:** With origins as old as pagan Andalusia, bullfighting is a pure expression of Spanish temperament and passion. Detractors call the sport cruel, bloody, and savage. Aficionados, however, view bullfighting as a microcosm of death, catharsis, and rebirth. If you strive to understand the bullfight, it can be a powerful and memorable experience. Head for the Plaza de Toros (bullring) in any major Andalusian city; the best *corridas* are in Seville. See chapter 5.

- **Feasting on Tapas in the Tascas:** Julia Child once said, "Tapas are reason enough to go to Seville." We agree wholeheartedly. These small plates of food can be washed down with wine or beer, but a true Andalusian will accompany them with a glass of sherry. These tasty treats can be almost anything, cured ham or chorizo (spicy

sausage); *gambas* (deep-fried shrimp) are always a favorite, as are marinated anchovies, even stuffed peppers or a hake salad—and most definitely a bowl of soothing gazpacho, a "liquid salad" for a hot summer day.

- **Getting Swept Up in the Passion of Flamenco:** Best heard in the old gypsy taverns of Seville and Granada, in such evocative neighborhoods as Seville's Barrio de Triana or Granada's Albaicín, flamenco traces its Spanish roots to Andalusia. From the poshest nightclub to the lowest taverna, you can hear the staccato sound of foot stomping, castanet rattling, hand clapping, and the sultry sound of an Andalusian guitar. Some critics say the origins of flamenco actually lie somewhere deep in the heart of Asia, but the Andalusian gypsy has given the art a special and distinctive regional interpretation. The flamenco dramatizes inner tension and conflict. Performed by a great *artista,* it can tear your heart out with its soulful, throaty singing. In all cities and towns, flamenco can be heard nightly.

2 The Best Luxury Hotels

- **Hotel Alfonso XIII** (Seville; ✆ **95-491-70-00**): This reproduction of a Spanish palace, a fixture in Seville since 1929, is a regal bastion of fine living. From its white marble courtyard to its Moroccan gardens, it is the grande dame of all the Andalusian hotels. The bedrooms in this superexpensive bastion of glamour are ultraspacious. See p. 67.

- **AC Palacio de Santa Paula** (Granada; ✆ **95-880-57-40**): It's not quite as magnificent as the Alhambra, but this post-millennium architectural monument to

grandeur is as good as it gets in Granada. The contemporary and the antique have been harmoniously blended, more so than anywhere else in the province. Many buildings, including a 15th-century medieval cloister and two 14th-century Arab houses, came together to create this deluxe hotel. It's both of the past, and as modern as tomorrow. See p. 169.

- **AC Quinta Canela Golf** (Ayamonte; ✆ **95-947-78-30**): The greatest resort living along the Costa de la Luz is found at this magnificent estate with an 18-hole

Andalusia

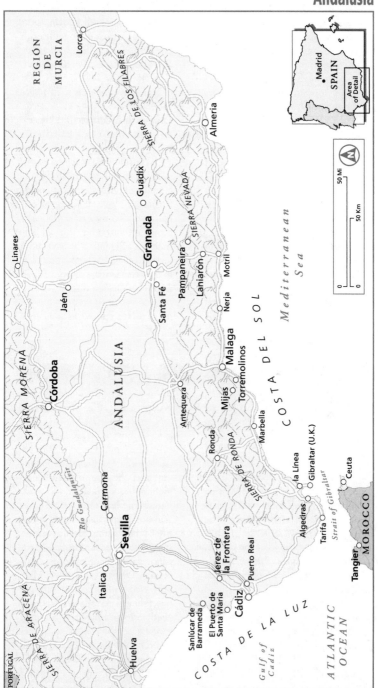

golf course built near an estuary of the Río Guadiana. Stunningly modern, it evokes an elegant Portuguese manor house but with Andalusian architectural motifs. Standing on landscaped grounds, it offers bedrooms both spacious and luxurious. See p. 290.

- **Marbella Club** (Marbella; ✆ 95-282-22-11): This is the grande dame of all Costa del Sol resorts, and the posh resort that made Marbella itself a player in world tourism. Since 1954 the rich and/or famous have flocked to its plush precincts. Boasting the most lavish hotel gardens along the coast, the club today is a hangout for movie stars, fading European aristocracy, and oil-rich sheiks. It's discreet, international, and an elegant bastion. See p. 317.

- **Kempinski Resort Hotel** (Estepona; ✆ 95-280-95-00): A justifiable member of "The Leading Hotels of the World," this is modern resort-hotel living at its most luxurious along the Costa del Sol. Not as well known as the Marbella Club, it is, nonetheless, a citadel of luxe living, with super, airy, and spacious bedrooms, first-class service, and some of the best cuisine along the coastal strip. See p. 310.

- **Duques de Medinacelli** (El Puerto de Santa María; ✆ 95-686-07-77): This tastefully converted 18th-century palace is one of the grandest hotels of Andalusia, the epitome of taste, style, and luxury. Set in beautifully landscaped gardens, it is imbued with the trappings of yesterday yet all the modern conveniences have been installed as well. Sherry producers in the area view this as one of their favorite addresses, not only for its public and private rooms, but for its first-rate cuisine as well. See p. 255.

3 The Best Paradors

- **Parador de Granada** (Granada; ✆ 95-822-14-40): This is the most famous parador in Spain. Naturally, it's the most sought after and hard to get into. Part of its allure is that it lies within the grounds of the Alhambra itself. With verdant gardens, splashing fountains, and Arab- and mudéjar-inspired architecture, the parador was converted from a former convent founded by Isabella and Ferdinand. The Catholic monarchs were once buried on its grounds. See p. 173.

- **Parador de Córdoba** (Córdoba; ✆ 95-727-59-00): Not all paradors are converted from ancient buildings. This parador, lying in a suburb of Córdoba called El Brillante, is modern with completely up-to-date amenities. However, it occupies the site of a former caliphate palace. It's known for its garden of orange trees and for the first palm trees planted in Europe. Bedrooms are spacious and luxurious, and the cuisine deserves its high praise. See p. 127.

- **Parador de Jaén** (Jaén; ✆ 95-323-00-00): This parador, 5km (3 miles) east of this historic former Muslim stronghold, opens onto the most panoramic view of any of its competitors. On the site of an old Muslim fortress from the 10th century, it is a showplace today. A citadel of good taste and baronial comfort, it offers bedrooms with balconies and canopied beds. See p. 152.

- **Parador de Ronda** (Ronda; ✆ 95-287-75-00): Sitting on a high cliff overlooking the fantastic gorge of Ronda, this parador offers beautifully furnished bedrooms that look down on the torrents of the Guadalevín River. Dramatically perched in this mountain town, it is a bastion of good taste and fine living. Modern amenities have been installed in all the rooms, and there's even an outdoor pool. See p. 220.

- **Parador de Cádiz** (Cádiz; © 95-622-69-05): This modern resort hotel opens onto one of the most beautiful beaches along the Bay of Cádiz outside this historic old port. Originally built as a private hotel in 1929, it has been extensively remodeled and updated.

Today it offers a luxurious setting, first-rate cuisine, and luxurious bedrooms, with both a health club and an outdoor pool. See p. 271.

- **Parador de Nerja** (Nerja; © 95-252-00-50): This parador is in a gem of a setting atop a bluff overlooking the Mediterranean, with one of the best beaches along the Costa del Sol only a short stroll away. It centers around a flower-filled courtyard with a splashing fountain. Bedrooms are spacious and bastions of comfort and good taste. The on-site restaurant features a top-notch international and Andalusian regional cuisine. See p. 352.

4 The Best Dining Experiences

- **Egaña Oriza** (Seville; © 95-422-72-11): Seville's best and most fashionable restaurant, set in a restored mansion near the Murillo Gardens, serves a savory mix of Basque and international specialties. Many of the ingredients, notably the wild game, originate in Andalusia. Try the woodcock flamed in Spanish brandy. See p. 80.

- **Bodegas Campos** (Córdoba; © 95-749-75-00): Not particularly elegant or grand, this restaurant has another allure: it serves the best food in Córdoba, with both Spanish and Andalusian dishes on its menu. Going strong since 1908, it uses market-fresh ingredients to concoct an array of the tastiest food in town. See p. 133.

- **Los Santanderinos** (Granada; © 95-812-83-35): In the newer part of Granada, this is a genuinely wonderful dining choice, serving the finest cuisine, a mixture of Spanish and Andalusian dishes, within the city proper.

Chef Jesús Diego Díaz is a media darling of the Spanish gastronomic press, and he deserves his acclaim. His tapas are among the tastiest in Granada. See p. 180.

- **La Meridiana** (Marbella; © 95-277-61-90): Sophisticated and fashionable, this deluxe restaurant in a romantic setting with a garden terrace delights the most discerning palates of the Costa del Sol. In a swank setting, with top-rate service, the chefs turn out the best Italian and international cuisine to be had in Marbella and beyond. Yes, foie gras, Beluga caviar, and freshly caught lobster—all those high-end favorites—are routinely dished up here. See p. 323.

- **Tragabuches** (Ronda; © 95-219-02-91): High in the mountains, chef/owner Daniel García turns out modern Spanish and Andalusian cuisine with sublime flavors from his inventive menu. His cooking technique is impeccably sharp and refined. See p. 224.

- **El Ventorillo del Chato** (Cádiz; © 95-625-00-25): In the ancient port city of Cádiz, this Andalusian restaurant has origins going back to 1780. But on the culinary front, it's stayed ahead of the times, turning out a virtual celebration of regional dishes. Sometimes, for added flavor, flamenco shows are also presented. Chefs have finely turned their time-tested recipes. See p. 272.

5 The Best Beaches

If you're from a country with terrific beaches, such as Australia or the United States, you probably won't be impressed with the beaches in Spain. But while you're vacationing along the Costa del Sol or Costa de la Luz, here's a preview of the best beaches, such as they are, that await you.

- **Playa Victoria,** Cádiz: One of the best beaches in Spain is found among the champagne-colored sands in this historic old port city. Local authorities work to keep the beach wide by pumping tons of sand here from points offshore. The beach stretches for 2km (1¼ miles), making it one of the finest beachfronts in southern Spain. Watersports galore are found along these sands, and the beach is flanked by dozens of restaurants, bars, and nightlife options. Drop in at any one of the *chiringuitos* (beach bars) that captures your fancy. Although richly built up, the *playa* still isn't junky. See p. 269.

- **Playa de la Caleta,** Cádiz: Locals call this beach **Baño de la Vina,** for the barrio that abuts it. In the old part of town, the beach forms a half-moon of golden sands to the immediate east of Castillo de Santa Catalina. To the immediate west is another fortification, Castillo de San Sebastián. The latter fortress lies on an islet reached by causeway. This beach and bay were once used by the Phoenicians, but it's kept up with the times, and is more favored by local residents than the tonier Playa Victoria. Watersports are popular, but many of the townspeople come here just to absorb the sun. If you want another beach in town, head over to the **Playa Santa María del Mar,** which is found just 500m (1,640 ft.) east of the Cathedral. For more information, see p. 269.

- **Playa Isla Canela:** The little town of Ayamonte lies 37km (22 miles) east of the provincial capital of Huelva where Columbus dared to dream "the impossible dream." One of the best beaches along the strip known as the Costa de la Luz is Playa Isla Canela. Expect tranquil waters protected by the sandbars 50 to 100m (164–328 ft.) found in the area. At low tide these sandbars become virtual islands. There's not a lot of tourist infrastructure here; it's a great place just to bask in the sun. When you tire of the sands, you'll find little kiosks on the beach renting water sports equipment or others hawking freshly cooked (or caught) seafood for your lunch. Coverage of Ayamonte begins on p. 290.

- **Playa Zahara,** near Tarifa: The little city of Tarifa is the southernmost town in continental Europe. Its windy beaches also make it the windsurfing capital of Europe. At the little fishing village of Zahara de los Atunes (p. 281) you'll come across some of the Costa de la Luz's most beautiful white sandy beaches. Here **Playa Zahara** stretches for a total of 8km (5 miles). If you don't mind the almost constant winds, these are fabulous beaches. The landscape is a bit savage here, and the panoramic views are of the coast of Africa. See p. 281.

- **Playa de la Carihuela,** Torremolinos: Even if the beach here is not among the world's greatest, you'll have a roaring good time on the sands of La Carihuela bordering the old fishing village of this wildly popular resort along the Costa del Sol. An expat population of Germans, Scandinavians, and Brits can be found playing volleyball or sunning themselves on the beige sands in skimpy suits. When you tire of the sands, a bevy of excellent seafood restaurants lines the waterfront. The beach has facilities for paragliding, windsurfing, water-skiing, and plain old sailing. For more on Torremolinos, see our coverage beginning on p. 298.

- **El Fuerte** and **La Fontanilla,** Marbella: On either side of the Costa del Sol's glossiest resort stretches the sands of these two good beaches, both famous and fashionable since the 1960s. The beaches are protected from the winds from the north by the mountains of Sierra Blanca, which can extend the bathing season from May to October. If you find the sands too crowded, you can also sample two of Marbella's other beaches, the **Playa de la Bajadilla** in the east and the amusingly named **Playa de Venus,** both of which lie between the resort's twin harbors. Many watersports such as sailing and water-skiing are possible from these beaches. See chapter 10.

6 The Most Charming Towns

- **Ubeda:** In Jaén province, this is the gem of the area, containing Plaza Vázquez de Molina, the most architecturally harmonious square in Andalusia. Its Moorish legacy lives on its *esparto* (grass) weaving and pottery making, but the town mainly evokes 16th-century Spain and the Renaissance. Ubeda is dramatically built over an escarpment overlooking the valley. Its palaces, churches, and mansions are best seen on a leisurely stroll. See p. 158.
- **Arcos de la Frontera:** The term *de la frontera* (frontier) dates from the days when this town marked the boundaries between the Muslim controlled territories and the encroaching Catholic-held lands. Hemmed in on three sides by the Guadalete River, Arcos is one of the most beautiful of the Pueblos Blancos (the white towns or villages of the interior of Andalusia).

This seemingly impregnable site was captured by King Alfonso X in 1250. A hair-raising terrace opens onto a valley of neatly cultivated green fields and flowering orchards. Except for the city of Ronda, Arcos has the best hotels you'll encounter on a driving tour of this area. See p. 233.
- **Mijas:** This Pueblo Blanco is the only white town that most visitors from the Costa del Sol drive up to see on a day's excursion. Even though mobbed, Mijas still retains its original charm. It occupies a panoramic site, welded to the side of a mountain. Its whitewashed houses look like a stack of sugar cubes. On a clear day you can enjoy stunning views of the Mediterranean and across the sea to the foreboding Rif Mountains of Morocco. To get around you can rent a *burro taxi* (guided donkey). See "Mijas" in chapter 8.

- **Jerez de la Frontera:** This is home base for Andalusia's distinctive fortified wine—sherry—which was received enthusiastically by English, Scottish, and Irish shippers in the 16th century. Touring and tasting wine in the wineries, or bodegas, is traditionally viewed as a prime attraction of Andalusia. There are more than 100 bodegas in all, with such famous names as Sandeman, González Byass, and Harvey. Jerez is also the center for the Real Escuela Andaluza del Arte Ecuestre, a rival to Vienna's renowned Spanish Riding School. These "dancing horses" are Jerez's other major attraction. See "Jerez de la Frontera" in chapter 8.

- **Nerja:** East of Málaga, this town of whitewashed buildings opens onto the "Balcony of Europe," a marble-paved projection above a headland jutting into the sea. Lying at the mouth of the Río Chillar, it stands on a sloping site beneath a wall of jagged coastal mountains. The town is filled with some sandy beaches and fishing boats bobbing at anchor. It's the perfect antidote to the tourist crowds in Torremolinos and Marbella in the west. See "Nerja" in chapter 10.

7 The Best Architecture

- **Seville Cathedral,** Seville: This is the largest Gothic structure on the planet and the third-largest church in Europe, topped only by St. Peter's in Rome and St. Paul's in London. "Let us build a cathedral so immense that everyone on beholding it will take us for madmen," the chaplain said when workers were tearing down an ancient mosque to erect this splendid edifice. This cathedral is one of the last to be built in the Gothic style but it also shows obvious Renaissance motifs. Works of art abound, including magnificent stained-glass windows from the 15th century. The Treasury contains art by such Spanish masters as Goya, Murillo, and Zurbarán. See p. 94.

- **Giralda Tower,** Seville: Next to the cathedral, this Muslim tower conjures up Seville, as the Eiffel Tower conjures up Paris. It was constructed in the 12th century, modeled after the Koutoubia in Marrakesh and the Hassan Tower in Rabat. Amazingly, the Christian overlords allowed this Moorish tower to stand with certain alterations. The top story, which has a Renaissance motif, was added in the 16th century. From its top, one of the great city views in all Spain is visible. See p. 94.

- **Alcázar,** Seville: Ordered constructed by Pedro the Cruel, this splendid 14th-century mudéjar palace is the oldest royal residence in Europe still in use. It lies north of the cathedral. Some remains of the original Alcázar of the Almohads can still be seen. Centuries of architects and builders have produced an ornate complex of pavilions, fountains, pools, patios, and ornamental gardens. Residents Ferdinand and Isabella, who received Columbus here, greatly influenced its architecture. Moorish influences join forces with Gothic, Renaissance, and baroque elements, yet it all comes together harmoniously with its own very particular charm. See p. 92.

- **Alcázar de los Reyes Cristianos,** Córdoba. One of Spain's greatest examples of military architecture was commissioned in 1328 by Alfonso XI. Ferdinand and Isabella lived here at this fortress on the

Río Guadalquivir as they made plans to send their armies to conquer Granada. The complex is distinguished by its towers, Torre de los Leones and Torre de Homenaje, the former containing intricately carved ogival ceilings that are the most notable examples of Gothic architecture in Andalusia. The gardens still show their Moorish origins, a vast architectural complex of landscaping, fountains, and pools. See p. 138.

- **Mezquita-Catedral de Córdoba,** Córdoba: This is a 1,200-year-old masterwork by a succession of caliphs that is one of the architectural wonders of Europe. Its interior is a virtual forest of pillars and red-and-white candy-striped Moorish horseshoe arches. The phantasmagoric rows of columns stretch in every direction. In the midst of it all, as impossible as it sounds, is a florid cathedral in a Gothic and Renaissance architectural motif. This wonder is the third-largest mosque in the world, even though it hasn't been used as such since 1236. This Great Mosque, the crowning glory of Muslim architecture in the West, is reason enough to visit Córdoba. See p. 139.

- **The Alhambra,** Granada: Set against the snowcapped peaks of the Sierra Nevada mountain range, the Alhambra is one of the most fabled landmarks in the world, evoking a fantasy of *1,001 Arabian Nights.* It is the single-most visited attraction in all of Andalusia. It was the last bastion of luxury living for the Nasrid kings, the last Muslim rulers of Spain, and their harems filled with dancing girls. The palace-fortress is girded by more than 1.6km (1 mile) of ramparts, enclosing a virtual royal city. Actually the Alhambra is a series of three palaces of architectural wonder, with courtyards, fountains, fanciful halls, and scalloped windows framing vistas. The oldest section is the Alcazaba, dating from the 9th century. See p. 189.

8 The Best Gifts & Souvenirs

- **Antiques:** Many avid shoppers land in Andalusia and go on shopping binges for antiques and accessories. Seville in particular offers antiques hunters some rare possibilities. There is a wide range of dealers throughout the province; you'll often find them in some of the smaller villages, stores marked just by a little sign. Many items purchased in these shops are small decorative pieces that can be shipped home easily. Some of the most popular "antiques" purchased in Andalusia are old posters, many from the 1800s. Posters advertising the famous Andalusian fairs or else the well-attended *corridas* (bullfights) sell the most copies.

- **Ceramics and Tiles:** Throughout the province, stores sell highly distinctive ceramics (each town or region has its own style) as well as *azulejos* (hand-painted tiles). For example, to suit the preferences of the many English expats who settled in and around Cádiz, florals and busy scenic designs became popular in this area. Many of these floral motifs, however, were rooted in Spanish cultural traditions from the 18th century. Other pieces have ancient geometric patterns inherited from the Arabs. Some wall plates are enameled and trimmed in 24-karat gold.

- **Clothing:** Flamenco dress, as it's often called, along with *feria* (fair or festival) clothing fill the stores of Granada and Seville, among other towns and cities of Andalusia. If you picture yourself as Carmen, in polka dots and a fan, snapping castanets, you have come to the right place. Clothing stores sell all sorts of traditional Andalusian dress for women to wear, some of it classical, not corny. You can purchase all the mantillas, hair ornaments, and Spanish fans you've dreamed about. It is a land of ruffled skirts, dangling earrings, and *mantoncillos* (flamenco scarves). Surprisingly, Seville has become a center of high fashion for the 21st century. Boutique after boutique sells stylish clothing. Seville hardly rivals Milan in fashion, but many of its young designers are garnering praise from the international fashion press. See chapters 5 and 7.

- **Guitars:** In the land of flamenco, guitars are highly prized by visitors. Artisans in Granada turn out top-quality, custom-made guitars. Of course, you can purchase ready-made guitars a lot more cheaply. We especially like to stroll Calle Cuesta de Gomérez, a narrow and sloping street uphill from the Alhambra in Granada. Artisans along this street turn out some of the world's finest instruments. Many of their guitars often end up in the possession of famed musicians. See chapter 7.

- **Leather Goods:** For centuries, leather products have been associated with Andalusia, especially Cordovan leather. Andalusian leather items are soft and supple, and are usually a good value. Unlike the softer leather from sheep, cow leather is of heavier quality and is often made into jackets and coats. In general, shoppers can tell the quality of the leather by its feel—the softer, of course, being the more expensive. Many outlets for leather goods are found in the old quarter of Seville, Barrio de Santa Cruz. Córdoba, in particular, is famed for its embossed leather products, including such items as cigarette boxes, jewel cases, attaché cases, book and folio covers, ottoman covers, and the like. See chapter 6.

- **Marquetry:** Marquetry has been a famous product of Granada since the Muslim empire. Artisans still make furniture and other items inlaid with ivory and colored woods in the Moorish design. Inlaid boxes are a particularly good item to take home as gifts, and they become lasting souvenirs. Throughout Granada, especially in the Albaicín, which is a virtual North African souk (marketplace), you will see shop after shop hawking this extremely delicate work. See chapter 7.

2

A Traveler's Guide to Southern Spain's Art & Architecture

Andalusia has a rich legacy in art and architecture, and some of the greatest achievements of the Muslim rule still remain—notably the Alhambra at Granada and the Mezquita (mosque) at Córdoba. Andalusia also claims as its native sons two of the greatest artists of all time: Diego Velázquez and Pablo Picasso.

This all-too-brief overview will give you a quick preview of what's left for you to see, after all the conquerors and armies marched through.

1 Art 101

In Andalusia the dawn of art actually began 25,000 years ago when prehistoric man decorated caves in the province, painting in charcoal, blood red, and a goldlike ocher. For a look at this prehistoric art, visit **Cueva de la Pileta** near Ronda (p. 219) or if open, **Cueva de Nerja** in Nerja (p 352).

On October 25, 1881, in the port city of Málaga along Andalusia's southern coast, an artist was born. **Pablo Picasso** went on to become the greatest master of 20th-century art. Andalusia doesn't just rely on Picasso's artistic legacy, however. Its many museums and churches overflow with treasures dating from Spain's golden age of art, a period when Seville stood at the center of an explosion of painting and sculpture.

Although hundreds of priceless images were demolished in various wars, notably the Napoleonic invasion and the Spanish Civil War of the '30s, much remains to delight the art lover today.

ROMANESQUE (10TH–13TH C.)

When the Moors subdued Andalusia back in the 8th century, they naturally came to dominate art in the province. As the Koran forbade them to create graven images (human figures, for example), they turned instead to decorative arts. Geometric designs and exaggerated Kufic inscriptions appeared on painted tiles—called *azulejos*—in stucco plasterwork, and in various woodcarvings. Other rich and varied artifacts from this Muslim era include wood strap work in geometric designs, weapons, small ivory chests, and brocades.

GOTHIC (13TH–16TH C.)

The schools of Catalonia (Barcelona) and France were the stars of this era in painting. Artists often worked on polyptyches and altarpieces, some reaching a height of 15m (50 ft.). Although influenced by the Italian, French, and Flemish schools, Gothic painting in Spain was distinctive in its interpretation. Colors such as deep red and lustrous golds were varied and vivid. Breaking from Romanesque, compositions became more complex. A sense of motion came into painting, as opposed to the more rigid forms of Romanesque.

The most notable of the Andalusian artists of this period was **Bartolomé Bermejo** (ca. 1440—died sometime after 1495), who was heavily influenced by van Eyck. The first Spanish painter to use oils, he became the leader of the Italianate Valencian school. He is believed to have been born in Córdoba. He wasn't influenced by the art of his native province at the time—nothing in the art in that period can explain the origin of Bermejo's style or his artistic technique. His paintings are characterized by a profound gravity, evoking Flanders where he once studied. Harmonious colors render some of his art splendidly decorative and some of his figures indicate strong sculptural modeling. His best work is in Madrid's Prado.

Pedro Berruguete (1450–1504) straddled the line between Gothic and the Renaissance during a transitional period. Berruguete became the forerunner of Spanish portraitists of the 17th century. For a good look at his achievements, visit the **Museo Provincial** in Jaén where you can see such paintings as *Christ at the Column.*

THE RENAISSANCE & BAROQUE (16TH–17TH C.)

By the 16th century, the Siglo de Oro (golden age) of art finally arrived in Spain. The Renaissance was a long time in coming. When it eventually began to replace Gothic works, the style, which had originated in Florence, had already mutated into the baroque in Spain. Some of the world's greatest artists rose out of Andalusia during this period. Seville in particular saw the rise of three great artists—Diego Velázquez, El Greco, and Francisco Goya—who are still hailed as among the greatest who ever lived.

In the golden age, **naturalism** came into bloom. A technique called *chiaroscuro,* evocative of that used by Italy's Caravaggio, contrasted light and shadow. Stern realism was often depicted. Portraiture and still life *(bodegón)* flourished.

The late Renaissance and baroque paintings became more theatrical and often decorative—"art for art's sake." Patrons, often with money they'd made from the New World, demanded paintings that were dynamic with realistic figures. A painter's easel was filled with vivid colors. No longer was the church the main patron of art. Rich merchants demanded that their own likenesses be captured on canvas, and also flattering images of their families, regardless of what they actually looked like. It was a new day in art, freeing it from the church and its draconian dictates. Artists no longer devoted themselves strictly to paintings of the Madonna and Child.

The most important painter to emerge from this era was **Diego Velázquez** (1599–1660), the leading artist in the court of King Philip IV. Born in Seville, he did not achieve his greatest fame until long after his death. In time, his works such as *Las Meninas,* painted in 1656, would influence Picasso himself and even Salvador Dalí. Go to the Prado in Madrid to see Velázquez in all his glory. It's hard to find many works by Velázquez in Andalusia. A notable exception is *Receiving the Chasuble* (ca. 1623) displayed at the Museo Provincial de Bellas Artes in Seville (p. 95). Although this painting has some emotional intensity, it is not one of the artist's greatest masterpieces.

While still young, **Francisco Zurbarán** (1598–1662) was sent to study art at the School of Juan de Roelas in Seville. He became the Spanish equivalent of Michelangelo da Caravaggio. The Museo Provincial de Bellas Artes de Sevilla (p. 95) contains several of his works for those who'd like to appreciate him today. He excelled in a forcible, realistic style and painted directly from nature. Most of his paintings focused on ascetic, religious motifs. His color is often bluish to excess. The light seems to come from within the subject of his paintings rather than from an external source.

Painting tender, intimate, even mystical scenes, **Bartolomé Esteban Murillo** (1617–82) was a leading rival of Zurbarán. The darling of Counter-Reformation art collectors, he is showcased at Museo Provincial de Bellas Artes in Seville (p. 95), and, of course, at El Prado in Madrid. At the age of 26, Murillo went to Madrid where he studied under Velázquez, but he returned to Seville in 1645. He excelled in the painting of flowers, water, light clouds, drapery, and in the use of color such as in his *The Little Fruit Seller* in 1670. Some critics dismiss Murillo as "tenderly sentimental—even saccharine."

The greatest Spanish sculptor of the 17th century, **Juan Martínez Montañés** (1568–1649) became hailed as *el dios de la madera* (the god of wood). For most of his life, he worked in Seville. The cathedral at Seville (p. 94) holds his masterpiece, *Christ of Clemency* (1603–06). In this polychromed wooden statue, he brought a new naturalism to church carving, tempering his "baroque emotionalism" with a classical sense of dignity. His polychrome wooden sculptures, and those of others, appealed to the Andalusian sense of drama and pathos. Martínez Montañés spread his carving style through a workshop he founded, teaching Cano (see below) among others. Curiously enough, Martínez Montañés is remembered today not for his own work but for a famous painting that Velázquez did of him, now in Madrid's Prado.

Architect, painter, and sculptor, **Alonso Cano** (1601–67) was often called the Spanish Michelangelo because of the diversity of his talents. In spite of his violent temper (he is rumored to have murdered his wife), his paintings for the most part are serene, even sweet. In Madrid he was hired by Philip IV to restore paintings in his royal collection. Here, Cano came under the influence of Venetian masters of the 16th century and used many of their techniques in his later works. He is celebrated today for designing the facade of the Cathedral in Granada in 1667 (p. 197). This is one of the grandest and boldest statements in Spanish baroque architecture. Today the cathedral owns several of Cano's paintings and sculptures, including a polychrome wooden statue of the Immaculate Conception from 1655 that is hailed as his masterpiece. Martínez Montañés and Cano in their wake left many devoted followers.

Another painter born in Seville was **Juan de Valdés Leal** (1622–90), who also worked in Córdoba. Along with Murillo (see above), he founded an academy of painting in Seville in 1660. When Murillo died in 1682, Valdés Leal became the leading painter of Seville. Valdés Leal was mostly a religious painter, although he took a radically different approach from Murillo, specializing in the macabre, even the grotesque. All of his works have vivid colors, dramatic light effects, and a sense of fluid movement. He sought with his powerful realism to challenge "earthly vanities."

BOURBON ROCOCO & NEOCLASSICAL (18TH–19TH C.)

With the coming of Bourbon rule to Spain, the monarchs set out to attract some of Europe's greatest painters to their court in Madrid. Painting came under the dictates of the Academy of San Fernando founded in 1752. **Francisco Goya** (1746–1828) dominated this lusty period in Spanish art, but Andalusia had its own homegrown stars.

Marching to a drummer only he heard, **Julio Romero de Torres** was born in Córdoba one sunny day on November 9, 1874. The son of a painter, Rafael Romero de Torres, Julio studied art from the age of 10. In time he became famous for his paintings of Andalusian beauties. We would consider many of their poses demure today, but they were regarded as provocative at the time. His most celebrated work, on display at the **Museo de Julio Romero de Torres** at Córdoba (p. 142) is *Naranjas y Limones (Oranges and Lemons)*. The dark-haired beauty in the portrait is bare breasted and holding oranges.

20TH CENTURY

After a period of "romantic decline" in the latter 19th century, Spain rose again in the art world at the turn of the 20th century, as Spanish artists helped develop Cubism and surrealism. A host of Spanish artists—not only Picasso—rose to excite the world. These included the great surrealist **Joan Miró** (1893–1983); **Juan Gris** (1887–1927), the purest of the cubists, and the outrageous **Salvador Dalí** (1904–89).

Pablo Picasso (1881–1973), of course, is known as one of the 20th century's greatest modern artists and the most famous founder of Cubism (along with Georges Braque). His body of work changed radically over the years, his most famous being the Blue Period in which he depicted harlequins, beggars, artists, and prostitutes among others. Although he experienced financial difficulties early in his life, his paintings now sell into the millions. *Les Noces de Pierrette (The Marriage of Pierrette)* fetched $51 million in 1999. Today visitors flock to Málaga, the town of his birth, to see the **Picasso Museum** (p. 345).

After producing some of Spain's greatest artists during the golden age, Andalusia became a backwater in art for most of the 1900s. **Rafael Zabaleta** (1907–60) rose from obscurity and became known for his popular scenes of rural life. Born in Jaén province to a family of rich landowners, he made his little Andalusian village of Quesada the subject of most of his work. His bucolic scenes are still a hot item on the art market today.

2 Architecture 101

Long before the Muslims crossed the Straits of Gibraltar in 711, Romans controlled Andalusia. Regrettably, not a lot remains of their architecture or monuments. For a look at what used to be, you can take a day trip to **Itálica,** the "noble ruins" of a Roman city founded at the end of the 3rd century B.C. by the Roman general, Scipio Africanus, lying 9km (5½ miles) northwest of Seville outside the small town of Santiponce.

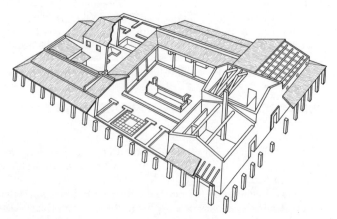

Roman House

Itálica (p. 120) was the birthplace of two of the most famous Roman emperors, Hadrian and Trajan. Still impressive, the major achievement here was a colossal amphitheater that held 25,000 spectators screaming for blood. At one time this amphitheater was one of the largest in the Roman Empire.

You can still see classic Roman architecture—or at least the foundations—of the Hadrianic baths as well as a well-preserved Roman theater. At the peak of its glory, Itálica was the third largest city in the world, surpassed only by Rome and Alexandria itself.

Of course, seeing the somewhat barren landscape today, you'll have to imagine much of the architecture of the once-fabled town and its grand buildings dripping in colored marble. Over the centuries, seemingly everyone in the area, including the invading Duke of Wellington during the Peninsula Wars, went digging for Roman treasures at Itálica, including statues, marble, rare marbles, and sculpture.

MOORISH ARCHITECTURE (8TH–15TH C.)

After the Muslims subdued Andalusia, following the departure of the Romans and Visigoths, these new conquerors began to influence the landscape with their new buildings, including aqueducts, baths, *alcázares* (palaces), and *alcazabas* (fortresses). Islamic architecture had come to Andalusia.

Although there was an earlier "pre-Caliphal period" (notably A.D. 710–929), the true glory of Moorish architecture came under the Cordovan Caliphate (929–1031). Begun in 785, the **Great Mosque of Córdoba** (p. 139) was lavishly and dramatically extended with horseshoe arches and ornate decoration. The most distinguishing feature of the architecture, the **arch,** reached its apogee here in both the horseshoe arch and the decorative multifoil arch. (Actually, the former rulers, the Visigoths, created the horseshoe arch.) The ornamental use of calligraphy and elaborate stuccowork are other distinctive and important aspects.

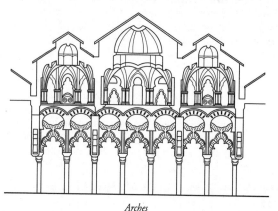

Arches

Even today many architectural influences are visible at the Great Mosque of Córdoba, in such features as its **Mihrab** (a richly ornamented prayer niche), and its **Puerta del Perdón** (a mudéjar-style entrance gate that was actually built during Christian rule). See below for more on mudéjar, a style reaching its zenith of expression in Andalusia. In the 16th century a cathedral was built in the heart of the reconsecrated mosque. Part of the Islamic architecture had to be destroyed to make way for this cathedral with its Italianate dome.

The Caliphal era ended to be replaced by the brief Taifa era (1031–91). It quickly gave way to new rulers, the Almoravid and Almohad dynasties (1091–1248). These austere Islamic fundamentalists brought a purer, less fanciful style of architecture, which can best be seen at **La Giralda** in Seville (p. 94). This minaret, which still graces the skyline, was completed in 1198. At the time of the Reconquista, the Muslim bronze spheres crowning it were replaced by Christian symbols, a bronze portraying Faith.

The Almohads did not eschew adornment completely; their artisans created the *artesonado* ceiling (paneled wood ceilings that were painted and intricately carved) and *azulejos* (glazed tiles beautifully painted with patterns). Although still using the horseshoe arch of the Visigoths, the Almohads introduced the narrow, pointy arch. To this day, the Giralda remains the most beautiful structure in Seville.

The flowering of Muslim architecture in Andalusia occurred during the Nasrid era (1238–1492), the last Moors to hold power before the Reconquista by the Catholic monarchs, Isabella and Ferdinand. These Sultans created one of the

La Giralda before and after the Reconquista

most magnificent palaces ever built: the **Alhambra** at Granada (p. 189). *Alhambra* means "the red" referring to the red walls of the fortress. In 1238 Muhammad ibn el-Ahmar ordered construction to begin on this impressive fortification. The site was developed over both the 13th and 14th centuries, so it represents a medley of styles. It is a vast complex of mosques, palaces, gardens, walls, towers, and residences. Restored after its discovery by writers and artists in the 19th century, including Washington Irving, the palace is filled with architectural wonders, including the Patio de los Leones. Its arcades are supported by 124 slender marble columns. At its center a fountain rests on 12 proud marble lions. The salons are stunning achievements, especially Salón de Embajadores, the sumptuous throne room from 1334 to 1354, its ceiling representing the seven heavens of the Muslim cosmos. For the various caliphs of the Nasrid dynasty, this palace represented an earthly paradise, even though modest material—tiles, plaster, and wood—were used.

MUDÉJAR OR POST-MOORISH ARCHITECTURE (MID–14TH TO LATE 15TH C.)

After the Muslims were ousted from power, Andalusia continued to mount churches on the sites of former mosques. Often original architectural motifs were incorporated into these Christian churches. Motifs included ornamental brickwork in relief alternating with stone, archways, and even roof tiles. Muslims who stayed on after the Reconquista created a virtually new style of architecture called mudéjar.

Since they were better builders, the *mudéjares* (Arabs) were employed to build the new churches and palaces in the reconquered territories. The word *mudéjar* literally means "those who were permitted to stay."

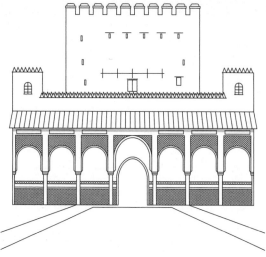

Alhambra

Their architecture was a hybrid style—a "bastard" style, as some critics called it. One of the best examples of the mudéjar style is the **Salón de Embajadores** in the Alcázar at Seville (p. 92). This Room of the Ambassadors forms part of the palace of King Don Pedro in the Alcázar. It is surmounted by a wood dome and flanked with double geminate windows, a stunning achievement. Dozens of churches and palaces in Andalusia still retain mudéjar architectural motifs. And the mudéjar tradition lives today in pottery made in Granada and Seville that still reflects Moorish design.

As you drive through the **Las Alpujarras region** (p. 211) of Granada province, the final bastion of the Moriscos (Muslims who were forced to convert to Christianity), you'll see the flat-roofed houses that evoke the Berber dwellings of the Moroccans who live in the Atlas mountains across the Straits of Gibraltar.

Not all Reconquista architecture was mudéjar. The first major style used by Catholic Andalusia was **Romanesque** (the term had not come into vogue at the time). For its inspiration, this style of architecture drew upon the rounded arches from the classical days of ancient Rome. Romanesque churches were dark and somber with small windows and large piers. There are few remnants of Romanesque in Andalusia.

GOTHIC (13TH–16TH C.)

Somehow the French Gothic style of architecture seems ill suited to the hot plains of Andalusia with its

Decorative Ceramic

almost desertlike landscape in some parts. But arrive it did in the form of the Cathedral of Seville (p. 94). The rounded arches of Romanesque gave way to pointed arches which could carry far more of the weight of a massive building such as a cathedral. Windows became larger and were filled with stained glass depicting scenes from the Bible. Peasants who could not actually read the Bible could see biblical scenes depicted in the glass panels.

Seville's cathedral was not built in a pure Gothic style; it also showed the Renaissance influence. It is characterized by massive column shafts that hold up mammoth arches. Its vaulting is splendid, constructed in the Flamboyant Gothic style and rising 56m (184 ft.) over the transept crossing. The bulk of this structure was constructed between 1401 and 1507. As styles changed, an altar was added in the late Gothic style (1496–1537). The Capilla Real (Royal Chapel; 1530–69), was actually Plateresque (see below).

By the end of the 15th century, Spain had developed its own unique style of Gothic architecture, calling it **Isabelline** in honor of the Catholic queen (1474–1504). This style's exuberant decoration covered entire facades of buildings, its rich, even lavish, ornamentation coming in the form of lacelike carvings and heraldic motifs. Foreign artists, such as Juan Guas, arriving in Spain labeled it "a fantasy."

Although the cathedral at Seville is the most outstanding Gothic building in all the province, there are dozens of other Gothic—or at least partially Gothic—churches in Andalusia. Many town mansions and small castles, which still survive, were also built in this elaborate style.

THE RENAISSANCE (16TH C.)

When the Renaissance finally came to Spain, it wasn't always known as that. The very early Renaissance in Spain was termed **Plateresque** because its fine detailing evoked the ornate work of a silversmith. In Spanish, *platero* means silversmith.

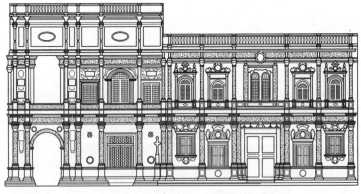

Ayuntamiento

The best example of the Plateresque style is the **Ayuntamiento (town hall)** in Seville (p. 101). Begun in 1527 and completed in 1534, the Plateresque style is best seen on the east side of the town hall opening onto Plaza de San Francisco. Plateresque was the style preferred by the architect Diego de Riaño.

A new style of Renaissance architecture arose in Spain at the end of the 16th century. Called the **Herreran style,** it was named for Juan de Herrera

(1530–97), the greatest figure of Spanish classicism. The favorite architect of Philip II, Herrera developed a style of building that was grand but austere as well as geometric in its effect. His greatest achievement was El Escorial, that mammoth royal palace outside Madrid. In Andalusia his work can be seen at the **Archivo de Indias** (p. 101) in Seville. Built between 1584 and 1598, the facade of this structure remains even today one of the most harmonious and classic in all of Seville.

Plateresque eventually gave way to what became known as the **High Renaissance** style, as exemplified by the **Palacio de Carlos V** in Granada. Begun in 1526, this palace was incongruously—even scandalously—placed in the heart of the Alhambra. Its elegant and grandiose style evokes the king's power as Holy Roman Emperor. If you can forgive where it was placed, the palace is a perfect architectural specimen with purely classical lines. Dignified in appearance, its layout was "a circle within a square." In Andalusia this palace is the crowning achievement of the High Renaissance style. See p. 193.

BAROQUE (17TH–18TH C.)

Baroque suggests flamboyance but early Spanish baroque was more austere in the 17th century. A family of architects led by José de Churriguera (1665–1725) pioneered the Churrigueresque style, a type of architecture noted for its sumptuousness and dense concentrations of ornaments covering entire facades of buildings. This style was later copied by his brothers, other Churriguera family members, and leading architects of the day. The best example of the Churrigueresque style in Andalusisa is the flamboyant, baroque sacristy of the **Monasterio de la Cartuja** (p. 199) in Granada.

Andalusia was the one province of Spain where the baroque blossomed most brilliantly. Seville has more baroque churches per square kilometer than any other city in the world, notably **Iglesia de San José** (p. 101), one of the most beautiful examples of a baroque church anywhere.

With the coming of neoclassicism and modernism, devotees of architecture turned to other parts of Spain, including Bilbao and especially Barcelona, to indulge their passions.

MODERN (20TH C.)

Modern architecture received a boost when Seville hosted Expo '92. Many innovative designs were introduced at this time, none more notable than the **five bridges** spanning the Río Guadalquivir. The most exceptional of these are the Puente de Chapina, with a geometrically designed canopy; the Puente del Alamillo, with a single upward arm holding its weight; and the Puente de la Barqueta, a suspension bridge held by one overhead beam.

The most dramatic modern structure in Andalusia is the deliberately leaning **Pabellón de Andalucía** on Isla de la Cartuja. Today it houses a movie theater and a 3-D laser show.

In the **Parque Científico y Tecnológico (Science and Technology Park),** Calle Leonardo da Vinci, you can take in some of the spectacular pavilions that are still standing. The buildings are owned by the Andalusian World Trade Center and used by private companies, but their architecture can be admired from the outside.

3

Planning Your Trip to Southern Spain

In this chapter you'll find everything you need to plan your trip—from descriptions of southern Spain's regions, to tips on when to go and getting the best airfare.

1 The Regions in Brief

In A.D. 711 Muslim armies swept into Iberia from strongholds in what is now Morocco. Since then, Spain's southernmost district has been enmeshed in the mores, art, and architecture of the Muslim world.

During the 900s, Andalusia blossomed into a sophisticated society—advanced in philosophy, mathematics, and trading—that far outstripped a feudal Europe still trapped in the Dark Ages. Moorish domination ended completely in 1492, when Granada was captured by the armies of Isabella and Ferdinand, but even today the region offers echoes of this Muslim occupation. Andalusia is a dry district that isn't highly prosperous and depends heavily on tourism.

The major cities of Andalusia deserve at least a week, with overnights in **Seville** (hometown of Carmen, Don Giovanni, and the barber); **Córdoba,** site of the Mezquita, one of history's most versatile religious edifices; and **Cádiz,** the seaport where thousands of ships embarked on their colonization of the New World. Perhaps most interesting of all is **Granada,** a town of such impressive artistry that it inspired many of the works by the 20th-century romantic poet Federico García Lorca.

CADIZ & THE COSTA DE LA LUZ Dotted with churches and monuments, the old port city of Cádiz lies on a limestone rock emerging from the sea at the end of a 9km-long (6-mile) promontory projecting into the Atlantic. This historic core of old Cádiz is linked to Andalusia by a bridge. Walls rising to a height of 15m (50 ft.) protect the center from the turbulent waves of the ocean.

Some claim that Cádiz is Europe's oldest city, citing Hercules as its founder. Actually the Phoenicians founded the city back in 1100 B.C. Wealth from the Spanish conquistadores arrived here, eventually attracting unwanted attention from Sir Francis Drake who raided the port in 1587. This was the first of many such attacks from the British fleets. In 1812 Spain's first constitution was declared here.

Two days are sufficient to explore the sights in Cádiz, a workaday port whose attractions do not equal those of Granada or Seville.

If you have extra time, you can retreat to the city's beaches, or those along the **Costa de la Luz,** which sprawls both east and west of Cádiz. On a clear day you can see across the water to Tangier, Morocco. The coast is riddled with beaches and fishing villages, many of which would be idyllic for a laid-back vacation. In particular, **Tarifa,** the windsurfing capital of Europe, comes to mind.

CORDOBA This ancient city, founded by the Carthaginians and later the Roman *Baetica,* reached its zenith in the 10th century as the capital of the great caliphate. It was also the greatest spiritual and scientific center of the Western world, with some 300 mosques and one of the world's greatest universities. Those glory days are long gone, but Córdoba's architecture still makes it one of the most appealing cities in Europe.

Today, with a population of some 310,000, Córdoba is visited mainly because of its celebrated mosque, La Mezquita, the world's third largest. Incidentally, it hasn't been used as a mosque since King Ferdinand and his armies attacked in 1236. After Córdoba fell, the mosque was reconsecrated as a Christian church. As amazing as it sounds, a cathedral was launched in 1523 within the walls of the original mosque—and it still stands today.

You can spend 2 to 3 days in Córdoba, wandering in its old quarter and exploring an *alcázar* (fortress) constructed by Christian kings in 1327.

COSTA DEL SOL What the Riviera is to France, the **Costa del Sol** is to Spain. The "Sun Coast" sprawls across the southernmost edge of Spain between Algeciras to the west—across from the rocky heights of British-controlled Gibraltar—and the rather dull Almería to the east. Think traffic jams, suntan oil, sun-bleached high-rises, and nearly naked flesh. The beaches here are some of the best and most popular in Europe, but this can also be an overly crowded, crime-filled region.

Once known for its scented orange groves and rolling fields of silvery olive trees, the Costa del Sol of today is an overdeveloped urban sprawl of housing developments, hotels, resorts, tourist complexes, and amusement centers, along with such better attractions as beaches and golf courses.

The tawdry, carnival-like atmosphere of the coast is a turnoff to many North American visitors who prefer to spend their time exploring the art cities of Andalusia, especially Seville and Granada.

Unless you travel by car or rail from Madrid, chances are you'll arrive by plane via **Málaga,** the district's most historic city and the capital of the Costa del Sol. Hans Christian Andersen praised it, and Pablo Picasso was born here. It is much more staid than Torremolinos, and is more of a workaday city than a sprawling resort. With its fortress, cathedral, and bullring, along with a Picasso Museum, it has more cultural attractions than any other place along the coast. Málaga also enjoys the best transportation links along the entire coast, both from the air and by rail from other leading Andalusian cities as well as Madrid and Barcelona.

If you're seeking pockets of posh and beach resorts that are still some of the greatest in Spain, anchor at **Marbella,** which in the 1960s, before it was overrun, was one of the chicest resorts in all of Europe. Frank Sinatra, Sophia Loren, and the Duke and Duchess of Windsor were once regulars. Today's star seekers may spot Antonio Banderas.

One modern development that has managed to remain distinctive and upmarket is **Puerto Banús,** a neo-Moorish village that curves around a sheltered marina where the wintering rich dock their yachts.

If **Torremolinos** was ever chic, it was early in the 1960s when two lovers, James Kirkwood *(A Chorus Line)* and James Leo Herlihy *(Midnight Cowboy),* lived here in a romantic little villa. Today the beautiful people are long gone, and Torremolinos gets the low-budget tours from the Midlands of England and other parts of northern Europe. Although some visitors like this urban sprawl of mediocre beaches; "lager life," after-dark diversions, and package tours galore, you should anchor here only if you want to be caught up in the human circus that descends during the summer months. If you're set on visiting, do so in June before the hordes arrive to dance the night away.

GIBRALTAR   Thrust up from the sea some 200 million years ago, Gibraltar is a tiny peninsula lying between the Spanish town of La Linea de la Concepción on the Costa del Sol and industrial Algeciras. It is just 6.4km (4 miles) long and 2km (1¼ miles) wide.

At 449m (1,476 ft.), the Rock of Gibraltar—known to the ancients—guards the entrance to the Mediterranean. Through its narrow strait, waters from the more turbulent Atlantic pass into the calmer Mediterranean.

We'll be really blunt: There is no compelling reason to visit this self-governing British colony, "Gib," as locals affectionately call it. Border crossings can be tedious. Except for a few attractions, such as the Upper Rock Nature Reserve and the famous Barbary Apes, there just isn't a lot to do. Sure, you can enjoy fish and chips and pints of bitter, but you'll find better versions of both in London. Many visiting journalists consider Gibraltar a tourist trap.

Often visitors go simply because Gibraltar is there. Visit if you must but don't expect a grand old time. When you cross the border, you leave Spanish culture behind, but what you find is not quite British either. It's . . . well, it's Gibraltar.

GRANADA   One of the hardest questions a travel writer to Andalusia

can be asked is: "If I don't have time for both, should it be Granada or Seville? Only if forced at gunpoint would we say Granada—and that's because of its **Alhambra,** resident palace of the Moorish rulers of the Nasrid dynasty. It is one of the world's greatest architectural treasures.

Granada, of course, has much more to offer. Much of its charm derives from a mellow blending of its Eastern and Western architectural influences and customs. Other major attractions include the Gothic **cathedral; Capilla Real (Royal Chapel),** burial place of the Catholic monarchs Ferdinand and Isabella, and the **Albaícin** quarter, a cone-shaped network of tightly packed white houses that was the heart of Muslim Granada. On a hot summer day there is no cooler place to be than the **Generalife,** the summer palace of the former sultans and their harems, standing on 30 hectares (75 acres) of grounds. Granada's prestigious festival of music and dance takes place here.

The capital of eastern Andalusia, Granada lies in the foothills of the Sierra Nevada, with a population of some 300,000. Allow at least 2 to 3 days for a proper visit.

JAEN   The capital of its own province, the ancient city of Jaén, and the even more interesting historic towns of Ubeda and Baeza, can be visited before you reach Córdoba—that is, if you're heading south from Madrid.

Jaén was called *Giyen* when it lay on the ancient caravan route used by the Arabs. At the time of the Christian Reconquest of southern Spain, the armies of Ferdinand and Isabella used it as their gateway to Andalusia. That's not a bad idea for today's visitor, who can spend a day exploring Jaén and another visiting the "twin" towns of Ubeda and Baeza.

Jaén is the center of one of the world's largest olive-growing districts, making it a virtual island in a sea of olive trees. Jaén's massive **cathedral** from the 16th century is one of the grandest examples of Spanish Renaissance architecture, and you can wander for hours in its **Old Town,** originally a Moorish settlement.

The town of **Ubeda** is known as the "Andalusian Salamanca" because of its numerous Renaissance buildings. It's a harmonious town filled with churches, monuments, and palaces. **Baeza,** too, is filled with elegant town houses and noble mansions, many constructed during its heyday in the 16th century. Olive groves and vineyards envelop Baeza.

NERJA East of Málaga, the town of Nerja—our favorite along the entire Costa del Sol—opens onto the "Balcony of Europe," a marble-paved projection towering over a headland and jutting out toward the sea. This seaside resort lies at the mouth of the Río Chillar on a site below the Sierra de Mihara.

Although the tourist boom has led to a mass of new buildings on its periphery, its historic core is still one of the coast's most charming, with whitewashed houses and narrow streets for rambling at leisure.

Nerja can be easily seen in a day. Its main attraction is the **Cuevas de Nerja,** caves with magnificent stalactites and bizarre rock formations.

RONDA & THE PUEBLOS BLANCOS/SHERRY TRIANGLE One of the leading attractions of southern Spain, Ronda, at an altitude of 698m (2,300 ft.), is a town built on a triangular plateau, with its apex pointing south. It is divided into two towns by the 150m (150-ft.) gorge of the Río Guadalevín. At the southern tip of Ronda is **La Ciudad** or the Old Town, which grew up on the Roman settlement of Arunda. A trio of bridges spanning the gorge links the old and new town.

Ronda deserves at least 2 days, which will allow you to explore its antique architecture, visit one of the oldest bullrings in Spain, and take in its Moorish and Roman ruins. Those with a car and an extra 2 days can explore the so-called **Pueblos Blancos (white towns)** of Andalusia in the hilly hinterland above the Costa del Sol. The houses in these agricultural villages are characterized by whitewashed walls. The higher you climb into the *sierras,* the prettier these villages grow. Favorite destinations are **Arcos de la Frontera, Olvera,** and **Sanlúcar.** Those with yet another day can do some wine tasting at the sherry-producing wine bodegas of **Jerez de la Frontera,** northeast of Cádiz. Jerez is also the equestrian center of Andalusia. Watching a "horse ballet" at a dressage school is one of the highlights of a visit to southern Spain.

SEVILLE Andalusia's grandest city links the heart of the province with its coastal plains and maritime routes. Standing on the Río Guadalquivir, it lies 80km (50 miles) north of the Atlantic Ocean with a Mediterranean climate but irregular rainfall, which means the sun shines 2,796 hours per year.

No longer Spain's most populous city, it is still an urban sprawl once you branch out from its historic core. The population numbers more than 800,000 Sevillanos.

Seville reached the zenith of its power in the 15th and 16th centuries when it was the gateway to the New World explored by Columbus. At that time Seville was the fourth-largest city on the globe, the place where treasure ships landed with their cargoes from the Americas.

Allow at least 3 or 4 nights to explore the capital of Andalusia, including such attractions as its world-famous cathedral, **La Giralda, Reales Alcázares,** and its **Museo de Bellas Artes,** along with its historic core, **Santa Cruz.**

2 Visitor Information & Entry Requirements

VISITOR INFORMATION

TOURIST OFFICES   Spain's tourist offices can be reached at the following addresses:

In the United States   Contact the **Tourist Office of Spain,** 666 Fifth Ave., 5th Floor, New York, NY 10103 (✆ **212/265-8822**), which can provide sightseeing information, events calendars, train and ferry schedules, and more. Elsewhere in the United States, branches of the Tourist Office of Spain are located at: 8383 Wilshire Blvd., Suite 956, Beverly Hills, CA 90211 (✆ **323/658-7188**); 845 N. Michigan Ave., Suite 915E, Chicago, IL 60611 (✆ **312/642-1992**); and 1221 Brickell Ave., Suite 1850, Miami, FL 33131 (✆ **305/358-1992**).

In Canada   Contact the **Tourist Office of Spain,** 102 Bloor St. W., Suite 3402, Toronto, ON M5S 1M9, Canada (✆ **416/961-3131**).

In Great Britain   Write to the **Spanish National Tourist Office,** 22–23 Manchester Sq., London W1M 5AP (✆ **020/7486-8077**).

WEBSITES   On the Net you can find lots of great information at the following sites:

Spain in General   Tourist Office of Spain (www.okspain.org), **All About Spain** (www.red2000.com), **Cybersp@in** (www.cyberspain.com).

Seville   Seville by All About Spain (www.red2000.com); **Sevilla On Line** (www.sol.com), **Seville Travel Guide** (www.aboutsevilla.com), **Andalucia.com** (www.andalucia.com), **Andalucía: There's Only One** (www.andalucia.org).

Málaga   Málaga Travel Guide (www.aboutmalaga.com), **Costa del Sol Tourist Board** (www.visitcostadelsol.com), **Costa del Sol Companion** (www.costaguide.com).

Granada   Granada en la Red (www.granadainfo.com), **Granada Travel Guide** (www.aboutgranada.com).

Cádiz   Andalusia.com (www.andalucia.com).

3 Entry Requirements & Customs

ENTRY REQUIREMENTS

Visas are not needed by U.S., Canadian, Irish, Australian, New Zealand, or British citizens for visits of less than 3 months. You do need a valid passport unless you're a citizen of another E.U. country (in which case you need only an identity card, although we always recommend you carry a passport anyway).

For information on how to get a passport, go to the "Fast Facts" section of this chapter—the websites listed provide downloadable passport applications as well as the current fees for processing passport applications. For an up-to-date country-by-country listing of passport requirements around the world, go to the "Foreign Entry Requirement" Web page of the U.S. State Department at **http://travel.state.gov**.

WHAT YOU CAN TAKE INTO SPAIN   You can take into Spain most personal effects and the following items duty-free: two still cameras and 10 rolls of film per camera, tobacco for personal use, 1 liter each of liquor and wine, a portable radio, a tape recorder, a typewriter, a bicycle, sports equipment, fishing gear, and two hunting weapons with 100 cartridges each.

WHAT YOU CAN TAKE HOME FROM SPAIN

Returning **U.S. citizens** who have been away for at least 48 hours are allowed to bring back, once every 30 days, $800 worth of merchandise duty-free. You'll be charged a flat rate of duty on the next $1,000 worth of purchases. Any dollar amount beyond that is dutiable at whatever rates apply. On mailed gifts, the duty-free limit is $200. Be sure to have your receipts or purchases handy to expedite the declaration process. *Note:* If you owe duty, you are required to pay on your arrival in the United States, either by cash, personal check, government or traveler's check, or money order, and in some locations, a Visa or MasterCard.

To avoid having to pay duty on foreign-made personal items you owned before you left on your trip, bring along a bill of sale, insurance policy, jeweler's appraisal, or receipts of purchase. Or you can register items that can be readily identified by a permanently affixed serial number or marking—think laptop computers, cameras, and CD players—with Customs before you leave. Take the items to the nearest Customs office or register them with Customs at the airport from which you're departing. You'll receive, at no cost, a Certificate of Registration, which allows duty-free entry for the life of the item.

With some exceptions, you cannot bring fresh fruits and vegetables into the United States. For specifics on what you can bring back, download the invaluable free pamphlet *Know Before You Go* online at **www.cbp.gov**. (Click on "Travel," then "Know Before You Go! Online Brochure.") Or contact the **U.S. Customs & Border Protection (CBP),** 1300 Pennsylvania Ave. NW, Washington, DC 20229 (© **877/287-8667**), and request the pamphlet.

For a clear summary of **Canadian** rules, write for the booklet *I Declare,* issued by the **Canada Customs and Revenue Agency** (© **800/461-9999** in Canada, or 204/983-3500; www. ccra-adrc.gc.ca). Canada allows its citizens a C$750 exemption, and you're

allowed to bring back duty-free one carton of cigarettes, one can of tobacco, 40 imperial ounces of liquor, and 50 cigars. In addition, you're allowed to mail gifts to Canada valued at less than C$60 a day, provided they're unsolicited and don't contain alcohol or tobacco (write on the package "Unsolicited gift, under $60 value"). All valuables should be declared on the Y-38 form before departure from Canada, including serial numbers of valuables you already own, such as expensive foreign cameras. *Note:* The C$750 exemption can only be used once a year and only after an absence of 7 days.

Citizens of the U.K. who are **returning from Spain** will go through a separate Customs Exit (called the "Blue Exit") especially for E.U. travelers. In essence, there is no limit on what you can bring back from an E.U. country, as long as the items are for personal use (this includes gifts), and you have already paid the necessary duty and tax. However, customs law sets out guidance levels. If you bring in more than these levels, you may be asked to prove that the goods are for your own use. Guidance levels on goods bought in the E.U. for your own use are 3,200 cigarettes, 200 cigars, 400 cigarillos, 3 kilograms of smoking tobacco, 10 liters of spirits, 90 liters of wine, 20 liters of fortified wine (such as port or sherry), and 110 liters of beer.

The duty-free allowance in **Australia** is A$400 or, for those under 18, A$200. Citizens can bring in 250 cigarettes or 250 grams of loose tobacco, and 1,125 milliliters of alcohol. If you're returning with valuables you already own, such as foreign-made cameras, you should file form B263. A helpful brochure available from Australian consulates or Customs offices is *Know Before You Go.* For more information, call the **Australian Customs**

Service at ℂ **1300/363-263,** or log on to www.customs.gov.au.

The duty-free allowance for **New Zealand** is NZ$700. Citizens over 17 can bring in 200 cigarettes, 50 cigars, or 250 grams of tobacco (or a mixture of all three if their combined weight doesn't exceed 250g); plus 4.5 liters of wine and beer, or 1,125 milliliters of liquor. New Zealand currency does not carry import or export restrictions. Fill out a certificate of export, listing the valuables you are taking out of the country; that way, you can bring them back without paying duty. Most questions are answered in a free pamphlet available at New Zealand consulates and Customs offices: *New Zealand Customs Guide for Travellers, Notice no. 4.* For more information, contact **New Zealand Customs,** The Customhouse, 17–21 Whitmore St., Box 2218, Wellington (ℂ **04/473-6099** or 0800/ 428-786; www.customs.govt.nz).

4 Money

Regrettably, Andalusia is no longer a budget destination. In such major cities as Seville or Granada, you can often find hotels charging the same prices as in London or Paris.

Taken as a whole, though, Andalusia remains slightly below the cost-of-living index of such countries as England, Italy, Germany, and France. Unless the current monetary situation is drastically altered, there is a very favorable exchange rate in Spain when you pay in U.S. dollars.

Prices are generally high, but you get good value for your money. Hotels are usually clean and comfortable, and restaurants, for the most part, offer good cuisine and ample portions made with quality ingredients. Trains are fast and on time, and most service personnel treat you with respect.

In Andalusia, many prices for children—generally defined as ages 6 to 17—are lower than for adults. Fees for children under 6 are generally waived.

It's a good idea to exchange at least some money—just enough to cover airport incidentals and transportation to your hotel—before you leave home (though don't expect the exchange rate to be ideal), so you can avoid lines at airport ATMs (automated teller machines). You can exchange money at your local American Express or Thomas Cook office or your bank. If you're far away from a bank with currency-exchange services, American Express offers traveler's checks and foreign currency, though with a $15 order fee and additional shipping costs, at www.americanexpress.com or ℂ **800/807-6233.**

ATMs

The easiest and best way to get cash away from home is from an ATM (automated teller machine). The **Cirrus** (ℂ **800/424-7787;** www.mastercard.com) and **PLUS** (ℂ **800/843-7587;** www.visa.com) networks span the globe; look at the back of your bank card to see which network you're on, then call or check online for ATM locations at your destination. Be sure you know your personal identification number (PIN) before you leave home and be sure to find out your daily withdrawal limit before you depart. Also keep in mind that many banks impose a fee every time a card is used at a different bank's ATM, and that fee can be higher for international transactions (up to $5 or more) than for domestic ones (where they're rarely more than $1.50). On top of this, the bank from which you withdraw cash may charge its own fee. To compare banks' ATM fees within the U.S., use www.bankrate.com. For international withdrawal fees, ask your bank.

You can also get cash advances on your credit card at an ATM. Keep in mind that credit card companies try to protect themselves from theft by

The Euro, the U.S. Dollar, the British Pound & the Canadian Dollar

Conversion ratios between the U.S. dollar and other currencies fluctuate, and their differences could affect the relative costs of your holiday. The figures reflected in the chart below were valid at the time of this writing, but they might not be valid by the time of your departure. This chart would be useful for conversions of small amounts of money, but if you're planning on any major transactions, check for more updated rates prior to making any serious commitments.

For American Readers At press time, US$1 was worth approximately .83€. (Inversely stated, that means that 1€ was worth approximately US$1.20.)

For British Readers At press time, £1 equaled approximately US$1.85 or approximately 1.50€.

For Canadian Readers At press time, C$1 equaled approximately US76¢ or approximately .61€.

Euro €	US$	UK£	C$	Euro €	US$	UK£	C$
1.00	1.20	0.67	1.63	75.00	90.00	50.25	122.25
2.00	2.40	1.34	3.26	100.00	120.00	67.00	163.00
3.00	3.60	2.01	4.89	125.00	150.00	83.75	203.75
4.00	4.80	2.68	6.52	150.00	180.00	100.50	244.50
5.00	6.00	3.35	8.15	175.00	210.00	117.25	285.25
6.00	7.20	4.02	9.78	200.00	240.00	134.00	326.00
7.00	8.40	4.69	11.41	225.00	270.00	150.75	366.75
8.00	9.60	5.36	13.04	250.00	300.00	167.50	407.50
9.00	10.80	6.03	14.67	275.00	330.00	184.25	448.25
10.00	12.00	6.70	16.30	300.00	360.00	201.00	489.00
15.00	18.00	10.05	24.45	350.00	420.00	234.50	570.50
20.00	24.00	13.40	32.60	400.00	480.00	268.00	652.00
25.00	30.00	16.75	40.75	500.00	600.00	335.00	815.00
50.00	60.00	33.50	81.50	1,000.00	1,200.00	670.00	1,630.00

limiting the funds someone can withdraw outside their home country, so call your credit card company before you leave home. And keep in mind that you'll pay interest from the moment of your withdrawal, even if you pay your monthly bills on time.

TRAVELER'S CHECKS

Traveler's checks are something of an anachronism from the days before the ATM made cash accessible at any time. Traveler's checks used to be the only sound alternative to traveling with dangerously large amounts of cash. They were as reliable as currency, but, unlike cash, could be replaced if lost or stolen.

These days, traveler's checks are less necessary because most cities have 24-hour ATMs that allow you to withdraw small amounts of cash as needed. However, keep in mind that you will likely be charged an ATM withdrawal fee if the bank is not your own, so if you're withdrawing money every day, you might be better off with traveler's checks—provided that you don't mind showing identification every time you want to cash one.

You can get traveler's checks at almost any bank. **American Express** offers denominations of $20, $50, $100, $500, and (for cardholders only) $1,000. You'll pay a service charge ranging from 1% to 4%. You can also get American Express traveler's checks over the phone by calling ℂ **800/221-7282;** Amex gold and platinum cardholders who use this number are exempt from the 1% fee.

Visa offers traveler's checks at Citibank locations nationwide, as well as at several other banks. The service charge ranges between 1.5% and 2%; checks come in denominations of $20, $50, $100, $500, and $1,000. Call ℂ **800/732-1322** for information. AAA members can obtain Visa checks without a fee at most AAA offices or by calling ℂ **866/339-3378. Master-Card** also offers traveler's checks. Call ℂ **800/223-9920** for a location near you.

Foreign currency traveler's checks are useful if you're traveling to one country, or to the Euro zone; they're accepted at locations such as bed-and-breakfasts where dollar checks may not be, and they minimize the amount of math you have to do at your destination. **American Express, Thomas Cook, Visa,** and **MasterCard** offer foreign currency traveler's checks. You'll pay the rate of exchange at the time of your purchase (so it's a good idea to monitor the rate before you take the plunge), and most companies charge a transaction fee per order (and a shipping fee if you order online).

If you choose to carry traveler's checks, be sure to keep a record of their serial numbers separate from your checks in the event that they are stolen or lost. You'll get a refund faster if you know the numbers.

CREDIT CARDS

Credit cards are a safe way to carry money. They also provide a convenient record of all your expenses, and they generally offer relatively good exchange rates. You can also withdraw cash advances from your credit cards at banks or ATMs, provided you know your PIN. If you've forgotten yours, or didn't even know you had one, call the number on the back of your credit card and ask the bank to send it to you. It usually takes 5 to 7 business days, though some banks will provide the number over the phone if you tell them your mother's maiden name or some other personal information. Keep in mind that when you use your credit card abroad, most banks assess a 2% fee above the 1% fee charged by Visa, MasterCard, or American Express for currency conversion on credit charges. But credit cards still may be the smart way to go when you factor in things like exorbitant ATM fees and higher traveler's check exchange rates (and service fees).

For tips and telephone numbers to call if your wallet is stolen or lost, see "Lost & Found" in the "Fast Facts" section of this chapter.

In Andalusia, the most commonly accepted credit cards are MasterCard and Visa. Of secondary importance are American Express and Diners Club.

(*Tips* **Small Change**

When you change money, ask for some small bills or loose change. Petty cash will come in handy for tipping and public transportation. Consider keeping the change separate from your larger bills, so that it's readily accessible and you'll be less of a target for theft.

Tips **Dear Visa: I'm Off to Granada!**

Some credit card companies recommend that you notify them of any impending trip abroad so that they don't become suspicious when the card is used numerous times in a foreign destination and block your charges. Even if you don't call your credit card company in advance, you can always call the card's toll-free emergency number (see "Fast Facts," later in this chapter) if a charge is refused—a good reason to carry the phone number with you. But perhaps the most important lesson here is to carry more than one card with you on your trip; a card might not work for any number of reasons, so having a backup is the smart way to go.

5 When to Go

CLIMATE

Spring and fall are ideal times to visit Andalusia. May and October are the best months, in terms of both weather and crowds. In our view, however, the balmy month of May (with an average temperature of 61°F/16°C) is the most glorious time for making your own discovery of Seville.

In summer, it's hot, hot, and hotter in Andaluisa, but especially in Seville and Córdoba. Seville has the dubious reputation of being the hottest part of Spain in July and August; the *average* temperature is 93°F (34°C).

August remains Europe's major vacation month. Traffic into the Costa del Sol from France, the Netherlands, Britain, and Germany becomes a veritable migration, and low-cost hotels along the coastal areas are virtually impossible to find. To compound the problem, many restaurants and shops in such inland cities as Seville also decide that it's time for a vacation, thereby limiting options for both dining and shopping.

Weather Chart for Andalusia

Granada	Jan	Feb	Mar	Apr	May	June	July	Aug	Sept	Oct	Nov	Dec
Temp (°F)	44	46	50	54	63	69	77	77	69	61	50	45
Temp (°C)	7	8	10	12	17	21	25	24	21	16	10	7
Rainfall (in.)	1.30	1.70	2.40	2.00	1.70	.80	.20	.10		1.90		1.90

Málaga	Jan	Feb	Mar	Apr	May	June	July	Aug	Sept	Oct	Nov	Dec
Temp (°F)	54	54	64	70	73	81	84	86	81	73	68	63
Temp (°C)	12	12	18	21	23	27	29	30	27	23	20	17
Rainfall (in.)	2.40	2	2.40	1.80	1	.20	.05	.10	1.20	2.50	2.50	2.40

Seville	Jan	Feb	Mar	Apr	May	June	July	Aug	Sept	Oct	Nov	Dec
Temp (°F)	59	63	68	75	81	90	97	97	90	79	68	61
Temp (°C)	15	17	20	24	27	32	36	36	32	26	20	16
Rainfall (in.)	2.60	2.40	3.60	2.30	1.60	.30	0	.20	.80	2.80	2.70	3.20

HOLIDAYS

Holidays include January 1 (New Year's Day), January 6 (Feast of the Epiphany), March 19 (Feast of St. Joseph), Good Friday, Easter Monday, May 1 (May Day), June 10 (Corpus Christi), June 29 (Feast of St. Peter and St. Paul), July 25 (Feast of St. James), August 15 (Feast of the Assumption), October 12 (Spain's National Day),

November 1 (All Saints' Day), December 8 (Immaculate Conception), and December 25 (Christmas).

No matter how large or small, every city or town in Spain also celebrates its local saint's day. In Seville, it's April 4 (St. Isidore). You'll rarely know what the local holidays are in your next destination in Andalusia. Try to keep money on hand, because you may arrive in town only to find banks and stores closed. In some cases, intercity bus services are suspended on holidays.

CALENDAR OF EVENTS

Some dates below are approximate, as exact days may not be announced until 6 weeks before the actual festival. Check with the Tourist Office of Spain (see "Visitor Information," earlier in this chapter) if you want to attend a specific event.

January

Granada Reconquest Festival, Granada. The whole city celebrates the Christians' victory over the Moors in 1492 and the highest tower at the Alhambra opens to the public. For information, contact the Tourist Office of Granada (© 95-824-71-28). January 2.

Día de los Reyes (Three Kings Day), throughout Andalusia. Parades are held all over the province on the eve of the Festival of the Epiphany. Various "kings" dispense candy to kids. January 6.

Andrés Segovia International Guitar Competition, Almuñecar. The great Segovia, who as a young man, fell in love with this part of Spain, created the "Andrés Segovia Award" in recognition of the importance of the Spanish guitar. Talented musicians from all over the world participate. Call © 95-883-86-04 (www.almunecar.com) for more information. For 5 days first week in January.

February

Carnavales de Cádiz, Cádiz. The oldest and best-attended carnival in Spain is a freewheeling event full of costumes, parades, strolling troubadours, and drum beating. Call © 95-621-12-56 or go to www.carnavaldecadiz.com for more information. Late February or early March.

March

Semana Santa (Holy Week), Seville. Although many of the country's smaller towns stage similar celebrations (especially notable in Málaga), the festivities in Seville are by far the most elaborate. From Palm Sunday until Easter Sunday a series of processions with hooded penitents moves to the piercing wail of the *saeta*, a love song to the Virgin or Christ. *Pasos* (heavy floats) bear images of the Virgin or Christ. Again, make hotel reservations way in advance. Call the Seville Office of Tourism for details (© 95-422-14-04). Usually last week of March.

April

Bullfights, all over Spain. Holy week traditionally kicks off the season all over Spain, especially in Seville.

Feria de Sevilla (Seville Fair). This is the most celebrated week of revelry in the country, with all-night flamenco dancing, merrymaking in *casetas* (entertainment booths), bullfights, horseback riding, flower-decked coaches, and dancing in the streets. Reserve a hotel early. For general information and exact festival dates, contact the Office of Tourism in Seville (© 95-422-14-04). Second week after Easter.

May

Jerez May Horse Fair. Jerez de la Frontera stages this spectacular equestrian event at Gonzalez Hontoria Park. Many of the greatest riders, certainly some of the world's finest horses, take part in various endurance trials, coach driving, and dressage competitions. Call ☏ **95-633-11-50** for more information. First week of May.

Festival de los Patios, Córdoba. At this famous fair residents decorate their patios with cascades of flowers. Visitors wander from patio to patio. Call ☏ **95-747-12-35** for more information. First 2 weeks of May.

Romería del Rocío (Pilgrimage of the Virgin of the Dew), El Rocío (Huelva). The most famous pilgrimage in Andalusia attracts a million people. Fifty men carry the statue of the Virgin 15km (9 miles) to Almonte for consecration. Third week of May.

June

Corpus Christi, all over Andalusia. A major holiday on the Spanish calendar, this event is marked by big processions, especially in Málaga, Seville, and Granada. First week of June.

International Music and Dance Festival, Granada. Granada's prestigious program of dance and music attracts international artists who perform at the Alhambra and other venues. It's a major event on Europe's cultural calendar; reserve well in advance. For schedule and tickets, contact El Festival Internacional de Música y Danza de Granada (☏ **95-822-18-44**). Last week of June to first week of July.

July

Fiesta de la Virgen del Carmen. In mid-July, the towns and fishing villages along the southern coast of Spain honor La Virgen del Carmen, the protector of seamen. An effigy of the virgin is paraded through the streets and taken for a sail on one of the gaily-adorned boats in the harbor. The best place to see this fiesta is Estepona, but other major events honoring the saint take place in Málaga, Nerja, Torremolinos, Benalmadena, Fuengirola, and Marbella. July 16.

August

Feria de Málaga (Málaga Fair). One of the longest summer fairs in southern Europe (generally lasting 10 days), this celebration kicks off with fireworks and is highlighted by a parade of Arabian horses pulling brightly decorated carriages. Participants are dressed in colorful Andalusian garb. Plazas rattle with castanets, and wine is dispensed by the gallon. For information, call ☏ **95-221-34-45.** Always the weekend before August 19.

Feria de Agosto, Málaga. Málaga celebrates its major fiesta of the summer honoring the reconquest of their city on August 19, 1487, from the Moors. The Old Town turns into one big street party with lots of entertainment. Locals dress up in the traditional costumes, and food and wine flow freely. At night the celebration moves to the city's fairgrounds in the suburbs. Call ☏ **95-205-86-94** for more information. August 19.

September

Fiero de Pedro Eomero, Ronda. This fair is famous for a bullfight on the first Saturday in September. The matadors dress in "suits of light" from the 18th and 19th centuries. Before they face the bulls, horse-drawn carriages parade through the town with participants in what Andalusians call "Goyesque costumes." The procession ends at the bullring. Call ☏ **95-289-12-72** for more information. First week in September.

Autumn Festival, Jerez de la Frontera. The whole sherry-producing town celebrates with a grape harvest parade, a "treading of the grapes" ceremony, a horse show, horse races, a locally staged opera, a flamenco festival, sports activities, and various religious observances honoring the town's patron saint. For more information, call ℭ **95-635-93-00.** All month.

October

Grape Harvest Festival, Jerez de la Frontera. Andalusia's major wine festival honors the famous sherry of Jerez, with 5 days of processions, flamenco dancing, bullfights, livestock on parade, and, of course, sherry drinking. For information, call ℭ **95-633-11-50.** Mid-October (dates vary).

November

All Saints' Day, all over Spain. This public holiday is reverently celebrated with relatives and friends laying flowers on the graves of loved ones. November 1.

December

Fiesta Mayor de Verdiales, outside Málaga. *Verdiales* are traditional forms of song and dance in Málaga province. On April Fool's Day, there's a competition staged at Venta San Cayetano del Puerto de la Torre on the outskirts of the city, to decide which village troupe can sing and dance the best. The party goes on all night, with music, food stalls, and lots of flowing wine. December 28.

6 Travel Insurance

Since Andalusia for most of us is far from home, and a number of things could go wrong—lost luggage, trip cancellation, a medical emergency—consider the following types of insurance.

Check your existing insurance policies and credit card coverage before you buy travel insurance. You may already be covered for lost luggage, canceled tickets, or medical expenses.

The cost of travel insurance varies widely, depending on the cost and length of your trip, your age and health, and the type of trip you're taking, but expect to pay between 5% and 8% of the vacation itself.

TRIP-CANCELLATION INSURANCE Trip-cancellation insurance helps you get your money back if you have to back out of a trip, if you have to go home early, or if your travel supplier goes bankrupt. Allowed reasons for cancellation can range from sickness to natural disasters to the State Department declaring your destination unsafe for travel. (Insurers usually won't cover vague fears.) In this unstable world, trip-cancellation insurance is a good buy if you're getting tickets well in advance—who knows what the state of the world, or of your airline, will be in 9 months? Insurance policy details vary, so read the fine print—and especially make sure that your airline or cruise line is on the list of carriers covered in case of bankruptcy. A good resource is **"Travel Guard Alerts,"** a list of companies considered high-risk by Travel Guard International (see website below). Protect yourself further by paying for the insurance with a credit card—by law, consumers can get their money back on goods and services not received if they report the loss within 60 days after the charge is listed on their credit card statement.

Note: Many tour operators, particularly those offering trips to remote or high-risk areas, include insurance in the cost of the trip or can arrange insurance policies through a partnering provider, a convenient and often cost-effective way for the traveler to obtain insurance. Make sure the tour company is a reputable one, however. Some experts suggest you avoid buying insurance from the tour or cruise company you're traveling with, saying it's better to buy from a "third party" insurer than to put all your money in one place.

For information, contact one of the following recommended insurers: **Access America** (© 866/807-3982; www.accessamerica.com); **Travel Guard International** (© 800/826-4919; www.travelguard.com); **Travel Insured International** (© 800/243-3174; www.travelinsured.com); and **Travelex Insurance Services** (© 888/457-4602; www.travelex-insurance.com).

MEDICAL INSURANCE For travel overseas, most health plans (including Medicare and Medicaid) do not provide coverage, and the ones that do often require you to pay for services upfront and reimburse you only after you return home. Even if your plan does cover overseas treatment, most out-of-country hospitals make you pay your bills upfront, and send you a refund only after you've returned home and filed the necessary paperwork with your insurance company. As a safety net, you may want to buy travel medical insurance, particularly if you're traveling to a remote or high-risk area where emergency evacuation is a possible scenario. If you require additional medical insurance, try **MEDEX Assistance** (© 410/453-6300; www.medexassist.com) or **Travel Assistance International** (© 800/821-2828; www.travelassistance.com; for general information on services, call the company's Worldwide Assistance Services, Inc., at © 800/777-8710).

LOST-LUGGAGE INSURANCE On international flights (including U.S. portions of international trips), baggage coverage is limited to approximately $9.07 per pound, up to approximately $635 per checked bag. If you plan to check items more valuable than the standard liability, see if your valuables are covered by your homeowner's policy, get baggage insurance as part of your comprehensive travel-insurance package, or buy Travel Guard's "BagTrak" product. Don't buy insurance at the airport, as it's usually overpriced. Be sure to take any valuables or irreplaceable items with you in your carry-on luggage, as many valuables (including books, money, and electronics) aren't covered by airline policies.

If your luggage is lost, immediately file a lost-luggage claim at the airport, detailing the luggage contents. For most airlines, you must report delayed, damaged, or lost baggage within 4 hours of arrival. The airlines are required to deliver luggage, once found, directly to your house or destination free.

7 Health & Safety

STAYING HEALTHY
Andalusia should not pose any major health hazards. The rich cuisine—garlic, olive oil, and wine—may give some travelers mild diarrhea, so take along some antidiarrhea medicine, moderate your eating habits, and even though the water is generally safe, drink bottled water only. Fish and shellfish from the horrendously polluted Mediterranean should only be eaten if cooked.

If you are traveling around southern Spain over the summer, limit your exposure to the sun, especially during the first few days of your trip and, thereafter, from 11am to 2pm. Use a sunscreen with a high protection factor and apply it liberally. Remember that children need more protection than adults do.

Before you go, contact the **International Association for Medical Assistance to Travelers (IAMAT;** © 716/754-4883, or in Canada 416/652-0137; www.iamat.org) for tips on travel and health concerns in the countries you're visiting, and lists of local, English-speaking doctors. The United States **Centers for Disease Control and Prevention** (© 800/ 311-3435; www.cdc.gov) provides up-to-date information on health hazards by region or country and offers tips on food safety.

WHAT TO DO IF YOU GET SICK AWAY FROM HOME

Andalusian medical facilities are top rate. If a medical emergency arises, your hotel staff can usually put you in touch with a reliable doctor. If not, contact the American embassy or a consulate; each one maintains a list of English-speaking doctors. Medical and hospital services aren't free, so be sure that you have appropriate insurance coverage before you travel.

If you get sick, consider asking your hotel concierge to recommend a local doctor—even his or her own. You can also try the emergency room at a local hospital; many have walk-in clinics for emergency cases that are not life-threatening; you may not get immediate attention, but you won't pay the high price of an emergency room visit. We list hospitals and emergency numbers under "Fast Facts" in the individual destination chapters.

If you suffer from a chronic illness, consult your doctor before your departure. For conditions like epilepsy, diabetes, or heart problems, wear a **MedicAlert Identification tag** (© 888/633-4298; www.medicalert. org), which will immediately alert doctors to your condition and give them access to your records through MedicAlert's 24-hour hot line.

Pack **prescription medications** in your carry-on luggage, and carry prescription medications in their original containers, with pharmacy labels— otherwise they won't make it through airport security. Also bring along copies of your prescriptions in case you lose your pills or run out. Don't forget an extra pair of contact lenses or prescription glasses. Carry the generic name of prescription medicines, in case a local pharmacist is unfamiliar with the brand name.

STAYING SAFE

Along with the United States, Spain, too, became a victim of terror on March 11, 2004, when terrorists attacked its rail system in Madrid.

While there is little you can do to protect yourself from random terrorist attacks, petty crime is much more common. Although most of the estimated one million American tourists have trouble-free visits to Andalusia each year, the principal tourist areas have been experiencing an increase in crime. Seville and Málaga, in particular, have reported growing incidents of muggings and attacks, and older tourists and Asian Americans seem to be particularly at risk. Criminals frequent tourist areas and major attractions such as museums, monuments, restaurants, hotels, beach resorts, trains, train stations, airports, subways, and ATMs. Travelers should exercise caution, carry limited cash and credit cards, and leave extra cash, credit cards, passports, and personal documents in a safe location. Crimes have occurred at all times of day and night.

Thieves often work in teams or pairs. In most cases, one person distracts a victim while the accomplice performs the robbery. For example, a stranger might wave a map in your face and ask for directions or "inadvertently" spill something on you. While your attention is diverted, an accomplice makes off with the valuables. Attacks can also be initiated from behind, with the victim being grabbed around the neck and choked by one assailant while others rifle through the belongings. A group of assailants may surround the victim, maybe in a crowded popular tourist area or on public transportation, and only after the group has departed does the person discover he/she has been robbed. Some attacks have been so violent that victims have needed to seek medical attention after the attack.

Theft from parked cars is also common. Small items like luggage, cameras, or briefcases are often stolen from parked cars. Travelers are advised not to leave valuables in parked cars and to keep doors locked, windows rolled up, and valuables out of sight when driving. "Good Samaritan" scams are unfortunately common. A passing car will attempt to divert the driver's attention by indicating there is a mechanical problem. If the driver stops to check the vehicle, accomplices steal from the car while the driver is looking elsewhere. Drivers should be cautious about accepting help from anyone other than a uniformed Spanish police officer or Civil Guard.

The loss or theft abroad of a U.S. passport should be reported immediately to the local police and the nearest U.S. embassy or consulate. U.S. citizens may refer to the Department of State's pamphlet, *A Safe Trip Abroad,* for ways to promote trouble-free journeys. The pamphlet is available by mail from the Superintendent of Documents, U.S. Government Printing Office, Washington, DC 20402, via the Internet at www.access.gpo.gov/su_docs, or via the Bureau of Consular Affairs home page at http://travel.state.gov.

8 Specialized Travel Resources

TRAVELERS WITH DISABILITIES

Because of Andalusia's many hill towns and endless flights of stairs, visitors with disabilities may have difficulty getting around the province, but conditions are slowly improving. Newer hotels are more sensitive to the needs of those with disabilities, and the more expensive restaurants, in general, are wheelchair accessible. However, since most places have limited, if any, facilities for people with disabilities, you might consider taking an organized tour specifically designed to accommodate travelers with disabilities.

Many travel agencies offer customized tours and itineraries for travelers with disabilities. **Flying Wheels Travel** (© 507/451-5005; www.flyingwheelstravel.com) offers escorted tours and cruises that emphasize sports and private tours in minivans with lifts. **Access-Able Travel Source** (© 303/232-2979; www.access-able.com) offers extensive access information and advice for traveling around the world with disabilities. **Accessible Journeys** (© 800/846-4537 or 610/521-0339; www.disabilitytravel.com) caters specifically to slow walkers and wheelchair travelers and their families and friends.

Organizations that offer assistance to travelers with disabilities include **MossRehab** (www.mossresourcenet.org), which provides a library of accessible-travel resources online and the **American Foundation for the Blind (AFB; © 800/232-5463;** www.afb.org), a referral resource for the blind or visually impaired that includes information on traveling with Seeing Eye dogs.

For British Travelers with Disabilities   The annual vacation guide *Holidays and Travel Abroad* costs £5 from **Royal Association for Disability and Rehabilitation (RADAR),** Unit 12, City Forum, 250 City Rd., London EC1V 8AF (© **020/7250-3222;** www.radar.org.uk).

GAY & LESBIAN TRAVELERS

In 1978, Spain legalized homosexuality among consenting adults. In April 1995, the parliament of Spain banned discrimination based on sexual orientation. In Andalusia the most popular resort for gay and lesbian travelers is Torremolinos, although there are gay bars in all the larger cities such as

Seville and Granada. Only problem is, many of them come and go with great frequency.

Before you go, consider picking up a copy of *Frommer's Gay & Lesbian Europe* (Wiley Publishing, Inc.), which contains chapters on Madrid, Barcelona, Sitges, and Ibiza, should you be planning to travel elsewhere in Spain after your visit to Andalusia.

The International Gay and Lesbian Travel Association (IGLTA; © 800/448-8550 or 954/776-2626; www.iglta.org) is the trade association for the gay and lesbian travel industry, and offers an online directory of gay- and lesbian-friendly travel businesses.

Many agencies offer tours and travel itineraries specifically for gay and lesbian travelers. **Above and Beyond Tours** (© 800/397-2681; www.abovebeyondtours.com) is the exclusive gay and lesbian tour operator for United Airlines. **Now, Voyager** (© 800/255-6951; www.nowvoyager. com) is a well-known San Francisco–based gay-owned and -operated travel service.

SENIOR TRAVEL

Mention the fact that you're a senior when you make your travel reservations. Many hotels offer discounts for seniors. In most cities, people over the age of 60 qualify for reduced admission to theaters, museums, and other attractions, as well as discounted fares on public transportation.

Members of **AARP** (formerly known as the American Association of Retired Persons), 601 E St. NW, Washington, DC 20049 (© 888/687-2277; www.aarp.org), get discounts on hotels, airfares, and car rentals. AARP offers members a wide range of benefits, including *AARP The Magazine* and a monthly newsletter. Anyone over 50 can join.

Many reliable agencies and organizations target the 50-plus market. **Elderhostel** (© 877/426-8056; www.elderhostel.org) arranges study programs for those 55 and over (and a spouse or companion of any age) in the U.S. and in more than 80 countries around the world, including Spain.

Recommended publications offering travel resources and discounts for seniors include the quarterly magazine *Travel 50 & Beyond* (www.travel50 andbeyond.com); *Travel Unlimited: Uncommon Adventures for the Mature Traveler* (Avalon); and *101 Tips for Mature Travelers,* available from Grand Circle Travel (© 800/221-2610 or 617/350-7500; www. gct.com).

FAMILY TRAVEL

Familyhostel (© 800/733-9753; www.learn.unh.edu/familyhostel) takes the whole family, including kids ages 8 to 15, on moderately priced domestic and international learning vacations. Lectures, fields trips, and sightseeing are guided by a team of academics.

Recommended family travel Internet sites include **Family Travel Forum** (www.familytravelforum.com), a comprehensive site that offers customized trip planning; **Family Travel Network** (www.familytravelnetwork.com), an award-winning site that offers travel features, deals, and tips; **Traveling Internationally with Your Kids**

Traveling with Minors
For changing details on entry requirements for children traveling abroad, go to the U.S. State Department website: http://travel.state.gov. Any questions parents or guardians might have can be answered by calling the **National Passport Information Center** at © 877/487-2778 Monday to Friday 9am to 8pm Eastern Standard Time.

(www.travelwithyourkids.com), a comprehensive site offering sound advice for long-distance and international travel with children; and **Family Travel** Files (www.thefamilytravelfiles.com), which offers an online magazine and a directory of off-the-beaten-path tours and tour operators for families.

9 Planning Your Trip Online

SURFING FOR AIRFARES

The "big three" online travel agencies, **Expedia.com, Travelocity.com,** and **Orbitz.com** sell most of the air tickets bought on the Internet. (Canadian travelers should try expedia.ca and Travelocity.ca; U.K. residents can go for expedia.co.uk and opodo.co.uk.) Each has different business deals with the airlines and may offer different fares on the same flights, so it's wise to shop around. Expedia and Travelocity will also send you **e-mail notification** when a cheap fare becomes available to your favorite destination. Of the smaller travel agency websites, **Side-Step** (www.sidestep.com) has gotten the best reviews from Frommer's authors. It's a browser add-on that purports to "search 140 sites at once," but in reality only beats competitors' fares as often as other sites do.

Also remember to check **airline websites,** especially those for low-fare carriers whose fares are often misreported or simply missing from travel agency websites. Even with major airlines, you can often shave a few bucks from a fare by booking directly through the airline and avoiding a travel agency's transaction fee. But you'll get these discounts only by **booking online:** Most airlines now offer online-only fares that even their phone agents know nothing about. For the websites of airlines that fly to and from your destination, go to "Getting There," p. 41.

Great **last-minute deals** are available through free weekly e-mail services provided directly by the airlines. Most of these are announced on Tuesday or Wednesday and must be purchased online. Most are only valid for travel that weekend, but some can be booked weeks or months in advance. Sign up for weekly e-mail alerts at airline websites or check megasites that compile comprehensive lists of last-minute specials, such as **Smarter Living** (www.smarterliving.com). For last-minute trips, **lastminute.com** in Europe often has better air-and-hotel package deals than the major-label sites. A website listing numerous bargain sites and airlines around the world is **www.itravelnet.com**.

If you're willing to give up some control over your flight details, use what is called an **opaque fare service** like **Priceline** (www.priceline.com; www.priceline.co.uk for Europeans) or its smaller competitor **Hotwire** (www.hotwire.com). Both offer rock-bottom prices in exchange for travel on a "mystery airline" at a mysterious time of day, often with a mysterious change of planes en route. The mystery airlines are all major, well-known carriers. The airlines' routing computers have gotten a lot better than they used to be. But your chances of getting a 6am or 11pm flight are pretty high. Hotwire tells you flight prices before you buy; Priceline usually has better deals than Hotwire, but you have to play their "name our price" game. If you're new at this, the helpful folks at **BiddingForTravel** (www.biddingfortravel.com) do a good job of demystifying Priceline's prices and strategies. Priceline and Hotwire are great for flights between the U.S. and Europe. *Note:* In 2004 Priceline added nonopaque service to its roster. You now have the option to pick exact flights, times, and airlines from a list of offers, or opt to bid on opaque fares as before.

For much more about airfares and savvy air-travel tips and advice, pick up a copy of *Frommer's Fly Safe, Fly Smart* (Wiley Publishing, Inc.).

SURFING FOR HOTELS

Shopping online for hotels is generally done one of two ways: by booking through the hotel's own website or through an independent booking agency (or a fare-service agency like Priceline; see below). These Internet hotel agencies have multiplied in mind-boggling numbers of late, competing for the business of millions of consumers surfing for accommodations around the world. This competitiveness can be a boon to consumers who have the patience and time to shop and compare the online sites for good deals—but shop they must, for prices can vary considerably from site to site. And keep in mind that hotels at the top of a site's listing may be there for no other reason than that they paid money to get the placement.

Of the "big three" sites, **Expedia** offers a long list of special deals and "virtual tours" or photos of available rooms so you can see what you're paying for (a feature that helps counter the claims that the best rooms are often held back from bargain booking websites). **Travelocity** posts unvarnished customer reviews and ranks its properties according to the AAA rating system. Also reliable are **Hotels.com** and **Quikbook.com.** An excellent free program, **TravelAxe** (www.travelaxe.net), can help you search multiple hotel sites at once, even ones you may never have heard of—and conveniently lists the total price of the room, including the taxes and service charges. Another booking site, **Travelweb** (www.travelweb.com), is partly owned by the hotels it represents (including the Hilton, Hyatt, and Starwood chains) and is therefore plugged directly into the hotels' reservations systems—unlike independent online agencies, which have to fax or

e-mail reservation requests to the hotel, a good portion of which get misplaced in the shuffle. More than once, travelers have arrived at the hotel, only to be told that they have no reservation. To be fair, many of the major sites are undergoing improvements in service and ease of use, and Expedia will soon be able to plug directly into the reservations systems of many hotel chains—none of which can be bad news for consumers. In the meantime, it's a good idea to **get a confirmation number** and **make a printout** of any online booking transaction.

In the opaque website category, **Priceline** and **Hotwire** are even better for hotels than for airfares; with both, you're allowed to pick the neighborhood and quality level of your hotel before offering up your money. Priceline's hotel product even covers Europe and Asia, though it's much better at getting five-star lodging for three-star prices than at finding anything at the bottom of the scale. On the down side, many hotels stick Priceline guests in their least desirable rooms. Be sure to go to the BiddingforTravel website (see above) before bidding on a hotel room on Priceline; it features a fairly up-to-date list of hotels that Priceline uses in major cities. For both Priceline and Hotwire, you pay upfront, and the fee is nonrefundable. *Note:* Some hotels do not provide loyalty program credits or points or other frequent-stay amenities when you book a room through opaque online services.

SURFING FOR RENTAL CARS

For booking rental cars online, the best deals are usually found at rental-car company websites, although all the major online travel agencies also offer rental-car reservations services. Priceline and Hotwire work well for rental cars, too; the only "mystery" is which major rental company you get, and for most travelers the difference between Hertz, Avis, and Budget is negligible.

Frommers.com: The Complete Travel Resource

For an excellent travel-planning resource, we highly recommend **Frommers.com** (www.frommers.com), voted Best Travel Site by *PC Magazine*. We're a little biased, of course, but we guarantee that you'll find the travel tips, reviews, monthly vacation giveaways, bookstore, and online-booking capabilities thoroughly indispensable. Among the special features are our popular **Destinations** section, where you'll get expert travel tips, hotel and dining recommendations, and advice on the sights to see for more than 3,500 destinations around the globe; the **Frommers.com Newsletter,** with the latest deals, travel trends, and money-saving secrets; our **Community** area featuring **Message Boards,** where Frommer's readers post queries and share advice (sometimes even our authors show up to answer questions); and our **Photo Center,** where you can post and share vacation tips. When your research is done, the **Online Reservations System** (www.frommers.com/book_a_trip) takes you to Frommer's preferred online partners for booking your vacation at affordable prices.

10 The 21st-Century Traveler

INTERNET ACCESS AWAY FROM HOME

Travelers have any number of ways to check their e-mail and access the Internet on the road. Of course, using your own laptop—or a PDA or electronic organizer with a modem—gives you the most flexibility. But if you don't have a computer, you can still access your e-mail from cybercafes.

WITHOUT YOUR OWN COMPUTER

It's hard nowadays to find a city that *doesn't* have a few cybercafes. Although there's no definitive directory for cybercafes—these are independent businesses, after all—three places to start looking are at **www.cybercaptive.com**, **www.netcafeguide.com**, and **www.cybercafe.com**. See "Fast Facts" in the individual destination chapters for cybercafes.

Aside from formal cybercafes, most **youth hostels** nowadays have at least one computer you can get to the Internet on. And most **public libraries** across the world offer Internet access

free or for a small charge. Avoid **hotel business centers,** unless you're willing to pay exorbitant rates.

Most major airports now have **Internet kiosks** scattered throughout their gates. These kiosks, which you'll also see in shopping malls, hotel lobbies, and tourist information offices around the world, give you basic Web access for a per-minute fee that's usually higher than cybercafe prices. The kiosks' clunkiness and high price means they should be avoided whenever possible.

To retrieve your e-mail, ask your **Internet service provider (ISP)** if it has a Web-based interface tied to your existing e-mail account. If your ISP doesn't have such an interface, you can use the free **mail2web** service (www.mail2web.com) to view and reply to your home e-mail. For more flexibility, you may want to open a free, Web-based e-mail account with **Yahoo! Mail** (http://mail.yahoo.com). (Microsoft's Hotmail is another popular option, but Hotmail has severe spam problems.) Your home ISP may be able to forward your e-mail to the Web-based account automatically.

WITH YOUR OWN COMPUTER

Wi-Fi (wireless fidelity) is the buzz-word in computer access, and more and more hotels, cafes, and retailers are signing on as wireless "hotspots" from where you can get high-speed connection without cable wires, net-working hardware, or, a phone line (see below). You sign up for wireless access service much as you do cell-phone service, through a plan offered by one of several commercial compa-nies that have made wireless service available in airports, hotel lobbies, and coffee shops.

There are also places that provide **free wireless networks** in cities around the world. To locate these free hotspots, go to **www.personaltelco.net/index. cgi/Wireless Communities**.

Most business-class hotels through-out the world offer dataports for lap-top modems, and a few thousand hotels in Europe now offer free high-speed Internet access using an Ether-net network cable. You can bring your own cables, but most hotels rent them for around $10. **Call your hotel in advance** to see what your options are.

In addition, major ISPs have **local access numbers** around the world, allowing you to go online by simply placing a local call. Check your ISP's website or call its toll-free number and ask how you can use your current account away from home, and how much it will cost.

Wherever you go, bring a **connec-tion kit** of the right power and phone adapters, a spare phone cord, and a spare Ethernet network cable—or find out whether your hotel supplies them to guests.

USING A CELLPHONE

The three letters that define much of the world's **wireless capabilities** are GSM (Global System for Mobiles), a big, seamless network that makes for easy cross-border cellphone use throughout Europe, including Spain. In the U.S., T-Mobile, AT&T Wire-less, and Cingular use this quasi-uni-versal system; in Canada, Microcell and some Rogers customers are GSM, and all Europeans and most Aus-tralians use GSM.

If your cellphone is on a GSM sys-tem, and you have a world-capable multiband phone such as many (but not all) Sony Ericsson, Motorola, or Samsung models, you can make and receive calls across civilized areas on much of the globe. Just call your wire-less operator and ask for "international roaming" to be activated on your account. Unfortunately, per-minute charges can be high—usually $1 to $1.50 in western Europe.

That's why it's important to buy an "unlocked" world phone from the get-go. Many cellphone operators sell "locked" phones that restrict you from using any other removable computer memory phone chip (called a **SIM card**) other than the ones they supply. Having an unlocked phone allows you to install a cheap, prepaid SIM card (found at a local retailer) in your des-tination country. (Show your phone to the salesperson; not all phones work on all networks.) You'll get a local phone number—and much, much lower calling rates. Getting an already locked phone unlocked can be a com-plicated process, but it can be done; just call your cellular operator and say you'll be going abroad for several months and want to use the phone with a local provider.

For many, **renting** a phone is a good idea. While you can rent a phone from any number of overseas sites, including kiosks at airports and at car-rental agencies, we suggest renting the phone before you leave home. That way you can give loved ones and busi-ness associates your new number, make sure the phone works, and take the phone wherever you go—especially helpful for overseas trips through several countries, where local phone-rental agencies often bill in local currency and may not let you take the phone to another country.

Phone rental isn't cheap. You'll usually pay $40 to $50 per week, plus airtime fees of at least a dollar a minute. If you're traveling to Europe, though, local rental companies often offer free incoming calls within their home country, which can save you big bucks. The bottom line: Shop around.

Two good wireless rental companies are **InTouch USA** (© **800/872-7626;** www.intouchglobal.com) and **Road-Post** (© **888/290-1606** or 905/272-5665; www.roadpost.com). Give them your itinerary, and they'll tell you

what wireless products you need. InTouch will also, for free, advise you on whether your existing phone will work overseas; simply call © **703/222-7161** between 9am and 4pm Eastern Standard Time, or go to http://intouchglobal.com/travel.htm.

For trips of more than a few weeks spent in one country, **buying a phone** becomes economically attractive, as many nations have cheap, no-questions-asked prepaid phone systems. Once you arrive at your destination, stop by a local cellphone shop and get the cheapest package; you'll probably pay less than $100 for a phone and a starter calling card. Local calls may be as low as 10¢ per minute, and in many countries incoming calls are free.

11 Getting There

BY PLANE

Any information about fares or even flights in the highly volatile airline industry is not written in stone; even travel agencies with banks of computers have a hard time keeping abreast of last-minute discounts and schedule changes. For up-to-the-minute information, including a list of the carriers that fly to Spain, check with a travel agent or the individual airlines.

FROM NORTH AMERICA
Flights from the U.S. East Coast to Spain take 6 to 7 hours. Spain's national carrier, **Iberia Airlines** (© 800/772-4642; www.iberia.com), has more routes into and within Spain than any other airline. It offers daily nonstop service to Madrid from New York, Chicago, Miami, and San Juan. Also available are attractive rates on fly/drive packages within Iberia and Europe; they can substantially reduce the cost of both the air ticket and the car rental.

A good money-saver to consider is **Iberia's EuroPass.** Available only to passengers who simultaneously arrange

for a transatlantic flight on Iberia and a minimum of two additional flights, it allows passage on any flight within Iberia's European or Mediterranean dominion for $139 to $169 per person one-way for each additional flight. This is especially attractive for passengers wishing to combine trips to Spain with, for example, visits to such far-flung destinations as Cairo, Tel Aviv, Istanbul, Moscow, and Munich. For details, ask Iberia's phone representative. The EuroPass can be purchased as a part of an Iberian Air itinerary from your home country only.

Iberia's main Spain-based competitor is **Air Europa** (© **888/238-7672;** www.aireuropa.com), which offers nonstop service from Newark Airport to Madrid, with continuing service to major cities within Spain. Fares are usually lower than Iberia's.

American Airlines (© **800/433-7300;** www.aa.com) offers daily nonstop service to Madrid from its massive hub in Miami.

Delta (© **800/241-4141;** www.delta.com) runs daily nonstop service from Atlanta (its worldwide hub) and New York (JFK) to both Madrid and Barcelona. Delta's Dream Vacation department has independent fly/drive packages, land packages, and escorted bus tours.

United Airlines (© **800/241-6522;** www.ual.com) does not fly into Spain directly. It does, however, offer airfares from the United States to Spain with United flying as far as Zurich, and then using another carrier to complete the journey. United also offers fly/drive packages and escorted motor coach tours.

Continental Airlines (© **800/ 525-0280;** www.continental.com) offers daily nonstop flights, depending on the season, to Madrid from Newark, New Jersey.

US Airways (© **800/428-4322;** www.usairways.com) offers daily non-stop service between Philadelphia and Madrid. The carrier also has connecting flights to Philadelphia from more than 50 cities throughout the United States, Canada, and the Bahamas.

FROM THE U.K.   British Airways (**BA;** © **0870/850-9850**) and **Iberia** (© **020/8222-8900** in London) are the two major carriers flying between England and Spain. More than a dozen daily flights, on either BA or Iberia, depart from London's Heathrow and Gatwick airports. The Midlands is served by flights from Manchester and Birmingham, two major airports that can also be used by Scottish travelers flying to Spain. There are about seven flights a day from London to Madrid and back and at least six to Barcelona (trip time: 2–2½ hr.). From either the Madrid airport or the Barcelona airport, you can tap into Iberia's domestic network, flying, for example, to Seville or the Costa del Sol. The best air deals on scheduled flights from England are those requiring a Saturday night stopover.

British newspapers are always full of classified advertisements touting "slashed" fares to Spain. A good source is *Time Out*. London's *Evening Standard* has a daily travel section, and the Sunday editions of most papers are full of charter deals. A travel agent can always advise what the best values are at the time of your intended departure.

Charter flights to specific destinations leave from most British regional airports (for example, to Málaga), bypassing the congestion at the Barcelona and Madrid airports. Figure on saving approximately 10% to 15% on regularly scheduled flight tickets. But check carefully into the restrictions and terms; read the fine print, especially in regard to cancellation penalties. One recommended company is **Trailfinders** (© **020/7937-5400** in London; www.trailfinder. com), which operates charters.

In London, there are many bucket shops around Victoria Station and Earls Court that offer cheap fares. Make sure the company you deal with is a member of the IATA, ABTA, or ATOL. These umbrella organizations will help you out if anything goes wrong.

CEEFAX, the British television information service, runs details of package holidays and flights to Europe and beyond. Just switch to your CEEFAX channel and you'll find travel information.

FROM AUSTRALIA   From Australia, there are a number of options to fly to Spain. The most popular is Qantas/British Airways (© **612/13-13-13**), which flies daily via Asia and London. Other popular and cheaper options are Qantas/Lufthansa via Asia and Frankfurt, Qantas/Air France via Asia and Paris, and Alitalia via Bangkok and Rome. The most direct option is on Singapore Airlines, with just one stop in Singapore. Alternatively, there are flights on Thai Airways via Bangkok and Rome, but the connections are not always good.

FLYING TO ANDALUSIA

Once you arrive in your gateway city to Spain—presumably Madrid if you're contemplating a trip to Andalusia—you can go the final lap of the journey by car, bus, or train. But the quickest way is a domestic flight. The major air gateways into Andalusia are Seville (number one), Granada, Málaga, and Jerez de la Frontera.

For most visits to the inland cities of Andalusia, Seville is the best gateway, unless you're visiting only Granada and saving Seville for another trip. For beach resorts along the Costa del Sol, Málaga is the principal gateway.

Seville is connected by direct flights to the Continent from Amsterdam, Brussels, Frankfurt, London, and Paris. But most visitors wing in from either Madrid (45 min.) or Barcelona (55 min.). There are at least six flights a day flying to Seville from either Barcelona or Madrid.

If **Granada** is your gateway to Andalusia, there are three flights per day from Barcelona (1 hr.) and four per day from Madrid (30 min.).

Most passengers fly to Seville and then journey to Jerez de la Frontera on a day trip either by car or train. However, Iberia has several flights a day to Madrid and Barcelona, the frequency depending on the time of the year.

For Costa del Sol visitors, **Málaga** is an international hub for flights, receiving planes from such destinations as London. Most major European capitals have direct flights to Málaga on their own national carriers. Or else you can fly on one of eight flights daily from Madrid (1 hr.) or on one of 3 flights from Barcelona (1½ hr.). There are also regular flights from many other Spanish cities such as Valencia.

For North American visitors, **Air Plus Comet** (✆ **212/983-1277**) flies once a week on a Thursday from New York to Málaga.

For complete information on Iberia flights, call ✆ **800/772-4642** in the U.S., or 902/400-500 in Spain.

GETTING THROUGH THE AIRPORT

With the federalization of airport security, security procedures at U.S. airports are more stable and consistent than ever. Generally, you'll be fine if you arrive at the airport **2 hours** before an international flight; if you show up late, tell an airline employee and she'll probably whisk you to the front of the line.

Bring a **current, government-issued photo ID** such as a driver's license or passport. Keep your ID at the ready to show at check-in, the security checkpoint, and sometimes even the gate. (Children under 18 need government-issued photo IDs for international flights.)

In 2003, the TSA phased out **gate check-in** at all U.S. airports. And **e-tickets** have made paper tickets nearly obsolete. Passengers with e-tickets can beat the ticket-counter lines by using airport **electronic kiosks** or even **online check-in** from your home computer. Online check-in involves logging on to your airline's website, accessing your reservation, and printing out your boarding pass—and the airline may even offer you bonus miles to do so! If you're using a kiosk at the airport, bring the credit card you used to book the ticket or your frequent-flier card. Print out your boarding pass from the kiosk and simply proceed to the security checkpoint with your pass and a photo ID. If you're checking bags or looking to snag an exit-row seat, you will be able to do so using most airline kiosks. Even the smaller airlines are employing the kiosk system, but always call your airline to make sure these alternatives are available. **Curbside check-in** is also a good way to avoid lines, although a few airlines still ban curbside check-in; call before you go.

Security checkpoint lines are getting shorter than they were during 2001 and 2002, but some doozies remain. If you have trouble standing for long periods of time, tell an airline employee; the airline will provide a wheelchair. Speed up security by **not wearing metal objects** such as big belt buckles. If you've got metallic body parts, a note from your doctor can prevent a long chat with the security screeners. Keep in mind that only **ticketed passengers** are allowed past security, except for folks escorting disabled passengers or children.

Federalization has stabilized **what you can carry on** and **what you can't.** The general rule is that sharp things are out, nail clippers are okay, and food and beverages must be passed through the X-ray machine—but that security screeners can't make you drink from your coffee cup. Bring food in your carry-on rather than checking it, as explosive-detection machines used on checked luggage have been known to mistake food (especially chocolate, for some reason) for bombs. Travelers in the U.S. are allowed one carry-on bag, plus a "personal item" such as a purse, briefcase, or laptop bag. Carry-on hoarders can stuff all sorts of things into a laptop bag; as long as it has a laptop in it, it's still considered a personal item. The Transportation Security Administration (TSA) has issued a list of restricted items; check its website (www.tsa.gov/public/index.jsp) for details.

Airport screeners may decide that your checked luggage needs to be searched by hand. You can now purchase luggage locks that allow screeners to open and relock a checked bag if hand-searching is necessary. Look for Travel Sentry certified locks at luggage or travel shops and Brookstone stores (you can buy them online at www.brookstone.com). These locks, approved by the TSA, can be opened by luggage inspectors with a special code or key. For more information on the locks, visit www.travelsentry.org. If you use something other than TSA-approved locks, your lock will be cut off your suitcase if a TSA agent needs to hand-search your luggage.

FLYING FOR LESS: TIPS FOR GETTING THE BEST AIRFARE

Passengers sharing the same airplane cabin rarely pay the same fare. Travelers who need to purchase tickets at the last minute, change their itinerary at a moment's notice, or fly one-way often get stuck paying the premium rate. Here are some ways to keep your airfare costs down.

- Passengers who can book their ticket **long in advance,** who can **stay over Saturday night,** or who **fly midweek** or **at less-trafficked hours** may pay a fraction of the full fare. If your schedule is flexible, say so, and ask if you can secure a cheaper fare by changing your flight plans.
- You can also save on airfares by keeping an eye out in local newspapers for **promotional specials** or **fare wars,** when airlines lower prices on their most popular routes. You rarely see fare wars offered for peak travel times, but if you can travel in the off-months, you may snag a bargain.
- Search **the Internet** for cheap fares (see "Planning Your Trip Online," earlier in this chapter).
- **Consolidators,** also known as bucket shops, are great sources for international tickets, although they usually can't beat the Internet on fares within North America. Start by looking in Sunday newspaper travel sections; U.S. travelers should focus on the *New York Times, Los Angeles Times,* and *Miami Herald.* For less-developed destinations, small travel agents

who cater to immigrant communities in large cities often have the best deals. *Beware:* Bucket shop tickets are usually nonrefundable or rigged with stiff cancellation penalties, often as high as 50% to 75% of the ticket price, and some put you on charter airlines, which may leave at inconvenient times and experience delays. Several reliable consolidators are worldwide and available on the Net. **STA Travel** is now the world's leader in student travel, thanks to their purchase of Council Travel. It also offers good fares for travelers of all ages. **ELTExpress** (**Flights.com;** © **516/228-4972;** www.eltexpress. com) started in Europe and has excellent fares worldwide, but particularly to that continent. It also has "local" websites in 12 countries. **FlyCheap** (© **800/FLY-CHEAP;** www.1800flycheap.com) is owned by package-holiday megalith MyTravel and so has especially good access to fares for sunny destinations. **Air Tickets Direct** (© **800/778-3447;** www.airtickets direct.com) is based in Montreal and leverages the currently weak Canadian dollar for low fares.

- Join **frequent-flier clubs.** Accrue enough miles, and you'll be rewarded with free flights and elite status. It's free, and you'll get the best choice of seats, faster response to phone inquiries, and prompter service if your luggage is stolen, your flight is canceled or delayed, or if you want to change your seat. You don't need to fly to build frequent-flier miles—**frequent-flier credit cards** can provide thousands of miles for doing your everyday shopping.

BY TRAIN

If you're already in Europe, you might want to go to Spain by train, especially if you have a Eurailpass. Even without a pass, you'll find that the cost of a train ticket is relatively moderate. Rail passengers who visit from Britain or France should make **sleeper reservations** as far in advance as possible, especially during the peak summer season.

Since Spain's rail tracks are of a wider gauge than those used for French trains (except for the TALGO and Trans-Europe-Express trains), you'll probably have to change trains at the border unless you're on an express train (see below). For long journeys on Spanish rails, seat and sleeper reservations are mandatory.

The most comfortable and the fastest trains in Spain are the **TER, TALGO,** and **Electrotren.** However, you pay a supplement to ride on these fast trains. Both first- and second-class fares are sold on Spanish trains. Tickets can be purchased in the United States or Canada at the nearest office of Rail Europe or from any reputable travel agent. Confirmation of your reservation takes about a week.

If you want your car carried aboard the train, you must travel **Auto-Expreso** in Spain. This type of auto transport can be booked only through travel agents or rail offices once you arrive in Europe.

To go from London to Spain by rail, you'll need to change not only the train but also the rail terminus in Paris. In Paris it's worth the extra bucks to purchase a **TALGO express** or a **"Puerta del Sol" express**—that way, you can avoid having to change trains once again at the Spanish border. Trip time from London to Paris is about 6 hours; from Paris to Madrid, about 15 hours or so, which includes 2 hours spent in Paris just changing trains and stations. Many different rail passes are available in the United Kingdom for travel in Europe, including Spain.

Once you arrive in such rail hubs as Madrid or Barcelona, you will find easy rail connections to the major cities of Andalusia, such as Seville or Málaga. See individual chapters for more details on traveling by train to your ultimate destination in southern Spain.

12 Packages for the Independent Traveler

Before you start your search for the lowest airfare, you may want to consider booking your flight as part of a travel package. Package tours are not the same thing as escorted tours. Package tours are simply a way to buy the airfare, accommodations, and other elements of your trip (such as car rentals, airport transfers, and sometimes even activities) at the same time and often at discounted prices—kind of like one-stop shopping. Packages are sold in bulk to tour operators—who resell them to the public at a cost that usually undercuts standard rates.

One good source of package deals is the airlines themselves. Most major airlines offer air/land packages, including **American Airlines Vacations** (© 800/321-2121; www.aavacations.com), **Delta Vacations** (© 800/221-6666; www.deltavacations.com), **Continental Airlines Vacations** (© 800/301-3800; www.coolvacations.com), and **United Vacations** (© 888/854-3899; www.unitedvacations.com). Among the airline packagers, **Iberia Airlines** (© 800/772-4642, or 90-240-05-00 in Spain; www.iberia.com) leads the way.

Several big **online travel agencies**—Expedia, Travelocity, Orbitz, Site59, and Lastminute.com—also do a brisk business in packages. If you're unsure about the pedigree of a smaller packager, check with the Better Business Bureau in the city where the company is based, or go online at www.bbb.org.

If a packager won't tell you where it's based, don't fly with them.

Solar Tours (© 800/388-7652; www.solartours.com) is a wholesaler that offers a number of package tours to Córdoba, Granada, Seville, and Andalusia, as well as to major beach resorts. Self-drive packages through Andalusia and other areas are also featured. A 9-day "Moorish Escapade" tour of Andalusia is its most popular jaunt. **Spanish Heritage Tours** (© 973/337-4012; www.shtours.com) is known for searching for low-cost airfare deals to Spain. It is especially good in putting together packages for the Costa del Sol, including 6-night deals that feature Córdoba, Seville, and Granada beginning at $839 per person. **Homeric Tours** (© 800/223-5570 or 212/753-1100; www.homerictours. com), the marketing arm of Iberia, is the most reliable tour operator and the agency used for air and land packages to some of Spain's highlights, including Córdoba, Seville, Granada, and the Costa del Sol. Naturally, round-trip airfares on Iberia are included in the deal. A recent offering (subject to change, of course) featured Madrid and the Costa del Sol in 8 days and 6 nights, including not only the transatlantic fare but 3 nights in a Madrid hotel, followed by 3 nights in a Costa del Sol hotel. Prices began at $649 per person. Several fly/drive packages are also offered.

13 Escorted General-Interest Tours

Escorted tours are structured group tours, with a group leader. The price usually includes everything from airfare to hotels, meals, tours, admission costs, and local transportation.

There are many escorted tour companies to choose from, each offering transportation to and within Spain, prearranged hotel space, and such extras as bilingual tour guides and lectures. Many Andalusian tours include excursions to Morocco.

Abercrombie & Kent International (© 800/323-7308 or 630/954-2944; www.abercrombiekent.com) runs some of Spain's most expensive and luxurious tours, including deluxe 9- or 15-day tours of the Iberian Peninsula by train. Guests stay in fine hotels, ranging from a late medieval palace to the exquisite Alfonso XIII in Seville.

American Express Vacations (© 800/941-2639 in the U.S. and Canada; www.travelimpressions.com) is one of the biggest tour operators in the world. Its offerings are comprehensive, and unescorted customized package tours to Andalusia are available, too.

Visit Spain Tours (© 866/878-4604) is a new tour operator featuring trips to Andalusia. Its packages include nonstop charter flights to Málaga, departing from New York's Kennedy Airport every Friday. Six-night packages run from $599 to $1,170 per person, based on double occupancy at first-class hotels. There are several optional trips available, taking in the cities of Granada, Seville, and Córdoba, even a trip across the straits to Morocco. A bus tour of Andalusia is also a feature.

Trafalgar Tours (© 800/854-0103 or 212/689-8977; www.trafalgartours.com) is cheaper, offering a number of tours of Spain. One of the most popular offerings is a 14-day trip, "Highlights of Spain and Portugal," costing from $1,499 per person and featuring such destinations as Córdoba, Granada, Seville, and the Costa del Sol, and even the self-governing British colony at Gibraltar.

Alternative Travel Group Ltd. (© 01865/315-678; www.atg-oxford.co.uk) is a British firm that organizes walking and cycling vacations, plus wine tours in Spain. One of its tours is devoted to Andalusia, an 8-day trip that includes 4 days of walking. Highlights include Seville, the "Pueblos Blancos" (white villages)—some in the heart of nature reserves—and lofty Ronda. Some of Andalusia's most charming villages or towns are featured on this trip, including Arcos de la Frontera, Zahara, and Grazalema.

Petrabax Tours (© 888/427-7246; www.petrabax.com) attracts those who prefer to see Spain by bus, although fly/drive packages featuring stays in paradors are also offered. A number of city packages are also available, plus an 8- or 9-day trip that tries to capture the essence of Spain, with stops in places ranging from Madrid to Granada, with stops in Córdoba and Seville.

Isramworld (© 800/223-7460; www.isram.com) sells both escorted and package tours to Spain. It can book you on bus tours as well as land and air packages. Devotees of southern Spain book its "Spanish Calvacade" tour, beginning in Madrid and journeying on to Seville and the Costa del Sol. Round-trip air transportation and 6 nights in hotel accommodations, along with six dinners, are included.

Many people derive a certain ease and security from escorted trips. Escorted tours—whether by bus, motor coach, train, or boat—let travelers sit back and enjoy their trip without having to spend lots of time behind the wheel or worrying about details. You know your costs upfront, and there are few surprises. Escorted tours can take you to the maximum number of sights in the minimum amount of time with the least amount of hassle—you don't have to sweat over the plotting and planning of a vacation schedule. Escorted tours are particularly convenient for people with limited mobility. They can also be a great way to make new friends.

On the downside, an escorted tour often requires a big deposit upfront, and lodging and dining choices are predetermined. You'll get little opportunity for serendipitous interactions with locals. The tours can be jam-packed with activities, leaving little room for individual sightseeing, whim, or adventure—plus they also often focus only on the heavily touristed sites, so you miss out on the lesser-known gems.

Before you invest in an escorted tour, ask about the **cancellation policy:** Is a deposit required? Can they cancel the trip if they don't get enough people? Do you get a refund if they cancel? If *you* cancel? How late can you cancel if you are unable to go? When do you pay in full? *Note:* If you choose an escorted tour, think strongly about purchasing trip-cancellation insurance, especially if the tour operator asks you to pay up front. See the section on "Travel Insurance," p. 32.

You'll also want to get a complete **schedule** of the trip to find out how much sightseeing is planned each day and whether enough time has been allotted for relaxing or wandering solo.

The **size** of the group is also important to know upfront. Generally, the smaller the group, the more flexible the itinerary, and the less time you'll spend waiting for people to get on and off the bus. Find out the **demographics** of the group as well. What is the age range? What is the gender breakdown? Is this mostly a trip for couples or singles?

Discuss what is included in the **price.** You may have to pay for transportation to and from the airport. A box lunch may be included in an excursion, but drinks might cost extra. Tips may not be included. Find out if you will be charged if you decide to opt out of certain activities or meals.

Before you invest in a package tour, get some answers. Ask about the **accommodations choices** and prices for each. Then look up the hotels' reviews in a Frommer's guide and check their rates online for your specific dates of travel. You'll also want to find out what **type of room** you get. If you need a certain type of room, ask for it; don't take whatever is thrown your way. Request a nonsmoking room, a quiet room, a room with a view, or whatever you fancy.

Finally, if you plan to travel alone, you'll need to know if a **single supplement** will be charged and if the company can match you up with a roommate.

14 Special-Interest Trips

Andalusia is one of the best destinations in Europe for enjoying the outdoors. Lounging on the beach tops the list of activities for most travelers, but there's a lot more to do. The province's mountains lure thousands of mountaineers and hikers, and fishing and hunting are long-standing Iberian obsessions. Watersports ranging from sailing to windsurfing are prime summer attractions.

In addition to sports and adventures, we've also detailed some of the best educational and cultural programs below.

BIKING

The leading U.S.-based outfitter is **Easy Rider Tours,** P.O. Box 228, Newburyport, MA 01950 (© **800/ 488-8332** or 978/463-6955; www. easyridertours.com). Their tours average between 48 and 81km (30–50 miles) a day.

One of the most intriguing bike tours is the *ruta de vino* (the wine route) in La Rioja country.

In England, the **Cyclists' Touring Club,** 69 Meadrow, Godalming, Surrey GU7 3HS, UK (© **0870/873-0060;** www.ctc.org.uk), charges £31

($51) a year for membership; part of the fee provides for information and suggested cycling routes through Spain, including Andalusia.

BIRDING

The Iberian Peninsula lies directly across migration routes of species that travel with the seasons between Africa and Europe. Some of the most comprehensive studies on these migratory patterns are conducted by Spain's **Centro de Migración de Aves,** SEO/BirdLife, Calle Melquiades Biencinto 34, 28053 Madrid (✆ **91-434-09-10;** www.seo.org). Based at a rustic outpost near Gibraltar, their summer work camps and field projects appeal to participants who want to identify, catalog, and "ring" (mark with an identifying leg band) some of the millions of birds that nest on Spanish soil every year. Participants are expected to pay for their "tuition," room, and board, but can often use the experience toward university credit, especially in such fields as zoology and ecology.

BOTANICAL TOURS

Travel specialist **Cox & Kings Travel,** Gordon House, 10 GreenCoat Place, London SW1P 1PH, UK (✆ **020/7873-5000;** www.coxandkings.co.uk), leads week-long treks that take in Granada, Seville, and Ronda, exploring their Moorish and Renaissance gardens and some of Southern Spain's architectural highlights. The tour is called "The Gardens of Andalusia."

GOLF

In recent decades, thousands of British retirees have settled in Spain, and their presence has sparked the development of dozens of new golf courses. More than a third of the country's approximately 160 courses lie within its southern tier, within a short drive of the Costa del Sol. In fact, Spain's two most talked-about golf courses are both in southern Spain. **Valderrama,**

11310 Sotogrande, Cádiz (✆ **95-679-12-00;** www.valderrama.com), is on the western tip of the Costa del Sol, a Robert Trent Jones–designed course carved out of an oak plantation in the 1980s. Hyatt's new **La Manga Club,** 30395 Los Belones, Cartagena (✆ **98-633-12-34**), is on the Costa Blanca near Murcia and is the site of three golf courses, one of which was recently remodeled by Arnold Palmer.

Packages that include guaranteed playing time on some of the country's finest courses, as well as airfare and accommodations, can be arranged through such firms as **Golf International** (✆ **800/833-1389** or 212/986-9176 in the U.S.; www.golfinternational.com), **Spanish Golf Adventures** (✆ **800/772-6465** in the U.S. and Canada; www.spanishgolf.com), **PGA Travel** (✆ **888/439-1831** in the U.S.; www.pgatravel.com), and **Comtours** (✆ **800/248-1331** in the U.S.; www.comtours.com).

HIKING & WALKING

To venture into the more rugged countryside of Andalusia's valley of the Guadalquivir, contact **Ramblers Holidays,** P.O. Box 43, Welwyn Garden AL8 6PQ, UK (✆ **01707/331-133;** www.ramblersholidays.co.uk). **Waymark Holidays,** 44 Windsor Rd., Slough SL1 2EJ, UK (✆ **01753/516-477;** www.waymarkholidays.co.uk), features tours of the Pueblos Blancos (white villages) of Andalusia, highlighting the limestone crags of the Grazalema National Park and the sandstone areas to the southwest of Ronda. In this part of Spain, which is on the major migratory pathway between Europe and Africa, some 250 species of birds can be spotted.

HORSEBACK RIDING

Andalusians are some of the world's greatest equestrians. **Al-Hazan Horse Riding** in Castellar de la Frontera (✆ **610-329-146**) offers the best tours. Its big feature is a 6-day, 7-night tour on horseback from Grazalema to Tarifa on the coast. You take bridle paths through the heart of the sierra, stopping off to dine in typical local restaurants or to stay at regional inns.

Rustic Blue, Barrio la Ermita, Bubión, Granada (© **958-76-33-81**), promotes walking, horseback riding, and other activities in Las Alpujarras, the southern slopes of the Sierra Nevada. Some of its horseback riding trails are among the most dramatic in Europe—one, in particular, taking you to Trevélez, at 1,550m (1,804 ft.), the highest village in Spain. You ride through fields of almonds, figs, and vineyards, with panoramic views in all directions. This is one of the friendliest and best outfitters we have found for specialized tours of the area.

SAILING

Alventus, an agency based in Seville, offers weeklong cruises along the coast of Andalusia and the Algarve in Portugal. Its three-masted, 13m (42-ft.) sailing yacht departs from the Andalusian port of Huelva. For reservations and information, contact Alventus at Calle Huelva 6, 41004 Sevilla (© **95-421-00-62;** www.alventus.com).

15 Getting Around

BY CAR

A car offers the greatest flexibility while you're touring, even if you're just doing day trips from Madrid. Don't, however, plan to drive in Seville or Granada for city sightseeing; it's too congested. Theoretically, rush hour is Monday through Saturday from 8 to 10am, 1 to 2pm, and 4 to 6pm. In reality, it's always busy.

CAR RENTALS Many of North America's biggest car-rental companies, including Avis, Budget, and Hertz, maintain offices throughout Andalusia. Although several Spanish car-rental companies exist, we've gotten lots of letters from readers telling us they've had a hard time resolving billing irregularities and insurance claims, so you might want to stick with the U.S.-based rental firms.

Note that tax on car rentals is a whopping 15%, so don't forget to factor that into your travel budget. Usually, prepaid rates do not include taxes, which will be collected at the rental kiosk itself. Be sure to ask explicitly what's included when you're quoted a rate.

Avis (© **800/331-1212;** www.avis.com) maintains about 100 branches throughout Spain, including in Cádiz, Granada, Seville, and Málaga. If you reserve and pay your rental by telephone at least 2 weeks before your departure from North America, you'll qualify for the company's best rate, with unlimited kilometers included. You can usually get competitive rates from **Hertz** (© **800/654-3131;** www.hertz.com) and **Budget** (© **800/472-3325;** www.budget.com); it always pays to comparison shop. Budget doesn't have a drop-off charge if you pick up in one Spanish city and return to another. All three companies require that drivers be at least 21 years of age and, in some cases, not older than 72. To be able to rent a car, you must have a passport and a valid driver's license; you must also have a valid credit card or a prepaid voucher. An international driver's license is not essential, but you might want to present it if you have one; it's available from any North American office of the American Automobile Association (AAA).

An auto supplier that might not automatically have come to mind is **Kemwel** (© **800/678-0678**), an auto rental broker that accumulates into one database the availability of rental cars in markets across Europe, including

Andalusia. Originally established in 1908, and now operating in close conjunction with its sister company, **Auto Europe** (© **800/223-5555**), it offers convenient and pre-paid access to thousands of cars, from a variety of reputable car rental outfits throughout Europe, sometimes at rates a bit more favorable than those you might have gotten if you had gone through the hassle of contacting those companies directly. Car rentals are reserved and pre-paid, in dollars, prior to your departure for Andalusia, thereby avoiding the confusion about unfavorable currency conversions and government tax add-ons that you might have discovered after your return home. You're given the option at the time of your booking as to whether or not you want to include collision-damage and other forms of insurance. Most car rentals can be picked up at either the airport or in the downtown offices of cities throughout Spain, and there's usually no penalty for one-way rentals.

Many packages include airfare, accommodations, and a rental car with unlimited mileage. Compare these prices with the cost of booking airline tickets and renting a car separately to see if these offers are good deals. Internet resources can make it easier to comparison shop. **Microsoft Expedia** (www.expedia.com) and **Travelocity** (www.travelocity.com) help you compare prices and locate car-rental bargains from various companies nationwide. They will even make your reservation for you once you've found the best deal. See "Planning Your Trip Online," earlier in this chapter, for tips.

DRIVING RULES Spaniards drive on the right side of the road. Drivers should pass on the left; local drivers sound their horns when passing another car and flash their lights at you if you're driving slowly (slowly for high-speed Spain) in the left lane. Autos coming from the right have the right-of-way.

Spain's express highways are known as *autopistas,* which charge a toll, and *autovías,* which don't. To exit in Spain, follow the *salida* (exit) sign, except in Catalonia, where the word to exit is *sortida.* On most express highways, the speed limit is 120kmph (75 mph). On other roads, speed limits range from 90kmph (56 mph) to 100kmph (62 mph). You will see many drivers far exceeding these limits.

The greatest number of accidents in Spain is recorded along the notorious Costa del Sol highway, the Carretera de Cádiz.

If you must drive through a Spanish city, try to avoid morning and evening rush hours. Never park your car facing oncoming traffic, as that is against the law. If you are fined by the highway patrol *(Guardia Civil de Tráfico),* you must pay on the spot. Penalties for drinking and driving are very stiff.

MAPS For one of the best overviews of the Iberian Peninsula (Spain and Portugal), get a copy of Michelin map number 990 (for a folding version) or number 460 for the same map in a spiral-bound version. For more detailed looks at Spain, Michelin has a series of six maps (nos. 441–446), showing specific regions, complete with many minor roads.

For extensive touring, purchase *Mapas de Carreteras—España y Portugal,* published by Almax Editores and available at most leading bookstores in Spain. This cartographic compendium of Spain provides an overview of the country and includes road and street maps of some of its major cities as well.

The **American Automobile Association** (© **800/222-4357;** fax 407/ 444-4300; www.aaa.com) publishes a regional map of Spain that's available free to members at most AAA offices in the United States. Also available free to members is a guide of approximately 60 pages, *Motoring in Europe,* that gives helpful information about road signs and speed limits, as well as insurance regulations and other relevant matters. Incidentally, the AAA is associated with the **Real Automóvil Club de España,** José Abascal 10, Madrid 28003 (© **91-594-74-00**). This organization can supply helpful information about road conditions in Spain, including tourist and travel data. It will also provide limited road service, in an emergency, if your car breaks down.

BREAKDOWNS   These can be a serious problem. If you're driving a Spanish-made vehicle, you'll probably be able to find spare parts, if needed. But if you have a foreign-made vehicle, you may be stranded. Have the car checked out before setting out on a long trek through Andalusia. On a major motorway you'll find strategically placed emergency phone boxes. On secondary roads, call for help by asking the operator to locate the nearest Guardia Civil, which will put you in touch with a garage that can tow you to a repair shop.

As noted above, the Spanish affiliate of AAA can provide limited assistance in the event of a breakdown.

BY PLANE
Two affiliated airlines operate within Spain: **Iberia** and its smaller cousin, **Aviaco.** (For reservations on either of these airlines, call © **800/772-4642.**) By European standards, domestic flights within Spain are relatively inexpensive, and considering the vast distances within the country, flying between distant points sometimes makes sense.

If you plan to travel to a number of cities and regions, **Iberia's "Visit Spain" ticket** can be a good deal. Sold only in conjunction with a transatlantic ticket and valid for any airport within Spain and the Canary or Balearic Islands, it requires that you choose up to four different cities in advance, in the order you'll visit them—perhaps

Seville, Cádiz, Granada, and Málaga. Restrictions forbid flying immediately back to the city of departure, instead encouraging far-flung visits to widely scattered regions of the peninsula. Only one change within the preset itinerary is permitted once the ticket is issued. The dates and departure times of the actual flights, however, can be determined or changed without penalty once you arrive in Spain. The actual costs depend on what kind of ticket you were issued—consult the folks at Iberia if you're interested in a multi-stopover ticket and see what the best deal is at the time of your visit. Children under 2 travel for 10% of the adult fare, and children 2 to 11 travel for 50% of the adult fare. The ticket is valid for up to 60 days after your initial transatlantic arrival in Spain.

BY TRAIN
Spain is crisscrossed with a comprehensive network of rail lines. Hundreds of trains depart every day for points around the country, including the fast TALGO and the newer, faster AVE trains, which reduced rail time between Madrid and Seville to only 2½ hours.

If you plan to travel a great deal on the European railroads, it's worth buying a copy of the *Thomas Cook Timetable of European Passenger Railroads.* It's available exclusively in North America from **Forsyth Travel Library,** 44 S. Broadway, White Plains, NY 10601 (© **800/FORSYTH;** www.forsyth.com), at a cost of $29, plus $4.95 postage priority airmail in the United States plus $2 for shipments to Canada.

The most economical way to travel in Andalusia is on the **Spanish State Railways (RENFE),** the national railway of Spain. Most main long-distance connections are served with night express trains having first- and second-class seats as well as beds and bunks. There are also comfortable high-speed daytime trains of the TALGO, TER, and Electrotren types. There is a general fare for these trains; bunks, beds, and certain superior-quality trains cost extra. Nevertheless, the Spanish railway is one of the most economical in Europe; in most cases, this is the best way to go.

SPANISH RAIL PASSES   RENFE offers several discounted rail passes. You must buy these passes in the United States prior to your departure. For more information, consult a travel agent or **Rail Europe** (© **800/4-EURAIL;** www.raileurope.com).

The **Iberic Railpass,** good for both Spain and Portugal, offers any 3 days of unlimited first-class train travel in a 2-month period for $249 (children 4–11 pay half-fare on any of these discount passes). An **Iberic Saverpass,** again including both Spain and Portugal, offers any 3 to 10 days unlimited, first-class train travel in a 2-month period starting at $219, and $30 for each additional day. A **Spain Flexipass** offers any 3 to 10 days unlimited train travel in a 2-month period. Three days in 2 months costs $225 in first class or $175 in second class. The pass can be extended to as much as any 10 days in 2 months, which costs $470 in first class or $385 in second class.

EURAILPASSES   In-the-know travelers take advantage of one of Europe's greatest travel bargains: the **Eurailpass,** which permits unlimited first-class rail travel in any country in western Europe except the British Isles (good in Ireland). Passes are sold only in North America and are nontransferable. A Eurailpass costs $588 for 15 days, $762 for 21 days, $946 for 1 month, $1,338 for 2 months, and $1,654 for 3 months. Children 3 and under travel free providing they don't occupy a seat (otherwise they're charged half-fare); children 4 to 11 are charged half-fare.

You can reduce costs with this means of transport by sharing your trip with another adult, who will receive a 50% discount on each of the above-mentioned fares.

Note: You can add what Europass refers to as an "associate country" (Austria, Benelux, Greece, or Portugal) to the reach of your Europass by paying a surcharge.

If you're under 26, you can purchase a **Eurail Youthpass,** entitling you to unlimited second-class travel for $414 for 15 days, $534 for 21 days, $664 for 1 month, $938 for 2 months, and $1,160 for 3 months. Seat reservations are required on some trains. Many of the trains have *couchettes* (sleeping cars), which cost extra. Obviously, the 2- or 3-month traveler gets the greatest economic advantages; the Eurailpass is ideal for such extensive trips. With the pass you can visit all of Spain's major sights, from Barcelona to Seville. Eurailpass holders are entitled to considerable reductions on certain buses and ferries as well.

If you'll be traveling for 2 weeks or a month, think carefully before you buy a pass. To get full advantage of a pass for 15 days or a month, you'll have to spend a great deal of time on the train.

⌒**Tips** **Have a Seat**

Remember that a train ticket does not guarantee you a seat; it merely gets you transportation from one place to another. On crowded trains and during busy times, you'll have to make a **seat reservation** (and pay for the privilege) if you want to be sure of sitting somewhere other than on top of your luggage. Seat reservations cost 8€ ($9.20) per person.

Riding the Rails in Style

Al Andalús Expreso (or simply Al Andalús) is a restored vintage train that travels through some of Andalusia's most historic destinations. The train retains an atmosphere and level of service you just don't see very often these days. The passenger and dining cars boast panels of inlaid marquetry, hardwoods, brass fittings, and etched glass that could well be found in the Edwardian parlor of a private mansion; beneath the antique veneers, state-of-the-art engineering maintains comfortably high speeds. The train offers fine dining and such amenities as individual showers.

Al Andalús consists of 13 carriages manufactured in Britain, Spain, or France between 1929 and 1930. These carriages were collected and restored by railway historians at RENFE. Included are two restaurant cars, a games and lounge car, a bar car where live piano music and evening flamenco dances are presented, five sleeping carriages, and two shower cars. All carriages (except the shower cars) are air-conditioned and heated.

For reservations, contact your travel agent. For additional brochures and information, contact **Marketing Ahead,** 381 Park Ave. S., Suite 718, New York, NY 10016 (© **800/223-1356** or 212/686-9213; www.marketing ahead.com).

Eurail Selectpass offers unlimited travel on the national rail networks of any three, four, or five bordering countries out of the 17 Eurail nations, including Spain, linked by train or ship. Two or more passengers can travel together for big discounts, getting 5, 6, 8, 10, or 15 days of rail travel within any 2-month period on the national rail networks of any three, four, or five adjoining Eurail countries linked by train or ship. A sample fare: For 5 days in 2 months you pay $356 for three countries.

Eurail Flexipass allows you to visit Europe, including Spain, with more flexibility. It's valid in first class and offers the same privileges as the Eurailpass. However, it provides a number of individual travel days you can use over a longer period of consecutive days. That makes it possible to stay in one city for a while without losing days of rail travel. There are two passes: 10 days of travel in 2 months

for $694, and 15 days of travel in 2 months for $914.

With many of the same qualifications and restrictions as the Flexipass is a **Eurail Youth Flexipass.** Sold only to travelers under 26, it allows 10 days of travel within 2 months for $488, and 15 days of travel within 2 months for $642.

WHERE TO BUY RAIL PASSES
Travel agents in all towns and railway agents in major North American cities sell all these tickets, but the biggest supplier is **Rail Europe** (© **800/848-7245;** www.raileurope.com), which can also give you informational brochures.

Many different rail passes are available in the United Kingdom for travel in Britain and continental Europe. Stop in at the **International Rail Centre,** Victoria Station, London SW1V 1JY (© **0870/5848-848** in the U.K.). Some of the most popular passes, including Inter-Rail and Euro

Youth, are offered only to travelers under 26 years of age; these allow unlimited second-class travel through most European countries.

BY BUS

Bus service in southern Spain is extensive, low priced, and comfortable enough for short distances. You'll rarely encounter a bus terminal. The station might be a cafe, a bar, the street in front of a hotel, or simply a spot at an intersection.

A bus may be the cheapest mode of transportation, but it's not really the best option for distances of more than 161km (100 miles). On long hauls, buses are often uncomfortable. Another major drawback is the lack of toilet facilities, although rest stops are frequent. It's best for 1-day excursions outside a major tourist center such as Seville. In the rural areas of the country, bus networks are more extensive than the railway system; they go virtually everywhere, connecting every village. In general, a bus ride between two major cities in Spain, such as from Córdoba to Seville, is about two-thirds the price of a train ride and a few hours faster. For bus information, contact ALSA (© **91-327-05-40;** www.ALSA.es).

16 Tips on Accommodations

From castles converted into hotels to modern high-rise resorts overlooking the Mediterranean, Andalusia has some of the most varied hotel accommodations in the world—with equally varied prices. Accommodations are broadly classified as follows:

ONE- TO FIVE-STAR HOTELS

The Spanish government rates hotels by according them stars. A five-star hotel is truly deluxe, with deluxe prices; a one-star hotel is the most modest accommodation officially recognized as a hotel by the government. A four-star hotel offers first-class accommodations; a three-star hotel is moderately priced; and a one- or two-star hotel is inexpensive. The government grants stars based on such amenities as elevators, private bathrooms, and air-conditioning. If a hotel is classified as a *residencia,* it means that it serves breakfast (usually) but no other meals.

HOSTALS

Not to be confused with a hostel for students, an hostal is a modest hotel without services, where you can save money by carrying your own bags and the like. You'll know it's an hostal if a small S follows the capital letter H on the blue plaque by the door. An hostal with three stars is about the equivalent of a hotel with two stars.

PENSIONS

These boardinghouses are among the least expensive accommodations, but you're required to take either full board (three meals) or half-board, which is breakfast plus lunch or dinner.

CASAS HUESPEDES & FONDAS

These are the cheapest places in Andalusia and can be recognized by the light-blue plaques at the door displaying CH and F, respectively. They are invariably basic but respectable establishments.

PARADORS

The Spanish government runs a series of unique state-owned inns called paradors (*paradores* in Spanish), which are found in parts of Andalusia. Deserted castles, monasteries, palaces, and other buildings have been taken over and converted into hotels. Today these paradors are documented in a booklet called *Visiting the Paradors,* available at Spanish tourist offices (see "Visitor Information," earlier in this chapter).

At great expense, modern bathrooms, steam heat, and the like have been added to these buildings, yet classic Andalusian architecture, where it existed, has been retained. Establishments are often furnished with antiques or at least good reproductions and decorative objects typical of the country.

Meals are also served in these government-owned inns. Usually, typical dishes of the region are featured. Paradors are likely to be overcrowded in the summer months, so advance reservations, arranged through any travel agent, are wise.

In addition, the government runs *refugios* (refuges), mostly in remote areas, attracting hunters, fishermen, and mountain climbers.

The central office of paradors is **Paradores de España,** Requeña 3, 28013 Madrid (© **91-516-66-66;** www.parador.es). The U.S. representative for the Paradores of Spain is **Marketing Ahead,** 381 Park Ave. S., New York, NY 10016 (© **800/223-1356** or 212/686-9213). Travel agents can also arrange reservations.

RENTING A HOUSE OR APARTMENT

If you rent a home or an apartment, you can save money on accommodations and dining and still take daily trips to see the surrounding area.

Apartments in Andalusia generally fall into two different categories: hotel *apartamentos* and *residencia apartamentos.* The hotel apartments have full facilities, with chamber service, equipped kitchenettes, and often restaurants and bars. The residencia apartments, also called *apartamentos turísticos,* are fully furnished with kitchenettes but lack the facilities of the hotel complexes. They are cheaper, however.

One rental company to try is **Hometours International** (© **866/ 367-4668** or 865/690-8484), which mainly handles properties in Andalusia. Call them and they'll send you a 40-page color catalog with descriptions and pictures for $5 to cover postage and handling. Units are rented for a minimum of 7 days.

Another agency is **ILC** (International Lodging Corporation; © **800/ SPAIN-44** or 212/228-2004; www. ilcweb.com), which rents privately owned apartments, houses, and villas, for a week or more. It also offers access to suites in well-known hotels for stays of a week or longer, sometimes at bargain rates. Rental units, regardless of their size, usually contain a kitchen. The company's listings cover accommodations in Seville and Granada.

17 Recommended Books

ECONOMIC, POLITICAL & SOCIAL HISTORY

Historically, Spain's golden age lasted from the late 15th to the early 17th century, a period when the country reached the height of its prestige and influence. This era is well surveyed in J. H. Elliot's *Imperial Spain 1469-1716* (New American Library).

If you like more contemporary history, read John Hooper's *The Spaniards* (Penguin). Hooper provides insight into the events of the post-Franco era,

when the country came to grips with democracy after years of fascism.

THE ARTS

The Moors contributed much to Spanish culture, leaving Spain with a distinct legacy that is documented in Titus Burckhardt's *Moorish Culture in Spain* (McGraw-Hill).

Spain's most famous artist was Málaga-born Pablo Picasso. The most controversial book about the late painter is *Picasso, Creator and*

Destroyer by Arianna Stassinopoulos Huffington (Simon & Schuster).

Andalusia (Evergreen Series), by Eliane Faure and Christian Sappa, is a great picture book on the province, covering major cities such as Seville along with popular customs and old traditions. *Andalusia (Art & Architecture)*, by Brigitte Hintzen-Bohlen, is good for an armchair tour, with drawings of architecture, along with brief narrative descriptions of the people and places of the province.

FICTION & BIOGRAPHY

Denounced by some as superficial, James A. Michener's *Iberia* (Random House) remains the classic travel log on Spain.

The latest biography on one of the 20th century's most durable dictators is *Franco: A Concise Biography,* which was released in the spring of 2002.

Gabrielle Ashford Hodges documents with great flair the Orwellian repression and widespread corruption that marked the notorious regime of this "deeply flawed" politician.

The most famous Spanish novel is *Don Quixote* by Miguel de Cervantes. Readily available everywhere, it deals with the conflict between the ideal and the real in human nature. Nicholas Wollaston's *Tilting at Don Quixote* (André Deutsch Publishers) takes us on a panoramic tour of Quixote's Spain, unfolding as a backdrop against Wollaston's own personal life journey. The writer has great sympathy for the half-crazed don and his illusions.

Driving Over Lemons: An Optimist in Andalucia, by Chris Stewart, is a charming book, telling the story of an English sheep shearer, Chris Stewart, who buys an isolated farmhouse in the mountains outside of Granada.

FAST FACTS: Spain

Business Hours Banks are open Monday to Friday 9:30am to 2pm and Saturday from 9:30am to 1pm. Most offices are open Monday to Friday 9am to 5 or 5:30pm; the longtime practice of early closings in summer seems to be dying out. In restaurants, lunch is usually from 1 to 4pm and dinner 9 to 11:30pm or midnight. There are no set rules for the opening of bars and taverns; many open at 8am, others at noon; most stay open until 1:30am or later. Major stores are open Monday to Saturday 9:30am to 8pm; smaller establishments, however, often take a siesta, doing business from 9:30am to 1:30pm and 4:30 to 8pm. Hours can vary from store to store.

Climate See "When to Go," earlier in this chapter.

Currency See "Money," earlier in this chapter.

Customs See "Visitor Information," earlier in this chapter.

Driving Rules See "Getting Around," earlier in this chapter.

Drugstores To find an open pharmacy outside normal business hours, check the list of stores posted on the door of any drugstore. The law requires drugstores to operate on a rotating system of hours so that there's always a drugstore open somewhere, even Sunday at midnight.

Electricity Most hotels have 220 volts AC (50 cycles). Some older places have 110 or 125 volts AC. Carry your adapter with you, and always check at your hotel desk before plugging in any electrical appliance. It's best to travel with battery-operated equipment or just buy a new hair dryer.

Embassies & Consulates If you lose your passport, fall seriously ill, get into legal trouble, or have some other serious problem, your embassy or consulate can help. But, regrettably, it's in Madrid. These are the Madrid addresses and hours: The **United States Embassy,** Calle Serrano 75 (© **91-587-22-00;** Metro: Núñez de Balboa), is open Monday through Friday from 9am to 6pm. The **Canadian Embassy,** Núñez de Balboa 35 (© **91-423-32-50;** Metro: Velázquez), is open Monday through Friday from 8:30am to 5:30pm. The **British Embassy,** Calle Fernando el Santo 16 (© **91-319-02-00;** Metro: Colón), is open Monday through Friday from 9am to 1:30pm and 3 to 6pm. The **Republic of Ireland** has an embassy at Paseo Castellana 46 (© **91-436-40-93;** Metro: Serrano); it's open Monday through Friday from 9am to 2pm. The **Australian Embassy,** Plaza Diego de Ordas 3, Edificio Santa Engracia 120 (© **91-441-60-25;** Metro: Ríos Rosas), is open Monday to Thursday 8:30am to 5pm and Friday 8:30am to 2:15pm. Citizens of **New Zealand** have an embassy at Plaza de la Lealtad 2 (© **91-523-02-26;** Metro: Banco de España); it's open Monday to Friday 9am to 1:30pm and 2:30 to 5:30pm.

Emergencies The national emergency number for Spain is © **006.**

Etiquette In Franco's day, many visitors would be arrested for the skimpy, revealing wear worn around the city streets of Andalusia today. Nonetheless, it is considered extremely rude for men to go bare-chested except at the beach or at poolside. Spaniards and church officials do object to your visiting churches and cathedrals if scantily clad even on the hottest day of summer. Casual dress is acceptable, but one should "cover up" as much skin as possible.

In spite of what you've heard in days of yore, when Spaniards showed up for appointments 2 or 3 hours late, most nationals now show up on time as they do in the rest of the E.U. countries. It's always wise for men to wear a suit for business meetings. Spanish speakers should address strangers with the formal *usted* instead of the more familiar *tú.*

Holidays See "Calendar of Events," earlier in this chapter.

Information See "Visitor Information," earlier in this chapter.

Language The official language in Spain is Castilian (or *Castellano*). Andalusians speak it with a southern accent. In shops, restaurants, hotels, and nightclubs catering to visitors, English is commonly spoken.

The best phrase book is *Spanish for Travellers* by Berlitz; it has a menu supplement and a 12,500-word glossary of both English and Spanish.

Liquor Laws The legal drinking age is 18. Bars, taverns, and cafeterias usually open at 8am, and many serve alcohol to 1:30am or later. Generally, you can purchase alcoholic beverages in almost any market.

Lost & Found Be sure to tell all of your credit card companies the minute you discover your wallet has been lost or stolen, and file a report at the nearest police precinct. Your credit card company or insurer may require a police report number or a record of the loss. Most credit card companies have an emergency toll-free number to call if your card is lost or stolen; they may be able to wire you a cash advance immediately or deliver an emergency credit card in a day or two. **Visa's** U.S. emergency number in Spain is © **90-099-11-24. American Express** cardholders and traveler's check holders should call ℂ **90-547-408-70. MasterCard** card-holders should call ℂ **90-097-12-31.**

If you've lost all forms of photo ID call your airline and explain the situation; they might allow you to board the plane if you have a copy of your passport or birth certificate and a copy of the police report you've filed.

Mail Airmail letters to the United States and Canada cost .75€ (85¢) up to 15 grams, and letters to Britain or other E.U. countries cost .50€ (60¢) up to 20 grams; letters within Spain cost .25€ (30¢). Postcards have the same rates as letters. Allow about 8 days for delivery to North America, generally less to the United Kingdom; in some cases, letters take 2 weeks to reach North America. Rates change frequently, so check at your local hotel before mailing anything. As for surface mail to North America, forget it. Chances are you'll be home long before your letter arrives.

Passports **For Residents of the United States:** Whether you're applying in person or by mail, you can download passport applications from the U.S. State Department website at **http://travel.state.gov/passport_services. html**. To find your regional passport office, either check the U.S. State Department website or call the **National Passport Information Center** toll-free number (ℂ **877/487-2778**) for automated information.

For Residents of Canada: Passport applications are available at travel agencies throughout Canada or from the central **Passport Office,** Department of Foreign Affairs and International Trade, Ottawa, ON K1A 0G3 (ℂ **800/567-6868;** www.ppt.gc.ca).

For Residents of the United Kingdom: To pick up an application for a standard 10-year passport (5-year passport for children under 16), visit your nearest passport office, major post office, or travel agency or contact the **United Kingdom Passport Service** at ℂ **0870/521-0410** or search its website at www.ukpa.gov.uk.

For Residents of Ireland: You can apply for a 10-year passport at the **Passport Office,** Setanta Centre, Molesworth Street, Dublin 2 (ℂ **01/671-1633;** www.irlgov.ie/iveagh). Those under age 18 and over 65 must apply for a €12 ($14) 3-year passport. You can also apply at 1A South Mall, Cork (ℂ **021/272-525**), or at most main post offices.

For Residents of Australia: You can pick up an application from your local post office or any branch of Passports Australia, but you must schedule an interview at the passport office to present your application materials. Call the **Australian Passport Information Service** at ℂ **131-232,** or visit the government website at www.passports.gov.au.

For Residents of New Zealand: You can pick up a passport application at any New Zealand Passports Office or download it from their website. Contact the **Passports Office** at ℂ **0800/225-050** in New Zealand, or 04/474-8100, or log on to www.passports.govt.nz.

Police The national emergency number is ℂ **006** throughout Spain.

Restrooms In Andalusia they're called *aseos* and *servicios* or simply *lavabos* and labeled *caballeros* for men and *damas* or *señoras* for women. If you can't find any, go into a bar, but you should order something.

Safety See "Health & Safety," earlier in this chapter.

Taxes The internal sales tax (known in Spain as *IVA*) ranges between 7% and 33%, depending on the commodity being sold. Food, wine, and basic necessities are taxed at 7%; most goods and services (including car rentals) at 13%; luxury items (jewelry, all tobacco, imported liquors) at 33%; and hotels at 7%.

If you are not a European Union resident and make purchases in Spain worth more than 90€, you can get a tax refund. To get this refund, you must complete three copies of a form that the store will give you, detailing the nature of your purchase and its value. Citizens of non-E.U. countries show the purchase and the form to the Spanish Customs Office. The shop is supposed to refund the amount due you. Inquire at the time of purchase how they will do so and discuss in what currency your refund will arrive.

Telephones If you don't speak Spanish, you'll find it easier to telephone from your hotel, but remember that this is often very expensive because hotels impose a surcharge on every operator-assisted call. In some cases it can be as high as 40% or more. On the street, phone booths (known as *cabinas*) have dialing instructions in English; you can make local calls by inserting a .25€ (30¢) coin for 3 minutes.

For directory assistance: Dial ✆ **1003** in Spain.

For operator assistance: If you need operator assistance in making an international call, dial ✆ **025**.

Toll-free numbers: Numbers beginning with **900** in Spain are toll-free, but calling an 800 number in the States from Spain is not toll-free. In fact, it costs the same as an overseas call.

In Andalusia many smaller establishments, especially bars, discos, and a few informal restaurants, don't have phones. Further, many summer-only bars and discos secure a phone for the season only, then get a new number the next season. Many attractions, such as small churches or even minor museums, have no staff to receive inquiries from the public.

In 1998, all telephone numbers in Spain changed to a nine-digit system instead of the six- or seven-digit method used previously. Each number is now preceded by its provincial code for local, national, and international calls. For example, when calling to Seville from Seville or another province within Spain, telephone customers must dial 95-000-00-00.

When in Spain, the access number for an **AT&T** calling card is ✆ **800/CALL-ATT**. The access number for **Sprint** is ✆ **800/888-0013**.

More information is also available on the Telefónica website at www.telefonica.es.

To call Spain from another country: Dial the international access code (U.S. or Canada 011, U.K., Ireland, or New Zealand 00, Australia 0011), followed by the country code 34, and then the city code and then the local number. If you're calling Spain from the United States the whole number you'd dial would be 011-34-93-000-0000.

To make international calls from Spain: Dial 00 and then the country code (U.S. and Canada 1, U.K. 44, Ireland 353, Australia 61, New Zealand 64). Next dial the area code and number. For example, if you wanted to call the British Embassy in Washington, D.C., you would dial 00-1-202-588-7800.

Time Spain is 6 hours ahead of Eastern Standard Time in the United States. Daylight saving time is in effect from the last Sunday in March to the last Sunday in September.

Tipping Don't overtip. The government requires restaurants and hotels to include their service charges—usually 15% of the bill. However, that doesn't mean you should skip out of a place without dispensing an extra euro or two. Here are some guidelines:

Your hotel porter should get .60€ (70¢) per bag. Maids should be given .85€ ($1) per day, more if you're generous. Tip doormen .75€ (85¢) for assisting with baggage and .50€ (60¢) for calling a cab. In top-ranking hotels the concierge will often submit a separate bill, showing charges for newspapers and other services; if he or she has been particularly helpful, tip extra. For cab drivers, add about 10% to the fare as shown on the meter. At airports, such as Barajas in Madrid and major terminals, the porter who handles your luggage will present you with a fixed-charge bill.

Service is included in restaurant bills. But it is the custom to tip extra—in fact, the waiter will expect a tip. That tip is left at your discretion. Some Spanish diners leave nothing if the service was outright bad. Other more generous diners tip as much as 5% to 10% if the service was good.

Barbers and hairdressers expect a 10% to 15% tip. Tour guides expect 2€ ($2.30), although a tip is not mandatory. Theater and bullfight ushers get from .50€ (60¢).

4

Settling into Seville

Sometimes a city becomes famous simply for its beauty and romantic aura. Seville (Sevilla in Spanish), the capital of Andalusia, is such a place. Despite its sultry summer heat and problems, such as high unemployment and street crime, it remains one of Spain's most charming cities. If you you're only going to see a few Spanish cities in your lifetime, make one of them Seville.

All the images associated with Andalusia—orange trees, mantillas, lovesick toreros, flower-filled patios, and castanet-rattling gypsies—come

alive in Seville. But this is no mere tourist city; it's also a substantial river port, and it possesses some of the most important artistic works and architectural monuments in Spain.

Unlike other Spanish cities, Seville fared rather well under most of its conquerors—the Romans, Arabs, and Christians. Rulers from Pedro the Cruel to Ferdinand and Isabella held court here. When Spain entered its 16th-century golden age, Seville funneled gold from the New World into the rest of the country, and Columbus docked here after his journey to America.

1 Orientation

GETTING THERE

BY PLANE   Iberia (© **800/772-4642** in the U.S., or 90-240-05-00 toll free in Spain) flies several times a day between Madrid (and elsewhere via Madrid) and Seville's Aeropuerto San Pablo, Calle Almirante Lobo (© **95-444-90-23**). It also flies several times a week to and from Alicante, Grand Canary Island, Lisbon, Barcelona, Palma de Majorca, Tenerife, Santiago de Compostela, and (once a week) Zaragoza. The airport lies about 9.6km (6 miles) from the center of the city, along the highway leading to Carmona. A bus run by **Amarillos Tour S.A.** (© **902-21-03-17**), meets all incoming flights and transports you into the center of Seville for 2.30€ ($2.75). For airport information, call © **95-444-9000.**

BY TRAIN   Train service into Seville is now centralized into the Estación Santa Justa, Av. Kansas City s/n (© **95-240-02-02** for information and reservations, or 95-454-03-03 for information). Buses C1 and C2 take you from this train station to the bus station at Prado de San Sebastián, and bus EA runs to and from the airport. The high-speed AVE train has reduced travel time from Madrid to Seville to 2½ hours. The train makes 17 trips daily, with a stop in Córdoba. Sixteen trains a day connect Seville and Córdoba; the AVE train takes 45 minutes and a TALGO takes 1½ hours. Three trains a day run to Málaga, taking 3 hours; there are also three trains per day to Granada (4 hr.).

BY BUS   Although Seville confusingly has several satellite bus stations servicing small towns and nearby villages of Andalusia, most buses arrive and depart from the city's largest bus terminal, on the southeast edge of the old city, at Prado de San Sebastián, Calle José María Osborne 11 (© **95-441-71-11**). Several different companies make frequent runs to and from Córdoba (2½ hr.),

Málaga (3½ hr.), Granada (4 hr.), and Madrid (8 hr.). For information and ticket prices, call Alsina Graells at © **95-441-88-11.** A newer bus station is at Plaza de Armas (© **95-490-80-40**), but it usually services destinations beyond Andalusia, including Portugal.

BY CAR   Seville lies 540km (341 miles) southwest of Madrid and 217km (135 miles) northwest of Málaga. Several major highways converge on Seville, connecting it with the rest of Spain and Portugal. During periods of heavy holiday traffic, the N-V (E-90) from Madrid through Extremadura—which, at Mérida, connects with the southbound N-630 (E-803)—is usually less congested than the N-IV (E-5) through eastern Andalusia.

VISITOR INFORMATION

The tourist office, **Oficina de Información del Turismo,** at Av. de la Constitución 21B (© **95-422-14-04**), is open Monday to Saturday from 9am to 7pm, Sunday and holidays from 10am to 2pm.

CITY LAYOUT

The heart of Seville lies along the east bank of the Guadalquivir River. This **Old Town** *(centro histórico)* once enclosed by walls, is fairly compact. The best, really the only, way to explore it is on foot. Today nearly all the sights lie between two of the major bridges of Seville: the Puente de San Telmo, to the south, and the Puente de Isabel II (also known as the Puente de Triana), an Eiffel Tower–like structure from the mid-1800s. Near Puente de San Telmo are such sights as the Torre del Oro, the University of Seville, and the Parque de María Luisa. Near the Puente de Isabel II are the Maestranza bullring, the major shopping streets, and the Museo de Bellas Artes. In the middle of the centro histórico is the cathedral and its adjoining Giralda tower, the Alcázar, and the colorful streets of the old Jewish quarter, the Barrio Santa Cruz.

MAIN STREETS, SQUARES & ARTERIES   The old **Paseo de Colón** is that part of Seville's historic core that opens onto the Guadalquivir River. Any number of streets, including Santander, lead to **Avenida de la Constitución,** where you'll find the major attractions of Seville, including the Alcázar and the cathedral. To the east of both the Alcázar and the cathedral lies the Barrio Santa Cruz. Major historic squares include Plaza Nueva, Plaza de El Salvador, Plaza de Jerez, and Plaza de Triunfo. From Plaza del Duque, the Museo de Bellas Artes is reached by heading west toward the river along Calle Alfonso XII. The best place to start your exploration of Seville is **Plaza Virgen de los Reyes.** From here many of the major attractions, including the Giralda, the Patio de los Naranjos, and the Archivo de Indias, are all close at hand. Directly south of the plaza is the Alcázar—the whole area, in fact, is historic Seville in a nutshell.

FINDING AN ADDRESS   Most of Seville's streets run one way, usually toward the Guadalquivir River. Individual buildings are numbered with odd addresses on one side of the street and even numbers on the opposite side, so no. 14 would likely fall opposite no. 13 and 15. Many addresses are marked s/n, which means the building has no number *(sin número)*. When this occurs, be sure to obtain the name of a cross street as a reference point.

MAPS   Even if you're in Seville for only a day or two, you'll need a detailed street map, not the general overview often handed out free at tourist offices. The best street maps of Seville are those published by **Euro City,** available at local newsstands and in bookstores. These maps contain not only a detailed street index, but also plot tourist information, places of interest, and even locations of vital services (such as the police station). You can more or less count on getting lost in the intricate maze of the Barrio Santa Cruz, for which no adequate map exists. A sketch map provided by the tourist office will help get you around the area, however.

THE NEIGHBORHOODS IN BRIEF

CENTRO HISTORICO This is the heart of historic Seville, and contains its most imposing sights. Of these the massive **cathedral** is the dominant attraction. It's the area where you'll want to spend the most time, and it's also where you'll find the finest hotels and restaurants.

BARRIO SANTA CRUZ This is an area of wrought-iron *cancelas* (gates), courtyards with Andalusian tiled fountains, art galleries, restaurants, cafes, *tabernas,* flowerpots of geraniums, and winding narrow alleyways. The former ghetto of Seville's Jews, it's today named after a Christian saint, and is the single most colorful part of the city. Exploring is best done during the day (muggings sometimes occur at night). Filled with interesting sights, such as Casa Murillo and some fascinating churches, it's one of Andalusia's architectural highlights.

LA MACARENA Thought to be named for a Roman, Macarios, and the site of his former estate, this is a famous quarter of Seville that seems sadly neglected by visitors, who spend most of their time in the two quarters discussed above. It's filled with interesting attractions such as the **Convento de Santa Inés** (reached along Calle María Coronel). According to legend, King Pedro the Cruel was so taken with Inés's beauty that he pursued her incessantly— until she poured boiling oil over her face to disfigure herself.

TRIANA & EL ARENAL These two districts were immortalized by Cervantes, Quevedo, and Lope de Vega, the fabled writers of Spain's golden age. They were the rough-and-tough seafaring quarters when Seville was a thriving port in the 1600s. In El Arenal, the 12-sided **Torre del Oro (Gold Tower),** built by the Almohads in 1220, overlooks the river on Paseo Cristóbal Colón. You can take the riverside esplanade, Marqués de Contadero, which stretches along the banks of the river from the tower. The **Museo Provincial de Bellas Artes** also found here houses Spain's best collection of Seville's painters, notably Murillo. Across the river, Triana was once the gypsy quarter but has now been gentrified.

2 Getting Around

BY BUS

You can actually walk most everywhere in Seville, although there are buses, used mainly for visiting the environs, which have little interest for most visitors. If you use a bus for getting around the city, you'll find that most lines converge at Plaza de la Encarnación, Plaza Nueva, or in front of the cathedral on Avenida de la Constitución. Bus service is daily from 6am to 11:15pm. The city tourist office will provide a booklet outlining bus routes. The best buses for circling through the center of town include C1 and C2 *(circulares interiores).* It costs 1€ ($1.20) for transit via bus between any two points in Seville. No buses go directly into the town's medieval core, since the streets are too narrow, but anyone can reach the approximate point of their intended address by getting out at

> *Tips* **Seville: A Driver-Unfriendly City**
>
> Be warned that driving here is a nightmare: Seville was planned for the horse and buggy rather than for the car, and nearly all the streets run one-way toward the Guadalquivir River. Locating a hard-to-find restaurant or a hidden little square will require patience and luck.

an appropriate point on the avenues that encircle the central core, then walking a short distance. If you plan on riding the bus frequently, consider buying a bus pass, known locally as a *Bonobus,* for 3.90€ ($4.70). It allows its holder ten rides on any bus in Seville, and because it's a bearer instrument, it can be transferred without penalty from one person to another. You cannot buy these passes on the bus: They're available at tobacco stands, news kiosks, and during any morning session at the Seville Tourist Office at Plaza Nueva. For general bus information, call © **90-245-99-54.** For lost objects, call © **95-442-04-03.**

BY BICYCLE

Although Seville is intensely hot in summer, bike rentals are possible, even though spring and autumn are better times—at least cooler—for cycling around. Rentals are available at **Cyclotour** (© **95-427-45-66**), with two locations: Paseo de Colón s/n next to Torre del Oro, and Avenida Hernán Cortez, Parque de María Luisa s/n. The shops are open 10am to 9pm. Rentals are 10€ ($12) for 4 hours, 18€ ($22) for 8 hours, 20€ ($24) for 24 hours, and 50€ ($60) for one week. A deposit of 100€ ($120) is required.

BY CARRIAGE

They're romantic, the echo of the horses' hooves makes an appealing clip-clop on the cobblestones, and the Giralda seems ever-so-evocative from behind a horse's rump. You'll find clusters of such carriages on the eastern side of the cathedral (Plaza del Triunfo), their official gathering place. In some circumstances, they'll crop up near the Alcázar and in the shadow of the Giralda as well. Don't expect uniform behavior or treatment from the many entrepreneurs who, with their horses, work the trade, but they tend to be available daily between 10am and 11pm. They charge between 35€ and 40€ ($42–$48) for a 35- to 40-minute clip-clop tour of the city's broader avenues, and the drivers are somewhat brusque.

BY TAXI

This is quite a viable means of getting around, especially at night, when streets are dangerous because of frequent muggings. Call **Tele Taxi** (© **95-462-22-22**) or **Radio Taxi** (© **95-458-00-00**). Cabs are metered and charge about .50€ (60¢) per kilometer at night and .40€ (45¢) during the day.

BY CAR

Chances are you arranged to rent a car before you got to Seville (rates are lower that way). However, if you didn't, you'll find **Avis** at the airport (© **95-444-91-21**), and at the train station (© **95-453-78-61**). **Hertz** is also at the airport (© **95-451-47-20**) and on Vía Santa Justa near the train station (© **95-442-61-56**).

FAST FACTS: Seville

American Express The American Express office, in the Hotel Inglaterra, Plaza Nueva 7 (© **95-421-16-17**), is open Monday to Friday 9:30am to 1:30pm and 4:30 to 7:30pm, Saturday 10am to 1pm.

Babysitters If you need a babysitter, ask the concierge or reception desk of your hotel. You will not always get an English-speaker, however.

Bookstore The **Beta Librería**, Av. de la Constitución 27 (© **95-45-607-03**), sells books in Spanish and to a lesser extent, English and French. It's the most centrally located of a large chain of bookstores with other branches throughout the city.

Consulates The **U.S. Consulate** is at Paseo de las Delicias 7 (© **95-423-18-85**), open Monday to Friday 10am to 1pm and 2 to 4:30pm. The nearest British Consulate is in Málaga, but there is an **Australian Consulate** at Federico Rubio 14 (© **95-422-09-71**), open Monday to Friday 10am to noon.

Currency Exchange There are many offices of these scattered within the neighborhood around the cathedral, but some of the biggest and busiest lie immediately adjacent to the Post Office. As for ATMs, there are dozens around Seville, especially near the cathedral.

Dentists If you have an emergency check at the reception desk of your hotel. There's also a large dental clinic with extended hours for emergencies. It's the *Centro Dentaire La Macarena,* Rondo Capucinos 8-10 (© **95-441-32-02**).

Doctors Your hotel can provide you with the names of doctors, but in an emergency, you should dial © **112** on any phone. Otherwise, contact the *Clínica Triana,* Av. Ronda de Triana 14A (© **95-433-48-28**).

Emergencies For the police or fire department call © **112.** For an ambulance, dial © **112** or 061.

Hospitals The city's biggest and best equipped is *Virgen del Rocío,* Av. Manuel Siurot s/n (© **95-501-20-00**), about 2km (1¼ miles) from the city center.

Internet Access The most convenient place is the **Sevilla Internet Center,** Calle Almirantazgo 2 (© **95-450-02-75**), open Monday to Friday 9am to 10pm, Saturday and Sunday 10am to 10pm. Charges are 3€ ($3.60) per hour. Another option is **The Email Place,** Calle las Sierpes 54 (© **95-421-85-92**), open June to September Monday to Friday 10am to 10pm and Saturday and Sunday noon to 9pm. October to May hours are Monday to Friday 10am to 11pm and Saturday and Sunday noon to 9pm. Charges are 2.20€ ($2.65) per hour.

Newspapers Newsstands in the center of the city as well as many first-class and deluxe hotels have kiosks selling English-language newspapers and magazines. Two locally edited daily newspapers of note include the somewhat to-the-right-of-center *ABC,* selling at newsstands for around 1€ ($1.20); and the Andalusian edition of *El País,* a centrist to slightly-left-of-center publication, selling for 1€ ($1.20).

Pharmacies One of the biggest is the *Pharmacia Puerta de la Carne,* Calle Demetrio de los Ríos 3 (© **95-441-44-53**). Check any pharmacy window for the name and address of the pharmacy open all night—pharmacies rotate that duty. You can also call **Farmacias de Guardia** at © **90-252-21-11** for the night-duty schedule.

Police The police station is located on Paseo de las Delicias (© **95-461-54-50**).

Post Office The post office is at Av. de la Constitución 32 (© **95-422-47-60**). It's open Monday to Saturday from 9am to 8:30pm.

Restrooms You'll find a few of these in Seville, including a much-overused cluster on the Paseo Colon. Each requires a deposit, in coins only, of around .20€ (25¢). You'll be better off doing as the locals do, and ducking into whatever bar or cafe looks amenable and—if you have the time, buying a bottle of mineral water, coffee, a drink, or whatever as part of the experience.

Safety With massive unemployment, the city has been hit by a crime wave in recent years. María Luisa Park is especially dangerous, as is the highway leading to Jerez de la Frontera and Cádiz. Dangling cameras and purses are especially vulnerable. Don't leave cars unguarded with your luggage inside. Regrettably, some attacks occur when passengers stop for traffic signals.

Taxis See "Getting Around," earlier in this section.

3 Where to Stay

During Holy Week and the Seville Fair, hotels often double, even triple, their rates. Price increases are often not announced until the last minute. If you're going to be in Seville at these times, arrive with an ironclad reservation and an agreement about the price before checking in.

VERY EXPENSIVE

Casa Imperial ✪✪✪   In the historic center, this hotel was launched in the mid-1990s near Casa Pilatos. The building dates from the 15th century, when it housed the butler to the Marquis of Tarifa. The interior is refined, and there are four Andalusian patios adorned with exotic plants. The beamed ceilings are original, and sparkling chandeliers hang from the ceilings. The rooms are large—many have small kitchens and ample terraces. The bathrooms are tastefully decorated with showers and luxurious tubs, some of which are antiques.

Calle Imperial 29, 41003 Seville. © **95-450-03-00.** Fax 95-450-03-30. www.casaimperial.com. 26 units. 240€ ($288) double; 305€ ($366) suite. AE, DC, MC, V. Limited free parking, otherwise 18€ ($22). Bus: 24 or 27. **Amenities:** Restaurant; bar; 24-hr. room service; babysitting; laundry service/dry cleaning. *In room:* A/C, TV, dataport, minibar, hair dryer, safe.

Hotel Alfonso XIII ✪✪✪   At a corner of the gardens fronting the Alcázar, this rococo building is one of Spain's three or four most legendary hotels and Seville's premier address. This splendid palace dwarfs the competition, and is now a Westin hotel. Built in the mudéjar/Andalusian revival style as a shelter for patrons of the Ibero-American Exposition of 1929 and named after the then-king of Spain, it reigns as a superornate and expensive bastion of glamour. Its rooms and hallways glitter with hand-painted tiles, acres of marble and mahogany, antique furniture embellished with intricately embossed leather, and a spaciousness nothing short of majestic. All rooms are beautifully kept, with bathrooms containing tub/shower combos.

Seville Accommodations

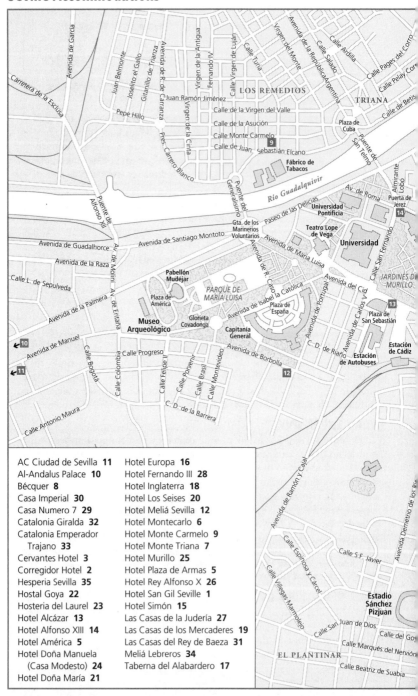

AC Ciudad de Sevilla **11**
Al-Andalus Palace **10**
Bécquer **8**
Casa Imperial **30**
Casa Numero 7 **29**
Catalonia Giralda **32**
Catalonia Emperador
   Trajano **33**
Cervantes Hotel **3**
Corregidor Hotel **2**
Hesperia Sevilla **35**
Hostal Goya **22**
Hosteria del Laurel **23**
Hotel Alcázar **13**
Hotel Alfonso XIII **14**
Hotel América **5**
Hotel Doña Manuela
   (Casa Modesto) **24**
Hotel Doña María **21**

Hotel Europa **16**
Hotel Fernando III **28**
Hotel Inglaterra **18**
Hotel Los Seises **20**
Hotel Meliá Sevilla **12**
Hotel Montecarlo **6**
Hotel Monte Carmelo **9**
Hotel Monte Triana **7**
Hotel Murillo **25**
Hotel Plaza de Armas **5**
Hotel Rey Alfonso X **26**
Hotel San Gil Seville **1**
Hotel Simón **15**
Las Casas de la Judería **27**
Las Casas de los Mercaderes **19**
Las Casas del Rey de Baeza **31**
Meliá Lebreros **34**
Taberna del Alabardero **17**

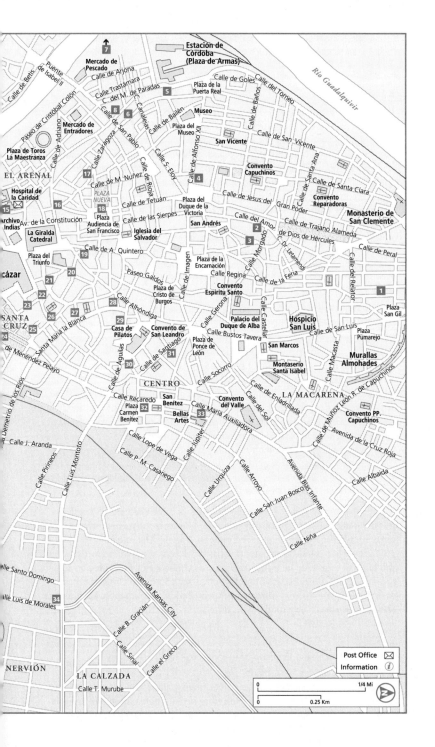

Estación de
Córdoba
(Plaza de Armas)

Río Guadalquivir

Mercado de
Pescado

Calle de Arjona

Calle de Betis

Puente
de Isabel II

Calle de Cristóbal Colón

Paseo de Cristóbal Colón

Calle Trastamara

C. del M. de Paradas

C. Canalejas

Calle de San Pablo

Calle de Bailén

Calle de Goles

Calle del Torneo

Plaza de la
Puerta Real

Calle de Baños

Museo

Plaza del
Museo XII

San Vicente

Calle de San Vicente

Calle de Santa Ana

Calle de Santa Clara

Paseo de Adriano

Mercado de
Entradores

Plaza de Toros
La Maestranza

Calle Zaragoza

Calle de Rioja

Calle de Alfonso XII

Convento
Capuchinos

EL ARENAL

Calle de M. Núñez

PLAZA
NUEVA

Hospital de
la Caridad

Calle de Tetuán

Plaza del
Duque de la
Victoria

Calle de Jesús del Gran Poder

Convento
Reparadoras

Monasterio de
San Clemente

Archivo
Indias

Av. de la Constitución

Plaza
Audiencia de
San Francisco

Calle de las Sierpes

San Andrés

Calle del Amor
de Dios de Hércules

Calle de Trajano Alameda

Iglesia del
Salvador

La Giralda
Catedral

Calle de A. Quintero

Calle Morgado

Calle de Peral

Plaza del
Triunfo

Plaza de la
Encarnación

Calle de la Feria

Calle del Relator

cázar

Paseo Galdos

Calle de Imagen

Calle Regina

Plaza de
Cristo de
Burgos

Convento
Espíritu Santo

Calle Gerona

Calle Castellar

Hospicio
San Luis

Plaza
San Gil

Calle Alhóndiga

SANTA
CRUZ

Casa de
Pilatos

Palacio del
Duque de Alba

Calle de Bustos Tavera

Calle de San Luis

Plaza
Pumarejo

Santa María la Blanca

Convento de
San Leandro

Plaza de
Ponce de
León

San Marcos

Murallas
Almohades

Calle de Menéndez Pelayo

Calle de Aguilas

Calle de Santiago

Montaserio
Santa Isabel

Calle Macasta

Calle de Muñoz León R. de Capuchinos

CENTRO

Calle Socorro

Calle de Enladrillada

LA MACARENA

Calle de los Ríos

Calle Recaredo

San
Benítez

Convento
del Valle

Calle del Sol

Calle J. Aranda

Plaza
Carmen
Benítez

Bellas
Artes

Calle María Auxiliadora

Convento PP.
Capuchinos

Calle de Avenida de la Cruz Roja

Calle Lope de Vega

Calle Júpiter

Calle Primos

Calle Luis Montoto

Calle P. M. Casariego

Calle Urquiza

Calle Arroyo

Avenida Bus Infante

Calle Albaida

Calle San Juan Bosco

Avenida Kansas City

Calle Niña

alle Santo Domingo

alle Luis de Morales

Calle B. Gracián

Calle Sinaí

Calle el Greco

NERVIÓN

LA CALZADA

Calle T. Murube

| Post Office | ✉ |
| Information | ⓘ |

0   1/4 Mi

0   0.25 Km

69

San Fernando 2, 41004 Seville. © **800/221-2340** in the U.S. and Canada, or 95-491-70-00. Fax 95-491-70-99. 146 units. 285€–598€ ($342–$718) double; from 850€ ($1,020) suite. AE, DC, MC, V. Parking 14€ ($17). **Amenities:** Restaurant; 2 bars; outdoor pool; tennis courts; car rental; 24-hr. room service; babysitting; laundry service/dry cleaning; nonsmoking rooms. *In room:* A/C, TV, minibar, hair dryer, safe.

EXPENSIVE

Al-Andalús Palace ★★   No hotel in Seville has a more avant-garde design than this palace just 5 minutes from the center in the Heliópolis district, an upmarket residential area. The front public rooms are suspended by cable, and the glass facade reflects both the blue skies of Seville and the marble floors. The large guest rooms are elegantly appointed, with big windows; some have balconies. The decor and furnishings are minimalist—functional but modern. Many accommodations have small living rooms and suites with their own breakfast bars. The bathrooms have showers, large tubs, and mirrors; the suites contain hydromassage.

Av. Palmera s/n, 41012 Seville. © **95-423-06-00.** Fax 95-423-02-00. www.hoteles-silken.com. 623 units. 237€ ($284) double; 1,095€ ($1,314) suite. AE, DC, MC, V. Parking 9€ ($11). Bus: 34. **Amenities:** 5 restaurants; 2 bars; outdoor pool; health spa; 24-hr. room service; babysitting; laundry service/dry cleaning; nonsmoking rooms; rooms for those w/limited mobility. *In room:* A/C, TV, dataport, minibar, hair dryer, safe (in some).

Casa Número 7 ★★ *Finds*   This is as close as you can get to staying in an elegant private home in Seville. Next to the Santa Cruz barrio, the little inn is in a beautiful, sensitively restored 19th-century mansion where you live in style, with a butler to serve you breakfast. Small in size, Casa Número 7 is big on style and grace notes, recapturing the aura of Old Seville. It thinks of itself, with justification, as a civilized oasis in the midst of a bustling city. The building envelops an old atrium, and is filled with such touches as family photographs, Oriental area rugs, a marble fireplace, and floral print love seats. Rooms are individually decorated in old Sevillano style, with impeccable taste and an eye to comfort. All come with good-size bathrooms with tub/shower combination. Our favorite is the spacious Yellow Room, with its "Juliet balcony" overlooking the street.

Vírgenes 7, 41004 Seville. © **95-422-15-81.** Fax 95-421-45-27. www.casanumero7.com. 6 units. 177€–275€ ($212–$330) double. Rates include breakfast. Bus: 10, 15, 24, or 32. **Amenities:** "Honesty" bar; laundry service. *In room:* A/C, hair dryer.

Hesperia Sevilla ★★   In the modern and commercial area of Seville, a 5-minute walk from the historical core, this contemporary chain-owned hotel ranks number three in town, bested only by Alfonso XIII and Meliá Colón. In a building that could be an international hotel almost anywhere in the world, the hotel is noted for such nice facilities as its pools and for its spacious bedrooms. Each is furnished comfortably, often with rich, dark wood pieces, and each comes with a tiled bathroom with tub/shower combination. Commercial travelers are particularly fond of this one.

Tips **Finding a Hotel in the City's Impossible Maze**

The tourist offices have made great efforts to signpost the location of every hotel. The moment a car enters town, yellow and black signs pop up, pointing the way to each individual hotel. Their placement respects one-way street routings, and, in most cases, they actually work, even in neighborhoods with streets that are impossibly narrow.

<Kids **Family-Friendly Hotels**

Hotel Doña María (p. 74)   Located behind the cathedral and the Giralda, this is one of the most gracious hotels in the old quarter of Seville. The garden courtyard and the rooftop pool delight adults and children alike. Rooms contain wide beds and bathrooms with dual sinks, and some rooms are large enough for the entire family.

Hotel Fernando III (p. 74)   This hotel lies in the medieval Barrio Santa Cruz, the old Jewish quarter. The helpful and polite staff speaks English and is welcoming to families, offering some guest rooms large enough to accommodate children and adults.

Hotel Meliá Sevilla (below)   On the outskirts of town, this 11-story structure offers many facilities appreciated by families, including a pool, fitness center, squash court, and parking garage. Families enjoy dining on a terrace alfresco, and there's also a snack bar on the grounds.

Av. Eduardo Data 49, 41018 Seville. ✆ **95-454-83-00.** Fax 95-453-23-42. www.hesperia-sevilla.com. 242 units. 185€ ($222) double; 191€–284€ ($229–$341) suite. AE, DC, MC, V. Free parking. Bus: 22, 23, 32, or 71. **Amenities:** 2 restaurants; 2 bars; 24-hr. room service; 2 pools (1 indoor); Jacuzzi w/solarium terrace; sauna; laundry service/dry cleaning; nonsmoking rooms; rooms for those w/limited mobility. *In room:* A/C, TV, dataport, minibar, hair dryer, safe (for a fee).

Hotel Los Seises   Once the 16th-century palace of the archbishop of Seville, this hotel is behind the cathedral in the old Jewish Quarter of Santa Cruz. Renovations have added modern amenities but many of the Andalusian touches have been retained. In this category of antique hotels, we prefer the Casa Imperial, but what you get here isn't bad. And hey, it was the pope's choice when he visited Seville. Traditional stucco walls are adorned with modern paintings that contrast with the antique tiles. The rooms range from small to spacious, each with a good bed and a restored bathroom with a tub/shower combo. Be sure to check out the stunning vista of La Giralda you can enjoy while sunbathing on the rooftop.

Calle Segovias 6, 41004 Seville. ✆ **95-422-94-95.** Fax 95-422-43-34. www.hotellosseises.com. 42 units. 189€–272€ ($227–$326) double. AE, DC, MC, V. Parking 17€ ($20). Bus: 10, 20, 41, or 42. **Amenities:** Restaurant; bar; outdoor pool; limited room service; babysitting; laundry service/dry cleaning; nonsmoking rooms. *In room:* A/C, TV, dataport, minibar, hair dryer, safe.

Hotel Meliá Sevilla ⭐⭐ <Kids   Located a short walk east of the Plaza de España, near the Parque María Luisa, this is the most elegant, tasteful, and international of Seville's modern skyscraper hotels. It opened in 1987, rising 11 floors. It incorporates acres of white marble as well as several dozen shopping boutiques and private apartments into its L-shaped floor plan. Bedroom decor is contemporary and comfortable, and each unit offers a private bathroom with a tub/shower, though rooms in the back lack a view. The Meliá was a favorite of the planners of the massive Expo, which transformed the face of both Seville and Andalusia. The hotel lacks the personal touch provided by the staff at Alfonso XIII, but its rooms are superior to those at the Inglaterra.

Doctor Pedro de Castro 1, 41004 Seville. ✆ **800/336-3542** in the U.S., or 95-442-26-11. Fax 95-442-16-08. www.solmelia.com. 364 units. 194€ ($233) double; from 313€ ($375) suite. AE, DC, MC, V. Parking 13€ ($15). Bus: 30, 31, 33, or 72. **Amenities:** 2 restaurants; bar; 24-hr. room service; outdoor pool; massage;

babysitting; laundry service/dry cleaning; nonsmoking rooms; rooms for those w/limited mobility. *In room:* A/C, TV, dataport, minibar, hair dryer, safe.

Las Casas del Rey de Baeza ⓐ   Less luxurious than its sibling, La Casa de la Judería (see below), this antique hotel close to the Casa de Pilatos is still a winning choice with its stone floors and 19th-century Andalusian architecture. A hotel since 1998, it has an interior patio surrounded by a cozy coterie of rooms and a long Andalusian balcony. Some of the beautifully furnished rooms have living rooms, and the decor is finely honed in marble and wood with comfortable furnishings. The bathrooms contain tub/shower combos.

Calle Santiago, Plaza Jesús de la Redención 2, 41003 Seville. ℂ **95-456-14-96.** Fax 95-456-14-41. www. hospes.es. 41 units. 142€–289€ ($170–$347) double; 195€–373€ ($234–$448) suite. AE, DC, MC, V. Parking 12€ ($14). Bus: 10, 15, 20, or 32. **Amenities:** Restaurant; bar; lounge; outdoor pool; babysitting; limited room service; laundry service/dry cleaning; nonsmoking rooms; rooms for those w/limited mobility. *In room:* A/C, TV, dataport, minibar, hair dryer, safe.

Meliá Libreros ⓐ   Enjoying a position as the fifth-best hotel of Seville, this government-rated four-star hotel is in a modern building with black glass walls. Last renovated in 2004, it is completely up to date and a rewarding choice, although it has little Andalusian style. Although it's the largest hotel in Seville, it still manages to offer good service, catering to both business and leisure travelers.

The refurbished bedrooms have a certain Mediterranean flair, with creamy colors, matching fabrics, plenty of mirrors, and lots of light. The bedrooms are spacious and comfortable, each with a tiled bathroom with tub/shower. For business clients, there is a "royal service floor." Most of the food served here is of an acceptable international standard; frankly, we prefer the breakfast buffet to the regular dining opportunities.

Luis Morales 2, 41018 Seville. ℂ **95-457-94-00.** Fax 95-458-23-09. www.melialebreros.solmelia.com. 431 rooms. 180€ ($216) double; 279€–357€ ($335–$428) suite. Free parking. Bus: 21. **Amenities:** 3 restaurants; 4 bars; 2 pools (1 indoor); Jacuzzi; 24-hr. room service; babysitting; laundry service/dry cleaning; dance club; nonsmoking rooms; rooms for those w/limited mobility. *In room:* A/C, TV, dataport, minibar, hair dryer, safe (for a fee).

Taberna del Alabardero ⓐⓐ *Finds*   This tavern now houses one of the single most charming places to stay in the city. Close to the bullring and a 5-minute walk from the cathedral, this restored 19th-century mansion has a spectacular central patio and a romantic atmosphere. The units on the third floor have balconies overlooking street scenes as well as whirlpool tubs. All the rooms are spacious and comfortable, each individually decorated in a specific regional style. The bathrooms contain tub/shower combos.

Zaragoza 20, 41001 Seville. ℂ **95-456-06-37.** Fax 95-456-36-66. 7 units. 145€–235€ ($174–$282) double; 178€–274€ ($213–$329) junior suite. Rates include continental breakfast. AE, DC, MC, V. Parking 12€ ($14). Bus: 21, 25, 30, or 43. **Amenities:** Restaurant; bar; lounge; 24-hr. room service; babysitting; laundry service/dry cleaning. *In room:* A/C, TV, minibar, hair dryer, safe.

MODERATE
AC Ciudad de Sevilla ⓐ *Finds*   At last a hotel with some 19th-century Andalusian styling. Last renovated in 2001, this charming, graceful hotel stands on one of the most prestigious residential streets of Seville, near Avenida de la Palmera. Although its architecture is in the old style, evoking in some parts a Spanish church, it is completely modernized. Bedrooms are beautifully maintained and well furnished; each is midsize with a tiled bathroom containing a tub and shower. On-site is a handsomely decorated and traditional restaurant with a succulent and varied menu based on market-fresh ingredients.

Av. Manuel Siurot 25, 41013 Seville. ✆ **95-423-05-05.** Fax 95-423-85-39. www.ac-hoteles.com. 94 units. 160€ ($192) double; 252€–384€ ($302–$461) suite. AE, DC, MC, V. Parking: 12€ ($14). Bus: 1, 6, 33, or 72. **Amenities:** Restaurant; bar; coffee shop; outdoor pool; gym; sauna; 24-hr. room service; laundry service/dry cleaning; nonsmoking rooms. *In room:* A/C, TV, dataport, minibar, hair dryer, beverage maker.

Bécquer *(Value* A short walk from the action of the Seville bullring and only 2 blocks from the river, Bécquer is on a street full of cafes where you can order tapas and enjoy Andalusian wine. The Museo Provincial de Bellas Artes is also nearby. Built in the 1970s, the hotel was enlarged and much renovated in the late 1980s. It occupies the site of a former mansion and retains many objets d'art rescued before that building was demolished. You register in a wood-paneled lobby before being shown to one of the functionally furnished rooms—a good value in a pricey city, as most units are at the lower end of the price scale. All have bathrooms with tub/shower combos.

Calle Reyes Católicos 4, 41001 Seville. ✆ **95-422-89-00.** Fax 95-421-44-00. www.hotelbecquer.com. 141 units. 124€–210€ ($149–$252) double; 250€–324€ ($300–$389) suite. AE, DC, MC, V. Parking 12€ ($14). Bus: C1, C2, or C4. **Amenities:** Restaurant; bar; lounge; spa; limited room service; babysitting; laundry service/dry cleaning. *In room:* A/C, TV, dataport, minibar, hair dryer, safe.

Catalonia Emperador Trajano In the center of the historic and shopping district of Seville, this hotel lies only 500m (1,640 ft.) from the AVE rail station at Santa Justa. A modern hotel, it was built in 1992 and last renovated in 1998. Bedrooms are midsize to spacious and are furnished comfortably in a modern but not spectacular style. Most of the rooms open onto a view. Each comes with a tiled bathroom with combination tub/shower. Although it's more functional than stylish, it's a good address to know about.

Calle José Laguillo 8, 41003 Seville. ✆ **95-441-11-11.** Fax 95-453-57-02. www.hoteles-catalonia. 76 units. 195€ ($234) double. Rates include continental breakfast. AE, DC, MC, V. Free parking. Bus: C1, C2, or 32. **Amenities:** Restaurant; bar; car-rental desk; room service (8am–11:30pm); babysitting; laundry service/dry cleaning. *In room:* A/C, TV, minibar, hair dryer, safe.

Catalonia Giralda ✦ In the heart of the historic core and the main shopping district, this government-rated four-star hotel is named after one of Seville's most famous monuments, La Giralda. The hotel is convenient to the Santa Justa rail station. First constructed in 1967, the hotel received a complete overhaul in 1999. The midsize bedrooms are spread over five floors, and each comes with a combination tub/shower. Bedrooms are bright with modern, comfortable furnishings. The on-site restaurant is standard but acceptable if you don't want to go out at night.

Sierra Nevada 3, 41003 Seville. ✆ **95-441-66-61.** Fax 95-441-93-52. 110 units. 170€–195€ ($204–$234) double. AE, DC, MC, V. Parking: 12€ ($14). Bus: C3, 24, or 27. **Amenities:** Restaurant; bar; babysitting; laundry service/dry cleaning. *In room:* A/C, TV, hair dryer.

Cervantes Hotel This balconied, government-rated three-star hotel lies in what locals call an *antigua casa sevillana,* meaning an antique house in the local style with wrought-iron-grille balconies. Last renovated in 2001, it opens onto a central courtyard, as in the typical style. Bedrooms are beautifully maintained and midsize for the most part, furnished with wooden pieces. Each is adjoined by a tiled bathroom with tub/shower combo. There is no restaurant on-site, but many lie within a few minutes' walk of the hotel.

Cervantes 10, 41003 Seville. ✆ **95-490-02-80.** Fax 95-490-05-36. www.hotel-cervantes.com. 48 units. 114€–189€ ($137–$227) double. AE, DC, MC, V. Parking: 11€ ($13). Bus: 2, 13, or 14. **Amenities:** Cafeteria; car-rental desk; 24-hr. room service; laundry service/dry cleaning. *In room:* A/C, TV, minibar, hair dryer, safe.

Corregidor Hotel ⚐ *Value*   This is a typical Andalusian hotel with colonial styling such as arches, balconies, tall windows, antiques, lamps, columns, and colorful tiles. In the local style, life revolves around a central patio. The hotel, constructed in 1977, was last renovated in 1992, a bit of a stretch, but there has been considerable maintenance since those days. The midsize bedrooms are comfortably and traditionally furnished with tiles and wooden furniture, each containing a bathroom with a tub/shower. The English bar is a popular gathering place for guests. The charming atmosphere makes this hotel a very good value.

Morgado 17, 41003 Seville. ℰ **95-438-51-11.** Fax 95-438-42-38. http://Seville.hotelsspainonline.com/ Corregidor. 76 units. 90€–142€ ($108–$170) double; 180€ ($216) suite. AE, DC, MC, V. Parking: 14€ ($17). Bus: B2, 10, 11, 12, 15, 20, 24, 27, or 32. **Amenities:** Restaurant; bar; car rental; babysitting; 24-hr. room service; laundry service/dry cleaning. *In room:* A/C, TV, safe.

Hotel Alcázar   On the wide and busy Boulevard Menéndez y Pelayo, across from the Jardines de Alcazon, this pleasantly contemporary hotel is sheltered behind a facade of brown brick. Built in 1964, the hotel was last renovated in 1991. Slabs of striated gray marble cool the reception area in the lobby. Above, three latticed structures resemble a trio of *miradores*. The medium-size guest rooms have functional modern furniture and private bathrooms with tub/shower combinations.

Menéndez y Pelayo 10, 41004 Seville. ℰ **95-441-20-11.** Fax 95-442-16-59. 93 units. 90€–160€ ($108–$192) double. Rates include breakfast. AE, DC, MC, V. Parking 14€ ($17). Bus: 21 or 23. **Amenities:** Bar; babysitting; laundry service/dry cleaning; nonsmoking rooms; rooms for those w/limited mobility. *In room:* A/C, TV, dataport, hair dryer.

Hotel Doña María ⚐ *Kids*   Highlights here include the Iberian antiques in the stone lobby and upper hallways and a location a few steps from the cathedral, which allows for dramatic views from the rooftop terrace. An ornate neoclassical entryway is offset with a pure white facade and iron balconies, which hint at the building's origin in the 1840s as a private villa. Amid the flowering plants on the upper floor you'll find garden-style lattices and antique wrought-iron railings. Each of the one-of-a-kind rooms has a bathroom with a tub/shower combo. Sizes range from small to large enough for the entire family. A few have four-poster beds, others a handful of antique reproductions. Light sleepers might find the noise of the church bells jarring. Breakfast is the only meal served. There's a garden courtyard and a rooftop pool.

Don Remondo 19, 41004 Seville. ℰ **95-422-49-90.** Fax 95-421-95-46. www.hdmaria.com. 64 units. 100€–220€ ($120–$264) double. AE, DC, MC, V. Parking 12€ ($14). **Amenities:** Breakfast room; 2 bars; outdoor pool; limited room service; babysitting; laundry service/dry cleaning. *In room:* A/C, TV, dataport, minibar, hair dryer, safe.

Hotel Fernando III *Kids*   You'll find the Fernando III on a narrow, quiet street at the edge of the Barrio Santa Cruz, near the northern periphery of the Murillo Gardens. Established in 1969, this hotel is warmer, much bigger, and more obviously "Andalusian" in its decor and presentation than the post-*movida* angularity of its sister hotel, the also-recommended Hotel Alfonso X, just across a narrow alleyway. With sweeping expanses of marble flooring in the lobby, a very plush and posh-looking cocktail bar, a uniformed staff, and a well-manicured and impeccably correct restaurant, it's rather "grand hotel" in its presentation. Its vast lobby and baronial dining hall are reminiscent of a luxurious South American hacienda. Many of the rooms—medium in size, comfortably furnished, and well maintained—offer balconies filled with cascading plants; all have private bathrooms with tub/shower combinations. The restaurant features regional Andalusian cuisine.

San José 21, 41001 Seville. (C) **95-421-77-08.** Fax 95-422-02-46. 157 units. 146€ ($175) double; 170€ ($204) suite. AE, DC, MC, V. Parking 13€ ($16). Bus: 21 or 23. **Amenities:** Restaurant; bar; rooftop pool; room service; laundry service/dry cleaning. *In room:* A/C, TV, minibar, hair dryer, safe.

Hotel Inglaterra ★★   This is a genuinely excellent and very comfortable hotel whose historical importance has been to some degree obscured behind contemporary-looking marble sheathing that was added in 1968 as part of a radical modernization. Inaugurated with pomp and circumstance in 1857, and still considered one of the finest hotels in Seville, it has hosted the monarchs of Spain and Belgium (in 1915 and 1921, respectively), Seville-born actress Penelope Cruz, and a wide assortment of Spanish and international luminaries. It occupies one side of a palm-lined plaza (Plaza Nueva) that's home to some of Seville's most upscale shops. Throughout, there's an elegant but unpretentious ambience that's established by a topnotch concierge staff. Bedrooms are plush, conservatively modern, and comfortable. In 2004, management embarked on a campaign to install some of the plushest accommodations in Seville on the uppermost floors; these rooms have views directly over the Giralda and many of the antique rooftops within the immediate neighborhood.

On-site is a richly decorated Irish pub, the Trinity. One floor above street level The Galería serves well-prepared food from a frequently changing international menu.

Plaza Nueva 7, 41001 Seville. (C) **95-422-49-70.** Fax 95-456-13-36. www.hotelinglaterra.es. 102 units. 118€–204€ ($142–$245) double; 173€–255€ ($208–$306) suite. Parking 14€ ($17) per day. Bus: 21, 23, 25, 26, or 40. **Amenities:** Restaurant; bar; limited room service; babysitting; laundry service. *In room:* A/C, TV, minibar, hair dryer, safe, radio.

Hotel Montecarlo   The government gives it only a two-star rating, but this stylish 18th-century house is a good choice for those seeking old-fashioned Seville atmosphere. The hotel, with its two main yards, was last renovated in 2002, and it lies within walking distance of the historic monuments in the center of Seville. In the typically Andalusian style, there is a fountain-studded central patio filled with plants. Long corridors, columns, colorful tiles, and arches set the architectural style. The bedrooms are midsize to spacious and are comfortably and attractively furnished, each with a combination tub/shower.

Calle Gravina 51, 41001 Seville. (C) **95-421-75-01.** Fax 95-421-68-25. www.hotelmontecarlosevilla.com. 49 units. 158€ ($190) double. AE, MC, V. Bus: B2, C4, 6, or 43. **Amenities:** Restaurant; room service (8am–11pm); babysitting; laundry service. *In room:* A/C, TV, hair dryer, safe.

Hotel Monte Carmelo *(Value)*   This building, last renovated in 2002 and a 10-minute walk from the historic district, has some good deals. The midsize bedrooms are decorated in a restrained modern style, often with painted wooden furniture, carpeting, and matching fabrics. Each comes with a tiled bathroom with a tub/shower. The staff is helpful. Beds come in various sizes: doubles, king size, and even some triples if you're traveling with family. The cafeteria serves an excellent buffet breakfast.

Virgen de la Victoria 7, 41011 Seville. (C) **95-427-90-00.** Fax 95-427-10-04. www.hotelmontecarmelo.com. 68 units. 120€ ($144) double. AE, MC, V. Parking: 9€ ($11). Bus: 10, 11, 12, 15, 20, 24, 27, or 32. **Amenities:** Breakfast lounge; bar; 24-hr. room service; babysitting; laundry service/dry cleaning; nonsmoking rooms. *In room:* A/C, TV, minibar, hair dryer, safe.

Hotel Monte Triana   In the Triana district, this government-rated three-star hotel lies a 15-minute walk from the commercial center and the historic monuments. A hotel since 1991, the building rises four floors behind a dull facade with large windows. Larger numbers of business travelers are drawn to the hotel than tourists, although it is perfectly reasonable for both. Most of the rooms are on the interior, away from street noises, and connected to a pleasant patio. They are functional rather than inspired, but comfortable. The housekeeping is first rate and the bathrooms are well equipped, coming with tub/shower combinations and complimentary toiletries. A cafeteria serves breakfast and assorted dishes throughout the day.

Clara de Jesús Montero 24, 41010 Seville. © **95-434-18-32.** Fax 95-434-33-28. www.hotelesmonte.com. 117 units. 134€ ($161) double. Rates include breakfast. AE, DC, MC, V. Parking 7€ ($8.40). Bus: 43. **Amenities:** Cafeteria; bar; limited room service; babysitting; laundry service/dry cleaning; nonsmoking rooms. *In room:* A/C, TV, dataport, minibar, hair dryer, safe.

Hotel Plaza de Armas   This glass-and-steel hotel is in direct contrast to the antique *casas* of Seville converted into hotels. Built in 1992 and renovated in 2003, it is the city's most modern-looking structure, lying in the center close to the Plaza de Armas and the cathedral. The interior design consists of architectural lines of almost Japanese simplicity intermixed with steel and wood. The rooms are airy and colorful in severe contemporary style, with roomy bathrooms containing tub/shower combos.

Av. Marqués de Paradas s/n, 41001 Seville. © **95-490-19-92.** Fax 95-490-12-32. www.nh-hoteles.es. 262 units. 101€–212€ ($121–$254) double. AE, DC, MC, V. Bus: 2, 4, or 43. **Amenities:** Restaurant; bar; outdoor swimming pool; room service (8am–noon, 1–4pm, and 8–11pm); babysitting; laundry service/dry cleaning. *In room:* A/C, TV, dataport, minibar, hair dryer, safe.

Hotel San Gil Seville ★★ *Finds*   This landmark building from 1901, in a setting of towering palm trees, captures some of the colonial style of Old Seville. As a guest, you can enjoy an aura of old Andalusia but can also take advantage of modern amenities. Lying near the historic Macarena Wall and the Santa Cruz barrio, the hotel has a rooftop swimming pool that opens onto vistas of the surrounding cityscape. Inside, the hotel is richly endowed with old Andalusian styling, including an elaborate use of tiles. Bedrooms are midsize for the most part and decorated in creamy colors with light wooden furnishings, plus tiled bathrooms with tub/shower combos.

Parras 28, 41002 Seville. © **95-490-69-39.** Fax 95-490-69-39. www.holidaycityeurope.com. 60 units. 97€–198€ ($116–$238) double; 113€–222€ ($136–$266) junior suite; 150€–320€ ($180–$384) suite. Rates include continental breakfast. AE, DC, MC, V. Parking: 11€ ($13). Bus: C3, 2, 13, or 14. **Amenities:** Restaurant; bar; outdoor pool; 24-hr. room service; laundry service/dry cleaning; solarium. *In room:* A/C, TV, kitchenette (in suite), minibar, hair dryer, iron/ironing board, safe.

La Casa de la Judería ★★ *Value*   In the Santa Cruz district, this hotel is installed in a palace from the 1600s once owned by the duke of Beja, a great character in the history of Spain's aristocracy and known as the patron of Cervantes. Within easy walking distance of the cathedral and other sights, the building has been a hotel since 1991. It's now one of the best places to stay in Seville, offering excellent bang for your euro. All the rooms, medium in size, are individually decorated and furnished in an antique style, sometimes with four-poster beds; all have balconies, some facing street scenes and others opening onto one of the four interior patios. Many units have living rooms, and all the suites contain whirlpool tubs. The bathrooms are beautifully maintained, with tub/shower combos.

Plaza Santa María la Blanca, Callejón de Dos Hermanas 7, 41004 Seville. © **95-441-51-50.** Fax 95-442-21-70. www.casasypalacios.com. 119 units. 128€–246€ ($154–$295) double; 218€–365€ ($262–$438) suite. AE, DC, MC, V. Parking 15€ ($18). Bus: 21 or 23. **Amenities:** Restaurant; bar; 24-hr. room service; babysitting; laundry service/dry cleaning; 2 rooms for those w/limited mobility. *In room:* A/C, TV, minibar, hair dryer, safe.

Las Casas de los Mercaderes ★ (Finds)   Charming and historic, this boutique-style hotel was built in the 18th century (with alterations in the 19th c.) as a patio-centered three-story private home that's about as Sevillian as you can get. Today, the patio that for many generations remained open to the sky is covered with a Victorian-inspired glass and iron canopy, allowing the courtyard to be plushly furnished with kilim carpets and wicker chairs that gracefully show off a ring of delicate granite columns. Bedrooms are cozy and relatively plush, with big curtains, carpets, coordinated color schemes that usually reflect the pink tones of the building's facade and courtyard, and tile-covered bathrooms, with tub/shower combos. The cathedral lies within a 4-minute walk and the staff is attentive.

Calle Alvarez Quintero 9–13. 41004 Seville. ℭ **95-422-58-58.** Fax 95-422-98-84. www.casasypalacios.com. 47 units. 105€–128€ ($126–$154) double. Parking 15€ ($18) per day. AE, DC, MC, V. Bus: 21, 23, 41, or 42. **Amenities:** 2 bars; coffee bar; limited room service; babysitting; laundry service; solarium. *In room:* A/C, TV, minibar, hair dryer, iron/ironing board, safe.

INEXPENSIVE

Hostal Goya   Its location in a narrow-fronted town house in the oldest part of the barrio is one of the Goya's strongest virtues, but the building's gold-and-white facade, ornate iron railings, and picture-postcard demeanor are all noteworthy. The rooms are cozy and simple. Guests congregate in the marble-floored ground-level salon, where a skylight floods the couches and comfortable chairs with sunlight. No meals are served. Reserve well in advance. Parking is often available along the street.

Mateus Gago 31, 41004 Seville. ℭ **95-421-11-70.** Fax 95-456-29-88. 20 units. 70€–85€ ($84–$102) double. MC, V. Bus: 10, 12, 41, or 42. *In room:* A/C, no phone.

Hostería del Laurel ★ (Finds)   Long one of our favorite dining taverns in Santa Cruz, this traditional inn, whose downstairs is hung with cured Andalusian hams and strings of fresh garlic, also offers bargain rooms. During his stay here in 1844, Don José Zorrilla, Spain's most romantic writer of the time, was so inspired by the atmosphere of the inn that he created his famous character, Don Juan Tenorio. Bedrooms are simply furnished and immaculately kept, opening onto one of the barrio's most delightful and time-mellowed squares. Each unit comes with a small bathroom equipped with tub/shower. The rooms are spread across several floors of restored old houses with their tiny patios and bubbling fountains. When you're hungry, just follow the yummy smells to the restaurant downstairs (see "Where to Dine," later in this chapter).

Plaza de los Venerables 5, 41004 Seville. ℭ **95-422-02-95.** Fax 95-421-04-50. www.hosteriadellaurel.com. 21 units. 70€–97€ ($84–$116) double. Rates include breakfast. AE, DC, MC, V. Bus: 21, 23, 41, or 42. **Amenities:** Restaurant; bar; 24-hr. room service for drinks; 1 room for those w/limited mobility. *In room:* A/C, TV, hair dryer, safe.

Hotel América   Built in 1976 and partially renovated in 1994, this hotel contains rather small bedrooms but the maids keep the place spick-and-span. Superior features include wall-to-wall carpeting and, in winter, individual heat controls that work. All units have well-kept bathrooms with tub/shower combinations. Near the hotel is a parking garage for 600 cars. There isn't a major restaurant, but the América does offer a tearoom and a cafeteria that serves regional and international cuisine. The hotel is set on the northern side of the Plaza del Duque. One of Spain's major department stores, El Corte Inglés, opens onto the same square.

Jesús del Gran Poder 2, 41002 Seville. ℭ **95-422-09-51.** Fax 95-421-06-26. 100 units. 80€–110€ ($96–$132) double. AE, DC, MC, V. Parking 8.50€ ($10) nearby. Bus: 2, 10, 20, or 32. **Amenities:** Cafeteria; lounge; laundry service/dry cleaning. *In room:* A/C, TV, dataport, minibar.

Hotel Doña Manuela (Casa Modesto)   This, one of Seville's newest hotels, owes its existence to the success and the recent expansion of a the Modesto, a restaurant recommended later in this chapter. The Modesto's outdoor tables fill most of the available space of a cobble-covered plaza near the northern edge of the Barrio de Santa Cruz. Its three-story facade, with heavy roof cornices and wrought-iron railings surrounding each of the ocher-trimmed windows, reflects the building techniques of the 19th century, as does its scarlet-colored, antiques-dotted lobby. However, despite its virtues as a building with a sense of history, this is a government-rated two-star hotel whose upstairs furnishings and amenities are less luxurious than the lobby implies. Rooms are small and relatively modest, with simple, angular furniture, flowered fabrics, and a sense of modernity inspired to some degree by the 1970s. The rooftop, however, boasts a tile-floored sun terrace, with views over the Murillo Gardens (Jardines de Murillo), which begin just across the avenue. The cathedral, accessible via a series of very narrow and colorful alleyways, lies within an 11-minute walk.

Paseo Catalina de Ribera 2, 41004 Seville. ⓒ **95-454-64-00**. Fax 95-454-64-20. donmanuela@andalunet.com. 19 units. 75€–100€ ($90–$120) double. Rates include breakfast. Parking 13€ ($15) per day. AE, DC, MC, V. Bus: 21 or 23. **Amenities:** Direct access to Casa Modesto's restaurant and bar; room service (during restaurant open hours only). *In room:* A/C, TV, safe.

Hotel Europa   Dating from the 18th century, this hotel lies next to La Giralda, the Cathedral and the once Jewish ghetto of Santa Cruz. It still retains much of its original character, though it has been modified over the years. The hotel is small but choice, with many Moorish architectural details still evident, including tall windows with iron grilles, wide stairs, marble floors, and wooden screens. Bedrooms for the most part are small, though comfortably furnished with rather dark, heavy wooden pieces and thick curtains. Each comes with a tiled bathroom with tub/shower combination.

Jimios 5, 41001 Seville. ⓒ **95-450-04-43**. Fax 95-421-43-05. www.hoteleuropasevilla.com. 25 units. 91€ ($109) double. MC, V. Parking 10€ ($12). Bus: 21, 23, 25, 26, 30, 31, 33, 34, or 40. **Amenities:** Room service (8am–11pm); babysitting. *In room:* A/C, TV.

Hotel Murillo   Tucked away on a narrow street in the heart of Santa Cruz, the Residencia Murillo (named after the artist who used to live in this district) is very close to the gardens of the Alcázar. Inside, the lounges harbor some fine architectural characteristics and antique reproductions; behind a grilled screen is a retreat for drinks. Many of the rooms we inspected were cheerless and gloomy, so have a look before checking in. All contain bathrooms with tub/shower combos. You can reach this *residencia* from the Menéndez y Pelayo, a wide avenue west of the Parque María Luisa, where a sign leads you through the **Murillo Gardens** on the left. Motorists should try to park in the Plaza de Santa Cruz. Then walk 2 blocks to the hotel, which will send a bellhop back to the car to pick up your suitcases. If there are two in your party, station a guard at the car, and if you're going out at night, call for an inexpensive taxi to take you instead of strolling through the streets of the old quarter—it's less romantic but a lot safer.

Calle Lope de Rueda 7–9, 41004 Seville. ⓒ **95-421-60-95**. Fax 95-421-96-16. www.hotelmurillo.com. 57 units. 50€–63€ ($60–$76) double; 63€–79€ ($76–$95) triple. AE, DC, MC, V. Parking 14€ ($17) nearby. Bus: 21 or 23. **Amenities:** Breakfast room; laundry service/dry cleaning; nonsmoking rooms. *In room:* A/C.

Hotel Rey Alfonso X ⚡   One of the newest and most arresting hotels in Seville occupies a triangle-shaped plaza from which it's easy to access, via a brisk 7-minute walk through impossibly narrow alleyways loaded with shops and tascas, the rear side of the cathedral. In 2002 this former office building was radically gutted and

stripped, replaced by an angular, glistening, architecturally dramatic and minimalist interior that's entirely sheathed, both in its bedrooms and public areas, with
slabs of beige-colored marble, dark-stained hardwoods, and white plaster walls.
The most interesting bedrooms directly overlook the animated plaza outside.
Additional bedrooms with less intriguing views overlook courtyards and the buildings of the surround neighborhood. Bathrooms have tub/shower combos.

Ximénez de Enciso 35, 41004 Seville. © **95-421-00-70.** Fax 95-422-02-46. www.reyalfonsox.com. 35 units.
80€ ($96) double; 175€ ($210) suite. Parking 13€ ($16). AE, DC, MC, V. Bus: 21, 23, 41, or 42. **Amenities:**
Bar; access to the rooftop pool at the Hotel Fernando III across the street; 24-hr. room service; laundry service. *In room:* A/C, TV, safe.

Hotel Simón *(Value)*   This 18th-century mansion next to the cathedral in the
Arenal district is a bargain hunter's delight. Within are a beautifully ornate staircase and a patio of tropical plants. The social areas are chic and comfortable, and
the lounge displays bric-a-brac belonging to the original mansion. Reservations
are recommended as far in advance as possible because the word is out that this
is a stylish establishment charging low prices. The rooms are medium to large,
each individually decorated in keeping with the history of this place, even with
antiques. All units contain bathrooms with tub/shower combos.

Calle García de Vinuesa 190, 41001 Seville. © **95-422-66-60.** Fax 95-456-22-41. 31 units. www.hotelsimon
sevilla.com. 70€–92€ ($84–$110) double; 100€–120€ ($120–$144) suite. DC, MC, V. Bus: 21, 23, 41, or 42.
Amenities: Breakfast room; lounge; laundry service/dry cleaning. *In room:* A/C, hair dryer.

WHERE TO STAY NEARBY

El Palacio de San Benito ★★★ *(Finds)*   The most exclusive B&B in southern
Spain, this treasure lies in a stunningly converted palace that represents the epitome of luxury living as practiced by Spanish dons in the 14th to 15th centuries.
You'll need a car to reach the little Moorish town of Cazalla de la Sierra, a 75km
(47-mile) drive north of the center of Seville. Seville's best-known decorator,
Manuel Morales de Jódar, is responsible for the restoration of the palace and for
its decoration, which is a medley of styles and eras. Somehow a look that encompasses everything from centuries-old Andalusian tiles to Baroque antiques manages to be beautifully harmonious. A patio of columns greets you, along with
fountains and landscaping. Various tapestries from Aubusson in France and
from Brussels decorate the palace. The library with its Carrara marble fireplace
evokes the best of 19th-century Victoriana. The bedrooms are sumptuous and
beautifully furnished, most often with 17th and 18th century pieces including
much from the reign of Queen Isabella II. The on-site restaurant offers market-
fresh ingredients turned into elegant and tasty dishes by a master chef.

Cazalla de la Sierra, 41370 Seville. © **95-488-33-36.** Fax 95-488-31-62. www.palaciodesanbenito.com. 9 units.
120€–210€ ($144–$252) double with breakfast; 240€–330€ ($288–$396) double with half-board. AE, DC,
DISC, MC, V. Parking 12€ ($14). **Amenities:** Restaurant; bar; outdoor pool; 24-hr. room service; laundry serv-
ice/dry cleaning; 1 room for those w/limited mobility. *In room:* A/C, TV, dataport, minibar, hair dryer.

Hacienda Benazuza/El Bulli Hotel ★★★ *(Finds)*   On a hillside above the
agrarian hamlet of Sanlúcar la Mayor, 19km (12 miles) south of Seville, this legendary manor house is surrounded by 16 hectares (40 acres) of olive groves and
farmland. The history of its ownership reads like roster of every major cultural
influence that has swept through Andalusia since the Moors laid its foundations
in the 10th century. After the Catholic conquest of southern Spain, the site
became a stronghold of the fanatically religious Caballeros de Santiago. In 1992,
Basque-born entrepreneur Rafael Elejabeitia bought the property and spent millions of pesetas to transform it into one of Andalusia's most charming hotels.

Careful attention was paid to preserving the ancient Moorish irrigation system, whose many reflecting pools nourish the gardens. All but a few of the rooms are in the estate's main building, each individually furnished with Andalusian antiques and Moorish trappings. All units contain neatly kept bathrooms with tub/shower combos. The kitchen is run by Ferran Adrià, the famous Catalonian chef who is hailed as one of the top two or three best chefs in the country. He's rarely on the premises but his recipes and cooking style are used. Even if you're not staying here, you might want to call for a dinner reservation. Chances are it'll be one of your finest meals in Seville.

Calle Virgen de las Nieves s/n, 41800 Sanlúcar la Mayor, Seville. ✆ **95-570-33-44.** Fax 95-570-3410. www. hbenazuza.com. 44 units. 310€–390€ ($372–$468) double; 435€–535€ ($522–$642) junior suite; 1,030€–1,130€ ($1,236–$1,356) suite. AE, DC, MC, V. Free parking. Closed Jan. From Seville, follow the signs for Huelva and head south on the A-49 Hwy., taking Exit 16. **Amenities:** 3 restaurants; bar; outdoor pool; tennis court; 24-hr. room service; babysitting; laundry service/dry cleaning; rooms for those w/limited mobility. *In room:* A/C, TV, dataport, minibar, hair dryer, safe.

4 Where to Dine

VERY EXPENSIVE

Egaña Oriza ✿✿✿ BASQUE/INTERNATIONAL   Seville's most stylish restaurant is within the conservatory of a restored mansion adjacent to the Murillo Gardens. Its reputation stems in large part from a game-heavy menu in a region otherwise devoted to seafood. The restaurant was opened by Basque-born owner/chef José Mari Egaña, who combines his passion for hunting with his flair for cooking. Many of the ingredients have been trapped or shot within Andalusia. The view from the dining room encompasses a garden and a wall that formed part of the fortifications of Muslim Seville. Specialties depend on the season but might include ostrich carpaccio, gazpacho with prawns, steak with foie gras in grape sauce, casserole of wild boar with cherries and raisins, duck *quenelles* in a potato nest with apple purée, and woodcock flamed in Spanish brandy. The wine list provides an ample supply of hearty Spanish reds. Dessert might feature a chocolate tart slathered with freshly whipped cream.

San Fernando 41. ✆ **95-422-72-11.** Reservations required. Main courses 20€–50€ ($24–$60). AE, DC, MC, V. Restaurant: Mon–Fri 1:30–3:30pm and 9–11:30pm, Sat 9–11:30pm; bar: daily 10am–midnight. Closed Aug. Bus: 21 or 23.

La Isla ✿ SPANISH/ANDALUSIAN   La Isla consists of two large Andalusian dining rooms (thick plaster walls, tile floors, and taurine memorabilia). The seafood is trucked or flown in from either Galicia or Huelva, one of Andalusia's major ports, and is always fresh. Menu items include *merluza a la primavera* (hake with young vegetables), *solomillo a la castellana* (grilled beefsteak with strips of Serrano ham), chicken croquettes, and shellfish soup. The restaurant is a short walk from the cathedral within a very old building erected, the owners say, on foundations laid by the ancient Romans.

Arfe 25. ✆ **95-421-26-31.** Reservations recommended. Main courses 22€–38€ ($26–$46). AE, DC, MC, V. Daily 1:30–5:30pm and 8pm–midnight. Closed Aug. Bus: 21, 25, 41, or 42.

Taberna del Alabardero ✿✿ ANDALUSIAN   One of Seville's most prestigious restaurants occupies a 19th-century town house 3 blocks from the cathedral. Famous as the dining choice of nearly every politician and diplomat who visits Seville, it has recently hosted the king and queen of Spain, the Spanish president and members of his cabinet, and dozens of well-connected but merely affluent visitors. Amid a collection of European antiques and oil paintings, you'll dine in any of two main rooms or three private ones, and perhaps precede your meal with a drink or tapas on the flowering patio. There's a garden in back with additional tables. Tantalizing menu items include spicy peppers stuffed with pulverized thigh of bull, Andalusian fish *(urta)* on a compote of aromatic tomatoes with coriander, cod filet with essence of red peppers, and Iberian beefsteak with foie gras and green peppers.

Calle Zaragoza 20, 41001 Seville. © **95-450-27-21.** Fax 95-456-36-66. Reservations recommended. Main courses 20€–30€ ($24–$36). AE, DC, MC, V. Daily 1–4pm and 8pm–midnight. Closed Aug. Bus: C1.

EXPENSIVE

Becerrita ⚐ *Finds* ANDALUSIAN/SPANISH   Frankly, Sevillanos would like to keep this cozy little trattoria to themselves, but slowly word is getting out to an international community. In an elegant setting near Plaza Carmen Benitez, the restaurant is decorated with colorful wallpaper, wooden columns, and a collection of drawings. Locals claim the chefs make the best bull's tail croquettes *(croquetas de cola de toro)* in Seville. Against a backdrop of ceramic walls and linen-covered tables, you can also order tamer fare like young sirloin steak, baked white prawns in garlic sauce with white beans, or cod stuffed with scallops and served in a pastry shell with pine nuts. Sea bass in a cockle sauce is another delight, as is the asparagus with strips of ham. Also look for the wide array of fresh, tasty tapas such as stuffed calamari. The chef's signature dish is an Iberian pork stew *(carrillada de Ibérico estofado).* If you like fish ask about the daily fresh catch.

Recaredo 9, Santa Catalina. © **95-441-20-57.** Reservations recommended. Main courses 12€–25€ ($14–$30). AE, V. Mon–Sat 1–4:30pm and 8pm–midnight; Sun 1–4:30pm. Closed Aug. Bus: A, A2, or C2.

Casa Robles *Overrated* ANDALUSIAN   Locals and major Spanish gourmet books laud this restaurant, but we have our doubts. It began life as an unpretentious bar and bodega in 1954 and over the years has evolved into a bustling two-floor restaurant in a building a short walk from the cathedral. In an all-Andalusian decor, you can order such standard dishes as fish soup in the Andalusian style, *lubina con naranjas* (whitefish with Sevillana oranges), hake baked with strips of Serrano ham, and many kinds of fresh fish. The dessert list is long and very tempting. If you opt for a meal at Robles, by all means, avoid the street-level tapas bar, where a drunk or two might wander in during mealtime, where the toilets seem as open and available as something at the local bus station, and where, even if you opt for a seat near the busy restrooms, you'll be charged the same inflated prices (with service that's much worse) as in the grander and more formal dining room upstairs.

Calle Alvarez Quintero 58. © **95-421-31-50.** Reservations recommended. Main courses 15€–21€ ($18–$25). AE, DC, MC, V. Daily 2–5pm and 9pm–1:30am. Bus: 41 or 42.

Corral del Agua ⚐ *Finds* SEVILLANA   In an ancient building with a central courtyard, this discovery is charmingly positioned in the old barrio of Santa Cruz. With its marble fountain and plants, it is a cozy, atmospheric choice. Once patronized by Don Juan himself (or so it's claimed), this building was originally a stable. Two recommend starters are the invigorating salad of lettuce hearts from Tudela with sautéed garlic and strips of ham, and the salmon pudding with mayonnaise. Among our favorite main courses is sea bass in a dry sherry sauce. Also terrific was a sirloin of veal cooked in the old Sevillana way (garlic, bay leaf, olive oil, and vegetables, and lots of black pepper). Aficionados order *cola de toro al estilo de Sevilla* (bull's tail in the style of Seville).

Seville Dining

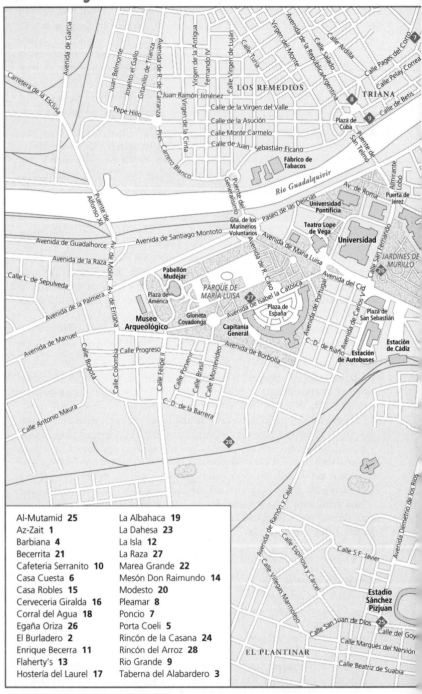

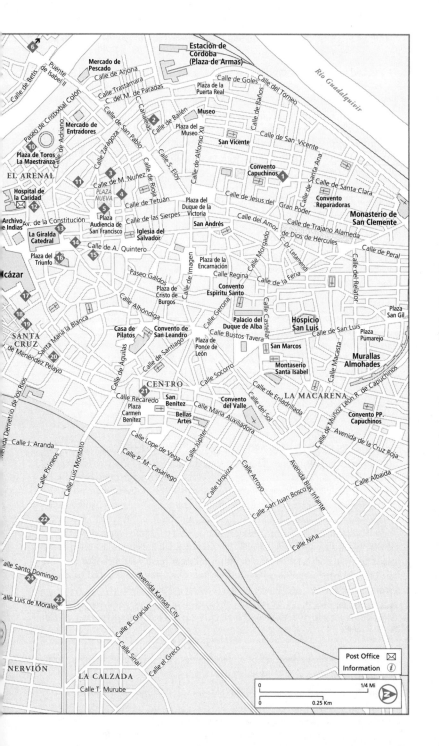

Estación de
Córdoba
(Plaza de Armas)

Río Guadalquivir

Mercado de
Pescado

Calle de Arjona

Calle de Goles

Calle del Torneo

Calle Trastámara

Plaza de la
Puerta Real

C. del M. de Paradas

Calle de Betis

Puente de Isabel II

Paseo de Cristóbal Colón

Calle de Adriano

Calle Tarazona

Calle de San Pablo

Calle Canalejas

Calle de Bailén

Museo

Plaza del
Museo

Calle de Baños

Calle de San Vicente

Calle de Santa Ana

San Vicente

Convento
Capuchinos

Calle de Santa Clara

Mercado de
Entradores

Plaza de Toros
La Maestranza

EL ARENAL

Calle S. Eloy

Calle de Alfonso XII

Calle de Jesús del Gran Poder

Convento
Reparadoras

Monasterio de
San Clemente

Hospital de
la Caridad

Calle de M. Nuñez

Calle de Rioja

PLAZA
NUEVA

Calle de Tetuán

Plaza del
Duque de la
Victoria

Calle del Amor

de Dios de Hércules

Calle de Trajano Alameda

Calle de Peral

Archivo
e Indias

Av. de la Constitución

Plaza
Audiencia de
San Francisco

Calle de las Sierpes

San Andrés

Calle del Relator

La Giralda
Catedral

Iglesia del
Salvador

Calle de A. Quintero

Plaza de la
Encarnación

C. D. Letanendi

Calle Morgado

Plaza del
Triunfo

Calle de Imagen

Calle Regina

Calle de la Feria

Plaza
San Gil

cázar

Paseo Galdós

Plaza de
Cristo de
Burgos

Convento
Espiritu Santo

Calle Alhóndiga

Calle Gerona

Palacio del
Duque de Alba

Hospicio
San Luis

Calle de San Luis

Plaza
Pumarejo

Calle Castellar

Casa de
Pilatos

Convento de
San Leandro

Calle Bustos Tavera

San Marcos

Murallas
Almohades

SANTA
CRUZ

Santa María la Blanca

Calle de Aguilas

Calle de Santiago

Plaza de
Ponce de
León

Montaserio
Santa Isabel

Calle Macasta

de Menéndez Pelayo

Calle Socorro

Calle de Enladrillada

LA MACARENA

Avenida Demetrio de los Ríos

CENTRO

Calle Recaredo

San
Benítez

Convento
del Valle

Calle de Muñoz León

R. de Capuchinos

Convento PP.
Capuchinos

Calle J. Aranda

Plaza
Carmen
Benítez

Bellas
Artes

Calle María Auxiliadora

Calle del Sol

Avenida de la Cruz Roja

Calle Luis Montoto

Calle Lope de Vega

Calle Júpiter

Avenida Blas Infante

Calle Albaida

Calle Pirineos

Calle P. M. Casariego

Calle Urquiza

Calle Arroyo

Calle San Juan Bosco Infante

Avenida Kansas City

Calle Niña

Calle Santo Domingo

Calle Luis de Morales

Calle B. Gracián

NERVIÓN

LA CALZADA

Calle Sinaí

Calle el Greco

Calle T. Murube

Post Office ⊠
Information ⓘ

0   1/4 Mi

0   0.25 Km

83

Callejón del Agua 6. ✆ **95-422-07-14.** Reservations recommended. Main courses 15€–18€ ($18–$22). Mon–Sat noon–4pm and 8pm–midnight. Closed Jan to mid-Feb. Bus: 21, 25, 26, 30, or 31.

El Burladero ✮ CONTINENTAL   This restaurant in one of Seville's most prominent hotels is awash in bullfighting memorabilia. The wall tiles were removed from one of the pavilions at the 1929 Seville world's fair, and the photographs adorning the walls are a veritable history of bullfighting. The restaurant boasts a popular bar, where Sevillanos meet and mingle before their meals. Menu specialties include upscale interpretations of local country dishes, with an attractive mix of items from other regions of Spain and Europe as well. Examples include *bacalao al horno con patatas* (baked salt cod with potatoes and saffron sauce), roasted shoulder of lamb stuffed with a deboned oxtail and served in a richly aromatic sauce, clams with white kidney beans, and *cocido* (a boiled amalgam of sausages, meats, chickpeas, and vegetables). Dishes from other parts of Europe include duck liver, truffled filet steak in puff pastry, and salmon cooked in lemon-flavored dill sauce.

In the Hotel Meliá Colón, Canalejas 1. ✆ **95-450-55-99.** Reservations recommended. Main courses 14€–22€ ($17–$26); fixed-price menus from 35€ ($42). AE, DC, MC, V. Daily 1:30–3:30pm and 9–11:30pm. Closed mid-June to Sept 2. Bus: 2 or 43.

Enrique Becerra ✮ ANDALUSIAN   Near the cathedral and Plaza Nueva, this popular tapas bar and dining spot has a cozy, intimate setting that makes you feel welcome and appreciated. While perusing the menu, you can sip dry Tío Pepe and nibble herb-cured olives with lemon peel. Specialties include gazpacho, sea bream Bilbao style, and a wide range of well-prepared meat and fish dishes. The ice-cold sangria is great for hot summer days. The wine list is one of Seville's best.

Gamazo 2. ✆ **95-421-30-49.** Reservations recommended. Main courses 12€–20€ ($14–$24); fixed-price menus 37€–43€ ($44–$52). AE, DC, MC, V. Mon–Sat 1–5pm and 8pm–midnight. Closed Aug. Bus: 21, 25, 30, or 40.

Hostería del Laurel ✮ *Finds* ANDALUSIAN   This hidden treasure is tucked in one of the most charming buildings on tiny, difficult-to-find Plaza de los Venerables in Barrio de Santa Cruz. When the 19th-century playwright José Zorilla rewrote Tirso de Molina's original *Don Juan,* he used the Hostería de Luarel as one of the settings for his rewrite. It has iron-barred windows stuffed with plants. Inside, amid Andalusian tiles, beamed ceilings, and more plants, you'll enjoy good regional cooking. The *hostería* has some of the best and freshest tapas in town, our favorite being a *zarzuelita de mariscos* (shellfish cocktail) appetizer. The catch of the day is flown in daily, and fish can be either grilled or fried. The chefs also turn out one of the town's best seafood-studded paellas. The *hostería* is attached to a well-recommended hotel; see "Where to Stay," earlier in this chapter.

Plaza de los Venerables 5. ✆ **95-422-02-95.** Reservations recommended. Main courses 12€–35€ ($14–$42); 3-course fixed-price menu 60€ ($72). AE, DC, MC, V. Daily noon–4pm and 8pm–midnight. Bus: 21, 23, 41, or 42.

⌒Finds Churros: Fit for a King

Calle Postigo is adjacent to Seville's Alcázar, site of the royal family's residence in Seville. Shops on this street sell *churros,* an unsweetened deep-fried pastry. Royalty-watchers have, during the family's rare residences in Seville, seen *el Rey* buying churros at some of the shops on this street. Bus: 41 or 42.

La Albahaca ★★ FRENCH/BASQUE   This elegant restaurant is in the Barrio de Santa Cruz, Seville's most evocative quarter. Juan Talavera, a celebrated architect, constructed this 1920s Andalusian mansion, and many of the original architectural features remain. Over the years the restaurant has attracted royals such as the king and queen of Spain, and visiting celebrities like Charlton Heston.

Lovely and graceful, it shuttles diners from a high-ceilinged central courtyard into one of several parlor-sized dining rooms each decorated in a smooth, nostalgic style that reflects the tastes and opulence of Spain's Victorian era. High quality ingredients go into the first-rate cuisine. Intriguing appetizers include a fresh goose liver and apple terrine in a pheasant jelly, and the baked sea bass with stir-fried plums, raisins, and almonds. Enduring main courses are roasted wild boar with fig marmalade, and a roasted pheasant breast with Iberian bacon. One of our favorites is veal sirloin with fresh gooseliver and a red-wine sauce. If we had to pick three desserts off a menu that's one of the best in town, we'd choose the fig soufflé, the bitter orange mousse, and the cottage cheesecake with walnuts.

Plaza Santa Cruz 12. ☏ **95-422-07-14.** Reservations required. Main courses 15€–30€ ($18–$36). AE, DC, MC, V. Mon–Sat 1–4pm and 8pm–midnight. Bus: 21 or 23.

La Dehesa ★ ANDALUSIAN   One of Seville's leading restaurants, La Dehesa is known for its regional decor and for serving some of the finest cuisine in town. It is decorated like an elegant bodega (wine tavern) with stucco walls and windows with potted plants. Each corner is a shrine to a particular bullfighter, all of whom have donated memorabilia. Some of the city's best chefs show off their prowess with market-fresh, perfectly prepared fish and seafood. Meats, such as the tender, garlic-flavored lamb cutlets, are a particularly good choice: Herbs and spices are used judiciously to bring out natural flavor. Our preferred appetizer is the flavorful *ensalada de La Dehesa* (shrimp, avocado, and green leaf salad). Desserts are homemade and sumptuous, including freshly baked tarts or a delightful platter of crepes stuffed with nuts and banana ice cream.

Calle Luis de Morales 2. ☏ **95-457-62-04.** Reservations required. Main courses 14€–23€ ($17–$28). AE, DC, MC, V. Daily 1:30–4pm and 8:30pm–midnight. Bus: 32, 70, or 71.

MODERATE

Al-Mutamid ★ ANDALUSIAN   Among the top 10 restaurants of Seville, this winner stands east of the Alcázar and the Parque de María Luisa. It is luxuriously decorated with maritime artifacts, creamy colors, sculptures, and modern lighting. We're still salivating at the memory of the sea bass with crab sauce and the rice "marine style" (very much like a paella using only shellfish). Meat fanciers will delight in the tender and beautifully seasoned entrecote of veal and also in the oven-roasted and well-seasoned ribs of lamb. A platter of fresh shellfish is one of the best dishes to order. The shellfish is freshly harvested each day from the coast near Huelva, and then perfectly grilled with fresh garlic and white wine. Finish off with an orange mousse with honey. You can dine in air-conditioned comfort or out on the terrace.

Gran Plaza 8. ☏ **95-492-55-04.** Reservations required. Main courses 9€–26€ ($11–$31). AE, MC, V. Daily noon–5pm and 8pm–1:30am. Bus: C or C3.

Az-Zait ANDALUSIAN/INTERNATIONAL   Next to the Convent of San Lorenzo, this charming, graceful restaurant has good service and inventive cuisine inspired by the classics. In air-conditioned comfort, you can order dishes that are often influenced by the Far East—the Spanish call it *gastronómica oriental*. Begin with a refreshing bowl of gazpacho, which, for a change of pace, is served with a carpaccio of shrimp. You can go on to such main dishes as codfish cooked in the regional style with fresh tomatoes and olives, or the grilled honey-glazed cuttle-fish, a preparation preferred by the former Moorish conquerors. Local gas-tronomes recommend the loin of sea bass in a velvety smooth cream sauce.

Plaza San Lorenzo 1. ✆ **95-490-64-75.** Reservations recommended. Main courses 9€–20€ ($11–$24). AE, MC, V. Mon–Sat 1–4pm and 8:30pm–midnight; Sun 1–4pm. Bus: C3, 6, 13, or 14.

Barbiana ✿✿ ANDALUSIAN/SEAFOOD   Close to the Plaza Nueva in the heart of Seville, this is one of the city's best fish restaurants. Chefs endeavor to secure the freshest seafood, even though Seville is inland. In the classic Andalusian architectural tradition, a tapas bar is up front. In the rear is a cluster of rustically decorated dining rooms. The trick here is not to consume so much wine and tapas in the front that you are too stuffed to enjoy the main courses. If you visit for lunch, the chef's specialty is seafood with rice (not available in the evening). We've sampled many items on the menu, often in the company of friends, and our hands down favorites are *ortiguilla,* a sea anemone fast fried in oil, and the *tortillitas de camarones,* chickpea fritters with bits of chopped shrimp and fresh scallions. If you're going to order shellfish, the specialty here, get it *a la plancha* (fresh from the grill). Fresh fish is also available grilled with a zesty sauce, or deep-fried. We always keep an eye out for the *sargo* (rockfish), which is grilled and flavored with garlic juice and served with sweet roasted red peppers.

Calle Albaredo 11. ✆ **95-421-12-39.** Reservations recommended. Main courses 9€–20€ ($11–$24). AE, DC, MC, V. Mon–Sat noon–4:30pm and 8pm–midnight; Sun 8pm–midnight. Bus: 21, 25, 30, or 40.

La Raza SPANISH/SEAFOOD   In business for more than half a century, this longtime favorite lies on the periphery of the Parque María Luisa. Shaded by palms or rubber trees, sidewalk tables are placed outside in fair weather. This modern restaurant also has a big bar with an outside patio. Natural flavors and robust spicing characterize the good-tasting main dishes. A local favorite is *cola de toro* (oxtail); tamer fare includes succulent prawns in garlic butter and flecks of freshly chopped parsley. Sirloin steak is made even more enticing with a fla-vorful whiskey sauce. A cooling bowl of gazpacho is an ideal summer starter.

Av. Isabel la Católica 2, off Plaza de España. ✆ **95-423-20-24.** Reservations recommended. Main courses 10€–25€ ($12–$30). AE, MC, V. Daily 9am–1am. Bus: C2, 1, 5, or 34.

Marea Grande ✿✿ SEAFOOD/ANDALUSIAN   One of Seville's top five restaurants, this Mediterranean-style place lies off Eduardo Data. Inside you'll sit by candlelight at discreetly separated tables surrounded by wooden furnishings and artwork. In fair weather you can also dine on the terrace. The chefs create high-quality dishes, some innovative, some traditional. King prawns with Béchamel sauce, and a tender sirloin steak with black peppercorns are two of the best options. Beef tacos come with a port-enriched salsa, but for something spicier, opt for the hake *(merluza)* in a pil-pil sauce (codfish gelatin and herbs whipped into a mayonnaise-like consistency with olive oil). A signature dish is octopus prepared with shrimp. For dessert, we'd recommend a caramel-flavored pastry with orange marmalade and both a white and dark chocolate sauce.

Diego Angulo Iñiguez 16. ✆ **95-453-80-00.** Reservations required. Main courses 8€–20€ ($9.60–$23); fixed-price menu 35€ ($42). AE, MC, V. Mon–Sat 1:30–4:30pm and 9pm–midnight. Closed Aug 15–30. Bus: 21 or 23.

Mesón Don Raimundo ANDALUSIAN/MOORISH   Near the cathedral and the landmark Virgen de los Reyes, this lunch restaurant is not only one of the best in the heavily trodden tourist district, but also one of the most convenient for sightseers. It is tucked away in an alleyway—a bit hard to find—lying off Calle Argote de Molina. Very cozy, with dark wooden furnishings, it evokes an old convent. The wine cellar is choice, and the welcome is warm. Dishes have a real taste of Andalusia, exemplified by the ribs of wild boar baked to perfection over firewood. Sherry from nearby Jerez de la Frontera flavors a sauce for the beef tenderloin. Some of the dishes display a Moorish influence, including the Mozarab-style wild duck braised in sherry. In fall look for the perfectly seasoned pheasant. Fish also appears; our favorite is the filets of sea bass with fresh prawns, lots of garlic and olive oil, and pine nuts.

Calle Argote de Molina 26, Santa Cruz. ✆ **95-422-33-55.** Reservations recommended. Main courses 6€–21€ ($7.20–$25). Daily 11:30am–4pm. Bus: 21, 23, or 25.

Modesto *Value* SPANISH   Belying its "modest" name, this place fills the ground floors of two antique buildings on opposite sides of a cobble-covered square in the Barrio de Santa Cruz. Established around 1900, it more than doubled in size in 2004 when it annexed a neighboring building. During clement weather, scores of local residents pack into the square to enjoy Modesto's good food and low prices. On warm nights, an army of black-vested, white-shirted waiters dashes about the square, delivering platters of fried fish, grilled meats, olives, salads, and soups. Fish and shellfish soup comes rich with saffron and seafood flavorings; a mixed platter of deep-fried fish relies on the Mediterranean's bounty. There are platters of Iberian ham, sole, hake *(merluza),* and pork in many different variations, flans, and a wide selection of Andalusian and Spanish wines.

Cano y Cueto 5. ✆ **95-441-68-11.** Main courses 6€–20€ ($7.20–$24). AE, DC, MC, V. Daily noon–5pm and 8pm–2am. Bus: 21 or 23.

Pleamar SEAFOOD/SPANISH/MEDITERRANEAN   Close to the Plaza de Cuba, this is a first-rate seafood restaurant, serving many specialties known along Spain's Costa del Sol. With its nautical decor, it's been in Seville for more than a quarter of a century. It has loyal devotees, and also attracts a discerning foreign clientele. Alongside a well-chosen *carte* of regional wines, the kitchen turns out dishes that are a celebration of forthright flavors and market-fresh ingredients. Its seafood paella is one of the best in Seville, or try a local favorite like noodles with anchovies or salted sea bass. An array of fresh shellfish can be either sautéed or grilled, and you can also order fish baked in a salt crust, a technique that keeps the fish moist and tender. (Both salt and skin are removed at table.) Save room for one of the special desserts, made fresh daily.

Gustavo Bacarisas 1. ✆ **95-427-79-80.** Reservations recommended. Main courses 8€–16€ ($9.60–$19). AE, MC, V. Daily 1–4pm and 8pm–midnight. Closed Aug 15–30. Buses: C3, 4, 5, 41, or 42.

Poncio *Finds* ANDALUSIAN   Even if your cabbie tells you that this relatively new dining room in the Triana district doesn't exist, press on and you'll discover some of Seville's finest food. Eat in style with Spanish dons and sherrymakers from Jerez de la Frontera who journey to Seville on business. Chef Willy Moya might have studied in Paris, but when he got back home, he invented his own dishes. We like to start with a platter of the tender, flavorful Jabugo ham, preceded, of course, by a glass of sherry. On our last visit our party ordered an array of tapas: baby broad beans with quail eggs and ham; fresh, salted anchovies; and steamed peppers stuffed with prawns and orange cream. Only the croquettes were disappointing, a bit heavy. That "thick tomato soup" on the English menu turns out to be one of Seville's most delightful gazpachos. Ask the waiter to describe the dish of the day—often the best choice on the menu—or stick to such favorites as tender lamb, aromatically roasted in a wood-burning stove or salt-encrusted sea bass in a delicate prawn oil served with olive caviar (not caviar, but minced olives). The desserts have never disappointed. Would you believe hot apple pie with ice cream? The wine list is short but refined.

Calle Victoria 8. ℰ **95-434-00-10**. Reservations required. Main courses 12€–24€ ($14–$29). AE, DC, MC, V. Mon–Sat 2–4pm and 9:30–11:30pm. Bus: 5 or 42.

Porta Coeli ✦✦ MEDITERRANEAN With one of Seville's most sophisticated decors, this is the finest hotel dining in the city. Even if you're not a hotel guest, consider reserving one of the 15 beautifully laid tables set against a backdrop of tapestry-hung walls. The flavor combinations are contemporary, and rely on fresh ingredients. The menu boasts a wide variety of dishes featuring duck with fried white beans and ham. Another savory offering is *ensalada de bacalao con tomate* (salt cod salad with tomatoes) and *arroz marinero con bogavante* (rice with crayfish). The locals rave about the *corazón de solomillo al foie con zetas al vino* (beef heart with liver and mushroom in red-wine sauce), though this might be an acquired taste. For dessert, nothing beats the luscious napoleon with fresh fruit.

In the Hesperia Sevilla, Eduardo Dato 49. ℰ **95-454-83-00**. Reservations recommended. Main courses 11€–29€ ($13–$35). AE, DC, MC, V. Mon–Sat 1:30–4pm and 9pm–midnight. Closed Aug. Bus: 23.

Río Grande *Kids* ANDALUSIAN This classic Sevillian restaurant is named for the Guadalquivir River, which its panoramic windows overlook. It sits near the Plaza de Cuba in front of the Torre del Oro. Some diners come here just for the view of the city monuments. Most dishes are priced at the lower end of the scale. A meal might include stuffed sweet pepper *flamenca,* fish-and-seafood soup seaman's style, salmon, chicken-and-shellfish paella, bull's tail Andalusian-style, or garlic chicken. A selection of fresh shellfish is brought in daily. Large terraces contain a snack bar, the Río Grande Pub, and a bingo room. You can often watch sports events on the river in this pleasant (and English-speaking) spot.

Calle Betis s/n. ℰ **95-427-83-71**. Reservations required. Main courses 15€–21€ ($18–$25). AE, DC, MC, V. Daily 1–4pm and 8pm–midnight. Bus: C3.

INEXPENSIVE

Cafetería Serranito SPANISH The venue is as low-key as anything we recommend within Seville, a cheap, bustling, workaday restaurant where portions are big, service is inscrutable and even gruff (certainly it's monolingual), and cuisine is mass-market but flavorful. Set deliberately near Seville's bullfight ring, this is the circa-1980 branch of an older restaurant that dates from 1923. Expect crowds on normal days, and mobs just before and after the fights. Torero memorabilia and at least eight stuffed bulls heads adorn the walls; bullfight fans remember some of these animals individually and distinctly from former fights. Fish dishes include *pijotas* (small fried hake); *cazón en adobo* (seasoned dogfish); *pez espada* (grilled swordfish); a house specialty known as *caldereta de toro* (bull-meat stew); *gambas al ajillo* (prawns fried with garlic); and *serranito de pollo* (cured ham with chicken filets, tomato sauce, and bread.) Come here for the sociology as much as for the dining—and bring your sense of humor.

Antonia Díaz 4. ℰ **95-421-12-43**. Reservations not accepted. Main courses 6€–14€ ($7.20–$17). Half-platters 3.60€–6.60€ ($4.30–$7.90). No credit cards. Daily 2:30–5pm and 9pm–midnight. Bus: 42, B2, or C4.

Casa Cuesta ✦ *Finds* SPANISH This is a fine choice in Triana, the pottery-making district across the river from the medieval core of Old Seville. The venue, which dates from 1880, is warm and old-fashioned. With its geometric tilework, checkerboard-patterned marble floors, high ceilings, and ornate, 19th-century bar, Casa Cuesta is a great place for lunch or dinner, or just for drinks and some tapas. The biggest of the dining room tables is round, and features a rough-hewn tree trunk rising from its center to support part of the massive ceiling and a wrought-iron lighting fixture. The well-prepared Spanish food includes Cured Iberian ham, fried meats and fish, *raciones* of potato salad flavored lightly with olive oil, and a variety of fried meats and fish. For a starter, we recommend *salmorejo* a thick Cordovan version of gazpacho. The ambience in Triana is less touristy, and a bit more workaday than its counterpart across the river.

Calle Castilla 1, Triana. © **95-433-33-35**. Main courses 10€–15€ ($12–$18); tapas 1.50€–2.50€ ($1.80–$3). AE, MC, V. Wed–Mon noon–1am. Bus: 43 or B2.

Cervecería Giralda SPANISH   There are at least a dozen popular tapas bars on the Calle Mateos Gagos, a picturesquely narrow street in the Barrio Santa Cruz that leads to the plaza beside the Cathedral. But this, one of our favorites in Seville, is also one of the most evocative. Established in 1934 atop what had been the ruins of a 10th-century Arab bathhouse, it retains the same four central columns, and the same elaborate system of domes and vaults as the bath's original construction. When we were last here, enjoying a beer near the sprawl of refrigerated fish displayed on the marble bar top, a group of flamenco singers rehearsed some of their music, giggling, in a distant corner, and lovers smooched in front of elaborate mudéjar-style tiles. Tapas are elaborate and often fish-based, while meals in the restaurant section might include salads, omelets, shellfish, codfish steaks with shellfish sauce, hake stuffed with squid, baked snapper, Iberian ham stuffed with foie gras, and filets of pork with roasted red peppers.

Calle Mateos Gagos 1. © **95-422-74-35**. Reservations recommended for dinner, not for tapas. Tapas 1.85€–2.10€ ($2.20–$2.50); main courses in restaurant 12€–17€ ($14–$20). Daily 1–4:30pm and 8pm–2am. AE, DC, MC, V. Bus: 41 or 42.

Flaherty's IRISH/INTERNATIONAL   Immediately adjacent to the rear of the cathedral and the entrance that leads into the Patio de los Naranjos, this is the biggest, busiest, loudest, and sudsiest Irish pub in Seville. Its premises were carved from a combination of at least two antique buildings, each with massive ceiling beams and very thick walls. The resulting labyrinth includes a vine-covered open-air patio, one end of which is devoted to the busy toilets, the other to an open grill on which burgers, sausages, and steaks sizzle and fry. There are more than a few big-screen TVs for sporting events, lots of beer, and a combination of Celtic influences (both Iberian and Irish) that any genealogist would find intriguing. The menu is based on sandwiches, burgers, and chicken burgers, plus platters of charbroiled chicken, lamb cutlets, steaks, and Caribbean-style jerk ribs. The staff is overwhelmingly international, comprising employees from Norway, Germany, the U.S., Canada, France, Argentina, Cuba, and, of course, Spain. Naturally, there are at least four kinds of beer on tap.

If you enjoy Irish pubs, and want something a bit more upscale, consider a wee dram or two at the more elegant Trinity Pub within the Hotel Inglaterra.

Calle Alemanes 7. © **95-421-04-51**. Tapas and raciones 2.50€–8€ ($3–$9.60); salads, sandwiches, and platters 5€–14€ ($6–$17). AE, DC, MC, V. Daily 11am–3am. Bus: 41 or 42.

Rincón de la Casana ℛ ARGENTINEAN/ANDALUSIAN   Close to the Old Town, this landmark wins new converts every year. Converted from an old building, it has a main door that's intricately carved and crafted, and its roof is red tiled in the traditional style. The two-story interior has one of the most interesting decors in the city, with antique tiles and typical Andalusian artifacts. At the entrance is the mounted head of the last bull killed by the famous matador José Luis Vásquez. On our last visit we savored *chuletón de buey* (ox steak) and *carne con chimichurri* (steak with chopped parsley and garlic dressing in virgin olive oil). Desserts are freshly made every day, including traditional puddings and tasty tarts, most often with fresh fruit.

Santo Domingo de la Calzada 13. 🕐 **95-453-17-10.** Reservations required. Main courses 9€–18€ ($11–$22); fixed-price buffet 10€ ($12). AE, DC, MC, V. Mon–Sat noon–5pm and 8:30pm–12:30am. Bus: 24, 27, or 32.

Rincón del Arroz ⭐ ANDALUSIAN/SEAFOOD   In the Heliópolis district, this restaurant lures diners with a lobster tank and some of the finest paellas and seafood in town. Meals are simultaneously inventive and classic but that's all that's fancy here. We like to start with the thin slices of cured, dried tuna, a local delicacy. Many Andalusian restaurants serve eggs scrambled with various vegetables and meats. Here the chef whips the eggs with bits of tiny fresh asparagus tips and throws in bits of shrimp and ham. Although we've never sampled anything better here than *arroz con Bogavante* (rice with lobster), the fresh crab is a fine runner up. A velvety pâté of duck, when featured, also gets our vote. On any night, the grilled fish with fresh herbs is reliable. Finish off with the chef's most luscious dessert: homemade walnut and raisin ice cream.

Av. Ramón Carande 19. 🕐 **95-462-81-72.** Reservations recommended. Main courses 7€–19€ ($8.40–$23). AE, DC, MC, V. Mon–Sat noon–5pm and 8pm–midnight; Sun noon–5pm. Bus: 30 or 31.

5

What to See & Do in Seville

With one of the richest cultural heritages of any city in Europe, Seville deserves at least 3 days of your time. Most of your time will be spent in the city's historic core, on the east bank of the Río Guadalquivir, which can be covered on foot.

Most visitors head for the Cathedral, La Giralda, the Alcázar, and the Museo de Bellas Artes, taking in the Renaissance Casa de Pilatos and Seville's bullring, Plaza de Toros de la Maestranza, if they have the time. Those on longer stays will find more than enough churches, palaces, parks, and other monuments to keep busy.

1 Sightseeing Suggestions for the First-Timer

The following suggested itineraries allow visitors to experience the highlights of Seville in only a few days.

IF YOU HAVE 1 DAY   Seville's two major sights, its world-famed **Cathedral** and **Giralda Tower,** and the **Alcázar** will take up the better part of your day. This Christian cathedral is the largest in Europe and takes a long time to explore. Climbing the Giralda Tower is one of the highlights of a visit to Seville; afterward be sure to spend some time relaxing among the orange trees and fountain of the peaceful Patio de los Naranjos. The royal residence of the Alcázar will occupy most of your afternoon. As night falls over Seville, do as the locals do and visit the *tascas* recommended below for some of the finest tapas in Andalusia.

IF YOU HAVE 2 DAYS   Follow the recommendations above on day 1. On day 2, go for an early morning stroll through the old, narrow streets of the **Barrio de Santa Cruz.** Once the Jewish Ghetto, it was restored in the early 20th century. Spend at least 2 hours here (more if you have time—it's easy to get lost in Murillo's former stamping ground), wandering ancient *calles* such as **Ximénes de Enciso** and **Santa Teresa.** Stay for lunch at one of the fine wine bars and restaurants the district is known for. After a siesta, visit the **Museo Provincial de Bellas Artes de Seville.** Finally, cap off your day with dinner in a typical Sevillana restaurant and take in a flamenco show if you're still standing on your feet.

IF YOU HAVE 3 DAYS   On your third day in Seville, visit the **Hospital de la Santa Caridad** of Don Juan fame in the morning, and the **Casa de Pilatos** in the afternoon. Before lunch wander through the colle **Parque María Luisa,** taking time out to see **Plaza de América,** the landmark square of Seville with its gardens and many attractions. For a final adieu to Seville, with a promise to return in the future, take a romantic carriage ride through the narrow streets of Old Seville. Of course, you can end this evening (or any evening) with many glasses of sherry from nearby Jerez de la Frontera and even more tapas.

2 Seeing the Sights

The only way to explore Seville is on foot, with a good map in hand—but stay alert for muggers.

THE TOP ATTRACTIONS

Alcázar ★★★ Pedro the Cruel built this magnificent 14th-century mudéjar palace north of the cathedral. It's the oldest royal residence in Europe still in use: On visits to Seville, King Juan Carlos and Queen Sofía stay here. From the Dolls' Court to the Maidens' Court through the domed Ambassadors' Room, it contains some of the finest work of Sevillian artisans. In many ways it evokes the Alhambra at Granada. Ferdinand and Isabella, who at one time lived in the Alcázar and influenced its architectural evolution, welcomed Columbus here on his return from America.

Allow at least 2 hours to go through the palace complex and visit the gardens with their fountains and pavilions. You'll enter through the Puerta del León (Lion's Door), which is flanked by two towers. Continue straight ahead into the Patio de la Montería, where the court once assembled. In the audience chamber here, you can see a replica of the *Santa María* and an impressive altarpiece, *Virgin of the Navigators* ★, which was painted by Alejo Fernández in 1531.

From this courtyard the facade of the **Palacio Pedro** ★★★ confronts you. Continue inside to reach the **Patio de las Doncellas (Court of the Maidens)** ★, which was decorated by the most skilled architects who worked on Granada's Alhambra. An upper story was added to this exquisite patio of Moorish arches in the 1500s.

Other landmarks in this palace include the Salón de Embajadores (Ambassadors' Hall), constructed in 1427 and dominated by an impressive cedarwood **cupola** ★★ that is often described as a "half orange." This hall also has a trio of symmetrically arranged and ornate arches, each with three horseshoe arches.

The Salón del Techo is notable for its coffered ceiling, and the Patio de las Muñecas (Doll's Court) is small, but splendidly and delicately ornamented; it was also designed by the Alhambra's craftsmen.

The **Salones de Carlos V** ★ lie to the immediate right (facing) Pedro's palace. These rooms are decorated with beautiful 16th-century *azulejos* (tiles), and contain a stunning collection of 16th-century **tapestries** ★★ from Brussels that depict the life of the emperor and his conquest of Tunis in 1535.

Save time for the **gardens** ★, a wonderful oasis from the heat of a summer day. The Jardín Inglés, modeled on 18th-century English gardens, dates to 1909, and the Jardín de los Poetas (Poets' Garden) features two ponds evocative of those once designed by the Arabs.

Plaza del Triunfo s/n. (✆ **95-450-23-23.** Admission 5€ ($5.75). Oct–Mar Tues–Sat 9:30am–6pm, Sun 9:30am–1:30pm; Apr–Sept Tues–Sat 9:30am–7pm, Sun 9:30am–5pm.

Archivo de Indias ★ The Archivo de Indias is said to contain some four million antique documents, including letters exchanged between patron Queen Isabella and explorer Columbus (he detailing his discoveries and impressions). These very rare documents are locked in air-conditioned storage to keep them from disintegrating. Special permission has to be acquired before examining some of them. Displayed in glass cases are other fascinating documents in which the dreams of the early explorers come alive.

Juan de Herrera, the great architect of Philip II's El Escorial, designed the building. It stands next to the cathedral and was originally the Lonja (Stock

Seville Attractions

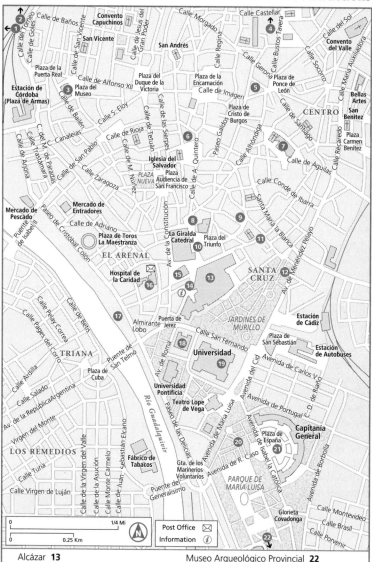

Alcázar **13**
Archivo General de Indias **14**
Barrio de Santa Cruz **9**
Basilica de la Macarena **2**
Casa de Murillo **11**
Casa de Pilatos **7**
Catedral de Sevilla and Giralda Tower **10**
Convento de Santa Paula **4**
Hospital de la Santa Caridad **16**
Isla Mágica **1**
Jardines de Murillo **12**
Giralda Tower **8**

Museo Arqueológico Provincial **22**
Museo de Arte Contemporáneo **15**
Museo de Artes y Costumbres Populares **22**
Museo Provincial de Bellas Artes de Sevilla **3**
Palacio de San Telmo **18**
Parque María Luisa **20**
Plaza de America **22**
Plaza de España **21**
Real Fábrica de Tabacos **19**
San Pedro **5**
San Salvador **6**
Torre del Oro **17**

Exchange). Construction on the Archivo de Indias lasted from 1584 to 1646. In the 17th century it headquartered the Academy of Seville, which was founded in part by the great Spanish artist Murillo. In 1785, during the reign of Charles III, the building became a general records office for the Indies.

Av. de la Constitución 3. ② **95-421-12-34.** Free admission. Mon–Fri 8am–3pm. Bus: 21, 22, 23, 25, 26, 30, 31, 33, 34, 40, 41, or 42.

Casa de Pilatos ⋆⋆ This 16th-century Andalusian palace of the dukes of Medinaceli recaptures the splendor of the past, combining Gothic, mudéjar, and Plateresque styles in its courtyards, fountains, and salons. According to tradition, this is a reproduction of Pilate's house in Jerusalem. Don't miss the two old carriages or the rooms filled with Greek and Roman statues. The collection of paintings includes works by Carreño, Pantoja de la Cruz, Sebastiano del Piombo, Lucas Jordán, Batalloli, Pacheco, and Goya. The museum's first floor can be seen by guided tour only, but the ground floor, patios, and gardens are self-guided. The palace is about a 7-minute walk northeast of the cathedral on the northern edge of Barrio de Santa Cruz, amidst a warren of labyrinthine streets whose traffic is funneled through the nearby Calle de Aguilas.

Plaza Pilatos 1. ② **95-422-52-98.** Museum 8€ ($9.60); patio and gardens 5€ ($6). June–Sept daily 9am–7pm; Oct–May daily 9am–6pm.

Catedral de Sevilla and Giralda Tower ⋆⋆⋆ The largest Gothic building in the world and the third-largest church in Europe (after St. Peter's in Rome and St. Paul's in London), the Catedral de Sevilla was designed by builders whose stated goal was that: "those who come after us will take us for madmen." Construction began in the late 1400s on the site of an ancient mosque and took centuries to complete. The cathedral claims to contain the remains of Columbus; his tomb is mounted on four statues. Works of art abound, many of them architectural, such as the 15th-century stained-glass windows, the iron screens *(rejas)* closing off the chapels, the elaborate 15th-century choir stalls, and the Gothic reredos above the main altar. During Corpus Christi and Immaculate Conception observances, altar boys with castanets dance in front of the high altar. In the Treasury are works by Goya, Murillo, and Zurbarán, and on the macabre side, a display of skulls.

After touring the dark interior, you'll emerge into the sunlight of the Patio of Orange Trees, with its fresh citrus scents and chirping birds. La Giralda, a Moorish tower next to the cathedral, is the city's most recognizable monument. Erected as a minaret in the 12th century, later additions include 16th-century bells. To climb it is to take the walk of a lifetime. There are no steps, but if you make it to the top of the seemingly endless ramp you'll have a dazzling view of Seville. Entrance is through the cathedral.

Av. de la Constitución s/n. ② **95-421-49-71.** Cathedral and tower 7€ ($8.40) adults, 1.50€ ($1.80) children under 17 and students, free for all Sun. Mon–Sat 11am–5pm; Sun 2:30–6pm (July–Aug 9:30am–3:30pm).

Hospital de la Santa Caridad ⋆ This 17th-century hospital is intricately linked to the legend of Miguel Manara, portrayed by Dumas and Mérimée as

---

> **Tips** **Cathedral Dress Code**
>
> Shorts and T-shirts are not allowed in the cathedral. Remember to dress appropriately before you set out so you're not turned away.

Discovering Murillo: The Great Painter of Sentiment

Why did Seville-born **Bartolomé Estéban Murillo** (1618–82) become so popular in the latter part of the 1800s? Partly because he painted the most beautiful and sentimental Madonnas of his era. But the very reason behind his success caused him to fall out of favor with critics during most of the 20th century. Today, some art historians are taking another look at Murillo, and his reputation is making a sort of comeback.

If you'd like to form your own opinion of Murillo, some of his most important works are at the **Museo Provincial de Bellas Artes** in Seville and at the **Prado** in Madrid.

The true devotee can also visit **Casa del Murillo,** Calle Santa Teresa 8, Alfalfa (© **95-422-94-15**). The house is not a museum, but contains the offices of the Andalusian Department of Culture. Nevertheless, you can wander into the courtyard and poke about on the lower floor. Most helpful to the true Murillo aficionado is a display on the ground floor that pinpoints the works that can be seen in Seville. Admission free, the casa is open Monday to Friday from 10am to 2pm and 4 to 7pm.

Finally you can stroll through the **Jardines de Murillo,** entering from Plaza Santa Cruz. On a hot day in Seville, a stroll among the shade trees here is restful.

the scandalous Don Juan. It was once thought that he built this institution to atone for his sins, but this has been disproven. The death of Manara's beautiful young wife in 1661 caused him such grief that he retired from society and entered the "Charity Brotherhood," burying corpses of the sick and diseased as well as condemned and executed criminals. Today, members of this brotherhood continue to look after the poor, the elderly, and the infirm who have no one else to help them. Nuns will show you through the festive orange-and-sienna courtyard. The baroque chapel contains works by the 17th-century Spanish painters Murillo and Valdés Leal. As you're leaving the chapel, look above the exit door for the macabre picture of an archbishop being devoured by maggots.

Calle Temprado 3. © **95-422-32-32.** Admission 4€ ($4.80) adults, free for children under 12. Mon–Sat 9am–1:30pm and 3:30–7:30pm; Sun 9am–1pm.

Museo Provincial de Bellas Artes de Sevilla ⊛⊛   This lovely old convent off Calle de Alfonso XII houses one of the most important collections of Spanish art. A whole gallery is devoted to two paintings by El Greco, and works by Zurbarán are on exhibit; however, the devoutly religious paintings of the Seville-born Murillo are the highlight. An entire wing is given over to macabre paintings by the 17th-century artist Valdés Leal. His painting of John the Baptist's head on a platter includes the knife—in case you don't get the point. The top floor, which displays modern paintings, is less interesting.

Plaza del Museo 9. © **95-422-07-90.** Admission 1.50€ ($1.80). Tues 3–8pm; Wed–Sat 9am–8pm; Sun 9am–2pm. Bus: C4.

Torre del Oro   The 12-sided Tower of Gold, dating from the 13th century, overlooks the Guadalquivir River. Originally it was covered with gold tiles, but someone made off with them long ago. The tower has been restored recently and turned into a maritime museum, the Museo Náutico, which displays drawings and engravings of the port of Seville in its heyday.

Paseo de Cristóbal Colón. © **95-422-24-19.** Admission 1€ ($1.20). Tues–Fri 10am–2pm; Sat–Sun 11am–2pm. Free on Tues. Closed Aug.

MORE TO SEE & DO

BARRIO DE SANTA CRUZ ✦✦✦   What was once a ghetto for Spanish Jews, who were forced out of Spain in the late 15th century in the wake of the Inquisition, is today Seville's most colorful district. Near the old walls of the Alcázar, winding medieval streets with names like Vida (Life) and Muerte (Death) open onto pocket-size plazas. Flower-filled balconies with draping bougainvillea and potted geraniums jut over this labyrinth, shading you from the hot Andalusian summer sun. Feel free to look through numerous wrought-iron gates into patios filled with fountains and plants. In the evening it's common to see Sevillanos sitting outside drinking icy sangria under the glow of lanterns.

To enter the Barrio Santa Cruz, turn right after leaving the Patio de Banderas exit of the Alcázar. Turn right again at the Plaza de la Alianza, going down Calle Rodrigo Caro to the Plaza de Doña Elvira. Use caution when strolling through the area, particularly at night; many robberies have occurred here.

BASILICA DE LA MACARENA   On the northern tier of the central city, this church possesses the most revered image in Seville, "The Virgin of Hope," which locals call La Macarena. It is strictly for Madonna worshippers (of Catholic, not Kabbalah ilk). She is the patron saint of matadors and a favorite of Spain's gypsies. The Seville-born matador Joselito was so taken with her that he spent a good hunk of his fortune to purchase four emeralds for her. When he died in the ring in 1920, the Macarena wore widow's weeds for a month.

The work, which may date as far back as the close of the 17th century, is attributed to the sculptor Pedro Roldán. The fraternity worshipping the Madonna appears in procession on Sacred Friday every year, leading "Christ's float" through the city streets, with the Madonna forever raining five tears of sadness.

Difficult to reach by public transportation, the church is best approached by taxi going along the outer ring from Colón to Torneo to Resolano Andueza. Also on-site is a treasury displaying rare ecclesiastical relics.

Puerta de la Macarena, La Macarena. © **95-490-18-00.** Free admission to basilica; treasury 2.70€ ($3.25). Basilica daily 9am–1pm and 5–8pm; treasury daily 9:30am–1pm and 5–8pm.

CONVENTO DE SANTA PAULA   There are 17 cloistered women's convents still functioning (in some cases, flourishing) in Seville today. Some are very small, some are in steep decline, and some are so obscure that their doors are almost always closed to casual visitors. But if a peek into this medieval lifestyle intrigues you, the most interesting (and most accessible) cloistered convent is **Santa Paula,** which offers infrequent but viable tours. A cloistered nun conducts the tours in Spanish.

Tips **Staying Safe at Night**

The most romantic time to stroll around Barrio Santa Cruz is at night, but it's also the most dangerous. Use caution in the evening as you walk along. Muggings are common.

The convent of Jerónimas nuns (followers of St. Jerome) dates from 1475, the facade—a stellar example of the so-called Catholic Monarch's style—from 1503. Gothic, mudéjar, and Renaissance decorations combine here. The single nave of the church is covered by a ceiling designed by Diego López de Arenas in 1623. The main altarpiece is in the Baroque style, the creation in 1730 of José Fernando de Medinilla. On-site is a small museum with various ecclesiastical art and sculpture mostly from the 16th to the 18th centuries. You can also admire the main cloister of the convent, which dates from the early 16th century.

Santa Paula. ℂ 95-453-63-30. Admission 2€ ($2.40). Tues–Sun 10:30am–1pm and 4:30–6:30pm. Bus: 10, 11, or 12.

PARQUE MARIA LUISA & PALACIO DE SAN TELMO 🎔🎔   Parque María Luisa, named for and dedicated to the sister of Isabella II, was once the grounds of the **Palacio de San Telmo.** The palace, whose baroque facade is visible behind the deluxe Alfonso XIII Hotel, today houses a seminary. While a bit difficult to visit, the palace has free guided tours Monday and Wednesday by appointment. Call ℂ 95-503-55-05 for more information. The entrance is at Avenida de Roma, El Arenal. Originally conceived as the University for Sailors (Universidad de Mareantes), the palace was named for St. Elmo, patron saint of navigation. A lavish celebration of the baroque style, it is largely the work of architect Leonardo de Figueroa and was constructed between 1682 and 1796. In time it became the mansion for the Dukes of Montpensier of the Bourbon dynasty. Today the palace is the seat of the Andalusian government. Its most outstanding feature is its elaborate and confectionary **Churrigueresque-style main portal** 🎔🎔, dating from 1734.

The former private royal park is now open to the public. In 1929, when Seville was to host the Spanish American Exhibition, many pavilions from around the world were erected here. The Depression put a damper on the exhibition, but the pavilions still stand. Running south along the Guadalquivir River, the park attracts those who want to take boat rides, walk along flower-bordered paths, jog, or go bicycling. The most romantic way to traverse it is by rented horse and carriage, but this can be expensive depending on what you manage to negotiate with your driver. Do stay alert while walking through this park, as many muggings have been reported.

PLAZA DE AMERICA   Another landmark Sevillian square, the Plaza de América represents city planning at its best: Here you can walk through gardens planted with roses, enjoying the lily ponds, fountains, and the protective shade of the palms. And here you'll find a trio of elaborate buildings left over from the world exhibition that never materialized—in the center, the home of the government headquarters of Andalusia; on either side, two minor museums worth visiting only if you have time to spare.

The **Museo Arqueológico Provincial,** Plaza de América s/n (ℂ 95-423-24-01), contains many artifacts from prehistoric times and the days of the Romans, Visigoths, and Moors. It's open Wednesday through Saturday from 9am to 8pm, Tuesday 3 to 8pm, and Sunday from 9am to 2pm. Admission is 1.50€ ($1.75) for adults and free for students and children. Bus nos. 30, 31, and 34 go there. Nearby is the **Museo de Artes y Costumbres Populares,** Plaza de América s/n (ℂ 95-423-25-76). In a mudéjar pavilion opposite this museum of archaeology is Seville's museum of folklore artifacts. On its ground floor you see traditional occupations, including a forge, a baker's oven, a wine press, a tanner's shop, and other occupations. More interesting on this floor is the stunning collection of ceramics. Upstairs

(*Moments*   **Hanging with Carmen in Old Seville**

While in Seville, you'll probably see flyers pasted to lamplights throughout the city's historic core, advertising **"Walking in Seville with Carmen."** Carmen (aka Johanna Vandenbussche), a raven-haired Bruger beauty, conducts an unusual, but brilliant tour that's part street theater and part "stand up tragedy." The flyer will advise you to assemble at the entrance to the Alcázar (near the corner of the Calle Santo Thomás and the Calle Miguel Mañara). In August tours leave at 7pm, from March to July and September and October at 6pm. In November tours are only on weekends and Monday. Times vary other months, so call first.

The fee is at your discretion but 5€ to 10€ ($6–$12) is reasonable. By the end of the tour, you'll probably be giggling, laughing, and moaning at the tempestuous events that befell Carmen. En route, you'll witness the bemused humor and grudging respect paid to the actress from the shopkeepers and local residents encountered along the way.

Carmen/Johanna's 90- to 120-minute performance incorporates a battered accordian, rolled in a shopping bag on wheels, wheezing out musical accompaniment. The tour is charming, funny, rich with anecdotal insights, and presented with a feminist slant.

For more information, call ℭ **66-067-57-48;** visit www.sol.com/carmen/index.htm or contact Johanna directly at johahaha@yahoo.com.hk. To reach the tour's point of departure, take bus no. 21, 23, 34, or 40.

is devoted to such exhibitions as the court dress of the 19th century as well as 18th-century fabrics and embroideries from the factories of Seville. One by Murillo, *Children Eating Grapes,* is particularly evocative. Gold works and a varied collection of paintings and musical instruments are also displayed on this floor. It's open Tuesday 3 to 8pm, Wednesday through Saturday from 9am to 8pm, and Sunday from 9am to 2pm. Admission is 1.50€ ($1.80) for adults and free for children and students.

PLAZA DE ESPAÑA   The major building left from the exhibition at the Parque María Luisa (see above) is the half-moon–shaped Renaissance-style structure set on this landmark square. The architect, Aníbal González, not only designed but also supervised the building of this immense structure; today it's a government office building. At a canal here you can rent rowboats for excursions into the park, or you can walk across bridges spanning the canal. Set into a curved wall are alcoves with tile murals focusing on the characteristics of Spain's 50 provinces.

REAL FABRICA DE TABACOS   When Carmen waltzed out of the tobacco factory in the first act of Bizet's opera, she made its 18th-century inspiration world-famous. This old tobacco factory was constructed between 1750 and 1766, and 100 years later it employed 10,000 *cigarreras,* of which Carmen was one in the opera. (She rolled cigars on her thighs.) In the 19th century, these tobacco women made up the largest female workforce in Spain. Many visitors arriving today, in fact, ask guides to take them to "Carmen's tobacco factory."

The building, located on Calle San Fernando near the city's landmark luxury hotel, the Alfonso XIII, is the second largest in Spain and is still here. But the Real Fábrica de Tabacos is now part of the Universidad de Sevilla. Look for signs of its former role, however, in the bas-reliefs of tobacco plants and Native Americans over the main entrances. You'll also see bas-reliefs of Columbus and Cortés. Then you can wander through the grounds for a look at student life, Sevillian style. The factory is directly south of the Alcázar gardens.

WALKING TOUR   THE OLD CITY

Start: At the Giralda by the cathedral.
Finish: At the Hospital de los Venerables in the Barrio Santa Cruz.
Time: 4 hours, including rapid visits to the interiors.
Best Times: Early morning (7–11am) and late afternoon (3–7pm).
Worst Times: After dark or during the heat of midday.

Seville is so loaded with architectural and artistic treasures that this brisk overview of the central zone doesn't begin to do justice to its cultural wealth. Although this walking tour includes the city's most obvious (and spectacular) monuments, such as the Giralda and the cathedral, it also visits lesser-known churches and convents, the city's most desirable shopping district, and the labyrinthine alleyways of the Barrio Santa Cruz.

Begin with a visit to the:

❶ Cathedral & Giralda

This Gothic structure is so enormous that even its builders recognized the folly and fanaticism of their dreams. Its crowning summit, the Giralda, one of Europe's most famous towers, was begun in the late 1100s by the Moors and raised even higher by the Catholic monarchs in 1568. Because of the position of these connected monuments near the summit of a hill overlooking the Guadalquivir, some scholars nostalgically refer to the historic neighborhood around them as the Acropolis.

After your visit, walk to the cathedral compound's northeastern corner for a visit to the:

❷ Palacio Arzobispal (Archbishop's Palace)

This 16th-century building rests on 13th-century foundations, with a 17th-century baroque facade of great beauty. Although designed to house the overseer of the nearby cathedral, it was sometimes pressed into service for secular visitors. One of these was Napoleon's representative, Maréchal

Soult, after he conquered Seville in the name of the Bonaparte family and France early in the 19th century.

From here, walk across the street, heading south, to Plaza Virgen de los Reyes, for a visit to the:

❸ Convento de la Encarnación (Convent of the Incarnation)

Its origins date from the 1300s, shortly after the Catholic reconquest of Seville. Part of its architectural curiosity includes the widespread use of the lobed, horseshoe-shape arches and windows traditionally used in mosques.

Exit the church, then walk eastward across Plaza del Triunfo into the entrance of one of the most exotic palaces in Europe, the:

❹ Reales Alcázar (Royal Alcázar)

The oldest royal seat in Spain was originally built for the Moorish caliphs in A.D. 712 as a fortress, then enlarged and embellished over the next thousand years by successive generations of Moorish and, beginning in 1248, Christian rulers. Its superimposed combination of Arab and Christian Gothic architecture makes for one of the most interesting monuments in Iberia. Lavish gardens, as exotic as what you'd expect in the Old Testament, sprawl in an easterly direction in back. More than any other monument on this tour, with the exception of the cathedral, the Alcázar deserves a second visit after the end of this walking tour.

Exit from the Alcázar back onto Plaza del Triunfo. At the plaza's southwestern edge rises the imposing bulk of the:

⑤ Archivo de Indias (Archive of the Indies)

Built as a commodities exchange, it was abandoned for a site in Cádiz when that port replaced Seville as the most convenient debarkation point for ships coming from the New World. In 1758 it was reconfigured as the repository for the financial records and political and cultural archives of anything concerning the development of the Western Hemisphere. Its closets and storerooms contain more than four million dossiers.

From here, walk a half-block west to the roaring traffic of Avenida de la Constitución, then turn north, bypassing the facade of the already-visited cathedral. The *avenida* will end within 2 blocks at the ornate bulk of Seville's:

⑥ Ayuntamiento (Town Hall)

Begun in 1527, and enlarged during the 19th century, this is the city's political showcase. To see its most interesting (Plateresque) facade, turn right (east) when you reach it, then flank the building's eastern edge for a view of the medallions and allegorical figures that kept teams of stonemasons busy for generations.

The town hall's northeastern facade marks the beginning of Seville's most famous shopping street:

⑦ Calle Sierpes

This street stretches north from the Town Hall. Its southern terminus, where you're standing, was once the site of a debtor's prison where Miguel de Cervantes languished for several years.

Walk along the western edge of this famous street, turning left (west) after 2 blocks onto Calle Jovellanos for a view of the:

⑧ Iglesia (Church) de San José

Named in honor of a famous carpenter (St. Joseph, husband of the Virgin), this lavish baroque chapel functioned as the seat of the carpenter's guild after its completion in 1747.

Retrace your steps along Calle Jovellanos to Calle Sierpes, traverse the busy street, and continue walking due east along Calle Sagasta. Within a block, Calle Sagasta will deposit you in Plaza del Salvador, in front of the elaborate facade of the:

⑨ Iglesia del Salvador (Savior)

One of the grandest churches of Seville, this is preferred by many visitors to the rather chilly pomposity of the previously visited cathedral. The enormous building was begun in 1674 on the site of one of the Muslim world's holiest sites, the mosque of Ibn Addabas. Beneath the Catholic iconography you can still make out the base of the Moorish minaret (converted long ago into a Christian belfry) and the Moorish layout of the building's courtyard.

TAKE A BREAK
You can sit at **La Antigua Bodeguita**, Plaza del Salvador 6 (✆ **95-456-18-33**), enjoying cold, refreshing drinks while admiring the facade of the old Iglesia del Salvador. If you're hungry, you can order a number of tasty, inexpensive tapas.

After your visit, walk 3 blocks north along Calle Cuna (a wide boulevard that Sevillanos usually refer to simply as "Cuna") for an exterior view of one of the most-envied private homes in town, at Calle Cuna 18:

⑩ Palacio de Lebrija (Casa de la Condesa de Lebrija)

Austere on the outside, lavish and mudéjar on the inside, the palace was built in the 1400s and managed to incorporate in its floors a series of ancient mosaics, dug up from the excavations in the nearby town of Itálica. Although it's closed to casual visits, it's

Walking Tour: The Old City

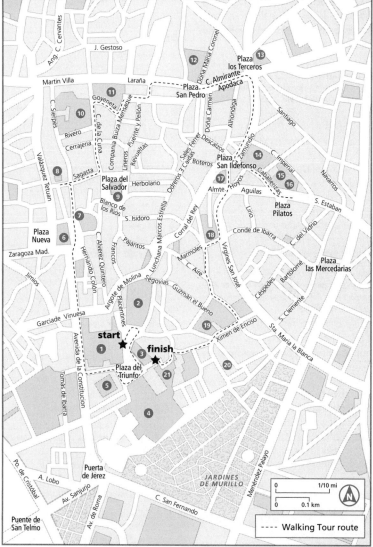

---- Walking Tour route

the most visible vestige of an aristocratic way of life that's rapidly fading.

From here, walk 2 short blocks east along
Calle de Goyeneta for a view of the:

⑪ Iglesia de la Anunciación
Built in 1565 with profits from the
New World, and associated for many
centuries with both the Jesuits and the
city's university, this church contains a
cold, rather macabre-looking crypt
(Panteón de Sevillanos Ilustres) where
many of the city's governors and their
families are buried.

From here, head east, passing through Plaza
de la Anunciación onto Calle del Laraña Imagen for a short 2 blocks. Rising ahead of you
from its position beside Plaza de San Pedro
is the:

⑫ Iglesia de San Pedro
Built in the mudéjar style in the 1300s,
with some portals and towers added in
the 1600s and 1700s, San Pedro is
famous as the site where Spain's greatest painter, Velázquez, was baptized in
1599. Coffered ceilings rise above the
building's main sanctuary and its eight
shadowy chapels. The site is available
for visits only during Mass.

From Plaza de San Pedro, adjacent to the
church's eastern entrance, walk east for 2
blocks along Calle del Almirante Apodaca
until you reach the:

⑬ Iglesia de Santa Catalina
This 14th-century Gothic-mudéjar
monument has endured many alterations and additions. Most significant
of these is a simple Gothic portal that
was moved into its present position in
1930 from another church. Make it a
point to walk around this medieval
hybrid for views of horseshoe (lobed)
arches that attest to the strong influence of Moorish design on its past.

After your visit, walk south for a block along
Calle Carrión, whose name will change after
a block to Calle Francisco Mejías. The massive and severe-looking building that rises in
about a block is the:

⑭ Convento de San Leandro
Although the building you see today
was begun around 1580, it replaced a

much older 13th-century church that
was the first to be constructed in Seville
after the Christian reconquest in 1248.
Severe and simple, with a single barrel
vault covering its single aisle, it's open
only during early morning (7am) Mass
and on some holy festival days.

Immediately to the southeast, opening off
Plaza de Pilatos, is the grandest and most
ornate palace that's open to view in Seville,
the:

⑮ Casa de Pilatos (Pilate's House)
One of the city's most frequently visited
museums, Pilate's House was built in
1521 by the Marquis de Tarifa after his
trip to the Holy Land where, according
to legend, he was inspired by the ruined
house in Jerusalem from which Pontius
Pilate is said to have governed. The
main entrance, modeled after an
ancient Roman triumphal arch, is fash-
ioned from bronze, jasper, and Carrara
marble, and the overall effect is one of
imperial Roman grandeur.

After your visit, walk less than a block
southeast for a view of the:

⑯ Iglesia de San Esteban
This is one of the finest examples
of mudéjar-Gothic architecture in
Andalusia. Constructed during the late
1300s and early 1400s, it combines
Moorish-style coffered ceilings with
Gothic ribbed vaulting.

From here, retrace your steps to Plaza de
Pilatos, then fork right onto Calle Caballer-
izas for a block until you reach Plaza de San
Ildefonso. Flanking its edge rises the:

⑰ Iglesia de San Ildefonso
This colorful and graceful small-scale
structure filled with artistic treasures is
one of the most charming baroque
churches in Seville. Regrettably, it's
open only during Mass, during which
discreet visitors can admire the interior.

From here, walk west for 2 short blocks south
along Calle Vírgenes until you reach the:

⑱ Iglesia de San Nicolás de Bari
Although the church was built in the
1700s, long after the departure of the

Moors, the forest of red-marble columns that support the five aisles of its interior evoke some aspects of a mosque. The eclectic, and somewhat cluttered, aspect of its baroque interior is particularly charming.

From here, walk south for a block along Calle de Federico Rubio until you reach the soaring walls of a building usually described as the gateway to one of Seville's most colorful antique neighborhoods, the:

⑲ Iglesia de Santa Cruz (Holy Cross)

Originally built between 1665 and 1728, and conceived as the parish church of the Barrio Santa Cruz, which you'll visit shortly, it's prefaced with a relatively new facade that was added in 1929. This is a particularly active church, servicing the spiritual needs of a congested neighborhood, and is normally open only during Mass.

At this point your tour will become less rigidly structured, and will allow you to wander through the narrow and labyrinthine alleyways of the:

⑳ Barrio Santa Cruz

Before 1492, when the Jews were driven from Spain by the repressive edicts of Ferdinand and Isabella, this was the Jewish ghetto of Seville. Today it's highly desirable real estate—thick-walled houses, window boxes studded with flowers, severe exteriors opening onto private patios that ooze Andalusian charm. Wander at will through the neighborhood, and don't be surprised if you quickly get lost in the maze of twisting streets. Know that your final destination lies uphill (to the southwest) at a point near the cathedral (discreet signs indicate its direction).

We recommend that you walk southwest along the relatively wide Calle Ximenes de Enriso, ducking into side alleyways at your whim for views of the streets that radiate out from there. At the barrio's southwestern edge, beside Plaza de los Venerables, you'll want to visit one of the barrio's greatest monuments, the:

㉑ Hospital de los Venerables (Hospice of the Venerable Ones)

It was founded in 1675 as a retirement home for aged priests, was completed 12 years later, and is maintained today as a museum.

TAKE A BREAK
Some of the best tapas in the old quarter is served at **Casa Román**, on Plaza de los Venerables (✆ **95-422-84-83**), which is also a good place to stop for a pick-me-up glass of regional wine.

3 Especially for Kids

The greatest thrill for kids in Seville is climbing **La Giralda,** the former minaret of the Great Mosque that once stood here. The view from this 20-story bell tower is certainly worth it, but most kids delight in the journey up. With some inclined ramps and some steps, the climb was originally designed to be ridden up on horseback. Little gargoyle-framed windows along the way allow you to preview the skyline of Seville.

With your family in tow, head for **Plaza de España;** you'll find rowboats as well as *pedaloes* (pedal boats) for rent. A collection of Andalusian donkey carts here adds to the fun, and there are ducks to feed on the Isla de los Patos.

The tourist office (see "Orientation," earlier in this chapter) can give advice on how to rent *pedaloes* (canoes) for trips along the Guadalquivir River. Or you can go to the riverbanks near the Torre del Oro and rent through the **Cruceros Turísticos Torre del Oro,** Paseo Marqués del Contadero (✆ **95-421-13-96**).

Isla Mágica, Pabellón de España, Isla de la Cartuga (✆ **90-216-17-16**), lies on the island of La Cartuga, across the river from the city's historic core. It's installed on the site of the 1992 world Expo grounds. Today the site has been transformed into a Disneyesque playground. There is a 16th-century motif to the whole park, in honor of the fact that Seville was the departure point for many of the great discoveries of that century. Like a Disneyland, the park is divided into a series of seven attractions, everything from Amazonia (an unknown forest) to The Pirates' Cove. There are also street performances, themed festivals—including one devoted to beer—and a film, *Piratas,* showing in a movie house where the seats shimmy and shake. Admission is 21€ ($25) for adults and 15€ ($17) for children 5 to 12; free for ages 5 and under. From April to November hours are daily 11am to midnight. The attraction lies across the bridge, Ponte de la Barqueta; take bus C2 from the center.

To cap a family trip to Seville, take one of the **horse-and-buggy rides** that leave from Plaza Virgen de los Reyes on Adolfo Rodríguez Jurado, or from the Parque de María Luisa at Plaza de España.

4 Organized Tours

There are two distinct independent companies that conduct tours of Seville, each with a recorded commentary about the sights you're passing, and each with a choice of at least six different languages, including English. We don't consider participation in one of these tours essential, but they will give you an overview of the town—especially the monuments around its historic medieval core—that would be hard to cover completely on your own. You'll see sights you might have otherwise overlooked, including the district associated with the 1929 World Exposition, the banks of the Guadalquivir, the inner avenues of the 1992 Expo, and the graceful symmetry of the Plaza de España. *Tip:* The upper deck of each of the buses offers views that are unobstructed, but if you plan this during the heat of midday, consider bringing a sunhat and sunglasses.

A local outfit that handles only the briefest of bus tours is **City Sightseeing,** Plaza de España (© **95-450-20-99**). Tours of Seville depart every 20 minutes, year-round, beginning at 10am, with the last departure scheduled for 10pm. The commentary is jaded and a bit blasé, and the overview is fairly superficial, but the cost of 11€ ($13) for adults, 5€ ($6) children is reasonable. You do not disembark the bus during this hour-long tour. Reservations aren't necessary. Departures are from Torre del Oro, Plaza de España, Isla Mágica, and la Cartuga.

More appealing are the 4-hour city tours conducted twice daily by **Visitours,** Calle Torricelli 32, Isla de la Cartuja (© **95-446-09-85**). Morning and afternoon tours leave daily at 9 and 9:30am, 3:45, 4, 4:30, 8, and 8:30pm, costing about 37€ ($44) each. Morning tours include a visit to the cathedral, Alcazar, and the Santa Cruz district, whereas the afternoon tour is a boat trip around the city and a visit to one museum.

A **boat trip** not known to many visitors allows you to sail along the Guadalquivir River from Seville to the famous old port of Sánlucar de Barrameda in Cádiz province. Departures are at 8:30am with a return at 5:30pm, costing 12€ ($14) per person. For more information, call © **95-456-16-92.**

ANDALUSIAN EXCURSIONS

In addition to being loaded with monuments of consuming historic and cultural interest, Seville is a good base for exploring Andalusia. Some of the best guided-tours in Andalusia are offered by **Visitours,** Américo Vespucio 61, Isla de la Cartuja (© **95-446-09-85**). These experienced travel professionals are well versed in the charm and lore of the region, and their buses, which hold between 8 and 48 passengers, always have the option of picking up and dropping off clients at their hotels. Reservations a day in advance are strongly recommended. Two of the company's most popular tours depart daily. A tour of **Granada** leaves Seville at 7am, explores all that city's major monuments and neighborhoods, and returns to Seville around 7pm. The price is 87€ ($104). A tour of **Córdoba** departs Seville at 8:30 and 9am, returns around 6 and 6:30pm, and costs 70€ ($84) per person.

Two other worthy tours depart 3 or 4 days a week, depending on the season. A visit to **Jerez de la Frontera** and **Cádiz** includes a visit to the riding school at Jerez, a tour of one of the city's most interesting wine bodegas, lunch in an Andalusian village (Puerto de Santa María), and a boat ride that begins on the Guadalete River and ends in Cádiz's Atlantic harbor. The tour, departing at 9 and 9:30am and returning at 6 and 6:30pm, costs 78€ ($94) per person. If at all possible, try to schedule your participation for a Thursday (or June–July, for Thurs or Sat), as participants attend a riding exhibition in Jerez that's conducted only on those days. A visit to the historic hamlet of **Ronda,** conducted several times a week, departing at 9am and 9:30am, returning at 6pm and 6:30pm, costs 78€ ($94) per person.

5 Staying Active

BOATING
Seville is hardly on the beach but the Guadalquivir River is used for cruises, canoeing, and paddle boating. Seville, perhaps, looks its most scenic from the river. Near Torre del Oro, you can get information and details, including prices, about boating. Check with **Cruceros Turísticos Torre del Oro,** Paseo Marqués de Contadero, Arenal (© **95-421-13-96**), about river cruises. Costing 12€ ($14) per person, these run every 30 minutes daily 11am to midnight from April to October. Off-season hours are daily from 11am to 9pm.

SWIMMING
To cool off in summer you may want to patronize one of the local swimming pools, known as *piscinas.* These include **Virgen de Los Reyes,** Av. Doctor Fedriani s/n (© **95-437-68-66**); **Mar de la Plata,** Calle Mar de la Plata s/n (© **95-445-40-95**), and **Guadalpark,** Polígono del Aeropuerto (© **95-440-66-22**). Most pools open in summer on weekdays from around noon to 7:30pm and on weekends from 11am to 7:30pm. Weekday prices are 2.80€ ($3.35) for adults and 1.60€ ($1.90) for children. On Saturday and Sunday prices rise to 4€ ($4.80) for adults and 2€ ($2.40) for children.

6 Spectator Sports

BULLFIGHTING
From Easter until late October, some of the best bullfighters in Spain appear at the **Plaza de Toros Real Maestranza,** on Paseo de Colón 12 (© **95-422-45-77**). One of the leading bullrings in Spain, the stadium attracts matadors whose fights often receive TV and newspaper coverage throughout Iberia. Unless there's a special festival going on, bullfights *(corridas)* occur on Sunday. The best are staged during April Fair celebrations.

Tickets should be purchased in advance at the ticket office *(despacho de entradas)* on Calle Adriano, beside the stadium. You'll also find many unofficial kiosks selling tickets placed strategically along the main shopping street, Calle Sierpes. However, they charge a 20% commission for their tickets—a lot more if they think they can get it. The prices vary, often beginning at 18€ ($22) for a nosebleed seat *(grado del sol),* which means you'll be at a hard-to-see elevation in the fierce sun. For a front-row seat in the shade—*barrera de sombra*—expect to pay from 75€ to 80€ ($90–$96).

The major bullfights are called *corridas de toros* and feature more experienced matadors. For apprentice bullfighters with younger bulls, the bullfights are advertised as *novilladas.* Because of the excessive heat in July and August, corridas most often occur on Thursday nights at 9pm. Posters around town advertise the various bullfights.

Even people not attending one of the *corridas de toros* like to see the bullring, arguably the most beautiful in Spain. It was constructed in the 1760s, lying across the river. It is oval in shape and holds some 14,000 spectators. You can tour the attraction with an English-speaking guide (you can find these independent guides at the entrance) daily from 9:30am to 2pm and 3 to 7pm for 4€ ($4.80). On bullfight days, hours are 9:30am to 3pm.

As part of the tour you can visit **Museo Taurino,** the bullfight museum. On display is a stunning collection of *trajes de luces,* those jazzy "suits of lights" as they are called. Look for bullfight memorabilia, along with pictures of famous matadors or even more famous fans such as Don Ernesto Hemingway. At the end of a tour you're taken into a chapel where matadors come to pray to their patron, La Macarena, before facing "death in the afternoon."

7 Shopping

The pedestrian strip of **Calle Sierpes** is the principal shopping street of Seville. Store after store stands side by side along this monument to 19th century architecture. Other great places for both window and actual shopping are the side streets branching off from Sierpes, especially **Calle Tetuán. Calle Cuna**—locals call it simply "Cuna"—is the third major shopping street. Calle Sierpes tends to attract the most dedicated local consumers, and its stores rarely include real cutting-edge or high-fashion shops. These tend to cluster near or at the edge of **Plaza Nueva.**

If you're seeking Andalusian handicrafts, head for the narrow streets of **Barrio de Santa Cruz.** For specific shopping streets in Santa Cruz, seek out **Rodrigo Caro** and **Mateos Gago.** You could fill many a mansion with the trinkets and antiques for sale here. Other antiques and handicraft shops are found in the sector lying west of the cathedral, including **El Arenal.** Major stores are open Monday to Saturday 9:30am to 8pm; smaller establishments, however, often take a siesta, doing business from 9:30 or 10am to 1:30 or 2pm and again from 4:30 or 5 to 8pm. Exceptions to this are listed below.

SHOPPING A TO Z
ANTIQUES
Félix   In the center of Seville, in front of the cathedral, this shop is the best outlet in Seville for antique Andalusian posters. Most popular are scenes, some in the Art Deco style, from the Feria de Abril (April Fair), from one of the *corridas* at the bullring, or from Semana Santa. Locals call these posters "propaganda" of major events. Av. de la Constitución 26. ✆ 95-421-80-26.

Félix e Hijo   This is a family affair (see above). Whereas Félix sells mostly antique posters, this outlet specializes in archaeological artifacts ranging from Greek vases to Roman mosaics. Much of the loot was dug up in the surrounding countryside. Surprisingly, many items are affordable. Av. de la Constitución 20. ✆ 95-422-33-34.

ART GALLERIES
Rafael Ortiz ⭐   This is one of Seville's most respected art galleries, specializing in contemporary paintings, usually by Iberian artists. Exhibitions change frequently and inventories sell out quickly. Marmoles 12. © **95-421-48-74.**

BOOKS
The English Bookshop   Smaller than many of the other book emporiums in Seville, this is the kind of place where you can find tomes on gardening, political discourse, philosophy, and pop fiction, all in one cozy place. Open Monday to Saturday from 10am to 1:45pm and 5 to 8:30pm, Saturday from 10am to 1:30pm. Eduardo Dato 36. © **95-465-57-54.**

Librería Vértice   Set conveniently close to Seville's university, this store stocks books in a polyglot of languages. Inventory ranges from the esoteric and professorial to Spanish romances. San Fernando 33. © **95-421-16-54.**

CERAMICS
El Postigo   Set in the town center near the cathedral, this shop contains one of the biggest selections of Andalusian ceramics in town. Some of the pieces are much, much too big to fit into your suitcase; others, especially the hand-painted tiles, make charming souvenirs that can easily be transported. Open Monday to Saturday 10am to 2pm, Monday to Friday 5 to 8:30pm. Arfe s/n. © **95-456-00-13.**

Martian   Set close to Seville's town hall, this outfit sells a wide array of painted tiles and ceramics. The inventory includes vases, plates, cups, serving dishes, and statues, all made in or near Seville. Many of the pieces exhibit ancient geometric patterns of Andalusia. Other floral motifs are rooted in Spanish traditions of the 18th century. Calle Sierpes 74. © **95-421-34-13.**

DEPARTMENT STORES
El Corte Inglés   This is the best of the several department stores clustered in Seville's commercial center. A well-accessorized branch of a nationwide chain, it features multilingual translators and rack after rack of every conceivable kind of merchandise for the well-stocked home, kitchen, and closet. If you're in the market for the brightly colored *feria* costumes worn by young girls during Seville's holidays, there's an impressive selection of the folkloric accessories that make Andalusia memorable. Plaza Duque 10. © **95-459-70-00.**

FANS
Casa Rubio   Carmen fluttered her fan and broke hearts. You can, too, if you pick up a traditional Andalusian fan here. This outlet stocks the best selection in town, ranging from the austere and dramatic to the florid and fanciful. Calle Sierpes 56. © **95-422-68-72.**

FASHION
Blasfor   This retail outlet sells and manufactures everything a well-dressed woman would need for the *feria* and fiestas of Seville, in a spectrum of colors, sizes, and degrees of ornamentation. Many of the mantillas, hair ornaments, and fans are made in Seville, and any would be absolutely splendid at the Rocio, at Holy Week, or at any particularly indulgent cocktail party in the U.S. where such exotic attire might be admired. Don't overlook the silver-framed religious icons of a lavishly suffering Christ in his torment: The somewhat bizarre combination of elaborate colors, fine workmanship, Andalusian splendor, and religious suffering might remind you of a richly inventoried sacristy of a church,

where all of the objects just happen to be for sale. Calle Sierpes 33 (② **95-422-76-61**) and Calle Sierpes 79 (② **95-421-40-50**).

Carolina Herrera   The boutique that bears Venezuela-born Carolina Herrera's name stands on Seville's stylish Plaza Nueva, selling high-priced scarves, shoes, belts, wallets, handbags, and luxury goods. It's supremely luxurious, and surprisingly macho, outfitted in tones of dark leather and dark woods, and permeated with rock music. Unfortunately, the staff is snooty, judgmental, and extravagantly unhelpful in any language. Plaza Nueva 8. ② **95-450-04-18**.

Coco-Sevilla   Staffed and managed by four artistic "collaborators" (two of them Spanish, the others French), this shop aims to outfit women with fiesta-inspired silk scarves, *feria* mantillas, and Andalusian jewelry. These can be coordinated in ways that might make any woman look like a modern-day version of Carmen. The vision of the accessories sold here falls midway between nostalgically old-fashioned and contemporary, and there's ample use of wild and passionate roses, many of them applied as batiks. The most expensive item of jewelry sells for around 145€ ($174); shawls and scarves go for around 150€ ($180) each. Open daily 11am to 7pm. Calle Ximénez de Enciso 28. ② **95-421-45-32**.

Dulce Flamenco   Come to this tiny boutique, just behind the rear side of the cathedral, for some of the most charming baby clothes in town. Priced at around 8€ ($9.60) each, the garments—mostly T-shirts and Andalusian *feria* dresses, are Sevillian inspired, Spanish in their trendiness and verve, and crafted in very small (and adorable) sizes. Also look for fans, priced at from 3.25€ to 94€ ($3.90–$113) each, and leather purses crafted into whimsical patterns, in some cases in very soft suede. There's also jewelry for sale. Open daily 11am to 8pm. Calle Ximénez de Enciso 1. ② **95-456-41-20**.

Iconos   This small, idiosyncratic boutique is loaded with fashion accessories that can be used by everyone from teenage girls to mature women. Silk scarves, costume jewelry, and an assortment of T-shirts with logos in varying degrees of taste—it's all here. Much of the merchandise represents the new, youthful perceptions of post-*movida* Spain. Open Monday to Saturday from 10am to 9pm, Sunday from noon to 5pm. Av. de la Constitución. ② **95-422-14-08**.

Lina   If you want to look like Carmen at the Sevilla Fair, head for Lina, which celebrates "fiesta de color" with a wide assortment of flamenco dresses (the ones with the polka dots and ruffled skirts), dangling earrings, *mantoncillos* (flamenco scarves), and elegant shawls. Open Monday to Friday 10am to 1:30pm and 5 to 8:30pm, Saturday 10:30am to 2pm. Calle Lineros 17. ② **95-421-24-23**.

Lio Sevilla   This gift shop sels *fiesta* and *feria* clothing for children. Here, for around 65€ ($78), you can outfit your 14-year-old (provided that she's cooperating) in an outfit reminiscent of Carmen. There are puffy and frilly mantilla skirts, and bullfighting memorabilia and T-shirts. Open Monday to Saturday 10am to 10pm, Sunday 11am to 9pm. Calle Mateos Gago 15A. ② **95-422-62-89**.

María Rosa ☙   This is the best outlet in Andalusia for flamenco dresses. In the heart of Seville, the shops offer exclusive models and textiles. Open Monday to Friday 10am to 1:30pm and 5 to 8:30pm, Saturday 10am to 2pm. Cuna 13. ② **95-422-21-43**.

MaxMara   There are only two branches of this hip and upscale store in all of Andalusia (the other one is in Marbella). MaxMara stocks both sportswear and elegant eveningwear for busy, hip, urban women. Lately, according to a spokesperson, the wives of many of the region's most visible politicians have been cropping up in MaxMara, seeking pantsuits and business suits in particular. The tones of pale gray and soft pink are popular. Plaza Nueva 3. © **95-421-48-25.**

Purificazione García   The designer (Purificazione García) of this sportswear and disco clothing line comes from Catalonia, but the clothes are actually assembled in northwestern Spain (Galicia). This outlet is cheaper than, and immediately adjacent to, the hyper-snobby Carolina Herrera boutique. The staff here is more approachable, the prices are a lot lower, and the ambience is less formal, more whimsical and comfortable. Plaza Nueva 8. © **95-450-11-29.**

Victorio & Lucchino 🎯🎯   This is the commercial headquarters of the most famous designers in Seville. Their names are known to virtually everybody in town, because of hot press they've generated and because of the cachet they've brought to the Sevillano's self-image. Even Penélope Cruz was one of their models before she emigrated to Hollywood. Fortunately, you don't have to be shaped like Penelope to wear these cutting-edge fashions. They stock garments up to size 46 (the rough equivalent of an American size 18) and have expanded their line to include both children's clothing and menswear.

Expect a starkly minimalist but glossy and very elegant showroom where the intricately tailored skirts, jackets, and bolero vests exert a powerful appeal on avid consumers. There aren't many clothes on display, but what there are are riveting. Some have hints of leather, some evoke an updated version of *feria* modish, and some focus exclusively on colors like magenta. Upstairs you'll find a jewelry boutique, a wedding salon, and a collection of housewares that a hyperwealthy homeowner in, say, the Balearics could use to furnish a hideaway villa. Plaza Nueva 10. © **95-422-79-51.**

FLEA MARKETS
"Los Hippies" sounds like something from the 1960s, but it actually is what Seville bargain hunters call their flea-market locations. On Wednesday and Thursday, the market takes place at **Plaza Magdalena** and **Calle Rioja;** on Friday at **Calle Feria** and **Calle Alameda,** and on Saturday at **La Plaza del Duque.** What's on sale? Almost anything from antiques (or *faux* antiques), lots and lots of junk, even some Cordovan leather goods, and clothes that John Lennon might have worn way back when. There are no set hours, but it's best to go before noon.

FOOD
La Delicia del Barrio   Tucked away within a cubbyhole, on a street that's otherwise devoted to tapas bars, this stylish boutique specializes in upscale food products of Andalusia. On display are a variety of olives, wines, cheeses, and most important of all, olive oils that, in their abundance and diversity, show off the fertility and rich culinary traditions of southern Spain.

If you want something really unusual, ask for a bottle of El Callejón Acebuchina, produced from wild olive trees (trees growing naturally on steep or impossibly rocky terrain that can't be cultivated in tracts). Despite its rarity, it sells for only 10€ ($12) for a half-liter bottle. Open daily 10:30am to 9pm. Calle Mateos Gagos 15. © **95-421-06-29.**

GIFTS
For another prestigious gift shop, see **Sevillarte** under "Porcelain," below.

El Azulejo   Bigger than most of its competitors within this crowded neighborhood near the cathedral, as well as classier and less claustrophobic, this shop sells upscale pottery, jewelry, and some of the most beautiful fans we've seen in

Seville. Priced at from 15€ to 160€ ($18–$192), they shimmer with hand-painted flowers or architectural renderings of actual sites within Seville. Open Monday to Saturday 9am to 7:30pm. Calle Mateos Gagos 10. ℭ **95-422-00-85.**

Matador   Souvenirs of the city, T-shirts, hammered wrought-iron whatnots, and ceramics—this store carries these and about a dozen other types of unpretentious gifts. Av. de la Constitución 28. ℭ **95-422-62-47.**

Snobismo   This shop manages to artfully crowd a wide array of merchandise into its precincts, everything from *sombreros* to *zapatos* (shoes). Tasteful scarves are sold, as is a good selection of leather bags and travel luggage. Top brand-name designers range from Armani to Alcocer. There is also a collection of splendid handcrafted jewelry from such places as Florence and Israel. Hours are Monday to Friday from 10am to 1:30pm and 5 to 8:30pm, Saturday from 10:30am to 2pm. Calle Jovellanos 11. ℭ **95-421-82-06.**

Tradiciones   Christmas and the Iberian interpretation of its traditions remain alive and well throughout the year in this boutique devoted to Nativity candles, carved figurines of the saints, and the decorative ribbons that make any gift, no matter how insignificant, look more substantial. Frankly, while we're not so keen on the candles and decorative gewgaws this place carries, the carved figures of the Virgin, Jesus, the Carpenter Joseph, the Saints, and the hosts of angels are worthwhile (albeit seasonal) souvenirs of your trip to Seville. Many figurines sell for 20€ ($24) or less; some go as high as around 75€ ($90). Open Monday to Saturday 10am to 2:30pm and 5:15 to 10pm, Sunday 10am to 3pm. Calle San José 18B. ℭ **95-421-10-50.**

JEWELRY

Agatha   This is the leading outlet for dramatic costume jewelry in Andalusia. From Seville, Agatha has branched out with outlets from Tokyo to Paris. The firm presents two major collections a year. Open Monday to Saturday 10am to 8:30pm. Closed on Saturday afternoon during July and August. Calle Tetuán 27. ℭ **95-456-39-45.**

Joyero Abrines   This is the kind of place where grooms have bought engagement and wedding rings for their brides for generations, and where generations of girlfriends have selected watches and cigarette lighters for the *hombre* of their dreams. There's another branch of this well-known store at Calle de la Asunción 28 (ℭ **95-427-42-44**). Both are open Monday to Saturday 10am to 1:30pm, Monday to Friday 5 to 8:30pm. Calle Sierpes 47. ℭ **95-427-42-44.**

Tous   This outlet celebrates "jewelry full of life" (in the owner's words), and displays some of the most innovative gems in Andalusia. Many of the designs are created by some of southern Spain's best artisans. Although there may be slight seasonal variations, regular hours are Monday to Friday 10am to 2pm and 5 to 8:30pm, Saturday 10am to 8pm. Calle Sierpes 8. ℭ **95-456-35-36.**

LEATHER

El Carambolo   The venue here is nonstandard leather goods, where artisans use traditional Andalusian leather-making techniques, with modern adaptations of color and design adding novel twists. (Ever seen a leather knapsack emblazoned with floral patterns, or with some of the architectural hallmarks of mudé-jar Spain?) It charges from 60€ to 140€ ($72–$168) for most of its leather wallets, purses, briefcases, and satchels, and a lot less for belts and keychain fobs. Open daily 11am to 9pm. Calle Santa Teresa 10. ℭ **95-422-78-77.**

Loewe ⚑★   This is the Sevillana branch of the oldest (established in 1856) and most famous purveyor of fine leather goods in Spain. You'll enter a big-windowed and sun-flooded store where topnotch leather goods are artfully displayed. Check out the new line of scarves, as designed by Oscar Marine, one of the graphic artists associated with Pedro Almodovar's films, which cost from 160€ to 180€ ($192–$216) each. Discerning women make a beeline for shoes they can really strut their stuff in, and the briefcases. Open Monday to Friday 10am to 8:30pm, Saturday 10am to 2pm. Plaza Nueva 12. ✆ 95-422-52-53.

MUSIC

Allegro   Next to the Teatro de la Maestranza, this is the best outlet in Seville for Spanish music, featuring *zarzuela* and flamenco songs along with the classics. You can listen before you buy. Open Monday to Friday 10am to 2pm and 5 to 8:30pm, Saturday 10am to 2pm. Closed August 15 to 30. Calle Dos de Mayo 37. ✆ 95-421-61-93.

PASTRIES

Confitería la Campana   This is one of the oldest and most respected pastry shops in Seville, with a pedigree going back to 1885, a sense of Victorian propriety, and a location near the beginning of an all-pedestrian street that's been considered a shopping mecca for years. They often provide the pastries at very grand and elegant diplomatic receptions. You'll select your caloric goodies beneath a splendid ceiling of white plaster and gilt. Look for the delightful tiled frieze of cherubs behind the counter. Locals flock in here in droves during Easter to buy *torrijas,* deep-fried, crustless bread soaked in honey. There's a cafe on the premises and takeaway service as well. Open daily 8am to 11pm. Calle Sierpes 1–3. ✆ 95-422-35-70.

PORCELAIN

Sevillarte   This is a glisteningly upscale gift shop that's the only officially authorized outlet for the full line of Lladró porcelain statues. Also in stock is an impressive array of silk "Manila" shawls—the kind of richly embroidered, jewel-toned shoulder wraps that no dignified Sevillana could live without. There's also a worthy display of porcelain, elaborately decorated fans (the kind that could transform virtually anyone into a hopeless flirt) and jewelry. Shawls, depending on their degree of embroidery, range from 28€ to 428€ ($34–$514); fans cost from 6€ to 81€ ($7.20–$97). Open Monday to Friday 10am to 7pm, Saturday 10am to 6pm, and Sunday 10am to 2pm. Calle Vida 17. ✆ 95-450-00-04.

SCENTS

Agua de Seville ⚑★⚑★   No scent emanating from Seville has elicited as much poetry as the blossoms from the city's 20,000 orange trees. In 1992, in honor of the Seville Expo, a team of designers came up with the world's ultimate orange-blossom-scented cologne, Agua de Seville, which today is a household name

---

Bitter Orange

There are more than 20,000 bitter orange trees in Seville, fruits of which are often exported to England for transformation into marmalade. The local name for these trees is **Azahar,** a word that translates directly from the Arabic as "white flower." For a brief period of 2 weeks in early April, the city is permeated with the scent of the Azahar, an intoxicating smell that everyone in Seville delights in.

---

throughout Andalusia. The bottle that contains it, shaped like the barrel of one of Napoleon's cannon, was inspired by the chimneys jutting skyward from the kilns of the Cartuja monastery on the site of Seville Expo. Both the men's and the women's version of the cologne is rich with the scents of jasmine and orange blossom, although the men's version has a stronger dose of sandalwood. The largest size (125 ml/4.2 oz.) of either version sells for 40€ ($48). Also on display are some carefully chosen gift items, housewares, and fashion accessories. Open Monday to Friday 10am to 2pm and 5 to 9pm, Saturday 10am to 2pm. Plaza Nueva 9. © 95-421-31-45.

TOBACCO

La Cava de Betis   One of the best outlets for smokers in Andalusia is this well-stocked "fumador," with its collection of handmade cigars. Coveted Cuban cigars as well as cigars from the Canary Islands and the Dominican Republic are sold here. The shop lies in the heart of Triana on the shores of the Guadalquivir River. Open July and August Monday to Friday 10am to 2pm, Thursday also 5 to 9pm. From September to May, hours are Monday to Friday 10am to 2pm and 5 to 9pm, Saturday from 10am to 2pm. La Calle Betis 36–39. © **95-427-81-85.**

8 Seville After Dark

Everyone from Lord Byron to Jacqueline Onassis has appreciated the unique blend of heat, rhythm, and sensuality that make up nightlife in Seville. If you're looking for a theme to define your nightlife wanderings, three of the most obvious possibilities might involve a bacchanalian pursuit of sherry, wine, and well-seasoned tapas. After several drinks, you might venture to a club whose focus revolves around an appreciation of flamenco as a voyeuristic insight into another era and the melding of the Arab and Christian aesthetic. And when you've finished with that, and if you're not wilted from the heat and the crowds, there's always the possibility of learning the intricate steps of one of southern Spain's most addictive dances, La Sevillana.

To keep abreast of what's happening in the arts and after dark in Seville, pick up a copy of the free monthly leaflet *El Giraldillo,* or consult listings in the local press, *Correo de Andalucía, Sudoeste, Nueva Andalucía,* or *ABC Sevilla.* Everything is listed here from jazz venues to classical music concerts and from art exhibits to dance events. You can also call the cultural hot line at © **010** to find out what's happening. Most of the staff speaks English.

Finds Flamenco, Concerts & Wine

Near Jardines de Murillo and Palacio de San Telmo stands **La Carbonería,** Calle Levíes 18 (© **95-421-44-60**), which is unique in Seville. A former charcoal factory has been converted into a concert hall and an array of local bars. It's really a big hall with whitewashed walls and a spectacular carved chimney. This is where the locals go to be entertained at night by a series of Andalusian-style concerts and flamenco shows at 10pm and midnight. You often sit on chairs placed on wooden floors at small wooden tables under low ceilings. In the rear is a large, plant-filled courtyard. Entrance is free and a beer or a glass of regional wine costs from 2.50€ ($3). Open daily 8pm to 2:30am. Bus: A3 or C3.

(*Finds* **A More Cultured Flamenco**

Most flamenco clubs in Seville are geared to tourists. If you'd like to see a more formal and academic presentation of this art form, visit **Casa de la Memoria,** Calle Ximenez de Enciso 28 (© **95-456-06-70**), in the Barrio de Santa Cruz. The price is only 11€ ($13) for adults or 9€ ($11) for students. The venue is a high-ceilinged Andalusian patio on a narrow street. Call for show times and a reservation. No alcohol is served.

Keep an eye out for classical concerts that are sometimes presented in the cathedral of Seville, the church of San Salvador, and the Conservatorio Superior de Música at Jesús del Gran Poder. Variety productions, including some plays for the kids, are presented at **Teatro Alameda,** Crédito (© **95-438-83-12**), but knowledge of Spanish is necessary. The venerable **Teatro Lope de Vega,** Avenida María Luisa (© **95-459-08-53**), is the setting for ballet performances and classical concerts, among other events. Near Parque María Luisa, this is Seville's leading stage.

OPERA

Teatro de la Maestranza 🐾🐾🐾   It wasn't until the 1990s that Seville got its own opera house, but it quickly became one of the world's premier venues for operatic performances. Naturally, the focus is on works inspired by Seville itself, including Verdi's *La Forza del Destino* and Mozart's *Marriage of Figaro.* Jazz, classical music, and even the quintessentially Spanish *zarzuelas* (operettas) are also performed. The opera house can't be visited except during performances. Tickets (which vary in price, depending on the event staged) can be purchased daily from 10am to 2pm and 6 to 9pm at the box office in front of the theater. Paseo de Colón 22. © 95-422-65-73.

FLAMENCO

When the moon is high in Seville, it's time to wander the alleyways of Santa Cruz in search of the sound of castanets. Or take a taxi, to be on the safe side.

Casa Anselma 🐾 *Finds*   If you're bored with touristy flamenco shows, seek out this little hideaway deep in the heart of Triana on the western bank of the river. The building, which is completely covered in decorative tiles called *azulejos,* is hard to miss. Inside it's wildly decorated with a lot of Spanish memorabilia, including bullfighting paraphernalia. The owner, Anselma, is the most celebrated flamenco performer in Sevilla, a secret the locals who flock here would like to keep to themselves. Flamenco performances are unrehearsed and spontaneous. Sometimes the joint jumps with communal singalongs or dancing with guitarists striking up their instruments. The club keeps no set hours, but it's usually packed and the action begins at midnight, Monday to Saturday. Instead of a cover, you're charged for what you have to drink. It's best reached by taxi, lying four blocks back from Calle Betis. Pagès del Corro 49, corner of Calle Antillano Campos. No phone.

El Arenal   The singers clap, the guitars strum, the tension builds, and the room fills with the ancient and mysterious magic of the flamenco. In the rear of a 17th-century structure, two shows are performed nightly at 9:30 and 11:30pm. Drinks and food are served at minuscule tables in a sweltering back room that evokes Old Andalusia. The location is between Varflora and Dos de Mayo in the vicinity of the Paseo Colón and the bullring. Cover 32€ ($38), including first drink, or 61€ ($73) for a fixed-price dinner. Calle Rodó 7. ℂ 95-421-64-92.

El Patio Sevillano In central Seville on the Guadalquivir riverbank between two historic bridges, El Patio Sevillano is a showcase for Spanish folk song and dance, performed by exotically costumed dancers. The presentation includes a wide variety of Andalusian flamenco and songs, as well as classical pieces by such composers as de Falla, Albéniz, Granados, and Chueca. From March to October, there are three shows nightly, at 7:30, 10, and 11:45pm. From November to February, there are two shows nightly, at 9 and 11:30pm. The cover 29€ ($35), includes the first drink. Paseo de Cristóbal Colón 11. ℂ 95-421-41-20.

Tablao Los Gallos Negotiating the labyrinth of narrow streets of the Barrio Santa Cruz somehow contributes to the authenticity of this intimate and high-energy flamenco club. The location is 2 blocks south of Ximénez de Enciso along Santa Teresa. No food is served during the shows, which begin every night at 9 and 11:30pm. Plaza de Santa Cruz 11. ℂ 95-421-69-81. Cover 27€ ($32), including 1st drink.

DANCE CLUBS

In Seville, some of these dance clubs have the life span of sickly butterflies. Check locally to see what's open at the time of your visit. Cover charges can vary depending on the night, but count on spending at least 6€ ($7.20) to get in, plus drinks.

Antique Teatro This is currently, one of the liveliest dance clubs in the city. Hours are Thursday to Saturday 11pm to 7am. In summer a terrace with torchlights opens up. Matemáticos Rey Pastor y Castor s/n, Pabellón Olímpico de Expo 92. ℂ 95-446-22-07.

Boss DJs rule the night at this favorite, which is open daily after midnight and usually rocks until the early hours. Betis 2. No phone.

Disco Catedral Playing the latest dance tunes, Disco Catedral is open Wednesday to Saturday at 11pm and usually shuts down at sunrise. Cuesta del Rosario 121. No phone.

TAPAS & DRINKS

Alianza Bar & Cafetería You'll follow narrow alleyways to reach this restaurant, the centerpiece of a hidden square in the Barrio de Santa Cruz. Cool tiles, marble surfaces, and air-conditioning are the perfect antidote to the heat of a

---

(Moments **Dancing the** *Sevillanas*

Flamenco is danced in solitary grandeur, but everyone joins in with the communal but complicated dance steps of the *sevillanas*. The best place to check it out is **El Simpecao,** Paseo de la O s/n (no phone). Beginning at 11pm every night of the year, recorded music presents four distinctly different facets of the complicated and old-fashioned dance steps in which dozens of everyday folk strut their Andalusian style in a way you'll rarely see outside of Spain. The setting is modern and just a wee bit battered. Entrance is free; bottled beer costs from around 2.50€ ($3) each.

sultry Sevillana midafternoon. The romantic-revival interior, festooned with photos of famous bullfighters and literati, is like something from a stage set for Pre-Franco Spain. And as the evening approaches, the tables on the square, close to a splashing fountain, evoke the scents and sounds of a Spanish garden. Come here for drinks, tapas, platters, and insight into the Spain of another era. Tapas cost 1.80€ to 2.50€ ($2.15–$3); sandwiches 3.50€ to 7€ ($4.20–$8.40); and platters 4€ to 12€ ($4.80–$14). May to October, open daily noon to midnight; November to April, daily noon to 8pm. Calle Rodrigo Caro 9. © 95-421-76-35.

Bodega Manola Blanco (Blanco Cerillo)   Although this place occupies an impossibly cramped triangle of a street corner just behind the Hotel Inglaterra and the Plaza Nueva, it seems as though everyone in the neighborhood, including the sales staffs at the upscale shops around the Plaza Nueva, crams in daily for drinks and tapas. There's even a rumor that the king of Spain, Juan Carlos, once dropped in for a nosh during the hubbub surrounding the Seville Expo of 1992. If you can handle the crowds, come by for coffee, priced at .90€ ($1.10); a platter of sliced Iberian ham, shrimp salad, or a platter of spinach studded with garbanzo beans; or even a beer or two. Tapas and raciones cost 1.30€ to 4.50€ ($1.55–$5.40). Open Monday to Friday 8am to 11pm, Saturday 8am to 4pm. Calle Madrid 8, corner of Calle Zaragoza, behind Plaza Nueva. © 95-422-57-22.

Casa Morales   Near the cathedral and Avenida de la Constitución, this is an old bodega dating from 1850 and decorated in a traditional Andalusian style with rustic wooden furniture. Its *auténtico* atmosphere is pretty much as it was when it welcomed the dons of the 19th century. Now women are invited as well, and you'll see them selecting the freshly made tapas of the day, often downed with blood-red rioja wine. The cook's specialties are sausages including spicy chorizo. Beer and wine are both popular here. Tapas begin at 2€ ($2.40). Open daily noon to 4pm and 8pm to midnight. García de Vinuesa 11. © 95-422-12-42.

Casa Román ⚘   Tapas are said to have originated in Andalusia, and this old-fashioned bar looks as if it has been dishing them up since day one (actually since 1934). Definitely include this place on your tasca-hopping through the old quarter of the Barrio Santa Cruz. Make your selection at the deli counter in front; you might even pick up the fixings for a picnic in the Parque María Luisa. Open Monday to Friday 9:30am to 4pm and 7pm to midnight, Saturday and Sunday 11am to 4pm and 7:30pm to midnight. Tapas are priced from 3.50€ ($4.20). Plaza de los Venerables. © 95-422-84-83.

Casa Ruitz   As you make the rounds of tapas bars, you'll discover treats like *pata negra* ham, made from a black-hoofed Iberian breed of pig. One of the world's great hams, the flavor is subtle and sweet instead of salty like Virginia ham. The pigs are fed on acorns. This tasca serves the best *pata negra* in Seville. The wine, too, is good here. Open Monday to Saturday 7:30am to 10:30pm. Calle Francos 59. © 95-422-86-24.

El Rinconcillo ⚘⚘   El Rinconcillo has a 1930s ambience, partly because of its real age and partly because of its owners' refusal to change one iota of the decor. This is the oldest and one of the most famous bars in Seville, with a history that dates from 1670. Amid dim lighting, heavy ceiling beams, and iron-based, marble-topped tables, you can enjoy a beer or a full meal along with the rest of the easygoing clientele. The bartender will mark your tab in chalk on a well-worn wooden countertop. El Rinconcillo is especially known for its salads, omelets, hams, and selection of cheeses. Look for the Art Nouveau tile murals. El Rinconcillo is at the northern edge of the Barrio Santa Cruz, near the Santa Catalina

Church. It's open Thursday to Tuesday from 1pm to 2am. A complete meal will cost around 20€ ($24). Gerona 40. ℂ 95-422-31-83.

Kios de la Flores Next to the Puente Isabel II, this is an enduring favorite in the Triana area across the river. With its typical tile floors and plastic tables and chairs, it is simplicity itself. In fair weather, the outdoor tables fill up quickly. The cook specializes in shellfish tapas. Try the delectable shellfish salad, the tiny sautéed clams known as *coquinas,* or the baby eels (not everyone's top choice, but a delight to gourmets). Tapas begin at 1.50€ ($1.80). Open daily 1pm to midnight. Plaza de Altozano s/n. ℂ 95-433-38-98.

La Alicantina ⭐ What is reported to be the best seafood tapas in town are served against a typically Sevillian, glazed-tile decor. Both the bar and the sidewalk tables are always filled to overflowing. The owner serves generous portions of clams marinara, fried squid, grilled shrimp, fried cod, and clams in béchamel sauce. Located about 5 blocks north of the cathedral, La Alicantina is open September to June daily noon to midnight; July and August daily 10:30am to 4pm and 8pm to 1am. Tapas range upward from 2€ ($2.40). Plaza del Salvador 2. ℂ 95-422-61-22.

La Antigua Bodeguita For as long as any of its neighbors in Seville can remember, the young and the restless have congregated every evening on the plaza outside of the pink-brick Baroque facade of the San Salvador church. The bar that attracts the majority of them is Antigua Bodeguita, a mellow place, loaded with the patina of years of hard living and cigarette smoke. It consists of two tile-sheathed rooms, each with a thick wooden bar for standing (there's not a single table). Guests carry their tapas and drinks into the square outside in a kind of revolving current that continues daily 2pm till 4am. Come here to see and be seen. Tapas cost 1.25€ to 4€ ($1.50–$4.80). Plaza del Salvador 6. ℂ 95-456-18-33.

La Bodega Some visitors, but mostly locals patronize this tiny bar with tasty tapas on a small street off San Eloy. It's a modest joint, with glaring neon lights at night that are unkind to all but those with perfect skin. The owner is helpful, and lovingly describes his tapas to every visitor—in Spanish. Along with a cold beer or a glass of Andalusian wine, you can sample *montaditos* (tiny sandwiches), savory prawns, fried anchovies, chorizo, and even baked salmon and various local cheeses. Shellfish tapas are a specialty. Tapas begin at 1.65€ ($2). Open Monday to Saturday noon to midnight. Fernan Caballero 6. ℂ 95-421-19-20.

La Tasca de El Burladero On the ground floor of the deluxe Hotel Colón, this is one of Seville's more sanitized tapas bars. Its long corridor looks like a bodega with arches, heavy lamps, wooden partitions, and dark colors, even a number of "squat tables." Both families and couples can be seen devouring the tapas, including some vegetable versions. A specialty is *espada casera* (swordfish). Tapas begin at 2€ ($2.40). Open daily 11am to 1am. Canalejas 1. ℂ 95-422-29-00.

Modesto At the northern end of Murillo Gardens, opening onto a quiet square with flower boxes and an ornate iron railing, Modesto serves fabulous seafood tapas. The bar is air-conditioned, and you can choose your appetizers just by pointing. Upstairs there's a good-value restaurant (see previous recommendation). Modesto is open daily from 8pm to 2am. Tapas are priced from 3€ ($3.60). Cano y Cueto 5. ℂ 95-441-68-11.

BARS, BEER HALLS & PUBS

Abades ⭐⭐ A converted mansion in the Barrio Santa Cruz has been turned into a rendezvous that's been compared to "a living room in a luxurious movie set." In the heart of the Jewish ghetto, this 19th-century house constructed around a central courtyard with a fountain, evokes the Spanish Romantic era. Drinks and low-key conversations are the style here, and since its opening in 1980 all the visiting literati and glitterati have put in an appearance. Young men and women in jeans also patronize the place, enjoying the comfort of the sofas and wicker armchairs.

The ingredients of a special drink called *aqua de Sevilla* are a secret, but we suspect sparkling white wine, pineapple juice, and eggs (the whites and yolks mixed in separately so that the whites achieve a meringue-like consistency). Classical music is played in the background. Take a taxi to get here at night, as it might not be safe to wander late along the narrow streets of the barrio. In summer, it's open daily from 8pm to 4am; in winter, daily from 8pm to 2:30am. Abades 1. © 95-571-82-79.

Bar Antigüedades   Set less than a block from the cathedral, within a timber-ceilinged triangular-shaped room lined with 18th-century brickwork, this is a fun, post-*movida* nightspot for 30- and 40-something Spaniards. Hanging from the ceiling is a pop-art theme that changes at least twice a year, for example, various body parts of plastic mannequins, each pierced with hundreds of toothpicks. The bar and its clients tend to be hip and international. Open nightly 9pm to 3am. Argote de Molina 40. No phone.

Bar Entrecalles   No matter how late it is, this place within the narrow and claustrophobic alleyways behind the cathedral is usually filled (sometimes mobbed) with hip and usually attractive people in their 20s and 30s. Don't overlook the satirical mural, in back, of a startled and outraged flamenco dancer who stares back at this late-night crowd in surprise. The site has seen many changes since it was originally established several generations ago as a store for milk and milk products. Its name ("between streets") derives from doors inside that open onto both the Calle Ximénez de Enciso and an even narrower street, the Lope de Rueda, in back. Tapas range from 2€ to 4.50€ ($2.40–$5.40). Open daily 1pm to 2:30am. Calle Ximénez de Enciso 14. © 61-786-77-52.

Cervecería de la Moneda   Beginning in 1936, this beer hall in the Arenal district did everything it could to exclude women, with plenty of collusion from the then-all-powerful Franco government. In 2001, many years after the death of the *generalissimo*, and after powerful lobbying from local feminists, it actually installed some women's toilets (thereby making newspaper stories about being one of the last beer halls in Seville to install them), and threw open the doors to persons of all genders and sexual persuasions. Today, within a baroque building that was famous during the 18th century as the site where coins were minted, you'll find a tempting array of tapas and endless streams of beer and wine. Daily 8am to 2am. In Casa de la Moneda (the city mint). Corner of Santander and Joaquín Hazanas. © 95-422-63-87.

Trinity Pub   There are several highly visible Irish pubs in Seville, but this one is the classiest, most elegant, and in some ways, most evocative of good times and the literary wealth of Ireland. Don't come looking for spilled beer and sawdust on the floor: Replicating a decor that evokes James Joyce's favorite hangout in Dublin, circa 1900, cost many thousands of euros. Most of the artwork and antiques, including the dartboards and their decorative boxes, derive from Celtic Ireland. Thanks to a pair of champion bartenders, it has produced more original cocktails than any other bar in Seville. If you're tired of Bushmill's and Guinness, ask for such original Trinity Bar prizewinners as a Trinity 2002 (dry vermouth, sweet vermouth, and gin) or a Manilva (a playful rum-based drink that tastes like tropical fruit punch). Open daily from 10:30am to 2am. In Hotel Inglaterra, Plaza Nueva. ✆ 95-422-49-70.

THE GAY & LESBIAN NIGHTLIFE SCENE

Seville has a large gay and lesbian population, much of it composed of foreigners and of Andalusians who fled here for a better life, escaping smaller, less tolerant towns and villages. Gay life thrives at the bars recommended below.

El Hombre y el Oso Founded in 1999 near the Alameda de Hercules, and with a gay underground following of men from throughout the region, this is the most popular and most frequently visited "bear bar" in Andalusia, with a decor that's loaded with depictions of bears of all shapes and sizes. How does its well-traveled owner define a bear? As a mature man, preferably gay, who's comfortable with his size, his age, and his worldview, and who tries, at least, to make friends and play happily with others. Shadowy and permissive, this bar, to an increasing degree, has established itself as an icon on Seville's relatively limited gay bar scene. Beer costs 3€ ($3.60). Open Sunday to Thursday 10:30pm to 2:30am, Friday and Saturday 10:30pm to 4am. Amor de Dios 32. ✆ 95-456-30-29.

Isbiliyya Café-Bar This is a popular meeting place and cruising grounds, mainly for young men, a lot of whom speak English and seem eager to meet foreigners. The bar is found across the street from the Puente Isabel II bridge. Outdoor tables are a magnet in summer. Open Monday to Wednesday 8pm to 5am and Thursday to Sunday 9am to 5am. Paseo de Colón 2. ✆ 95-421-64-00.

Itaca Technically, this place admits women, but since females are not admitted beyond the modest-size front bar, most of the inner workings of this dance club are reserved for men. The venue is weekends-only, when it tends to be very crowded with high-testosterone 20- and 30-somethings who come to dance, dance, dance. Clients seem to thrive on impossibly late hours, so a predisco nap is usually an excellent idea. It lies a few steps from El Hombre y el Oso (above). Open Friday and Saturday 10:30pm to 4am. Calle Amor de Dios 31. No phone. Cover 6€ ($7.20).

9 Side Trips from Seville

CARMONA ✦
34km (21 miles) E of Seville

An easy hour-long bus trip from the main terminal in Seville, Carmona is an ancient city dating from Neolithic times. It grew in power and prestige under the Moors, establishing ties with Castile in 1252.

Surrounded by fortified walls, Carmona has three Moorish fortresses—one a parador, the other two the **Alcázar de la Puerta de Córdoba** and **Alcázar de la Puerta de Sevilla.** The top attraction is **Seville Gate,** with its double Moorish arch, opposite St. Peter's Church. Note too, **Córdoba Gate** on Calle Santa María de Gracia, which was attached to the ancient Roman walls in the 17th century.

The town itself is a virtual national landmark, filled with narrow streets, whitewashed walls, and Renaissance mansions. **Plaza San Fernando** is the most important square, with many elegant 17th-century houses. The most important church is dedicated to **Santa María** and stands on the Calle Martín López. You enter a Moorish patio before exploring the interior with its 15th-century white vaulting.

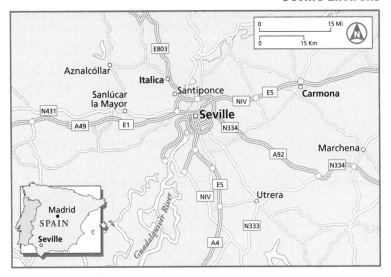

At Calle Emmedio there's a **Roman amphitheater** as well as a **Roman necropolis** containing the remains of 1,000 families that lived in and around Carmona 2,000 years ago. Of the two important tombs, the **Elephant Vault** consists of three dining rooms and a kitchen. The other, the **Servilia Tomb,** was the size of a nobleman's villa.

Carmona can be viewed relatively easy on a day trip from Seville, but because it has some of the most romantic and evocative hotels in the area, many visitors try to schedule an overnight visit.

GETTING THERE   If you're driving to Carmona, exit from Seville's eastern periphery onto the N-V superhighway, following the signs to the airport, then to Carmona on the road to Madrid. The Carmona turnoff is clearly marked.

WHERE TO STAY

Alcázar de La Reina ★★   After the parador, this is the second most important hotel in town, superior to the also-recommended Casa de Carmona. Known for its elegance, the hotel is stylish with an interior inspired by the mudéjar architecture. With a sleek but inviting decor, it offers a warm welcome and friendly service. The decoration is very personalized; no two rooms are the same. All the midsize to spacious bedrooms have flair, often with canopied or four-poster beds. Each comes with a luxurious marble-clad bathroom with a tub and shower. The suites are exceptional, especially El Mirador, which features a Jacuzzi and opens onto a panoramic view over the Vega de Carmona landscape. Even if you're just passing through Carmona for the day, consider eating at the first-class restaurant, which is warmly decorated and serves a market-fresh cuisine, with meals costing from 25€ to 32€ ($30–$38).

Plaza de Lasso 2, 41410 Carmona. (C) **95-419-62-00.** Fax 95-414-01-13. www.alcazar-reina.es/ingles/hotel/presenta.htm. 64 units. 119€–129€ ($143–$155) double; 281€ ($337) suite. Rates include breakfast. AE, DC, MC, V. **Amenities:** Restaurant; bar; outdoor pool; limited room service; babysitting. *In room:* A/C, TV, dataport, minibar, safe.

Casa de Carmona ★ *Finds*   One of the most elegant and intimate hotels in Andalusia, this plushly furnished hideaway was originally built as the home of the Lasso family during the 1500s. Several years ago, a team of entrepreneurs added the many features required for a luxury hotel while retaining the marble columns, massive masonry, and graceful proportions of the building's original construction. The most visible public room still maintains vestiges of its original function as a library. Each bedroom is a cozy enclave of opulent furnishings, with distinct decor inspired by ancient Rome, medieval Andalusia, or Renaissance Spain. All units have bathrooms with tub/shower combinations.

On the premises is an outdoor restaurant serving modern interpretations of Andalusian and international cuisine. Set at the edge of the village, the hotel also has a flowery terrace and an inner courtyard covered against the midsummer heat with canvas awning.

Plaza de Lasso 1, 41410 Carmona. © 95-419-10-00. Fax 95-419-01-89. www.casadecarmona.com. 32 units. 120€–270€ ($144–$324) double; from 500€–900€ ($600–$1,080) suite. Add about 30% for Feria de Sevilla and Easter (Semana Santa). AE, DC, MC, V. Free parking. **Amenities:** Restaurant; bar; outdoor pool; limited room service; babysitting; laundry service/dry cleaning. *In room:* A/C, TV, minibar, hair dryer, safe.

Parador de Carmona ✸✸✸   This looks more like a fortress than a parador, with windows opening on wide vistas of the River Corbones plains. In fact, it's one of the best paradors in Andalusia, offering plenty of charm and atmosphere, beautiful landscaping, a grand swimming pool, an Andalusian patio with a mudéjar fountain, and panoramic terraces. The parador has a slight edge over its nearby competitors, Alcázar de La Reina and Casa de Carmona. The foundations of the hotel date from the 14th century, and it was last renovated in 1998.

Bedrooms are bright and spacious, and furnished in a classical style, with Sevillano tiles and luxury bathrooms with tub/shower combination. The former refectory has been turned into an elegant dining room, serving local specialties such as *caruja de perdiz* (partridge), codfish pies, and a rich buffet of desserts. The parador hires the finest chefs in towns, with meals costing from 25€ ($30).

Alcázar s/n, 41410 Carmona. © 95-414-10-10. Fax 94-414-12-12. www.parador.es. 63 units. 120€ ($144) double. AE, DC. Free parking. **Amenities:** Restaurant; bar; outdoor pool; room service (8am–midnight); babysitting; 1 room for those w/limited mobility. *In room:* A/C, TV, minibar, hair dryer, safe.

WHERE TO DINE

San Fernando INTERNATIONAL/ANDALUSIAN   Outside of the luxury dining rooms of the hotels, this is the best restaurant in town. Dating from the 1700s, it is decorated with fabrics and wooden furnishings. Entered from a side street, the old-fashioned restaurant is on the second floor of an antique building, its windows opening onto the landmark square, Plaza de San Fernando, from which it takes its name. This is good local cooking, the type that's been served in the region for years. Classic soups include gazpacho and *ajo blanco*, a garlic soup flavored with almonds. Although it's an inland town, fresh fish reaches Carmona daily. Both cod and hake *(merluza)* appear perfectly grilled and spiced.

Calle Sacramento 3. © 95-414-35-56. Reservations recommended. Main courses 9€–18€ ($11–$22). AE, DC, MC, V. Tues–Sat 1:30–4pm and 9–11pm; Sun 1:30–4pm.

ITALICA
9km (5½ miles) NW of Seville

Lovers of Roman history will flock to Itálica (© **95-599-73-76**), the ruins of an ancient city northwest of Seville on the major road to Lisbon, near the small town of Santiponce.

After the battle of Ilipa, Publius Cornelius Scipio Africanus founded Itálica in 206 B.C. Two of the most famous Roman emperors, Trajan and Hadrian, were

Travel Tip: He who finds the best hotel deal has more to spend on facials involving knobbly vegetables.

Hello, the Roaming Gnome here. I've been nabbed from the garden and taken round the world. The people who took me are so terribly clever. They find the best offerings on Travelocity. For very little cha-ching. And that means I get to be pampered and exfoliated till I'm pink as a bunny's doodah.

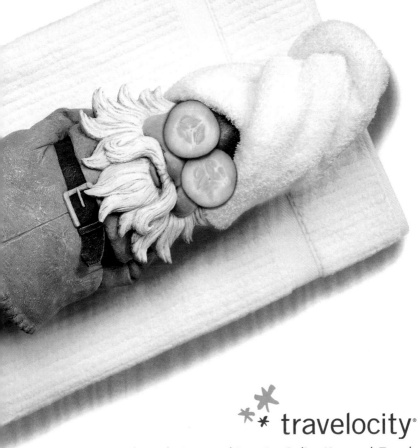

** travelocity

born here, and indeed, master builder Hadrian had a major influence on his hometown. During his reign, the **amphitheater,** the ruins of which can be seen today, was among the largest in the Roman Empire. Lead pipes that carried water from the Guadalquivir River still remain. A small **museum** displays some of the Roman statuary found here, although the finest pieces have been shipped to Seville. Many mosaics, depicting beasts, gods, and birds, are on exhibit, and others are constantly being discovered. The ruins, including a Roman theater, can be explored for 1.50€ ($1.80). The site is open April through September, Tuesday to Saturday from 9am to 8pm and Sunday from 9am to 3pm. From October through March, it's open Tuesday to Saturday from 9am to 5:30pm and Sunday from 10am to 4pm.

Itálica is best visited on a day trip. You can explore the sights in about 2½ hours.

GETTING THERE   If you're driving, exit from the northwest periphery of Seville, following the signs for highway E-803 in the direction of Zafra and Lisbon. A bus marked M-172 goes to Itálica and departures are from the Estación de Autobuses at Plaza de Armas. Buses depart every hour for the 30-minute trip.

6

Córdoba

Ten centuries ago, Córdoba was the capital of Muslim Spain. With a population of 900,000 it was Europe's largest city and a worldwide cultural and intellectual center. Later, greedy hordes sacked the city, tearing down ancient buildings and carting off many art treasures. Despite these assaults, Córdoba still retains traces of its former glory—in fact, of the three great medieval cities of Andalusia, Córdoba best preserves its Moorish legacy.

Today this provincial capital is known chiefly for its mosque, the world-famous Mezquita, but it abounds with other artistic and architectural riches, especially its lovely homes. The old Arab and Jewish quarters are famous for their narrow streets lined with whitewashed houses boasting flower-filled patios and balconies. Córdoba has recently joined the ranks of UNESCO's World Heritage sites, so you'll want to spend at least 2 days here.

From the 8th to the 11th centuries, the Umayyad caliphs brought an opulent lifestyle and great learning and culture to Córdoba while most of the rest of Europe languished in the Dark Ages. In those days, Córdoba—not Madrid—was the capital of Iberia. In its heyday, a pilgrimage to the Great Mezquita in Córdoba by a Muslim was said to have equaled a journey to Mecca.

Prior to the arrival of the Arabs, Córdoba had prospered in Roman times. Seneca the Elder (4 B.C.–A.D. 65), one of the greatest philosophers of the ancient world, lived here.

After the fall of the Romans, the city declined when it was taken over by the Visigoths who in turn gave way to the more cultured Arabs. The invaders brought in scientists, scholars, and philosophers, while at the same time generating great prosperity based on trade.

Córdoba became known for its pleasure palaces, including harems and luxurious baths. But it also boasted a library with 400,000 hand-copied books. The city was host to the first university established in Europe and Cordovan silverwork and tooled leathers became famous around the world.

Infighting among the Muslims led to the collapse of Córdoba in 1031, when it disintegrated as a center of the caliphate. Seville replaced Córdoba at that time as the capital of Iberia.

Even in this period of decline, Córdoba saw the birth of Moisés Maimónides (1135–1204), the fabled Jewish philosopher and Talmudist, who was born in the Judería (Jewish ghetto). In time he was driven from the city by the Almohads and sought refuge in the Ayyubid court in Egypt. There he became the physician to Saladin, and penned a number of works that still have a profound impact on world thought.

The Reconquista, the recapturing of Muslim Andalusia by the Christians, occurred in 1236 long before Ferdinand and Isabella took back Granada in 1492. Under various Catholic monarchs, Córdoba went into a decline that lasted for centuries.

Today, Córdoba's glory is long gone, but you can wander its streets and see what used to be. There's a lot more here than the Mezquita: You can stroll for hours in the Judería with its narrow, cobblestone streets and flower-filled patios; wander through Queen Isabella's garden in the Alcázar; visit Renaissance churches and palaces; explore some of Andalusia's finest museums; and even visit the nearby excavations of Madinat Al-Zahra, a country palace and royal city built by a 10th-century caliph.

Córdoba is also a modern city with broad, tree-lined boulevards and an up-to-date business community with computers and cellphones. You can live in modern chain hotels of a high international standard, but if you prefer the old-fashioned Andalusian lifestyle, in certain restaurants and palaces you can also truly live in the past.

1 Orientation

GETTING THERE

BY TRAIN   This is the most convenient and most popular means of transport to Córdoba, as the city is a rail junction for routes to the rest of Andalusia and is on the vital rail link between Madrid and Seville. The most popular line is the **AVE high-speed train** racing between Madrid and Córdoba or Córdoba and Seville. These days the travel time between Seville and Córdoba has been cut to just 25 minutes, which is why travelers with tight schedules visit Córdoba on a day trip from Seville. Amazingly, the AVE train ride between Madrid in the north and Córdoba in the south takes just 1½ hours. There are much slower trains but because vacation time is precious we don't recommend them.

There are between 22 and 31 trains per day arriving from Madrid, costing 47€ ($56) for a one-way ticket. A one-way ticket between Córdoba and Seville sells for 24€ ($28). If you're on the Costa del Sol and want to visit Córdoba, you can take one of the 10 to 12 trains per day from Málaga. Depending on the train, the trip takes 2 to 3 hours, costing from 13€ to 19€ ($16–$23) for a one-way ticket.

The main train station at Córdoba is on the town's northern periphery, at Glorieta de las Tres Culturas, off Avenida de América. Bus no. 3 runs between the rail station and the historic core of the city. For rail information, call © 90-224-02-02; for AVE schedules or information call © 90-224-02-02. The RENFE advance ticket office in Córdoba is at Ronda de los Tejares 10 (© 95-747-58-84). To reach the heart of the city from the station, head south on Avenida de Cervantes or Avenida del Gran Capitán.

BY PLANE   Air is not the best way to reach Córdoba. It does have a municipal airport lying 9km (5½ miles) from town. But it's mainly for private planes. Most visitors arriving by air from other parts of Spain or the continent fly to Seville, Málaga (capital of the Costa del Sol), or Granada, then travel by rail or car to reach Córdoba.

BY BUS   Córdoba is also served by buses but we don't recommend them for long-distance travel. If you're in some small town in Andalusia, however, without a good rail link, it may be your only means of transport if you're dependent on public transportation.

Confusingly, there are eight different bus terminals in the city. Note that you won't necessarily know which terminal you'll be arriving at, as each local bus line has its own station.

Most arrivals are on a bus operated by **Alsina Graells Sur** (© **95-727-81-00**), coming into Diego Serrano 14, lying on the outskirts of the city near Paseo de la Victoria. The most popular routes are between Córdoba and Seville, with 10 to 13 buses per day. The trip takes 2 hours and costs 8.55€ ($10) for a one-way ticket. Another popular run is between Granada and Córdoba, where eight to nine buses per day make the 3-hour run, costing 10€ ($12) for a one-way ticket.

The second most used terminal is operated by **Transportes Ureña** (© **95-740-45-58**). Its buses arrive at the terminal on Av. de Cervantes 22, a few blocks south of the train station. If you're visiting Jaén (see later in this chapter), you'll find a bus connection between that city and Córdoba. The trip takes 2 hours; there are six to eight trains per day, and the cost of a one-way ticket is 6.70€ ($8).

If you're on the tightest of budgets, you can call **Secorbus** (© **90-222-92-92**), which offers the least expensive bus runs between Madrid and Córdoba. But the trip takes 4½ hours. There are about seven buses a day making this long haul, a one-way ticket going for 11€ ($13).

BY CAR   Many visitors opt to drive to Córdoba from Seville. If you do, take the N-IV (E-5) south from Madrid, veering right (west) at the town of Bailén. Córdoba is well signposted, and the toll-free trip takes (roughly) about 3 hours. The same national highway continues west directly into Seville. Córdoba is 105km (65 miles) west of Jaén and 419km (260 miles) southwest of Madrid. It is also 166km (103 miles) northwest of Granada, and 129km (80 miles) east of Seville.

VISITOR INFORMATION

The **tourist office,** Calle Torrijos 10 (© **90-201-77**; www.andalusia.org), is open Monday to Friday 9:30am to 6:30pm, Saturday 10am to 2pm and 5 to 7pm, Sunday and holidays 10am to 2pm.

CITY LAYOUT

Córdoba is roughly divided into two different sectors, the old city consisting of the **Judería (Jewish Quarter)** and the area around the **Mezquita,** plus the newer section with broad, tree-lined boulevards. This modern city, the commercial part, extends from the **rail station** on Avenida de América down to the **Plaza de las Tendillas** (most often called Plaza Tendillas today), which is the heart of Córdoba.

Most of your time will be spent in the *centro* (historic center), which borders the Río Guadalquivir, the river that flows through Córdoba. From Tendillas square, a maze of narrow streets extends to the banks of the river.

Puente Romano, the Roman bridge, spans the Guadalquivir linking the "right bank" of Córdoba with the "left bank."

In the course of your visit to Córdoba you'll inevitably come to a major city square, **Plaza Campo Santo de los Mártires.** Directly east of this square is Córdoba's primary attractions, the **Mezquita** and the **Cathedral.** To the southwest of this square stands the **Alcázar de los Reyes Cristianos** and the adjacent **Jardines del Alcázar.** These attractions are all many visitors ever see of Córdoba.

Barrio de la Judería lies directly to the northwest of Campo Santo de los Mártires. Arabs and Jews once lived in harmony in this medieval quarter. About a third of a mile of restored town wall runs beside a moat and gardens along Calle Cairuán at the ghetto's western edge. At the northern end of the wall you'll see a bronze statue of a former resident, the philosopher, Seneca, standing beside the Puerta de Almodóvar, a gate that once protected the old quarter and which is even today the principal western entrance to the Judería.

From Puente Romano you can walk along Ronda de Isasa, which becomes Paseo de la Rivera. This will take you to another cluster of attractions, including **Iglesia de San Francisco, Museo de Bellas Artes, Posada del Potro,** and **Museo Julio Romero de Torres.** These attractions center on another landmark square, **Plaza del Potro.**

GETTING AROUND

The historic core of Córdoba is relatively small, and the best way to get around it is to walk. In fact, many of its labyrinthine and cobblestone streets such as those around the Mezquita and in the Judería (the old Jewish Quarter) are pedestrian only.

BY BUS   You can cover the relatively compact historic district on foot, but if you want to branch out to bordering areas, you can take a city bus. If you're staying on the outskirts, three main buses run into the historic core: bus nos. 1, 3, and 4. Most of our recommendations in the area north of the historic core can be reached by bus nos. 4, 5, 11, and 12. For bus information, call ℂ **95-725-57-00.**

BY TAXI   A typical fare—say, from the Mezquita to the train station—can range from 3€ to 5€ ($3.60–$6) depending on traffic. **Radio Taxi** (ℂ **95-776-44-44**) has taxi stands at most busy intersections, including Avenida del Gran Capitán, Plaza Colón, Plaza Tendillas, Calle Cañero, Calle Ciudad Jardín, Calle Arcos de la Frontera, and Calle Agustín Moreno.

BY CAR   Don't enter the complicated maze of streets in the Old Town with a car. You'll inevitably get lost and be unable to find parking. There are two small public parking lots outside the Old Town, one on Calle Robledo and the other on Calle Aeropuerto. Both are well positioned, well marked, and easy to find.

If you plan to tour the countryside around Córdoba, a car is the most useful, albeit expensive, way to do so. Major car-rental companies in Córdoba include **Avis,** Plaza de Colón 32 (ℂ **95-747-68-62**), and **Hertz** at Av. América s/n (ℂ **95-740-20-60**).

BY HORSE & CARRIAGE   *Coches de caballo* are for rent around the Mezquita and the Alcázar, and this is the most romantic and old-fashioned way to see Córdoba. However, some of the alleyways in the Judería are so tiny that even carriages can't fit. You'll find specific stops at Calle Torrijos adjoining the Mezquita and Campo Santo de los Mártires next to the Alcázar. The actual price depends on a negotiation between you and the driver: Agree on terms before hopping aboard. Prices may vary but an average cost is 25€ ($30) per hour.

FAST FACTS: Córdoba

Currency Exchange   Banks and ATMs are in the sector surrounding the mosque and Plaza Tendillas and also along Avenida Gran Capitán in the modern commercial section of town. Otherwise, you can go to the most central **Banco Santander Central Hispano,** Plaza Tendillas 5 (ℂ **95-749-70-00**), open Monday to Friday 8:30am to 2:30pm.

Emergency   For medical assistance dial ℂ **061.** For an ambulance call ℂ **95-729-44-70.** To report a fire call ℂ **080.** For a police emergency, phone ℂ **091.**

Hospital The most central is the **Red Cross Hospital,** Paseo de la Victoria (✆ **95-722-22-22**). Other hospitals include **Hospital Reina Sofía** at Av. Menéndez Pidal s/n (✆ **95-721-70-00**) and **Hospital Los Morales,** Sierra de Córdoba s/n (✆ **95-727-56-50**).

Internet Access In the Judería, try **NavegaWeb,** Plaza Judá Leví (✆ **95-729-30-89**). The charge is 1.20€ ($1.45) per hour. Open daily 10am to 10pm.

Maps If you need more detailed maps than the general one provided by the tourist office, go to the book department of **El Corte Inglés,** Ronda de los Tejares 32 (✆ **95-722-28-81**), the city's leading department store. It sells a superb and easy-to-use map for 3.10€ ($3.70). Store hours are Monday to Saturday 10am to 10pm.

Police The main station lies at Av. Doctor Fleming 2 (✆ **95-759-45-80**). Another major station is at Campo Madre de Dios s/n (✆ **95-723-37-53**).

Post Office The main post office is at Calle Cruz Conde 15 (✆ **95-747-97-67**), open Monday to Friday 8:30am to 8:30pm, Saturday and Sunday 9:30am to 2pm.

Safety Córdoba is safer than Seville but beware of muggers. Unemployment is high, and thousands of tourists are arriving with bulging wallets, cellphones, cameras, whatever. The police presence is strongest around the Mezquita and in the Judería district. A particularly dangerous strip is the section west of Calle de San Fernando, which should be avoided at night. Of course, it's wise to lock valuables in the safe in your room or in your main hotel safe and venture forth with only what you'll need for the day to cut down your loss in case you become the victim of a mugging.

2 Where to Stay

At the peak of its summer season, Córdoba has too few hotels to meet the demand, so reserve as far in advance as possible.

EXPENSIVE

El Conquistador Hotel ✦ Built centuries ago as a private villa, this hotel is tastefully renovated and one of the most attractive in town, with triple rows of stone-trimmed windows and ornate iron balustrades. It sits opposite an unused rear entrance to the Mezquita. The marble-and-granite lobby opens into an interior courtyard filled with seasonal flowers, a pair of splashing fountains, and a symmetrical stone arcade. The quality and comfort of the rooms—each with a black-and-white marble floor and a private bathroom—earn the hotel four government-granted stars. But for us, the rooms are too small.

Magistral González Francés 15, 14003 Córdoba. ✆ **95-748-11-02.** Fax 95-747-46-77. www.hotelconquistador cordoba.com. 128 units. 104€–168€ ($125–$202) double; from 218€ ($262) suite. AE, DC, MC, V. Parking 12€ ($14). Bus: 3. **Amenities:** Restaurant; bar; lounge; limited room service; babysitting; laundry service/dry cleaning; nonsmoking rooms; rooms for those w/limited mobility. *In room:* A/C, TV, dataport, minibar, hair dryer, safe.

Hespería Córdoba ✦ One of the four or five leading hotels of Córdoba, this first-class member of a chain stands near the city close to the Guadalquivir River. Built in 1993, it was last renovated in 2003. Impressive architecturally, its rooms open onto attractive cityscape vistas. Its most alluring feature, especially in summer, is a swimming pool set within an Andalusian courtyard. We're not too fond of the place when there's a convention going on, but when not over-burdened, the staff is most helpful and knowledgeable about Córdoba. Bed-rooms are midsize and attractively furnished in a mix of Andalusian traditional and contemporary, with much use of blue tiles and wooden furnishings. Each comes with a tiled bathroom containing a tub/shower combo. If you're staying in for the night, the on-site restaurant, Córdoban, serves a first-class medley of Spanish and international specialties, and the garden bar is idyllic for a drink before or after dinner.

Av. Fray Albino 1, 14009 Córdoba. ✆ **95-742-10-42.** Fax 95-729-99-97. www.hesperia-cordoba.com. 106 units. 140€–152€ ($168–$182) double; 233€ ($280) suite. Rates include breakfast. AE, DC, MC, V. Parking: 12€ ($14). Bus: 3. **Amenities:** Restaurant; bar/cafeteria; outdoor pool; laundry service/dry cleaning; non-smoking wing; rooms for those w/limited mobility. *In room:* A/C, TV, minibar, hair dryer, safe.

NH Amistad Córdoba ★★   In the heart of the Judería (old Jewish Quarter) a 4-minute walk from the mosque, this hotel is one of the most desirable in town. It opened in 1992 after renovations combined two existing 18th-century mansions, next to a synagogue that dates from 1314. The houses face each other and are linked by a small patio of beautiful Andalusian arches and colorful Span-ish tiles. The spacious rooms come with neat bathrooms containing tub/shower combos, and excellent beds, and the design is a tasteful combination of wood and fabric. In 1998, a more modern wing opened.

Plaza de Maimónides 3, 14004 Córdoba. ✆ **95-742-03-35.** Fax 95-742-03-65. www.nh-hoteles.com. 84 units. 140€–153€ ($168–$184) double. AE, DC, MC, V. Parking 14€ ($17). Bus: 2, 3, 5, or 6. **Amenities:** Restaurant; bar; 24-hr. room service; babysitting; laundry service/dry cleaning; nonsmoking rooms. *In room:* A/C, TV, dataport, minibar, coffeemaker, hair dryer, safe (in some).

Parador de Córdoba ★★ *(Value)*   Found inconveniently 4km (2½ miles) out-side town in a suburb called El Brillante, this parador, named after an Arab word meaning "palm grove," offers the conveniences and facilities of a luxurious resort hotel at reasonable rates. Occupying the site of a former caliphate palace, it's one of the finest paradors in Spain. Its most recent feature is a garden, Los Naranjos (the orange trees), where the first palm trees planted in Europe can be found. The spacious guest rooms have been furnished with fine dark-wood pieces, and some have balconies for eating breakfast or relaxing over a drink. All have bath-rooms with tub/shower combos. The dining room offers two classic Andalusian soups, both served cold. Try either *salmorejo cordobés* (vegetable soup) or *gazpa-cho blanco de almendras* (almond soup). To follow, try the delectable steak in green sauce.

Av. de la Arruzafa 33, 14012 Córdoba. ✆ **95-727-59-00.** Fax 95-728-04-09. www.parador.es. 94 units. 113€–130€ ($136–$156) double; 156€ ($187) suite. AE, DC, MC, V. Free parking. **Amenities:** Restaurant; bar; outdoor pool; tennis court; fitness center; sauna; limited room service; babysitting; laundry service/dry cleaning; nonsmoking rooms; rooms available for those w/limited mobility. *In room:* A/C, TV, dataport, mini-bar, hair dryer, safe.

Tryp Córdoba ★   Michelin rates this 1956 hotel (last renovated in 1992) as the best in Córdoba, but NH Amistad Córdoba has it beat by a mile. Nonethe-less, it's been a long and enduring workhorse over the years, and has such allur-ing features as an outdoor summer-only swimming pool, plus an array of other amenities. A further grace note: Many of its bedrooms open onto vistas of the Mezquita and the Jewish Quarter. If you're seeking a big-city hotel with no par-ticular Andalusian charm, this is a consideration. And the price is right. You can stay here in a suite for what you'd pay for a routine B&B in a city such as Zurich.

Córdoba

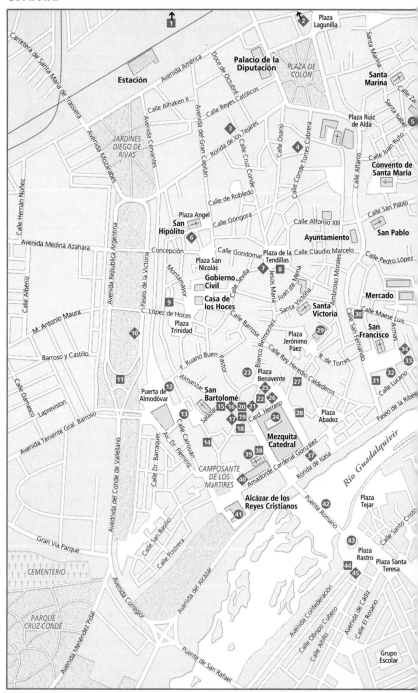

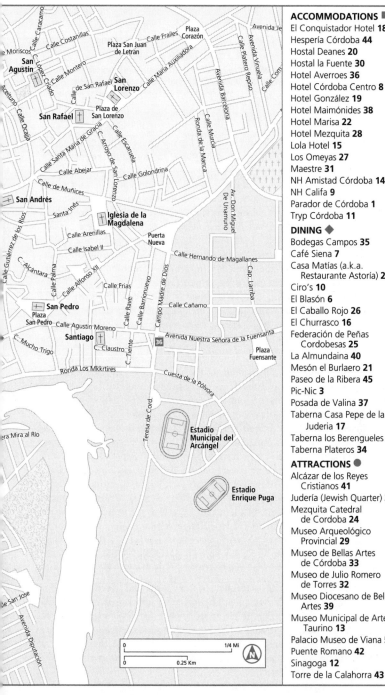

ACCOMMODATIONS ■
El Conquistador Hotel **18**
Hespería Córdoba **44**
Hostal Deanes **20**
Hostal la Fuente **30**
Hotel Averroes **36**
Hotel Córdoba Centro **8**
Hotel González **19**
Hotel Maimónides **38**
Hotel Marisa **22**
Hotel Mezquita **28**
Lola Hotel **15**
Los Omeyas **27**
Maestre **31**
NH Amistad Córdoba **14**
NH Califa **9**
Parador de Córdoba **1**
Tryp Córdoba **11**

DINING ◆
Bodegas Campos **35**
Café Siena **7**
Casa Matías (a.k.a.
   Restaurante Astoría) **2**
Ciro's **10**
El Blasón **6**
El Caballo Rojo **26**
El Churrasco **16**
Federación de Peñas
   Cordobesas **25**
La Almundaina **40**
Mesón el Burlaero **21**
Paseo de la Ribera **45**
Pic-Nic **3**
Posada de Valina **37**
Taberna Casa Pepe de la
   Juderia **17**
Taberna los Berengueles **4**
Taberna Plateros **34**

ATTRACTIONS ●
Alcázar de los Reyes
   Cristianos **41**
Judería (Jewish Quarter) **23**
Mezquita Catedral
   de Cordoba **24**
Museo Arqueológico
   Provincial **29**
Museo de Bellas Artes
   de Córdoba **33**
Museo de Julio Romero
   de Torres **32**
Museo Diocesano de Bellas
   Artes **39**
Museo Municipal de Arte
   Taurino **13**
Palacio Museo de Viana **5**
Puente Romano **42**
Sinagoga **12**
Torre de la Calahorra **43**

Its bedrooms are furnished in a standard international style, but are comfortable and spacious, each with a tiled bathroom with tub/shower combination. The reception desk and concierge are to be applauded for arranging virtually anything—tickets to flamenco shows, sightseeing excursions, car rentals, whatever.

Av. Jardines de la Victoria s/n, 14004 Córdoba. (*C*) **95-729-80-66.** Fax 95-729-81-47. www.solmelia.com. 147 units. 105€ ($126) double; 145€ ($174) suite. AE, DC, MC, V. Parking: 12€ ($14). Bus: 3. **Amenities:** Restaurant; bar; outdoor pool; room service (7am–10:30pm); babysitting; laundry service/dry cleaning. *In room:* A/C, TV, minibar, hair dryer (in some), safe.

MODERATE

Hotel Córdoba Centro   Most clients are business travelers, many of whom seem to return regularly to these premises in the 19th- and 20th-century neighborhood of Córdoba north of the Mezquita, perhaps grateful not to be constricted by the narrow alleyways of the city's early medieval core. The entrance is a bit tricky to find, positioned as it is at the end of a long passageway leading in from a shopping street that's mostly limited to pedestrian traffic. (If you phone in advance, a staff member will describe the location of the nearest parking garage.) It's a well-conceived but somewhat staid modern construction crafted from beige and white polished marble. Rooms are clean, streamlined, quiet, comfortable, and unpretentious, with very modern tiled bathrooms, angular furniture, and in almost every case, without particularly noteworthy views. The landmark Plaza de Tendillas is a few steps away, and a coffee shop and cafe, under separate management, occupies the building's ground floor.

Calle Jesús y María 8, 14003 Córdoba. (*C*) **95-749-78-50.** Fax 95-749-78-51. www.hotel-cordobacentro.com. 31 units. 100€ ($120) double. MC, V. Parking 9€ ($11) per day. Bus: 1, 3, 4, or 7. **Amenities:** TV lounge; room service (7am–10:30pm); laundry service/dry cleaning. *In room:* A/C, TV, minibar, safe.

Hotel Maimónides ★★   This is one of the best government-rated three-star hotels. Set within a few steps from the entrance to the Mezquita, it's the kind of place which probably deserves a four-star government rating, and which might indeed receive one during the lifetime of this edition. Resulting from the radical overhaul in 1976 of an antique building, it was renovated again in 2000. The result is a lovely enclave of Andalusian tilework set out in geometrical patterns, a splashing fountain, a friendly, hardworking staff, and an appealing mix of old-fashioned mudéjar-inspired touches and modern comforts. Bedrooms are clean, streamlined, sunny, and comfortable, each with a writing table, medium-to-large-size bathrooms, and lots of glossily polished stone and marble. As you might expect, a marble portrait bust of the hotel's namesake, the Arabic philosopher and mathematician Maimónides (1135–1204), accents a corner of the lobby.

Calle Torrijos 2, 14003 Córdoba. (*C*) **95-747-15-00.** Fax 95-748-38-03. www.hotel-maimonides.com. 82 units. 95€ ($114) double; 130€ ($156) suite. AE, DC, MC, V. Bus: 1, 3, or 7. **Amenities:** Restaurant; bar; room service (during in-house restaurant open hours only); babysitting. *In room:* A/C, TV, dataport, minibar, safe, hair dryer.

NH Califa *Value*   Attracting a mainly Spanish crowd, this central hotel is a short walk northwest of the Mezquita. Though rather impersonal and a bit austere, it's generally a good value. It has russet-colored marble floors, velour wall coverings, a spacious lounge, and a TV that seems to broadcast soccer matches nonstop. The midsize rooms are reasonably comfortable and furnished in a functional modern style. The bathrooms come with tub/shower combos. Parking is available along the street.

Lope de Hoces 14, 14003 Córdoba. (*C*) **95-729-94-00.** Fax 95-729-57-16. www.nhhoteles.es. 65 units. 117€ ($140) double; 162€ ($194) suite. AE, DC, MC, V. Bus: 12. **Amenities:** Bar; lounge; limited room service; laundry service; nonsmoking rooms; rooms for those w/limited mobility. *In room:* A/C, TV, dataport, hair dryer.

INEXPENSIVE

Hostal Deanes *Value*   A traditional Moorish house, lying only 50m (164 ft.) from the Mezquita, this former private home dates from the 16th century. In 1997 it was turned into a little inn. If you're seeking old-fashioned Andalusian charm, you'll be happy here. The bedrooms surround a busy patio cafe open daily from 9am to 10:30pm. In an adjoining bar you can see photographs of the many well-known bullfighters who have stayed or eaten here. The bedrooms are small but the bathrooms with shower are spacious. This is one of Córdoba's true bargains. There are no TVs in the rooms.

Calle Deanes 6, Judería, 14003 Córdoba. ⒸⒸⒸ **95-729-37-44.** 5 units. 31€ ($37) double. No credit cards. Parking 9€ ($11) nearby. Bus: 3. **Amenities:** Tapas bar. *In room:* No phone.

Hostal La Fuente   This is not a high-end recommendation: Your fellow lodgers are likely to be hard-partying students from other points within Spain and Europe, and the staff seems to revel in the fact that they speak not a solitary word of anything except local dialect. But the setting within two floors of a once-palatial mid-19th-century private home, centered around a tile-sheathed and plant-filled courtyard, is charming. Rooms, although simple and not overly large, are comfortable and clean, and recently renovated into angular, earth-toned enclaves of anonymous international styling. But there are lots of tables in the courtyard for contemplation, enough plants to evoke the Amazon rainforest, and overall, a feeling of somnolent, old-fashioned Andalusia at cost-conscious and completely unpretentious prices. A terrace overlooks Iglesia de San Francisco.

Calle San Fernando 51, 14003 Córdoba. ⒸⒸⒸ **95-748-78-27.** Fax 95-748-78-27. www.hostallafuente.com. 40 units. 78€ ($94) double. MC, V. Bus: 16. **Amenities:** Restaurant and cafe next door. *In room:* A/C, TV.

Hotel Averroes ⭐   This hotel expanded in 1999, adding 20 more rooms after renovating the house next door, and now the two buildings are linked by an impressive patio with potted plants and wrought-iron work. With its characteristic tiled walls and classic arches, the patio is a social area with tables where you can relax after a day of sightseeing. The medium-size rooms are comfortable, with marble floors, pastel walls, and good-size beds. All have bathrooms with tub/shower combos. The bus that stops in front will take you to the town center in just 15 to 20 minutes.

Campo Madre de Dios 38, 14002 Córdoba. ⒸⒸⒸ **95-743-59-78.** Fax 95-743-59-81. www.hotelaverroes.com. 79 units. 71€–90€ ($85–$108) double; 100€ ($120) junior suite. AE, DC, MC, V. Bus: 3. **Amenities:** Restaurant; bar; lounge; outdoor pool; rooms available for those w/limited mobility. *In room:* A/C, TV, hair dryer, safe.

Hotel González *Value*   In the heart of the Judería, only 40m (131 ft.) from the Mezquita, this is a small town palace that dates from the 16th century. In the mid-1980s it was successfully converted into a charming little hotel. All the bedrooms overlook either Plaza Judá Leví, one of the Jewish Quarter's most charming squares, or the inner Andalusian courtyard. The central hall and corridors are decorated with original artwork. Bedrooms are small and furnished in a bland, functional way with light wooden furnishings, but they are well maintained and comfortable. Bathrooms are also small and equipped with showers. If there is no room at this inn, try the owners' other bargain hotel, Hotel Mezquita (see below).

Calle Manríquez 3, 14003 Córdoba. ⒸⒸⒸ **95-747-98-19.** Fax 95-748-61-87. 41€–91€ ($49–$109). AE, DC, MC, V. Parking: 9€ ($11). Bus: 3. **Amenities:** Restaurant. *In room:* A/C, TV.

Hotel Marisa *Value*   In front of the Mezquita, this modest hotel is not only one of the most centrally located in Córdoba but also one of the city's best values.

Completed in the early 1970s, ongoing renovations have kept it in good shape. Most recent improvements have been to the bathrooms with showers, where the plumbing was renewed. The rooms are small but cozily comfortable. Ask for one with a balcony overlooking either the statue of the Virgin of Rosales or the Patio de los Naranjos. The architecture and furnishings are in a vague Andalusian style.

Cardenal Herrero 6, 14003 Córdoba. ✆ **95-747-31-42.** Fax 95-747-41-44. 28 units. 63€–66€ ($76–$79) double. AE, DC, MC, V. Parking 12€ ($14). Bus: 3 or 16. **Amenities:** Cafeteria; limited room service; laundry service/dry cleaning; rooms available for those w/limited mobility. *In room:* A/C.

Hotel Mezquita ⟨Value⟩   This hotel faces the east side of the Mezquita and is closer than any other to the mosque. In 1998, it was constructed on the site of two old houses, which are now connected by a patio. The decor includes tastefully arranged antiques throughout. The architecture is typically Andalusian—arches, interior patios, and hand-painted tiles, along with old mirrors and chandeliers. The small but comfortable rooms are painted pastels to contrast with the dark oak furnishings. The bathrooms come with tub/shower combos. Naturally, the rooms overlooking the Mezquita are the first to be booked.

Plaza Santa Catalina 1, 14003 Córdoba. ✆ **95-747-55-85.** Fax 95-747-62-19. hotelmezquita@wanadoo.es. 31 units. 41€–94€ ($49–$113) double. AE, DC, MC, V. Parking nearby 14€ ($17). Bus: 3 or 16. **Amenities:** Breakfast room; rooms for those w/limited mobility. *In room:* A/C, TV, dataport.

Lola Hotel ⟨★★⟩   If you're looking for a small and intimate boutique hotel in the shadow of the Mezquita, this is as good as it gets. The most surprising thing about this hotel, inaugurated in 2000, is that it's here at all, set behind the thick masonry walls of what was originally built as a private home in 1888. You'll register, relax, chitchat with your fellow guests, eat breakfast, and order drinks from the bar—all within the same cramped but convivial area: a small but cozy courtyard ringed with stone columns and open to the skies above Córdoba. At the touch of a button, an electric motor pulls a plastic canopy over the opening to shelter the furnishings from the cold and rain. Bedrooms inside are larger, more plush, and with more opulent bathrooms—each has gorgeous tilework—than you might have expect. Each bears a name popular for Muslim women during the 19th century: Aixa, Aida, Alzára, Jasmina, and Suleima. There are also rooms named after María and the hotel's owner, Lola (aka Dolores Cabezas-Morales).

Calle Romero 3, 14003 Córdoba. ✆ **95-720-03-05.** Fax 95-742-20-63. www.hotelconencantolola.com. 8 units. 76€–109€ ($91–$131) double. Rates include breakfast. AE, DC, MC, V. Bus: 1, 3, or 7. **Amenities:** Large open-air rooftop terrace w/view over the city's core. *In room:* A/C.

Los Omeyas ⟨★⟩   If you want to stay in the very heart of Córdoba, you can't find a better location than this hotel nestled in the Jewish Quarter. The name comes from the Umayyad dynasty that ruled the Muslim empire of al-Andalús (the Arab tradition is still clearly visible in white marble and latticework). The hotel receives natural light through a central colonnaded patio furnished with tables. Although in no way grand, the rooms are extremely comfortable and tasteful and have bathrooms with tub/shower combos; those on the top floor offer a panoramic view of the ancient tower of the mosque, which is literally around the corner.

Calle Encarnación 17, 14003 Córdoba. ✆ **95-749-22-67.** Fax 95-749-16-59. www.hotel-losomeyas.com. 33 units. 52€–64€ ($62–$77) double; 62€–74€ ($74–$89) triple; 72€–84€ ($86–$101) quad. AE, DC, MC, V. Parking 12€ ($14). Bus: 3 or 16. **Amenities:** Hotel restaurant nearby; cafeteria; bar; lounge. *In room:* A/C, TV, safe.

Maestre ⟨Value⟩   In the center of Córdoba, near the Guadalquivir River, this old house with traditional Moorish architecture has an interior courtyard with arches, white walls, red tiles, columns, and corridors. The location is convenient, a 10-minute stroll from the Judería and the Mezquita. Dating from 1992, the small-to-midsize bedrooms are hardly exciting but are simply, yet comfortably, furnished with wooden pieces and carpeted floors. Each comes with a small bathroom with shower stall. Management also operates the even less expensive **Hostal Maestre** nearby, where doubles rent for a mere 35€ ($42). If you're going to be in Córdoba for a few days with your family, ask about their self-catered apartments down the street. These are real bargains at only 55€ ($66) for a double, which can hold four comfortably (five if the child is small).

Romero Barros 4–6, San Pedro, 14003 Córdoba. (**95-747-24-10.** Fax 95-747-53-95. www.hotelmaestre. com. 29 units. 30€–50€ ($36–$60) double. Bus: 3 or 7. **Amenities:** Breakfast lounge; rooms for those w/limited mobility. *In room:* A/C, TV, safe.

3 Where to Dine

By all means, shake free of your hotel for at least one meal a day in Córdoba. The restaurants may combine food with flamenco—so make an evening of it.

Córdoba, incidentally, is well equipped to deal with caffeine addicts. Seek out local coffee shop chain, **Confitería Serrano.** The most central and convenient for most visitors is the branch at Calle Jesús María 8 ((**95-747-14-00**), occupying the ground floor of the also-recommended Hotel Córdoba Centro, very close to the landmark Plaza Tendillas. The venue also includes a deli where take-away pastries are a popular item. There's a brightly lit counter area, as well as banquettes. Platters cost from 8€ to 12€ ($9.60–$14).

Heladería Roldan, Paseo de la Victoria at Ronda de la Victoria ((**95-747-33-65**), is the most plush, elegant, and upscale pastry shop, bakery, and ice-cream shop in Córdoba, with an enviable position between two modern and monumental fountains. Rows of sidewalk tables ramble off toward the busy boulevard in a modern residential neighborhood north of the Mezquita. The cakes and pastries produced by this place are delicious and in some cases, visually superb, and include confections that display an entire football (that is, soccer) field, replete with goalies, nets, and even some players. After dark on nice evenings, it doubles as one of the most popular cafes in a neighborhood loaded with contenders.

EXPENSIVE

Bodegas Campos ★★ SPANISH/ANDALUSIAN   You'll eat one of your best meals in Córdoba at this local favorite on a narrow cobblestone street in a residential neighborhood 10-minutes from the Mezquita. In front is one of Córdoba's hippest and most crowded tapas bars. It's filled with attractive singles, some more interested in the scene than the food. Bodegas Campos has a welcoming rustic atmosphere and has been going strong since 1908 as both a wine cellar (bodega) and a tavern. The well-chosen menu prepared from fresh ingredients consists of local fare like salt cod salad with orange dressing, *frituritas de la casa con salmorejo* (tiny fried fish served with thick Andalusian gazpacho), and *escabeche de perdiz* (pickled pieces of partridge). Other specialties are *merluza rellena con verduritas* (hake stuffed with julienne vegetables) and an Iberian pig's cheek casserole. One of the noteworthy desserts is sorbet made with local oranges, and doused with the finest olive oil, the subtle and "almost tasteless" Arberquina oil. You can also retreat to the cozy Sacristy, a bar in back, past a wall of wine vats autographed by celebrity visitors. The restaurant offers one of the best selections of wine in town—try the house wine, *montilla viejo.*

Calle de los Lineros 32. ✆ **95-749-75-00.** Reservations recommended. Main courses 14€–19€ ($17–$23); gastronomic menu 37€ ($44). DC, MC, V. Mon–Sat 1–4pm and 8pm–midnight; Sun 1–4pm. Closed Dec 25 and 31. Bus: 1, 3, or 7.

Casa Matías/Restaurante Astoría ✦ *Finds* CONTINENTAL   In a quiet residential neighborhood of private apartments and long expanses of concrete, sits this quiet oasis. Set behind a facade that's painted ocher yellow with forest-green trim, it's the kind of hip, modern, fashionable place a Spanish businessman might take one of his clients from out of town. Because of its location just beyond the perimeter roads north of the city, it's rarely frequented by foreign visitors.

One habitué told us he comes here every week. When asked why, he explained that the food is lively and colorful and recommended the savory meatballs that come with three different sauces, including a creamy version called "grandmother's gravy." A casserole of well-flavored cod appears bubbling hot with potatoes. Locals favor the thick soup (actually a potage) of garbanzos and fresh spinach. However, we always go for the tasting menu, which changes nightly.

El Nogal 16. ✆ **95-727-76-53.** Reservations required. Main courses 12€–18€ ($14–$22); menú degustación 33€ ($40). AE, DC, MC, V. Daily 1–5pm and 8:30pm–midnight. Closed Sun July–Sept. Bus: 5.

Ciro's ✦✦ CONTINENTAL   This is the most famous and visible of the cafes and restaurants that line the wide promenades of the Paseo de la Victoria. Its excellent and upscale food is well known within Córdoba's gastronomic circles. Established in 1969 in a functional, all-purpose environment combining outside tables with a middle-bracket indoor *cafetería* (coffee shop) and tapas bar, it also offers fine dining within two formal dining rooms. One of these is *faux-baroque* and outfitted in tones of turquoise, the other is warmly contemporary in tones of brown. Neither of the rooms is immediately obvious to newcomers when they first enter. Spanish celebrities who have opted for meals here have included some well-known names, including the bullfighter Julio Albericio and pop singer Enrique Iglesias.

Food is delicious and ambitious, including hake or codfish prepared any way you like; Iberian beefsteak with pepper sauce; fish baked in a salt crust; *chuletillas* (sausages) grilled over charcoal; Segovia-style suckling pig; a mushroom pudding; a magnificent foie gras of duckling; and turbot served with *cava* (Catalonian sparkling wine) sauce.

Paseo de la Victoria 19–21. ✆ **95-729-04-64.** Reservations for restaurant recommended, not necessary in *cafetería*. *Platos combinados (cafetería)* 11€ ($13); main courses (restaurant) 13€–17€ ($15–$20); set-price menus 30€ ($36). AE, DC, MC, V. *Cafetería* daily 8am–midnight; restaurant daily 1–4pm and 8pm–midnight.

La Almudaina ✦✦✦ SPANISH/FRENCH   The owners of this historic restaurant near the Alcázar deserve as much credit for their renovations of a decrepit 15th-century palace as they do for the excellent cuisine produced in their bustling kitchen. Fronting the river in the old Jewish Quarter, La Almudaina is one of the most attractive eateries in Andalusia; you can dine in one of the lace-curtained salons or on a glass-roofed central courtyard. Nearly all the chef's dishes are based on fresh produce that's purchased that day at local markets. Many foodies lead off their meals with local favorites like a tasty *salmorejo* (a soup made with bread, tomato, fresh garlic, Iberian ham, and virgin olive oil). Anglerfish filets with a frothy seafood-brandy sauce taste ultrafresh. A tenderloin of pork is cooked to perfection and served with a delicate wine sauce. A favorite dessert is Cordovan quince pastry prepared according to a 19th-century recipe.

Jardines Plaza de los Santos Mártires 1. ✆ **95-747-43-42.** Reservations required. Main courses 12€–18€ ($14–$22); fixed-price menu 21€ ($25). AE, DC, MC, V. Mon–Sat noon–4pm and 8:30–11pm; Sun noon–4pm. Closed Sun June 15–Sept 1. Bus: 3 or 16.

Mesón el Burlaero ⭑ MEDITERRANEAN/ANDALUSIAN   In a 16th-century house that belonged to the first bishops of Córdoba, this restaurant in the Jewish Quarter is in the center of the tourist area. The *mesón* offers seven dining areas, along with balconies and a central patio adorned with antique-style murals. The whole place has been lovingly restored and tastefully decorated. The most lavish way to dine here is to order the *menú gastronómico de degustación,* a selection of various house specialties. From the a la carte menu you can begin with *salmorejo* (thick Andalusian gazpacho), and then follow with *rabo de toro en salsa* (bull's tail in savory tomato sauce) or *dorada a la sal* (gilthead sea bream that has been baked in a salt crust to retain its juices). On a hot day, the best dessert is the cold soufflé with vanilla ice cream.

Calle de la Hoguera 5. ☎ **95-747-27-19.** Reservations recommended. Main courses 12€–18€ ($14–$22); set menus 18€–30€ ($22–$36). AE, DC, MC, V. Daily 11am–4pm and 7:30pm–midnight. Bus: 3.

Pic-Nic ⭑ CONTINENTAL   Trekking out to the city's northern tier will convince visitors there's a lot more to Córdoba than medieval neighborhoods. The restaurant occupies the most distant corner of a long, narrow, and slightly battered square. It was created as part of the courtyard that fronts a residential apartment complex, whose entranceway opens onto the busy traffic of the Ronda de la Terrera. It sits, in a style that evolved in the late 1970s, behind a *moderno* entrance of varnished pine. Popular with Córdoba's business community, the superb cuisine here makes it one of the finest restaurants in the city. The cooking technique is impeccably sharp and precise. Some of the best examples include filets of pork in sherry sauce, a divine foie gras of goose, and an extraordinary magret of duckling flavored with port. For dessert, we are particularly fond of the *tareta de chocolate y naranja* (an orange-flavored chocolate tart).

Ronda de los Tejares 16. ☎ **95-748-22-33.** Reservations required. Main courses 16€–20€ ($19–$24). AE, MC, V. Mon 1:30–4pm; Tues–Sat 1:30–4pm and 9pm–midnight. Bus: 4, 5, 11, or 12.

MODERATE

El Blasón *Value* ANDALUSIAN/MOORISH   The tab, without wine, rarely exceeds 30€ ($36) at El Blasón, a restaurant in a relatively modern building near the Gran Teatro. You'll dine in any of four separate rooms, each evoking the mid–19th century, thanks to formal crystal chandeliers and a scattering of antiques. Especially appealing is an enclosed patio where ivy creeps up walls and the noises from the city outside are muffled. The cuisine is well prepared and in some cases described in terms that verge on the poetic. Examples are salmon with oranges from the mosque, and goose thigh in fruited wine. Braised oxtail is always a good bet, as well as any of the roasted lamb dishes redolent with the scent of olive oil and herbs.

José Zorrilla 11. ☎ **95-748-06-25.** Reservations recommended. Main courses 8€–21€ ($9.60–$25). AE, DC, MC, V. Daily noon–11:30pm. Closed Dec 24.

El Caballo Rojo ⭑⭑ SPANISH   Within walking distance of the Mezquita in the Old Town, this restaurant is the most popular in Andalusia, and with the exception of La Almudaina (see above), the best in Córdoba. The place has a noise level no other restaurant here matches, but the skilled waiters manage to cope with all demands. Stop in the restaurant's popular bar for a pre-dinner drink, then take the iron-railed stairs to the upper dining room, where a typical meal might include gazpacho, a main dish of chicken, then ice cream (often homemade pistachio) and sangria. An interesting variation on the typical gazpacho is an almond-flavored broth with apple pieces. In addition to Andalusian dishes, the chef offers both Sephardic and Mozarabic specialties, an example of the latter being monkfish prepared with pine nuts, currants, carrots, and cream. A local favorite is *rabo de toro* (stew made with the tail of a bull).

Cardinal Herrero 28, Plaza de la Hoguera. ℂ 95-747-53-75. Reservations required. Main courses 12€–20€ ($14–$24). AE, DC, MC, V. Daily 1–4:30pm and 8pm–midnight. Bus: 2.

El Churrasco ⊕ ANDALUSIAN   Housed in an ancient stone-fronted building in the Jewish Quarter northwest of the Mezquita, El Churrasco serves elegant meals in five dining rooms. You'll pass a bar and an open grill before reaching a ground-floor dining room that resembles a Moorish courtyard with rounded arches and a fountain. Upstairs, more formal rooms display the owner's riveting collection of paintings. You can enjoy such specialties as grilled filet of beef with whiskey sauce, succulent roast lamb, grilled salmon, and monkfish in pine-nut sauce—all accompanied by good service—but the signature dish is the charcoal-grilled pork loin.

Romero 16. ℂ **95-729-08-19.** Reservations required. Main courses 13€–25€ ($16–$30). AE, DC, MC, V. Daily 1–4pm and 8pm–midnight. Closed Aug. Bus: 2 or 6.

Federación de Peñas Cordobesas ANDALUSIAN   Built in a historical house that dates from 1900, this restaurant nestles in the old Judería, about midway between the Mezquita and the landmark Plaza Tendillas. In fair weather tables are placed outside around an old fountain in a courtyard surrounded by horseshoe arches. Inside the traditional Andalusian atmosphere is cozy. In business for 2 decades, the restaurant serves reliable regional favorites with a *carte* featuring affordable regional wines. Our favorite dish is the *zarzuela de pescado* (an assorted kettle of fresh fish cooked in their own juices). The sirloin *a la serrana,* another favorite, stuffs a sirloin with Serrano ham and serves it with a white sauce alongside mushrooms and fresh asparagus. Homemade desserts are prepared daily.

Conde y Luque 8, Judería. ℂ **95-747-54-27.** Main courses 11€–15€ ($13–$18). AE, DC, MC, V. Thurs–Tues 1–4pm and 8–11pm. Bus: 3.

Taberna Casa Pepe de la Judería ⊕ CORDOVAN   Around the corner from the mosque, this is one of the best-located restaurants in this ancient city. It lies on the route to the Judería, the old Jewish ghetto. A series of little rooms, decorated in a typical Andalusian style, are spread over three floors. From May to October, tables are placed on the rooftop where meats such as chicken and pork are barbecued, and an Andalusian guitarist entertains. The hearty, regional fare includes combinations like cod cooked with raisins, pine nuts, and mussels that may date back to recipes from the days when the Arabs controlled Córdoba. The chef prepares excellent soups such as a typical Andalusian gazpacho or one made with fresh fish and shellfish. We are especially fond of the *merluza* (hake) prepared Cordobesa style with sweet peppers, garlic, and onions; and the baked lamb, another specialty.

Calle Romero 1 ℂ **95-720-07-44.** Reservations recommended. Fixed-price menu 11€–18€ ($13–$22). Sun–Thurs 1–4pm and 8:30–11:30pm; Fri–Sat 1:30–4:30pm and 8:30pm–midnight.

Taberna los Berengueles SPANISH/SEAFOOD   The dignified and elegant 19th-century building housing this seafood restaurant is similar to many of its neighbors in this quiet residential neighborhood north of the Mezquita, but has the distinction of sitting across the street from the birthplace of Spain's most famous bullfighter, Manolete (Manuel Rodríguez Sancho, born here July 4, 1917). Inside, you'll find some spectacular mudéjar-style tilework, a series of cozy dining rooms, and a plant-studded patio good for romantic dining. The best dishes on the regular menu include *salmorejo,* the thick tomato soup of Andalusia; broad beans with strips of cured Iberian ham; spicy sausages with potatoes; braised pork chops braised over charcoal; succulent veal steaks; pasta with codfish; and a savory hake and shellfish stew. A separate fish menu reflects the array of seafood hauled in daily from the fishing port of Almuñecar.

Calle Conde de Torres Cabrera 7. ℂ 95-747-28-28. Reservations recommended. Main courses 8€–22€ ($9.60–$26). AE, MC, V. Mon–Sat 1–4pm and 8:30–11:30pm. Bus: 3.

INEXPENSIVE

Café Siena SPANISH   The layout of Córdoba makes it far too easy to get enmeshed in the medieval neighborhood around the Mezquita, and not venture anywhere else. This big, angular, and *moderno* cafe is the most appealing of those that ring the centerpiece of Córdoba's 19th- and early-20th-century commercial core, the Plaza de las Tendillas. In nice weather, most diners and drinkers opt for an outdoor table on the square. As day turns to evening, the clientele morphs from shoppers and local office workers to night owls on the make. The food is fairly standard, a litany of the country's favorite dishes, but the ingredients are fresh. The daily menu reflects the market shopping that morning.

Plaza de las Tendillas s/n. ℂ 95-747-30-05. Tapas 3€–9€ ($3.60–$11); main courses 9€–13€ ($11–$16); menu del día 11€ ($13). AE, DC. MC, V. Mon–Sat 9am–2am. Bus: 1, 3, 4, or 7.

Paseo de la Ribera *(Kids* ANDALUSIAN/MEDITERRANEAN   This has been a popular choice since being established in the closing months of the 20th century. It's known for affordable, traditional food and a reasonably priced wine *carte.* Fish lovers will enjoy the hearty, flavorful seafood rice prepared with small squid, and the perfectly prepared swordfish with prawn sauce. For meat eaters there are flavorful beef ribs; pork tenderloin with three sauces, including a green one; and a tender and well-flavored grilled steak. The grottolike decor tries to evoke a Roman cave, and the walls are covered with plaster, the chairs and tables set on wooden floors. Special platters costing from 7.50€ ($9) can be prepared for children.

Moments A Moroccan Teahouse Salon

Salon de Thé, Calle Buon Pastor 13 (ℂ 95-748-79-84; daily 11am–11pm), is an idyllic spot. On a hot summer day you might not immediately think of drinking tea, but the cool, Moroccan-style setting here, and the way it presents tea as refreshment for the senses might tempt you. The setting, within a labyrinth of impossibly narrow alleys near the Mezquita in the Judería, is a small-scale arcaded courtyard of a once-private home that was originally built in the 14th century, with low-slung (and somewhat uncomfortable) divans covered with Moroccan carpets, overstuffed cushions, and low low tables. The menu lists more than 30 kinds of tea, as well as coffee and fruited drinks made, Moroccan style, from condensed syrups mixed with crushed ice and water. A small fountain splashes fitfully in the courtyard's center, and the background music is rooted in the early Arabic roots of old Córdoba. The place, as you might expect, is busiest every day between 4 and 7pm. Pots of tea cost from 1€ ($1.20) for one person or 4€ ($4.80) for two to three people, with tapas and pastries ranging from 1.50€ to 6€ ($1.80–$7.20).

Plaza Cruz del Rastro 3. *©* **95-747-15-30.** Main courses 5.50€–13€ ($6.60–$15). DC, MC, V. Mon–Sat 10:30am–midnight; Sun 10:30am–5:30pm. Bus: 15 or 16.

Posada de Valina *(Value* ANDALUSIAN/CORDOVAN   Facing the south wall of the Mezquita, this restaurant is built on foundations that are among the oldest in Córdoba, with a history going back some 16 centuries. From a much later date, remnants of Roman columns and an ancient wall can still be seen. The restaurant itself lies in the inner courtyard of a little hotel below the balconies and gallery of the second floor. The chef proudly calls his food *la cocina cordobesa,* and so it is. Delicious treats appear on the menu, like *salmorejo* (cold tomato soup) or artichokes vinaigrette. We also recommend the fresh baked hake served in a sauce made with clams and shrimp and the savory oxtail. Desserts are home-made. Most main courses are priced at the lower end of the scale.

Corregidor Luis de la Cerda 83, Judería. *©* **95-749-87-50.** Reservations recommended on weekends. Main courses 6€–19€ ($7.20–$23). AE, DC, MC. Mon–Sat 1–4pm and 8pm–midnight; Sun 1–4pm. Bus: 3.

Taberna Plateros ANDALUSIAN   Dating from 1872, though previous owners claimed its origins might go as far back as the 1600s, this is one of the oldest establishments in Córdoba. Tables are placed in a spacious courtyard that leads to more dining rooms. The traditional marble bar is a rendezvous point for area workers, who gather and chatter with great animation when the nearby stores close for the evening. Pictures of the famous hometown bullfighter, Manolete, line the walls, and the decor is one of Andalusian tiles and red brick.

Dishes have authentic flavor. As one businessman at the bar told us, "The cooking is just what my grandmother fed me when I was a boy." The appetizers are very large, some so big in fact they will completely satisfy a person with a small appetite. Frequently changing main dishes might feature grilled swordfish or grilled cuttlefish. The cooks turn out several versions of *bacalao* (dried cod-fish). A local favorite, oxtail stew, in the words of one diner, "will put hair on your chest." Um, maybe you don't want that.

San Francisco 6, San Pedro. *©* **95-747-00-42.** Reservations recommended on weekends. Main courses 6.50€–10€ ($7.80–$12). AE, DC, MC, V. Tues–Sun 8am–4:30pm and 8pm–midnight. Bus: 3 or 7.

4 Seeing the Sights

Córdoba Visión, Av. Doctor Marañón 1 (*©* **95-776-02-41**), conducts the best English-language walking tours. These 4-hour-long guided tours are a great introduction to what can be a confusing maze of a city, with its treasures often hidden down narrow alleyways. Costing 25€ ($30) per person, tours are con-ducted Tuesday to Sunday at 10:30am.

Among Córdoba's many sights is the **Puente Romano (Roman bridge),** dat-ing from the time of Augustus and crossing the Guadalquivir River about 1 block south of the Mezquita. It's hardly Roman anymore because not one of its 16 supporting arches is original. The sculptor Bernabé Gómez del Río erected a statue of St. Raphael in the middle of the bridge in 1651.

Plaza de Toros, on Gran Vía del Parque, stages its major bullfights in May, although fights are presented at other times of the year. Watch for local announce-ments. Most hotels will arrange tickets for you, ranging in price (in general) from 20€ to 95€ ($24–$114). Call *©* **95-232-507** for information.

Alcázar de los Reyes Cristianos *★★*   Commissioned in 1328 by Alfonso XI, the Alcázar of the Christian monarchs is a fine example of military architecture. Ferdinand and Isabella governed Castile from this fortress on the Río Guadalquivir as they prepared to reconquer Granada, the last Moorish stronghold in Spain.

Columbus journeyed here to fill Isabella's ears with his plans for discovery. And it was at the Alcázar that Ferdinand and Isabella bade Columbus farewell as he set out to chart unknown territory and discover what (for Europeans) was a new world.

On a less happy note, the Alcázar was the headquarters of the dreaded Spanish Inquisition for 3 centuries. A former Arab bathhouse in the basement was turned into a Counter-Reformation interrogation center.

Originally, the Alcázar (Fortress) was the abode of the Umayyad caliphs. Of their former palace, little remains except ruins. You can see some Moorish courtyards with ornamental basins and some cooling pools and baths. Also on view are some impressive **Roman mosaics** ✿ from the time of the Emperor Augustus. One of them has alternating geometrical motifs, and yet another depicts Polyphemus and Galatea. A **Roman sarcophagus** ✿ is representational of 2nd- and 3rd-century funereal art.

If they are open, you can climb the towers, **Tower of the Lions (Torre de los Leones)** and **Tower of Homage (Torre de Homenaje).** The Tower of the Lions contains intricately carved **ogival ceilings** ✿ that are one of the most notable examples of Gothic architecture in Andalusia. At the top a panoramic vista unfolds, taking in the Alcázar gardens, the river, Puente Romano, and Torre de la Calahorra.

The **Gardens of the Alcázar** ✿✿ display their Arabic origins, complete with terraces, pools, and cooling fountains. Cypresses stud the earth, as do towering palms and orange trees. The Cordobeses themselves use these magnificent gardens on a summer day to escape the unbearable heat that descends on their city.

The centerpiece of the fortress, The **Patio Morisco (Court of the Moors)** is another lovely spot, with twin pools and an ivy-covered grotto, and pavement decorated with the coats-of-arms of León and Castile.

Caballerizas Reales. ℰ **95-742-01-51.** Admission 3€ ($3.60) adults (2€/$2.40 for gardens), free for children under 18 with parent. May–Sept Tues–Sat 8:30am–2pm and 6–8pm, Sun 10am–2pm; Oct–May Tues–Sat 10am–2pm and 4:30–6:30pm, Sun 9:30am–2:30pm. Gardens illuminated July–Sept 10pm–noon. Bus: 3 or 12.

Mezquita-Catedral de Córdoba ✿✿✿   In the 8th century, this Mezquita (Great Mosque) became the crowning glory of Muslim architecture in the West. With its fantastic labyrinth of red-and-white candy-striped Moorish horseshoe arches, it remains one of the grandest attractions in Europe. Not even the Catholic cathedral placed in its center can destroy the impact of this "forest" of architectural pillars. We suggest that you visit the phantasmagoric rows of columns and arches first, saving the florid cathedral for last.

The caliph of Córdoba, Abd el-Rahman I, built this place of worship in 785. To do so, he razed an earlier Visigothic basilica, which itself had replaced a Roman temple. Initially, the Great Mosque covered 23,400 sq. m (251,000 sq. ft.). The Mezquita was built in various stages, following an overall plan of a crenellated square perimeter enclosing **El Patio de los Naranjos (Court of Orange Trees)** ✿✿, which is one of the principal entrances to the mosque. This courtyard was redesigned following the Reconquista. Still visible are the irrigation channels dug by the Muslims. **Puerta del Perdón (Gate of Forgiveness),** on the north wall, is the former entrance into the mosque.

Before the Catholic takeover, the mosque had a total of 900 pillars. Remarkably, **856 pillars** ✿✿✿ are still standing. Their red-and-white peppermint stripes are formed in large part by white stone and red brick *voussoirs.* The pillars are also built of onyx, granite, marble, and jasper, filling a total of 19 aisles. A second row of arches set above the first almost doubles the height of the ceiling.

(*Tips* **Visiting the Mezquita**

Audio guides, giving elaborate commentary—sometimes more than you might have wanted—about the Mezquita in any of a half-dozen different languages, are available from a separate kiosk outside the mosque's main entrance. They rent for 3€ ($3.60) each and require a cash deposit of 20€ ($24), or some valid credit card or document left as insurance that you'll return the equipment. Photographs are allowed, but not if you use a tripod. And there are strict security regulations (no big bags or suitcases allowed) at the entrance.

Some of the most interesting pillars came from the ancient Visigothic basilica. You can pick these out by the impressive carvings on their capitals. Since some of the pillars brought in were taller than others, they had to be sunk into the floor of the mosque. The oldest known pillar came from Egypt and dates from the reign of Amenophis IV.

In the very heart of the Mezquita lies the **Mihrab** 𝒜𝒜𝒜, where the faithful gathered for ritual prayers. Bordered by Koranic sculptures and with carved stucco adorning its upper walls, the Mihrab was the holy sanctuary where the Koran was kept. It was also said to have another precious treasure, a bone from the arm of the prophet Muhammad. The bejeweled Koran was copied by the caliph's own hand and anointed with his blood. This sanctum is covered by a scallop-shaped dome, which is richly decorated with beautiful colored mosaics and gilded tiles.

In this area you can see the **Maksura** 𝒜, the enclosure reserved for the caliph and his entourage. This most sacred part of the architectural ensemble is roofed by a trio of ribbed domes resting on interweaving multifoil arches. One might call such florid and flamboyant architecture "Islamic baroque"; it features golden mosaics, arabesque, carvings, cupolas, palm-leaf motifs framed by Sufic script, and marble panels. The **Byzantine mosaics,** which have hundreds of pieces of tiny gold, glass, and ceramic tiles, were a gift of the 10th-century emperor of Constantinople. The **frieze** in gold and blue that runs all the way around the Mihrab lists the 99 names of Allah.

In later years, the addition of Christian chapels destroyed the architectural harmony of the Mezquita. At the far end of the mosque stands the **Capilla Villaviciosa** 𝒜, which was completed in 1371. The chapel features a stalactite ceiling and stunning plaster lacework. Also added was the **Chapel Royal** 𝒜 decorated in the 1200s with mudéjar stucco.

Although the people of Córdoba rallied against the idea, Emperor Carlos V ordered that part of the mosque be torn down to make way for the **Catedral** 𝒜𝒜, which disfigured the mosque. Later he regretted his decision, saying to his architects, "What you are building here can be found anywhere, but what you have destroyed exists nowhere." Construction began in 1523 in the Gothic style, although later additions were in the Plateresque and baroque styles, and even the Renaissance shows up in decorative figures in the medallions in the apsidal vaulting in 1560.

The greatest achievement is the baroque **choir stalls** 𝒜𝒜𝒜 by Pedro Duque Cornejo, the Andalusian sculptor, around 1750. He depicted on either side of the stalls the Ascension and scenes from the lives of Jesus and the Virgin Mary in lifelike detail. Almost equally stunning are two **pulpits** 𝒜𝒜 in marble, mahogany, and jasper. One of the pulpits rests on a pink marble ox.

Located in the Sacristy, next to the Mihrab, is the **Treasury,** displaying beautiful examples of Cordovan silver and gold artistry.

Calles Torrijos and Cardenal Herrero s/n (south of the train station, just north of the Roman bridge). ℂ **95-747-05-12.** Admission 6.50€ ($7.80) adults, 3.25€ ($3.90) children under 14. Nov and Feb daily 10am-5:30pm; Dec–Jan daily 10am–5pm; Apr–June daily 10am–7pm; Mar and July–Oct daily 10am–6:30pm (Sun 9–10:15am and 2–5:30pm). Bus: 3.

JUDERIA (JEWISH QUARTER)

North and west of the Mezquita is one of the most intriguing medieval ghettos remaining in Europe. Two of the world's greatest thinkers, the Jewish philosopher Maimónides and the Arab philosopher and mathematician Averroès, once called the **Judería** ✦✦✦ home.

No longer Jewish or even Arab, the neighborhood has been restored and makes for one of the most fascinating strolls in Andalusia. (Don't forget to bring along a good pair of walking shoes.) The only physical evidence left of its former Jewish population is the synagogue (p. 143). You can spend at least 2 hours here wandering about—and be prepared to get lost. Many upper middle class Cordobeses now occupy these old whitewashed houses and have restored them. You can enter the area through the Puerta de Almódovar, at the western frontier.

The Judería reached the zenith of its prosperity under the Moorish occupation (believe it or not), especially during the caliphate (929–1031). A great Talmudic school was founded here in an era of tolerance.

If there is one street you should seek out, it's **Calleja de las Flores** ✦✦, little street of flowers. Actually, it's little more than an alleyway lying off Calle Victor Bosco and Calle Blanco Belmonte. Somehow the wrought-iron grilles, potted flowers, and window boxes filled with geraniums appear more adorable here than elsewhere. Certainly the patios of the various houses deserve some prize, and it's perfectly acceptable to walk along gazing into the courtyards. The citizens of Córdoba take pride in showing off their patios as part of the city's tradition.

The Judería is also filled with delightful little squares that you'll stumble into after wandering down a dark alleyway into the bright sunshine of Andalusia.

Museo Arqueológico Provincial ✦ Córdoba's archaeological museum, 2 blocks northeast of the Mezquita, is one of the most important in Spain. Housed in a palace dating from 1505, it displays artifacts left behind by the various peoples and conquerors that swept through the province. There are Paleolithic and Neolithic items, Iberian hand weapons and ceramics, and Roman sculptures, bronzes, ceramics, inscriptions, and mosaics. Especially interesting are the Visigothic artifacts. The most outstanding collection, however, is devoted to Arabic art and spans the entire Muslim occupation. Take a few minutes to relax in one

---

Moments **Reviving Moorish Customs: Baños Arabes**

A popular Moorish custom survives at **Hamman Arabic Baths,** Corregidor Luí de la Cerda 51 (ℂ **95-748-47-46**), which lies next to the Mezquita. Taking the baths here is (probably) as close as you'll come to experiencing life as the ancient sultans lived it. You need to bring a swimming suit and you cannot wear shoes or sandals inside. Every bath lasts 1½ hours and includes a massage and Morocco tea for 24€ ($29). Sometimes belly dancers perform. Hours are daily from 10am to midnight; make a reservation and be sure to show up on time.

of the patios with its fountains and ponds. Right next door to the museum you can view the ruins of a Roman theater, which was discovered only in 2000.

Plaza Jerónimo Páez 7, Judería. ✆ 95-747-40-11. Admission 1.50€ ($1.80). Tues 2:30–8:30pm; Wed–Sat 9am–8:30pm; Sun and public holidays 9am–2:30pm.

Museo de Bellas Artes de Córdoba   As you cross the Plaza del Potro to reach the Fine Arts Museum, notice the fountain at one end of the square. Built in 1557, it shows a young stallion with forelegs raised, holding the shield of Córdoba. Housed in an old charity hospital on the plaza, the Fine Arts Museum contains medieval Andalusian paintings, examples of Spanish baroque art, and works by many of Spain's important 19th- and 20th-century painters, including Goya, Sorolla, Zurbarán, Murillo, and Valdés Leal. Of particular interest on the ground floor are sculptures by Juan de Mesa and Mateo Inurria, Spanish artists. Ferdinand and Isabella themselves founded this former Hospital de la Caridad, and twice they received Columbus here. The museum is east of the Mezquita, about a block south of the Church of St. Francis (San Francisco).

Plaza del Potro 1. ✆ **95-747-13-14.** Admission 1.50€ ($1.80) adults, free for children under 12. Tues 3–8pm; Wed–Sat 9am–8pm (June 15–Sept 15 8:30am–2:30pm); Sun and public holidays 9am–3pm. Bus: 3, 4, or 7.

Museo de Julio Romero de Torres   Across the patio from the Fine Arts Museum, this museum honors Julio Romero de Torres, a Córdoba-born (1874) artist who died in 1930 and was known for his sensual portraits of women. He caused the greatest scandal with his "hyper-realistic nudes," and in 1906 the National Exhibition of Fine Arts banned his *Vivadoras del amor.* On display is his celebrated *Oranges and Lemons,* and other notable works such as *The Little Girl Who Sells Fuel, Sin,* and *A Dedication to the Art of the Bullfight.* A corner of Romero's Madrid studio has been reproduced in one of the rooms, displaying the paintings left unfinished at his death.

Plaza del Potro 2. ✆ **95-749-19-09.** Admission 3€ ($3.60). Oct–Apr Mon–Fri 10am–2pm and 4:30–6:30pm, Sat–Sun 9:30am–2:30pm; May–Sept Tues–Sat 10am–2pm and 5:30–7:30pm.

Museo Diocesano de Bellas Artes   While the Inquisition was raging at the Alcázar (see above), this was the lavish home of the bishops of Córdoba, who might be called hangmen by today's standards. Facing the Mezquita, their former palace has been turned into a museum of religious art, with illustrated prayer books, tapestries, sculpture, and paintings. To our surprise, we discovered some works here by Julio Romero de Torres. These paintings are tame, however, in comparison to some of his more controversial work (see above). The wood sculptures of the Middle Ages are the best of the lot, along with a vast array of art from the Renaissance and baroque periods.

Calle Torrijos 12. ✆ **95-749-60-85.** Admission 1.20€ ($1.45). Free for children under 12. July–Aug Mon–Sat 9:30am–3pm; Sept–June Mon–Fri 9:30am–1:30pm and 2–6pm, Sat 9:30am–1:30pm. Bus: 3.

Museo Municipal de Arte Taurino   Memorabilia of great bullfights are housed here in a 16th-century building that was inaugurated in 1983 as an appendage to the Museo Municipal de Arte Cordobesa. Its galleries recall Córdoba's great bullfighters with suits of light, pictures, trophies, posters, even stuffed bulls' heads. You'll see a wax likeness of Manolete in repose and the blood-smeared uniform of El Cordobés—both of these famous matadors came from Córdoba. Of macabre interest is a replica of the tomb of the dashing Manolete, and even the hide of the bull that killed him. The museum is about a block northwest of the Mezquita, midway between the mosque and the synagogue.

Finds **A Stately Pleasure Dome: The Moorish Versailles**

The **Conjunto Arqueológico Madinat Al-Zahra**, a kind of Moorish Versailles just outside Córdoba, was constructed in the 10th century by the first caliph of al-Andalús, Abd ar-Rahman III. Thousands of workers and animals slaved to build this mammoth pleasure palace, said to have contained 300 baths and 400 houses. The Berbers sacked the place in 1013.

Over the years the site has been plundered for building materials. Some of these, it's said, went to build the Alcázar in Seville. Today, the **Royal House,** rendezvous point for the ministers, has been reconstructed. The principal salon remains in fragments, so you have to imagine it in its majesty. Just beyond the Royal House are the ruins of a **mosque** constructed to face Mecca.

It's at Carretera Palma de Río Km 8 (📞 **95-732-91-30**). Admission is 1.50€ ($1.80). Hours are from May 1 to September 30, Tuesday through Saturday from 10am to 8:30pm, Sunday from 10am to 2pm; from October 1 to April 30, Tuesday through Saturday from 10am to 6:30pm, Sunday from 10am to 2pm. Buses leave from Paseo de la Rivera and Av. de la Victoria (📞 **90-220-17-74**).

Plaza de las Bulas (aka Plaza Maimónides). 📞 **95-720-10-56**. Admission 3€ ($3.60), free for children under 18. May–Sept Tues–Sat 8:30am–2:30pm and 5:30–7:30pm, Sun 9:30am–3pm; Oct–Apr Mon–Sat 10am–2pm and 5:30–7:30pm, Sun 9:30am–2:30pm. Bus: 3.

Palacio Museo de Viana ⭐⭐ *(Finds*   Few of Córdoba's palaces have been open to the public in the past, but that's changed with the opening of this museum. Visitors are shown into a carriage house, where the elegant vehicles of another era are displayed. Note the intricate leather decoration on the carriages and the leather wall hangings, some of which date from the period of the Reconquest. There's also a collection of leather paintings. You can wander at leisure through the **garden and patios** ⭐⭐. These patios, 14 in all, are particularly stunning. The palace is 4 blocks southeast of the Plaza de Colón on the northeastern edge of the old quarter.

Plaza de Don Gome 2. 📞 **95-749-67-41**. Palace admission 6€ ($7.20); patios 3€ ($3.60). June–Sept Mon–Sat 9am–2pm; Oct–May Mon–Fri 10am–1pm and 4–6pm, Sat 10am–1pm. Closed June 1–15.

Sinagoga   In Córdoba you'll find one of Spain's three remaining pre-Inquisition synagogues, built in 1315 in the Barrio de la Judería (Jewish Quarter), 2 blocks west of the northern wall of the Mezquita. The synagogue is noted particularly for its stuccowork; the east wall contains a large orifice where the Tabernacle was once placed (inside, the scrolls of the Pentateuch were kept). Note the various adornments of *mozárabe* patterns and Hebrew inscriptions. You can still see the balcony where women were sequestered during worship. After the Jews were expelled from Spain, the synagogue was turned into a hospital, until it became a Catholic chapel in 1588.

Calle de los Judíos 20. 📞 **95-720-29-28**. Admission .30€ (35¢). Tues–Sat 9:30am–2pm and 3:30–5:30pm; Sun 9:30am–1:30pm. Bus: 3.

Torre de la Calahorra The Tower of Calahorra stands across the river at the southern end of the Roman bridge. Commissioned by Henry II of Trastamara in 1369 to protect him from his brother, Peter I, it now houses a town museum, Museo Vivo de Al-Andalús, where visitors can take a self-guided tour with headsets. One room holds wax figures of Córdoba's famous philosophers, including Maimónides. Other rooms exhibit a miniature model of the Alhambra at Granada, complete with water fountains; a miniature Mezquita; and a display of Arab musical instruments. You can climb to the top of the tower for some panoramic views of the Roman bridge, the river, and the cathedral/mosque.

Av. de la Confederación, Puente Romano. ℂ 95-729-39-29. Admission to museum 4€ ($4.80) adults, 2.50€ ($3) children under 8. Admission to Multivision 1.20€ ($1.40). May–Sept daily 10am–2pm and 4:30–8:30pm; Oct–Apr daily 10am–6pm. Tours daily 11am, noon, 3, and 4pm. Last tour 1 hr. before closing time. Bus: 16.

5 Shopping

In Moorish times, Córdoba's leather workers were legendary. Highly valued in 15th-century Europe, their leather was studded with gold and silver ornaments, then painted with embossed designs *(guadameci)*. Large panels often took the place of tapestries. Although the industry has fallen into decline and the market is filled mostly with cheap imitations, you can still find excellently crafted embossed leather as well as other Cordovan handicrafts at **Artesanía Andaluza,** Tomás Conde 3 (no phone), near the bullfight museum. Look also for filigree silver from the mines of Sierra Morena. The shop is open Monday to Saturday 9am to 5pm. **Taller Meryan** (see below) has perhaps the best embossed leather in the city.

Córdoba has a branch of Spain's major department store, **El Corte Inglés,** at Ronda de los Tejares 32 (ℂ 95-722-28-81). Some of the staff speaks English. It's open Monday to Saturday 10am to 10pm.

The other shops listed below can be reached via bus no. 1, 3, or 7. Most are open Monday to Saturday 9:30am to 8pm; smaller establishments, however, often take a siesta, doing business from 9:30 or 10am to 1:30 or 2pm and again from 4:30 or 5 to 8pm. Exceptions are listed below.

Aldefa Campos This gift and souvenir shop is trendier, glossier, and a bit more urban in its selection of porcelain and gift items than many of the more folklore-oriented shops that surround it. It's especially strong on housewares. Velásquez Bosco 8. ℂ 95-748-24-52.

Arte Zoco This is the largest association of craftspeople in Córdoba. Established in the Jewish Quarter in the mid-l980s, it assembles on one site the creative output of about a dozen artisans whose mediums include leather, wood, silver, crystal, terra cotta, and iron. About a half-dozen of the artisans maintain their studios on the premises, so you can visit and check out the techniques and tools they use to pursue their crafts. You'll find everything from new, iconoclastic, and avant-garde designs to pieces that honor centuries-old traditions. Of special interest is the revival of the Califar pottery first introduced to Córdoba during the regimes of the Muslim caliphs. The shop is open Monday to Friday 9:30am to 8pm, Saturday and Sunday 9:30am to 2pm. The workshops and studios of the various artisans open and close according to the whims of their occupants but are usually maintained Monday to Friday 10am to 2pm and 5:30 to 8pm. Calle de los Judíos s/n. No phone.

Artesanía Cordobesa There are many other shops selling porcelain flanking this place, but this is the only shop we found in Córdoba that specializes in the all-black ceramics made in Pueblo de la Rambla, a village about 40km (24 miles) away. Their manufacture incorporates a technique that has been used almost without variation since the 10th century. The pieces are pierced or cut, while the clay is still soft and wet, with filigreed patterns that show the light (from a candle inside) in particularly intriguing ways. Calle Deanes 1. ℭ 95-748-68-75.

Bodegas Mezquita Tienda   Come into the cool, masonry-lined premises of this upscale and well-organized delicatessen for one of the most complete collections of Andalucian olive oils, pastries, cheeses, wines, and cured meats anywhere. There are at least 13 kinds of olive oil here. You can also pick up bottles of *montilla* (dry sherry) and other regional wines. The location is just behind the Mezquita. Corregidor Luis de la Cerda 73. ℭ 95-749-81-17.

Galerías Turísticas, S.L.   Set very close to the main entrance of the Mezquita, this is the biggest, most upscale, and most "blockbuster-ish" of the gift and jewelry and souvenir stands in Córdoba's medieval quarter. Within a sprawling stone-and-masonry-sheathed environment that might remind you of the ground floor of a large U.S.-based department store, you'll find lots of sales clerks, plus glass display cases containing Majorca pearls, Feria dolls from Cádiz, castanets, inlaid marquetry boxes from Morocco, jewelry, handpainted fans, and some very tasteful and upscale gift items. Calle Torrijos 8. ℭ 95-748-56-02.

Joyería Manuel J. Regalos   Large, expensively outfitted, and elegant, with many of its more upscale gift items showcased within glass-fronted display cases, this store has a particularly appealing collection of Mantones de Manila (Manila shawls), many of them lavishly embroidered, and *feria* accessories. No self-respecting Andalusian woman would do without these shawls to ward off an evening chill. There are also *faux* tortoise-shell hair combs, some imperious enough to transform a Carmen wannabe into a Carmen clone in just a few passes of a hairbrush. Cardenal Herrero 30–32. ℭ 95-748-41-97.

Plata Natura   In the field of hyper-contemporary, one-of-a-kind body ornaments crafted from massive silver (sometimes accented with chunks of coral, strips of lizard skin, topaz, amber, jade, or shards of antique ceramics), this place is unique in Córdoba. It evokes a state-of-the-art showcase in, say, a posh but funky neighborhood of Madrid. Calle Lucano 22. ℭ 95-748-83-01.

Selene Arte Etnico   Directly across the street from the Mezquite's main entrance, this shop sells fine Moroccan crafts. Come here for mirrors set into intricately crafted frames made from polished pieces of camel and cow's bone, exotic hardwoods, and hammered silver. Most are priced at under 300€ ($360) and are laid out in the geometric patterns that would have been appreciated by the builders of the mosque itself. There are also elaborate embroideries, lamps made from iron, silver, and/or brass, and ceramics. Cardenal Herrero 20. ℭ 95-749-10-47.

Taller Meryan ✦   Alejandro and Carlos López Obrero operate out of this 250-year-old building. The street it's on is so enchanting you might want to come here even if you don't want to shop (check the information on Calleja de Las Flores in "Seeing the Sights, earlier in this chapter, for details). This is the best store in Córdoba for embossed leather products. You can see artisans plying their trades; although most items must be custom-ordered, some ready-made pieces are for sale, including cigarette boxes, jewel cases, attaché cases, book and folio covers, and ottoman covers. It's open Monday to Friday 9am to 8pm, Saturday 9am to 2pm. Calleja de Las Flores 2. ℭ 95-747-59-02.

6 Córdoba After Dark

You can certainly check out the flamenco clubs, but most Cordobeses roam around at night, sampling the tapas and drinking regional wine in the various taverns. There are worst ways to spend an evening.

TAPAS & WINE

You can begin your tapas crawl at the previously recommended **Bodegas Campos** (p. 133), which has some of the classiest tapas in town. But there are many other options, particularly if you find yourself wandering the streets of the Judería, which is particularly colorful in the evening. The best place to visit here, and one of the most authentic, is **Taberna Casa Pepe de la Judería** (p. 136).

El Caballo Rojo (p. 135) is another first-class restaurant with a good supply of tapas, which it serves on a leafy Andalusian patio. One specialty we recently enjoyed here was *alboronia,* a cold salad of stewed vegetables with saffron, honey, and aniseed flavoring.

Our other favorite *tascas* include these listed below. Tapas usually cost from 1€ to 3€ ($1.20–$3.60).

Añil   This tasca is different from the rest in that it specializes in the north's *cocina vasca* (Basque cuisine), paying special attention to its *bacalao* (dried cod) dishes. There is a summer terrace opening onto vistas of the city. Favorites include platters of baby squid, steak tartare, tenderloin of beef with Roquefort sauce, and perfectly grilled codfish. Open Tuesday to Saturday 1 to 4:30pm and 8:30pm to midnight. Mayoral 21. ✆ **95-727-79-07.**

Bar Círculo Taurino   This is the bar where aficionados meet to debate—often loudly—the relative merits (or lack thereof) of Andalusian bullfighters. In between a lot of wine or beer, Andalusian olives and hunks of cheese are consumed, among other tapas. The bar is small, cramped, and loaded with bullfighting memorabilia. The location is convenient in the vicinity of the Plaza Colón. Open daily 1 to 4pm and 8:30 to 11:30pm. Calle Manuel María Arcona 1. ✆ **95-748-18-62.**

Casa Miguel   This is the oldest bodega in Córdoba, some say it dates from 1812, some 1880. It is certainly one of the most authentic of all the *tabernas.* Each of the small rooms has a different theme. *Azulejos* (earthenware tiles) form a large part of the decor, as do wine barrels, photographs of bullfighters, and even guitars and lanterns. Cooks prepare a series of some of the best and freshest tapas in town. Open daily from 1 to 4pm and 8 to 11:30pm. Plaza San Miguel 7. ✆ **95-747-83-28.**

Casa Pepe   Lying in the Judería, close to the Mezquita, this is an atmospheric old hideaway in an antique building where many generations have lifted a glass of wine. Try a glass of *montilla* (a regional version of dry sherry) along with some Serrano ham. Open Monday to Thursday 1 to 4pm and 8:30 to 11:30pm, Friday to Sunday 1 to 4pm and 8:30pm to 12:30am. Calle Romano 1. ✆ **95-720-07-44.**

Casa Rubio   Push back a thick curtain to enter this dimly lit tasca where you'll find a gruff but accommodating welcome at the rectangular bar or in either of a pair of rooms partially covered with Andalusian tiles. We like the leafy inner courtyard where iron tables and a handful of chairs wobble slightly on the uneven floor. Open daily 1 to 4pm and 8:30 to 11:30pm. Puerta de Almódovar 5. ✆ **95-742-08-53.**

El Juramento   This tasca is old-fashioned enough to be cozy and crowded enough to be convivial. It attracts a wide-ranging age group, and there are 18 tables for patrons who actually want to sit. The cooks whip up everything from a *rabo de toro* (bull's tail simmered in tomato sauce) to fried slices of hake. Open Wednesday to Monday 1:15 to 4pm and 9:15pm to midnight. Calle Juramento 6. ℂ **95-748-54-77.**

Taberna Casa Salinas   Near Casa Pepe, this is another atmospheric old dive, offering glasses of sherry and plates of freshly made tapas along with spicy Andalusian sausages and buckets of olives. Pepe Salinas is now in his fourth decade of running this crowded bar and old-fashioned dining room. In fair weather the action spills onto a romantic Andalusian courtyard. Sometimes spontaneous flamenco shows are staged here. Open Monday to Saturday 11:30am to 4:30pm and 8:30pm to midnight (closes at 5:30pm Sun). Puerto de Almodóvar s/n. ℂ **95-729-08-46.**

FLAMENCO CLUBS & MORE

Tablao Cardenal at Calle Torrijos 10 (ℂ **95-748-31-12**) is Córdoba's most popular and dynamic flamenco club. Just across from the Mezquita, you can enjoy a show featuring international and award-winning flamenco artists. Some of the purest styles of Andalusian flamenco—*soleá, bulerías,* and *alegrías*—are showcased here. Shows are presented Tuesday to Saturday at 10:30pm, with a cover of 18€ ($22) that includes your first drink.

For an even more authentic flamenco venue, head for **Mesón Flamenco La Bulería,** Pedro López 3 (ℂ **95-748-38-39**), close to the Plaza de la Corredera on the outskirts of the old part of town. This is one of the most reasonably priced flamenco shows in Andalusia, considering the class of its talent. The cover of 11€ ($13) includes your first drink. Most shows start nightly around 10:30pm. The club is generally closed from December to February.

For more formal entertainment, check out the listings at the city's theatrical grande dame, the early-1900s **Gran Teatro de Córdoba,** Av. Gran Capitán 3 (ℂ **95-748-02-37**), site of most of the ballet, opera, chamber music, and symphony performances in town.

NIGHTCLUBS

Jazz Café   Don't even think of coming here until very late; most of the jazz acts begin around 1am, and the doors only open (reluctantly) at around 11pm. You have to ring a bell to gain entrance to this club that sits on a steeply sloping street behind fortresslike iron gates. Inside, tiny marble tables and spinning ceiling fans evoke colonial Havana. In addition to regularly scheduled music featuring local and visiting musicians, management encourages anyone with musical talent to participate in the frequent jam sessions. Cover charges range from 3€ to 7€ ($3.60–$8.40), depending on the night of the week. Open Tuesday to Saturday 11am to 4am. Calle Rodríguez Marín s/n, corner of Calle Espartaría. ℂ **95-747-19-28.**

La Comuna   Lots of students on the make show up here hoping to score. High energy and a hot DJ keep the place electric. Pop and funk dominate. Beer goes for 2€ ($2.40), with mixed drinks costing 4€ ($4.80). Open Thursday to Saturday midnight to 5am. Calle del Caño 1. ℂ **95-571-55-63.**

La Moncloa   Named for the presidential palace outside Madrid (why no one knows), this spot mostly attracts student for dancing, pickups, and Spanish pop. A DJ plays house, hip-hop, and a variety of Latin music. A cover charge that's imposed only on weekends ranges from 5€ to 10€ ($6–$12). The club is open nightly June to September 9pm to 6am. Closed October to May. Beer costs

2.50€ ($3), with mixed drinks priced from 3€ to 5€ ($3.60–$6). Av. del Brillante s/n. © **95-727-23-11.**

7 On the Way to Granada: Jaén, Baeza & Ubeda

International visitors discovered the province of Jaén, and its three principal cities—**Jaén** (the capital), **Baeza,** and **Ubeda**—in the 1960s. For years, visitors whizzed through Jaén on the way south to Granada or bypassed it altogether on the southwest route to Córdoba and Seville. But the government improved the province's hotel outlook with excellent paradors, which now provide some of the finest accommodations in Andalusia.

Since that time, new and charming boutiques have opened up, and old monuments have been dusted off. For those who have at least a day, a detour through these towns is rewarding. If you have time for only one stop, make it ancient Ubeda, which has the most charm.

If you're visiting Granada after a previous stopover in Córdoba, you can head east along N-IV (E-5) to the turnoff town of Bailén. If you're going on to Granada without stopping over, you can head straight south along N-323, which will take you to the city of Jaén. You can stop off in Jaén for the night or else bypass the city and follow the signs to E-902 into Granada.

Back at Bailén if you want to visit Ubeda and Baeza (or both), get onto N-322 and head east, following the signs to either Ubeda or Baeza. Ubeda is on the main route, N-322. Baeza, however, lies a short drive southwest of Ubeda and is reached by taking a secondary route, N-321.

JAEN
97km (60 miles) E of Córdoba

In the center of Spain's major olive-growing district, **Jaén** is sandwiched between Córdoba and Granada and has always been a gateway between Castile and Andalusia. This city lies east of Córdoba and can be reached from that city in less than an hour. It's also possible to drive down from Madrid, visiting Jaén (and subsequently Ubeda or Baeza) before visiting either Granada or Córdoba. The drive south via E-5 or N-IV to Jaén is 338km (210 miles) from Madrid.

Jaén's bustling modern section is of little interest to visitors, but the **Moorish Old Town,** where narrow cobblestone streets hug the mountainside, is reason enough to visit. A hilltop castle, now a first-rate parador, dominates the city. On a clear day you can see the snow-covered peaks of the Sierra Nevada.

The city of Jaén is the center of a large province of 13,491 sq. km (5,189 sq. miles) framed by mountains: the Sierra Morena to the north, the Segura and Cazorla ranges to the east, and those of Huelma, Noalejo, and Valdepeñas to the south. To the west, plains widen into the fertile Guadalquivir Valley. Jaén province comprises three well-defined districts: the Sierra de Cazorla, a land of wild scenery; the plains of Bailén, Ajona, and Arjonilla, filled with wheat fields, vineyards, and old olive trees; and the valleys of the tributaries of the Guadalquivir.

Life in Jaén revolves around the landmark **Plaza de la Constitución.** From here, take Calle Bernabé Soriano uphill to the **cathedral** and the **Old Town.**

ESSENTIALS
GETTING THERE   If you're **driving,** see routing details above. You can also drive north from Granada along E-902, a distance of 93km (58 miles). If you're taking the **train** from Córdoba in the west, it takes only 1½ hours to reach Jaén

Jaén

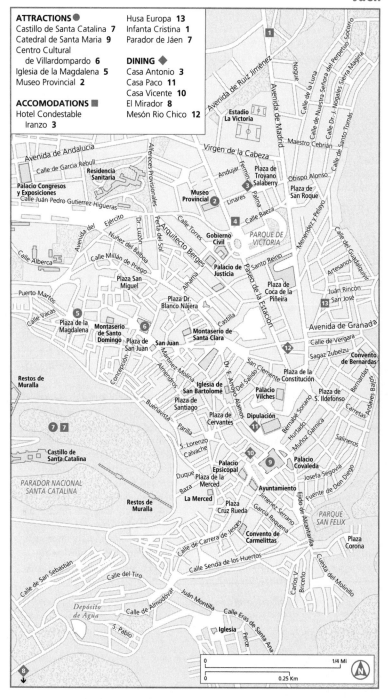

ATTRACTIONS ●
Castillo de Santa Catalina **7**
Catedral de Santa Maria **9**
Centro Cultural
  de Villardompardo **6**
Iglesia de la Magdalena **5**
Museo Provincial **2**

ACCOMODATIONS ■
Hotel Condestable
  Iranzo **3**

Husa Europa **13**
Infanta Cristina **1**
Parador de Jáen **7**

DINING ◆
Casa Antonio **3**
Casa Paco **11**
Casa Vicente **10**
El Mirador **8**
Mesón Rio Chico **12**

0   1/4 Mi
0   0.25 Km

from there. There is only one train per day, leaving at 8am daily, costing 7.55€ ($9.05) for a one-way ticket. There are two trains per day from Madrid, taking 4 to 5 hours and costing 20€ ($23) for a one-way ticket. Trains arrive in Jaén at the RENFE station on Paseo de la Estación (℃ **90-224-02-02**), north of the center of town.

If you are coming north from Granada, **Alsina Graells** runs 15 **buses** per day from Granada, taking 1½ hours and costing 6.25€ ($7.50) for a one-way ticket. Buses arrive in Jaén at Plaza Coca de la Piñera (℃ **95-325-50-14**), a block south of Parque de la Victoria.

VISITOR INFORMATION   The **tourist office,** Calle Maestra 13 (℃ **95-324-26-24;** www.andalusia.org), is open September to June Monday to Friday from 10am to 7pm, Saturday and Sunday from 10am to 1pm. Open July to October Monday to Friday 10pm to 8pm; Saturday and Sunday from 10am to 1pm.

EXPLORING JAEN

Castillo de Santa Catalina ⟨ᵰ⟩   On a rocky crag, lying 5km (3 miles) from the center of Jaén, this restored castle dominates the city. Today it is the site of the Parador de Jaén, reason enough for many visitors to stop over here. Originally the Moors constructed the fortress, although it is said that Hannibal's men built the first watchtower here. The Nasrid caliph, Alhamar, builder of the Alcázar at Granada, ordered construction of the castle. Later King Ferdinand III captured it and took the Castillo in 1246 in time to celebrate the Feast Day of patron saint, Santa Catalina (St. Catherine). Of course, you can stay or dine at the parador, but the reason many sightseers trek up here is to enjoy the finest and most panoramic view in the province.

Castillo de Santa Catalina. ℃ **95-312-07-33.** Admission 3€ ($3.60). June–Sept Tues–Sun 10am–2pm and 5:30–9:30pm; Oct–May Tues–Sun 10am–2pm and 3:30–7:30pm.

Catedral de Santa María   The formality and grandeur of Jaén's cathedral bears witness to the city's past importance. Begun in 1555, on the site of a former mosque, and completed in 1802, it's a honey-colored blend of Gothic, baroque, and Renaissance styles, with an emphasis on the latter. The original architect was Andrés de Vandelvira (1509–75), who designed many buildings at Baeza and Ubeda. A huge dome dominates the interior with its richly carved choir stalls. The **cathedral museum** ⟨ᵰ⟩ contains an important collection of historical objects in two underground chambers, including paintings by **Jusepe de Ribera,** the baroque painter. Its most celebrated relic is the Santo Rostro (Holy Face). According to legend, this cloth was used by Veronica to wipe Jesus' face on his way to Calvary. Evocative of Italy's Shroud of Turin, the image of Christ is said to have imprinted on the fabric. The cathedral stands southwest of the Plaza de la Constitución.

Plaza de Santa María. ℃ **95-323-42-33.** Free admission to cathedral; museum 5€ ($6). Cathedral daily 8:30am–1pm and 5–8pm (closes at 7pm in winter); museum Tues–Sat 9am–1pm and 4–7pm. Bus: 8, 10, or 16.

Centro Cultural Palacio de Villardompardo   This is a three-in-one attraction, including some former Arab baths (known as *hamman*) and two museums, the Museo de Artes y Costumbres Populares and the Museo Internacional de Arte Naif.

Underneath the palace, near Calle San Juan and the Chapel of Saint Andrew (San Andrés), are the former **Arab baths.** They represent some of the most important Moorish architecture from the 11th century ever discovered in Spain. You can visit a warm room, a hot room, and a cold room—the last with a barrel vault and 12 star-shaped chandeliers.

The **Museo de Artes y Costumbres Populares** houses a collection of primarily 19th-century folkloric artifacts, including costumes, dolls, ceramics, and even photographs documenting former days in Andalusia. The **Museo Internacional de Arte Naif** features a changing art exhibit featuring the work of artists from around the globe who have created professional, skilled paintings without any formal art instruction.

Plaza de Santa Luisa de Marillac s/n. ℂ **95-324-80-68.** Free admission. Tues–Fri 9am–8pm; Sat–Sun 9:30am–2:30pm. You must go on foot: In the old quarter of Jaén, follow signs indicating either BAÑOS ARABES or BARRIO DE LA MAGDALENA.

Iglesia de la Magdalena   Of the many churches worth visiting in Jaén, La Magdalena is the oldest and most interesting. This Gothic church was once an Arab mosque. The minaret of the former mosque is now the bell tower of the church. If you wander to the back of the church you can see a courtyard that was used by Arab worshippers for ritualized ablutions. In the cloisters are several tombstones from the era of the Roman occupation of Andalusia.

Calle de la Magdalena. ℂ **95-319-03-09.** Free admission. Tues–Sat 9am–12:30pm; Sun 5am–8pm.

Museo Provincial 🏛   In this dusty, offbeat, and little-visited museum, one of the finest Spanish collections of pre-Roman artifacts is found, along with other treasures. The collection, housed in a 1547 mansion, includes Roman mosaics, a mudéjar arch, and many ceramics from the early Iberian, Greek, and Roman periods. On the upper floor is an exhibit of Pedro Berruguete paintings, including *Christ at the Column.* Look for a Paleo-Christian sarcophagus from Martos. In the most modern section stand nearly a dozen life-size Iberian sculptures that were unearthed in 1975 near the village of Porcuna. The museum is between the bus and train stations.

Paseo de la Estación 29. ℂ **95-325-06-00.** Admission 1.50€ ($1.80). Tues 2:30–8:30pm; Wed–Sat 9am–8pm; Sun 9am–2:30pm.

WHERE TO STAY

Hotel Condestable Iranzo *(Value*   There's no old-fashioned Andalusian charm here. This large hotel occupying an entire corner of the main square is no beauty, but it is well located, has a good view of the castle and the mountains, and offers a wide range of facilities. The midsize rooms are functional and comfortable, all with bathrooms containing tub/shower combos. The on-site restaurant serves good, inexpensive Andalusian food with main courses priced at 6€ to 15€ ($7.20–$18).

Paseo de la Estación 32, 23008 Jaén. ℂ **95-322-28-00.** Fax 95-326-38-07. 165 units. 79€–90€ ($95–$108) double; 128€–138€ ($154–$166) suite. AE, MC, V. Parking 7€ ($8.40). **Amenities:** Restaurant; bar; disco; limited room service; babysitting; laundry service/dry cleaning. *In room:* A/C, TV, dataport, hair dryer.

Husa Europa *(Value*   In the commercial and historical center of Jaén, this little hotel became a winner after a massive renovation that brought everything up to date. Although the avant-garde decor is a little severe, it manages to be cozy and contemporary at the same time. The medium-size rooms have been spruced up and the sparkling clean bathrooms have tub/shower combos.

Plaza de Belén 1, 23001 Jaén. ℂ **95-322-27-00.** Fax 95-322-26-92. www.husa.es. 37 units. 57€ ($68) double; 70€ ($84) triple. Rates include continental breakfast. AE, DC, MC, V. Parking 7€ ($8.40). **Amenities:** Cafeteria; lounge; bicycles; nonsmoking rooms; rooms for those w/limited mobility. *In room:* A/C, TV, dataport, hair dryer, safe.

Infanta Cristina   After the parador, this hotel is the best place to stay in Jaén, as long as your expectations aren't too high. Instead of a dramatic mountaintop perch like the parador, Infanta Cristina lies in the modern part of the city near the train station. It's the most convenient choice for arriving rail passengers. This corner hotel is serviceable and well run, its spacious bedrooms have modern wooden furniture and views, and its tiled bathrooms are equipped with tub/shower combos. The on-site restaurant, Az-zait, attracts nonresidents as it's known for its regional specialties. A complete meal costs 36€ ($43).

Av. de Madrid, 23009 Jaén. ⓒ **95-326-30-40.** Fax 95-327-42-96. www.hotelinfantacristina.com. 83 units. 119€ ($143) double; 175€ ($210) suite. AE, DC, MC, V. Parking 7€ ($8.40). **Amenities:** Restaurant; cafeteria; room service (8am–10:30pm); babysitting; laundry service; rooms for those w/limited mobility. *In room:* A/C, TV, dataport, minibar, hair dryer.

Parador de Jaén ⭐⭐⭐   Five kilometers (3 miles) to the east on the hill overlooking the city, this castle is one of the government's showplace paradors. In the 10th century, the castle was a Muslim fortress surrounded by high protective walls and approached only by a steep winding road. The castle is still reached by the same road; you enter through a three-story-high baronial hallway, and the polite staff will show you to your balconied midsize room (doubles only), tastefully furnished and comfortable, with canopied beds and spick-and-span tile bathrooms equipped with tub/shower combos. The most charming feature of the bedrooms are the panoramic views of mountains. Make reservations well in advance as this place books quickly.

Castillo de Santa Catalina, 23001 Jaén. ⓒ **95-323-00-00.** Fax 95-323-09-30. www.parador.es. 45 units. 114€ ($137) double; 142€ ($170) suite. AE, DC, MC, V. Free parking. **Amenities:** Restaurant; bar; seasonal outdoor pool; limited room service; laundry service/dry cleaning; nonsmoking rooms. *In room:* A/C, TV, dataport, minibar, hair dryer, safe.

WHERE TO DINE

Consider a meal in the luxurious hilltop parador commanding a view of Jaén (see above). It's one of the loveliest spots in the area.

Casa Antonio ⭐⭐ ANDALUSIAN   Some of the best Andalusian food in the province is served here in a traditional setting. A trio of tiny dining rooms is decorated with contemporary paintings and dark wood paneling. Recommended items include mushrooms in a well-flavored cream sauce served with prawns and black olives, scallops with mashed potatoes, and a tender roast sucking pig baked with potatoes, in the Castilian style.

Calle Fermín Palma 3. ⓒ **95-327-02-62.** Reservations recommended. Main courses 15€–21€ ($18–$25). AE, DC, MC, V. Tues–Sun 1:30–4:15pm and 9–11:30pm. Closed Aug.

Casa Paco 🄥𝘃𝘢𝘭𝘶𝘦 ANDALUSIAN   In the center of Jaén, this is a simple place with wood panels and a few tables favored by blue collar workers with big appetites and small budgets. The food isn't haute, but in the words of the chef, "it's honest and true food, even noble." Try his oven-baked hake *(merluza)* or a particularly delightful trout grilled with lemon grass Thai style. A well-flavored tenderloin of beef is also featured, as are omelets, a favorite being one made with fresh mushrooms, ham, and prawns. If you're going to have dinner here, you have to arrive before 6pm.

Flores 4. ⓒ **95-325-54-41.** Reservations required. Main courses 7€–12€ ($8.40–$14). AE, DC, V. Tues–Sat 10am–6pm. Closed Aug.

Casa Vicente ⭐ ANDALUSIAN   Near the cathedral in the historic district, this restaurant is part of a palace dating from the 16th century, complete with a central patio ringed by the dining areas. It's praised locally for the quality of its tapas and its wine. The area surrounding the town is known for its vegetables, which are showcased in such dishes as *espinaca esparragada* (spinach with vegetable sauce) and *alcachofa natural* (artichokes in garlic). For a main dish, we recommend the *lomo de orsa mozárabe* (lamb in sweet-and-sour sauce) or *bacalao encebollado* (salt cod sautéed with onions and sweet peppers). Two local desserts are rice pudding and *manjarblanco mozárabe* (Moorish-style fudge).

Francisco Martín Mora 1. ℂ **95-323-22-22.** Reservations recommended. Main courses 12€–18€ ($14–$22); set menu 21€ ($25); tasting menu 36€ ($43). DC, MC, V. Thurs–Tues 1:30–4pm and 8:30–11:30pm; Sun noon–5pm. Closed Aug.

El Mirador INTERNATIONAL/ANDALUSIAN   Decorated like a Swiss chalet, this local favorite serves the best barbecue in town. Patrons opt for a seat on its big terrace where they can enjoy the specialties of the evening, in big portions at affordable prices. For starters, there are two versions of the cold tomato soups that are famous in Andalusia. Take your pick: gazpacho or salmorejo. You might also begin the fresh anchovies marinated with onion and green pepper or a homemade pâté of partridge. Most diners select one of the barbecue meats as their main course; the roast suckling pig is particularly popular. The place has lots of character and when there's a full house, it feels like a party.

Carretera Los Villares Km 5. ℂ **95-323-51-31.** Reservations recommended. Main courses 6€–15€ ($7.20–$18). AE, DC, MC, V. Tues–Sun 1:30–4pm and 9–11pm. Closed Aug 15–Sept 7.

Mesón Río Chico ⟨Value⟩ ANDALUSIAN   Serving authentic regional cuisine, this informal restaurant has been around since 1962 in a simple modern building in the heart of Jaén. Menu items include strongly flavored versions of hake, beefsteak, roasted pork, and chicken. Because there's room for only 45 diners at a time, it's important to reserve in advance. Many locals call this their favorite restaurant in town, even though many recipes and dishes haven't been changed since the 1960s.

Calle Nueva 12. ℂ **95-324-08-02.** Reservations recommended. Main courses 8€–16€ ($9.60–$19). AE, MC, V. Tues–Sat 2–4pm and 9–10pm; Sun noon–3:30pm.

JAEN AFTER DARK

For a night of Andalusian flamenco, head uphill from the cathedral to **Peña Flamenca Jaén,** Calle Maestra 11 (ℂ **95-323-17-10**). Some rising flamenco artists strut their stuff here before they move on to the tourist joints of Seville and the Costa del Sol. Mixed drinks cost 3€ ($3.60) and beyond, or else you can try a local drink—*manzanillo,* the province's specialty apple liqueur. Artists perform on a wood stage that's overly adorned with regional artifacts, and there's a wooden bar. Hours are Monday to Friday 8pm to 1am, Sunday midday to 11am. There is no cover, and tapas range from 1€ to 5€ ($1.20–$6).

A hip bar, **Moët,** Avenida de Andalucía (ℂ **95-327-30-94**), near the train station, attracts a young crowd, especially students, with its DJ-spun Iberian pop. On the weekend it turns into a disco. There's no cover but mixed drinks cost 4€ ($4.80) and up. Beer is only 1.80€ ($2.15). Tapas cost from 2€ to 6€ ($2.40–$7.20). Open Monday to Wednesday 4pm to 4:30am, Thursday to Saturday from 4pm until "we have to toss out the last drunk," as the waiter put it.

BAEZA ✸✸
45km (28 miles) NE of Jaén

Historic Baeza (known to the Romans as *Vilvatia*), with its Gothic and Plateresque buildings and cobblestone streets, is one of the best-preserved old towns in Spain. At twilight, when lanterns hanging from walls of plastered stone light the narrow streets, you might feel you've stumbled back into the 15th century. The town's heyday was in the 16th and 17th centuries. Even if you don't go inside many specific monuments—and, indeed, many of the most charming buildings aren't open to the public—you can still get a good idea of the architecture by strolling through the *barrio monumental* and admiring the old buildings.

ESSENTIALS

GETTING THERE   The nearest important rail junction, receiving **trains** from Madrid and most of Andalusia, is the **Estación Linares-Baeza** (© **90-224-02-02**), 14km (8½ miles) west of Baeza's center. There is one train per day from Córdoba and two per day from Madrid arriving at Estación Linares-Baeza.

There are 10 **buses** a day from Ubeda; the ride is 15 minutes long, costing 1€ ($1.20) one-way. From Jaén, there are 14 buses per day (trip time: 45 min.), costing 3.10€ ($3.70) one-way. For more information, call © **95-374-04-68.**

To reach Baeza from Jaén (see above), follow Route N-321 northeast for 45km (28 miles). The town lies 308km (191 miles) south of Madrid.

VISITOR INFORMATION   The **tourist office,** at the Plaza del Pópulo s/n 23440 (© **95-374-04-44;** www.andalusia.org), is open in winter Monday to Friday from 9:30am to 2:30pm and 4 to 6pm, Saturday from 10am to 2pm, Sunday from 10am to 1pm. Summer hours are Monday to Friday from 9:30am to 7pm, Saturday and Sunday 10am to 1pm and 5 to 7pm.

EXPLORING BAEZA

Baeza's main square, the **Plaza del Pópulo** ⚲, is a two-story open colonnade. The buildings here date in part from the 16th century, and the tourist office, where you can get a town map, is housed in one of the most interesting. Look for the fountain containing four half-effaced lions, the **Fuente de los Leones,** which may have been brought here from the Roman town of Cantulo.

Head south along the Cuesta de San Gil to reach the Gothic and Renaissance **Santa Iglesia Catedral** ⚲, Plaza de la Fuente de Santa María (© **95-374-41-57**), built in the 16th century on the foundations of an earlier mosque. Look for the **Puerta de la Luna (Moon Door),** and in the interior, remodeled by Andrés de Vandelvira (architect of Jaén's cathedral) and his pupils, the carved wood and the brilliant painted *rejas* (iron screens). The **Gold Chapel** is especially stunning. The edifice possesses one of the most important Corpus Christi icons in Spain, *La Custodia de Baeza.* Climb the clock tower for a panoramic view of town. The cathedral is open October to May daily from 10:30am to 1pm and 4 to 6pm, June to September 10:30am to 1pm and 5 to 7pm; admission is 2€ ($2.40).

After leaving the cathedral, continue up the Cuesta de San Felipe to the **Palacio de Jabalquinto** ⚲, a beautiful example of civil architecture in the Flamboyant Gothic style, built by Juan Alfonso de Benavides, a relative of King Ferdinand. Its facade is filled with interesting decorative elements, and there's a simple Renaissance-style courtyard with marble columns. Inside, two lions guard the ornate baroque stairway. The building is currently closed for restoration.

With your back to the tourist office (see above) on Plaza del Pópulo, head up the stairs to your immediate right and go left on Calle Conde de Romanones. At the end of the street you'll see the old university of Baeza, **Antigua Universidad.** It was founded back in 1595 and is one of the oldest in the area. The poet, Antonio Machado, taught French here from 1912 to 1919; his fans request a key from the custodian to visit his classroom. Entrance to the school is on Beato Juan de Avila s/n (© **95-374-01-50**). From April to September visits are possible Thursday to Tuesday 10am to 1pm and 5 to 7pm; October to March Thursday to Tuesday 10am to 1pm and 4 to 6pm. Admission is free.

When you've seen the university, continue down Calle Conde Romanones until you reach **Iglesia de Santa Cruz.** Built sometime in the 1200s, this is the town's oldest church and one of the few Romanesque buildings still standing in Andalusia. Inside you can see frescoes of the Virgin Mary, San Sebastián, and St. Catherine. Admission is free and hours are usually Monday to Saturday 11am to 1pm and Sunday noon to 2pm.

Next door you'll see an entrance to a little **museum** displaying florid icons, ornately gilded carriages, and regional artifacts of the area. Its most interesting exhibits are bizarre costumes worn in the annual procession of the religious brotherhood of Santa Vera Cruz at the time of the Semana Santa. Don't make a special point of visiting the museum, but if the doors are open you might pop in for a look. Admission free, it is usually open daily from 11am to 1:30pm and 4:30 to 7pm. But don't count on those hours being honored.

Before leaving Baeza, you might take in the facades of two more buildings, one the **Ayuntamiento** at Plaza Cardenal Benavides, lying north of the landmark Plaza del Pópulo. It was designed by the same Andrés de Vandelvira who worked on the cathedral and the facade is a stellar example of the Plateresque style. Between the balconies you'll note the coat-of-arms of Philip II, among others. Sometimes a custodian will let you in for a look at the *Salón de Plenos,* the primary hall of the building, noted for its carved and painted woodwork.

Just a short stroll west of the Ayuntamiento is the **Convento de San Francisco,** Calle de San Francisco, another of Vandelvira's architectural masterpieces, dating from the 16th century. In the 1800s an earthquake struck the building, partially destroying it; it was further damaged when the French army came through. Although it's been partially restored, a quick look is probably sufficient.

To cap your visit to Baeza, head for the park atop the old city wall. To reach it, stroll along Paseo de las Murallas. Once here, you can take in the **panoramic view** ⊛ of the Guadalquivir Valley, a carpet of green studded with olive trees.

WHERE TO STAY

Confortel Baeza   Back in the 16th century this was a convent for the Clarisas order. Today it's a government-rated three-star hotel opening onto a large square in the heart of the Old Town. Traditionally furnished midsize bedrooms are comfortable, each with a private tiled bathroom with tub or shower. Antiques are scattered throughout, and there is much use of wooden furniture. All the floors are reached by elevator. The hotel is also a good choice for dining, as it operates a restaurant specializing in regional food and international specialties, as well as a snack bar.

Calle Concepción 3, 23440 Baeza. © 95-374-81-52. Fax 95-374-25-19. www.trhhoteles.com. 84 units. 81€–95€ ($97–$114) double; 126€–140€ ($151–$168) suite. AE, DC, MC, V. Parking: 8€ ($9.60). **Amenities:** 2 restaurants; bar; babysitting; laundry service; rooms for those w/limited mobility. *In room:* A/C, TV, minibar, hair dryer.

El Patio ⟨Value⟩   With a convenient location near the Plaza del Pópulo and the town monuments, this unusual place offers you a chance to stay in a restored 16th-century palace for a ridiculously low price. Of course, it's no Palace of Versailles; but this window into yesterday looks like an old summer house with an interior patio of arches, columns, and corridors. Bedrooms open onto the central court-yard. They are small, with standard but comfortable furnishings, and a cramped bathroom with shower stall. Breakfast at 4€ ($4.80) is the only meal served.

Calle Conde Romanones 13, 23440 Baeza. © **95-374-02-00.** Fax 95-374-82-60. www.baeza.net/guia/hospedarse.htm. 12 units. 28€ ($34) double. MC, V. Parking 6€ ($7.20). **Amenities:** Breakfast room. *In room:* No phone.

Hospedería Fuentenueva ★ *Finds* You wouldn't believe it to look at this lit-tle boutique hotel today, but it was once a women's prison. Lying near the Puerta de la Luna and most of the town monuments, it is warm and hospitable. Bed-rooms are attractively and comfortably furnished and are midsize for the most part, each equipped with a well-kept modern bathroom with a tub/shower combo. Furnishings are mostly wood, and many rooms open onto attractive vis-tas of the town. The hotel has a garden, and there is an on-site shop selling gifts, mostly pottery. A fountain bubbles away in the interior courtyard in the typical Andalusian style. All rooms are nonsmoking.

Paseo Arca del Agua, 23440 Baeza. © **95-374-31-00.** Fax 95-374-32-00. reserves@fuentenueva.com. 12 units. 68€–80€ ($82–$96) double. AE, MC, V. Free parking. **Amenities:** Restaurant; bar; outdoor pool; room service (8am–10pm); laundry service. *In room:* A/C, TV, hair dryer.

La Loma *Value* This small, traditional Andalusian house is generally conceded to be the town's best bang for the buck, considering its comfort and its low prices. The rooms are modernized, exceedingly comfortable, and pleasant enough, and the hospitable owners are friendly. Bedrooms are a bit small with wooden furniture resting on tiled floors. More tiles are used in the well-main-tained and tidy little bathrooms, each with a tub/shower combo. Many bed-rooms open onto beautiful views of the Guadalquivir River.

Carretera de Ubeda, 234040 Baeza. © **95-374-33-02.** Fax 95-374-82-66. 10 units. 50€–56€ ($60–$67) double. AE, DC, MC, V. Free parking. **Amenities:** Restaurant. *In room:* A/C, TV.

Palacete Santa Ana ★★ In the very heart of Baeza, near the town hall, this restored 16th-century mansion is the best place in town to spend the night. There is much Andalusian character here, and a strong Moorish influence as seen in the blue tiles and stones. Naturally, there's an interior patio with a bub-bling fountain. More than any other place in town, you get the feeling of really living in a noble Andalusian house of some long departed don. The attractively decorated and comfortably furnished bedrooms are midsize, each with a small tiled bathroom with tub and shower. The town's attractions and some good restaurants are nearby.

Santa Ana Vieja 9, 23440 Baeza. © **95-374-16-57.** Fax 95-374-16-57. www.palacetesantana.com. 13 units. 75€ ($90) double. AE, DC, MC, V. **Amenities:** Restaurant; laundry service. *In room:* A/C, TV.

WHERE TO DINE

Casa Juanito ★ *Finds* ANDALUSIAN Owner Juan Luis Pedro Salcedo is a devotee of the lost art of Jaén cookery and revives ancient recipes in his fre-quently changing specials. He runs a small olive oil outlet and meals use only his own produce. Game is served in season, and many vegetable dishes incorporate ham. Among the savory and well-prepared menu items are *habas* (beans), filet of beef with tomatoes and peppers, partridge in pastry crust, house-style cod, and venison.

In the Hotel Juanito, Plaza del Arca del Agua s/n. © **95-374-00-40.** Reservations required on weekend Main courses 15€–30€ ($18–$36). MC, V. Sun–Mon 1:30–3:30pm; Tues–Sat 1:30–3:30pm and 8–10:30pm. Closed 1st week of July.

Cusco ANDALUSIAN   Believe it or not, this simple place is the only restaurant the Michelin guide people recommend in Ubeda. While it's a reliable choice in the city center, it's hardly the only acceptable restaurant in town. We especially like fish platters like the perfectly grilled sea bass with a basil sauce or hake *(merluza)* in a saffron sauce. As is the Andalusian custom, many diners begin their meal, especially in summer, with a soothing bowl of gazpacho.

Parque de Vandelvira 8. (C) **95-375-34-13.** Main courses 9€–15€ ($11–$18). AE, MC, V. Sun 1–4pm; Mon–Sat 1–4pm and 8–11pm.

El Sali SPANISH/ANDALUSIAN   This restaurant is set in a modern building erected in the 1970s in the town center, adjacent to the Plaza del Pópulo. In air-conditioned comfort, you can enjoy what many locals regard as the most reasonable set menu in town, and in summer you can sit on a terrace overlooking the city's Renaissance monuments. The owners are known for their fresh vegetables, as exemplified by *la pipirana,* a cold medley of vegetables with tuna, accented with boiled eggs, tomatoes, onions, and spices (only in summer). The atmosphere is relaxed, the service cordial, and the portions generous.

Pasaje Cardenal Benavides 15. (C) **95-374-13-65.** Main courses 8€–16€ ($9.60–$19); fixed-price menu 12€ ($14). AE, DC, MC, V. Wed 1–4pm; Thurs–Tues 1–4pm and 8:30–11:30pm. Closed Sept 24–Oct 20.

La Gondola ANDALUSIAN   In the very heart of the Renaissance town, this is one of the most convenient places to dine when you're exploring the town's monuments. The decor is in a traditional regional style, warm and inviting. The staff is cordial and helpful in guiding you through the menu of regional dishes. We were especially pleased with the fresh fish dishes, especially the salmon with a champagnelike wine sauce and the grilled hake *(merluza)* with fresh, locally grown vegetables. Main dishes such as pork cutlets and barbecued entrecote of veal with green peppers are also satisfying. Desserts are made fresh daily.

Portales Carbonería 13. (C) **95-374-29-84.** Reservations recommended. Main courses 9€–17€ ($11–$20). AE, DC, MC, V. Daily 8am–4:30pm and 8pm–midnight.

Museo Agrícola-Restaurante ANDALUSIAN   This restaurant could practically rely on its decor to attract diners, but happily it also serves good, hearty food. The walls are hung with a virtual museum's worth of agricultural tools and other regional artifacts. The chef is known locally for his succulent barbecued meat roasted over olive branches or almond tree leaves. A signature dish is the oven-baked baby goat, which is beautifully spiced. For a fish course, we recommend a platter of the king prawns in white sauce, and for an appetizer, a traditional local soup, *ajo blanco* (white garlic).

Calle San Cristóbal 17. (C) **95-379-04-73.** Reservations recommended. Main courses 9€–17€ ($11–$20). AE, DC, MC, V. Mon–Sat 1–4pm and 8:30pm–midnight. Closed 15 days in Aug (dates vary).

Vandelvira (★) (*Finds*) ANDALUSIAN   A 16th-century former convent has been converted into this citadel of good cooking and affordable prices. Similar to a cathedral in size, the building still contains much of its original architecture and conventual furnishings. The summer terrace is one of the most popular night bars and taverns in town. The chefs have a few fish dishes, including *bacalao* (cod), but mostly their meats are the way to go. Milk-fed lamb is one of their finest options, but the veal dishes are also outstanding. One of their more exotic specialties is pigs' knuckles stuffed with *perdiz* (partridge) and spinach. They also prepare an excellent appetizer of partridge pâté with virgin olive oil.

Calle de San Francisco 14. (C) **95-374-81-72.** Reservations recommended. Main courses 12€–23€ ($14–$28). AE, DC, MC, V. Sun 1:30–4pm; Tues–Sat 1:30–4pm and 8:30–11pm.

UBEDA ★★
57km (35 miles) NE of Jaén

A former stronghold of the Arabs, which today is often called the "Florence of Andalusia," Ubeda is a Spanish National Landmark filled with golden-brown Renaissance palaces and tile-roofed whitewashed houses. The best way to discover its charm is to wander the narrow cobblestone streets of the *casco antiguo* **(Old Town)** ★★★. The government long ago created a parador here in a renovated ducal palace—you might stop in for lunch. Allow time for a stroll through Ubeda's shops, specializing in crafts like esparto grass carpets or pottery.

ESSENTIALS
GETTING THERE   For information on **trains** serving the area, see "Getting There" under "Baeza," above.

There are 10 **buses** daily to Baeza, less than 10km (6¼ miles) away, and to Jaén. Seven buses per day go to the busy railway station at Linares-Baeza, where a train can take you virtually anywhere in Spain. Bus service to and from Córdoba, Seville, and Granada is also available. Ubeda's bus station is in the heart of the modern town, on Calle San José (© **95-375-21-57**), where signs will point you on a downhill walk to the *zona monumental*.

To **drive** here, turn off the Madrid-Córdoba road and head east for Linares, then on to Ubeda, a detour of 42km (26 miles). The turnoff is at the junction with N-322. From Jaén, the capital of the province, take N-321 northeast for 57km (35 miles).

VISITOR INFORMATION   The **tourist office,** Calle Baja del Marques 4 (© **95-375-08-97;** www.andalusia.com), is open Monday to Friday 9am to 2:45pm and 4 to 7pm (June–Sept 5–8pm), Saturday and Sunday 10am to 2pm.

EXPLORING UBEDA
Begin your tour at the centrally located **Plaza de Vázquez de Molina** ★★, the most harmonious square in Andalusia, which is flanked by several mansions, including the **Palacio de las Cadenas,** now the town hall. The mansions have been decaying for centuries, but many are now finally being restored. The famous Spanish architect, Andrés de Vandelvira, designed the interior patio of the slender arches of the town hall and many of the most impressive mansions of old Ubeda. The architect's crowning achievement is the privately owned **Palacio de Vela de los Cobos,** which you can admire on Plaza del Ayuntamiento. It was designed in the mid-1500s for Francisco de Vela de los Cobos, the town's magistrate. Its impressive facade is surmounted by an arcaded gallery. The L-shaped architecture of the building is most unusual.

You can pick up a map from the tourist office and set out. Most of the buildings aren't open to the public, including many by Vandelvira himself, but at least you can admire the facades, which in many cases are the most interesting elements.

Palacio de las Cadenas (Palace of Chains) takes its name from the decorative iron chains once affixed to the columns of its main portal. Today it can be entered from either Plaza Vázquez de Molina or Playa Ayuntamiento. After a look-see, you can go around the corner to Callejón de Jesús, which will take you into vaulted stone-built cellars, and the very minor **Museo de Alfarería.** This museum has an excellent collection of the green glaze ceramics Ubeda is famous for. Some of the pieces are quite stunning. Charging 1.85€ ($2.20) for admission, it is open May to September Tuesday to Saturday 10:30am to 2pm and 5:30 to 8pm. Off-season hours are Tuesday to Saturday 4:30 to 7pm.

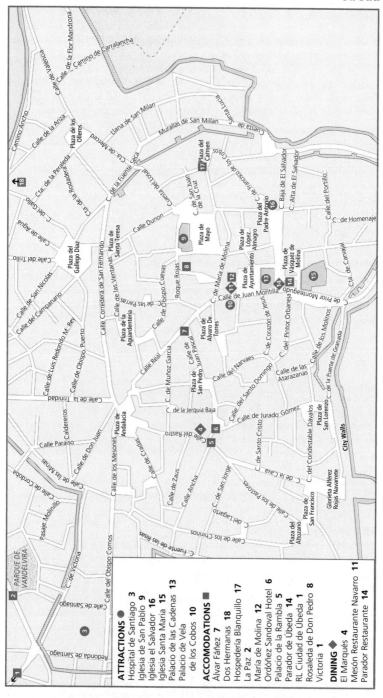

Ubeda

ATTRACTIONS ●
Hospital de Santiago **3**
Iglesia de San Pablo **9**
Iglesia el Salvador **16**
Iglesia Santa Maria **15**
Palacio de las Cadenas **13**
Palacio de Vela
de los Cobos **10**

ACCOMODATIONS ■
Álvar Fáñez **7**
Dos Hermanas **18**
Hospedería Blanquillo **17**
La Paz **2**
Maria de Molina **12**
Ordóñez Sandoval Hotel **6**
Palacio de la Rambla **5**
Parador de Úbeda **14**
RL Ciudad de Úbeda **1**
Rosaleda de Don Pedro **8**
Victoria **1**

DINING ◆
El Marqués **4**
Mesón Restaurante Navarro **11**
Parador Restaurante **14**

Also opening onto Plaza Vázquez de Molina is **Iglesia Santa María,** mainly from the 17th century, although its cloisters predate the building by at least a century. Inside you can visit a series of beautiful **chapels** ✦, which are protected by stunning **wrought-iron grilles** ✦, most of them created by Master Bartolomé. The church is usually open during the day.

Before the completion of Plaza Vázquez de Molina, a nearby square, **Plaza Primero de Mayo,** was the heart of the Old Town. Today it is the scene of an outdoor market. So-called heretics were burned here during the Inquisition.

Hospital de Santiago   On the western edge of town off Calle del Obispo Coros stands the Hospital of Santiago, built by Andrés de Vandelvira and completed in 1575, and still in use today. Over the main entryway is a carving of St. James "the Moorslayer" in a traditional pose on horseback. Note the monumental staircase leading upstairs from the inner patio. In the chapel are some marvelous woodcarvings. Today the hospital is a cultural venue, hosting concerts and containing a minor modern art museum.

Av. Cristo Rey. ⓒ **95-375-08-42.** Free admission. Mon–Fri 8am–3pm and 4–10pm; Sat–Sun 11am–3pm and 6–10pm.

Iglesia de San Pablo ✦   This Gothic church in the center of the Old Town is almost as fascinating as the Iglesia El Salvador (below). The Gothic San Pablo is famous for its 1511 **south portal** ✦ in the Isabelline style and for its **chapels** ✦ decorated with beautiful wrought-iron grilles. Vandelvira himself designed the "Heads of the Dead Chapel," the most stunning. You might also seek out the richly carved Chapel of Las Mercedes in the florid Isabelline style.

Plaza 1 de Mayo. ⓒ **95-375-06-37.** Free admission. Mon–Sat 5:30–8:15pm; Sun 11am–1:45pm (and 7–9pm in summer).

Iglesia El Salvador ✦✦   One of the grandest examples of Spanish Renaissance architecture, this church was designed in 1536 by Diego de Siloé as a family chapel and mausoleum for Francisco de los Cobos, secretary of the Holy Roman Emperor Charles V. The richly embellished portal is mere window dressing for the wealth of decoration on the **interior** ✦ of the church, including a **sacristy** ✦✦ designed by Andrés de Vandelvira with medallions, caryatids, *atlantes,* and coffered decorations and ornamentations. The many sculptures and altarpieces and the spectacular rose windows are also of special interest.

Calle Francisco de los Cobos. ⓒ **95-375-81-50.** Admission 2.25€ ($2.70) adults, 1€ ($1.20) children. Mon–Sat 4:30–7pm; Sun 10:45am–2pm and 4:30–7pm.

SHOPPING

Ubeda is hailed as "the crafts capital of Andalusia" and many visitors come here just to shop. Walk its ancient streets and you'll come upon shop after shop where artisans sell stained glass, stone carving, basket weaving, wrought iron, and more.

Pottery is king, however, and **Calle Valencia** is known as "pottery row." The town's legendary pottery was by Pablo Tito, whose works are highly valued collector's items today. He left his trade secrets to his offspring, who still carry on in his tradition.

Friendly, outgoing **Juan Tito,** is behind the potter's wheel at Playa del Ayuntamiento 12 (ⓒ **95-375-13-02**). His display of ceramics is most impressive. Another son, **Paco Tito,** Calle Valencia 22 (ⓒ **95-375-14-96**), will also try to lure you to his lair. His specialty is making clay sculptures based on characters from *Don Quixote.* Yet a third potter drawing upon the Tito legend is **Melchor**

Tito at Calle Valencia 44 (© **95-375-33-65**). He was actually the son-in-law of the fabulous Pablo and specializes in a stunning green glaze pottery. All of these shops are open Monday to Friday 8am to 2pm and 4 to 8:30pm, Saturday 8am to 2pm and 5 to 8pm. Another specialist in the green glaze pottery identified with Ubeda is **Antonio Almazara,** Calle Valencia 34 (© **95-375-12-00**). The best shop for esparto ware, including baskets, mats, and even rugs, is **Artesanía Blancho,** Calle Real 47 (© **95-375-04-56**). At both of these last two shops the owner lives at the same address, so hours are daily 9am to 8pm.

WHERE TO STAY

Alvar Fáñez ★ *Finds*   This cozy and thoughtfully executed hotel resulted from the radical overhaul of a 16th-century building in the late 1990s. There's a cozy cafe and bar on the street level, and a restaurant whose tables spill into the hotel's glass-covered courtyard. The upper floors of the arcades around the courtyard have mirador-style glass windows around the perimeter, making the place cozy, weather tight, and very charming. Check out the covered veranda on the building's third (top) floor, where cane and rattan chairs provide deep seating amid sputtering candles set on marble-topped tables—perfect for watching an Andalusian sunset. Bedrooms contain comfortable, blandly contemporary furniture and simple bathrooms with tubs and showers.

Calle Juan Pasquau 5, 23400 Ubeda. ©/fax **95-379-60-43**. www.alvarfanez.com. 11 units. 80€–120€ ($96–$144) double. AE, DC, MC, V. **Amenities:** Restaurant; bar. *In room:* A/C, TV, minibar, safe.

Dos Hermanas   This little inn, a hotel since the mid-1980s, has two things going for it: extremely agreeable prices, and fine and decent rooms. Think of it as a good, safe haven with a fine bed for the night and not as a place at which you'd want to hang your hat for a long time. Built along straight, functional lines, it is not big on architectural details, but has been much improved following a 2003 renovation. The small bedrooms are furnished in a standard way, mainly with wooden pieces. Each has a somewhat cramped private bathroom with tub and shower. "We are modest but no one ever accused us of overcharging," one of the staff members told us.

Risquillo Bajo 1, 23400 Ubeda. © **95-375-21-24**. Fax 95-379-13-15. 30 units. 38€ ($46) double. MC, V. Parking 5€ ($6). **Amenities:** Breakfast lounge. *In room:* A/C, TV.

Hospedería Blanquillo ★ *Finds*   This is a real discovery that opened in 2004. A stone-built, two-story house, it is an elegant Renaissance structure that in the 16th century was built by a prominent Jewish family. It has been beautifully restored and converted into a charming inn filled with architectural character. The midsize bedrooms are handsomely decorated and comfortably furnished, with adjoining tiled bathrooms with tub/shower combos. The more expensive bedrooms are a bit larger and contain private balconies opening onto views of olive trees. Like most buildings of this era, the hotel boasts a central columned courtyard with a fountain.

Plaza del Carmen 1, 23400 Ubeda. © **95-379-54-05**. Fax 95-379-54-06. www.elblanquillo.com. 17 units. 62€–82€ ($74–$98) double; 180€–200€ ($216–$240) suite. Rates include continental breakfast. MC, V. Free parking. **Amenities:** Restaurant; bar; 24-hr. room service; babysitting; laundry service; rooms for those w/limited mobility. *In room:* A/C, TV, dataport, minibar (suites only), hair dryer, safe.

La Paz *Value*   This hotel is so reasonably priced and agreeable that it's often filled with a diverse collection of value-seekers. It was built in 1971 but considerably upgraded and improved in 2004. In the heart of the commercial district opposite the statue of a military hero, the architecture has a certain Andalusian character. Bedrooms are midsize and decorated in a simple Iberian fashion with dignified wooden furniture and papered walls. Each comes with a small, tiled bathroom with a tub/shower combo. The traditional dark wood furnishings contrast with the stark white walls.

Calle Andalucía 1, 23400 Ubeda. © **95-375-21-40.** Fax 95-375-08-48. www.hotel-lapaz.com. 40 units. 56€ ($67) double. AE, DC, MC, V. Parking: 9€ ($11). **Amenities:** Bar; laundry service. *In room:* A/C, TV, hair dryer.

María de Molina ★ *Finds* The parador (below) is still the number-one place to stay, but this hotel gives it serious competition. In a beautifully restored and once-decaying palace, the three-story hotel lies in the center of the historic district. Much of the past, including stone vaulted ceilings downstairs, was retained by the modern architects. The hotel opens onto a marble columned atrium in which chairs are placed in the center, with a skylight overhead. Wherever you look you'll find grace notes such as hand-carved wooden doors and marble arches over stairwells. In contrast, the bedrooms are thoroughly modernized, ranging from rather cramped to spacious suites. We prefer the rooms with terraces or balconies, but these need to be booked well in advance. Each room comes with a small bathroom covered in Andalusian tiles and equipped with tub and shower. Try to have at least one dinner at the restaurant, enjoying not only its fine Andalusian cuisine, but also its mellow ambience, particularly inviting at night.

Plaza del Ayuntamiento, 23400 Ubeda. © **95-379-53-56.** Fax 95-379-36-94. www.hotel-maria-de-molina.com. 26 units. Sun–Thurs 72€ ($86) double; Fri–Sat 84€ ($101) double; Sun–Thurs 92€ ($110) suite; Fri–Sat 122€ ($146) suite. AE, DC, MC, V. **Amenities:** Cafeteria; lap pool; limited room service; laundry service; rooms for those w/limited mobility. *In room:* A/C, TV, dataport, minibar, safe.

Ordóñez Sandoval Hotel ★ *Finds* This hotel was created in 2003, when Amalía Peres Ordóñez commissioned a team of contractors to upgrade three rooms within her ancestral private home. The result is a miniboutique hotel with accommodations shoehorned into the antique framework of a medieval house rebuilt in the mudéjar-romantic style in 1889. You'll enter the place through elaborate wrought-iron gates, passing lavish blue and white "romantic revival" tilework en route. Inside, are wide stone staircases, a stunningly small-scale courtyard, family antiques, and a sense of old-fashioned hospitality. Breakfast is served in what was originally conceived as the family chapel, and accommodations are comfortable and large, with upscale and carefully tiled bathrooms with tub and shower. Rooms don't contain the lavish historical overlay of the Palacio de la Rambla, but in light of the more intimate and very congenial setting, they're well worth the money.

Calle Antonio Medina 1, 23400 Ubeda. © **95-379-51-87.** 3 units. 70€ ($84) double. AE, DC, MC, V. *In room:* A/C, TV, minibar, safe.

Palacio de la Rambla ★★ *Finds* When the Marquesa de la Rambla arrives in town, she stays here at her ancestral 16th-century home. The front entrance is fortresslike, with color tiles in the mudéjar style. Inside, the cloistered courtyard, an ideal retreat on a hot day, has Plateresque and Renaissance-style carvings, granite columns, flocks of nesting birds, and forests of ivy. Eight of its rooms are open to paying guests. The spacious manorial rooms under soaring ceilings boast many of their original furnishings, but everything has been supplemented with modern conveniences. Each has a tiled, very large bathroom with a tub/shower combo and is individually furnished, often with grand antiques, tapestries, objets d'art, and other remnants of old Spain's aristocratic life. The venue is so charming as to be almost spooky—you're literally living with the accumulated memories and ghosts of a very old family mansion. You can still visit two incredibly formal salons, each outfitted as if awaiting a visit from Philip II.

Plaza del Marqués 1, 23400 Ubeda. © **95-375-01-96.** Fax 95-375-02-67. 8 units. 100€ ($120) double; 112€ ($134) suite. Rates include buffet breakfast. AE, MC, V. Parking 5€ ($6). Closed July 15–Aug 15. **Amenities:** Laundry service. *In room:* A/C, TV, minibar, hair dryer, iron/ironing board.

Parador de Ubeda ★★★
On the town's central square stands this 16th-century palace turned parador, which shares an old paved plaza with the Iglesia El Salvador and its dazzling facade. The formal entrance to this Renaissance palace leads to an enclosed patio, encircled by two levels of Moorish arches, where palms and potted plants stand on the tile floors. The rooms are nearly two stories high, with beamed ceilings, tall windows, and antiques and reproductions; the beds are comfortable, and the bathrooms come with tub/shower combos.

Plaza Vázquez de Molina 1, 23400 Ubeda. © **95-375-03-45.** Fax 95-375-12-59. www.parador.es. 36 units. 120€–132€ ($144–$158) double; 180€ ($216) suite. AE, DC, MC, V. **Amenities:** Restaurant; bar; sauna; limited room service; babysitting; laundry service/dry cleaning; nonsmoking rooms. *In room:* A/C, TV, dataport, minibar, hair dryer, safe.

RL Ciudad de Ubeda ★★ *(Value*
In terms of government ratings, this city center hotel is quite luxurious and rated second only to the parador. Up to date with a full range of amenities, it is also elegant architecturally, studded with beautiful, large windows, plus peek-a-boo dormers jutting out of its roof. Inside, it's all four-star luxury. Expensive materials went into the creation of the elegant public rooms. The spacious bedrooms reflect the same good taste, with an emphasis on comfort. The decor is filled with adornments, the furniture mostly wooden and modern, and thick carpets rest on the floors. Each comes with a good-size tiled bathroom with a tub/shower combo. Built in the late '90s, the hotel added a new wing and rooms in 2004. For what it offers, its rates are very low.

Cronista Juan de la Torre s/n, 23400 Ubeda. © **95-379-10-11.** Fax 95-379-10-12. www.rlhoteles.com. 92 units. 96€ ($115) double; 156€ ($187) suite. Free parking. **Amenities:** Restaurant; bar; outdoor pool; room service (8am–10pm); babysitting. *In room:* A/C, TV, dataport, minibar, hair dryer, safe.

Rosaleda de Don Pedro
In the *zona monumental,* the attraction-rich center of town, this former family mansion has been virtually rebuilt and turned into a three-story hotel with a facade studded with balconies. The building goes back to the 16th century, but it only became a hotel in 2001. Government-rated three stars, it is one of the better and more agreeable midbracket hotels in town. Bedrooms are a bit small but tastefully and comfortably furnished, each with a bathroom, also small, that is tiled, conveniently laid out, and equipped with shower and tub.

Obispo Toral 2, 23400 Ubeda. © **95-379-61-11.** Fax 95-379-51-49. 30 units. 72€–110€ ($86–$132) double. MC, V. Parking 8€ ($9.60). **Amenities:** Restaurant; bar; outdoor pool; 24-hr. room service; rooms for those w/limited mobility. *In room:* A/C, TV, dataport, minibar, hair dryer.

Victoria *(Value*
Near Plaza de Toros stands the town's rock-bottom bargain. A 2003 renovation upgraded furnishings in the rather small but comfortably furnished bedrooms, each with a little attached tiled bathroom with shower. The rooms are adequately comfortable, but it's not a hotel to hang out in. But for an affordable room for the night, it's fine. All rooms come with a small balcony, but there are no real hotel amenities to speak of.

Alaminos 5, 23400 Ubeda. © **95-375-29-52.** 15 units. 34€ ($41) double. AE, DC, MC, V. *In room:* A/C, TV.

WHERE TO DINE

El Marqués *Value* SPANISH   At the edge of a small, charming square a few steps from the also-recommended Palacio de la Rambla, this is one of the best-managed and most highly recommended restaurants in town. In a setting of immaculate napery and bright lighting, uniformed waiters will bring you tempting platters of Iberian cured ham, salads, grilled steaks or fish, soups, and desserts such as ice creams and flans. Especially memorable are the salmon in wine sauce and the veal stew with mushrooms. Notice the stained-glass depiction of a farmer sowing seed in a corner of the restaurant.

Plaza Marqués de la Rambla 2. (C) **95-375-72-55**. Main courses 10€–18€ ($12–$22); fixed-price menu 16€ ($19). MC, V. June–Sept Sun 1:30–4pm, Mon–Sat 1:30–4pm and 8:30–11:30pm.

Mesón Restaurante Navarro NAVARRESE/ANDALUSIAN   Set at the edge of one of Ubeda's largest squares, this amicable and sometimes animated restaurant does a thriving business selling beer and tapas every evening till about midnight. There are a handful of dining tables on the square outside, and more in a back room, which seems like something of an afterthought to the heavy bar trade that packs in lots of locals throughout the evening. Hearty, flavorful fare includes roast goat with tomatoes, roast chicken with potatoes, hake medallions, and grilled swordfish.

Plaza Ayuntamiento 2. (C) **95-379-06-38**. Main courses 9€–16€ ($11–$19); tapas 1.35€–6€ ($1.60–$7.20). AE, DC, MC, V. Daily 11am–4pm and 8pm–2am.

Parador Restaurante ★ SPANISH/ANDALUSIAN   This parador is the best place to dine for miles around. Although the cuisine isn't the most creative, it's made with market-fresh ingredients prepared from decades-old recipes. The menu is wide ranging. Start with a typical dish of the area, such as cold soup with almonds, delightful on a hot day. Partridge is a local favorite—appetizers might include stuffed green peppers with partridge, stewed partridge with plums, or a refreshing salad with marinated partridge. The best fish dishes are the grilled monkfish in saffron sauce and the grilled sole with garlic and apple-vinegar sauce. Meat eaters might be tempted by the regional dishes, such as oxtail in red-wine sauce and stewed kid with pine nuts. The *menú del parador* is a good bet, including an appetizer plus fish or meat for a main course and then dessert. The tasting menu for two showcases four typical regional dishes nightly.

Plaza Vazques de Molina 1. (C) **95-375-03-45**. Reservations recommended. Main courses 9€–21€ ($11–$25); menú del parador 26€ ($31); tasting menu 48€ ($58) for 2 people or 24€ ($29) per person. AE, DC, MC, V. Daily 1:30–4pm and 8:30–11pm.

7

Granada

About 660m (2,200 ft.) above sea level in the foothills of Sierra Nevada, Granada sprawls over two main hills, the Alhambra and the Albaicín, and is crossed by two rivers, the Genil and the Darro. This former stronghold of Moorish Spain is full of romance and folklore.

Granada's Alhambra, the hilltop fortress palace of the Nasrid kings, the last Muslim rulers of Spain, is one of the world's fabled landmarks. This monumental edifice arguably is Spain's greatest attraction. (Castilians claim that the Prado in Madrid is *número uno*.)

Washington Irving *(Tales of the Alhambra)* used the symbol of this city, the pomegranate *(granada)*, to conjure a spirit of romance. In fact, the name probably derives from the Moorish word *karnattah*. Some historians have suggested that it comes from Garnatha Alyehud, the name of an old Jewish ghetto.

Washington Irving may have helped publicize the glories of Granada to the English-speaking world, but in Spain the city is known for its ties to another writer: Federico García Lorca. Born in 1898, this Spanish poet/dramatist was shot by soldiers in 1936 in the first months of the Spanish Civil War. During Franco's rule, García Lorca's works were banned in Spain, but today he's once again honored in Granada, where he grew up.

Granada came to prominence in the 1200s at the peak of Muslim power. Even after Seville and Córdoba had fallen to the Catholic monarchs, Granada stood as the last surviving Islamic capital in Spain. It's where the sultans took their last stand against the Catholic invaders.

Fleeing Seville and Córdoba to the west, thousands of Moors flocked to this last stronghold. Many of them were artisans, and the Alhambra and other buildings testify to their skills.

On January 2, 1492, Granada fell to the Catholics when Boabdil, the last of the Moorish kings, turned his beloved city over to Ferdinand and Isabella. Isabella immediately began to "Christianize" Granada, ordering the construction of a cathedral and its adjoining royal chapel. She also ordered that Muslim mosques be repurposed as churches or for other Christian use. Although some great architectural monuments were destroyed in the process, the Moorish district of the Albaicín fortunately remains more or less intact, allowing a peek at the architectural glory that existed during the Middle Ages.

Under subsequent Catholic monarchs, Granada prospered until the 1500s when it fell into a decline that lasted many years.

Today Granada is back, with an economy fueled not only by tourism, but also by light industry. The University of Granada is one of the finest in Spain, and there is a young, vibrant population.

Budget at least 2 days—preferably 3—to see this city of the pomegranate.

1 Orientation

GETTING THERE

BY PLANE   **Iberia** flies to Granada from Barcelona and Madrid, and several times a week from Palma de Majorca. Three planes a day land from Barcelona (trip time: 1 hr.); four planes fly in from Madrid, taking only a half-hour. Granada's **Armilla Airport** is 16km (10 miles) west of the center of town on Carretera Málaga; call ✆ **95-824-52-00** for information. Other than a minor tourist information booth and an ATM, there are few services. A convenient Iberia ticketing office is 2 blocks east of the cathedral at Plaza Isabel Católica 2 (✆ **90-240-05-00**). A bus departs several times daily connecting this office with the airport, costing 4.40€ ($5.30) one-way. The bus runs Monday to Saturday at 8:15am, 9:15am, and 5:30pm; Sunday at 5:30 and 7pm. Trip time is 45 minutes. Taxis line up outside the terminals at the airport, charging about 16€ ($19) to the center of the city.

BY TRAIN   The train station is **Estación de RENFE de Granada,** Av. Andaluces s/n (✆ **95-827-12-72;** www.renfe.es), although the main ticket office is at Calle de los Reyes Católicos 45 (✆ **95-822-31-19**).

Granada is well linked with the most important Spanish cities, especially those of Andalusia. Four trains per day arrive from Seville, taking 4 to 5 hours, depending on the train, and costing 17€ ($20) for a one-way ticket. From Madrid, two daily trains arrive in Granada, taking 5 to 6 hours and costing 28€ to 44€ ($34–$53) per one-way ticket. From Barcelona, there is a daily train, taking 12 to 13 hours and costing 49€ ($59) one-way.

BY BUS   Granada is served by far more buses than trains. It has links to virtually all the major towns and cities in Andalusia, even to Madrid. The main bus terminal is **Estación de Autobuses de Granada,** Carretera de Jaén s/n (✆ **95-818-54-80**). One of the most heavily used bus routes is the one between Seville and Granada. Ten buses run per day, costing 16€ ($19) for a one-way ticket. The trip is 3 hours. You can also reach Granada in 3 hours on a bus from Córdoba, which costs 10€ ($12) for a one-way ticket. There is also a fleet of 10 buses per day. If you're on the Costa del Sol, the run is just 2 hours, costing 8.05€ ($9.65) per one-way ticket. This is a very popular routing with 17 buses going back and forth between Granada and the coast per day. For bus information call **Alsina Graells** at ✆ **95-818-54-80.**

BY CAR   Granada is connected by superhighway to Madrid, Málaga, and Seville. Many sightseers prefer to make the drive from Madrid to Granada in 2 days, rather than one. If that is your plan, Jaén makes a perfect stopover. See chapter 6.

From Seville in the west, head east along N-334, which becomes N-342 on its final run into Granada. Many visitors head to Granada from Málaga (capital of the Costa del Sol). Take N-331 north from Málaga, cutting northeast onto N-321 and hooking into the N-342 for its final run into Granada. From Madrid, head south on N-IV (also called E-5) until you reach the town of Bailén. Once here, continue south onto N-323 toward Jaén. After leaving Jaén, the road becomes E-902 for its tortuous, mountainous descent south into Granada.

The city of Granada is located 415km (258 miles) south of Madrid, 122km (76 miles) northeast of Málaga, 261km (162 miles) east of Córdoba, and 250km (155 miles) east of Seville.

VISITOR INFORMATION

The **tourist office,** Calle de Santa Ana 4 (© **95-822-59-90;** www.andalusia. com), is open Monday to Saturday 9am to 7pm, Sunday 10am to 2pm.

CITY LAYOUT

One of the best maps of Granada, for those who plan to explore the city in some depth, is available for 2.85€ ($3.40) at **El Corte Inglés,** Calle Gentil 20–22 (© **95-822-32-40**), open Monday to Saturday 10am to 10pm.

Essentially Granada is divided into **upper and lower towns.** Crowning the city is the **Alhambra district,** dominated by—you guessed it—the fortress palace of the Alhambra. The upper city is composed of two hills facing each other across the narrow gorge of the Río Darro. On the southern hill stands the Alhambra itself and the nearby summer palace of the **Generalife,** also once the gardens of the Nasrid kings.

The old Arab quarter occupies the second or northern hill, the **Albaicín,** a former ghetto that's now a rapidly gentrifying district with many fashionable restaurants and boutique hotels. Expect tiny alleyways, otherwise known as streets, and whitewashed houses. Ancient Arab baths and the remains of the old Moorish walls can still be seen.

Another satellite hill leads off from the Albaicín, wandering into the **Sacromonte district,** long a haven for Granada's famous gypsies. A warren of little whitewashed homes trails out to a rocky mountainside riddled with caves.

Cuesta de Gomérez is one of the most important streets in the lower town, often called the **Cathedral district.** This is **centro Granada,** or "downtown," as Americans say. Congested, compact, it is relatively easy to navigate. This is Granada's business center, home to most of its restaurants, shops, and hotels. It climbs uphill from the Plaza Nueva, the center of the modern city, to the Alhambra. At the Plaza Nueva the east-west artery, **Calle de los Reyes Católicos,** goes to the heart of the 19th-century city and the towers of the cathedral. Granada's principal north-south artery is the **Gran Vía de Colón.**

Calle de los Reyes Católicos and the Gran Vía de Colón meet at the circular **Plaza de Isabel la Católica,** graced by a bronze statue of the queen offering Columbus the Santa Fe agreement, which granted the rights to the epochal voyage to the New World. Going west, Calle de los Reyes Católicos passes near the cathedral and other major sights in the downtown section of Granada. The street runs to **Puerta Real,** Granada's commercial hub with many stores, hotels, cafes, and restaurants.

2 Getting Around

Granada is extremely congested and also compact. Once you're in the district of your choice, you can walk along to most points of interest. Don't even attempt to drive here.

BY BUS

Buses in Granada tend to be painted red, carry lots of advertising on their sides, and are small enough, and lean enough, to navigate some of the narrow streets leading from the town's commercial center to the Alhambra. A single ride costs .90€ ($1.10), a booklet of nine bus tickets goes for 5€ ($6), and a booklet of 20 bus tickets sells for 20€ ($24). Buy any of these tickets directly from the driver, who will accept bills of up to 10€ ($12). For short-term visitors, bus **no. 32** is the best choice, since it makes frequent runs from Old Granada to the

Alhambra. Another good one is **no. 30,** or "Destination Alhambra," running from Plaza Nueva to the Alhambra. A final pick is **no. 31,** which also leaves from Plaza Nueva and runs to the old ghetto, the Albaicín. To hit the major boulevards, which are good for shopping, the **no. 3** bus runs from the terminal to Avenida de la Constitución, Gran Vía, and Plaza Isabel la Católica. For information about public transportation, call ☎ **900-71-09-00.**

BY TAXI
Most trips in the city cost around 6€ ($7.20). Taxis can be hailed in the streets; a green dome light indicates the vehicle is free. Taxis often line up outside first-class hotels, in the vicinity of the Alhambra, and at the landmark Plaza Nueva. To summon a cab, call **Radio Taxi** at ☎ **95-828-06-54.**

BY CAR
It's impossible to get around Granada by driving. A rented car is best left for exploring the surrounding Sierra Nevada mountain range. Rental prices vary greatly, depending on the time of the year and the agency, but count on shelling out around 300€ ($360) per week, including unlimited mileage and insurance. For most rentals, you must be 21 or older and have had a valid national drivers license for at least a year.

Major car-rental agencies include **Atasa,** Plaza Cuchilleros 1 (☎ 95-822-40-04); **Hertz,** Luis Braille 7 (☎ 95-825-24-19); **Budget,** Recogidas 35 (☎ 95-825-05-554); **Avis,** Recogidas 31 (☎ 95-825-23-58); and **Europcar,** Av. del Sur 2 (☎ 95-829-50-65). Europcar, Hertz, and Avis also maintain kiosks at the airport.

ON FOOT
This is about the only way to get around most neighborhoods, especially the hilly Albaicín and the Alhambra. For Greater Granada, a bus or taxi will have to do.

FAST FACTS: Granada

American Express The office is at Calle Reyes Católicos (☎ **95-822-45-12**). Hours are Monday to Friday 9am to 1:30pm and 2 to 9pm; Saturday 10am to 2pm.

Babysitters The best way to find a sitter is to ask the concierge or receptionist at your hotel. For a fee of 6€ ($7.20) per hour, you can also contact **La Cabaña del Dormilón,** Cortijo Argaz, Calle Alhami 6, Carretera de Huetor Vega (☎ **95-812-33-55**), which is located on the southern outskirts of Granada, but which can send a staff member directly to your hotel. The hours are rather rigid: only Monday to Friday 7:30am to 9pm.

Bookstore The best English-language outlet is **Metro,** Calle Gracia 31 (☎ **95-826-15-65**), which has a large section, including travel guides and maps, in its English language department. Open Monday to Friday 10am to 2pm and 5 to 8:30pm, Saturday 11am to 2pm.

Consulates The nearest are in Seville. See chapter 4.

Currency Exchange The best and most central office is the **Banco Santander Central Hispano,** Gran Vía 3 (☎ **95-821-73-00**), open May to September Monday to Friday 9am to 2pm; October to April Monday to Saturday 9am to 2pm. You'll find 24-hour ATM machines at Puerta Real and Plaza de Isabel la Católica.

Emergencies For emergencies involving the police, the fire department, or an ambulance, dial ℂ **112.**

Hospital The town's biggest is the **Hospital Clínico,** Av. de Madrid s/n (ℂ **95-802-30-00).**

Internet Cafe One of Granada's largest and best maintained is **Navegaweb Café,** Calle de los Reyes Católicos 55 (ℂ **95-821-05-28).** Large, high-ceilinged, and airy, it has a staff that's helpful about getting your Web session up and running quickly. Internet access costs 1€ ($1.20) for 30 minutes. A leading competitor, **Internet Redisis,** calle Veronica de la Magdalena 1 (ℂ **95-853-50-86),** charges the same fee.

Newspapers Daily newspapers edited and published in Granada sell for around 1€ ($1.20), and include the right-of-center *Ideal* and *La Opinión,* and the slightly left-of-center *Granada Hoy.* For listings of the cultural events being presented in and around Granada, pick up, for 1.50€ ($1.80), in any newspaper kiosk, a copy of *Guía de Granada del Ocio.*

Pharmacy A large 24-hour pharmacy in the town center is **Farmacia Tallon,** Recogides 48 (ℂ **95-825-12-90).** A slightly smaller option is **Farmacia Oeste,** Av. Olorez 1 (ℂ **95-828-75-75).**

Post Office Called **Correos Granada,** the main post office is at Puerta Real s/n (ℂ **95-219-71-97),** open Monday to Friday 8:30am to 8:30pm, Saturday 9:30am to 2pm.

Restrooms There are a handful of public toilets in Granada, but fewer than you might wish. Most lie along the Paseo Violon, near Congress Hall. Their doors open with the insertion of a .20€ (25¢) coin. Otherwise, duck into the nearest bar or cafe with the intent of buying a coffee or bottle of water as part of the process.

Telephones Pay phones are scattered throughout Granada, a local call requiring .20€ (25¢) for the first 3 minutes. Many of them also accept phone cards, available at local tobacco stands and news kiosks in increments of 6€ ($7.20), 10€ ($12), and 20€ ($24). For directory assistance for phone numbers within Spain, call either ℂ **11818,** 11835, or 11843.

3 Where to Stay

EXPENSIVE

AC Palacio de Santa Paula ✦✦✦ One of Granada's grandest and most unusual hotels opened in 2001 behind the very large sienna-colored facade of what had been built in the 19th century as Jerónimos Convent. Inside, you'll find one of the most imaginative combinations of modern and antique architecture in Spain, a brilliantly schizophrenic integration of buildings that incorporates a 15th-century medieval cloister, two 14th-century Arab houses, a deconsecrated baroque chapel, and many high-ceilinged vestiges of Granada's Catholic Reconquista. All of these structures are interlinked with a sophisticated ultramodern shell of glass, steel, aluminum, and polished stone. Even the simplest units are hypermodern, soothing, comfortable, and well designed, with soundproof windows protecting sleepers from the busy traffic of the Gran Via Colón. Each room comes with a luxurious tiled bathroom with tub and shower.

Granada Accommodations & Dining

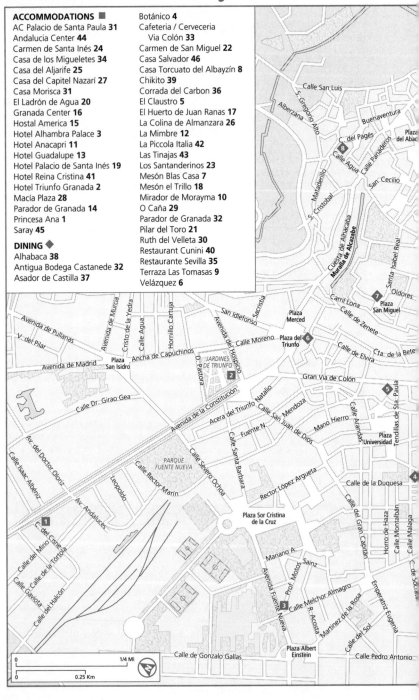

ACCOMMODATIONS ■
AC Palacio de Santa Paula **31**
Andalucia Center **44**
Carmen de Santa Inés **24**
Casa de los Migueletes **34**
Casa del Aljarife **25**
Casa del Capitel Nazarí **27**
Casa Morisca **31**
El Ladrón de Agua **20**
Granada Center **16**
Hostal America **15**
Hotel Alhambra Palace **3**
Hotel Anacapri **11**
Hotel Guadalupe **13**
Hotel Palacio de Santa Inés **19**
Hotel Reina Cristina **41**
Hotel Triunfo Granada **2**
Macía Plaza **28**
Parador de Granada **14**
Princesa Ana **1**
Saray **45**

DINING ◆
Alhabaca **38**
Antigua Bodega Castanede **32**
Asador de Castilla **37**

Botánico **4**
Cafeteria / Cerveceria
   Via Colón **33**
Carmen de San Miguel **22**
Casa Salvador **46**
Casa Torcuato del Albayzín **8**
Chikito **39**
Corrada del Carbon **36**
El Claustro **5**
El Huerto de Juan Ranas **17**
La Colina de Almanzara **26**
La Mimbre **12**
La Piccola Italia **42**
Las Tinajas **43**
Los Santanderinos **23**
Mesón Blas Casa **7**
Mesón el Trillo **18**
Mirador de Morayma **10**
O Caña **29**
Parador de Granada **32**
Pilar del Toro **21**
Ruth del Velleta **30**
Restaurant Cunini **40**
Restaurante Sevilla **35**
Terraza Las Tomasas **9**
Velázquez **6**

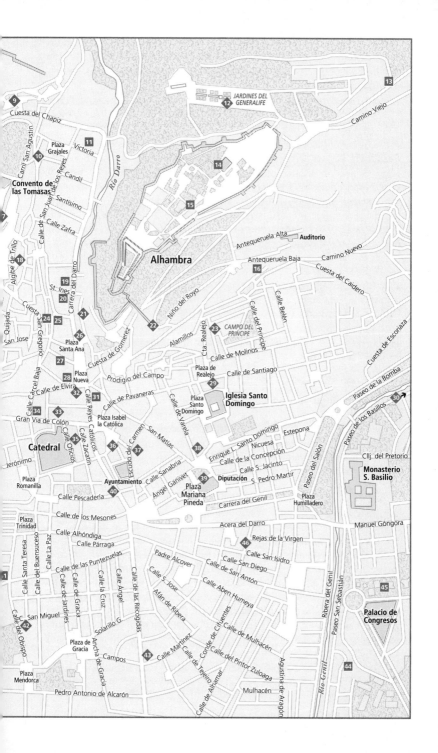

Cuesta del Chapiz

JARDINES DEL GENERALIFE

Camino Viejo

Plaza Grajales

Victoria

Río Darro

Convento de las Tomasas

Carril San Agustín

Calle de San Juan de los Reyes

Candil

Santísimo

Calle Zafra

Algibe de Trillo

Calle del Darro

St. Inés

Carrera del Darro

Cuesta de San Gregorio

Quijada

San Jose

Plaza Santa Ana

Cuesta de Gomérez

Alhambra

Antequeruela Alta

Auditorio

Antequeruela Baja

Camino Nuevo

Cuesta del Caidero

Niño del Royo

Calle Belén

Calle del Príncipe

Cuesta de Escoriaza

Cta.-Realejo

CAMPO DEL PRINCIPE

Alamillos

Calle de Molinos

Paseo de la Bomba

Prodigio del Campo

Plaza de Realejo

Calle de Santiago

Plaza Santo Domingo

Iglesia Santo Domingo

Paseo de los Basillos

Calle de Pavaneras

Calle de Varela

Plaza Isabel la Católica

Calle Cárcel Baja

Calle de Elvira

Calle Reyes Católicos

San Matías

Enrique L. Santo Domingo

Nicuesa

Estepona

Gran Via de Colón

Calle Zacatín

Calle del Carmen

Calle de la Concepción

Paseo del Salón

Monasterio S. Basilio

Cllj. del Pretorio

Catedral

Calle Oficios

Escudo del Carmen

Calle Sanabria

Calle S. Jacinto

S. Pedro Martír

Jerónimo

Plaza Romanilla

Ayuntamiento

Angel Ganivet

Plaza Mariana Pineda

Diputación

Carrera del Genil

Plaza Humilladero

Manuel Góngora

Calle Pescadería

Calle de los Mesones

Acera del Darro

Plaza Trinidad

Calle Alhóndiga

Calle Párraga

Rejas de la Virgen

Calle Santa Teresa

Calle del Buensucceso

Calle La Paz

Calle de las Puntezuelas

Padre Alcover

Calle San Diego

Calle de San Antón

Calle San Isidro

Ribera del Genil

Palacio de Congresos

Calle del Obispo

San Miguel

Calle de Gracia

Calle de Jardines

Calle de la Cruz

Calle Angel

Calle la Angel

Calle de las Recogidas

Calle S. Jose

Afán de Ribera

Calle Aben Humeya

Conde de Cifuentes

Calle de Mulhacén

Paseo San Sebastián

Agustina de Aragón

Plaza de Gracia

Solarillo G.

Ancha de Gracia

Campos

Calle Martínez

Calle de Tejeiro

Calle del Pintor Zuloaga

Río Genil

Plaza Mendorca

Pedro Antonio de Alcarón

Calle de Alhamar

Mulhacén

Somewhat more upscale units and suites occupy the site of the Moorish houses and the cloister. Scattered throughout the premises are a half-dozen imaginative suites. The staff is particularly charming. The in-house restaurant, **El Claustro,** is separately recommended later in this chapter.

Gran Vía de Colón 31, 18001 Granada. © **95-880-57-40.** Fax 95-880-57-41. www.ac-hotels.com. 75 units. 175€–225€ ($210–$270) double; 310€ ($372) junior suite. Parking 15€ ($18) per day. Bus: 3, 9, 6, or 11. AE, DC, MC, V. **Amenities:** Restaurant; gym; sauna; 24-hr. room service; babysitting; nonsmoking rooms. *In room:* A/C, TV, dataport, minibar, safe.

Andalucía Center ☆

One of Granada's newest hotels, and a member of the same chain as the also-recommended Granada Center, this hotel lies near the Convention Center, a 25-minute walk from the historic core. This is a hip and hypermodern hotel and—in its own restrained and tasteful way—a very luxurious choice. Imagine an Italian-style Milanese *moderno* hotel with a post-*movida* Iberian twist, all of it unified with an acre of glistening beige stone, lots of dark hardwoods, and theatrical lighting fixtures. There's a first-class restaurant and a stylish and macho-looking bar—the kind that makes you want to linger—on the lobby level; a rooftop pool and sun terrace, and a breakfast buffet that, by anyone's estimate, is generous. Bedrooms, scattered over five floors, are large and comfortable, adjoining first-class bathrooms with tub and shower.

Since parking in the center of Granada is hard to find, leave your car in this hotel's garage, then taxi to any point near the center.

Av. de América s/n, 18006 Granada. © **95-818-15-00.** Fax 95-812-94-84. www.hotelescenter.es. 115 units. 140€–160€ ($168–$192) double; 200€–390€ ($240–$468) suite. AE, DC, MC, V. Parking 13€ ($16). Bus: 3, 9, 11, or 33. **Amenities:** Restaurant; bar; outdoor pool; room service (8am–11:30pm); laundry service; solarium. *In room:* A/C, TV, dataport, minibar, hair dryer, safe.

Casa de los Migueletes ☆☆ *(Finds)*

Renovated at huge expense in 2003, this is the best-accessorized and plushest of the crop of new boutique hotels that has opened within medieval houses of the Albaicín. Rates are higher than at some of the less highly recommended boutique hotels in the neighborhood, but the venue is richer and more substantial. Although it has a three-star government rating, it contains many accessories associated with four-star hotels. The structure was built in 1642, and used by the local police force (then known as *Los Migueletes* for the weapons they carried) throughout most of the 1800s. After collapsing into a virtual ruin, it was rescued by Norway-born Karl Otto Skogland and his wife, Lise. Some of the rooms, especially the spectacular suite, feel baronial, thanks to high ceilings, majestic proportions, some of the best mattresses available, and flagstone or tile-covered floors. All bedrooms are different in size and layout, some opening onto the interior courtyard, whereas others have a view of the Alhambra, which is especially dramatic when floodlit at night. Public areas are graceful and museumlike. A fountain splashes in the courtyard, wraparound verandas above the stone-floored patio are supported by delicate granite columns, and breakfast is served in a vaulted white-brick cellar with sophisticated Scandinavian touches. Note that the elevator grants access to only about 80% of the rooms. All rooms are nonsmoking.

Calle Benelua 11, 18010 Granada. © **95-821-07-00.** Fax 95-821-07-02. www.casamigueletes.com. 25 units. 129€–199€ ($155–$239) double; 229€–499€ ($275–$599) suite. Parking 9€ ($11) per night. Bus: 30, 31, or 32. **Amenities:** Breakfast room; laundry service. *In room:* A/C, TV, dataport, minibar, safe.

Granada Center ☆☆

Come here if you want a slick, marble-clad hotel rather than something more evocative of Andalusia. In overall luxury, only the Saray does it (slightly) better. A sleek, modern urban hotel, Granada Center is surrounded by beautiful gardens and has harmonious, though severe, exterior lines. Its ivy-draped balconies soften this severity, as does the interior use of warm decorations and colors. The dramatic triangular atrium evokes a Hyatt hotel. Midsize to spacious guest rooms are among the city's best, with rich upholstery, contemporary prints, bedside controls, laminated desks, and a medley of coordinated pastels and tasteful wooden furnishings in a mix of dark and light colors. Each unit comes with a tiled bathroom with a tub/shower combination. There are facilities galore, including a garden-style cafe in front of the building, a salon, and a pub.

Av. Fuentenueva s/n, 18002 Granada. ☎ **95-820-50-00.** Fax 95-828-96-96. www.hotelescenter.es. 171 units. 160€–231€ ($192–$277) double; 457€ ($548) suite. AE, DC, MC, V. Bus: 11. **Amenities:** Restaurant; cafe; bar; car-rental desk; hairdresser; 24-hr. room service; laundry service/dry cleaning. *In room:* A/C, TV, dataport, minibar, safe.

Hotel Alhambra Palace ★

Evoking a Moorish fortress complete with a crenellated roofline, a crowning dome, geometric tile work, and the suggestion of a minaret, this legendary hotel is a good choice. It was built by Duke San Pedro de Galatino in 1910 in a secluded spot just a 10-minute walk from the Alhambra. The private rooms don't live up to the drama of the public areas. Most rooms are spacious and quite comfortable, but a few small ones are in need of restoration. All contain bathrooms with tub/shower combos. Try for one with a balcony opening onto a view of the city of Granada, but avoid the court rooms, which lack double-glazing. Most readers like the old-world aura here, but a few have found the hotel so unsatisfactory they didn't want to check in after seeing their room. If at all possible, ask to see your room before agreeing to a booking.

Plaza Arquitecto García de Paredes 1, 18009 Granada. ☎ **95-822-14-68.** Fax 95-822-64-04. www.h-alhambra palace.es. 126 units. 185€ ($222) double; 262€ ($314) suite. Rates include breakfast. AE, DC, MC, V. Free parking. Bus: 30. **Amenities:** Restaurant; bar; business center; 24-hr. room service; babysitting; laundry service; rooms for those w/limited mobility. *In room:* A/C, TV, dataport, minibar, hair dryer, safe.

Parador de Granada ★★★

This most famous parador in Spain—and the hardest to get into—is within the grounds of the Alhambra. It's rich with mudéjar- and Arab-inspired architectural touches, including splashing fountains, wraparound loggias, gardens laden with wisteria, and aromatic herbs. Unfortunately, it is consistently booked, so reserve as far as possible in advance. The decor is tasteful, and the rich Andalusian ambience evokes a lot of history. From the terrace you have views of the Generalife gardens and the Sacromonte caves. The guest rooms are roomy and comfortable and have bathrooms with tub/shower combos. Ask for a room in the older section, which is furnished with antiques; rooms in the more modern wing are less inspired.

The parador itself is within a former convent founded by the Catholic monarchs after they conquered the city in 1492. Before that, the building was part of the Muslim complex that included the Alhambra and a mosque built in the mid-1300s by Caliph Yusuf I. The bodies of Ferdinand and Isabella were placed here until their tombs could be readied in the cathedral.

Real de la Alhambra s/n, 18009 Granada. ☎ **95-822-14-40.** Fax 95-822-22-64. www.parador.es. 36 units. 214€ ($257) double. AE, DC, MC, V. Free parking. Bus: 30. **Amenities:** Restaurant; bar; limited room service; laundry service/dry cleaning; currency exchange; rooms for those w/limited mobility. *In room:* A/C, TV, dataport, minibar, hair dryer.

Royal Burials, Royal Ironies

Even if you're not staying at the **Parador de Granada** (see above), try to make a detour into gardens. During its role in the 16th century as a Franciscan monastery, it adapted an existing Muslim structure as the temporary burial chamber of the ardently catholic Queen Isabella (1451–1504), whose body rested here for 17 years. A few years later when Ferdinand (1452–1516) died, he, too, was interred here temporarily. Eventually, both Isabella and Ferdinand were disinterred and moved to more luxurious digs in the Capilla Real, now an annex of Granada's enormous cathedral. The Capilla Real was originally envisioned as a royal mausoleum for the descendants of the Catholic kings, but it had not been completed at the time of Ferdinand and Isabella's death.

Today, within the parador's gardens, birds twitter and flowers bloom. A simple plaque denotes the former burial site of the Catholic monarchs. Ironically, the surrounding motifs were developed by their hated enemies, the Muslims, and some of the lavish calligraphy that sheathes the walls of the burial chamber refer to Allah. One wonders if Isabella–who generally tended to shun excess luxury of any type—ever realized this. If she had, would her spirit have rested peacefully?

Saray 🐦🐦 Stay here if you want the most comfortable and best-run hotel in town. In terms of room size, amenities, and luxuries, this hotel is *número uno* in Granada, although it lacks the personal charm of the boutique hotels. Built in 1991, next to the Palacio de Congresos, it is much more modern than the Alhambra Palace, which is the place to stay if you're seeking grand, old Granada tradition. The Saray rises nine floors and is U-shaped, with a trio of exterior elevators. In honor of Granada's former conquerors, postmodern Arabesque overtones are evoked, including a Moorish garden, various mosaics, plaster fretwork, and fountains, Fine furnishings and the rare antique add grace notes to the public lounges. Plenty of mirrors, wooden furniture, overstuffed armchairs, and elegant fabrics enhance the luxe touches throughout.

Bedrooms are midsize to spacious, and superior in most ways with plenty of amenities and lots of stylish comfort, offering everything from bedside controls to mirrored closets, from double-glazed windows to tiled bathrooms with tub/shower combo and robes. We prefer the alcove accommodations, which have more space and charming loveseats. You might not feel quite like a sultan here, but the staff tries to provide the services and comfort of a deluxe palace.

Paseo de Enrique Tierno Galván, 18006 Granada. ✆ **95-813-00-09.** Fax 95-812-91-61. www.h-santos.es. com. 230 units. 175€ ($210) double; from 260€ ($312) suite. AE, DC, MC, V. Bus: 11. **Amenities:** Restaurant; cafeteria; bar; outdoor pool; 24-hr. room service; babysitting; laundry service/dry cleaning; nonsmoking rooms. *In room:* A/C, TV, dataport, minibar, hair dryer, safe.

MODERATE

Carmen de Santa Inés 🐦 *Value* Graciously restored, Carmen de Santa Inés will house you stylishly, comfortably, and affordably. Lying in the historical Albaicín section, this was an old Moorish house on a quiet street. Much of yesterday has been retained, including original wooden beams, a private patio, Arab fountains, a marble staircase and columns—all very romantic. Bedrooms are small but filled with comfort and character. If you've got a few extra bucks to spare, rent "El Mirador," with its balcony terrace opening onto panoramic views of the Alhambra and the cityscape. There is no elevator, and only breakfast is served.

You could also stay at the parent hotel, the first-class **Hotel Carmen** at Acera del Darro 62 (© **95-825-83-00**). Because it's more tranquil, this inn has a slight edge on its sibling, Palacio de Santa Inés (see below), which is only 2 blocks away.

Placeta de Porras 7, 18018 Granada. © **95-822-63-80.** Fax 95-822-44-04. 9 units. 95€–125€ ($114–$150) double; 200€ ($240) suite. AE, DC, MC, V. Parking: 11€ ($13). Bus: 30, 31, or 32. **Amenities:** Laundry. *In room:* A/C, TV, minibar, hair dryer, safe.

Casa Morisca ★★ *(Finds)*   We thought we couldn't top the charms of the two Ineses: Carmen de Santa Inés and Palacio de Santa Inés. Then we slept at Casa Morisca and fell in love again, fickle us. In the historic lower district of Albayzin, at the foot of the Alhambra, this house dates from the end of the 15th century. In the patio you can still see the remains of a Moorish pool and galleries supported by pilasters and columns. The interior was kept and restored, although the facade was given a 17th-century overlay. Bedrooms are individually decorated in an old style but with all modern comforts such as private bathrooms equipped with showers and tubs. No hotel in Granada has been restored with such respect for its past life. For example, a turret lookout above the upper floor, which appeared in an 1859 photograph, was reconstructed accurately in 1998. All the 17th-century iron and carpentry work has been cleaned and restored. Local craftsmen worked only with the original materials of the building, including clay tiles and lime mortar.

Cuesta de la Victoria 9, 18010 Granada. © **95-822-11-00.** Fax 95-821-57-96. www.hotelcasamorisca.com. 14 units. 140€ ($168) double; 190€ ($228) suite. AE, DC, MC, V. Free parking. Bus: 31 or 32. **Amenities:** Breakfast room; limited room service; laundry service/dry cleaning; rooms for those w/limited mobility. *In room:* A/C, TV, dataport, minibar, hair dryer, safe.

El Ladrón de Agua   Set behind a frescoed 16th-century Italianate facade on one of Granada's impossibly narrow, evocative streets, this is the newest (2004) of the historic "boutique" hotels of the Albaicín. It's simpler, more stripped down, and less plush than these competitors. The name, El Ladrón de Agua (The Water Thief), references a collection of poems by Nobel Prize–winning Andalusian poet Juan Ramón Jiménez. Some of his verses are stenciled or highlighted in the form of metallic cutouts, or projected with laser beams onto the stark white walls of the hotel's artfully minimalist interior. You'll also find high-tech lighting and fountains from which—in a nod to the hotel's name—water dribbles out imperceptibly and is "stolen" away into drains virtually concealed from view. Whereas each of the bedrooms is comfortable and tasteful, with high ceilings, tiled bathrooms with shower, and a combination of modern and antique accents; eight also have views over the Alhambra, which is perched high atop a forested hilltop, on the opposite side of the river. Each room is named after a poem, or a snippet of a poem, by either Jiménez or his hosts during his sojourns in Granada, artistic luminaries Federico García Lorca or Manuel de Falla.

Carrera del Darro 13, 18010 Granada. © **95-821-50-40.** www.ladrondeagua.com. 15 units. 90€–135€ ($108–$162) double; 175€ ($210) suite. AE, DC, MC, V. Bus: 30 or 32. **Amenities:** Breakfast room; laundry service. *In room:* A/C, minibar, TV, dataport, safe.

Hostal América ★★ (Value) This is one of only two hotels on the actual grounds of the Alhambra, the other being the much more expensive (and much better accessorized) Parador de Granada, whose garden gates lie a few steps away. Overall, it's a fun, charming, and very unusual place to stay, far from the cacophony of Granada's commercial core, and curiously, almost eerily, quiet after the daily hordes depart from the grounds of the Alhambra.

Hostal América was built in the mid–19th century as a private home, then transformed in 1928 into the charming, intimate, small-scale Victorian-era hotel you see today. Queen Sofía paid a visit here in 1992. There's a courtyard in back that's festooned with grapevines and dotted with blue-and-white ceramic tiles. Antiques, curios, and photos of past literati who have stayed here abound, especially in the hotel's eccentric, intensely personalized and cozily cluttered living room. Although small, the rooms are comfortably and decently furnished, and well-maintained, with compact bathrooms with tile sheathings and shower stalls. None has its own TV.

Real de la Alhambra 53, 18009 Granada. © **95-822-74-71.** Fax 95-822-74-70. www.hotelamericagranada. com. 17 units. 107€ ($128) double; 135€ ($162) suite. DC, MC, V. Parking nearby 12€ ($14). Bus: 30. **Amenities:** Restaurant (breakfast and lunch only); outdoor patio and bar; room for those w/limited mobility. *In room:* A/C, hair dryer.

Hotel Palacio Santa Inés ★★ This *antigua casa,* consisting of two small mudéjar buildings constructed in the first third of the 16th century, is one of the most enchanting places to stay in Granada. It's in the colorful Albaicín district, about a 5-minute walk from the Alhambra. The painstakingly restored little palace was in complete ruins until the mid-1990s. Today it's a lovely, graceful inn, even a bit luxe. A 16th-century courtyard, time-aged wooden beamed ceilings, and silver chandeliers take you back to yesterday, as do the restored frescoes on the walls of the patio (said to have been painted by a student of Raphael). The rooms are medium-size, some have small sitting rooms, and several open onto views of Granada. Much of the furniture is antique, and the modern bathrooms have tub/shower combos. The hotel is a block northwest of Carrera del Darro and Iglesia de Santa Ana.

Cuesta de Santa Inés 9, 18010 Granada. © **95-822-23-62.** Fax 95-822-24-65. www.palaciosantaines.com. 35 units. 125€–155€ ($150–$186) double; 240€ ($288) suite. AE, DC, MC, V. Parking 16€ ($19). Bus: 30 or 32. **Amenities:** Breakfast room; babysitting; laundry service/dry cleaning; nonsmoking rooms. *In room:* A/C, TV, minibar, hair dryer, safe.

Hotel Reina Cristina In the center of the city, a 3-minute walk from the cathedral in a renovated 19th-century mansion called a *casa granadina,* this hotel had a role in a dark moment of Granada's history. Here, the right-wing forces of Generalísimo Franco abducted one of the nation's greatest writers and Granada's favorite son, the poet/playwright Federico García Lorca. He was taken 3km (2 miles) away and executed. The family-operated hotel now exudes grace, charm, and tranquillity, and the service is helpful. All the small rooms have undergone extensive renovation, although many of the original furnishings remain. The bathrooms have been renewed, all with tub/shower combos.

Calle Tablas 4, 18002 Granada. © **95-825-32-11.** Fax 95-825-57-28. www.hotelreinacristina.com. 43 units. 106€ ($127) double; 130€ ($156) triple. Rates include breakfast buffet. AE, DC, MC, V. Parking 12€ ($14). Bus: 5. **Amenities:** Restaurant; bar; limited room service; laundry service/dry cleaning; rooms for those w/limited mobility. *In room:* A/C, TV, dataport, minibar, hair dryer, safe.

Hotel Triunfo Granada ★ Set immediately adjacent to the early medieval stone archway known as the Puerto de Elvira, in the 19th-century commercial core of Granada, this is a relatively staid, comfortably upscale, and much-modernized hotel. Its facade is about a century old. The interior is much more modern than the exterior implies, thanks to a 1989 renovation that left most of the public and private surfaces shimmering with thousands of slabs of glossy marble and stone. The staff at this small-scale hotel is uniformed, efficient, and very polite. Bedrooms are conservatively furnished in a contemporary style. Mostly midsize, they are comfortable, with occasional touches of luxury; each comes with a medium-size bathroom in beige marble equipped with tub and shower. The clientele? A Spanish hotel critic recently referred to them as "business drones"—a bit harsh, perhaps, although the Triunfo does attract a huge percentage of clients in Granada for commercial interest.

Plaza del Triunfo 10, 18010 Granada. ✆ **95-820-74-44.** Fax 95-827-90-17. www.h-triunfo-granada.com. 37 units. 130€ ($156) double. Rates include breakfast. Bus: 3 or 33. **Amenities:** Restaurant next to hotel; room service (8am–11:30pm); laundry service/dry cleaning; nonsmoking rooms; rooms for those w/limited mobility. *In room:* A/C, TV, dataport, minibar, hair dryer, safe.

Princesa Ana ⭐   Lying only 200m (656 ft.) from the train station, this four-story, government-rated four-star hotel is one of the leading choices of Granada, yet charges reasonable rates. Devotees consider it much better than its competitor, Reina Christina, and on par with the Inglaterra; the latter is slightly more cutting edge. The styling throughout is vaguely neoclassical, and dates from 1988. The hotel received its last major overhaul in 1996. Bedrooms are midsize and furnished in both traditional and modern pieces, with fabrics coordinated on the beds and the draperies, the floors softly carpeted. Contemporary and tasteful wooden furnishings are used throughout, and the bathrooms come with a combination tub/shower. All in all, this hotel is serviceable and reliable, but not spectacular.

Moments **Cave Living near the Alhambra**

Usually when searching for accommodations, "cave" isn't one of the options at the top of your list. Surprisingly, however, this offbeat living arrangement appeals to hundreds of visitors to Granada.

In the mid–20th century, the caves were viewed as hangouts for disreputable schemers who fed off the tourist trade. Today, however, staying in one of the caves is viewed as a fun adventure and an option possibility for the general public.

A cave has little in common, of course, with a conventional hotel, which is why we don't recommend first-time visitors stay in one. But if you're on a second or third visit, and you're intrigued by the novelty of a cave, you can contact **La Glicinia,** Camino Nuevo del Cementerio, Cuesta de la Glicinia, 18009 Granada (✆ **95-822-17-20),** about renting one of these dwellings. The couple that runs this agency, Alberto and Rosa, rent out caves on a short-term basis, charging 121€ ($145) for two persons, with breakfast included. Only cash is accepted.

Each of the apartments is fully furnished, containing a bedroom, working kitchen, fireplace, and the memorabilia of a family that might have lived there. These apartments is near the Alhambra Palace Hotel and within walking distance of the Alhambra itself. Bus no. 34 from Plaza Nueva in the lower town runs here every hour.

Av. de la Constitución 6, 18014 Granada. ✆ **95-828-74-47.** Fax 95-827-39-54. 61 units. 135€ ($162) double; 235€ ($282) suite. AE, DC, MC, V. Bus: 15 or 18. **Amenities:** Restaurant; bar; room service (8am–noon); babysitting; laundry service/dry cleaning; nonsmoking rooms. *In room:* A/C, TV, dataport, minibar, hair dryer, safe.

INEXPENSIVE

Casa del Aljarife 🐾 *Finds*   In the Albaicín district 4 blocks from the Plaza Santa Ana, this little nugget is known only to a few discerning travelers. In a recently renovated 17th-century structure, it has a large patio with trees and a Moorish fountain with views of the Alhambra. A family concern, the *casa* is well cared for and has a welcoming atmosphere. Each medium-size or spacious room has its own unique style, with a tasteful Andalusian style. The bathrooms have shower stalls. Owner Christian Most is gracious, apologizing for the lack of luxuries by pointing out that "everything you need" is virtually outside the door.

Placeta de la Cruz Verde 2, 18010 Granada. ✆/fax **95-822-24-25.** www.granadainfo.com/most. 4 units. 89€ ($107) double; 108€ ($130) triple; 124€–168€ ($149–$202) suite. MC, V. Bus: 31 or 32. **Amenities:** Breakfast room; TV salon. *In room:* A/C.

Casa del Capitel Nazari 🐾 *Value*   This is one of at least four boutique hotels that opened during the early millennium within the cramped but evocative medieval neighborhood known as the Albaicín, a few steps uphill from the Plaza Nueva. Situated within a private, patio-centered home built at least 400 years ago, and the beneficiary of a river of funds spent on renovations and modern comforts like plumbing, it's a cozy, appealing mixture of antique and modern. The hotel's name derives from the oldest of the stone columns that support the two stories of wraparound balconies. Carved during the Nasrid (in Spanish, *Nazari*) dynasty, before the reconquest of the city by Ferdinand and Isabella, it's at least a thousand years old. Of the many columns within the building's structure it has by far the most ornate carving. Bedrooms are simple, not overly large, and accented with many hand-hewn antique features, including beams. All are nonsmoking.

Cuesta Aceituneros 6, 18010 Granada. ✆ **95-821-52-60.** Fax 95-821-58-06. www.hotelcasacapitel.com. 17 units. 70€–95€ ($84–$114) double. AE, DC, MC, V. Parking 10€ ($12) per day. Bus: 31 or 32. **Amenities:** Breakfast room; laundry service. *In room:* A/C, TV, dataport, minibar, hair dryer.

Hotel Anacapri   In the center of Granada next to the cathedral, the unpretentious Anacapri lies a 10-minute walk from the Alhambra. The rooms are a bit small, but the medley of old furniture with modern touches is comfortable. The best units have antique windows, jutting beams, and terraces overlooking street scenes. The bathrooms are equipped with showers and tubs. The Salón Social is a public area with tiled walls where you can relax while contemplating an 18th-century patio with a central fountain.

Calle Joaquín Costa 7, 18010 Granada. ✆ **95-8222-74-77.** Fax 95-822-89-09. www.hotelanacapri.com. 49 units. 72€–98€ ($86–$118) double. AE, DC, MC, V. Parking 16€ ($19). Bus: 31 or 32. **Amenities:** Bar; laundry service/dry cleaning. *In room:* A/C, TV, safe.

Hotel Guadalupe   This building sits beside an inclined road leading up to the Alhambra. Rising five floors, it uses lots of marble and stonework to add architectural character. Built in 1969, the hotel is rated three stars by the government. Its major drawback is that it's an oasis for the tour bus set. Nonetheless, it remains one of the better choices in this price range, a feeling enhanced by such rustic decor as arches, a beamed lobby, wrought iron, marble floors, and a fireplace. The better bedrooms lie within the hotel's main core, the less desirable assigned to an annex a few yards away. Furnishings evoke a large, low-key country hotel, with built-in closets, plus rustic tile floors or carpeting. The most desirable accommodations open onto private balconies or terraces. The compact bathrooms come with tub and shower and, usually, a Jacuzzi.

Paseo de la Sabica s/n, 18009 Granada. © **95-822-34-23.** Fax 95-822-37-98. www.hotelguadalupe.es. 58 units. 96€ ($115) double. AE, DC, MC, V. Parking 11€ ($13). Bus: 30. **Amenities:** Restaurant; bar; limited room service; babysitting; laundry service/dry cleaning. *In room:* A/C, TV, minibar, hair dryer.

Macía Plaza   This attractive 1970s hotel at the bottom of the hill leading up to the Alhambra is a real bargain for a government-rated three-star. The location on the heartbeat Plaza Nueva is definitely for those who want to be in the eye of the storm. All the small guest rooms are functionally but comfortably furnished with good beds and bathrooms that are tiled and come with shower stalls. Standard wood furniture is used throughout the three-story building, which is graced with balconies and wide windows, making it look like an antique house. Following a thorough 2002 renovation, the hotel is much improved.

Plaza Nueva 4, 18010 Granada. © **95-822-75-36.** Fax 95-822-75-33. www.maciahoteles.com. 44 units. 68€ ($82) double. AE, DC, MC, V. Parking 16€ ($19). Bus: 3. **Amenities:** Breakfast lounge; laundry service; nonsmoking rooms; rooms for those w/limited mobility. *In room:* A/C, TV, dataport, safe.

4 Where to Dine

EXPENSIVE

Asador de Castilla CASTILIAN   In the Cathedral district, this longtime favorite stands on a small square near the old town hall (Ayuntamiento). It's an authentic Castilian *asador* (barbecue) restaurant patronized by many of the city's leading politicians and journalists, and Andalusian families celebrating rites of passage. It lies behind a solid stone facade, with medieval coats-of-arms and stone carvings. The chefs are famous locally for their roast lamb with herbs, their refried beans with strips of Iberian ham, and for their various *guisos caseros,* which are homemade stews, mostly meat, but also containing plenty of fresh vegetables. Even though Granada is inland, the chefs also manage to serve fresh fish.

Calle Escudo del Carmen 17. © **95-822-29-10.** Reservations recommended. Main courses 18€–21€ ($22–$25). AE, DC, MC, V. Wed–Mon 1–4pm and 9pm–midnight. Closed Aug. Bus: 4 or 6.

Carmen de San Miguel ANDALUSIAN   On the hill leading up to the Alhambra, this likable restaurant offers spectacular views over the city center. Meals are served in a glassed-in dining room and patio-style terrace, where the banks of flowers are changed seasonally. Specialties include grilled hake, a pâté of partridge with a vinaigrette sauce, Iberian ham with Manchego cheese, and a casserole of monkfish and fresh clams. The food, although good, doesn't quite match the view. The wines are from throughout the country, with a strong selection of Riojas.

Plaza de Torres Bermejas 3. © **95-822-67-23.** Reservations recommended. Main courses 15€–20€ ($18–$24); menú del día 30€–44€ ($36–$53). AE, DC, MC, V. Mon–Sat 1:30–4pm and 8:30–11:30pm; winter Sun 1:30–4pm. Bus: 30 or 32.

El Claustro ⭐ SPANISH/CONTINENTAL   This stylish and soothing restaurant is set within what was originally built in 1540 as a cloister for nuns. Its soaring and heavily beamed ceiling exudes Renaissance artistry, and windows overlook the graceful symmetry of an arcaded courtyard where nuns used to pray. Some diners come here for the chance to view the unusual hotel that contains it (see "Where to Stay," earlier in this chapter). Others come with the understanding that the place has become an "important" dining venue for the political and media *grandées* of Granada since its opening late in 2001.

Menu items are savory, well conceived, and imaginative, and include such starters as a salad of marinated rabbit; red lentils with razor shell clams; Granada-style salad of cod with oranges; and pickled sardines served with a cream of asparagus soup. Main courses change several times a year, but we've enjoyed roasted mackerel with a chop suey of cod; angler fish with foie gras and marrow; and roasted baby goat with potatoes. There's even a filet of kangaroo with pink peppercorns and sweet tomato sauce. Dessert might be banana fritters with coconut sorbet, or a sublime tiramisu.

In the AC Hotel Palacio Santa Paula, Gran Vía de Colón 31, 18001 Granada. ℂ **95-880-57-40.** Reservations recommended. Main courses 19€–24€ ($23–$29). AE, DC, MC, V. Daily 1:30–4pm and 8:30–11pm. Bus: 3, 6, 9, or 11.

Las Tinajas ✦ ANDALUSIAN   This restaurant, a short walk from the cathedral, is named for the huge amphorae depicted on its facade. For more than 3 decades it has been the culinary showcase of José Alvarez. The decor is classical Andalusian, with wood walls adorned with ceramic tiles and pictures of old Granada. Diners are surrounded by antique ornaments interspersed with modern elements and fixtures. There's a convivial but crowded bar where both locals and visitors order Andalusian wines and a wide variety of delicious tapas. To start, try the cold zucchini-and-almond cream soup or the white beet stuffed with ham and cheese. Follow with a delectable monkfish cooked with local herbs or the peppered sirloin steak. Desserts include Moorish cake with almonds and raspberries, made from a recipe left over from the days of the sultan, and a hearty regional pudding with coffee-flavored cream.

Martínez Campos 17. ℂ **95-825-43-93.** Reservations recommended. Main courses 8€–22€ ($10–$26); set menu 28€–32€ ($34–$38). AE, DC, MC, V. Daily noon–5pm and 8pm–midnight. Closed July 15–Aug 15. Bus: 4 or 6.

Los Santanderinos ✦✦ SPANISH/ANDALUSIAN   This is arguably the best restaurant in Granada, lying in the new part of town near the Palacio des Congregos. It is a genuinely wonderful dining choice. Don't be disappointed by its location on a banal-looking expanse of concrete, within a modern-day apartment complex that's a universe away from the touristy neighborhoods around the cathedral and the Alhambra. Inside, the venue is charming, with a small tapas bar near the entrance, an immaculate and rather formal dining room that's packed with members of the local bourgeoisie and business community, and a charming and attentive staff.

Chef Jesús Diego Díaz, whose name crops up frequently in Spain's gastronomic press, prepares dishes that include green asparagus "in the style of Santanderinos" that's artfully interspersed with Iberian ham, shavings of cheese, and ingredients we couldn't even guess at. A platter of braised exotic mushrooms with Iberian ham sets a perfect autumn tone. Tasty main courses include stuffed squid covered with a squid-ink-based black sauce, as well as a wide medley of beef, lamb, and other fish dishes. Even if you order something as simple as a green salad it will resemble a work of art, laboriously arranged like a sculpture and perfectly dressed. Come here distinctly for the food and the insight into modern-day, nontouristic Granada. It's worth the trip.

Albahaca 1 (Urbanización Jardín de la Reina, near the Puente del Genil). ℂ **95-812-83-35.** Main courses 13€–22€ ($15–$26); set-price menus 29€–32€ ($34–$39). MC, V. Mon–Sat 1–3:30pm and 8–11:30pm. Bus: 1 or 3.

Ruta del Velleta ✦✦ ANDALUSIAN   Despite its 1976 origins as an unpretentious roadhouse restaurant, this place rapidly evolved into what's usually decreed the best restaurant in or around Granada. It's in the hamlet of Cenés de la Vega, about 6km (3½ miles) northwest of Granada's center, and has six dining rooms of various sizes, each decorated with a mix of English and Andalusian furniture and accessories. (They include a worthy collection of hand-painted ceramics from the region, many of which hang from the ceilings.) The owners are a pair of Granada-born brothers, Miguel and José Pedraza, who direct the impeccable service rituals. Menu items change with the season but are likely to include roast suckling pig; roasted game birds like pheasant and partridge, often served with Rioja wine sauce; preparations of fish and shellfish, including monk-fish with Andalusian herbs and strips of Serrano ham; filet steak in morel-studded cream sauce; and a dessert specialty of frozen rice pudding on a bed of warm chocolate sauce. The wine list is one of the region's most comprehensive.

Carretera Vieja de la Sierra Nevada Km 5.5, Cenés de la Vega. ℭ **95-848-61-34.** Reservations recommended. Main courses 15€–22€ ($18–$26); fixed-price menus 45€ ($54) without wine. AE, DC, MC, V. Sun 1–4pm; Mon–Sat 1–4pm and 8pm–midnight. Bus: 13 or 33.

MODERATE

Alhabaca ✮ *Finds* ANDALUSIAN/SPANISH   You'd have to be in Granada for quite a while to discover this local favorite, a little *mesón* (inn) in a century-old building. Owner Javier Jiménez seats 30 diners at 10 tables in an old-fashioned restaurant decorated in a rustic style with bare white walls. The traditional dishes he serves are unpretentious and tasty, especially the *salmorejo* (creamy tomato gazpacho) and *ensalada de dos salsas* (a green salad with two dressings). The stuffed salmon is marvelous, as is *pastel de berenjena con salmón marinado* (layered pastry with eggplant and marinated salmon). For dessert, we recommend the velvety yogurt mousse.

Calle Varela 17. ℭ **95-822-49-23.** Reservations recommended on weekends. Main courses 8€–15€ ($10–$18); *menú del día* 15€ ($18). MC, V. Tues–Sat 1–4pm and 8–11pm; Sun 1–4pm. Closed Aug. Bus: 8, 13, or C.

Corrada del Carbón ANDALUSIAN   A cozy, convivial place whose interior resembles the slightly cluttered patio of a prosperous farmhouse deep in the Iberian countryside, this restaurant is one of the town center's busiest. You'll pass through a busy tapas bar before hitting a dining room ringed with multilevel verandas whose heavy timbers are softened by hand-painted porcelain and potted verdant plants. Many menu items are grilled, each well-prepared and succulent and redolent of the herbs and other bounty of the Spanish countryside. Beef sirloin with cheese, and oxtail are two of the most popular items.

Mariana Pineda 8. ℭ **95-822-38-10.** Main courses 12€–17€ ($15–$21); AE, DC, MC, V. Sun 1–4pm; Mon–Sat 1–4pm and 8:30pm–midnight. Bus: 4 or 11.

El Huerto de Juan Ranas ✮ *Finds* HISPANO/ISLAMIC   Come when the restaurant is closed and you'll see nothing more than a blank white wall pierced by the outline of a forbidding door. Return at night when the candles are lit and floodlights shine across the ravine upon the Alhambra. This restaurant was established in the late 1990s within what had been a dignified and antique private home. Today, mudéjar-inspired tilework and playful streams of water create a Hispano-Moorish environment of enormous charm. Members of the family of King Fahd of Saudi Arabia are said to have abandoned their vacation home in Marbella once or twice for meals here.

The easier dining venue here involves remaining upstairs on the vine-covered tapas terrace, where views of the floodlit Alhambra sweep outward into the night. Gastronomes, good friends, and romantics, however, descend into the dining room. Clients are encouraged to remain as long as they like, without worrying about giving up their tables for a second seating. Dishes incorporate the Spanish and Arab traditions, and might include Iberian steak with caramelized onions; a Moroccan version of *pastela* (meat cakes with eggplant); lamb couscous with vegetables; rack of lamb with crackling herbs; eggplant with honey sauce; and scrambled eggs with eggplant and fresh salmon. Unless you're familiar with the upper reaches of the Albaicín neighborhood after dark, we advise traveling to and from this difficult-to-find restaurant by taxi.

Calle de Atarazana 8 (Mirador de San Nicolás). (✆) **95-828-69-25.** Reservations recommended for the restaurant, not necessary for the tapas terrace. Tapas and *raciones* 4.50€–15€ ($5.40–$18); main courses 14€–24€ ($16–$29); set-price menus 50€ ($59). AE, DC, MC, V. Tues–Sun 8–11:30pm. Bus: 32.

La Mimbre ANDALUSIAN/GRANADINO   While exploring the Alhambra and the summer palace of Generalife, there is no more conveniently located dining spot than this little eatery that is tucked, surprisingly, right into the walls of the sultan's palace itself. Over the years it has been a popular place for many poets and artists who have flocked to Granada. The building itself dates from the end of the 19th century and has a traditional decor. The garden with its old Andalusian fountain is a romantic choice for dining on a summer evening. The menu is backed by a good and affordable selection of regional wines. Oxtail is one of the chef's specialties. He also features cod in a smoked cod appetizer platter and as a main dish served with a succulent shellfish sauce. Another of our favorite dishes, the salad of string beans and slices of cooked ham, has competition in the form of *choto al ajillo* (braised kid studded with garlic) that we sampled on a recent visit.

Av. del Generalife, Alhambra. (✆) **95-822-22-76.** Main courses 12€–20€ ($14–$24). AE, MC, V. Oct–Apr daily noon–4pm; May–Sept daily 8:30–11:30pm. Closed part of Jan. Bus: 1, 6, or 7.

La Piccola Italia ITALIAN   This elegantly decorated and inviting restaurant several blocks south of Plaza de la Trinidad and the Cathedral is Granada's best Italian restaurant and a nice change of pace from Spanish food. Tables are set with beautiful linens, drawings adorn the walls, and there is much use of glass and wooden furniture. The waiters are among the more skilled in Granada. Many families come here for pizzas straight from the ovens, but the pasta dishes are also good, especially the ravioli filled with fresh spinach and a regional cheese. The chefs are also adept at such dishes as a perfectly fried and seasoned chicken cutlet or salmon in a creamy white sauce. Desserts are homemade and luscious.

Obispo Hurtado 3. (✆) **95-825-96-78.** Reservations required. Main courses 12€–24€ ($14–$29). Daily 1:30–4:30pm and 8:30pm–midnight. Bus: 2, 7, or 11.

Parador de Granada ★★ ANDALUSIAN/SPANISH   Even if you can't afford to stay at this luxurious parador (see "Where to Stay," earlier in this chapter), the most famous in Spain, consider heading here for a tranquil retreat after you've battled the tourist hordes in the Alhambra itself. The dining room is spacious, the service is polite, and you gaze upon the rose gardens and a distant view of the Generalife. Lunch is the best time to dine here, because the terrace overlooking the palace is open then. A light outdoor lunch of sandwiches and salads can be ordered on the a la carte menu if you're not up for heavy Spanish food in the heat of the day. The cuisine is competent in every way, although at no point rising to any culinary achievement. When in doubt, order the Andalusian specialties rather than the Spanish national dishes, as most of the chefs are Andalusian.

Moments   Tea, Chocolate-Dipped Doughnuts & More

The people of Granada are rediscovering their Islamic roots in laid-back lounges that serve mint tea, traditional Arab pastries, and tapas. The best of these is **Al-Andalús,** Calle Calderería Vieja 34 (© **95-822-46-41**), where patrons even pass a traditional water pipe. Our favorite time to visit is late afternoon and early evening, when, against a backdrop of blue tiles and wooden furniture, you can order their fresh salad made with oranges and lemon or a bowl of gazpacho. More filling selections include honey-coated Moroccan lamb and *pinchitos monunos* (pieces of pork on a skewer with vegetables). Main plates cost from 9€ to 18€ ($11–$22). The salon is open daily from 11:30am to 2am.

López Mezquita Café Pastelería, Calle de los Reyes Católicos 3941 (© **95-822-12-05**), is in the center of the city. With its rustic decor, the cafe has a warm, inviting ambience. You can enjoy various cheeses from the province of Granada, along with spicy chorizo sausage pies. Pasty specialties, costing from 2€ ($2.40), include *pastela monunos,* which can be filled with many different ingredients—meat, chicken, prunes, dried grapes, nuts, and more. Our favorite is *cuajado de carnaval,* a mousselike concoction made with seasonal fruit. The turnovers filled with fish or chicken are another tasty specialty. Hours are Monday to Saturday 9am to 11pm.

At around 6pm, many locals indulge in *chocolate con churros* (doughnut sticks dipped in hot chocolate). Although this may be an acquired taste for some, chocoholics will love it. Many little cafes around the cathedral serve this treat, but you can also enjoy it at virtually any cafe within the city limits.

Real de la Alhambra. © **95-822-14-40.** Main courses 10€–18€ ($12–$22); fixed-price menu 25€ ($30). AE, DC, MC, V. Daily 1–4pm and 8:30–11pm. Bus: 30 or 32.

Restaurante Cunini SEAFOOD/SPANISH   The array of seafood specialties served at Cunini, perhaps 100 in all, starts with the tapas served at the long stand-up bar. Many guests move on after a drink or two to the paneled ground-floor restaurant. Meals often begin with soup—perhaps *sopa sevillana* (with ham, shrimp, and whitefish). Also popular is a deep fry of small fish called a *fritura Cunini,* with other specialties including rice with seafood, *zarzuela* (seafood stew), smoked salmon, and grilled shrimp. The Plaza de la Pescadería is adjacent to the Gran Vía de Colón just below the cathedral. Outdoor tables fill part of a lovely old square, and they are protected with canvas canopies from the wind and rain.

Plaza de la Pescadería 14. © **95-825-07-77.** Reservations recommended. Main courses 13€–33€ ($16–$40); fixed-price menu 19€ ($23). AE, DC, MC, V. Tues–Sat noon–4pm and 8pm–midnight; Sun noon–4pm. Bus: 5 or 11.

Velázquez ANDALUSIAN/GALICIAN   This restaurant was founded in 1989 by the Gastronomic Society of Andalusia. Named for Spain's greatest golden age artist, it lies near two landmark squares, Puerta de Elvira and Plaza del Triunfo. The decoration is in the typical Spanish style with a wood-beamed dining room upstairs and hams hanging from the ceiling at the bodega on the ground floor. Foodies who like to eat well and affordably, but not flashily, appreciate the chef's brand of cooking. Offerings change with the season, but we recently enjoyed a pâté of pheasant liver as an appetizer. One of the chef's signature dishes has Moroccan overtones: honey-coated baked lamb. Also in the Moroccan style is oven-baked lamb flavored with mint. Fish fanciers will also like the braised medallions of monkfish *(lomitos de rape).* Desserts are luscious but tend to be very, very sweet (the way locals prefer them).

Emilio Orozco 1, Triunfo. ℭ **95-828-01-09**. Reservations recommended. Main courses 13€–15€ ($16–$18). MC, V. Mon–Sat 1–4pm and 8–11:30pm. Closed Aug. Bus: 3, 10, or 20.

INEXPENSIVE

Antigua Bodega Castanede ⭐ *(Finds* ANDALUSIAN   More and more discerning visitors are going to Andalusia wanting to dine in *típico* joints that rarely see a foreigner. Our nomination for the most rustic local bodega in Granada is the Castanede. It's been here for more than a century and is the oldest of its type in the colorful Albaicín barrio, only a 10-minute walk from the Alhambra, just off the Plaza Nueva. A convivial spot, it's crowded with locals who know they can get tasty but unpretentious food here at low, low prices. Winning high praise is the wide range of tapas—there are 18 stuffed versions of the humble potato alone. Other meals include a variety of thick stews served in traditional clay bowls, ideal if you're visiting on a cold day. You can order a *tabla ibérica,* a selection of small dishes featuring cheese, ham, crab, shrimp, and venison. If you've got a sweet tooth, go for the chocolate mousse or one of the homemade tarts. There are only 11 tables for a proper sit-down meal on these clay floors resting under wooden beams, but many patrons crowd in at the bar.

Calle Elvira 5. ℭ **95-822-63-62**. Main courses 8€–12€ ($10–$14). MC, V. Daily 12:30–5pm and 8pm–1:30am. Bus: 30 or 31.

Botánico VEGETARIAN/ANDALUSIAN   In front of the Botanical Gardens of the University of Granada, this minimalist restaurant is known for vegetarian dishes influenced by the cooking of Asia and North Africa. It's especially popular with university students. The ingredients that go into the dishes are extremely fresh, and the staff works hard to please. We opted for a quichelike "cheese cake" as a savory appetizer. The chefs are known for their creative salads that feature many different flavors and combinations, including mushrooms, sweet red peppers, and dozens of other ingredients; and every day there are about three vegetarian casserole offerings, such as meatless lasagna. Among the more challenging selections is a Moorish-inspired cakelike dish filled with chicken, meat, and cinnamon. A typical Mediterranean salad is served with feta cheese, black olives, roast chicken, and fresh vegetables. The signature dish here is oven-baked duck with couscous. There is a limited but good selection of homemade desserts as well.

Málaga 3. ℭ **95-827-15-98**. Reservations recommended. Main courses 6€–15€ ($7.20–$18). V. Mon–Fri noon–1am; Sat–Sun noon–2am. Bus: 4, 7, or 13.

Cafetería/Cervecería Vía Colón *(Kids* SPANISH   We—and scores of local residents—think it's worth knowing about the good, inexpensive food you can get at this place. In fact, this is one of the best spots behind the cathedral for fast but traditional Spanish food. Although less than a decade old, the restaurant looks much older, thanks to marble countertops, faux baroque decorations, and elaborate ceiling moldings. In summertime, outdoor tables are set up within the shadow of the cathedral's foundations. Perhaps best of all, the salads, burgers, omelets, crepes, and sandwiches available at this well-intentioned, bustling place can give you a break from too much heavy Spanish food. A series of *platos combinados* (pork steaks with rice and vegetables, fish with trimmings) are a good value at 8€ ($9.60) each. Don't come here for a leisurely meal; the setting isn't conducive to lingering and tables turn over quickly.

Gran Vía de Colon 13. © 95-822-07-52. Reservations not accepted. Sandwiches, salads, crepes, burgers, omelets, and platters 2.50€–8€ ($3–$9.60). MC, V. Mon–Fri 8am–2am; Sat 8am–1am. Bus: 30 or 31.

Casa Salvador GRANADINO   A third-generation family restaurant, this tavern has been feeding locals ever since it opened in 1947. Traditional in style, it is decorated with brick walls and Andalusian tiles. Nearby residents flock here for *platos típicos de Granada,* which needs no translation. The chefs specialize in choice cuts of meat and fresh fish. Two of the best main courses are fried swordfish in a shrimp sauce and a platter of savory barbecued meats. For a local favorite, try the oxtail.

Duende 6. © 95-826-19-55. Reservations recommended. Main courses 8€–15€ ($9.60–$18). DC, MC, V. Tues–Sat 1–4pm and 8–11:30pm; Sun 1–4pm. Closed mid-July to Aug 1. Bus: 3, 6, or 12.

Casa Torcuato del Albayzín *Value* ANDALUSIAN   Near Plaza Carniceros, this rustic, Moorish-style restaurant is treasured by Albaicín foodies, who come here for some of the best and the most affordable dishes served in the area. In a simple interior or, at times, on an outdoor terrace you can enjoy traditional recipes dating back many years. Try an appetizer of broad beans and strips of ham, then move on to the sirloin steak stuffed with cheese and ham, or the pastry shell filled with swordfish, very traditional. Looking for something more unusual? Get the lamb omelet.

Pagés 31. © 95-520-28-18. Reservations recommended. Main courses 6€–12€ ($7.20–$14). Sun 11am–4pm; Mon–Sat 11am–4pm and 8pm–midnight. Closed Sun in summer. Bus: 3, 6, or 12.

Chikito SPANISH   Chikito is across from the famous tree-shaded square where García Lorca met with other members of El Rinconcillo (The Little Corner), a group of young men who brought a brief but dazzling cultural renaissance to their hometown in the 1920s. The cafe where they met has now changed its name, and today is a bar/restaurant. In fair weather, guests enjoy drinks and snacks on tables placed in the square; in winter they retreat inside to the tapas bar. Specialties include *sopa sevillana,* shrimp cocktail, Basque hake, baked tuna, oxtail, *zarzuela* (seafood stew), grilled swordfish, and Argentine-style veal steak.

Plaza del Campillo 9. © 95-822-33-64. Reservations recommended. Main courses 12€–22€ ($14–$26); fixed-price menu 19€ ($23). AE, DC, MC, V. Thurs–Tues 1–4pm and 8–11:30pm. Bus: 1, 2, or 7.

La Colina de Almanzara GRANADINO/ANDALUSIAN   Lying in a restored *carmen* (a villalike house) at the foot of the hill leading to the Alhambra, this restaurant is right off Plaza Santa Ana. The multifloored dining room belongs to a culinary group that is dedicated to preserving the traditional recipes of Granada province. Decoration is in a typical Moorish style, with wood and stucco carved ceilings along with wooden artifacts and furnishings. Expect inventive cooking and fresh flavors, such as wild boar with a peach sauce. In the Moroccan tradition, fresh tuna is flavored with mint, and chicken comes with a cinnamon sauce. The signature dish is oven-baked lamb served in its own *jus.*

A first for many diners might be the honeyed eggplant *(berenjenas a la miel)*. If they're on the menu, definitely order the fresh artichokes harvested from neigh-boring fields, served with a savory house vinaigrette.

Santa Ana 16, Albaicín. ✆ **95-822-95-16.** Reservations recommended. Main courses 9€–13€ ($11–$16). MC, V. Daily 1–4pm and 8pm–midnight. Bus: 1, 8, or 22.

Mesón Blas Casa ANDALUSIAN   On its choicest square of the Albaicín, this old favorite is staunchly traditional and housed in an antique structure that was once a private home. It's now been successfully converted to this relatively undiscovered dining room decorated with wooden furniture and tile floors. When the snow starts falling, the fireplace is lit, and the place is enveloped in a warm, cozy ambience.

The chef consistently turns out delicious garlic-studded lamb or leg of pork from a wood-burning stove. The signature dish is swordfish Mosarabe (with prunes, dried grapes, pine nuts, clams, and shrimp). Another intriguing platter is *antología de salmón y gulash* (a goulash of salmon au gratin). That classic local dish, *rabo de toro* (oxtail) also appears.

Plaza San Miguel Bajo 15, Albaicín. ✆ **95-827-31-11.** Reservations recommended. Main courses 8€–10€ ($9.60–$12). MC, V. Tues–Sun noon–5pm and 8pm–midnight. Closed 10 days in Jan. Bus: 1, 8, or 10.

Mesón el Trillo *(Kids (Value* BASQUE   In a typical *carmen,* near Placeta de Car-vajales, this little secret hideaway is treasured by local foodies for its intimate, homey atmosphere and succulent cuisine. To make it even more enticing, it offers a garden terrace with a view of the Alhambra. Mesón el Trillo is also a fam-ily favorite, and, if asked, the chefs will prepare special plates for children, most often a platter of spaghetti or perhaps a chicken dish. Devotees demand that cer-tain favorites stay on the menu, including cod pil-pil with olive oil and garlic and a really fresh-tasting and well-flavored spinach salad with a house-made yogurt dressing. For meat eaters, one of the best dishes is a tender and perfectly grilled sirloin steak with mustard sauce. One specialty you might like to try, especially if you're vegetarian, is a pastry filled with celery and cheese with a quichelike consistency. This undiscovered restaurant is also one of the most affordable in Granada.

Callejón del Aljibe de Trillo 3. ✆ **95-822-51-82.** Reservations recommended. Main courses 9€–12€ ($11–$14). DC, MC, V. Wed–Mon noon–4pm and 8pm–midnight. Bus: 1, 5, or 12.

Mirador de Morayma ANDALUSIAN/SPANISH   Don't expect subtlety or big-city sophistication here—what you'll get is generous portions of good cook-ing and a deep pride in the region's rural traditions. Facing the Alhambra in an antique Renaissance era house in the Albaicín, this is a large, rambling restaurant—really a *carmen*—with a half-dozen dining rooms and three outdoor terraces. According to tradition, Morayma, the wife of Boabdil, last of the Mus-lim kings, was born here. The hardworking staff prepares dishes like gazpacho, roasted goat in wine sauce, slabs of beefsteak with a sauce of aromatic herbs, grilled Spanish sausages, and roasted lamb.

Calle Pianista García Carrillo 2. ✆ **95-822-82-90.** Reservations recommended. Main courses 10€–18€ ($12–$22). AE, MC, V. Mon–Sat 1:30–3:30pm and 8:30–11:30pm; Sun 1:30–3:30pm. Bus: 31 or 32.

O Caña SPANISH   Behind a mosaic-sheathed facade in an antique building in Granada's Jewish Quarter, this restaurant offers a long bar, a salon where you sit down before a meal with a glass of sherry, and a well-managed dining room. The portions are generous, well flavored, and authentic to the old-time traditions of

Andalusia. Since it opened in 1905, the site has turned out endless versions of its specialties (oxtail, grilled *solomillo* of beefsteak, Spanish sausages, grilled duck breast, and endless amounts of suckling pig and roasted lamb). It has earned the loyalty of generations of local families, many of which arrive en masse to dine together, especially on Sundays.

Plaza de Realejo 1. ✆ **95-825-64-70.** Main courses 6€–12€ ($7.20–$14); fixed-price menu 10€ ($12). AE, DC, MC, V. Daily 7am–midnight. Bus: 7, 11, or C.

Pilar del Toro SPANISH/ANDALUSIAN   A particularly evocative place for drinks, tapas, or a full-fledged meal is Pilar del Toro, a multipurpose drinking and dining venue whose charms and diversity only become visible if you take a tour through the labyrinth of its upper dining rooms. The building that houses it is a private home dating from 1879. The interior patio looks like something from a Cuban hacienda, complete with deeply upholstered chairs and sofas. Above you'll find at least three charming dining areas, including a sheltered garden with dining tables and two romantic and intimate candlelit dining rooms. You can enjoy dishes like puff pastry filled with spinach and ham; codfish with a mousseline of avocado; roasted striped bass with mushroom sauce; and sliced or roasted lamb with fig sauce. Dessert might include a chocolate soufflé.

Hospital de Santa Ana 12. ✆ **95-822-38-47.** Reservations recommended for the restaurant, not for the tapas bar. Main courses 9.60€–17€ ($12–$20). AE, DC, MC, V. Daily 1–4pm and 8–11:30pm. Bus: 31 or 32.

Restaurante Sevilla SPANISH/ANDALUSIAN   Attracting a mixed crowd of all ages, the Sevilla is definitely *típico,* but with an upbeat elegance. The "great broads" and "fabulous studs" of the '50s and '60s who came here included Ava Gardner, Marlon Brando, Savador Dalí, André Segovia, Gene Kelly, and Ingrid Bergman. Even before them, the place was discovered by García Lorca, a patron in the 1930s, and Manuel de Falla. Most dishes are at the lower end of the price scale. Our most recent meal here included gazpacho, Andalusian veal, and caramel custard, plus bread and the wine of Valdepeñas. To break the gazpacho monotony, try *sopa virule,* made with pine nuts and chicken breast. For a main course, we recommend the *cordero a la pastoril* (lamb with herbs and paprika). The best dessert is bananas flambé. You can dine inside, which is pleasantly decorated, or on the terrace. The restaurant is opposite the Royal Chapel, near the Plaza Isabel Católica.

Calle Oficios 12. ✆ **95-822-12-23.** Reservations recommended. Main courses 12€–24€ ($14–$29); menú del día 15€ ($18). AE, DC, MC, V. Mon–Sat 1–4:30pm and 8–11:30pm. Bus: 39 or 32.

Terraza Las Tomasas ANDALUSIAN   Very traditionally Moorish in style, this is a tasteful and elegant choice, with beautiful china, crystal, and expensive linen and a panoramic location at the edge of the Sacromonte district. We recommend taking a taxi here, as the alleyways leading to this place are impossibly narrow. The chef applies his own creative touch to traditional favorites, and diners instinctively warm to such fine dishes as smoked octopus Galician style, or veal sirloin with a black pepper sauce and three different types of mustard. Veal might also appear with fresh foie gras and a sauce made of tangerine and prunes. An especially delightful dish is hake with Swiss chard and a shrimp sauce. For dessert, we recommend the chocolate soufflé with orange sauce.

Carril de San Agustín 4. ✆ **95-822-41-88.** Reservations recommended. Main courses 6€–12€ ($7.20–$14). June 1–Sept 30 Mon–Sat 9am–11:30pm; Oct 1–May 31 Tues 8:30–11pm, Wed–Sat 1:30–3:30pm and 8:30–11pm, Sun 1:30–3:30pm. Closed mid-Jan to mid-Feb. Bus: 32.

5 Exploring Granada

Try to spend some time walking around Old Granada. About 3 hours will allow you to see the most interesting sights. No reservations are needed to take a **Guided Walking Tour** through the historical heart of the city. Departures are daily at 10:30am from Plaza del Carmen by the town hall. The cost is 10€ ($12); children under 14 go for free. For more information, call ✆ **600-41-20-51.**

Puerta de Elvira is the gate through which Ferdinand and Isabella made their triumphant entry into Granada in 1492. It was once a grisly place, with the rotting heads of executed criminals hanging from its portals. The quarter surrounding the gate was the Arab section *(morería)* until all the Arabs were driven out of the city after the Reconquest.

One of the most fascinating streets is **Calle de Elvira;** west of it the Albaicín (old Arab quarter) rises on a hill. In the 17th and 18th centuries, many artisans occupied the shops and ateliers along this street and those radiating from it. On Calle de Elvira stands the **Iglesia de San Andrés,** begun in 1528, with a mudéjar bell tower. Much of the church was destroyed in the early 19th century, but several interesting paintings and sculptures remain. Another old church in this area is the **Iglesia de Santiago,** constructed in 1501 and dedicated to St. James, patron saint of Spain. Built on the site of an Arab mosque, it was damaged in an 1884 earthquake. The church contains the tomb of architect Diego de Siloé (1495–1563), who did much to change the face of the city.

Despite its name, the oldest square is the **Plaza Nueva,** which, under the Muslims, was the site of the bridge of the woodcutters. The Darro was covered over here, but its waters still flow underneath the square (which in Franco's time was named the Plaza del General Franco). On the east side of the Plaza Nueva is the 16th-century **Iglesia de Santa Ana,** built by Siloé. Inside its five-nave interior you can see a Churrigueresque reredos and coffered ceiling.

The *corrida* isn't really very popular here, but if you want to check out a bullfight anyway, they're usually limited to the week of the Fiesta de Corpus Christi from May 29 to June 6, or the Día de la Cruz (Day of the Cross) observed on May 3. There's also a fight on the last Sunday in September. **Plaza de Toros,** the bullring, is on Avenida de Doctor Olóriz, close to the soccer stadium. For more information, call ✆ **95-827-24-51.**

Abadía del Sacromonte   Crowning the Sacromonte (Sacred Hill) is this dilapidated abbey. Originally, this was a Benedictine monastery, and inside the ashes of San Cecilio, the patron saint of Granada, are stored.

Camino del Sacromonte, Sacromonte. ✆ **95-822-14-45.** Admission 1.80€ ($2.15). Tues–Sat 11am–1pm and 4–6pm; Sun noon–1pm and 4–6pm. Guided tours every 30 min.

⟨Moments Strolling Andalusia's Most Romantic Street

The most-walked street in Granada is **Carrera del Darro,** running north along the Darro River. It was discovered by the Romantic artists of the 19th century; many of their etchings (subsequently engraved) of scenes along this street were widely circulated, doing much to spread the fame of Granada throughout Europe. You can still find some of these old engravings in the musty antiques shops. Carrera del Darro ends at Paseo de los Tristes (Avenue of the Sad Ones), so named for the funeral corteges that used to go by here on the way to the cemetery.

(*Value* **Bargain Pass**

The **Bono Turístico Pass,** costing 18€ ($22) and good for 1 week, allows culture vultures to see Granada's major attractions for one bargain price. You can visit not only the Cathedral and the Alhambra, but Generalife, Monasterio Cartuja, and Monasterio de San Jerónimo. Passes are available at Caja Général de Ahorros de Granada, at Plaza Isabel la Católica, and the tourist office. For more information, call © **902-10-00-95.**

Albaicín 👁👁   This old Arab quarter on one of Granada's two main hills doesn't belong to the city of 19th-century buildings and wide boulevards. It, and the surrounding gypsy caves of Sacromonte, are holdovers from an older past. The Albaicín once flourished as the residential section of the Moors, but it fell into decline when the Christians drove them out. This narrow labyrinth of crooked streets escaped the fate that befell much of Granada, being torn down in the name of progress. Preserved are its alleyways, cisterns, fountains, plazas, whitewashed houses, villas, and the decaying remnants of the old city gate. Here and there you can catch a glimpse of a private patio filled with fountains and plants, a traditional elegant way of life that continues.
Bus: 31 or 32.

Alhambra and Generalife 👁👁👁   One of Europe's greatest attractions, the stunningly beautiful and celebrated **Calat Alhambra (Red Castle)** is perhaps the most remarkable fortress ever constructed. Muslim architecture in Spain reached its apogee at this pleasure palace once occupied by Nasrid princes and their harems. Although later Moorish occupants turned the Alhambra into a lavish palace, it was originally constructed for defensive purposes on a rocky hilltop outcropping above the Darro River. The modern city of Granada was built across the river from the Alhambra, about .8km (½ mile) from its western foundations.

When you first see the Alhambra, its somewhat somber exterior may surprise you. The true delights of this Moorish palace lie within. Tickets are sold in the office at the Entrada del Generalife y de la Alhambra. Enter through the incongruous 14th-century **Puerta de la Justicia (Gateway of Justice)** 👁. Most visitors don't need an expensive guide but will be content to stroll through the richly ornamented open-air rooms, with their lacelike walls and courtyards with fountains. Many of the Arabic inscriptions translate to "Only Allah is conqueror."

The tour begins in the **Mexuar,** also known as Palacio Nazaríes (Palace of the Nasrids), which is the first of the trio of palaces that compose the Alhambra. This was the main council chamber where the sultan's chief ministers met. The largest of these chambers was the Hall of the Mexuar, which Spanish rulers converted to a Catholic chapel in the 1600s. From this chapel a panoramic view spreads over the rooftops of the Albaicín.

Pass through another chamber of the Sultan's ministers, the Cuarto Dorado (Golden Room), and you'll find yourself in the small but beautiful **Patio del Mexuar.** Constructed in 1365, this is where the Sultan sat on giant cushions and listened to the petitions of his subjects or else met privately with his chief ministers. The windows here are surrounded by panels and richly decorated with tiles and stucco.

Granada Attractions

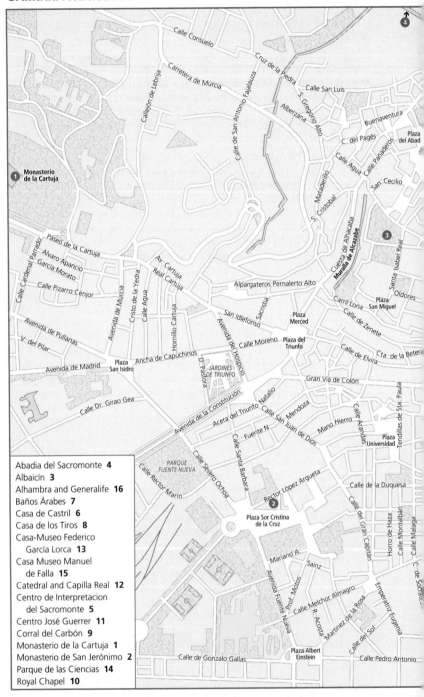

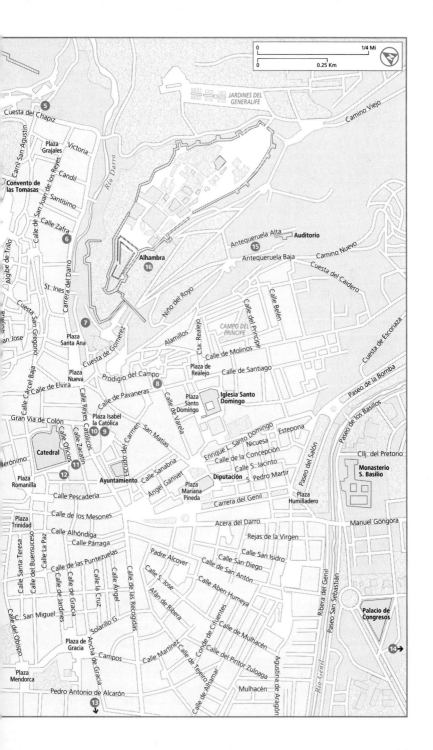

0   1/4 Mi

0   0.25 Km

JARDINES DEL GENERALIFE

Camino Viejo

⑤ Cuesta del Chapiz

Carril San Agustín

Plaza Grajales   Victoria

Calle de San Juan de los Reyes

Candil

Convento de las Tomasas

Santísimo

Algibe de Trillo

Calle Zafra

⑥

Río Darro

Antequeruela Alta   **Auditorio**

⑮

Antequeruela Baja   Camino Nuevo

Alhambra   **⑯**

Cuesta del Caldero

St. Ines

Carrera del Darro

Cuesta San Gregorio

an Jose

Niño del Royo

⑦

Calle del Príncipe

Calle Belén

Plaza Santa Ana

CAMPO DEL PRINCIPE

Cuesta de Gomérez

Cuesta de Escoriaza

Cta. Realejo

Paseo de la Bomba

Alamillos

Calle de Molinos

Prodigio del Campo

Plaza de Realejo   Calle de Santiago

Plaza Nueva

Calle de Pavaneras   **⑧**

Calle de Elvira

Plaza Santo Domingo   **Iglesia Santo Domingo**

Paseo de los Basilios

Gran Via de Colón

Calle Reyes Católicos

Plaza Isabel la Católica   **⑩** **⑨**

Escudo del Carmen San Matías

Calle de Varela

Calle Sanabria

Enrique L. Santo Domingo

Nicuesa   Estepona

Paseo del Salón

Clj. del Pretorio

Catedral

erónimo

Calle Oficios

Calle Zacatín

⑪

⑫

Ayuntamiento

Angel Ganivet

Calle de la Concepción

Calle S. Jacinto

Diputación S. Pedro Martír

Monasterio S. Basilio

Plaza Romanilla

Plaza Mariana Pineda

Carrera del Genil

Plaza Humilladero

Calle Pescadería

Calle de los Mesones

Acera del Darro

Manuel Góngora

Plaza Trinidad

Calle Alhóndiga

Calle Párraga

Rejas de la Virgen

Calle Santa Teresa

Calle del Buensuceso

Calle la Paz

Calle de las Puntezuelas

Padre Alcover

Calle San Isidro

Calle San Diego

Calle de San Antón

Ribera del Genil

Calle S. Jose

Calle Aben Humeya

Calle de Gracia

Calle de la Cruz

Calle Angel

Calle de las Recogidas

Afán de Ribera

Paseo San Sebastián

C. San Miguel

Calle de Jardines

Solarillo G.

Calle de Cifuentes

Calle de Mulhacén

Palacio de Congresos

Calle del Obispo

Plaza de Gracia

Ancha de Gracia

Campos

Calle Martínez

Calle de Tejeiro

Conde del Pintor Zuloaga

Agustina de Aragón

⑭→

Plaza Mendorca

Pedro Antonio de Alcarón

Calle de Alhamar

Mulhacén

Río Genil

⑬ ↓

191

The Palace of the Nasrids, Mexuar, was constructed around two courtyards, the **Patio de los Arrayanes (Court of the Myrtles)** and the **Patio de los Leonares (Court of the Lions)** ✦✦✦. The latter was the royal residence.

The Court of the Myrtles contains a narrow reflecting pool banked by myrtle trees. Note the decorative and rather rare tiles, which are arguably the finest in the Alhambra. Behind it is the **Salón de Embajadores (Hall of the Ambassadors),** with an elaborately carved throne room that was built between 1334 and 1354. The crowning cedar wood dome of this salon evokes the seven heavens of the Muslim cosmos. Here bay windows open onto **panoramic vistas** ✦✦ of the enveloping countryside.

An opening off the Court of the Myrtles leads to the greatest architectural achievement of the Alhambra, the **Patio de los Leonares (Court of Lions)** ✦✦✦, constructed by Muhammad V. At its center is Andalusia's finest fountain, which rests on 12 marble lions. These marble lions represent the hours of the day, the months of the year, and the signs of the zodiac. Legend claims that water flowed from the mouth of a different lion each hour of the day. This courtyard is lined with arcades supported by 124 (count them) slender marble columns. This was the heart of the palace, the most private section where the sultan enjoyed his harem, which included both male and female beauties.

At the back of the Leones courtyard is the **Sala de los Abencerrajes** ✦, named for a noble family who were rivals of the last emir, Boabdil. This hall has a richly adorned honeycombed ceiling. To get rid of his rivals, Boabdil invited them to a banquet. In the middle of the banquet, his guards entered and massacred his guests.

Opening onto the Court of Lions are other salons of intrigue, notably the Hall of the Two Sisters, **Sala de las Dos Hermanas,** where the sultan kept his "favorite" of the moment. The Hall of the Two Sisters takes its name from the two large white marble slabs, each identical, in the pavement. Boabdil's stern, unforgiving mother, Ayesha, once inhabited the Hall of the Two Sisters. This salon has a honeycomb dome and is celebrated as the finest example of Spanish Islamic architecture.

The nearby **Sala de los Reyes (Hall of Kings)** was the great banqueting hall of the Alhambra, site of parties, orgies, and feasts. Its ceiling paintings are on leather and date from the 1300s. Eunuchs guarded the harem but not always well. According to legend, one sultan beheaded 36 Moorish princes here because one of them was suspected of being intimate with his favorite.

A gallery leads to the **Patio de la Reja (Court of the Window Grille).** This is where Washington Irving lived in furnished rooms and where he began to write his famous book, *Tales of the Alhambra.* The best-known tale is the legend of Zayda, Zorayda, and Zorahayda, the three beautiful princesses who fell in love with three captured Spanish soldiers outside the Torre de las Infantas. Irving credits the French with saving the Alhambra for posterity, but in fact they were responsible for blowing up seven of the towers in 1812, and it was a Spanish soldier who cut the fuse before more damage could be done. When the duke of Wellington arrived a few years later, he chased out the chickens, the gypsies, and the transient beggars who were using the Alhambra as a tenement and set up housekeeping here himself.

Before going on to the Emperor Charles V's palace, there are some other gems around the Court of Lions, including the **Baños Reales (Royal Baths),** with their lavish decorations in many colors. Light enters through star-shaped apertures. To the immediate east of the baths lies the **Daraxa Garden,** and to its

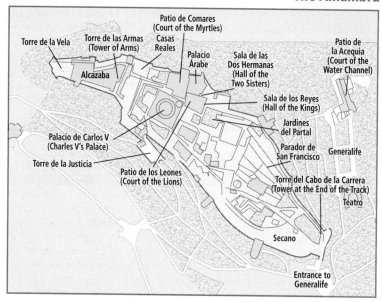

immediate south the lovely and resplendent **Mirador de Daraxa,** the sultana's private balcony onto Granada.

To the immediate southeast of these attractions are the **Jardines del Partal** ★★ and their perimeter towers. The beautiful gardens occupy a space that once was the kitchen garden, filled with milling servants preparing the sultan's banquets. These gardens are dominated by the **Torre de Las Damas (Ladies' Tower).** This tower and its pavilion, with its five-arched portico, are all that are left of the once-famous Palacio del Partal, the oldest palace at the Alhambra. Of less interest are the perimeter towers, including the Mihrab Tower, a former Nasrid oratory; the Torre de las Infantas (Tower of the Princesses) and Torre de la Cautiva (Tower of the Captive). Like the Damas tower, these towers were also once sumptuously decorated inside; today only some decoration remains.

Finally you can move to the immediate southwest to visit **Emperor Charles V's Palace (Palacio de Carlos V)** ★, where the Holy Roman emperor lived. Charles may have been horrified when he saw a cathedral placed in the middle of the great mosque at Córdoba, but he's also responsible for some architectural confusion in Granada. He literally built a Renaissance palace in the middle of this Moorish stronghold. It's quite beautiful, but terribly out of place in such a setting—Charles V did not consider the Nasrid palaces grand enough. In 1526 he ordered Pedro Machuca, a student of Michelangelo, to design him a fitting royal residence. He financed the palace by levying a tax on the Muslims. In spite of its incongruous location, the final result is one of the purest examples of classical Renaissance in Spain.

The square exterior opens to reveal a magnificent circular two-story courtyard that is open to the sky. Inside the palace are two museums. The first, **Museo de la Alhambra** (© **85-822-62-70**), is a museum of Hispano-Muslim Art, its salons opening onto the Myrtle and Mexuar Courts. They display artifacts retrieved from the Alcázar, including fragments of sculpture, but also unusual braziers and even perfume burners used in the harems. The most outstanding exhibit is a **blue amphora** ⚝ that is 132 centimeters (52 in.) high. This precious object stood for years in the Hall of the Two Sisters. Also look for an ablutions basin dating from the 10th century and adorned with lions chasing stags and an ibex. The museum is open Tuesday to Saturday 9am to 7:15pm and Sunday 9am to 5:45pm.

The palace also houses the **Museo Bellas Artes en la Alhambra** (✆ **95-822-48-43**), open Tuesday to Saturday 9am to 8pm, Sunday 9am to noon. Of minor interest, it displays mostly religious paintings and sculpture from the 16th to the 18th centuries.

Before leaving the Alhambra precincts, try to see the **Alcazaba,** which dates from the 9th century and is the oldest part of the complex. This rugged Middle Ages fortress was built for defensive purposes. For a spectacular **view** ⚝⚝, climb the **Torre de la Vela (Watchtower).** You look into the lower town onto Plaza Nueva, and you can also see the snow-capped Sierra Nevada in the distance. From the tower you can also view the Generalife (see below), the "gypsy hill" of Sacromonte.

Exit from the Alhambra via the Puerta de la Justicia, then circumnavigate the Alhambra's southern foundations until you reach the gardens of the summer palace, where Paseo de los Cipreses quickly leads you to the main building of the **Generalife** ⚝⚝, built in the 13th century to overlook the Alhambra and set on 30 lush hectares (75 acres). The sultans used to spend their summers in this palace (pronounced "heh-neh-rah-*lee*-feh"), safely locked away with their harems. Don't expect an Alhambra in miniature: The Generalife was always meant to be a retreat, even from the splendors of the Alhambra. Lying north of the Alhambra, this country estate of the Nasrid emirs was begun in the 13th century, but the palace and gardens have been much altered over the years. The palace is mainly noted for its beautiful courtyards, including **Patio de Polo,** where the visitors of yore would arrive on horseback.

The highlight of the Generalife is its **gardens** ⚝⚝⚝, begun in the 13th century but much modified over the years. Originally, they contained orchards and pastures for domestic animals. Highlights include **Escalera del Agua (The Water Staircase)** with water flowing gently down. An enclosed Oriental garden, **Patio de la Acequía,** was constructed around a long pool, with rows of water jets making graceful arches above it. The **Patio de la Sultana** (also called the

---

⌐Tips **Walking to the Alhambra**

Many visitors opt for a taxi or the bus to the Alhambra, but some hardy souls enjoy the uphill climb from the cathedral at the Plaza de la Lonja (signs indicate the winding roads and the steps that lead to the Alhambra). If you decide to walk, enter the Alhambra via the Cuesta de Gomérez, which, although steep, is the quickest and shortest pedestrian route. It begins at the Plaza Nueva, about 4 blocks east of the cathedral, and climbs steeply to the Puerta de las Granadas, the first of two gates to the Alhambra. The second, another 183m (600 ft.) uphill, is the Puerta de la Justicia, through which 90% of visitors enter the Alhambra. Watch out for so-called "guides" milling around the parking lot; they may just be interested in picking your pocket.

Tips The Alhambra: Saving Time & Hassles

The Alhambra is the most-visited monument in Spain, receiving 3.2 million visitors a year, more than the Prado. Only 7,700 tickets (pre-established quota) are sold per day, at a rate of 350 per half-hour. Each ticket indicates the 30-minute block of time during which you're granted access. Make the Alhambra your first stop of the day, and arrive at 7am, when the lines begin to form. By 11am these lines will resemble something at DisneyWorld.

You can avoid the long lines entirely by purchasing advance tickets through any worldwide branch of the **BBVA (Banco Bilbao & Vizcaya;** www.BBVA.es). You'll pay a service charge of just .90€ ($1.05) on top of the official rate of 10€ ($12) each. You can visit a branch of the BBVA yourself or call for advance bookings at *©* **90-222-44-60.**

Often, the day's quota of tickets are exhausted by 1pm, forcing gatekeepers to turn many hopefuls away, especially during the peak season of spring and summer.

After the day's allotment of 7,000 tickets has been sold, the curators will begin selling tickets just to the gardens and the fortress. These are not particularly desirable, and some visitors feel they've been ripped off. The gardens you'll have access to are relatively small and creations of the late 19th and early 20th centuries. And the fortress, a ruin that survives without many changes from the Arab era, is big, sprawling, and austere, without the joy and architectural verve of the Palace, which is the most-photographed, most charming, and most evocative part of the Alhambra.

Another way to avoid standing in line to buy tickets is to take a **guided tour.** Most of the travel agencies in Granada charge between 38€ and 40€ ($46–$48) for a 3- to 4-hour visit, per person. It's proba-bly worth the extra few euros, since agencies prebuy huge blocks of Alhambra tickets, sparing you the inconvenience of waiting in line.

Tours can be arranged through a company we've found reliable: **Central Servicio Turísticos,** Calle Estribo 2 (*©* **90-246-20-46**).

Rates for private, officially sanctioned guides who will purchase your ticket in advance are between 120€ ($144) and 140€ ($168) for a 3- to 4-hour tour. Central Servicio Turísticos can arrange one for you, although they will probably request an advance deposit, payable by credit card over the phone.

Renting an audio guide costs 3€ ($3.60) and requires a security deposit of 50€ ($60).

Experts recommend spending at least 3 hours for even the briefest visits to the Alhambra.

There are sprawling expanses of **free parking lots** near the base of the Alhambra, but if, on your way to them, you're stopped by some-one claiming you owe a fee, don't be fooled. They are frauds, and this is an ongoing piece of larceny that local authorities are trying to sup-press.

Patio de los Cipreses) was the secret rendezvous point for Zoraxda, wife of Sultan Abu Hasan, and her lover, the chief of the Abencarrajes.

Palacio de Carlos V. © **95-822-09-12.** Comprehensive ticket, including Alhambra and Generalife (below), 10€ ($12); Museo Bellas Artes 1.50€ ($1.80); Museo de la Alhambra 1.50€ ($1.80); illuminated visits 6.75€ ($8.10). Mar–Oct daily 9am–7:45pm, floodlit visits daily 10pm–midnight; Nov–Feb daily 9am–5:45pm, floodlit visits daily 8–10pm. Bus: 2.

Baños Arabes   Remarkable, these "baths of the walnut tree" as they were known by the Moors escaped destruction during the reign of the Reyes Católicos (Ferdinand and Isabella). Among the oldest buildings still standing in Granada, and among the best-preserved Muslim baths in Spain, they predate the Alhambra. Visigothic and Roman building materials are supposed to have gone into their construction.

Carrera del Darro 31. © **95-802-78-00.** Free admission. Tues–Sat 10am–2pm. Bus: 31 or 32.

Casa de Castril   This building has always been one of the most handsome Renaissance palaces in Granada. The Plateresque facade of 1539 has been attributed to Diego de Siloé. In 1869, it was converted into a museum with a collection of minor artifacts found in the area. The most outstanding exhibit here is a collection of Egyptian alabaster vases that were dug up in a necropolis in Almuñécar. Look especially for the figure of a bull from Arjona. There is also a selection of decorative Moorish art that the Arabs left behind as they retreated from Granada.

Museo Arqueológico, Carrera del Darro 41. © **95-822-56-40.** Admission 1.50€ ($1.80). Tues 3–8:30pm; Wed–Sat 9am–8:30pm; Sun 9am–2pm. Bus: 31 or 32.

Casa de los Tiros   The "House of Shots" is a fortresslike palace that is Renaissance in its architecture, dating from the 1500s. Its name comes from the musket barrels protruding from its facade. Once it was owned by a noble family who was given the Generalife after the Reconquest of Granada. Their proudest possession was the sword of Boabdil, the last Muslim king. A carving of that sword can be seen in the facade of the building along with statues of Mercury, Theseus, Hercules, Hector, and Jason.

Inside you'll find intriguing portraits of Catholic monarchs, including Ferdinand, Isabella, and even Philip IV. Each royal looks rather dour. The major feature of the house is the **Cuadra Dorada (Hall of Gold),** which is decorated with gold lettering and more royal portraits. Various photos, engravings, and centuries-old lithographs depict Granada in the 19th and early 20th century.

Plaza Padres Suarez, Realejo. © **95-822-10-72.** Free admission. Mon–Fri 2:30–8pm. Bus: 23 or 32.

Casa-Museo Federico García Lorca (Huerta de San Vicente) ★ *Finds* Poet/dramatist Federico García Lorca, author of *Blood Wedding, The House of Bernarda Alba,* and *A Poet in New York,* spent many happy summers with his family here at their vacation home. He moved to Granada in 1909, a dreamy-eyed schoolboy, and was endlessly fascinated with its life, including the Alhambra and the gypsies, whom he later described compassionately in his *Gypsy Ballads.* The house is decorated with green trim and grillwork and filled with family memorabilia like furniture and portraits. You can look out at the Alhambra from one of its balconies. You may inspect the poet's upstairs bedroom and see his oak desk stained with ink. Look for the white stool that he carried to the terrace to watch the sun set over Granada. The house is in the Fuentevaqueros section of Granada, near the airport.

Moments Andalusia's Greatest View

It's a tradition at sunset to flock to the **Mirador de San Nicolás** for what is arguably the greatest view in Andalusia. Tiled rooftops drop to the Darro River. On the far side stands the Alhambra, which, if the night is right, seems so red in the dying glow it almost appears in flames. In the distance loom the snowcapped peaks of the Sierra Nevada. To reach this spot from Peso la Harina, head northwest along Calle Salvador until you reach Calle Abad. At his point, turn left (west), which will lead into San Nicolás.

Calle de la Virgen Blanca s/n, Parque Federico García Lorca. (*Ⓒ*) **95-825-84-66**. Admission 2.10€ ($2.50). Apr 1–June 30 daily 10am–1pm and 5–7pm; July–Aug daily 10am–2:30pm; Sept daily 10am–1pm and 6–8pm; Oct 7–Mar 31 Tues–Sun 10am–1pm and 4–7pm.Bus: 6.

Casa Museo Manuel de Falla   The composer Manuel de Falla (1876–1946) lived in this charming whitewashed house on the Alhambra hill. His villa—called a *carmen*—is pretty much as he left it and is filled with memorabilia. You can see his piano and his original furniture, along with photographs, manuscripts, and other mementos. The garden is awash with roses, and you can stand at the same spot the composer did to enjoy the panoramic view. The location is across from the Alhambra Palace Hotel.

Calle Antequerela Alta 11. (*Ⓒ*) **95-822-21-89**. If the building is closed (highly likely) you can admire it from the outside. Admission 2€ ($2.40). Daily 10am–1:30pm. Bus: 5 or 32.

Catedral and Capilla Real ✦✦✦   This richly ornate Renaissance cathedral with its spectacular altar is one of the country's architectural highlights, acclaimed for its beautiful facade and gold-and-white interior. It was begun in 1521 and completed in 1714.

Enrique de Egas created the original Gothic-style plans, but it was Renaissance maestro Diego de Siloé who designed the facade and the chief attraction inside the cathedral, the **Capilla Mayor** ✦✦, a rotunda circled by an ambulatory. Capilla Mayor is surmounted by a 45m (150-ft.) dome. The graceful rotunda has two architectural layers, the upper one adorned by art by Alonso Cano depicting the life of the Madonna along with stunning stained glass that dates from the 1500s. At the entrance to the rotunda is a pair of panels, one depicting Ferdinand and Isabella in prayer, the other by Alonso Cano depicting Adam and Eve.

Several glittering side chapels also decorate the cathedral, and one is especially extravagant, the carved and gilded Capilla de Nuestra Señora de la Antigua, also known as the Capilla Dorada on the north wall. Before leaving the area, and once outside, note the Puerta del Perdón, a notably elaborate side entrance facing north on Calle de la Cárcel.

Behind the cathedral (entered separately) is the flamboyant Gothic and Plateresque **Royal Chapel,** where the remains of Queen Isabella and her husband, Ferdinand, lie. It was their wish to be buried in recaptured Granada, not Castile or Aragón. Work was begun by Enrique Egas in 1506 but completed in 1521 when Charles V reigned as emperor. Nonetheless, the chapel still has a unity of architectural style. Visitors enter through the Lonja (Exchange House), which is an adjoining structure on Calle de los Oficios, a narrow pedestrian street that runs alongside the cathedral.

Inside, the chapel is a virtual celebration of the Isabelline style, with its ribbed vaulting along with walls emblazoned with the arms of Isabella and Ferdinand, the conquerors of Granada.

A highlight is a visit to the chancel, enclosed by a **screen** ⊛ by Master Barolomé. This adornment contains the **mausoleums** ⊛⊛ of Ferdinand and Isabella on the right. You may be surprised by how short they were. Occupying much larger tombs are the remains of their daughter, Joanna the Mad, and her husband, Philip the Handsome. Domenico Fancelli of Florence sculpted the recumbent Carrera marble figures of the Catholic monarchs in 1517 and Bartolomé Ordóñez the figures of Juana la Loca and Felipe el Hermoso, the parents of Charles V, in 1520.

Look for the stairs at the royal feet of the sculptures. These lead to a crypt that contains a quartet of lead caskets where the royal ashes actually lie, including a very small casket for one royal grandchild. Of special interest is the **high altar retablo** ⊛ dating from 1520. This was one of the first *retablos* in Spain to show no Gothic influence. If you head for the north transept you will encounter the most celebrated triptych in Granada (much reproduced on postcards). By Fleming Thierry Bouts, it is called the *Triptych of the Passion.*

In the sacristy you can view Isabella's personal **art collection** ⊛⊛, many by Flemish masters and various Spanish and Italian artists, including Rogier Van der Weyden and Botticelli. Some of the most outstanding pieces of art are by Memling, Bartolomé, and Bermejo. A glass case contains Ferdinand of Aragón's sword, Isabella's scepter and crown, as well as a reliquary and a missal. You can also see the queen's ornate jewel chest. Church vestments are also on display in the sacristy. Above the chapel's exit doorway is a copy of the famous painting of Boabdil's surrender to Isabella. She is depicted wearing her filigree crown, the one you've just seen.

The cathedral is in the center of Granada off two prominent streets, Gran Vía de Colón and Calle de San Jerónimo. The Capilla Real abuts the cathedral's eastern edge.

Plaza de la Lonja, Gran Vía de Colón 5. ⓒ **95-822-29-59.** Cathedral 3€ ($3.60); chapel 3€ ($3.60). Daily 10:30am–1:30pm and 3:30–6:30pm (4–8pm in summer). Bus: 6, 9, or 11.

Centro de Interpretación del Sacromonte   For decades under Franco's rule, gypsies and the caves and the architecture on their hill, Sacromonte, were scorned. Seen as "undesirables" gypsies were often persecuted. Times have changed. Today their flamenco music is taken seriously, regarded as an art form and approached with a high degree of scholarship. And at this center, Granada celebrates gypsies and their origins.

Combining 10 separate caves, each a former residence or crafts studio, along with common exposition areas and a botanical garden, this is a living, breathing museum of a formerly vital but now-dying way of life. Each of the caves sports whitewashed walls. Many tools are displayed, including a formidable-looking loom and a carpenter's studio. There's also a kiosk selling flamenco recordings and gift items, plus a staff who works to produce an ongoing series of cultural and ecological events that change on a rotating basis.

To reach it, you can walk the steep uphill cobble-covered paths from a point near the top of the Río Darro, from Paseo de los Tristes. This is a continuation of the much-visited Carrera del Darro, just across the ravine from the Alhambra. Or you can take bus no. 31 or 32 from the Plaza Nueva, at the bottom of the hill.

The museum lies at Barranco de los Negros s/n. ℂ **95-821-51-20.** Admission 4€ ($4.80) including guided tour. Access to outdoor areas (miradors, walkways, and communal gardens) 1€ ($1.20). Bus: 31 or 32.

Centro José Guerrer   The artist José Guerrero was born in Granada in 1914. By the time of his death in 1991, his paintings were owned by some of the most important Spanish museums of contemporary art. The collection at this center covers the entire scope of his life, with a representation of his key works and milestones in his artistic production. This museum displays some of his best works.

Calle Oficios 8. ℂ **95-822-51-85.** Free admission. Tues–Sat 11am–2pm and 5–9pm. Bus: 6, 9, or 11.

Corral del Carbón   Built in 1336, and formerly an Arab guesthouse, the Coal House (its English name) was indeed used as a coal storage warehouse in the 19th century. Long since restored, it is today one of the oldest Moorish buildings remaining in Granada. It is the only Muslim inn that remains in Spain. At one time there were dozens. In time the Christians used it as a theater before it degenerated into an industrial site. The rooms are spread around a central patio. The building is in the shape of a quadrangle and is entered through a large horseshoe arch leading into the main hall, capped with a dome. The center today houses a number of artisans' shops.

Calle Mariana Pineda. ℂ **95-822-59-90.** Free admission. Mon–Sat 9am–8pm; Sun 10am–2pm. Bus: 3, 9, or 11.

Monasterio de la Cartuja ⭐   This 16th-century monastery, off the Albaicín on the outskirts of Granada, is sometimes called the Christian answer to the Alhambra because of its ornate stucco and marble and the baroque Churrigueresque fantasy in the sacristy. Its most notable paintings are by Bocanegra, its outstanding sculpture by Mora. The church of this Carthusian monastery was decorated with baroque stucco in the 17th century, and its 18th-century sacristy is an excellent example of latter-day baroque style. Napoleon's armies killed St. Bruno here. Sometimes one of the Carthusian monks will take you on a guided tour.

Paseo de Cartujar s/n. ℂ **95-816-19-32.** Admission 3€ ($3.60). Mon–Sat 10am–1pm; Sun 10am–noon and 4–8pm (closes at 6pm in winter). Bus: 8 from cathedral.

Monasterio de San Jerónimo   Following the Reconquest of Granada by Ferdinand and Isabella, this was the first monastery to be founded. Dating from the 16th century, the restored monastery-church is one of the grandest buildings designed by Diego de Siloé. Its public cloister represents a magnificent use of space, with double tiers of arcaded ambulatories enveloping an orange grove. The monastery was severely damaged by the troops of Napoleon.

Calle Rector López Argüeta. ℂ **95-827-93-37.** Admission 3€ ($3.60). Daily 10am–1:30pm and 3–6:30pm. Bus: 6, 9, or 11.

Parque de las Ciencias *Kids*   Across from the convention center of Granada, this science park is a vast array of attractions, embracing everything from a Biosphere Room to a Planetarium, from the Explora Room to a Butterfly Park. Dominating the park is an observation tower, soaring 50m (165 ft.) with panoramic views over Granada. The on-site museum has interactive exhibits and conducts scientific experiments.

Av. del Mediterráneo, Zaidín. ℂ **95-813-19-00.** Park 3.60€ ($4.30) park; planetarium 1.60€ ($1.90). Tues–Sat 10am–7pm; Sun 10am–3pm. Bus: 1 or 5.

6 Shopping

Alcaicería ⊛, once the Moorish silk market, is next to the cathedral in the lower city. The narrow streets of this rebuilt village of shops are filled with vendors selling the arts and crafts of Granada province. For the souvenir hunter, the Alcaicería offers one of the most splendid assortments in Spain of tiles, castanets, and wire figures of Don Quixote chasing windmills. Lots of Spanish jewelry can be found here, comparing favorably with the finest Toledan work.

Handicrafts stores virtually line the main shopping arteries, especially those centered on **Puerta Real,** including **Gran Vía de Colón, Reyes Católicos,** and **Angel Ganivet.** For the best selection of antiques stores, mainly selling furnishings of Andalusia, browse the shops along **Cuesta de Elvira.**

ART

Galería de la Cueva   This is not the most prestigious, or even the most famous, art gallery in Granada. Instead, you'll find a well-meaning and slightly academic administration whose goal involves encouraging young, sometimes relatively unknown artists to sell their paintings at cost-effective prices that range from 100€ to 300€ ($120–$360) each, far less than what you'd find in more stylish galleries. Inventories include many charming landscapes and architectural renderings of buildings you might recognize from your treks through Andalucia. Calle Tinajilla 8. ② **95-820-69-32.**

FASHION

Dely's   At this shop downhill from the cathedral, on a narrow street with the most dense pedestrian traffic in the Old Town, you'll find stylish women's clothing, the kind a post-*movida* hipster might wear to a hot dance club or date. Garments are slinky but relatively formal, many embroidered with silk into flowered patterns that are part East Indian, part flamenco. Calle Mesones 1. ② **95-826-01-75.**

Ôxia   If you happen to have teenage children of your own, the merchandise in this shop might remind you of exactly what you *don't* want them to wear. The place defines itself as a repository for "urban fashion." Calle Gracia 21. ② **95-825-84-49.**

Marquetry the Old-Fashioned Way

Connoisseurs of the fine art of marquetry (the craft in which tiny pieces of bone and colored hardwoods are arranged into geometric patterns and glued into wooden frames) may be interested in the demonstration of this art form in the Alhambra at **Laguna Taracea,** Real de la Alhambra 30 (② **95-822-90-19;** www.laguna-taracea.com).

The company was established by the ancestors of today's owner, Miguel Laguna, in 1877. Know before you buy that prices vary with the percentage of real bone in the raw materials. Marquetry work that's crafted from authentic hardwoods and bone sell for up to three times as much as clones made from colored plastic. After a few moments under the tutelage of this place, you'll be able to recognize the difference.

For sale in the shop are elaborately patterned, and very beautiful, trays, boxes, chess sets, picture frames, and more, as well as large, heirloom-quality chests of drawers, each emulating a different 17th-century Iberian design and each selling for several thousand euros.

Shopping for Spanish Guitars

Granada and the art of guitar-making have always been intricately intertwined. Even if you don't want to haul a guitar back from Andalusia, you might want to check out the neighborhood where they're manufactured.

Calle Cuesta de Gomérez, a narrow and steeply sloping street that runs uphill to the Alhambra from a point near the Plaza Nueva, in Old Granada, is the centerpiece of the city's guitar-making trade. Today, there are at least five guitar-making studios—usually small shops with no more than two, and usually only one, artisan per cubbyhole. Prices for one of the laboriously crafted instruments might, in a pinch, begin at 195€ ($234). Costs for some of the most resonant guitars can easily exceed 2,000€ ($2,400).

The oldest studio, **Casa Ferrer,** 26 Calle Cuesta de Gomérez (✆ **95-822-18-32**), was established in 1875. Competitors include **Guitarrería Antonio Morales,** at no. 9 (✆ **95-881-88-20**); and **José López Bellido,** at no. 36 (✆ **95-822-27-41**). At least one additional craftshop, **Germán Pérez Barranco,** still maintains a presence at 6 Calle Cuesta de Gomérez (✆ **95-822-70-33;** www.guitarreria.com). Most business is conducted from premises at Reyes Católicos 47; the the cubbyhole on Calle Cuesta de Gomérez is maintained primarily as a prestigious and highly visible link to the company's origins.

In most places along Calle Cuesta de Gomérez expect gruff but courteous responses to your questions. Settings are unpretentious, usually within a working crafts studio littered with gluepots and tools for fine woodworking.

GIFTS

El Zoco Nazari This small but choice shop is packed, cheek-by-jowl, against junkier-looking competitors on either side. Much of what it sells is carefully chosen and attractive, but of particular interest are Art Deco–era (1930s) replicas of posters advertising the glories of flamenco in Andalusia; Moroccan mirror frames set with bone; porcelain, sometimes with silver appliqués, that emulate the *La Loza Dorada* motifs of the 10th-century Nazari dynasty; and some very fine leather goods. The Swiss-born staff speaks English, and a bit of everything else as well. Reyes Católicos 50. ✆ **95-822-59-77.**

MOROCCAN CRAFTS

Bazar Abdel You can't leave this shop without a distinct sense of Granada's Moorish antecedents, and the vivid tradition of craftsmanship that flourishes in Morocco, a short distance across the Straits of Gibraltar. Come here for inlaid boxes, chastened copper and brassware, porcelain in the jewel tones of the sub-Sahara, and for some genuinely intriguing mirror frames crafted from hammered silver and mosaics of exotic hardwoods and bone. Carrera del Darro 47. ✆ **95-822-23-29.**

Tienda "Morocco" On display within this relatively new store are mirror frames crafted from bone, copper, and silver and parchment lamps, porcelain, marquetry-inlaid boxes, and gift items. Carrera del Darro 15. ✆ **95-822-13-71.**

A Shopping Secret

There is a street in Granada that every local shopper of artifacts and cheap clothing knows about: **Calle Calderería Nueva**. Too narrow for cars, and evoking an Arab souk, it slopes abruptly from the Albaicín into the more modern neighborhoods of the town, a point that's close to Plaza Nueva. Either side is thickly populated with stores of all degrees of junkiness. Some of the crafts stores, especially those selling Moroccan handicrafts, are genuinely upscale.

A particularly charming shop, positioned near the bottommost elevation of this narrow street, is **Karaván**, Calle Calderería Nueva 3 (✆ **95-822-69-71**), where some genuinely lovely Berber and Moroccan crafts from North Africa's High Atlas mountains, crafted from bone and exotic hardwoods, can be found.

SILVER

Rafael Moreno Orfebre   This is one of the most important silversmiths in Granada. Look for chandeliers, religious votive objects, boxes, tableware, and sculptures. Reyes Católicos 28A. ✆ **95-822-99-16.**

7 Granada After Dark

In addition to its vast array of tapas bars, flamenco shows, and dance clubs, Granada is also a major center of Andalusian culture. Ask at the tourist office at the time of your visit for a current brochure of cultural presentations, including dance, concert, and theater performances.

THE BEST TAPAS BARS

Bar La Mancha   This little tasca in an old house decorated with antiques and lots of wood is one of the livelier ones in Granada. Some locals come here nightly to fill up on the tasty tapas, with portions costing from 2.50€ to 6.50€ ($3–$7.80). Open nightly from 8:30pm until the last customer staggers out at four in the morning. Calle Joaquín Costa 10. ✆ **95-822-89-68.**

Bar Pilar del Toro ⚐   Near the cathedral and the central Plaza Nueva, this tasca is attached to an even more famous restaurant. Many of the hottest-looking young men and women of Granada head here nightly to the lovely covered patio with its fountain and rattan sofas. The building itself is from the 1600s and the restaurant is upstairs. There's also a tearoom in the courtyard in the afternoon. Tapas are extremely good and fresh, ranging from 8€ to 15€ ($9.60–$18). Open daily 9am to 2am. Entrance on Plaza Santa Ana 12. ✆ **95-822-38-47.**

Bodega Castaneda ⚐   In back of the landmark Plaza Nueva, this tapas tavern is justifiably one of the most popular in Granada. Its array of tapas is so mouthwatering you may want to spend a couple of hours snacking and drinking the affordable Riojas. The waiters will indicate the selection of tapas for the evening; they often recommend some of the sausages such as spicy *chorizo* or salami. Our favorite is *jamón de Trevelez and de Bellota* (this ham comes from acorn-fed pigs, which makes the meat taste sweeter than regular ham). Fish fanciers will gravitate to the slices of tuna or salmon. Another delight is the manchego cheese of the area. Tapas range in price from 1.50€ to 2.90€ ($1.80–$3.50). This 1936 tavern has dark colors, wooden furnishings, and brick walls.

Open daily 11:30am to 4pm and 7pm to 1am. Almireceros 1–3. ⓒ **95-822-32-22.**
Bus: 4, 5, 20, or 22.

Casa de Vinos La Brujidera   A great variety of regional wine and special
tapas are served at this *típico* tavern between Plaza Isabel la Católica and Plaza
Nueva in the center of the lower town. Most of the clients are locals, not tourists,
and they flock here for one of the best choices of affordable wine from all over
Spain. The best tapas is a series of particularly choice cuts of cold meats. In fair
weather umbrella-shaded chairs are placed outside. In the background you'll
usually hear jazz playing. Hours are daily from 12:30 to 4pm and 8pm to 2am.
Monjas del Carmen 2. ⓒ **95-822-25-95.**

Casa Henrique ⓖ   Near Puerta Real in the center of Granada, this is arguably
Granada's most famous tasca dive. Antique and looking it, it's an old-fashioned
masonry-sided hole-in-the-wall—and very cramped. For decor, it relies on
antique barrels of wine and sherry. It's known for its *vino costa,* a smooth little
wine that seems to go well with almost any of the delicious array of tapas served
here. A specialty is thin-sliced Serrano ham, and heaping platters of steamed
mussels flavored with fresh herbs and white wine. You might also try the goat
cheese with fresh anchovies. Portions range from 6€ to 12€ ($7.20–$14). Open
noon to 4pm and 8pm to midnight Monday to Saturday. Calle Accero de Darro 8.
ⓒ **95-812-35-08.**

Casa Vino del Agua   This is a well-maintained and popular bar hidden away
in the heart of the Albaicín. It has an adjoining restaurant in a small garden. The
lure here are the small portions of cheeses, pâtés, and salads, ranging in price
from 5€ to 7€ ($6–$8.40). Unusual for Andalusia, fondue is also a specialty, as
is smoked fish and even caviar. Some of the food is "cooked on the stone," meaning on a hot stone brought to your table. Open Thursday to Monday 1 to
3:30pm and daily 8pm to midnight. Calle Algibe de Trillo 7. ⓒ **95-822-43-56.**

La Gran Taverna   In the very center of Granada, this modern and very popular tasca attracts both coffee-drinkers and wine-tasters, as well as lovers of sliced
Serrano ham, fondues, and liqueurs. Rich and dark, the wooden bar was
installed in the building back in the 19th century. A chunk of regional cheese
from Granada province, a few snails, or else just some olives and nuts—and the
evening is yours. Open daily 8pm to 2am. Plaza Nueva 2. ⓒ **95-822-88-46.**

La Taberna de Tiacheta   On a sloping, cobble-covered square or in the rustic interior you can enjoy platters of smoked fish or cured ham, artichokes with
cured ham, red peppers stuffed with pulverized cod, selected cheeses, or deer-
meat stew. Prices range from 3.75€ to 8.40€ ($4.50–$10). The location is
across the narrow river (the Darro) from the crushing mass of other nightclubs.
Its view is from the river's opposite side. Open daily 6pm to 2am. Puente 1, Carrera del Darro. ⓒ **95-822-13-71.**

Tasca Hopping

Calle Navas is loaded with tapas bars (tascas) and favored by office workers who toil within the bureaucracies of Granada. *Habas con jamón*
(broad beans with strips of Iberian ham) is especially popular. Another
good place to begin your tasca crawl is along **Campo del Príncipe,** where
at least seven old-fashioned tapas bars do a rollicking business during the
cool of the evening.

The Gypsy Caves of Sacromonte

These inhabited gypsy caves near the Albaicín are the subject of much controversy. Admittedly, they're a tourist trap, one of the most obviously commercial and shadowy rackets in Spain. Still, they can be a potent enough attraction if you follow some rules.

Once, thousands of gypsies lived on **Sacromonte (Holy Mountain)** named for several Christians martyred here. However, many of the caves were heavily damaged by rain in 1962, forcing hundreds of occupants to seek shelter elsewhere. Nearly all the gypsies remaining are involved one way or another with tourism. (Some don't even live here—they commute from modern apartments in the city.)

When evening settles over Granada, loads of visitors descend on these caves. From each one, you'll hear the rattle of castanets and the strumming of guitars, while everybody in the gypsy family struts his or her stuff. Popularly known as the *zambra,* this is intriguing entertainment only if you have an appreciation for the grotesque. Whenever a gypsy boy or girl comes along with genuine talent, he or she is often grabbed up and hustled off to the more expensive clubs. Those left at home can be rather pathetic in their attempts to entertain.

One of the main reasons for going is to see the caves themselves. If you're expecting primitive living, you may be in for a surprise—many are quite comfortable, with conveniences like telephones and electricity. Often they're decorated with copper and ceramic items—and the inhabitants need no encouragement to sell them to you.

If you want to see the caves, you can walk up the hill by yourself. Your approach will already be advertised before you get here. Attempts will be made to lure you inside one or another of the caves—and to get money from you. Alternatively, you can book an organized tour arranged by one of the travel agencies in Granada. Even at the end of

FLAMENCO SHOWS

Sala de Fiesta Alhambra   The best flamenco shows are staged here nightly at 10pm in a garden. The acts are a bit racy. In addition to flamenco, performers attired in regional garb do folk dances and play guitar. The cover charge of 25€ ($30) includes your first drink. It's best to take a taxi here. Carretera de Jaén, Polígono Industrial Olinda. (C) 95-841-22-69.

NIGHTCLUBS

Most of these nightclubs begin slowly revving their engines at 11pm, but don't really wake up until around midnight. They really get percolating around 2am, continuing on until at least 4am or even sunrise. If you're an absolute nightlife fanatic, you might then consider going out to any of the coffee bars of the city for omelets and breakfast fare beginning around 6:30am.

Camborio   Lying a 20-minute walk uphill from Plaza Nueva, this is a particularly popular address with students. Many of these young people stand on the rooftop terraces for a panoramic view of the Alhambra at sunrise, one of the most striking vistas in all of Andalusia. Each of the four bars plays different one of these group outings—with all expenses theoretically paid in advance—there's likely to be an attempt by the cave dwellers to extract more money from you. As soon as the *zambra* ends, hurry out of the cave as quickly as possible. *Be warned:* Many of our readers have been critical of these tours.

A visit to the caves is almost always included as part of the morning and (more frequently) afternoon city tours offered every day by such companies as **Grana Visión** (𝒞 **95-853-58-75**). Night tours (when the caves are at their most eerie and evocative) are usually offered only to those who can assemble 10 or more people into a group. The cost ranges from 25€ to 28€ ($30–$34). This might have changed by the time of your visit, so phone a reputable tour operator such as Grana Visión to learn if any other options are available.

You can, of course, visit the *cuevas* on your own. The clubs below offer a package deal including transportation to and from your hotel and your first drink. Most of these caves lie along **Camino del Sacromonte.** The best of these *zambras* include **Cueva María La Canastera (Cueva Museo)** at Camino del Sacromonte 81 (𝒞 **95-812-11-83**), which charges an admission of 22€ ($26). Shows are at 10:30pm. Three other leading Sacromonte clubs incude **Cueva La Rocío,** Camino del Sacromonte 70 (𝒞 **95-822-71-29**), with shows at 10 and 11pm. The entrance, including bus and drink, is 23€ ($28). **Venta El Gallo,** Barranco de los Negroes 5 (𝒞 **95-822-05-91**), offers a show at 10pm nightly, including the bus and a first drink for 23€ ($28). If you want dinner, too, the total cost is 45€ ($54). Finally, **Cueva Los Tarantos,** Camino del Sacromonte 9 (𝒞 **95-822-45-25**), features shows at 9:30 and 11pm. Bus fare is included in the cover of 23€ ($28), which includes your first drink, or 50€ ($60) if you want dinner.

music. A 4.50€ ($5.40) cover charge is imposed only on Friday and Saturday nights. Beer ranges in price from 1.80€ to 3€ ($2.15–$3.60). Open Tuesday to Saturday 11pm to 7am. Camino del Sacromonte 48. 𝒞 **95-822-12-15.**

Copas La Fontana   This is one of the biggest and (in our opinion) hippest of the bodegas lining the edge of the Carrer del Darro, a street that's legendary for its nightlife and its sense of medieval history. The interior is a sprawling labyrinth of ocher-colored rooms, each with lots of wood trim, terra-cotta floors, and ongoing surges of recently released music from Madrid, Los Angeles, New York, London, and Havana. The paintings decorating the walls include some interesting portraits—and they're all for sale. And amid the permissive madness, you'll see age-old artisans' tools artfully displayed on the thick masonry walls. Cocktails cost 4.30€ ($5.15). Daily 4pm to 4am. Carrera del Darro 19. 𝒞 **95-822-77-59.**

Disco Zoo   This dance bar occupies the deep deep cellar of a building close to the Melia Hotel, in the commercial heart of modern-day Granada. It's so dark, and the lighting so eerie, that the only thing you'll be able to distinguish amid the shadows are the faces and forms of the young, the energetic, and the sexually ambiguous patrons who call this place their own. By 3am, the dance floor is packed. The cover is 8€ ($9.60), and hours are Thursday to Sunday midnight to 6am. Calle Mora 2. No phone.

El Príncipe   This very late-night disco doesn't really get going until at least 2am. Clients are stylish and well-dressed. The setting is beneath the very high timbered ceiling of what was originally a grain warehouse. The sound system is sophisticated and up-to-date, sending waves of house and garage music reverberating down to the dance floor from the ceiling above. If you happen to get hungry with all this dance, dance, dance, consider any of the selection of tapas that are sold until the wee early hours. El Campo del Príncipe. ⓒ **95-822-80-88.**

Granada 10   Beginning around 2am, the club is abuzz with the dance moves of hip 30-somethings and Spanish soap opera stars. The dress code is a bit posh—hopefuls in sweatsuits have been turned away. The sometime-movie theater that houses this place has a cruciform-shaped floor plan and you'll probably be sandwiched into areas that aren't otherwise devoted to movie seats. It's close to the Gran Vía and the cathedral. A cover charge of 10€ ($12) includes a first drink. Open Monday to Friday 12:30am to 5am, Saturday and Sunday 12:30am to 7am. Carcel Baja 10. ⓒ **95-822-40-01.**

Kasbah   This is like a candlelit cafe you might come across in the sub-Sahara, with silk embroidered and overstuffed pillows and cozy nooks. On Thursday, Saturday, and Sunday nights at 10:30pm, a belly dancer performs. A huge selection of Moroccan teas costs from 1.80€ ($2.15). Hours are Monday to Friday noon to 1:30am, Saturday and Sunday noon to 3:30am. Calle Calderería Nueva 4. ⓒ **95-822-79-36.**

Planta Baja   Live bands from Spain and all over Europe regularly play at this techno dance club. In a central lower-town location, this club is heavily patronized by university students. Look for the listing of bands and their performance times in the front window. From 10pm, live music is presented. After midnight, a hot DJ takes over. The 5€ ($6) cover includes a first drink. The club is open Thursday to Saturday 10pm to 6am, but closed in July and August. Calle Horno de Abad 11. ⓒ **95-825-35-09.**

GAY & LESBIAN BARS

Granada has the largest and most concentrated gay scene in inland Andalusia. For coastal gay life, head for Torremolinos. See chapter 10.

El Angel Azul   Rainbow flags proclaim this late-late-nightclub's gay tolerance, which after a glimpse of its guests, might be defined as *very* tolerant. But in the universe of the hopelessly trendy of Andalusia, no one cares about labels like gay, straight, or slightly bent. The dance music is disco, the cover charge is 8€ ($9.60), and hours are Thursday to Saturday midnight to 6am. Calle Lavadero de Tablas 15. No phone.

El Rincón de San Pedro ⚓   The most appealing gay-friendly bar in Granada occupies a 400-year-old building whose foundations rise, high and fortress-like, above the trickle of cold water known as the Río Darro, just across the ravine from the Alhambra. You'll enter a room illuminated with flickering candles perched high on candelabras, near an illuminated polychrome copy of a medieval statue devoted to San Pedro. Add lots of shimmering gilt (it contributes to the venue's sense of camp) and enough brushed aluminum and industrial-looking hardware to appeal to the butch crowd, and you have El Rincón de San Pedro.

In midsummer, come here before midnight, after which the staff is required to close the French doors looking over the Alhambra. The music after that hour gives the neighbors reason to complain to the police. From the premises, look out the open windows high above the ravine. With drink in hand and with music playing in the background, you can take in the floodlit towers of the Alhambra. Beer costs from 2.50€ ($3). The club is usually open daily 5pm to 4am. Closed Monday to Wednesday October to June. Carrera del Darro 12. No phone.

La Puerta del Vino   The staff is gruff and jaded, the beer is cold, the tapas come in generous portions, and there's a very discreet rainbow flag stuck somewhere near the cash register. The photos and memorabilia in this family-style, Art Nouveau dining room pay tribute to such former counterculture patrons as García Lorca, Manuel de Falla, and a host of other young Spaniards with romantic ideals. Maybe the place is gay (its name appears on all the right lists), maybe it's not, or perhaps it's all a function of when you happen to show up. Paseo de Los Tristes 5. ℂ 95-821-00-26.

Pub Fondo Reservado   Woodsy-looking and battered, this is the leading gay and lesbian pub in the Albaicín, with a strict policy of not even opening its doors till around midnight. Once you're inside, you'll be within a group of people who seem to have known a lot about one another for dozens of years. Nonetheless, the ambience is laidback, and the clientele can easily direct you to more current, and trendier, gay venues in other parts of the Albaicín. Its entrance opens onto a very small, very charming plaza that it shares with the also-recommended hotel, Palacio de Santa Inés. Cuesta de Santa Inés. No phone.

8 Side Trips from Granada

The snowcapped peaks of the **Sierra Nevada** surround the city of Granada, and a number of intriguing excursions exist in several directions. From the top of the highest peak you can see the African coast, and on the clearest of days, even Castilla la Mancha in the central part of eastern Spain. The mountain range is also the home of the Spanish ibex. For those who like to go on trekking jaunts, the Sierra Nevada is the most rewarding territory in all of Andalusia.

The province of Granada is filled with other attractions. You can visit **Guadix,** known for its cave dwellers, and **Las Alpujarras,** one of the most remote—and most fascinating parts of Andalusia. But first, here's a trip closer to Granada.

SANTA FE: THE "CRADLE OF AMERICA"

If you head southwest of Granada along N-342, you come to the little town of Santa Fe, lying 8km (5 miles) from the city. This unimpressive-looking town looms large in history: It was here in the winter of 1491 that Isabella and Ferdinand summoned some 150,000 Spanish troops to besiege Granada, the last territory in Spain under Muslim control.

After the Moorish armies were defeated, it was at Santa Fe that a document of surrender was signed between the Catholic monarchs and the last sultan, Boabdil. These terms of surrender were known as "The Capitulation of Santa Fe," the final act of the Reconquista. When Isabella learned that the Turks had closed the Gibraltar Straits, denying Spain access to the silk route, an alternative route had to be found to the East. In an appendix to the capitulation document, the monarchs agreed to a "wild dream" proposed by an explorer from Genoa and sent Cristóbal Colón (Christopher Columbus) on a journey to the New World. That's why the little town of Santa Fe today is known as the "Cradle of America."

Santa Fe has long spread beyond its original cross-shaped boundaries. At each of the four ends of the "cross" was a gate, emblazoned with the initials of the Catholic monarchs. The gates remain and you can explore or photograph them. In the center of the Old Town is a church that may or may not be open.

FUENTE VAQUEROS

Fans of Federico García Lorca (1898–1936) can journey 17km (11 miles) northwest of Granada to call upon the **Casa-Museo Federico García Lorca,** García Lorca 4 (© **95-851-64-53**), where the poet-playwright was born on June 5, 1898. He lived in this village until age 6. There are many photographs of the artist, posters of his plays, and costumes that bring back his spirit. The house contains many of the original family furnishings. A short video at the end of a visit shows Lorca in action and on tour with the Teatro Barraca.

The museum was opened in 1986 in honor of the 50th anniversary of the assassination of the artist by Franco's troops during the Spanish Civil War. These fascist assassins cited homosexuality as the reason for Lorca's death, but the real reason for his death was his outspoken defense of the Republic, and his criticisms of monarchism, Catholicism, and fascism.

Today Spain has restored Lorca to his rightful place in Spanish letters. A highly revered poet and dramatist, he is viewed by scholars as one of the two greatest poets Spain has produced in the 20th century, and is certainly one of the country's greatest dramatists since the golden age.

Temporary art shows are presented in the former barn and stables. Charging an admission of 1.20€ ($1.45), the house is open July to September Tuesday to Sunday 10am to 1pm and 6 to 8pm; October to March, Tuesday to Sunday 10am to 1pm and 4 to 6pm; April to June daily 10am to 1pm and 5 to 7pm. Guided tours are conducted daily.

True Lorca fans can also visit the village of **Viznar,** 9km (5½ miles) northeast of Granada. Head out the N-342 and follow the signs for the turnoff to Viznar. It was here that the fascists brought Lorca to be beaten and shot in 1936 when they took over Granada. Friends had urged him to flee Spain and escape to France or even America but he refused.

Outside the village on the road to Alfacar is the **Federico García Lorca Memorial Park,** lying 3km (2 miles) from Viznar. A marker pinpoints the spot where the poet was assassinated. Lorca's body was never recovered, so there is no grave for pilgrims to seek out.

GUADIX

If you continue east of Granada for 58km (36 miles), you'll reach the old mining town of Guadix, a land of cave communities perched on a 304m (1,000-ft.) plateau. The town is one of the oldest in Spain and has been inhabited for centuries. Amazingly, half of its estimated population of 20,000 souls inhabits troglodyte cave houses, known as *casas cueva* in Spanish.

Your tour can begin in the center of town at the dignified **cathedral** built between 1594 and 1706. Designed by Diego de Siloé, the architect who helped change the face of Granada, the cathedral is open Monday to Saturday 11am to 1pm and 4:30 to 7pm, Sunday 10:30am to 2pm. Admission is free.

The other town landmark is the nearby **Alcazaba Arabe,** an 11th-century Muslim fort opening onto panoramic views of the Ermita Nueva. It is open Tuesday to Saturday 11am to 2pm and 4 to 6:30pm, Sunday 11am to 2pm. Admission is 1.20€ ($1.45). Facing the cathedral, head up any of the slanting side streets to the left to reach the hilltop fortress with its series of turrets.

Another 10-minute walk uphill from the cathedral will deliver you to the **Barriada de Cuevas** ✦✦, site of some 2,000 cave dwellings which were carved out of the soft sandstone mountains and have existed for half a millennium. Most of these *cuevas* are still occupied by families. From the street about all you'll see is a whitewashed front door. Almost every cave, however, has a TV antenna. Amazingly these caves are often comfortably furnished, and have pleasant year-round temperatures despite the scalding heat that descends in July and August. A few also operate as boardinghouses and will rent you a room.

For visits, call at the doorway to the **Cueva-Museo de Alfarería,** Calle San Miguel 47 (© **95-866-47-67**), which contains a water well dating from the mid–17th century. On display is a collection of domestic and decorative ceramics, many of them antique. Open Monday to Saturday 10am to 2pm and 5 to 7pm, Sunday 11am to 2pm, admission is 2€ ($2.40).

Another attraction is the **Cueva-Museo de Costumbres Populares,** lying off Calle Canada de las Perales (no phone). You can go inside to see a completely preserved cave house, furnished with artifacts. You could actually imagine living here. Open Monday to Saturday 10am to 2pm and 5 to 7pm, Sunday 10am to 2pm, charging an admission of 1.30€ ($1.55).

Maestra buses (© **95-866-06-57**), depart from Granada to Guadix at the rate of 11 per day Monday to Saturday. On Sunday only six buses make the run. It costs 3.95€ ($4.75) for a one-way ticket. A train connection from Granada costs 5.25€ ($6.30) one-way. Either trip takes an hour.

Once you arrive at Guadix, there is a small **tourist office** on Avenida Mariana Pineda (© **95-866-26-65**), open Monday to Friday 8am to 3pm.

WHERE TO STAY & DINE

Cuevas Pedro Antonio de Alarcón It's back to being a cave-dweller here, although conditions are far from prehistoric. At this *aparthotel,* you live not in the main *cueva* district but in a cave right outside town. Each sleeps anywhere from two to five guests for the night and comes complete with kitchenette. If you would like to honeymoon here, you can rent a suite with a romantic whirlpool bath. There are furnishings, but this ain't the Ritz. The decor relies partly on crafts and hand-woven Alpujarras tapestries and rugs; these tapestries often serve as doors between rooms. White walls, wooden furniture, bricks, and ceramic tiles provide the backdrop. Most rooms are spacious, complete with a bathroom with tub and shower. You can enjoy Andalusian specialties in the subterranean restaurant. The caves are near the train station, about 1km (⅔ mile) from Guadix's historical core. Its entrance is on N-342 between the town and the motorway.

Barriada San Torcuato, 18500 Guadix. ✆ **95-866-49-86.** Fax 95-866-17-21. www.andalusia.com/cavehotel. 20 units. 52€–62€ ($62–$74) double; 88€–110€ ($106–$132) suite. MC, V. **Amenities:** Restaurant; outdoor pool; tennis court; laundry service. *In room:* A/C, TV, minibar, hair dryer.

Hotel Comercio   Near Placeta de Los Naranjos and Plaza de Las Américas in the center of town, this is the leading hotel in town—admittedly, king of a lackluster pack. Built a century ago, the building was last renovated in 2004. It is family-run, warm and inviting. Once a private home, the two-story hotel contains an internal patio with beautiful stairs, corridors, and arches. Bedrooms are small to midsize, filled with dark wood furnishings and marble floors. Each comes with a well-maintained private bathroom with tub or shower. In the public area is a music concert room along with a small art gallery. Even if you're not staying here, you can visit the award-winning restaurant, the finest in the area. Specialties like roast lamb with pine nuts and raisins seem to hark back to the Moorish invasion.

Calle Mira de Amezcua 3, 18500 Guadix. ✆ **95-866-05-00.** Fax 95-866-50-72. www.hotelcomercio.com. 40 units. 65€ ($78) double; 240€ ($288) suite. AE, DC, MC, V. Parking 6€ ($7.20). **Amenities:** Restaurant; bar; outdoor pool; gym; Jacuzzi; laundry service; rooms for those w/limited mobility. *In room:* A/C, TV, safe.

SIERRA NEVADA ✦✦✦

A summer hiking center and a vast winter ski resort, the snowcapped Sierra Nevada mountain range is where locals go to play any season of the year. Only an hour's drive from Granada, its dramatic centerpiece, **Mulhacén,** is the highest peak in Spain, rising 3,478m (11,410 ft.). Many other peaks reach a height of 3,000m (9,842 ft.) or more. This vast mountain range extends some 75km (47 miles) west to east. Most of the 1,710 sq. km (660 sq. miles) of wilderness are part of the **Parque Nacional.**

Many visitors elect to explore **Pico de Veleta,** the third highest mountain in the country at 3,390m (11,125 ft.). The view from its **summit** ✦✦ is one of the most panoramic in all of Spain, sweeping over the vast range of Las Alpujarras (the southern slopes of Sierra Nevada) and all the way to the sea. On a clear day you can even see the coast of North Africa. In July and August, microbuses run to the summit along the highest road in Europe. This dangerous road runs past the ski resort of Solynieve at 2,100m (6,890 ft.) and skirts both Mulhacén and Pico de Veleta. Even on the hottest day in August it's cold at the top: Bring a sweater.

In 1986 UNESCO declared the Sierra Nevada to be a biosphere reserve. Because of the mountain range's proximity to the Mediterranean, there is a great diversity of flora and fauna. There are more than 2,100 catalogued flora species, 175 native to Iberia and 65 native to the Sierra Nevada. In spring you can see birds like the common chaffinch and the kinglet, and in fall you can observe the ringed ouzel. The rare golden eagle is also found here.

For more information on trails to the summits of Mulhacén and Pico de Veleta, get in touch with the National Park Service information office at Pampaneira (✆ **95-876-31-27**). For information on the town of Pradollano, contact the **Sierra Nevada Tourist Office** at Pradollano in the Edificio Telecabina (✆ **95-824-91-00**), 33km (21 miles) southeast of Granada. In winter call ✆ **95-824-91-19** for snow and road conditions.

Pradollano is the country's southernmost ski resort and the largest and busiest in Andalusia, a province not normally associated with snow. The resort has 45 downhill runs, for a total of 61km (38 miles), plus 19 lifts. Some of the runs practically start at the peak of Pico de Veleta. The ski season begins in December and normally lasts until April, although in some years it's been known to last into early June. Pradollano also offers four ski schools. In winter **Autobar Bonal** (© 95-846-50-22) operates buses from Granada to Pradollano, leaving daily at 8am with a return at 6:30pm. In summer, departures are daily at 9am, with a return at 5pm. A round-trip ticket costs 5.50€ ($6.60).

WHERE TO STAY & DINE

El Lodge   This is the finest hotel in the Sierra Nevada, and in peak season reservations should be made far in advance. Otherwise, you may find yourself staying in a Granada hotel and commuting to the Sierra Nevada on day trips. In a three-story wooden building, the ski lodge lies at El Balcón de Pradollano at a height of 2,100m (6,889 ft.). There is an alpine quality, and an intimate, cozy atmosphere in winter. Rooms tend to be very small, however, almost ship cabin size. Completely encased in wood, they come with equally small bathrooms, each with a tub and shower. The on-site restaurant serves regional specialties.

Calle Pradollano s/n, 18196 Pradollano. © **95-848-06-00.** Fax 95-848-13-14. www.ellodge.com. 16 units. 198€–230€ ($238–$276) double; 302€–437€ ($362–$524) suite. AE, DC, MC, V. Closed May–Oct. **Amenities:** Restaurant; bar; spa; Jacuzzi; room service (8am–11pm). *In room:* A/C, TV, hair dryer.

LAS ALPUJARRAS ✈

At the southern flank of the Sierra Nevada, where deep ravines split arid hillsides, lies what was for centuries one of Spain's most remote and isolated corners. A journey here is like a journey back into time. Muslim shepherds and farmers lived here until being replaced by Christian settlers in the 1500s.

In the wake of the Reconquista in Seville in 1248 and Granada in 1492, Moors fled to the area to stake out a new life. Ill-fated Boabdil, last emir of Granada, fled here with his mother when Isabella and Ferdinand defeated his armies.

Isolated for centuries from the rest of the world, most of the Alpujarreños still cling to their old rural way of life. You'll see, for example, communal laundry troughs where women gather to wash the family clothing. Writers like Richard Ford and Washington Irving have been attracted by the rural idyll of this district.

Las Alpujarras is like a piece of the Orient located in the western extreme of Europe. Whitewashed cubic houses, terrace farming, towns hugging the contours of mountains, and incredible scenery await you at every turn. The scenery is dotted with the evocative remains of fortresses and fortified towers, most erected during the period of Islamic domination.

The donkey is still used as a beast of burden and a means of transport. In the high range live the mountain goat and other species such as the fox, badger, and genet. Wildcats still call Las Alpujarras home, as does the jeweled lizard.

By the mid–20th century, struggling artists, writers, poets, and hippies settled in the area, along with many expats. Islamic influences have remained strong in the area, particularly in the Berber style villages and the terraced and irrigated landscape.

Some of the architecture of Las Alpujarras still shows a marked Moorish influence, especially in the clay roofs with chimneys. In little villages, narrow streets wind between the houses built one above the other. Most houses are constructed of local materials such as stone, mud, slate, gray clay, or *launa* (wood from the chestnut tree). Houses are almost always whitewashed, and are cubic in shape with few exterior openings.

Alpujarras handicrafts, once in danger of extinction, have been revived. In fact, some visitors tour the region merely to shop. Embroidery, *esparto* work, silverwork, basket weaving, wrought iron, pottery, and leather goods, among other items, are just part of the wide range of crafts for sale from village to village. Alpujarras blankets are highly coveted.

GETTING THERE & EXPLORING

To explore the area you can drive on the E902 to the town of **Lanjarón,** 46km (29 miles) southeast of Granada. This spa town is known for its mineral waters. Continue from here to Orgiva, which is the best center for the western Alpujarras. **Orgiva** is the largest town of the region. It's known for its baroque church on the main street and a lively Thursday market (best in the morning).

At Orgiva, you can leave the C-332, following the signs to the village of **Pampaneira** along a road that winds in serpentine curves. At 1,059m (3,474 ft.), this hamlet overlooks the Poqueira Gorge, a mammoth ravine carved by the Río Poqueira. The town's craft looms are well known, as are its fountains, springs, and tiny squares. Pampaneira lies 14km (8½ miles) northeast of Orgiva.

From Pampaneira you can climb to two of the best-known villages. It takes about an hour to reach **Bubión,** about two to reach **Capileira.** The latter lies at 1,436m (4,711 ft.) and also overlooks the Poqueira Gorge. At its Plaza Mayor, you can visit a little museum with an excellent display of Alpujarras handicrafts. It's open Tuesday to Sunday 11:30am to 2pm. Bubión, on the other hand, is best for its village charm and Berber architecture, with dozens of artisan shops.

If you follow the signposts to the end of the trail, you reach the little village of **Treveléz,** as you climb one of the highest roads in Europe (see "Sierra Nevada," above). This village, known for its *jamón serrano* (Serrano ham), is Spain's second highest community at 1,476m (4,842 ft.). It lies on the slopes of Mulhacén, and many hikers use it as their base for ascending the mountain. After finishing your tour in Treveléz, you work your way back to Orgiva and Lanjorán (the original gateway), connecting to the E902 that will take you north back to Granada.

It's best to explore Las Alpujarras by car, although buses run by **Alsina Graells** (© **95-878-50-02**) leave Granada daily at 10:30am, noon, and 5:15pm for the most scenic of the villages. Buses return to Granada from Alcutar, the farthest town out, at 5am and 5pm. Ask at the Granada bus station for a schedule.

WHERE TO STAY & DINE

Albergue de Mecina   Lying only 200m (656 ft.) from the center of Fondales, this little hotel dates from the dawn of the millennium. Its traditional Alpujarras architecture blends in smoothly with the other buildings in this tiny hamlet. You enter into an enclosed courtyard capped by a glass dome. Bedrooms are small with whitewashed walls, comfortable furnishings, and a little adjoining bathroom with tub and shower. Some of the accommodations open onto a private balcony or terrace. The nearby restaurant, L'Atelier, serves vegetarian and Mediterranean specialties, including vegetarian sausages and white garlic soup. Main courses cost from 9€ to 12€ ($11–$14), and it makes a good luncheon stopover if you're touring in the area. Hours are Thursday to Sunday 1 to 4pm and 7 to 11pm.

Calle La Fuente s/n, Mecina Fondales 18416. © **95-876-62-41.** Fax 95-876-62-55. www.ocioteca.com/hoteldemecina. 21 units. 65€ ($78) double. AE, DC, MC, V. Free parking. **Amenities:** Restaurant; outdoor pool; babysitting; laundry service; rooms for those w/limited mobility. *In room:* A/C, TV.

Hotel Taray *(R)* *Value*   An ideal base for exploring Las Alpujarras, this hotel lies in Orgiva, the largest town in the region. It's only a decade or so old, but looks much older. The place is very cozy, with mainly wooden furnishings and a decor that incorporates regional ornaments and crafts, including hand-woven bed-spreads and curtains. The best rooms are the three opening onto rooftop terraces with views of the hotel gardens. All guests share a panoramic terrace. Rooms for the most part are midsize, each comfortably and tastefully furnished and equipped with a tub/shower combo in the private bathrooms.

This is one of the better places for dining in the area, even if you aren't a hotel guest. The Taray operates its own farm, and much of the ingredients, including alpinelike lamb, trout, berries, and oranges, originate here.

Carretera Tablate-Albuñol Km 18, Orgiva 18400. © **95-878-45-25.** Fax 95-878-45-31. www.hoteltaray.com. 15 units. 85€ ($102) double. AE, DC, MC, V. Free parking. **Amenities:** Restaurant; babysitting; laundry service. *In room:* A/C, TV, minibar.

La Fragua   In a characteristic village home near the town hall, this two-story house, built of stone with whitewashed walls, is the finest address in the little hamlet of Trevélez high in the mountains. The inn dates from 1991 and was last renovated in 2002. The rooms are slightly better, though more expensive, in an adjoining newer structure. Most are midsize, each tastefully and comfortably furnished, and with a tub/shower combo in the bathroom. A comfortable guest lounge is found in each of the hotels' two buildings. Guests head for the rooftop terrace for panoramic views of the surrounding area.

A family-run enterprise, the hotel generates more business for its cafe/bar/restaurant than it does for its rooms. With panoramic mountain views from the dining room, an excellent regional menu of specialties is presented, along with a *carte* of affordable regional wines. Meat fanciers will do fine here if they order the herb-flavored loin of pork or suckling pig in a garlic sauce.

San Antonio 4, Barrio Medio, 18417 Trevélez. © **95-885-86-26.** Fax 95-885-86-14. www.hotellafragua.com. 14 units. 33€–40€ ($40–$48) double. MC, V. Free parking. **Amenities:** Restaurant; laundry service; rooms for those w/limited mobility. *In room:* A/C, TV.

8

Ronda & the Pueblos Blancos/Sherry Triangle

There's a lot more to inland Andalusia than Granada, Seville, and Córdoba. Although not in their league, the tiny city of Ronda enjoys an incomparable setting, perched high above the Tajo Gorge where political prisoners were once thrown to their deaths. Ronda also has beautiful and historic art and architecture, with one of the oldest bullrings in the country and plenty of Roman and Moorish ruins.

Ronda is the best known of Spain's Pueblos Blancos (white towns), so called for their whitewashed houses built closely together. Visitors with more time can visit the other Pueblos Blancos in and around Ronda. Below we describe a 2-day driving tour that will take you to our favorite (and

the most beautiful) of these towns, including Arcos de la Frontera. This is one of Spain's most scenic routes and has plenty of fascinating stops along the way.

Another wonderful series of towns are those that make up the famous "Sherry Triangle": Jerez de la Frontera, El Puerto de Santa María, and the port of Sanlúcar de Barrameda. These towns are known for their, yes, sherry (*jerez* in Spanish). Indulging in a wine-tasting tour in their vineyards is one of the best ways to experience these towns. If you have time for only one, make it Jerez de la Frontera, with the best bodegas (wineries) and the world headquarters of the sherry industry. In Jerez you can also see "The Dancing Horses of Andalusia."

1 Ronda ★/★

102km (63 miles) NE of Algeciras, 97km (60 miles) W of Málaga, 147km (91 miles) SE of Seville, 591km (367 miles) S of Madrid

This little town high in the Serranía de Ronda Mountains (698m/2,300 ft. above sea level) is one of the oldest and most aristocratic places in Spain. Ronda's near impregnable position kept the Catholic troops at bay until 1485. The main attraction is a deep gorge, spanned by three bridges over the Guadelevín River. On both sides of this hole in the earth are houses clinging to the cliff that look as though they might plunge into the chasm at the slightest push.

Ronda is an incredible sight. The town and the surrounding mountains were legendary hideouts for bandits and smugglers, but today the Guardia Civil has just about put an end to that. The gorge divides the town into an older part, the Moorish and aristocratic quarter, and the newer section south of the gorge, built principally after the Reconquest.

The old quarter is by far the more fascinating; it contains narrow, rough streets and buildings with a marked Moorish influence (watch for the minaret). After the lazy resort living of the Costa del Sol, make a side excursion to Ronda; its unique beauty and refreshing mountain air are a tonic.

Ronda

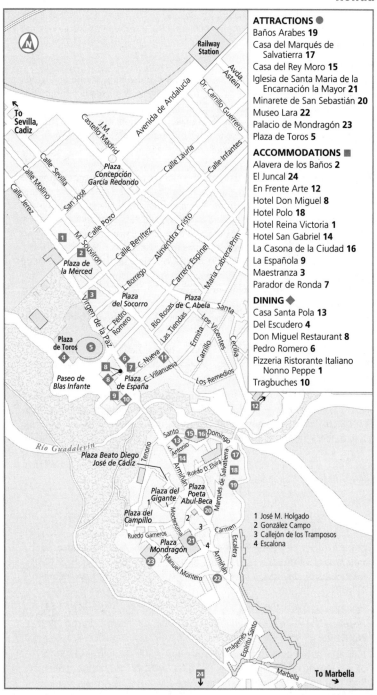

ATTRACTIONS ●

Baños Arabes **19**
Casa del Marqués de Salvatierra **17**
Casa del Rey Moro **15**
Iglesia de Santa Maria de la Encarnación la Mayor **21**
Minarete de San Sebastián **20**
Museo Lara **22**
Palacio de Mondragón **23**
Plaza de Toros **5**

ACCOMMODATIONS ■

Alavera de los Baños **2**
El Juncal **24**
En Frente Arte **12**
Hotel Don Miguel **8**
Hotel Polo **18**
Hotel Reina Victoria **1**
Hotel San Gabriel **14**
La Casona de la Ciudad **16**
La Española **9**
Maestranza **3**
Parador de Ronda **7**

DINING ◆

Casa Santa Pola **13**
Del Escudero **4**
Don Miguel Restaurant **8**
Pedro Romero **6**
Pizzeria Ristorante Italiano Nonno Peppe **1**
Tragbuches **10**

1 José M. Holgado
2 González Campo
3 Callejón de los Tramposos
4 Escalona

Note that local children may attach themselves to you as guides. For a few euros, it's not a bad idea to hire one since it's difficult to weave your way in and out of the narrow streets.

ESSENTIALS

GETTING THERE   Most visitors take a **train** to the main station at Avenida La Victoria (© 95-287-16-73). Three trains arrive from Granada per day. The trip takes 3 hours and costs 10€ ($12) one-way. You can also visit Ronda from the Costa del Sol where one daily train makes the 2-hour trip from Málaga to Ronda, costing 7.55€ ($9.05) one-way. Two trains daily connect Ronda and Madrid. The trip takes 4½ hours and costs 49€ ($58) one-way.

The main **bus** station is at Plaza Concepción García Redondo 2 (© 95-218-70-61). There are five buses a day from Seville, taking 2½ hours and costing 9€ ($11) one-way. There is also service from Málaga, taking 2½ hours and costing 7.55€ ($9.05) one-way. Also on the Costa del Sol, Marbella runs 5 buses per day to Ronda, taking a half-hour and costing 4.30€ ($5.15) one-way.

Major highways circle Ronda, but you'll have to take winding, circuitous, and secondary routes to reach the town itself. From Seville, take N-334 southwest. When you reach the small town of El Arahal, continue south into Ronda along C-339. If you're in Granada, take N-342 west to the junction with N-332, then take N-332 southwest to the junction with C-339, which eventually winds its way southeast into Ronda. If you're on the Costa del Sol you can reach Ronda from Málaga traveling northwest via the scenic C-344, or from Marbella northwest on C-339.

VISITOR INFORMATION   The **tourist office,** Plaza de España 9 (© 95-287-12-72; www.turismoderonda.es), is open Monday to Friday 9am to 7:30pm, Saturday and Sunday 10am to 2pm.

GETTING AROUND   The town is small so you can walk to most places of interest. If you have to go farther afield, you can call **Parada de Taxis** at © 95-287-23-16. Taxis are usually found in front of the Plaza de Toros, the bullring. A typical fare—say, from the train station to Plaza de España—costs 4€ ($4.80).

If you arrived in Ronda by train or bus and want to explore the environs, perhaps taking a driving tour of the Pueblos Blancos, you can rent **cars** at **Velasco,** Lorenzo Borrego 11 (© 95-287-27-82).

FAST FACTS: **Ronda**
_____

Currency Exchange The most central bank, with ATMs, is **Banco Santander Central Hispano,** Carretera Espinel 17 (© 95-902-24-24), near Calle los Remedios. Open Monday to Friday 8:30am to 2pm, Saturday 8:30am to 1pm.

Emergency Dial © 092. For a medical emergency, call © 95-287-17-73.

Hospital The main hospital is **Centro de Salud,** Carretera El Burgo (© 95-287-56-75).

Internet Access Head for **Planet Adventure,** Calle Molino 6 (© 95-287-52-49), open daily 9am to 10pm, charging 1.80€ ($2.15) per hour 9am to 3pm or 2.40€ ($2.90) per hour 3 to 10pm.

Pharmacy The most central is **Farmacia Homeopatia,** Plaza de España 5 (© 95-287-52-49), open Monday to Friday 9:30am to 2pm and 5 to 8:30pm.

EXPLORING RONDA

It takes a half-day at most to see Ronda, but if you have more time, spend a full day or even two wandering the narrow streets of the walled Old Town and exploring the Moorish ruins. The best time to visit is in the spring when the orange and almond trees are in bloom.

Ronda was precariously erected at the edge of the mountain range of the Serranía de Ronda on a **platform site** 🏵🏵 that was cut by the Guadalevín River in prehistoric times. **El Tajo,** a 100m (328-ft.) ravine divides Ronda into two distinct parts, including **La Ciudad** 🏵🏵🏵, the Moorish Old Town with a labyrinth of streets and alleyways, flanked by whitewashed houses with wrought-iron balconies. La Cuidad lies on the south side of El Tajo ("the ravine" in English).

The newer town, **El Mercadillo** 🏵, is to the north. This town sprang up after the Christian Reconquest and is filled with a number of attractions, including the Plaza de Toros or bullring (see below).

Three bridges cross the gorge, the main one being **Puente Nuevo** 🏵, from which you can enjoy a panoramic view of Ronda and its countryside. This is Ronda's most famous bridge and was an architectural marvel when it was constructed between 1755 and 1793. A lantern-lit parapet graces the bridge. Over the years many people have fallen to their deaths from here, even the original architect did so during an inspection. During the bitter Spanish Civil War, it was a place of execution for Franco's troops or the rebels, depending on which group was controlling Ronda at the time. Ernest Hemingway in *For Whom the Bell Tolls* recorded how prisoners were thrown alive into this deep gorge.

Ronda's two other bridges are both north of Puento Nuevo. These include **Puente Viejo (Old Bridge),** dating from 1616, and the single-span Moorish bridge, **Puente de San Miguel.**

Ronda is still entered by two ancient gates, the 13th-century **Puerta de Almocobar** and the 16th-century **Puerta de Carlos V.**

In the center of the Moorish quarter stands **Iglesia de Santa María de la Encarnación la Mayor,** Plaza Duquesa de Parcent s/n (✆ **95-287-22-46**), a collegiate church that acts as a cathedral. The landmark square it opens on to is Ronda's most central. Like many churches in Andalusia, Santa María is a reconstruction of a former mosque, in this case, the Great Mosque of Ronda. As a result, both the interior and exterior feature a medley of architectural styles. Outside you see Moorish, Gothic, and Renaissance influences, with a belfry constructed on top of the old Moorish minaret. Inside you'll find naves in the late Gothic style, a main altar heavy with baroque gold leaf, a Plateresque chancel, and an arch still covered with Arabic calligraphy. You can still see an old Muslim *mihrab* (prayer niche) in front of the current street door. The two-tiered balcony on the facade was a gallery where notables could watch special events staged on the square below. Admission free, the church is open daily May to October 10am to 8pm (daily 10am–6pm in the off season).

East of the church if you follow Callejón de los Tramposos, you can see a Moorish tower, **Minarete de San Sebastián** part of the original Great Mosque of Ronda dating to the 14th century.

The still-functioning **Baños Arabes** ⚑, in a ravine below the Palacio del Marqués de Salvatierra (✆ **95-287-38-89**), are reached from the turnoff to Puente San Miguel. Dating from the 13th century, the baths have glass roof-windows and hump-shaped cupolas. Still well preserved, they are the finest example of Moorish baths in Spain. The star-shaped vents in the roof were modeled after the ceiling of the more famous bathhouse at the Alhambra in Granada. Note the beautiful octagonal brick columns supporting horseshoe arches. A channel from the nearby river carried water into the complex which once was surrounded by landscaped Moorish gardens. Admission is free, and the baths are open Wednesday to Saturday 9:30am to 3pm, Tuesday 10am to 1:30pm and 4 to 6pm, and Sunday 10am to 2pm.

Palacio de Mondragón, Plaza de Mondragón (✆ **95-287-84-50**), was once the 14th-century private home of the Moorish king, Abomelic. But after the Reconquista, it was renovated to receive King Ferdinand and Queen Isabella who stayed here. Inside you can see a trio of courtyards and a collection of Moorish mosaics. There is also a beautiful carved wooden ceiling. A small museum houses artifacts devoted to regional archaeology. Better than the museum is the restored mudéjar courtyard where you can take in a panoramic view of El Tajo with the Serranía de Ronda looming in the background. Flanked by two mudéjar towers, the building now has a baroque facade. It's open Monday through Friday from 10am to 7pm, Saturday and Sunday 10am to 3pm; admission is 2€ ($2.40), free for children under 14.

Another aristocratic home is **Casa del Marqués de Salvatierra,** on Marqués de Salvatierra s/n (✆ **95-287-12-06**), a noble Renaissance mansion with a rather grotesque frieze of Adam and Eve on its portal. An international traveler, the original marquis decorated his minipalace with the figures of two Inca Indian couples holding up a triangular pediment and other architectural curiosities. A wrought-iron balcony and detailed low reliefs form yet another part of his decorative overlay. Some of the pre-Columbian figures are sticking their tongues out. The palace was formed by combining two Moorish houses from the 1400s, a gift from the throne to the marqués after the Reconquista. You can also explore the gardens of the mansion. The mansion has been owned by the same family since 1475; they stay here in August, but the home is open other months. Hours are Friday to Wednesday 11am to 2pm and 4 to 7pm (but usually closed Sun 4–7pm). Admission is 3€ ($3.60). Because this is still a private residence, don't count on it always being open.

(Finds) When Curses Become a Blessing

On a hot day, and summers are very hot in Ronda, you can retreat to the town's loveliest spot, the gardens of **Alameda del Tojo** ⚑, lying beyond the Plaza de Toros in El Mercadillo, the New Town. This park dates from the heyday of the British invasion in the 19th century. The city fathers at the time raised money to create the gardens by heavily fining citizens who used obscene language in public. Apparently, there was a lot of cussing going on because the park is truly beautiful. If you walk to the end of the gardens, a panoramic balcony emerges from the face of the cliff. If you don't have vertigo, you can take in a vast sweep of the countryside beyond and the views of Serrenía de Ronda in the distance. A cliff-top walk leads to the Hotel Reina Victoria.

> ## *Moments* Prehistoric Cave Paintings
>
> Near Benaoján, the **Cueva de la Pileta** ☆ (℃ **95-216-73-43**), 25km (16 miles) southwest of Ronda, plus a 2km (1¼-mile) hard climb, has been compared to the Caves of Altamira in northern Spain, where prehistoric paintings were discovered toward the end of the 19th century. In a wild area known as the Serranía de Ronda, José Bullón Lobato, grandfather of the present owners, discovered this cave in 1905. More than a mile in length and filled with oddly and beautifully shaped stalagmites and stalactites, the cave also contained five fossilized human skeletons and two animal skeletons.
>
> In the mysterious darkness, **prehistoric paintings** depict animals in yellow, red, black, and ocher, as well as mysterious symbols. One of the highlights of the tour is a trip to the chamber of the fish, containing a wall painting of a great black seal-like creature about 1m (3 ft.) long. This chamber, the innermost heart of the cave, ends in a precipice that drops vertically nearly 75m (250 ft.). In the valley just below the cave lives a guide who'll conduct you around the chambers, carrying artificial light to illuminate the paintings. Plan to spend at least an hour here. Tours are given daily from 10am to 1pm and 4 to 6pm (Sept–June 10am–1pm and 4–5pm). Admission, including the hour tour, is 6.50€ ($7.80) adults, 3€ ($3.60) children 10 to 13, and 2.50€ ($3) children 5 to 10.
>
> It's easiest to get here by car from Ronda, but you can also take the train to Benaoján. The cave, whose entrance is at least 6.5km (4 miles) uphill, is in the rocky foothills of the Sierra de Libar midway between two tiny villages: Jimera de Libar and Benaoján. Ronda and the cave are in parallel valleys, separated by a steep range of hills. Reaching the cave requires a rather complicated detour to either the south or the north of Ronda, then doubling back.

Casa del Rey Moro, Cuesta del Santo Domingo (℃ **95-218-72-00**), is misnamed, as this House of the Moorish King was actually built in 1709. However, it's believed to have been constructed over Moorish foundations. The interior is closed, but from the garden you can take an underground stairway, called La Mina, which leads you to the river, a distance of 365 steps. Christian slaves cut these steps in the 14th century to guarantee a steady water supply in case Ronda came under siege. The owners of the Casa Imperial in Seville are turning this building into a sumptuous luxury hotel. When completed, perhaps in the lifetime of this edition, it is anticipated this will become Ronda's high-end luxury address.

Ronda has the oldest bullring in Spain. Built in 1785, the **Plaza de Toros** ☆☆ is the setting for the yearly Corrida Goyesca in honor of Ronda native son Pedro Romero, one of the greatest bullfighters of all time. The bullring is a work of architectural beauty, built of limestone with double arches and 136 Tuscan-like columns. The town is still talking about the music video Madonna and entourage staged here. If you want to know more about Ronda bullfighting, head for the **Museo Taurino,** Calle Virgen de la Paz (℃ **95-287-41-32**), reached through the ring. It's open daily March to October 10am to 8pm and November to February 10am to 6pm. Admission is 5€ ($6). Exhibits document the exploits of the noted Romero family. Francesco invented the killing sword and the *muleta,* and his grandson, Pedro (1754–1839), killed 5,600 bulls during his 30-year career. Pedro was the inspiration for Goya's famous *Tauromaquia* series. There are also exhibits devoted to Cayetano Ordóñez, the matador immortalized by Hemingway in *The Sun Also Rises.*

One of Ronda's newest museums is **Museo Lara,** Calle Armiñan 29 (*©* **95-287-12-63**), which contains the private art collection of a well-known local, Juan Antonio Lara. He started collecting "things" when he was a young boy, and this extensive museum is filled with what he accumulated in his lifetime—some 5,000 artifacts in all. These are divided into seven different compartments—galleries devoted to bullfighting, archaeology, weapons, antique clocks, knives, musical instruments, and early cameras and cinematographic equipment. Admission is 2.50€ ($3) for adults, and 2€ ($2.40) for students, children, and seniors. Hours are daily 10:30am to 7pm.

SHOPPING

Crafts, antiques, and some gift items are available, but save your serious shopping for Granada or Seville. **Muñoz Soto,** San Juan de Dios de Córdoba 34 (*©* **95-287-14-51**), has a range of decorative accessories, antiques, drawings of local scenes, and various souvenirs. Open Monday to Saturday 10am to 2pm and 4 to 7:30pm. Another good address for shoppers is **El Pensamiento Ronda,** Calle Espinel (*©* **95-287-21-93**), in a small shopping center. It has a wide range of merchandise from antiques to china, from paintings and pottery to glass and gift items. Open Monday to Saturday 10am to 8:30pm.

WHERE TO STAY
EXPENSIVE

El Juncal ★★ *(Finds)*   Tiny, quirky, and delightful, this is a real discovery. Manuel María Lopez and Lola Jiménez, who also operate Ronda's Michelin-starred restaurant, Tragabuches, are the entrepreneurs who created this gem of an inn. A 5-minute ride from the town center, it is surrounded by vineyards. An old Spanish *finca* (a kind of farmhouse) has been beautifully converted with furniture by Philippe Starck, contemporary rugs, even antique lace. The comfortable, midsize bedrooms have cool parquet flooring and modern decor. Bathrooms are immaculate with marble floors and tub/shower combos. The double rooms and suites are spread over two stories, some with private terraces or patios. Each unit is individually decorated. A lovely swimming pool is set in landscaped gardens. Although not as good as Tragabuches, there is an on-site Spanish restaurant with a fixed-price menu and fine regional wines.

Carretera El Burgo Km 1, 29400 Ronda. *©* **95-216-11-70.** Fax 95-216-11-60. www.eljuncal.com. 11 units. 110€–240€ ($132–$288) double; 165€–240€ ($198–$288) suite. AE, DC, MC, V. **Amenities:** Restaurant; lounge; outdoor pool; solarium; sauna; 24-hr. room service; babysitting; laundry service/dry cleaning; rooms for those w/limited mobility. *In room:* A/C, TV, dataport, hair dryer, safe.

Parador de Ronda ★★★   This parador is the grandest accommodation in the area. It sits on a high cliff overlooking the fantastic gorge that cuts a swath more than 150m (500 ft.) deep and 90m (300 ft.) wide through the center of this mountain town. Stretching along the edge of the gorge to a bridge, the Puente Nuevo, the parador is surrounded by a footpath with scenic views of the gorge and the Guadalevín River below. The good-size rooms are beautifully furnished, each containing a bathroom with a tub/shower combo; many open onto

---

Finds **Where Lemons Are Sweet**

Rondeños flock to **Confitería Harillo,** Carretera Espinel 36 (© **95-287-13-60**), for the best-tasting sweets in the area. Near the Plaza de Toros, the pastry chefs here still follow some recipes based on traditional Moorish treats—and they left centuries ago. Their fruit confections are made from ingredients grown in and around Ronda, including strawberries, lemons, and oranges. They taste divine but are extremely rich and sugary. Sugar-cooked egg yolks is a typical dessert, as are various nougats or sweets made with a mixture of almonds and pistachios. Some of the Arabic confections are really marzipan made with nuts other than almonds. Pastries begin at 2€ ($2.40). The cakes here are very good, nice to bring with you for a picnic in the hills. Open daily 10am to 9pm.

---

balconies with views of the peaks surrounding Ronda. Even if you don't stay here, consider eating in the first-class dining room with its dramatic views. Chef's specialties include roast kid, stewed partridge, rabbit *a la rondeña,* almond soup, cold garlic soup, and noteworthy desserts such as honey cake or sweet egg yolk flans. An average multicourse meal costs around 30€ ($36).

Plaza de España s/n, 29400 Ronda. © **95-287-75-00.** Fax 95-287-81-88. www.parador.es. 78 units. 119€–220€ ($143–$264) double; 184€–240€ ($221–$288) suite. AE, DC, MC, V. Parking 10€ ($12). **Amenities:** Restaurant; bar; outdoor pool; limited room service; laundry service/dry cleaning. *In room:* A/C, TV, minibar, coffeemaker (in some), hair dryer, safe.

MODERATE

En Frente Arte ⭐ *Value*   Lying on Ronda's oldest paved street and surrounded by historic buildings, this little inn faces the natural park, Sierra de las Nieves. The mansion has been beautifully decorated and handsomely restored, with whitewashed walls and a roof of red tiles. Its bedrooms, as evidenced by the difference in rates, range from small to spacious. Each room has a different decorative theme, ranging from Arabic to Spanish to French. Our favorite is the dramatic tower room, which has the best views. The atmosphere is casual. Above the intimate bar and informal restaurant, the hotel has a recreation room with pool table, TV, and library as well as a computer with free access to the Internet. A subtropical garden has exotic plants, and the courtyards and terraces open onto views of the Old Town and the countryside.

Calle Real 40, 29400 Ronda. © **95-287-90-88.** Fax 95-287-72-17. www.enfrentearte.com. 14 units. 78€–100€ ($94–$120) double. Rates include all drinks, breakfast, and a lunch buffet. MC, V. Free parking. **Amenities:** Restaurant; bar; outdoor pool; sauna; room service (8am–11pm); babysitting; laundry service. *In room:* A/C, TV, dataport, minibar, hair dryer, safe.

Hotel Reina Victoria ⭐   On the eastern periphery of town, this country-style hotel dates from 1906, when it was built by an Englishman in honor of Queen Victoria. It's near the bullring, with terraces that hang right over a 147m (490-ft.) precipice. Hemingway frequently visited, but the Reina Victoria is known best as the place where poet Rainer María Rilke wrote *The Spanish Trilogy.* His third-floor room has been set aside as a museum with first editions, manuscripts, photographs, and even a framed copy of his hotel bill. A life-size bronze statue of him stands in a corner of the garden. In fact, its critics claim that the somewhat dusty and dilapidated Reina Victoria is more museum than hotel. But its gardens and terraces have an enduring appeal for us, as does the old-fashioned

Victorian architecture with towering chimneys and sloping roofs. The rooms are big and airy, some with living rooms and many with private terraces. The beds are sumptuous, and the bathrooms boast tub/shower combos. The location is in the modern section of Ronda, about a 10-minute stroll west of the gorge.

Paseo Doctor Fleming 25, 29400 Ronda. ℂ **95-287-12-40.** Fax 95-287-10-75. www.hotelreina-victoriaronda. com. 89 units. 100€–124€ ($120–$149) double; 140€–160€ ($168–$192) suite. AE, DC, MC, V. Free parking. **Amenities:** Restaurant; bar; outdoor pool; limited room service; babysitting; laundry service/dry cleaning; rooms for those w/limited mobility. *In room:* A/C, TV, minibar, hair dryer, safe.

La Casona de la Ciudad ✿   Next to Plaza del Gigante in the old quarter, this former 16th-century private home became a hotel in 2004. Beyond the reception foyer, a central courtyard leads to the elegant drawing room and library as well as the breakfast room and gardens. Two bedrooms are on the ground floor. The beautifully restored and comfortably furnished accommodations are midsize, each coming with a combination tub/shower in the tiled bathroom. A bygone age is re-created with rich fabrics, antique furnishings, wooden floors, and Arab carpets. You'll feel you're in a minipalace with columns, high ceilings, balconies, and corridors. Only breakfast is served, but many good restaurants are nearby.

Marqués de Salvatierra 5, 29400 Ronda. ℂ **95-287-95-95.** Fax 95-216-10-95. www.lacasonadelaciudad. com. 9 units. 100€–115€ ($120–$138) double; 135€ ($162) junior suite; 165€ ($198) suite. AE, DC, MC, V. Parking 12€ ($14). **Amenities:** Breakfast lounge; outdoor pool; rooms for those w/limited mobility. *In room:* A/C, TV, dataport, minibar, hair dryer, safe.

Maestranza ✿ *Value*   This modern hotel grew up on the site of a villa once inhabited by Pedro Romero, a legendary bullfighter. In the center of town, it faces the oldest bullring in the world. Today all traces of the former villa are gone. In its place is one of the best and most contemporary hotels in town. The bedrooms are small to midsize, but have been designed for comfort, with modern furnishings, carpets, and draperies, each accommodation coming with a private bathroom with tub and shower. The public rooms are both tasteful and graceful, and the staff is helpful and the service excellent. Clients can use the facilities of a private country club nearby, with a swimming pool and tennis courts.

Calle Virgen de la Paz 24, 29400 Ronda. ℂ **95-218-70-72.** Fax 952-19-01-70. www.hotelmaestranza.com. 54 units. 92€–111€ ($110–$133) double; 128€–147€ ($154–$176) suite. AE, DC, MC, V. Parking 9€ ($11). **Amenities:** Restaurant; bar; limited room service; babysitting; laundry service/dry cleaning; nonsmoking rooms; rooms for those w/limited mobility. *In room:* A/C, TV, dataport, minibar, hair dryer, safe.

INEXPENSIVE

Alavera de los Baños ✿ *Finds*   In the San Miguel quarter of Ronda, formerly the Jewish ghetto, this hotel stands near the Baños Arabes (Arab baths). Dating from the 17th century, it was last renovated in 1999. An atmospheric place with great character, it has low ceilings and wooden beams. The inn was featured as a backdrop in *Carmen,* the movie classic. The bedrooms have panoramic views of the enveloping Serranía de Ronda as well as of the city walls. In the rear of the hotel is a garden with chairs and a pool. Bedrooms are small but comfortably and tastefully furnished with little shower-only bathrooms. Guests can enjoy the library and the on-site restaurant, where most of the food is organically grown.

Hoyo San Miguel, 29400 Ronda. ℂ **95-287-91-43.** Fax 95-287-91-43. www.andalucia.com/alavera. 10 units. 80€–100€ ($96–$120) double. AE, DC, MC, V. Free parking. **Amenities:** Restaurant; outdoor pool. *In room:* No phone.

Hotel Don Miguel ✿ *Value*   From the narrow street leading to it, this hotel presents a severely dignified white facade very similar to that of its neighbors.

From the back, however, some of its rooms look out over the river gorge of a steep ravine. Set a few steps east of the Plaza de España and composed of several interconnected houses, it offers a vine-strewn patio above the river, a modernized interior accented with exposed brick and varnished pine, and simple but comfortable small rooms. Overflow guests are housed in a building (no. 13) across the street. Rooms here have the same dramatic views and are comparable to the main building. All bathrooms come with tub/shower combos. The on-site restaurant with a balcony clinging to the cliff doesn't just rely on its view, but it also serves good food. See review below.

Plaza de España 4, 29400 Ronda. © **95-287-77-22.** Fax 95-287-83-77. www.dmiguel.com. 30 units. 85€ ($102) double. Rates include breakfast. AE, DC, MC, V. Parking 9€ ($11). **Amenities:** Restaurant; bar; lounge; rooms for those w/limited mobility. *In room:* A/C, TV, dataport (in some), safe (in some).

Hotel Polo *(Value* The hotel in its present incarnation dates from 1973 but the building itself has been housing frugal travelers for a century or more. Today the Puya brothers are in charge of this family business, running a well-maintained and decent four-story corner building right in the center within walking distance of the Puente Nuevo. The facade is from the 19th century, and the hotel was last renovated in 1999. The bedrooms are small with white walls and carpeting, along with tiled bathrooms with tub/shower combos. The hotel is especially popular with young people.

Maríano Soubiron 8, 29400 Ronda. © **95-287-24-47.** Fax 95-287-24-49. www.hotelpolo.net/hotel.html. 36 units. 55€–80€ ($66–$96) double. AE, DC, MC, V. Parking 10€ ($12). **Amenities:** Restaurant; bar; laundry service. *In room:* A/C, TV, hair dryer.

Hotel San Gabriel *★★ (Finds* This charming 1736 mansion—also called Su Casa en Ronda—stands in the historic core a 5-minute walk from the gorge. The building was painstakingly renovated by the owner and his sons and daughter, who give guests Ronda's warmest welcome. Inside, all is stylish and homelike, filled with antiques, stained-glass windows, a Spanish-style billiard table, a *cine* salon (with seats taken from the city's old theater), and even an old library. Each room is spacious and well appointed, all with exterior views, individual decoration, and bathrooms with tub/shower combos. Try for no. 15, a cozy top-floor nest on two levels. You can relax on the patio and take in the surroundings.

Marqués de Moctezuma 19 (just off Calle Armiñán), 29400 Ronda. © **95-219-03-92.** Fax 95-219-01-17. www.hotelsangabriel.com. 16 units. 70€–80€ ($84–$96) double; 92€–102€ ($110–$122) suite. AE, MC, V. **Amenities:** Breakfast room; bar; game room. *In room:* A/C, TV, minibar, hair dryer, safe.

La Española *(Value* A 2-minute walk from the gorge and next to the Plaza de Toros (the bullring), this two-story family-style house attracts bargain hunters. The small bedrooms are relatively simple, albeit comfortable, but at these prices, you can't expect dramatic views of the gorge. Rooms do, however, open onto the landscaped grounds and the Sierras in the distance and have full bathrooms with tub and shower. Every nook and cranny of the public areas has been decorated in a typical Andalusian style. The on-site restaurant offers typical dishes from the mountains of Ronda. Tables are placed on a covered terrace where live music can sometimes be heard. The government-rated two-star hotel lies between Puente Nuevo (the new bridge) overlooking the Tajo River, and Paseo de Blas Infante gardens.

José Aparicio 3, 29400 Ronda. © **95-287-10-51.** Fax 95-287-80-01. www.ronda.net/usuar/laespanola. 16 units. 70€–88€ ($84–$106). Rates include continental breakfast. AE, DC, MC, V. **Amenities:** Restaurant; bar; room service (8am–11pm). *In room:* A/C, TV.

ON THE OUTSKIRTS

El Molino del Santo ⭐ *Finds* This is one of the best country hotels in Andalusia, a real discovery. It adjoins a rushing stream outside Benaoján, an easy 10km (7-mile) drive west of Ronda. It's a great place for escapists—even Ronda can get overcrowded in summer. The landscaped inn was converted from an old olive and flower watermill set in the mountains within the Natural Park of Grazalema. Once a private home, it opened as a British-managed hotel in 1987. Guests relax in the gardens near the solar-heated pool, enjoying willow or fig trees for shade. Later they can wander through the flower-filled terrace, perhaps enjoying outside dining from May to October. Each of the good-size bedrooms is comfortably and tastefully furnished. Some are large enough for one or two extra beds, making them suitable for families. Most of the accommodations open onto terraces with views. Each room comes with a tiled bathroom with tub and shower. In the main lounge is a log fireplace for chilly nights in winter, and upstairs is a well-stocked library. The chefs specialize in regional dishes, and the menu varies according to the seasons. Breakfast is buffet style.

Estación de Benaoján, 29370 Benaoján. ℭ **95-216-71-51.** Fax 95-216-73-27. www.andalucia.com/Molino. 15 units. 134€–179€ ($161–$215) double. AE, DC, MC, V. Closed mid-Nov to mid-Feb. **Amenities:** Restaurant; bar; pool. *In room:* A/C, TV, minibar, beverage maker.

WHERE TO DINE
EXPENSIVE

Del Escudero ⭐ ANDALUSIAN The second-finest restaurant in town occupies a baronial-looking 19th-century villa which originally functioned as a private house. Inside, in a location very close to the town's *Plaza de Toros,* you'll find three separate dining rooms, each with white walls and lots of very large windows overlooking the jagged nearby mountains. There's also a well-tended dining terrace that the well-trained staff opens in nice weather. Dishes are defined as uptown and upscale Andalusian, including a house-made version of gooseliver pâté sweetened with the local Pedro Ximénez, which is usually defined as a reddish-colored dessert wine; filets of freshwater trout served with almond sauce and strips of Iberian ham; grilled filets of Andalusian pork with a truffle sauce; and slices of chocolate tart served with mango-flavored sherbet. If you opt to dine here, you'll be following in the steps of good company. Former clients have included a former president of Spain.

Paseo Blas Infante 1. ℭ **95-287-15-67.** Reservations recommended. Main courses 12€–18€ ($14–$22). AE, DC, MC, V. Sun noon–5pm; Mon–Sat noon–5pm and 7–10pm.

Tragabuches ⭐⭐⭐ MODERN SPANISH/ANDALUSIAN Chef/owner Daniel Garcia serves the finest and most creative cuisine in Ronda. There are two dining rooms, each with a stylish contemporary decor. Against a typical backdrop of white walls, tables are decked out with pastel cloths and seat covers. The inventive menu is likely to feature well-crafted dishes like *cochinillo asado* (grilled suckling pig) or *rape en salsa de vinagreta, pulpo y verdura* (monkfish in a vinaigrette sauce with octopus and fresh vegetables). Begin perhaps with a cheese taco or the tasty liver pâté. The excellent desserts include a range of homemade cakes and ice cream.

José Aparicio 1 (between Plaza de España and Plaza de Toros). ℭ **95-219-02-91.** Reservations recommended on weekends. Main courses 11€–25€ ($13–$30); set menu 64€ ($74). AE, DC, MC, V. Sun 1:30–3:30pm; Mon–Sat 1:30–3:30pm and 8:30–10:30pm.

MODERATE

Casa Santa Pola INTERNATIONAL/ANDALUSIAN   Constructed in the
19th century but altered and rebuilt over the years, this building on the outskirts
of the city opens onto views of the gorge. It's composed of three levels built onto
the mountainside; access is through the third floor. The interior is a mix of Moorish, rococo, and contemporary, with a decor of antique ornaments, wooden
floors, archways, terra-cotta walls, and red bistro-style tablecloths. Many of the
meals are cooked in a traditional brick oven. Excellent meals include *cochinillo*
(roast suckling pig), *lomo asado* (grilled filet beef steak), and the savory *rabo de
toro* (roast oxtail). Desserts are homemade and traditional to the area. On certain nights, diners are treated to flamenco shows organized by owner Tomás
Mayo.

Calle Santo Domingo 3. ℰ **95-287-92-08.** Main courses 10€–20€ ($12–$24); set menu 20€ ($24). AE, DC,
MC, V. Daily 11:30am–5pm and 7:30–11pm.

Don Miguel Restaurant ✿ ANDALUSIAN   At the end of the bridge facing
the river, this restaurant offers diners views of the upper gorge. It has enough
tables set outside on two levels to seat 300 people. The food is good, and the
waiters are polite and speak some English. There is a pleasant bar for drinks and
tapas. Try one of the seafood selections or the house specialty, stewed oxtail. The
also-recommended Hotel Don Miguel (see "Where to Stay," above) runs the
restaurant.

Plaza de España 3. ℰ **95-287-10-90.** Main courses 12€–18€ ($14–$22). AE, DC, MC, V. Daily 12:30–4pm
and 7:30–10:30pm.

INEXPENSIVE

Pedro Romero SPANISH/ANDALUSIAN   Named after the famed bullfighter, this restaurant attracts aficionados of that sport. It's opposite the bullring
and on bullfighting days it's almost impossible to get a table. While seated under
a stuffed bull's head, surrounded by photographs of young matadors, you might
begin your meal with the classic garlic soup, then follow with a well-prepared
array of meat or poultry dishes.

Virgen de la Paz 18. ℰ **95-287-11-10.** Reservations required on day of *corrida* and weekend. Main courses
6€–20€ ($7.20–$24). AE, DC, MC, V. Daily 12:30–4pm and 7:30–11pm.

Pizzeria Ristorante Italiano Nonno Peppe *(Kids)* PIZZA/ITALIAN   In
front of Plaza Nueva, this joint makes the best pizzas in town as well as homemade pastas—and its prices are affordable. Many of the ingredients are imported
from Italy. A young crowd and families patronizes the place. The lasagna is excellent, and there's pizza for vegetarians. Salads are fresh and crisp with tantalizing
dressings, and there is a friendly spirit of camaraderie. A good choice of freshly
made Italian desserts is on the menu, and the tiramisu is especially luscious.

Calle Nueva 18. ℰ **95-287-28-50.** Reservations recommended. Pizzas 3.50€–8€ ($4.20–$9.60); pastas
3.50€–6€ ($4.20–$7.20); main courses 5€–7€ ($6–$8.40). MC, V. Daily noon–4:30pm and 8pm–1am.

RONDA AFTER DARK

Wandering the streets of the Old Town and dropping into various tapas bars is
a good way to spend the early part of the evening. Try the **Relax Bar,** which also
has a restaurant at Calle los Remediois 27 (ℰ **95-287-72-07**). The place is popular with English-speaking visitors. Sit at one of the wooden tables and order
tapas for only 1€ ($1.20). There is a lot of vegetarian food here, and the wine
is affordable. Open daily 1 to 4pm and 8pm to midnight.

A good tapas and wine bar is **La Gota de Vino 13,** Calle Sevilla 13 (© **95-287-57-16**), attracting a young crowd that consumes massive quantities of Andalusian wine priced from 1.80€ ($2.15) per glass. Tapas range from 5€ to 7€ ($6–$8.40). Open Tuesday to Sunday 7pm to 2am.

Café de Ronda, Calle Tenorio 1 (© **95-287-40-91**), across the Puente Nuevo, occupies the first floor of a large mansion. Its main feature is a plant-filled courtyard with lots of outdoor seating. Try one of the specialty coffees, priced from 1.50€ ($1.80), or a sandwich, costing from 3€ ($3.60). Open Monday to Thursday 9am to 9pm and Friday to Sunday 9am to midnight.

Later that night there are various *discotecas* that come and go with the seasons. Along with a collection of routine pubs, they are found along **Calle Jerez** and in back of **Plaza del Socorro. Plaza de Abela** is another center of after dark bars and activities, as are the streets across from **Plaza de España** and **Plaza de Toros.** Favorites in this area include **Huskies Sport Bar,** Calle Molino 1 (no phone), where beer costs 1.20€ ($1.45). Open Monday at 8:30pm and Tuesday to Sunday at 5:30pm. Closing time depends on business and can get very late during the busy summer months. Another bar favored by young locals is **Bar Antonio,** Calle San José 4 (no phone), with some of the cheapest beer and tapas in town, both costing .80€ (95¢) a glass. Open Monday to Friday 7am to 11pm, Saturday 9am to 4pm.

2 Mijas ⭐

30km (19 miles) W of Málaga, 18km (11 miles) W of Torremolinos, 585km (363 miles) S of Madrid

Just 8km (5 miles) north of coastal road N-340/E-15 is a village known as "White Mijas" because of its marble-white Andalusian-style houses. **Mijas** is at the foot of a mountain range near the turnoff to Fuengirola, and from its lofty height—450m (1,476 ft.) above sea level—you get a panoramic view of the Mediterranean.

Celts, Phoenicians, and Moors preceded today's tourists to Mijas. The main allure here is the setting and the town itself, with its narrow streets, whitewashed houses draped in bougainvillea and jasmine, and panoramic views. Regrettably, because of the influx of tour groups, it is now overrun with tacky souvenir and crafts shops. And while it's as close as most Costa del Sol beachgoers come to a typical Andalusian village, that's something it hasn't actually been for a long time.

ESSENTIALS
GETTING THERE   From the Costa del Sol (the usual approach to Mijas) buses leave from the terminal at Fuengirola every 30 minutes during the day for the 8km (5 miles) trip north. Motorists in Fuengirola on the coast can follow the signs north into the hills, leading directly to Mijas. The hair-raising drive takes only 20 minutes. *Tip:* Try to arrive in Mijas at 4 o'clock in the afternoon when all the Costa del Sol tour groups have departed.

VISITOR INFORMATION   Buses arrive at a central square, **Plaza Virgen de la Peña,** which is also the site of the local tourist office (look for the sign; © **95-248-58-20**). Hours are Monday to Friday 9am to 3pm and 4 to 7pm, Saturday 10am to 2pm. The tourist office will provide you with leaflets outlining scenic walks in the surrounding hills.

EXPLORING MIJAS
The town's **location** ⭐⭐ alone continues to draw visitors, even if much of the town's original charm has been erased by tourism. The overgrown village is

welded to the side of a mountain. The easiest way to get around the cobblestone streets is to rent a burro taxi. Its whitewashed houses make it look like a stack of sugar cubes set against the mountain, which is heavy with pine trees. From many points in Mijas, there are lookout points. On a clear day you can see across the Mediterranean to the Rif Mountains in Morocco in North Africa. The best platform for a view is called *cuesta de la villa* (slope of the town).

The most delightful church is **Iglesia Parroquial de la Inmaculada Concepción (Church of the Immaculate Conception),** found at Plaza Constitución, site of Plaza de Toros (the bullring). The church is not rich in treasures but it has a beautiful terrace and gardens, from which you can enjoy panoramic views.

Many Costa del Sol visitors come here to watch *corridas* taking place at **Plaza de Toros,** Plaza Constitución (© **95-248-52-48**), the country's only square bullring (bullsquare?) at the old village plaza. Most bullfights take place on Sunday at 4:30pm. If you just want to check out the ring from June to September, it's open daily 10am to 10pm; October to February daily 9:30am to 6:30pm; March daily 10am to 7:30pm; and April and May 10am to 8:30pm. Admission is 3€ ($3.60).

To show how corny Mijas has become in its manmade attractions, it even has a museum of curiosities, **Carromato de Max,** Avenida del Compás (no phone; daily 10am–7pm; admission 3€/$3.60). Inside, you can gaze upon Leonardo's *The Last Supper* painted on a grain of rice, Abraham Lincoln painted on a pinhead, the shrunken head of a white man retrieved from South American Indians, and even fleas wearing clothes.

If Mijas is too overrun with souvenir shops for your tastes, head for the park at the top of Cuesta de la Villa, where you'll see the ruins of a **Moorish fortress** dating from 833.

WHERE TO STAY

Hotel Mijas 🏠🏠   One of the most charming hotels on the Costa del Sol dates from 1970 when it was built on steeply sloping land in the center of town. This Andalusian-inspired block of white walls and flowering terraces is sun flooded and comfortable. There are sweeping views over the Mediterranean from most of the public areas and the tiny but comfortable rooms. Bathrooms have tub/shower combos. The staff is tactful and hardworking. There is no elevator.

Urbanización Tamisa 2, 29650 Mijas. © **95-248-58-00.** Fax 95-248-58-25. www.hotasa.es. 204 units. 81€–113€ ($97–$136) double; 160€–240€ ($192–$288) suite. AE, DC, MC, V. Free parking. **Amenities:** Restaurant; bar; outdoor pool; health club; sauna; Jacuzzi; salon; limited room service; babysitting; laundry service/dry cleaning; nonsmoking rooms; rooms for those w/limited mobility. *In room:* A/C, TV, dataport, hair dryer, safe.

La Cala Resort 🏠🏠   Golfers journey to Mijas just to stay at this stylishly contemporary inland resort. The two golf courses at La Cala are its main attraction, including La Cala North (par 73) and La Cala South (par 72). Both were designed by the noted golf architect, Cabell B. Robinson, who cited the Costa del Sol terrain as his most challenging project. Even if you're not a golfer, this is one of the finest accommodations in the area, unless you prefer to be right on the sea rather than 7km (4⅓ miles) away. Bedrooms are midsize to spacious, each attractively furnished in a contemporary mode, with superb bathrooms with tub and shower. Every accommodation opens onto a large balcony overlooking the fairways and greens and the Mijas hills beyond. The food here, a medley of Spanish and Continental dishes, is first rate and uses quality ingredients.

La Cala de Mijas, 29649 Mijas. ☏ **95-266-90-00.** Fax 95/266-90-39. www.lacala.com. 107 units. 151€–237€ ($181–$284) double; 228€–303€ ($274–$364) junior suite. Rates include breakfast. AE, DC, MC, V. **Amenities:** 2 restaurants; bar; 2 pools (1 indoor); 2 tennis courts; squash; Jacuzzi; sauna; fitness center; 24-hr. room service; babysitting; laundry service/dry cleaning; nonsmoking rooms; rooms for those w/limited mobility. *In room:* A/C, TV, minibar, hair dryer, safe.

WHERE TO DINE

El Capricho ✿ SPANISH/ANDALUSIAN/INTERNATIONAL   In the old part of the city, this restaurant operates out of a house whose age even the owners don't know. It's in the typical Andalusian style with a wooden roof and interior whitewashed walls decorated with regional ceramics and drawings. If the weather is right, the beautiful terrace is the place to be. Prices do tend to be high since the restaurant caters to tourists. The cooks make the best shellfish paella in town, and the sautéed prawns zestily flavored with fresh parsley and pepper are also winners. The grilled tenderloin of beef is perfectly cooked but the honey sauce served with it comes as a surprise. Baked chicken stuffed with mushrooms is usually available. Desserts are homemade and luscious.

Los Caños 5. ☏ **95-248-51-11.** Reservations recommended. Main courses 26€–33€ ($31–$40). AE, MC, V. Thurs–Tues noon–4pm and 7–11pm. Closed Wed and Nov 15–Dec 15.

El Olivar INTERNATIONAL   Next to the town hall in the very center of town, this tavern serves some of Mijas's best tapas. Dishes may not be unusual but they are delicious. They are prepared fresh daily, and are offered along with an affordable selection of regional Andalusian wines. Rabbit from the nearby mountains—appearing on the menu as *conejo sierra de mijas*—is frequently featured. On a hot August day, we happily settle for a soothing bowl of gazpacho followed by a Spanish omelet made with potatoes. The chefs also prepare a tantalizing array of recently harvested *mariscos* (shellfish) from the coast, and they also do a perfectly grilled filet of sole. The decor is rustic with whitewashed walls, handcrafted local furniture, and, best of all, a terrace.

Av. Virgen de la Peña, Edificio El Rosario. ☏ **95-248-61-96.** Reservations recommended. Main courses 16€–28€ ($19–$34). Sun–Fri 1–4pm and 7–11pm. Closed Feb.

El Padrastro ✿ INTERNATIONAL   Part of the fun of dining at the town's best restaurant is getting here. You go to the cliff side of town and, if you're athletic, walk up 77 steps; if you're not, take the elevator to the highest point. El Padrastro serves international cuisine on its covered terraces with panoramic views of the coast. You can choose whether to eat inexpensively (stick with the regional dishes) or elaborately (break the bank and go for the chateaubriand with a bottle of the best Spanish wine).

Av. del Compás 20–22. ☏ **95-248-50-00.** Reservations recommended. Main courses 12€–30€ ($16–$39). AE, DC, MC, V. Daily 12:30–4pm and 7–11:30pm.

Mirlo Blanco ✿ BASQUE   In the center of town, this rustically decorated house is a century and a half old. Today, it's one of the better restaurants in Mijas. The Basque cooks of Spain are celebrated as the finest chefs in the country, and after devouring a delectable fish stew here, made with the fresh catch of the day, we agree. The Basques are also known for their delicious *merluza* (hake) dishes, and the cooks here prepare the fish with pepper, paprika, bay leaf, and cream, a perfect sauce for the dish. Other recommendations are the aromatic lamb dish flavored with honey, and the perfectly grilled tenderloin studded with peppercorns.

Plaza Constitución 2. ☏ **95-248-57-00.** Reservations recommended. Main courses 23€–30€ ($28–$36). AE, MC, V. Daily 1–3:30pm and 8–11:30pm. Closed Jan 10–30.

Valparaíso INTERNATIONAL   The decor is rustic but not the cuisine. As a summer treat, live music is played on the terrace as you dine. The menu is surprisingly varied and unusual, ranging from a garlic-studded roast leg of lamb, to breast of ostrich with a rose pepper sauce. Since Mijas is so close to the coast, seafood is another option. Fish selections don't get any more elegant than filet of sea bass with oysters and a champagne sauce.

Carretera de Mijas-Fuengirola Km 4. © **95-248-59-96.** Reservations recommended. Main courses 19€–23€ ($23–$28). AE, DC, MC, V. Daily 7:30pm–midnight. Closed Sun in winter.

Villa Paradiso INTERNATIONAL   This restaurant is particularly popular with British expats and others now living permanently in the area. Lamb shanks are aromatically baked in the oven until fork tender and served with a fresh fruit sauce. *Lubina* (sea bass) is baked in a salt crust, its aromas bursting forth when the crust is peeled back. Every day different specialties are featured. On our most recent visit, we enjoyed tender medallions of baby pork, and in fall, venison usually appears on the menu.

Centro Comercial El Zoco. © **95-293-12-24.** Reservations recommended. Main courses 8€–27€ ($9.60–$32). AE, DC, MC, V. Daily 9am–1pm and 7pm–midnight.

3 Antequera ★

48 km (29 miles) N of Málaga, 99 km (61 miles) E of Granada, 164 km (101 miles) SE of Seville

Celebrated for its Moorish castle and its dozens of antique churches, Antequera is one of Andalusia's most historic, yet undiscovered, towns. Recent excavations indicate that it was populated as early as the 1st century A.D. Christian settlers who moved in after the Reconquista left a legacy of two dozen historic churches.

This market town and industrial city with a population of 40,000 straddles two hills in the valley of the River Guadalhorce. No remote corner, Antequera lies on the main rail route to Granada and at the junction of three arteries leading to the most important cities of Andalusia: Seville, Granada, and Córdoba. It's also a convenient day trip from Málaga.

Allow at least a half-day to see the highlights of Antequera; set aside more time if you wish to explore the rugged, mountainous country to its south and east.

ESSENTIALS

GETTING THERE   Six **trains** per day arrive from Granada taking 2 hours and costing 5.75€ ($6.90) one-way; four trains pull in from Seville, taking 2½ hours and costing 10€ ($12) one-way. There is also service from Ronda, with three buses a day making the 1-hour trip, costing 4.90€ ($5.90) one-way.

Anywhere from 9 to 12 **buses** per day make the run from Málaga. The trip takes 45 minutes and costs 3.25€ ($3.90) one-way. There are also two buses per day from Córdoba taking 1¼ hours and costing 7.50€ ($9) one-way; five per day from Granada taking 2 hours and costing 6.20€ ($7.45) one-way; and five per day from Seville taking 2¼ hours and costing 9.95€ ($12) one-way.

GETTING AROUND   You can walk around the center of Antequera, but you may need public transportation to get from the train station to your hotel, or to sights in the outlying areas. **Taxi Radio Antequera** (© **95-284-55-30**) services the area, with most fares averaging 4€ ($4.80). Taxis meet all arriving trains and buses.

VISITOR INFORMATION   For information, go to the **Tourist Office,** Plaza de San Sebastián 7 (© **95-270-25-05**). From June 15 to September 15, the office is open Monday to Saturday from 11am to 2pm and 5 to 8pm, Sunday from

11am to 2pm. In off season, hours are Monday to Saturday from 10:30am to 1:30pm and 4 to 7pm, Sunday from 11am to 2pm.

FAST FACTS: Antequera

Currency Exchange For an ATM head to **Banco Santander Central Hispano,** Calle Infante Don Fernando 51 (© **90-224-24-24**). Open Monday to Friday from 8:30am to 2pm, Saturday from 8:30am to 1pm.

Emergency Dial © **112.** In an **medical** emergency, call © **95-284-19-66.**

Hospital The local **Hospital Comarcal** is at Calle Polígono Industrial 67 (© **95-284-62-63**).

Pharmacy **Antequera Farmacia** is at Plaza de San Francisco. It's open Monday to Friday from 9am to 1:30pm and 5 to 8:30pm, Saturday from 10:30am to 1:30pm. Come in person rather than trying to call.

Police The station is on Avenida de la Legión (© **95-270-81-04**).

Post Office The main branch is on Calle Nájera (© **95-284-20-83**). It's open Monday to Friday from 8am to 2pm, Saturday from 9:30am to 1pm.

EXPLORING ANTEQUERA

The core of the white-walled town was made for walking; as you stroll, you can explore ancient churches and cobblestone alleyways, and see windows pierced with the characteristic wrought-iron grilles of Andalusia.

Head up Cuesta de los Rojos to reach the **Alcabaza (Fortress).** This is where the Moors staged their last defense before being conquered by Catholic troops in 1410. The fortress then became a military base for the reconquest of Granada.

Today you can wander among the meager ruins that have been turned into a garden within the ancient walls. From the main tower, **Torre del Homenaje,** you can take in a panoramic **view** ✯ of the town; note the unusual roofs with their colored tiles. The view goes beyond the town to take in the surrounding plains and **Peña de los Enamorados (Lover's Rock),** from which two lovers— one a Christian, the other a Muslim—are said to have committed suicide when their parents forbade them to marry. The Alcazaba gardens are always open, although it's best to go during the day so that you can take in the views. Torre del Homenaje, however, is open Tuesday to Friday from 10:30am to 2pm and 4:30 to 6:30pm, Saturday and Sunday from 10:30am to 2pm. Admission is free.

The town is riddled with churches, but one is more notable than the rest. If you go through the 16th-century arch, **Arco de los Gigantes (Arch of the Giants),** to the far end of Plaza Alta, you'll come to **Colegiata de Santa María la Mayor** at Plaza Santa María, near the castle. Dating from 1514, it has a facade with geometric motifs, which is said to have been the first example of Renaissance-style architecture in the province. Actually the monument betrays several architectural influences, including mudéjar, Plateresque, and Gothic styles. The church (no phone) is open July to September 15, Tuesday to Friday from 10:30am to 2pm and 8 to 10pm; September 16 to June, Tuesday to Friday from 10:30am to 2pm and 4:30 to 7:30pm. It's also open year-round Saturday from 10:30am to 2pm, Sunday from 11:30am to 2pm. Admission is free.

If you are facing the church, on the left you can see the ruins of **Las Termas de Santa María,** a Roman thermal bath that was excavated in 1988. Some mosaic tiles and meager ruins remain, but that's about it.

Another attraction is the **Museo Municipal,** Calle Nájera (© 95-270-40-51), housed in the 18th-century Palacio de Nájera. Roman artifacts unearthed in the area are the chief attraction. The major exhibit is the *Efebo de Antequera* ★★, a Roman statue about 1.4m (5 ft.) high. Discovered outside of town in the 1970s, it is a stunning bronze statue of a boy dating from Roman times. Another notable sculpture is an eerily lifelike woodcarving by Pedro de Mena, a well-known 17th-century Andalusian sculptor, of **St. Francis of Assisi.** On an unusual note, the museum exhibits the avant-garde 1970s art of native son Cristóbal Toral. Charging 3€ ($3.60) for admission, the museum is open Tuesday to Friday from 9am to 2:30pm, Saturday from 10am to 1:30pm, and Sunday from 11am to 1:30pm. A guided tour is mandatory; tours leave every half-hour from the entrance.

One final notable church is **Iglesia del Carmen (Church of Our Lady of Carmen),** lying east of the Postigo de la Estrella, approached by heading up Cuesta de los Rojas. This is a rare 17th-century mudéjar church. Behind a plain facade lies a lavish interior with a coffered ceiling from the 18th century. Its greatest treasure—found at the main altar—is a *retablo* (altar) ★★. This is one of the finest of its kind in all the province, a masterpiece of late Baroque extravaganza. In the center, carvers Diego Márquez and Antonio Primo created a Madonna flanked by several polychromed saints and angels. Normal visiting hours are Monday to Tuesday from 10:30am to 2pm and 5 to 8pm; Wednesday and Friday from 10am to 2pm and 5 to 11pm, Saturday from 10am to 2pm and 5 to 8pm, and Sunday from 10am to 2pm. Admission is 1.50€ ($1.80).

ON THE OUTSKIRTS

The best day trip in the area is to **El Torcal** ★★, a natural park consisting of a strangely shaped series of limestone rocks. Some visitors have compared its surface to the landscape of an otherworldly planet. Towering over the park is a 1,370m (4,494 ft.) peak. Several trails circle this dramatic summit; in fact trails cross the entire park, stretching out for 12km (7¼ miles). You can take the path marked with a green arrow on your own for 1.5km (just under a mile). However, to venture on the other trails, you need to hire a guide from the **Centro de Información** in the park (© 95-203-13-89), which is open daily from 10am to 5pm. El Torcal lies 16km (10 miles) south of Antequera. Take Carretera de Malada out of Antequera and follow the signs to the site. Admission is free.

Lying only 1km (½ mile) east of Antequera, on the northern outskirts of town, is one of the most important prehistoric discoveries in Europe: **Viera, Romeral,** and **Menga** are funerary chambers dating from 2,500 to 1,800 B.C. and known for their Cyclopean size. The chambers were carved out of massive slabs of stone, including a 180-ton monolith.

The best preserved of the *cuevas* is Menga, which is also the oldest and largest of the trio. At one time these chambers were filled with great riches, but of course, this treasure has long since been looted. Romeral consists of a long corridor leading to two round chambers. Small flat stones are laid out so as to produce a trapezoidal section in the corridor. Viera starts out with a narrow passageway that leads deep into the bowels of the earth. It's an eerie and strangely evocative prehistoric site.

From the center of Antequera, follow signs out of town toward Granada. Past a gas station, watch for a small sign directing you to **Los Dólmenes.** This will lead you to Menga and Viera. To reach Romeral, continue along the road to Granada for another 3km (1¾ miles) until you see a sign. The caves are open Tuesday from 10am to 2pm, Wednesday to Saturday from 9am to 3pm, and Sunday from 9:30am to 2pm. Admission is free.

WHERE TO STAY

La Posada del Torcal ★★★ *(Finds)*   A real discovery, this small hotel lies in the lunarlike landscape of El Torcal (see "Exploring Antequera," above). This Andalusian *cortijo,* a farmhouse from the early part of the 20th century, was converted in 2004 and stands on a hill overlooking a 4.4-hectare (11-acre) estate of almond groves, with panoramic views of the rock formations in the park. For luxury and comfort, it even outclasses the Parador (see below). The spacious bedrooms are beautifully designed with tasteful, comfortable furnishings and luxurious tiled bathrooms with tub and shower. All the units have underfloor heating and a fireplace. A roaring log fire greets you in the wintertime. In fairer weather, you can enjoy dining alfresco on the panoramic terraces. All the modern amenities have been installed, including a Finnish sauna and a Jacuzzi.

Pardido de Jeva-Carretera de Villanueva de la Concepción, 29230 La Joya. © **95-203-11-77.** Fax 95-203-10-06. www.eltorcal.com/posadatorcal. 10 units. 125€–180€ ($150–$216) double; 190€–260€ ($228–$312) suite. AE, MC, V. Closed Jan. **Amenities:** Restaurant; bar; outdoor pool; tennis court; sauna; fitness center; spa; 24-hr. room service; babysitting; laundry service. *In room:* A/C, TV, minibar, hair dryer, safe.

Parador de Antequera ★★ *(Value)*   Surrounded by lush gardens and a swimming pool, this is an oasis in Antequera. Its rooms, public and private, open onto views of the *vega,* the fertile valley that envelops Antequera. This white-painted hostelry is on a hill and easy to spot, lying within walking distance of the Old Town. Last renovated in 2003, it offers midsize to spacious bedrooms, most with twin beds. The large bathrooms are state of the art and tiled, each with a tub/shower combo. Leather-covered furniture, wooden floors, and Andalusian artifacts create the aura of a big, sprawling hacienda. Even if you're not a guest, you can eat at the first-class restaurant that specializes in Andalusian dishes, many made with codfish.

Paseo García del Olmo, 29200 Antequera. © **95-284-02-61.** Fax 95-284-13-12. www.parador.es. 55 units. 85€–95€ ($102–$114) double. AE, DC, MC, V. Free parking. **Amenities:** Restaurant; bar; outdoor pool; room service (8am–11:30pm); babysitting; laundry service. *In room:* A/C, TV, minibar, hair dryer.

WHERE TO DINE

El Angelote SPANISH/ANDALUSIAN   Many guests prefer to dine at the Parador (see above), but this is a good choice within the town itself. Across the square from the Museo Municipal, it is decorated in the rustic bodega style, with brick walls, heavy wooden furniture, and antiques. The two wood-beamed dining rooms were originally part of a 17th-century private home that stood here. Chefs are big on flavor, and portions are hearty. The regional fare is well selected and uses local produce when available. Start with a creamy gazpacho, and follow (on a hot day) with such dishes as a codfish salad flavored with onions and dressed with virgin olive oil. Local foodies swear by the oxtail and the partridge with almonds and white wine. The signature dessert is *bienmesabe,* a sponge cake with almonds and a sugar and cinnamon "dusting."

Plaza Coso Viejo. © **95-270-34-65.** Reservations recommended. Main courses 9€–21€ ($11–$25). DC, MC, V. Tues–Sat 8–11:30am and noon–5pm; Sun noon–5pm. Closed 15 days in Aug (dates vary).

4 · A Driving Tour of the Pueblos Blancos

The brilliantly whitewashed villages and towns of inland Andalusia are called Pueblos Blancos. These are archetypal towns and villages that dot the steep slopes of the mountains, which extend north of Gibraltar. They occupy that part of Andalusia that lies between the Atlantic in the west and the Mediterranean extending eastward. One of the most traveled routes through the towns is the road that stretches from Arcos de la Frontera all the way to Ronda in the east.

Many towns have "de la Frontera" as part of their name, an ancient reference to the frontier towns that formed a boundary between Christian-held territories and Muslim towns and villages in the Middle Ages. Although the Catholic troops eventually triumphed, it is often the Moorish influence that makes these towns architecturally interesting, with their labyrinths of narrow, cobblestone streets, their fortresslike walls, and their little whitewashed houses with the characteristic wrought-iron grilles.

If you take the drive we've outlined below, you'll pass some of the great scenic landscapes of Spain, various thickly wooded areas that are often the home to some rare botanical species, including the Spanish fir, *Abies pinsap,* which only grows in four locations at more than 1,000m (3,281 ft.). As you drive along you'll approach limestone slopes that might rise as high as 6,640m (5,000 ft.). Castle ruins and old church bell towers also form part of the landscape. For those who have been across the sea to North Africa, much of the landscape of the Pueblos Blancos will evoke Morocco. The white towns sprawl across the provinces of Cádiz and Málaga, lying east of Seville, which is often the gateway for tours of this landscape.

The ideal time to drive through the Pueblos Blancos is spring, when all the wildflowers in all the valleys burst into bloom. Fall is another good time. Allow at least a day for Ronda, covered in detail at the beginning of this chapter. You can pass through the other villages on this tour, admiring the life and the architecture, and then moving on. The best hotels and restaurants along the entire stretch of the Pueblos Blancos are found in Ronda and Arcos de la Frontera. Elsewhere accommodations and restaurants are very limited, although we have included some recommendations along the way.

These whitewashed villages are fairly close together, so driving times, as indicated below, are fairly short. From Seville, you can begin your tour by heading to the Pueblos Blancos along A-4, which becomes N-IV. Continue southeast along N-IV until you come to the turnoff for C-343. At this point our first stopover on the tour, Arcos de la Frontera, will be signposted. Follow C-343 south into Arcos de la Frontera. The first part of the tour from Arcos to Ronda can be done in 1 day, with an overnight in Ronda.

The second part of the tour, from Ronda to Jerez de la Frontera in the west, can also be done in a day. However, those with more time can extend this tour to 3 or 4 days. In the towns along the way, we have recommended the best places to stay and dine: If you find a place that enchants you and your schedule allows it, you can stop over rather than pressing on to Ronda.

ARCOS DE LA FRONTERA 🕉🕉

Along with Ronda, this old Arab town is a highlight of the Pueblos Blancos and the center of the best inns along the route. Now a National Historic Monument, Arcos de la Frontera was built in the form of an amphitheater. The major attraction here is the village itself. Wander at leisure and don't worry about skipping a particular monument.

Once under the control of the Caliphate of Córdoba, Arco's period of glory came to an end when the kingdom collapsed in the 11th century. Arcos fell to Seville. By 1264, the Catholic troops had moved in, signaling the end of Muslim rule forever. Nearly all that interests the casual visitor will be found in the elevated **Medina (Old Town)** 👁️👁️, towering over the flatlands. The Old Town is huddled against the crenellated castle walls. You park your car below and walk up until you reach the site built on a crag overlooking a loop in the Guadalete River.

Pick up a map at the **Tourist Office** (© **95-670-22-64**), at the main square Plaza del Cabildo. Open Monday to Friday from 9am to 2pm and 5:30 to 7:30pm, Saturday 10am to 2pm, and Sunday 10:30am to 2:30pm. Start your visit at the **Balcon de Arcos,** at the same square. Don't miss the **view** 👁️👁️ from this rectangular esplanade overhanging a deep river cleft. You can see a Moorish castle, but it's privately owned and not open to the public. The main church on this square is **Iglesia de Santa María,** constructed in 1732 in a blend of Renaissance, Gothic, and baroque styles. Its **western facade** 👁️, in the Plateresque style, is its most stunning achievement. The interior is a mix of many styles— Plateresque, Gothic, mudéjar, and baroque. Look for the beautiful star-vaulting and a late Renaissance altarpiece. Open daily 10am to 1pm and 4 to 6:30pm, charging 2€ ($2.40).

You can head down the main street out of Plaza del Cabildo to **Iglesia de San Pedro,** with its baroque bell tower. It is on the other side of the cliff and approached through a charming maze of narrow alleys evocative of Tangier. You can climb the tower, but there are few guard rails. It's not for those with vertigo. Paintings here include *Dolorosa* by Pacheco, the tutor of the great Velásquez, and works by Zurbarán and Ribera. Open Monday to Saturday 10am to 3pm and 4 to 7pm, Sunday 10am to 1:30pm. Admission is 1.50€ ($1.80).

Another panoramic lookout point is **Mirador de Abades** 👁️, at the end of Calle Abades.

WHERE TO STAY

Cortijo Fain 👁️ *Finds*   A real discovery, this 17th-century farmhouse has been turned into a hacienda hotel lying 3km (2 miles) southeast of Arcos near the hamlet of Algar (reached via CA-52). Draped with purple bougainvillea, the house is warm and inviting with arches, white walls, a stone footpath, and Andalusian courtyards. Last renovated in 1999, the inn offers small, comfortably and rather charmingly furnished bedrooms, each with a tub/shower combo in its tiny bathrooms. Two suites have fireplaces. The setting is in a vast olive grove, and the inn has a swimming pool and a library. You can explore the countryside on a horseback ride arranged by the inn.

Carretera Arcos-Algar Km 3, 11630 Arcos de la Frontera. © **95-670-41-31.** Fax 95-671-79-32. http://cortijo fain.en.eresmas.com. 15 units. 72€–80€ ($86–$96) double; 96€–100€ ($115–$120) suite. AE, DC, MC, V. **Amenities:** Restaurant; outdoor pool; room service (8am–11pm); babysitting. *In room:* A/C, TV, minibar, hair dryer.

El Convento   Near Santa María Church, this was originally Convento Las Mercedarías, but was turned into an inn in 1987 and last renovated in 2004. The hotel is reached via a tiny cobblestone alleyway in back of the parador (see below). In a classic style, with a red-tile roof and wrought-iron grilles, the hotel is a snug nest. It is furnished with rustic wooden pieces, and is beautifully maintained. Its bedrooms are midsize, inviting and comfortable enough to make you want to linger. Each comes with a small tiled bathroom with a tub/shower

combo. El Convento also has the best hotel restaurant in town if you're just passing through (see below).

Maldonado 2, 11630 Arcos de la Frontera. ℂ **95-670-23-33.** Fax 95-670-41-28. www.webdearcos.com/elconvento. 11 units. 50€–81€ ($60–$97) double. AE, DC, MC, V. Parking 3€ ($3.60) nearby. **Amenities:** Restaurant; bar; room service (8am–11pm); solarium. *In room:* A/C, TV, dataport (in some), hair dryer.

Los Olivos   This former private home received a massive overhaul in 2002 and is now one of the town's most inviting stopovers. With its whitewashed walls, its yellowish tile roofs, its internal courtyard, it is built in the traditional Andalusian style and studded with balconies and wide windows. The small bedrooms are simply furnished with wooden bed frames and tile floors. Wicker chairs, long curtains, and a few drawings complete the decor. The bathrooms, also small, come with tub/shower combos. Some of the bedrooms open onto the vistas of the countryside, studded with olive trees.

Paseo de Boliches 30, 11630 Arcos de la Frontera. ℂ **95-670-08-11.** Fax 95-670-20-18. www.hotel olivosarcos.com. 19 units. 60€–70€ ($72–$84) double. AE, DC, MC, V. Parking 5€ ($6). **Amenities:** Bar; laundry service. *In room:* A/C, TV, minibar, hair dryer.

Marqués de Torresoto   At the center of Arcos, at the landmark Plaza del Cabildo, this is a converted palace dating from the 17th century, with its original chapel still intact. It was a private family home built by a local nobleman, Marqués de Torresoto. Turned into a hotel in 1994, it is graced with interior patios, corridors, columns, and arches in the typical Andalusian style. Rooms, mostly small, are a bit minimalist, evocative of a monastery, with white walls and wooden furniture, each room with a tiled bathroom with a tub/shower combination.

Marqués de Torresoto 4, 11630 Arcos de la Frontera. ℂ 95-670-07-17. Fax 95-670-42-05. www. hmdetorresoto.com. 13 units. 56€–64€ ($67–$77) double; 98€–114€ ($118–$137) suite. Rates include breakfast. Parking 3€ ($3.60) nearby. **Amenities:** Restaurant; bar; room service (8am–11pm); babysitting; laundry service. In room: A/C, TV, minibar, hair dryer.

Parador Casa del Corregidor ★★   In the old part of the city, this is the kind of first-class place that's more typical of Ronda than the other Pueblos Blancos. Originally the house of the *corregidor* (king's magistrate), it dates from the 18th century. From its balconies are panoramic views of the Guadalete River and the plains and farms beyond. Evocative of a chalet, the inn rises three floors with outside corridors, wooden columns, and a big terrace with a vista. Last renovated in 2003, the midsize bedrooms are traditionally and comfortably furnished, matching the style of the house. Many open onto views, and each comes with a small, tiled bathroom equipped with tub and shower. There is an on-site restaurant, serving dishes typical of the Sierra region (there's that oxtail again), but there are many other good options, including pork in a red-wine and fresh tomato sauce.

Plaza del Cabildo s/n, 11630 Arcos de la Frontera. ℂ **95-670-05-00.** Fax 95-670-11-16. www.parador.es. 20 units. 125€ ($150) double. Free parking nearby. **Amenities:** Restaurant; bar; room service (8am–11pm). In room: A/C, TV, minibar, hair dryer.

WHERE TO DINE

El Convento Restaurant ANDALUSIAN   This typical Andalusian restaurant is the best in town. Masses of flowers are inviting, and there are arches, columns, and arabesques, with heavy iron lamps, a holdover from the palace's 17th-century heyday. Highly recommended choices include fresh asparagus soup, meat and vegetable stew, and grilled partridge caught in the nearby countryside and baked and served with almond sauce. Another excellent dish is oven-baked and aromatically seasoned leg of lamb with fresh herbs and plenty of garlic. For dessert, try Tocino del Cielo, a cake marinated in sweet milk and covered with meringue.

Maldonado 2. ℂ **95-670-32-22.** Reservations recommended. Main courses 10€–18€ ($12–$22). AE, MC, V. Daily 1–4pm and 7–10pm. Closed Jan 7–22 and 15 days in July (dates vary).

El Lago ANDALUSIAN   El Convento is better, but this is a reliable choice, serving predictable but good food. The setting is rustic with wooden columns, a bar, heavy furniture, and the typical white walls. The service is simultaneously friendly, efficient, and welcoming. Chefs turn out classic recipes like oven-baked lamb flavored with garlic and fresh herbs. One casserole is made of fresh tomatoes and the extremely delectable Jabugo ham. A tender loin of beef appears with a zesty pepper sauce. The home-baked bread is fresh and aromatic, and the soups are filling and good-tasting. Desserts, however, are nothing special.

Carretera A-382 Este Km 1. ℂ **95-670-11-17.** Reservations recommended. Main courses 10€–15€ ($12–$18). AE, DC, MC, V. Daily 1–5pm and 8pm–midnight.

ZAHARA DE LA SIERRA ★
From Arcos de la Frontera, take the A-383 northeast, following the signs to Algodonales. Once you reach this town, head south at the junction with CA-531 to Zahara de la Sierra, the most perfect of the province's fortified hilltop *pueblos*. Trip time from Arcos is about 35 minutes, and the distance is 51km (32 miles).

Zahara lies in the heart of the **Natural Park Sierra de Grazalema** ⭐⭐, a 50,590-hectare (125,000-acre) park. An important reserve for griffon vultures, among other creatures, the park is studded with pine trees and oak forests. The **Parque Natural Information Office** (© **95-612-30-04**) lies at Calle San Juan (the eastern end of main street). Hours are open Monday to Saturday 9am to 2pm and 4 to 7pm, Sunday 9am to 2pm. It dispenses information and maps for those who'd like to go for walks in the park. There are five major routes in the park, and for most you'll need to seek permission at the office, which also organizes horseback riding, canoeing, and bike trips.

The white village of Zahara itself zigzags up the foot of a rock topped by a reconstructed *castillo.* Houses covered in characteristic red tiles huddle up to the ruined castle. Count on a 15- to 20-minute climb to reach what was once a 10th-century Muslim fortress constructed on Roman foundations 511m (1,676 ft.) above sea level.

Zahara was, in fact, so prized by the Moors that the ruler, Abu al'Hasan of Granada, recaptured it in 1481 from the Catholic troops. But with the fall of Granada at the Reconquista, Zahara once again fell into the hands of the Catholic monarchs. You can visit the Moorish castle, which is always open, offering **panoramic views** ⭐ of the surrounding countryside.

The cobbled main street, Calle San Juan, links the two most important churches, **Iglesia San Juan** and **Iglesia Santa María de la Mesa.** The latter is an 18th-century baroque church worth a look inside if it's open. It displays an impressive retable with a 16th-century image of the Madonna. The best time to be here is in June (annual dates vary) for the Corpus Christi celebration. Streets and walls seem to disappear under a mass of flowers and greenery.

WHERE TO STAY & DINE

Arco de la Villa   In business since 1998, this rural inn is a rustic stone house resting under a low roof and set near a promontory in front of the castle. It's modern and minimally decorated with whitewashed walls and light wooden furnishings. It's a safe, well-maintained nest that despite its modesty, is the best place in Zahara to stay. Bedrooms are small, simply but comfortably furnished, with little tile bathrooms with tub/shower combos. A reasonably good meal costing 15€ ($18) is served in the on-site restaurant if you're just passing through Zahara and need lunch.

Paseo Nazari, 11688 Zahara de la Sierra. © **95-612-32-30.** Fax 95-612-32-44. www.tugasa.com. 17 units. 53€–61€ ($64–$73) double. DC, MC, V. Free parking. **Amenities:** Restaurant; bar; limited room service; rooms for those w/limited mobility. *In room:* A/C, TV, dataport (in some).

Los Tadeos   This inn, launched at the beginning of the 21st century, is a family-run business, lying in a two-story structure outside of town near the municipal swimming pool. Its restaurant is more popular than its hotel rooms. Tables are placed on the terrace, and the food is typically Andalusian and budget priced, depending on the menu featured that day. Bedrooms are comfortable but small, each with a little tiled bathroom with tub and shower. They're decorated rustically, soberly, and simply. The best, and the most expensive, open onto private balconies with views. No one puts on airs here.

Paseo de la Fuente, 11688 Zahara de la Sierra. © **95-612-30-86.** www.zaharadelasierra.com. 10 units. 40€–50€ ($48–$60) double. MC, V. Free parking. **Amenities:** Restaurant; bar. *In room:* A/C, TV.

Marqués de Zahara   This rural inn is a 17th-century structure, a former private home, that has been converted to receive guests on its three floors. The location is central, and the decoration is very rustic with heavy curtains and dark colors. Furnishings are a bit of a disappointment, rather flea-markety, but they're comfortable enough for a night. Each of the small rooms comes with a shower bathroom, and the most expensive doubles contain private balconies. The handsomest feature is an attractive courtyard and delightful bar and dining room, where non-guests can enjoy regional meals usually costing under 15€ ($18).

Calle San Juan 3, 11688 Zahara de la Sierra. ℂ **95-612-30-61.** Fax 95-612-32-68. www.marquesdezahara. com. 11 units. 40€–52€ ($48–$62) double. MC, V. Free parking. **Amenities:** Restaurant; bar; laundry service; library. *In room:* A/C, TV.

OLVERA

From Zahara, return to CA-531 and follow the signs north to A-382. Once on A-382 head northeast to the village of Olvera. The distance between towns is only 24km (15 miles), usually taking only 15 minutes for the transfer.

Declared a national monument, Olvera was another Moorish stronghold. It played a major role in the defense of Granada, until it too fell to troops of the Catholic monarchs. Its two chief monuments are its castle and its cathedral, but even better is the view of the town and the surrounding countryside. Olvera comes at you like an explosion of whitewashed little houses tumbling down a hill crowned by the twin towers of its church and ancient castle. Climb the hill by walking up the town's long running main street.

In the town's Muslim heyday, **El Castillo de Olvera,** Plaza de la Iglesia 3, was one of the most impregnable fortresses in Andalusia. But even such a mighty bastion fell to the troops of King Alfonso XI in 1327. After the citadel was conquered, the castle and the surrounding village became part of the feudal estate of Pérez de Guzmán, a local nobleman. As late as the 19th century, the castle was still in private hands, the home of the dukes of Osuna. The castle is open Tuesday to Sunday 10am to 2pm and 5:30 to 8:30pm. Admission is free but donations are accepted.

Adjoining the castle is **Iglesia de San José,** an 18th-century church with a clock tower. It deserves only a passing look.

The village is known for its handicrafts, and you can see little shops on the narrow streets selling *esparto* and other hand-woven straw products. Foodies may want to stock up on Olvera's pure virgin olive oil. Its *aceite de oliva virgen* is among the best in Andalusia.

You can stop in at the **Oficina de Turismo,** Plaza de la Iglesia s/n (ℂ **95-612-08-16**), for what little information is needed. Hours are Monday to Friday 9:30am to 2pm. It can be open at other times as well, so check locally.

WHERE TO STAY

Hotel-Mesón Fuente del Pino   Standing at the entrance to town, this large, two-story house was turned into a hotel in 1992 and last renovated in 2000. It is one of the town's better addresses, ideal for a 1-night stopover. Rather extravagantly decorated in its public rooms, it is imbued with a real Andalusian aura with its flowery curtains, local tiles, wooden furniture, and whitewashed walls. Bedrooms are small and simply furnished, each comes with a little bathroom with shower. The on-site restaurant serves a varied cuisine based on regional products.

Av. Julián Besteiro s/n, 11690 Olvera. ℂ **95-613-02-32.** Fax 95-613-13-96. www.hotelfuentedelpino.com. 36 units. 50€–60€ ($60–$72) double. MC, V. Free parking. **Amenities:** Restaurant; bar; outdoor pool; laundry service; nonsmoking rooms; rooms for those w/limited mobility. *In room:* A/C, TV.

Sierra 7 Cal   Near Parque Entre Caminos, a 10-minute walk from the center, this is a large two-story modern building. It's been going strong since 1989, and was last renovated in 2003. The rooms here are small and fairly standard, but are well maintained and reasonably comfortable. The tile bathroom adjoining each unit contains a tub and shower. Expect tile floors, iron frames, and whitewashed walls. There is a tea salon plus a terrace with a view. Guests will find an affordable restaurant on-site, specializing in regional dishes.

Av. Nuestra Señora de los Remedios s/n, 11690 Olvera. (℃ **95-613-05-42.** www.tugasa.com/sierraycal.htm. 53€ ($64) double. AE, DC, MC, V. Free parking. **Amenities:** Restaurant; bar; outdoor pool; babysitting; non-smoking rooms; rooms for those w/limited mobility. *In room:* A/C, TV.

WHERE TO DINE

Linos ANDALUSIAN   In front of the local hospital in the newer part of town, this is one of the best places for regional Andalusian platters. Very typical of the area is a casserole, made from locally grown asparagus. They also do a peppery baked veal that is quite tasty, as is their garlic-flavored and perfectly roasted suckling pig. Even though inland, the kitchen manages to get fresh fish. Often it is served *a la sal,* which means it was cooked coated in salt, the skin removed at the last minute. The salt coating seals in the juices. Desserts are rather standard.

Av. Julián Besteiro 54. (℃ **95-613-03-75.** Reservations recommended. Main courses 5€–13€ ($6–$16). DC, MC, V. Wed–Mon 9am–midnight.

Sierra 7 Cal ANDALUSIAN   In the hotel of the same name recommended above, this is a rustically decorated restaurant that serves the finest food in the area. It is open to non-guests as well, most of whom are passing through Olvera for the day and stopping for lunch. In business since 2002, it takes market-fresh ingredients and with a minimum of artifice transforms them into flavorful dishes. Start, perhaps, with the house specialty, a bowl of *Pega con Bolos,* asparagus soup with homemade bread. Enticing fish dishes include sole in meunière sauce and trout in a sauce made with fresh prawns and ham. Meat eaters will delight in a tender and juicy Iberian sirloin of beef prepared with sausages.

Av. Nuestra Señora de los Remedios s/n. (℃ **95-613-05-42.** Reservations recommended. Main courses 8€–15€ ($9.60–$18). MC, V. Daily 1:30–3:30pm and 8:30–10:30pm.

SETENIL DE LAS BODEGAS ★★

From Olvera follow the signs to CA-4222, which will take you southeast to Setenil de las Bodegas. This winding road stretches for 13km (9 miles), taking you by olive groves and farming valleys. You'll pass through the town of **Torre Alhaquime** after 4km (2½ miles). Allow 15 to 30 minutes for this trip.

Setenil is one of the most bizarre of the Pueblos Blancos. The Río Trejo carved itself through the tufa rock to make room for the town, which is literally crammed into clefs of rock, its cavelike streets formed from the overhanging ledge of a gorge. Houses rise two or three floors, using the natural rock as their roofs. One street of town is actually a tunnel.

Other than the town itself, there are no specific attractions. The 16th-century Gothic church, **Iglesia La Encarnación,** stands on a rock in the center of the village next to an Arab tower, and the ruins of a **Muslim castle** are nearby. Another building, the **Ayuntamiento (town hall),** boasts a magnificent mudéjar *artesonado* ceiling. Of all the streets in town, **Calle Herreria** is the oldest, its houses wedged into the massive rock.

Chances are you'll press on and not spend the night. However, if you do there is one place to stay, the **Hotel El Almendra** (℃ **95-613-40-29;** fax 95-613-44-44; www.tugasa.com). This is a little *pensión* (boardinghouse) nestled under rock ridges. The very small rooms are simply furnished with wooden pieces, including decent beds. Each comes with a little tiled bathroom with shower and tub. The on-site restaurant serves very simple meals. The hotel is at Carretera Setenil-Puerto del Monte, has 28 units and charges 57€ to 65€ ($68–$78) for a double room.

CONTINUING ON TO RONDA

To reach Ronda, the capital of the white towns, return to CA-4222 and head southeast following the signs. The route will become CA-4211 as you continue south by the town of Arriate then change to MA-428, which takes you into Ronda. In all this is a distance of only 18km (11 miles), taking about 15 to 20 minutes. Spend at least one night in Ronda before continuing the driving tour the next day. Or else you can end the tour in Ronda if you feel you're going blind from seeing too many white villages glistening in the bright Andalusian sun. For more on Ronda, including its sights and where to stay and dine, see p. 214.

GRAZALEMA 👤

After visiting Ronda, head to the village of Grazalema, by taking A-376 northwest. At the junction with A-372, follow signs southwest to Grazalema. Travel time for the 33km (20-mile) drive is about a half-hour.

This is the whitest of the white towns—perhaps a *pueblo blanquísimo* (extraordinarily white town). It's also one of the best centers for exploring the **Parque Natural** of the Sierra de Grazalema. This charming village nestles under the craggy peak of San Cristóbal at 1,525m (5,003 ft.). As you wander its sloping, narrow streets, you'll pass house after house filled with summery flowers.

You will easily find the main square, with the **Grazalema Parque Natural Information Office,** Plaza de España (© 95-613-22-25), open Tuesday to Sunday 10:30am to 2pm and 5 to 6pm. Information is provided here about walks in the park and local activities like horseback riding.

Towering limestone crags overlook the town. For the best view, climb to a belvedere near the 18th-century chapel of San José. From here, you're rewarded with a panorama.

The town has two beautiful old churches, **Iglesia de la Aurora** on Plaza de España and the nearby **Iglesia de la Encarnación.** Both date from the 17th century.

Grazalema is also known for its local products, especially pure wool blankets and rugs. You may want to spend some time shopping here. The best place to purchase blankets is **Artesanía Textil de Grazalema,** Carretera de Ronda (© 95-613-20-08), a 5-minute walk from Plaza de España. It also sells souvenirs, handicrafts, and traditional gifts. At this small factory, open to the public, you can buy blankets and ponchos made from local wool using hand-operated looms and antique machinery. Open Monday to Friday 8am to 2pm and 3 to 6:30pm. Closed in August.

WHERE TO STAY

Casa de las Piedras   The building housing this 30-year-old inn, last renovated in 2002, dates from the 19th century. It stands on one of the oldest streets of the little town, only 50m (164 ft.) from the central square. It is a traditional Andalusian house spread across two floors. The bedrooms themselves are small and simple yet with a certain comfort, containing whitewashed walls, small lamps, a desk, and heavy wooden beds. Each comes with a little bathroom with shower. The hotel's dining room is one of the best in town for food (see below).

Las Piedras 40, 11610 Grazalema. © **95-613-20-14.** Fax 95-613-20-14. www.casadelaspiedras.net. 16 units. 43€ ($52) double. DC, MC, V. **Amenities:** Restaurant; laundry service. *In room:* A/C, TV.

Hotel El Horcajo ★ *Kids*   Set on a working estate in the Natural Park, this is a traditional Spanish colonial style farmhouse with whitewashed walls and iron grilles at the windows. The building dates from the 19th century, and the bedrooms have been installed in what were once stables. The main country house, still with its vaulted arches and wood beamed ceilings, is more than 170 years old. It has retained much of its original character, and offers an intimate family atmosphere. The very sober but cozy bedrooms, furnished with tiles and light wooden pieces, come with tiled bathroom with tub/shower combos. Constructed near the main building are 10 family units with a large double bed plus two single beds upstairs. These are built in a traditional style that blends in with the older structures. Many accommodations open onto a private terrace overlooking the estate. Rooms are decorated with locally crafted materials, and there is a comfortable lounge for guests. Typical local food is served, including some produce grown on the estate.

Carretera Ronda, 29400 Grazalema. ℭ 95-218-40-80. Fax 95-218-41-71. www.elhorcajo.com. 24 units. 61€–75€ ($73–$90) double; 68€–89€ ($82–$107) suite; 111€ ($133) triple; 133€ ($160) quad. AE, MC, V. **Amenities:** Restaurant; pool; room service (8am–11pm); laundry service; nonsmoking rooms. *In room:* A/C, TV, hair dryer.

Villa Turística de Grazalema *Kids*   One of the finest accommodations is found in this big chalet, built country style across two floors with white walls and wooden columns. Dating from 1990, it lies across the valley from the center of Grazalema. It's really a complex with semi-detached apartments that sleep from two to six guests. Most of the rooms open onto vistas of Grazalema or the *sierra* beyond. Families often book these rooms especially during the summer season, and the noise level may be uncomfortably high at the time. Bedrooms are small and furnished with light wooden pieces, tile floors, and summery colors, each with a tiled bathroom with tub/shower combo. Regional specialties are served at the villa's restaurant.

El Olivar s/n, 11610 Grazalema. ℭ **95-613-21-36.** Fax 95-613-13-22. www.tugasa.com. 24 units. 48€–82€ ($58–$98) double. MC, V. Free parking. **Amenities:** Restaurant; outdoor pool; rooms for those w/limited mobility. *In room:* A/C, TV, hair dryer, safe.

WHERE TO DINE

Cádiz El Chico ANDALUSIAN   The best restaurant in town stands right on the main square. In an antique building, it's typically decorated, even using blankets made in town. The simplified classic cuisine is inexpensive and good. There are some unusual dishes on the menu, notably *tagarnina* soup (made with an edible kind of cactus). Shoulder of lamb is studded with garlic and cooked over firewood. Oven-baked deer is another signature dish, most often served in a red-wine sauce. Of course, you find that Andalusian favorite, oxtail. Desserts are simple, nothing special.

Plaza de España 8. ℭ **95-613-20-27.** Reservations recommended. Main courses 9€–18€ ($11–$22). AE, MC, V. Daily 1–4pm and 8–11pm.

Casa de Las Piedras ANDALUSIAN   In this previously recommended hotel, near the central square, authentic, full-flavored regional dishes are presented in a 19th-century house. It's decorated in (what else?) a typical Andalusian regional style. Under beamed ceilings, you sit at wooden tables on wooden chairs and peruse the menu. Perhaps you'll begin with *Grazalema* (tomato) soup and follow with the delicious shredded veal with vegetables. Sea bass is perfectly sautéed and served with a mass of home-cut french fries. A signature dish is the oven-baked wild boar with spices. Prices are extremely reasonable considering the quality of the food, and the generous portions.

Las Piedras 40. © **95-613-20-14.** Main courses 5€–15€ ($6–$18). DC, MC, V. Tues–Sun 1:30–4pm and 8–11pm.

GAUCIN

From Grazalema, take A-374 southwest to Ubrique. From here, get on A-373 south. The route will curve east to Cortez de la Frontera. Once you reach this town, continue along the same A-373 south to Algatocin. At this point, connect with the A-369 and follow it southwest until you connect with the A-377 into Gaucín. (Look for signs.) Allow at least an hour for the 63km (39-mile) trip.

This mountain white town is perched on a ridge below a former Muslim fortress, which opens onto a panoramic vista of the countryside. Many expats, but Brits in particular, live here.

At the eastern edge of the village head up to the **Castillo del Aguila,** the Moorish castle. From its battlements you can look out over the countryside and on a clear day see all the way to the Rock of Gibraltar. Open daily 11am to 1pm and 4 to 6pm; admission is free.

The best place to stay and dine is **La Fructuosa** (© **95-215-10-72;** fax 95-215-15-80; lafructuosa@yahoo.es) in the center of Gaucín. Its bedrooms are simply but comfortably furnished, each with a tiled bathroom with tub and shower. Rooms go for 92€ ($110) double. The hotel restaurant, serving meals for 18€ ($22), is open only Wednesday to Saturday 8 to 10pm. The style of cooking is typically Andalusian, and portions are generous. The hotel is at Convento 67.

JIMENA DE LA FRONTERA ⚜

To reach this white town from Gaucín, take the winding A-369 out of town, traveling southwest for some 30 minutes, a distance of 23km (14 miles). Enveloped by Los Alcornocales Natural Park, Jimena was built 200m (656 ft.) above sea level. It lies so close to San Roque on the Costa del Sol and its string of beaches that it gets a lot of visitors on day trips, especially from the exclusive golf and polo belt of the coast. Chic Sotorgrande, an upmarket resort, is just a short drive to the south.

You enter Jimena through a gateway of three arches. Over the years the town has known many rulers, from the Phoenicians and Romans to the Moors and ultimately the Christian armies.

It's a delight to walk the steep and narrow cobblestone streets of Jimena, one of the more stunning of the Pueblos Blancos. It takes about 15 minutes to ascend to the highest point, the castle-fortress built on Roman ruins. Today the **Castillo-Fortaleza** is in ruins but still impressive. Inside the castle enclosure, you can take in one of the most panoramic **views** ⚜ of the Costa del Sol, including the Rock of Gibraltar and the port of Algeciras, where ferries depart for Morocco.

Visitors with more time will find that Jimena is the gateway to the **Parque Natural de los Alcornocales** ⚜⚜, stretching south to the Mediterranean and north to one of the white towns, El Bosque. The park is named for its cork oaks *(alcornocales),* which are among the largest in the world, but is also home to the gall and the holm oak as well as wild olive trees. Creatures such as the Egyptian mongoose, the royal eagle, eagle owls, lion buzzards, and the roebuck also inhabit the park. The park is one of the most heavily forested in Spain, and will give you a sense of what Iberia used to look like before being deforested.

At one of the tourist offices in one of the Pueblos Blancos that actually has tourist offices, inquire about a booklet, *Junta de Andalucía,* detailing eight walks through the park, ranging from 2 to 7km (1.25–4.35 miles).

WHERE TO STAY

Casa Grande *(Kids)*   If you'd like to overnight in Jimena, this little guesthouse is your best bet. It lies near Puerto Gales in the Barrio de Arriba and is an old Andalusian house in the traditional architectural style, with an internal courtyard. It rises two floors and is laced with corridors. Bedrooms are small and very basic, with traditional wooden furniture. Rooms here are among the most affordable along the trail of Pueblos Blancos. Families often book an apartment here complete with kitchen. Half the bedrooms have little private bathrooms with showers; the rest share a public bathroom in the corridor.

Calle Fuente Nueva 42, 11330 Jimena de la Frontera. ☏ **95-664-05-78.** www.posadalacasagrande.net. 7 units. 35€ ($42) double without bathroom; 45€ ($54) double with bathroom; 60€ ($72) apt. DC, V. Free parking. **Amenities:** Bar; laundry service; nonsmoking rooms; solarium. *In room:* A/C, no phone.

WHERE TO DINE

Mesón Restaurante Campoy ANDALUSIAN   Near the train station, this is a rustic old building with wooden furniture and a series of colored regional blankets for decor. The cook here prepares some of the most typical dishes of the surrounding area, using locally grown produce whenever possible. In spring, you might be able to order *revuelto de esparragos* (asparagus with scrambled eggs), or *chantarella* (a type of wild mushroom) will appear in one of the dishes. The cookery is robust and bursts with flavor. Good examples include an oven-baked lamb studded with garlic and heavily spiced or fish casserole studded with shellfish and flavored with a red sauce. The dessert specialty of the area, which might or might not be on the menu, is *piñonate,* which has been handed down from the Arabs. It's made of olive oil, honey, almonds, orange peel, and cinnamon.

Mesa de Los Angeles 36. ☏ **95-664-10-60.** Main courses 10€–14€ ($12–$17). DC, MC, V. Thurs–Tues 10am–11:30pm. Closed June 20–July 10.

Restaurante El Anon INTERNATIONAL/ANDALUSIAN   This restaurant serving a savory and affordable cuisine lies in the Hostal El Anon, which was formed when a series of small houses and stables were blended seamlessly together. There is an inviting Andalusian courtyard here along with a comfortable restaurant and even a rooftop pool. The style is predictably rustic with wooden furniture, antique ceramics, and copper ornaments. Parts of the building are 3 centuries old, and the restaurant itself opened in the late 1970s. Begin, perhaps, with the kidney pâté and follow with the freshly arrived catch of the day hauled up from the Costa del Sol. It can be grilled to your specifications. Many savvy locals prefer it just with olive oil and lemon. Local chicken is tantalizingly prepared with grapes, and a tender sirloin of beef appears on a platter with a blue cheese sauce.

Calle Consuelo 36. ☏ **95-664-01-13.** Reservations recommended. Main courses 9€–12€ ($11–$14). DC, MC, V. Thurs–Tues 1–3:30pm and 8–11:30pm. Closed 2 weeks in Nov (dates vary).

MEDINA SIDONIA

From Jimena, take C-333 northwest until you come to the junction with A-375 heading southwest to the junction with A-381. Once on A-381 continue northwest into Medina Sidonia. This hour-long trip takes you across 86km (54 miles).

Medina Sidonia fell to Catholic troops in 1264 under King Alfonso X. It was an ancient hilltop Muslim fortress. In the Middle Ages it became a famous seat of the Duke de Medina Sidonia, a title bestowed on the heirs of Guzmán El Bueno who helped recapture the town from the Moors.

The title today is held by the Duquesa de Medina Sidonia, known as *la duquesa roja* (the red duchess), for her left-wing political views. She is a champion of the poor and downtrodden, and her politics have even landed her in jail.

This village has seen better days, but wandering its cobbled and narrow streets is still an evocative experience, a bit like stepping back into the Middle Ages. Start at the central square, **Plaza de España.** The most impressive architecture here is the Renaissance facade of the 17th-century **Ayuntamiento (town hall).**

Nearby is the town's second most beautiful square, **Plaza Iglesia Mayor.** Here you can visit **Santa Iglesia Santa María La Coronada,** open daily 9:30am to 2:30pm and 4:30 to 9:30pm; admission is 2€ ($2.40). Built on the foundations of a former mosque, it is celebrated for its stunning *retablo* ★★, standing 15m (49 ft.) high. The *retablo* depicts scenes from the life of Jesus and is a piece of master work in polychrome wood achieved by the artisans of the Middle Ages.

After the church you can visit the **Roman Sewers** entered at Calle Espíritu Santo 3, open Tuesday to Sunday 10am to 1:30pm and 6 to 8pm, costing 3€ ($3.60) for admission. They date from the 1st century A.D. With the same ticket you can also see the ruins of a well-preserved **Roman road** nearby. More Moorish architecture is seen in a trio of gates, the best preserved of which is **Arco de la Pastora,** lying close to the Carretera de Jerez.

For information about the area, head to the local **Tourist Office,** Plaza Iglesia Mayor (✆ **95-641-24-04**), open Monday to Friday 10am to 1:30pm and 5 to 8pm.

If you find yourself in Media for lunch, consider stopping at **Venta La Duquesa** (✆ **95-641-08-36**), lying along A-393 3km (1¾ miles) to the southeast. The food is good and well prepared, without rising to any spectacular heights. Try the loin of pork, which is well spiced and tasty, or else a more local dish, partridge baked with onions and mushrooms. The restaurant is on Carretera de Jerez A-393, and main courses cost 11€ to 15€ ($13–$18).

VEJER DE LA FRONTERA ★

From Medina Sedonia follow the C-393 south to Vejer de la Frontera, a distance of 26km (17 miles), usually taking 20 minutes. This is one of the more dazzling Pueblos Blancos. Like most of the other towns we've visited, this *pueblo blanco* also reflects its Moorish history.

Vejer, still partially walled, lies in a deep cleft between two hills on the road between Tarifa (southernmost point in Spain) and the port of Cádiz, 10km (6¼ miles) inland. Dominated by its castle and a Gothic church, it looks like a town you'd find in the Greek islands.

For orientation, head to the **Tourist Office** at Calle Marqués de Tamarón 10 (✆ **95-645-01-91**). Hours are June to August Monday to Friday 9am to 2pm and 6:30 to 8pm. In August, it is also open on Saturday 10:30am to 2pm. In other months, it keeps no set hours.

You can skip most of the monuments, enjoying the beauty of the town. Or else you can duck into **Iglesia del Divino Salvador,** the major church, lying in back of the Tourist Office. Its doors may or may not be open. It's a mix of styles, including Romanesque, mudéjar, and Gothic.

Castillo Moro or the Moorish castle is reached by heading down Calle Ramón y Cajal from the church. The castle keeps such erratic, changing hours it's best to inquire at the tourist office. Over the years it's been altered drastically, but by 1000 B.C. it is known to have been some sort of fortress, standing watch over the fishing grounds and factories along the coast for the approach of an enemy vessel by sea. The site was also used by the Phoenicians and Carthaginians long before the coming of the Romans. Even if you can't see the castle, you can admire the panoramic **view** ★.

WHERE TO STAY & DINE

El Cobijo de Vejer   This Moorish-style house with an Andalusian courtyard is a much-restored 250 years old. In 1999 it opened as a hotel and was renovated in 2002. Its flower-filled patio is a delight, and it has individually decorated bedrooms that are midsize and vary in quality. The best open onto vistas of the town and countryside. Each bedroom comes with a tiled bathroom with shower. Some of the accommodations also come with small kitchen units and private sitting rooms.

Calle San Filmo 7, 11150 Vejer de la Frontera. ✆ **96-545-50-23**. 7 units. 62€ ($74) double. Rates include continental breakfast. DC, MC, V. Free parking. **Amenities:** Breakfast lounge. *In room:* A/C, TV, fridge.

Hotel Convento de San Francisco ★   Once a convent for the Clarias order, this restored 17th-century structure is on the smaller of the town's two main squares. Within its intact, ancient stone walls, you'll enjoy rustic charm and comfort. The furniture is mostly wood, often antiques. Bedrooms are midsize and each equipped with a small tiled bathroom with tub and shower. The former chapel holds a cafeteria serving one of best breakfasts in town. The restaurant is also an excellent choice for regional specialties; a complete lunch or dinner costs 22€ to 32€ ($26–$39).

La Plazuela, 11150 Vejer de la Frontera. ✆ **95-645-10-01**. Fax 95-645-10-04. www.tugasa.com. 25 units. 55€–64€ ($66–$77) double. AE, DC, MC, V. Free parking. **Amenities:** Restaurant; bar; laundry service. *In room:* A/C, TV, dataport, hair dryer.

CONTINUING ON TO THE SHERRY TRIANGLE

After your tour of Vejer, you can take N-340 northwest. At the junction with N-IV, continue northeast into Jerez de la Frontera. The distance from Vejer to Jerez is 62km (39 miles). The trip takes 45 minutes. Once in Jerez, you'll be in the center of the sherry-producing district of Andalusia, the Sherry Triangle.

Three cities make up this region: **Jerez de la Frontera,** plus the port cities of **El Puerto de Santa María** and **Sanlúcar de Barrameda.** If you have time to visit only one, make it Jerez because it has the best bodegas where you can see how sherry is produced and taste samples.

Jerez also gets the nod because it is a great equestrian center, known for its Carthusian horses, and it is also one of the best places to hear authentic flamenco.

Visitors flock to Sanlúcar de Barrameda for its beaches and also for its sherry bodegas. Those arriving at Puerto de Santa María find a dilapidated but intriguing little fishing port with lovely beaches nearby. Columbus once lived here. It deserves at least a day as you visit its sherry and brandy bodegas and sample its *marisco* (shellfish) bars along the water.

5 Jerez de la Frontera ★

87km (54 miles) S of Seville, 593km (368 miles) SW of Madrid, 34km (21 miles) NE of Cádiz

Over the centuries, the charming little Andalusian town of Jerez de la Frontera has shipped thousands of casks of golden sherry around the world. Dating back nearly 3,000 years, Jerez is today a modern, progressive town with wide boulevards and an interesting old quarter. Busloads of visitors pour in every year to get free drinks at one of the bodegas where wine is aged and bottled.

The name of the town is pronounced "heh-*res*" or "heh-*reth,*" in Andalusian or Castilian, respectively. The French and the Moors called it various names, including Heres and Scheris, which the English corrupted to Sherry.

ESSENTIALS

GETTING THERE   Iberia and Avianco offer **flights** to Jerez daily from Barcelona and Zaragoza; four daily flights from Madrid; and several flights a week to and from Germany, London, and in the summer Grand Canary Island. The airport at Carretera Jerez-Sevilla is about 11km (7 miles) northeast of the city center (follow the signs to Seville). Call © **95-615-00-00** for information.

Most visitors take one of 12 **trains** per day from Seville, taking 1¼ hours and costing 5.75€ ($6.90) one-way. Trains from Madrid also arrive daily. A ticket from Madrid to Jerez on the TALGO costs 55€ ($66), and the trip takes 4½ hours. The railway station in Jerez is at the Plaza de la Estación s/n (© **90-224-02-02**) at the eastern end of Calle Medina.

Bus connections are more frequent than train connections, and the location of the bus terminal is more convenient. You'll find it on Calle Cartuja at the corner of Calle Madre de Dios, a 12-minute walk east of the Alcázar. About 17 buses arrive daily from Cádiz (1 hr. away) and three buses per day travel from Ronda (2¾ hr.). Seven buses a day arrive from Seville (1½ hr.). Call © **95-634-52-07** for more information.

Jerez lies on the highway (E-5) connecting Seville with Cádiz, Algeciras, Gibraltar, and the ferryboat landing for Tangier, Morocco. There's also an overland road connecting Jerez with Granada and Málaga.

VISITOR INFORMATION   The **tourist office** is at Paul s/n, Edificio Senitium (© **95-635-94-50;** www.webjuarez.com). It's open Monday to Friday 9:30am to 2:30pm and 4:30 to 6:30pm, Saturday and Sunday 9:30am to 3:30pm. The English-speaking staff can provide directions, transportation suggestions, open hours, and so on for any bodega you might want to visit. You'll also be given a map pinpointing the location of various bodegas.

FAST FACTS   The most convenient location to **exchange money** is **Banco Santander Central Hispano,** Calle Larga 1 (© **90-224-24-24**), where you'll find ATMs. Open Monday to Friday 8:30am to 1:30pm. In case of an **emergency** dial © **061;** for the **police** call © **091.** If you need a **hospital** head to **Ambulatorio de la Seguridad Social,** Calle José Luis Díez (© **95-632-32-02**). For **Internet access** try **The Big Orange,** Calle Antonia de Jesús Tirado (© **95-635-01-01**), near the bus station. The charge is 1.80€ ($2.15) per hour. Open Sunday to Thursday 11am to 1am, Friday and Saturday 11am to 3am. The main branch of the **post office** is at Calle Cerrón 2 (© **95-634-22-95**), open Monday to Friday 8:30am to 8:30pm, Saturday 9am to 2pm.

EXPLORING THE AREA
TOURING THE BODEGAS 🐾🐾

Jerez is not surrounded by vineyards as you might expect. Instead, the vineyards lie to the north and west in the "Sherry Triangle" marked by Jerez, Sanlúcar de Barrameda, and El Puerto de Santa María (the latter two towns are on the coast). This is where top-quality *albariza* soil is found; the highest quality contains an average of 60% chalk, which is ideal for the cultivation of grapes used in sherry production, principally the white Palomino de Jerez.

Jerez de la Frontera

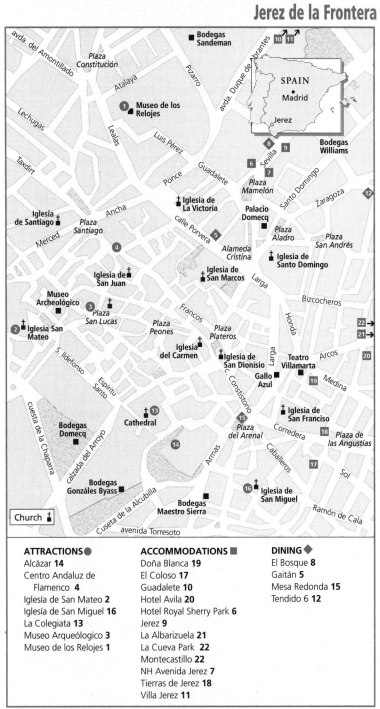

ATTRACTIONS ●
Alcázar **14**
Centro Andaluz de
  Flamenco **4**
Iglesía de San Mateo **2**
Iglesía de San Miguel **16**
La Colegiata **13**
Museo Arqueólogico **3**
Museo de los Relojes **1**

ACCOMMODATIONS ■
Doña Blanca **19**
El Coloso **17**
Guadalete **10**
Hotel Avila **20**
Hotel Royal Sherry Park **6**
Jerez **9**
La Albarizuela **21**
La Cueva Park **22**
Montecastillo **22**
NH Avenida Jerez **7**
Tierras de Jerez **18**
Villa Jerez **11**

DINING ◆
El Bosque **8**
Gaitán **5**
Mesa Redonda **15**
Tendido 6 **12**

Moments   The Dancing Horses of Jerez

A rival of sorts to Vienna's famous Spanish Riding School is the **Escuela Andaluza del Arte Ecuestre (Andalusian School of Equestrian Art)**, Av. Duque de Abrantes s/n (© **95-631-96-35**). In fact, the long, hard schooling that brings horse and rider into perfect harmony originated in this province. The Viennese school was started with Hispano-Arab horses sent from this region, the same breeds you can see today. Every Thursday at noon, crowds come to admire the **Dancing Horses of Jerez** 🐴🐴 as they perform in a show that includes local folklore. Lanes 1 and 2 (the lanes are rows for seating) sell for 21€ ($25), lanes 3 and 4 sell for 17€ ($20), and lanes 5 and 6 go for 13€ ($16). When performances aren't scheduled, you can visit the stables and tack room, observing as the elegant horses are being trained. Hours are Monday to Wednesday and Friday from 10am to 1pm, costing 6€ ($7.20) adults, 3€ ($3.60) children and seniors. On the grounds of the school you can visit **Museo del Enganche,** the harness museum, displaying antique carriages. Entrance is 3€ ($3.60). Bus no. 18 goes here.

In and around Jerez there must be more than 100 bodegas where you not only can see how sherry is made, bottled, and aged but also get free samples. Among the most famous producers are **Sandeman, Pedro Domecq,** and **González Byass,** the maker of Tío Pepe. On a typical visit, you'll be shown through several buildings in which sherry and brandy are manufactured. In one building, you'll see grapes being pressed and sorted; in another, the bottling process; in a third, thousands of large oak casks. Then it's on to an attractive bar where sherries—amber, dark gold, cream, red, sweet, and velvety—can be sampled. If offered, try the very dry La Ina sherry or the Fundador brandy, one of the most popular in the world. *Warning:* These drinks are more potent than you might expect.

Most bodegas are open Monday to Friday from 10:30am to 1:30pm. Regrettably, many of them are closed in August, but many do reopen by the third week of August to prepare for the wine festival in early September, which is an ideal time to visit. Regardless of when you come, you can count on the finest in hospitality since Jerez is widely known for welcoming visitors warmly.

Of the dozens of bodegas you can visit, the most popular are listed below. Some charge an admission fee and require a reservation.

A favorite among British visitors is **Harveys of Bristol,** Calle Pintor Muñoz Cebrian s/n (© **95-634-60-00**), which doesn't require a reservation. An English-speaking guide leads a 2-hour tour. Tours are Monday to Friday at 10am and noon, costing 4.50€ ($5.40).

Williams & Humbert Limited, Carretera Nacional IV Km 641.75, Puerto Santa María (© **95-635-34-06**), offers tours from 10 and 11am, noon, and 1:30pm Monday to Friday, charging 5€ ($6). Their premium brands include the world-famous Dry Sack Medium Sherry, Canasta Cream, Fino Pando, and Manzanilla Alegría, in addition to Gran Duque de Alba Gran Reserva Brandy. It's wise to reserve in advance.

Another famous name is **González Byass,** Manuel María González 12 (© **95-635-70-16**); admission is 8€ ($9.60), and reservations are required. Tours in English depart at 11:30am, 12:30, 1:30, 2:00, 3:30, 4:30, 5:30 and 6:30pm daily. Equally famous is **Domecq,** Calle San Ildefonso 3 (© **95-615-15-00**).

Reservations are required, and admission is 5€ ($6). Tours start at 10 and 11am, noon, and 2pm Monday to Friday (Sat tours May–Sept at 2pm).

Since many people go to Jerez specifically to visit a bodega, August or week-end closings can be very disappointing. If this happens to you, make a trip to the nearby village of Lebrija, about halfway between Jerez and Seville, 14km (8½ miles) west of the main highway. A good spot to get a glimpse of rural Spain, Lebrija is a local winemaking center where some very fine sherries originate. At one small bodega, Juan García, the owner courteously escorts visitors around. There are several other bodegas in Lebrija, and the locals will gladly point them out to you. It's all very casual, and much more informal than Jerez.

OTHER ATTRACTIONS

Aside from the bodegas, the chief attraction is the **Alcázar,** the former residence of the caliph of Seville, complete with an octagonal mosque and ancient baths. The complex was taken by Christian knights in the Reconquista in 1255. The walls of the old Moorish fortress are now surrounded by gardens through which you can stroll, south of Plaza del Arenal. The planting here has been modeled as closely as possible to the original gardens. Inside you can view a well-preserved mosque with a *mihrab.* The baths were constructed by the Almohads and based on Roman designs. In the complex stands the 18th-century **Palacio de Villavi-cencio,** Alameda Vieja (© **95-631-97-98**), constructed on the site of the origi-nal Muslim castle. Inside is a *cámara obscura,* that lens-and-mirrors device that projects views of the major landmarks of Jerez onto a large indoor screen. Views of the sherry vineyards and the sea beyond are also projected. Admission is 1.50€ ($1.80), 3.25€ ($3.90) including *cámara obscura.* Open May to mid-September daily 10am to 8pm; mid-September to April daily 10am to 6pm.

La Colegiata or Cathedral of San Salvador, Plaza de Arroyo, is primarily an 18th-century baroque structure with five aisles and both Renaissance and baroque adornments. Some of the building, however, dates from the 16th and 17th centuries. Inside you can see such treasures as Zurbarán's *The Sleeping Girl* in the sacristy. The transept crossing is covered by a dome. The cathedral lies at the top of a wide baroque flight of stairs. Set slightly apart is a 15th-century mudéjar belfry. Admission is free. The cathedral is open Monday to Friday 11am to 1pm and 6 to 8pm, Saturday 11am to 2pm and 6 to 8pm, and Sunday 11am to 2pm and 5:30 to 8pm.

Museo de los Relojes (Clock Museum) ⊛, in the Palacio de Atalaya, Cervantes 3 (© **95-618-21-00**), is across from the Royal Equestrian School. This treasure trove of 300 British and French timepieces includes many dating from the 1600s. They come in all shapes and sizes, as well as designs, their chimes ringing out in "concert" at noon. This may be the world's largest collection of fully functioning timepieces and antique clocks. Outside peacocks walk the grounds. Open Monday to Saturday 10am to 2pm; admission is 2€ ($2.40).

One of the oldest churches is **Iglesia de San Miguel,** a 15th-century Gothic structure lying to the south of Plaza del Arenal. Its ornate facade was added 3 centuries later. The bell tower is decorated with blue-and-white Andalusian tiles and the interior is a medley of Gothic architecture over different periods. Some of the architecture is in the Isabelline Gothic style. Note the magnificent stained-glass windows. In all, this is one of the area's most beautiful churches. It lies at Plaza de San Miguel (© **95-634-33-47**) and is open Tuesday to Friday 10am to 1:30pm, costing 1.80€ ($2.15) to enter. On weekends you can attend Mass here.

A modern flamenco museum, **Centro Andaluz de Flamenco,** Palacio Pemartín 1, Plaza San Juan (© **95-632-11-27**), is a busy place, complete with a multimedia show plus an audio and visual library devoted to the art of flamenco. Admission free, and it is open Monday to Friday 9am to 2pm.

If you still have time for a stroll, head for the old quarter, **Barrio de Santiago** 𝒜, which stretches uphill from the cathedral. Wander its labyrinthine maze of narrow lanes and alleyways. If you want to have a goal, seek out **Iglesía de San Mateo,** on Plaza del Mercado, noted for its mudéjar chapels. Look for its impressive retable and the beautiful vaulting over its chapels. It is open only for services daily 7 to 9am and 7 to 8pm. Facing the church, also on Plaza del Mercado, is the **Museo Arqueológico,** housed inside an 18th-century town mansion. It offers such treasures as a 7th century B.C. Greek helmet found in the Guadalete River. Other pieces include a ram's head from the 3rd century B.C. and some fine Roman heads. Many artifacts unearthed at the ancient town of Hasta Regia are also on display. There is even a Visigothic collection and treasures from the heyday of the Cordovan Emirate. Upstairs is a collection of Muslim and medieval artifacts, including Moorish ceramics and a Caliphal bottle vase with Kufic script from the 10th century. Open June to August Tuesday to Sunday 10am to 2:30pm; September to May Tuesday to Friday 10am to 2pm and 4 to 7pm, Saturday and Sunday 10am to 2:30pm. Admission is 1.50€ ($1.80).

WHERE TO STAY
VERY EXPENSIVE

Montecastillo 𝒜𝒜𝒜   Giving the NH Avenida Jerez serious competition is this deluxe country club in the rolling hills of the sherry *campiña* (wine country). The area's most tranquil retreat, it has rooms with balconies overlooking the plush, scenic landscape. The hotel, a 10-minute ride from the center of Jerez, is elegantly furnished and professionally run. The spacious rooms are decorated in a provincial French style with elegant fabrics, beautiful linens, and large beds. The marble bathrooms come with tub/shower combinations.

Carretera de Arcos, 11406 Jerez de la Frontera. © **95-615-12-00.** Fax 95-615-12-09. www.montecastillo. com. 120 units. 153€–295€ ($184–$354) double; from 554€ ($665) suite. Rates include breakfast. AE, DC, MC, V. Free parking. **Amenities:** Breakfast room; bar; 3 pools (2 outdoor, 1 indoor); golf course; health spa; Jacuzzi; sauna; business center; babysitting; laundry service/dry cleaning. *In room:* A/C, TV, dataport, minibar, hair dryer.

Villa Jerez 𝒜𝒜𝒜   This is a little gem, a pocket of posh that invites luxurious living and also offers top-rate regional and international cuisine in its restaurant, Las Yucas. While it's Jerez's best boutique hotel, Villa Jerez is very small and doesn't compete with the NH Avenida Jerez in terms of amenities and facilities. You'll find well-heeled guests drinking sherry in the lush gardens surrounding the hotel. Each room is individually decorated like a room in a Spanish mansion; all open onto views of the garden or pool. Bedrooms are spacious and tastefully and comfortably furnished, with luxe tiled bathrooms, including hydromassage baths and separate showers.

Av. de la Cruz Roja 7, 11407 Jerez de la Frontera. © **95-608-83-30.** 18 units. 236€–329€ ($283–$395) double; 294€–446€ ($353–$535) suite. AE, DC, MC, V. Free parking. **Amenities:** Restaurant; bar; outdoor pool; gym; sauna; 24-hr. room service; babysitting; laundry service/dry cleaning; nonsmoking rooms; rooms for those w/limited mobility. *In room:* A/C, TV, dataport, minibar, hair dryer, iron/ironing board, safe.

EXPENSIVE

Guadalete ⭐   In a tranquil exclusive area north of Jerez, this first-class hotel lies a 15-minute walk from the historic core. It may not be as good as the Royal Sherry Park but is still one of the town's leading hotels, often hosting business travelers dealing with the sherry industry. A marble-floored lobby, spacious and contemporary public rooms, and palm tree gardens give this place somewhat of a resort aura. The rooms are medium in size to spacious and have state-of-the-art bathrooms with tub/shower combos. The hotel is decorated with original watercolors and lithographs painted by local artists in the 1970s.

Av. Duque de Abrantes 50, 11407 Jerez de la Frontera. © **95-618-22-88.** Fax 95-618-22-93. 137 units. 110€–145€ ($132–$174) double; 235€–305€ ($282–$366) suite. Rates include breakfast. AE, MC, V. Free parking. **Amenities:** Restaurant; bar; outdoor pool; sauna; limited room service; laundry service/dry cleaning; rooms for those w/limited mobility. *In room:* A/C, TV, dataport, minibar, hair dryer, safe.

Hotel Royal Sherry Park ⭐⭐   Especially noted for its setting within a palm-fringed garden whose tiled borders attract many sun-loving guests, this is one of the best modern hotels in Jerez. It's located on a wide boulevard north of the historic center of town and contains a marble-floored lobby, modern public rooms, and fairly standard but comfortable guest rooms, each with a bathroom containing a tub/shower combo. The uniformed staff lays out a copious breakfast buffet and serves drinks at several hideaways, both indoors and within the garden.

Av. Alcalde Alvaro Domecq 11 bis, 11405 Jerez de la Frontera. © **95-631-76-14.** Fax 95-631-13-00. www.sherryparkhotel.com. 173 units. 128€–250€ ($154–$300) double; 251€–327€ ($301–$392) suite. AE, DC, MC, V. Free parking. **Amenities:** 3 restaurants; bar; 2 pools (1 indoor); health club; indoor sauna; salon; car rental; limited room service; babysitting; laundry service/dry cleaning. *In room:* A/C, TV, dataport, minibar, hair dryer, safe.

Jerez ⭐⭐⭐   All things considered, the Jerez has the edge over its nearest—and slightly more charming—competitor, Villa Jerez. This is the preferred address of the sherry-bottling crowd. The bedrooms are warmly decorated and stylish. All rooms open onto views of the landscaped gardens or a large pool. The bathrooms come with Jacuzzi baths and shower massages. You have a choice of standard doubles or deluxe doubles, or superior suites overlooking the pool and gardens from private balconies. The dining is deluxe with luxurious ingredients used in the top-rated cuisine. You can sample a glass of sherry by the pool or on a patio surrounded by fragrant orange trees.

Av. Alcalde Alvaro Domecq 35, 11405 Jerez de la Frontera. © **95-630-06-00.** Fax 95-630-50-01. www.jerezhotel.com. 129 units. 120€–150€ ($144–$180) double; 445€ ($534) suite. AE, DC, MC, V. Free parking. **Amenities:** Restaurant; bar; 2 pools (1 indoor); 2 tennis courts; gym; sauna; bike rentals; barber and salon; 24-hr. room service; babysitting; laundry service/dry cleaning; nonsmoking rooms; rooms for those w/limited mobility. *In room:* A/C, TV, dataport, minibar, hair dryer, iron/ironing board, safe.

NH Avenida Jerez ⭐⭐   Very close to the commercial heart of Jerez, this hotel occupies a modern balconied structure and is the best hotel within the center of Jerez itself, although Montecastillo (see above) on the outskirts is a serious challenger. Inside, cool polished stone floors, leather armchairs, and a variety of potted plants create a restful haven. The good-size rooms are discreetly contemporary and decorated in neutral colors, with big windows, comfortable beds, and private bathrooms equipped with tub/shower combos.

Av. Alcalde Alvaro Domecq 10, 11405 Jerez de la Frontera. © **95-634-74-11.** Fax 95-633-72-96. www.nh-hoteles.es. 95 units. 99€–218€ ($119–$262) double. AE, DC, MC, V. Parking 9€ ($11). **Amenities:** Restaurant; bar; limited room service; babysitting; laundry service/dry cleaning. *In room:* A/C, TV, dataport, minibar, hair dryer.

MODERATE

Doña Blanca   A serviceable, adequately comfortable hotel, this middle-bracket choice has been in business since 1994 and was last renovated in 2002. It lies in the very center of Jerez, within walking distance of both the Alcázar and cathedral. The structure is in the typical Andalusian style with wrought-iron balconies and grills. The staff is welcoming and the midsize bedrooms are furnished simply but comfortably with hardwood floors and minimal decorations. All accommodations are attached to private tiled bathrooms with tub/shower combos.

Calle Bodegas 11, 11402 Jerez de la Frontera. (*) **95-634-87-61.** Fax 95-634-85-86. www.hoteldonablanca. com. 30 units. 70€–142€ ($84–$170) double. AE, DC, MC, V. Parking 8.50€ ($10). **Amenities:** Breakfast room; bar; babysitting; laundry service; nonsmoking rooms. *In room:* A/C, TV, minibar, hair dryer, iron/ironing board, safe (in some), beverage maker.

La Albarizuela   Just a 5-minute walk from the bus station, this is a modern hotel that will not blow you away with charm and character, but it is comfortable. Last renovated in 2001, it has midsize rooms that are rather simple in their decoration and standard in their furnishings. Each comes with a tiled bathroom with tub and shower. In this price range we prefer Doña Blanca, but La Albarizuela is certainly serviceable. Bedrooms have a choice of a double bed (called matrimonial) or twins. A wide range of regional sherries awaits in the bar.

Honsario 6, 11402 Jerez de la Frontera. (*) **95-634-68-62.** Fax 95-634-66-86. www.hotelalbarizuela.com. 17 units. 99€–139€ ($119–$167) double. MC, V. Parking 9€ ($11). **Amenities:** Bar; cafeteria; limited room service; laundry service; rooms for those w/limited mobility. *In room:* AC, TV, dataport, hair dryer.

La Cueva Park   This charming hotel in a century-old building 6.5km (4 miles) from the center of town attracts motorists. It's also a convenient half-mile from the bus station. The architecture is typical of Andalusia, with a tiled roof overhanging thick brick walls. Gardens surround the hotel. All the units are medium-size and comfortably furnished. There are nine white-walled bungalow-style apartments classified as suites, each with its own cooking area, living room, and terrace. All units come with bathrooms containing tub/shower combos.

Carretera de Arcos Km 10, Apartado 536, 11406 Jerez de la Frontera. (*) **95-618-91-20.** Fax 95-618-90-20. www.hotellacueva.com. 58 units. 72€–110€ ($86–$132) double; 210€–330€ ($252–$396) suite. AE, DC, MC, V. Parking 10€ ($12). **Amenities:** Restaurant; bar; outdoor pool; limited room service; laundry service/dry cleaning; rooms for those w/limited mobility. *In room:* A/C, TV, dataport, minibar, safe.

Tierras de Jerez   This government-rated four-star hotel is slightly less alluring than Doña Blanca and more appealing than the more basic La Albarizuela. A four-story building, it was renovated in 2002 and enjoys a central location immediately east of the church of San Miguel. Bedrooms have traditional Andalusian furnishings and are completely modernized. Each is midsize and comes with a tiled bathroom with tub and shower. There's no hotel restaurant, but many decently priced choices lie within a short walk of the hotel.

Calle Corredera 58, 11402 Jerez de la Frontera. (*) **95-634-64-00.** Fax 95-632-11-13. www.intergrouphoteles. com. 30 units. 75€–140€ ($90–$168) double. AE, DC, MC, V. Parking 6€ ($7.20). **Amenities:** Breakfast room; cafeteria; limited room service; laundry service; nonsmoking rooms; rooms for those w/limited mobility. *In room:* A/C, TV, dataport, minibar, hair dryer.

INEXPENSIVE

El Coloso *(Value* A few steps from the Plaza de las Angustias in the historic center, this is one of the best bargains in town, modest but worth recommending. The decor is in the conventional local style with whitewashed walls and a trio of Andalusian-style patios with balconies opening onto street scenes of Jerez. The hotel opened in 1969 and was last renovated in 1998. The rooms are a bit cramped but beautifully maintained, with good beds and bathrooms containing tub/shower combos. Breakfast is the only meal served.

Calle Pedro Alonso 13, 11402 Jerez de la Frontera. ℭ/fax **95-634-90-08.** www.elcolosohotel.net. 25 units. 45€–82€ ($54–$98) double. MC, V. Parking 5€ ($6). *In room:* A/C, TV, hair dryer.

Hotel Avila   One of the better bargains in Jerez, the Avila is a modern building erected in 1968 and renovated in 1987. It's near the post office and the Plaza del Arenal in the commercial center of town. Its rooms are clean, comfortable, and well maintained, although not special in any way. The beds, however, are quite comfortable and the bathrooms are equipped with shower stalls.

Calle Avila 3, 11401 Jerez de la Frontera. ℭ **95-633-48-08.** Fax 95-633-68-07. www.hotelavilaonline.com. 33 units. 54€–74€ ($65–$89) double. DC, MC, V. Parking 7€–10€ ($8.40–$12) nearby. **Amenities:** Cafeteria; lounge; laundry service/dry cleaning. *In room:* A/C, TV, hair dryer.

WHERE TO DINE

El Bosque ✪ SPANISH/INTERNATIONAL   Less than 1.6km (1 mile) northeast of the city center, El Bosque opened after World War II and is the city's most elegant restaurant. A favorite of the sherry-producing aristocracy, it retains a strong emphasis on bullfighting memorabilia, which makes up most of the decor. Get the excellent *rabo de toro* (oxtail stew) if you want to dine like a native. You could also begin with a soothing gazpacho, then try one of the fried fish dishes, such as hake Seville style. Rice with king prawns and baby shrimp omelets are popular. Desserts are usually good, especially the pistachio ice cream.

Av. Alcalde Alvaro Domecq 26. ℭ **95-630-70-30.** Reservations required. Main courses 15€–28€ ($18–$34). AE, DC, MC, V. Mon–Sat 1:30–5pm and 8:30pm–midnight.

Gaitán ANDALUSIAN   Owner Juan Hurtado continues to win acclaim for the food served here at his small restaurant near the Puerta Santa María. Surrounded by celebrity photographs, you can enjoy such Andalusian dishes as garlic soup, various stews, duck a la Sevillana, and fried seafood. One special dish is lamb cooked with honey, based on a recipe so ancient it dates from the Muslim occupation of Spain. For dessert, the almond tart is a favorite.

Calle Gaitán 3. ℭ **95-634-58-59.** Reservations recommended. Main courses 13€–20€ ($16–$24); fixed-price menu 30€ ($36). AE, DC, MC, V. Sun 1–4:30pm; Mon–Sat 1–4:30pm and 8:30–11:30pm.

Mesa Redonda ✪✪ *Finds* TRADITIONAL SPANISH   This restaurant is a rare treat. Owner/chef José Antonio Romero and his wife, Margarita, have sought out traditional recipes once served in the homes of the aristocratic sherry dons of Jerez. They serve them in a setting like a private residence, complete with a library filled with old recipe books and literature about food and wine. The 10 tables fill quickly. The menu is ever changing; try the *albondiguillas marineras* (fish meatballs in shellfish sauce) and *hojaldre de rape y gambas* (a pastry filled with monkfish and prawns). Our highest recommendation goes to the *filetes de lenguado con zetas* (filet of sole with mushrooms) and *cordero asado* (grilled lamb). For dessert, there's nothing finer than the lemon-and-almond cake.

Manuel de la Quintana 3. ℭ **95-634-00-69.** Reservations required. Main courses 12€–15€ ($14–$18). AE, DC, MC, V. Mon–Sat 1:30–4pm and 9–11:30pm. Closed last week in July and 1st 3 weeks in Aug.

Tendido 6 ✪ ANDALUSIAN   Since 1960 this well-run local restaurant has been serving good, affordable food. It started out as a small wine shop serving olives and chicken with garlic and gradually expanded. A bar with an open-air terrace was added, and soon it was a full-fledged restaurant. The tapas and regional wines are among the best in Jerez, and they're served in a typically Andalusian setting. Since Jerez is fairly near the sea, the fresh catch of the day is brought in. One day it might be anglerfish in a savory green sauce, the next perfectly grilled swordfish cooked over firewood. Also recommended are grilled sirloin with pepper sauce, and artichoke with clams and wild asparagus croquettes.

Calle Circo 10. ℭ **95-634-48-35.** Reservations recommended. Main courses 9€–18€ ($11–$22). AE, DC, MC, V. Mon–Sat 1–4pm and 8–11:30pm. Closed 2nd week of Aug.

JEREZ DE LA FRONTERA AFTER DARK

A great way to start your evening is with local sherry and the best tapas in town at **Las Botas,** Santo Domingo 8 (ℭ **95-633-89-77**). In business since the mid-1970s, it offers a delectable display of food, including Spanish tortillas (thick omelets with layers of potato), cured jams, regional cheese, mushrooms, and shrimp or bull meat marinated in sherry. Plates cost from 4.80€ to 6€ ($5.75–$7.20). Open Monday to Saturday from noon to 5pm and 8pm to 1am.

Only 3 blocks from Plaza del Arenal, **Bar Alegría,** Calle Corredera 30 (ℭ **95-633-80-70**), is patronized by savvy locals. We'd come just for the *croquetas de pollo* (chicken croquettes), the best in the city. A friendly crowd, often young, congregates here at night. Tapas sell for 1.50€ ($1.80) and up, *raciones* for 6€ ($7.20). Open Monday to Saturday 8am to 11pm.

Jerez is known for its flamenco. The best shows—very untouristy—are at **El Lagá de Tío Parrilla,** Plaza del Mercado (ℭ **95-633-83-34**). Monday to Saturday shows begin at 10:30pm and 12:30am. The cover of 12€ ($14) includes the first drink, and reservations are requested.

6 El Puerto de Santa María

610km (379 miles) S of Madrid, 22km (14 miles) NE of Cádiz, 12km (7½ miles) S of Jerez de la Frontera, 102km (63 miles) S of Seville.

Part of the "Sherry Triangle," this old, dilapidated port is most easily reached from Cádiz (see chapter 9) but it's also within easy reach of Jerez de la Frontera (see above). A historic port, it opens onto the northern shores of the Bay of Cádiz. Nearby are some choice white sandy beaches of the Costa de la Luz. The Terry and Osborne sherry and brandy bodegas dominate the town. Many summer visitors come just to patronize the seafood bars (see "Where to Dine," below).

ESSENTIALS

GETTING THERE If you're already in Cádiz, the easiest way to get here is to take **El Vaporcito** (ℭ **95-687-02-70**), a **ferry** departing from a dock behind Estación Marítima near the Transportes Generalics Comes station at Plaza de la Hispanidad. There are four to six ferries leaving per day, taking 30 to 45 minutes and costing 2.50€ ($3) per ticket. Departures are between 10am and 8:30pm, with a return at 9am and 7:30pm.

There is also direct service by **train** from Seville, or suburban trains from Jerez de la Frontera or Cádiz. For information and schedules, call RENFE at ℭ **90-240-20-20.**

If you have a **car** and are in Jerez, just follow the signs south. There are two arteries going into Puerto de Santa María (the N-IV is faster).

VISITOR INFORMATION The local **tourist office** is at Luna 22 (ℭ **95-654-24-13**), open Monday to Friday 9am to 2pm and 4 to 6pm (hours subject to change).

EXPLORING THE TOWN

Columbus once lived in a house at Cristóbal Colón. Look for a marker. The author, Washington Irving, spent the fall of 1828 here at Calle Palacios 57. These houses can be viewed only from the outside.

Although Jerez is a far more appealing destination for bodega hopping, you can also visit **Terry** at Calle Tonelernos 1 (© **95-685-77-00**). Wine tastings are only conducted Monday to Friday 10am and noon. Admission is 4.50€ ($5.40). Another sherry bodega of interest is **Osborne-Bodega de Mora,** Calle Los Moros 7 (© **95-686-91-00**), open Monday to Friday 10:30am to 12:30pm, charging 5€ ($6) for entrance.

On the site of an old mosque, **Castillo de San Marcos,** Plaza de Alfonso s/n (© **95-685-17-51**), was built in the 13th century. It was ordered constructed by Alfonso X against future Muslim invasions from North Africa. Later it was the address of the duke of Medinaceli who welcomed Columbus here, but refused to finance his journey, thinking it impractical. It was within these walls that Juan de la Cosa drew the first map ever to include the New World. Charging 3€ ($3.60) for admission, hours are Tuesday, Thursday, and Saturday from 11am to 2pm.

The port also has a historic bullring, the neo-mudéjar **Plaza de Toros,** Los Moros, dating from 1880. It was the gift of a local sherry producer, Thomas Osborne, who designed it to seat 12,816 people, the exact population of the town in those days. It is open for viewing April to October Thursday to Tuesday 11am to 1:30pm and 6 to 7:30pm. From November to March it is open Thursday to Tuesday 11am to 1:30pm and 5:30 to 7pm. Closed bullfight days.

WHERE TO STAY

Del Mar   Near the center of town, west of the bullring, this hotel is one of the more affordable in a town known for its deluxe hostelries. Built in 1994 and last renovated in 2003, its midsize bedrooms are like those in a simply but comfortably furnished private home, with an adjoining tiled bathroom with tub and shower. The hotel is agreeable and unpretentious, the staff welcoming and helpful.

Av. Marina de Guerra, 11500 El Puerto de Santa María. © **95-687-57-00.** Fax 95-685-87-16. www.delmar hotel.org. 40 units. 58€–98€ ($70–$118). AE, MC, V. Parking 5€ ($6). **Amenities:** Cafeteria; limited room service; babysitting; laundry service; rooms for those w/limited mobility. *In room:* A/C, TV, minibar.

Duques de Medinacelli 🌟🌟🌟   One of the grandest hotels in all of Andalusia, this converted 18th-century palace is the epitome of taste, style, and luxury. It's elegant and occasionally grand, but the atmosphere is warm and inviting. Last renovated in 2002, it has many trappings of yesterday, including the town's most impressive Andalusian courtyard with columns and a fountain. Bedrooms are large and beautifully furnished with antiques or tasteful reproductions. There are many traces of mudéjar and beautiful gardens. Each room comes with a tiled and rather luxurious private bathroom with tub and shower. The on-site restaurant, Reina Isabel, a favorite of sherry producers, has first-rate meals.

Plaza de los Jazmines 2, 11500 El Puerto de Santa María. © **95-686-07-77.** Fax 95-654-26-87. www.jale. com/dmedinaceli/h_ab.htm. 28 units. 157€–244€ ($188–$293) double; 215€–312€ ($258–$374) junior suite; 272€–374€ ($326–$449) suite. AE, MC, V. Free parking. **Amenities:** Restaurant; bar; outdoor pool; sauna; 24-hr. room service; babysitting; laundry service/dry cleaning; rooms for those w/limited mobility. *In room:* A/C, TV, minibar, hair dryer, safe.

Los Cántaros   If you want to save money, try to stay at this modest but appealing choice in the center of the city near the riverbanks of Guadalete. The section is called Ribera del Marisco and its bars and restaurants make it *the* place to be at night. The building was constructed in 1983 over the site of a women's prison, the old jail giving way to attractively decorated and comfortable rooms. A series of 17th-century urns were uncovered; a few are on display in the hotel lounge. Bedrooms are midsize and come with tiled bathrooms with tub/shower combos. Renovations in 2004 made the hotel more inviting than ever.

Calle Curva 6, 11500 El Puerto de Santa María. ℂ **95-654-02-40.** Fax 95-654-11-21. www.hotelloscantaros. com. 39 units. 62€–103€ ($74–$124) double. AE, DC, MC. Parking 6€ ($7.20). **Amenities:** Cafeteria; bar; limited room service; laundry service; nonsmoking rooms. *In room:* A/C, TV, minibar, hair dryer, safe.

Monasterio de San Miguel ☆☆☆ If this hotel had a more tranquil location (it's in the center of town), it would equal Duques de Medinacelli. Regardless, it's a sumptuous place to stay—or so the Spanish royal family thought when they visited. Originally an 18th-century Capuchin convent and church, the hotel has been meticulously renovated, with much of the original design left intact. Bedrooms are midsize and beautifully and tastefully furnished, with luxuriously tiled bathrooms with tub and shower. They open onto private balconies overlooking a luxe swimming pool. You can wander through the hotel's gardens, stopping for drinks in the Andalusian courtyard with a bubbling fountain.

The on-site restaurant is one of the best in the area, the tables placed in a large, vaulted hall. The chef specializes in local seafood.

Virgen de los Milagros 27, 11500 El Puerto de Santa María. ℂ **95-654-04-40.** Fax 95-654-26-04. www.jale. com/monasterio. 165 units. 137€–167€ ($164–$200) double; 193€–222€ ($232–$266) junior suite; 242€–280€ ($290–$336) suite. AE, MC, V. Parking 12€ ($14). **Amenities:** Restaurant; cafeteria; bar; outdoor pool; 24-hr. room service; babysitting; laundry service/dry cleaning; nonsmoking rooms; rooms for those w/limited mobility. *In room:* A/C, TV, minibar, hair dryer, safe.

WHERE TO DINE

Many residents of Cádiz come over just for the evening to sample the *marisco* bars along Ribera de Marisco (Shellfish Way). The tourist office (see above) will provide you with a list of six different tapas routes, taking in more than three-dozen different bars, each with its own specialties. Along Ribera de Marisco, our favorite is **Romerijo** (ℂ **95-654-12-54**), although there are many nearby almost as good, including **Además Tapía, Casa Paco, Paco Ceballos, El Pijota,** and **Bar Jamón.** No phones, no reservations—just show up at night and start eating.

El Faro de El Puerto ☆ ANDALUSIAN/SEAFOOD Slightly outside of town, this converted villa is the best restaurant in the town. In typically Andalusian surroundings, El Faro uses market-fresh ingredients to showcase local food. The sherry producers of the area always take their best clients here. Our party was recently delighted with the roast suckling pig and tender, garlic-studded baby lamb, another classic. A signature platter is beef roulades with foie gras, mushrooms, and goat cheese. A wide selection of fish based on the catch of the day is featured nightly. We practically wanted to write a love note to the chef after sampling his grilled calamari. Grilled medallions of monkfish are another treat.

Carretera de Fuentebravia Km 0.5. ℂ **95-685-80-03.** Reservations recommended. Main courses 14€–21€ ($17–$25); menú degustación 36€ ($43). AE, DC, MC, V. Year-round daily 12:30–4pm; Sept–July Mon–Sat 7:30pm–midnight; Aug daily 7:30pm–midnight.

Los Portales SEAFOOD/ANDALUSIAN This nautically decorated restaurant is our pick for more formal dining in the Ribera del Marisco area. Since 1978, this back-street eatery has been heavily patronized by *gaditanas* (locals), who swear by its offerings and often take their out-of-town visitors here. With some of the most professional service in the area, the staff is dedicated to turning out market-fresh cuisine that's hearty and full of flavor. Try the garlic-doused lamb chops grilled with potatoes or fresh sea bass in lobster sauce. A tender grilled entrecote is served for the meat eater, or else there is always an offering of baby beef in a tangy mustard sauce. The catch of the day can be grilled or prepared almost any way you desire it. A local specialty is *ortiguillas* or fried sea anemones.

Ribera del Río 13. ② 95-654-21-16. Reservations recommended. Main courses 13€–20€ ($16–$24). AE, DC, MC, V. Daily noon–4:30pm and 7:30pm–12:30am.

7 Sanlúcar del Barrameda

24 km (15 miles) NW of Jerez de la Frontera

This port, though relatively unimportant today, lives on in nautical history. Columbus sailed from here on his historic third voyage to the New World in 1498. In 1519, Magellan set out from Sanlúcar to launch his circumnavigation of the globe.

At the mouth of the Río Guadalquivir, Sanlúcar borders the Parque Nacional Cota de Doñana (p. 292) and is a good base from which to explore this wilderness. There is a wide range of sandy beaches around the port, part of the Costa de la Luz, but many visitors come to visit the sherry bodegas. Along with Jerez de la Frontera and El Puerto de Santa María, Sanlúcar is the third section of the famous "Sherry Triangle."

ESSENTIALS

GETTING THERE If you're arriving by public transport, you can take a bus operated by **Transportes Los Amarillos** (② **95-638-50-60**). From Monday to Friday buses arrive from Jerez every hour, taking 45 minutes, or every 2 hours on weekends, costing 1.45€ ($1.75) for a one-way ticket. There are 6 to 12 buses a day from Seville, taking 2 hours and costing 6.25€ ($7.50) for a one-way ticket. Tickets can be purchased on the bus.

From Jerez or El Puerto de Santa María, signs point motorists northwest to Sanlúcar. Driving time from either town is about 20 minutes.

VISITOR INFORMATION The local **tourist office** is on Calzada del Ejército s/n, lying a block inland from the beach (② **95-636-61-10**). Open Monday to Friday 10am to 2pm and Saturday and Sunday 10am to 2pm and 6 to 8pm. At this office you can pick up information about tours of the park and can also inquire about which sherry bodegas might be open at the time of your visit.

EXPLORING THE TOWN

Sanlúcar is known for its distinctive *manzanilla* wine, the driest of all sherries, which acquires a dry, slightly salty tang from the winds blowing across the sea from North Africa. The town is also known for having some of Spain's best seafood. Many Andalusians come here just to dine.

Start your exploration on the landmark **Plaza del Cabildo,** a delightful square ringed with palm trees, very Moroccan in appearance. After that, consider a river cruise. **Los Cristóbal,** Avenida Bajo de Guía (② **95-696-07-66**), runs 3-hour cruises with an on-board cafe. Prices and timetables are subject to change, so call to check the schedule during your visit.

A 4-hour cruise is available through **Real Fernando** $\mathcal{F}$, Bajo de Guía (© **95-636-38-13**), for 15€ ($18) per passenger. This cruise heads up the Guadalquivir River, and makes various stops in the Doñana National Park. Cruises operate April to October daily from 9am to 8pm and November to March daily from 9am to 7pm.

Among Sanlúcar's many churches, a highlight is the 14th-century **Iglesia de Nuestra Señora de la O,** Plaza de la Paz (© **95-636-05-55**), open a half-hour before and after each Mass conducted Monday to Friday at 8pm and Sunday at 9am, noon, and 8pm. Admission is free. Although much altered over the years, this is Sanlúcar's greatest church. It has an impressive interior with a Gothic and mudéjar portal that depicts lions bearing coats-in-arms.

Also intriguing is **Iglesia de la Trinidad,** dating from the 15th century and lying just off Plaza del Cabildo in the heart of town. It's open Monday to Saturday 10am to 1:30pm. Today the *palacio* is the home of the duchess of Medina Sidonia. You're taken on a guided tour of the mansion and its beautiful gardens and shown through salons filled with antiques and the works of such Spanish masters as Goya and Morales. Since this is a private residence, it may be shut down at any time without notice. Check with the tourist office before coming.

Finally, pay a visit to one of Sanlúcar's famous bodegas where the delicate *manzanilla* is produced. Unlike Jerez, there are few to choose from. The best is also the home of the major producer of manzanilla: **Antonio Barbadillo,** Calle Sevilla 25 (© **95-638-55-00**), open Monday to Saturday for visits at noon and 1pm, costing 3€ ($3.60) for admission.

WHERE TO STAY

Hotel Los Helechos *(Kids* This former family villa has been successfully converted into one of the most desirable hotels in the area. A large building with a central Andalusian patio with fountain, corridors, and very old tiles, it is inviting and homelike, with some of the most affordable prices in town. The midsize bedrooms have been modernized yet they are traditional in decor, with heavy curtains; tasteful, comfortable furnishings; and tiled bathrooms with tub and shower. Accommodations range from singles to doubles, from triples to quads, the latter two categories ideal for families. A special feature is a balcony solarium with panoramic vistas of the ancient quarter of town. The staff will help you arrange excursions to the Doñana National Park.

Plaza Madre de Dios 9, 11540 Sanlúcar de Barrameda. © **95-636-13-49.** Fax 95-636-96-50. www.hotel loshelechos.com. 54 units. 40€–56€ ($48–$67) double; 55€–77€ ($66–$92) triple; 60€–98€ ($72–$118) quad. AE, MC, V. Free parking. **Amenities:** Bar; 24-hr. room service; babysitting; solarium; rooms for those w/limited mobility. *In room:* A/C, TV.

Posada de Palacio $\mathcal{F}$ *(Value* Don't be misled by the name. This is no grand palace but a boardinghouse on two floors converted from a 17th-century private family home. Opened as a hotel in 1986, it was last renovated in 2003. The building opens onto a central Andalusian patio with corridors and the characteristic arches. Under high ceilings, the furniture is a mixture of original antiques and contemporary pieces. Bedrooms are attractively and comfortably furnished. Regional artifacts add to the homey atmosphere. Each accommodation comes with a small tiled bathroom with tub and shower.

Caballeros 1, 11540 Sanlúcar de Barrameda. © **95-636-48-40.** Fax 95-636-50-60. www.posadadepalacio. com. 26 units. 75€–120€ ($90–$144) double; 95€–135€ ($114–$162) suite. AE, DC, MC, V. Free parking. **Amenities:** Breakfast lounge; bar; room service (8am–11pm); laundry service; nonsmoking rooms. *In room:* A/C, TV, hair dryer.

WHERE TO DINE

Bigote ⟨★⟩ SEAFOOD/SPANISH   Right on the beach, this place is known for the best shellfish paella at the port. With its maritime decor and wide windows, it is imbued with a bodega atmosphere. In summer it's packed, so reservations are imperative. Even with a reservation, you may still have to wait for a table. At the fish market, you may have seen crabs with enormous white claws, known locally as *bocas de las islas* (mouths of the islands). They are served here, as are clams with fine shells, which are marinated or cooked with paprika, rice, or noodles. Sea snails and razor clams also appear. Signature dishes are baby shark with seafood sauce, red snapper in vinaigrette, and various fried fish. Fried *acedias* (a type of delectable small sole) and *langostinos* are other specialties.

Bajo de Guía s/n. ⟨C⟩ **95-636-26-96.** Reservations recommended. Main courses 6€–15€ ($7.20–$18). AE, DC, MC, V. Mon–Sat 1:30–4pm and 8:30–11:30pm. Closed Nov.

Los Corrales ⟨★⟩ SEAFOOD/SPANISH   Right on Pileta Beach, this nautically decorated restaurant serves the best seafood from the Bay of Sanlúcar. Their rice dishes are also good, notably paella with pork, chicken, and shellfish, or a slightly different version—maritime-style rice—prepared with fish and shellfish. The grilled king prawns are the best we've enjoyed in the area, served simply with garlic butter and parsley. Artichokes and peas harvested in the nearby fields appear in various dishes. The oven-baked red snapper cooked with shrimp is a signature dish. The fruit trees around Sanlúcar are famous, and in summer, fresh apricots, pears, plums, and peaches turn up in various desserts.

Av. Calzada del Ejército s/n. ⟨C⟩ **95-636-49-06.** Reservations recommended. Main courses 9€–24€ ($11–$29). AE, DC, MC, V. Daily 1:30–5pm and 8–11pm. Closed Nov 2–25.

Venta Antonio ⟨★⟩ SEAFOOD/SPANISH   Outside of town, this family business has been luring seafood lovers since it opened in 1966. Spacious and bright, it is a comfortable restaurant attracting a family business to its location on the bay. The ever-changing menu uses the best fish and shellfish caught that day and on sale at local markets. The fish can be cooked more or less to your specifications— that is, grilled, oven-baked, or fried. The list of seafood is always impressive, including crabs, sea snails, fresh shrimp, sea-bullock, lobster and even *percebes* (goose barnacles). Fish platters come with servings of mashed potatoes, special sauces such as tomato or béchamel, and fresh vegetables.

Carretera Jerez-Sanlúcar Km 5. ⟨C⟩ **95-614-05-35.** Reservations recommended. Main courses 12€–24€ ($14–$29). AE, DC, MC, V. Daily 1:30–4:30pm and 8–11pm.

9

Cádiz & the Costa de la Luz

Although foreign visitors often overlook the southwestern corner of Spain, it is a prime destination for Spanish visitors from other regions of the country.

Beaches of all kinds have put this coastal area on the tourist maps. The province of Cádiz alone has 260km (161 miles) of coast and 138km (85 miles) of beaches, including coves, inlets, sandy stretches, and isolated strips. Neighboring Huelva province, associated with Columbus, has beaches that stretch from its eastern border to its frontier with Portugal in the west.

The two major cities, each capital to the province of the same name, are Cádiz and Huelva. Huelva can be skipped if you're pressed for time, but Cádiz is one of Andalusia's hidden gems. Long known as a seafaring port, it once dominated trade between Spain and the New World.

Much of modern Cádiz can be passed by, but the seaside promenades

and its Old Town can easily take up a day or more of your time. With its sailors' alleyways and high turreted houses, this is a remnant of the great days of the Spanish empire.

Heading east from Cádiz you can visit Europe's southernmost port city, Tarifa, for a day or overnight. Cádiz is also convenient for visiting El Puerto de Santa María, part of the fabled "Sherry Triangle" (see chapter 8).

Even if you don't fall in love with large, sprawling, and industrialized Huelva, you can use it as a base for exploring the province's many riches. In addition to living it up at the region's first-class and deluxe coastal resorts, you can explore Cota de Doñana National Park, sited at the estuary of the River Guadalquivir, and the country's largest wildlife reserve. Visitors often stay 2 days, then wish they'd budgeted more time.

1 Cádiz

122km (76 miles) S of Seville, 625km (388 miles) SW of Madrid, 32km (20 miles) SW of Jerez de la Frontera

At the end of a peninsula, Cádiz separates the Bay of Cádiz from the Atlantic. It was here that Columbus set out on his second and fourth voyages.

Cádiz (pronounced "*cah*-deeth") was founded, according to legend, by Hercules himself some 3,000 years ago. The seafaring Phoenicians settled here around 1100 B.C. and in 501 the conquering Carthaginians landed. They were followed by the Romans in 206 B.C. Cádiz was to see other conquerors, notably the Visigoths and the Muslims. The rule of the Moors came to an end in 1262 when King Alfonso X brought the port under the yoke of Spanish rule.

In 1587, Sir Francis Drake, whom Spaniards still refer to as a *pirata,* sailed into Cádiz and caused much damage in a raid. The attack of the British forces delayed the Armada. In 1596 Cádiz suffered its most devastating attack yet when combined Anglo and Dutch ships arrived at harbor to burn the city to the ground.

Cádiz

ATTRACTIONS ●
Ayuntamiento **19**
Castillo de Santa Catalina **12**
Catedral de Cádiz **16**
El Oratorio de la Santa Cueva **4**
Hospital de Mujeres **9**
Iglesia de Santa Cruz **17**
Museo de las Cortés de Cádiz **8**
Museum de Cádiz **1**
Oratorio de San Felipe Neri **7**
Parque Genovés **10**
Teatro Romano **18**
Torre Tavira Cámara Obscura **6**

ACCOMMODATIONS ■
Hospederia las Cortes de Cádiz **3**
Hotel de Francia y Paris **2**
Parador de Cádiz **11**

DINING ◆
Achuri **20**
Bar Zapata **14**
Comedor & Terrazo Joselito **15**
El Aljibe **21**
El Faro **13**
Restaurant San Antonio **5**

Cádiz bounced back and in the 1700s reached the zenith of its power and prestige—enough so that it attracted Napoleon's greedy eye. French troops invaded and Cádiz became the capital of occupied Spain. In the 19th century, the loss of the American colonies, on which the prosperity of Cádiz depended, plunged the port into a long slumber, from which it only started to recover in the 1970s. Long a bastion of liberal thought and tolerance, Cádiz saw more bloodshed during the Spanish Civil War in the 1930s when its townspeople fought—but lost—in their struggle against Franco's Fascists.

Today, this modern, bustling Atlantic port is a melting pot of Americans, Africans, and Europeans who are docking or passing through. The old quarter teems with local characters, little dives, and seaport alleys. The narrow cobblestone streets, which open onto charming small plazas, evoke an old city in North Africa. Despite its vibrancy and diverse influences, however, Cádiz isn't of major interest for most visitors. What the visitor confronts today is an industrial hub of activity with one of the busiest ports in Spain, dominated by its shipbuilding and naval dockyards. Cádiz is also a big fishing center, and also a major departure point for ships sailing to the Canary Islands, a Spanish possession. It is regrettable that many foreigners have yet to discover the charm of Old Cádiz.

When visitors, mostly Spanish, do flock to Cádiz, it is for the summer beaches and for the famous *Carnaval* in February, one of the most extravagant in Europe. Music fills the air from mandolins, tambourines, guitars, and even whistles. Seemingly everybody in town parades through the streets in costumes. Singing, dancing, and riotous street behavior characterize the event, which lasts all night long, ending when revelers flood the cafes for freshly cooked *churros* (like doughnut sticks), which they dunk into steaming hot cups of chocolate. The Cádiz carnival usually takes place during the second week of February.

ESSENTIALS

GETTING THERE   Twelve daily **trains** arrive from Seville (taking 2 hr.), Jerez de la Frontera (40 min.), and Córdoba (3 hr.). A one-way fare from Seville costs 8.25€ ($9.90), from Córdoba 15€ ($19), and from Jerez 3.05€ ($3.65). The train station is on Avenida del Puerto (© **90-224-02-02**), on the southeast border of the main port.

Six daily nonstop **buses** run from Madrid to Cádiz. Trip time is 7 hours and 45 minutes, costing 22€ ($26) for a one-way ticket. The bus from Madrid is run by **Secorbus** (© **95-625-74-15**) at Avenida José León de Carranza (N-20). However, most bus riders arrive from Seville on a vehicle run by **Transportes Generales Comes,** Plaza de la Hispanidad 1 (© **95-622-78-11**). Arrivals are at the rate of 11 to 14 per day, taking 2 hours and costing 9.30€ ($11) for a one-way ticket. These buses arrive at a terminal on the north side of town, a few blocks west of the main port.

Driving from Seville, the A-4 (also called E-5), a toll road, or N-IV, a toll-free road running beside it, will bring you into Cádiz.

VISITOR INFORMATION   The **tourist office,** Av. Ramón de la Carranza s/n (© **95-625-86-46;** www.cadizturismo.com), is open Monday to Friday 9am to 7pm, Saturday 10am to 1:30pm.

GETTING AROUND   Cádiz is well served by a network of **buses,** which are certainly the cheapest means of getting about. A single ride on any city bus costs .85€ ($1). Most residents save money by buying a **Bonobus Pass** for 5.55€ ($6.65), valid for 10 rides. It's sold at news kiosks and tobacco stands. Bus nos. 1 and 7 travel frequently between New Town and Old Town, and nos. 2 and 7

Playa Victoria

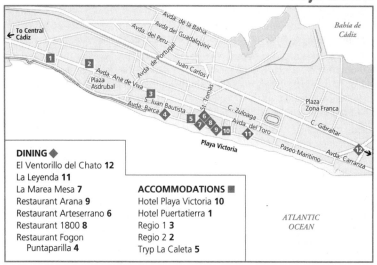

DINING ◆
El Ventorillo del Chato **12**
La Leyenda **11**
La Marea Mesa **7**
Restaurant Arana **9**
Restaurant Arteserrano **6**
Restaurant 1800 **8**
Restaurant Fogon
  Puntaparilla **4**

ACCOMMODATIONS ■
Hotel Playa Victoria **10**
Hotel Puertatierra **1**
Regio 1 **3**
Regio 2 **2**
Tryp La Caleta **5**

make constant runs around the Old Town's seafronting periphery. Most of the inland streets of the Old Town are, however, much too narrow for bus access. For more information about routes, call ℂ **95-628-38-04.**

Motorists who arrive in Cádiz have generally rented a **car** in Seville (see chapter 4), to drive south. Once in Cádiz, you'll have to cope with the parking. Many hotels have parking garages in their basements, charging from approximately 9€ to 14€ ($11–$17) per day. If you're driving a lot in a rented car, the convenience of parking at your hotel is definitely worth it. As for parking within the old city, you'll find underground parking garages scattered judiciously throughout the Old Town, each of them charging around 1€ ($1.20) per hour of parking time. Unless you're a very experienced European driver, we advise you not to venture too agressively into the center of the old city with your car, since roads are unbelievably narrow—stick to the peripheral avenues flanking the seafronts instead. Should you happen to see an available parking spot on the ring road encircling the old city, either deposit coins into the local meter, or into any of the blue-sided computerized boxes scattered throughout the town, then display the ticket that emerges on the dashboard of your car to avoid getting a ticket. The charge is 1€ ($1.20) per hour. Once you're in Cádiz, you can also rent a car. The two best agencies are **ATESA,** Av. Puerto de Sol 1 (ℂ **95-665-80-99**), open Monday to Friday 8am to 9pm, Saturday and Sunday 9am to 2pm and 4 to 9pm, and **Avis,** Av. Libertad 15 (ℂ **95-686-10-21**), open Monday to Friday 9am to 1pm and 4:30 to 7pm, Saturday and Sunday 9:30am to 1pm.

You can walk around the Old Town on foot, which is about the only way to see it. To go farther afield, call a **taxi** at ℂ **95-621-21-21.**

FAST FACTS: Cádiz

Currency Exchange ATMs are scattered throughout the city with a cluster of banks around Plaza San Juan de Dios in the center and along Avenida Ramón de Carranza facing the port. The most central bank with ATMs is

Banco Santander Central Hispano, Calle Columela 13 (© **95-224-24-24**), open Monday to Friday 8:30am to 2pm and Saturday 8:30am to 1pm.

Dentists If you have a dental emergency, ask at your hotel or the local tourist office, which has been known to make emergency phone calls around town for visitors in dental pain. Two local dental clinics are **Urgencia Dental Avenida,** Av. Ana de Viya 32 (© **95-620-00-82**); and the **Clínica Dental,** Calle Brasil 8 (© **95-626-24-69**).

Emergencies To summon the police, dial © **091**. To report a fire or call an ambulance, dial © **085** or 95-627-00-80.

Hospital The biggest and best-accessorized of the local hospitals is **Hospital Universitario Puerto del Mar,** Av. Ana de Viya 21 (© **95-600-21-00**).

Internet Cafe You'll find a battery of computers at **Novap,** Cuesta de las Calesas 45 (© **95-626-44-68**), across from the railway station, in Old Cádiz. It charges 1.20€ ($1.45) per hour for access. You'll also find a local branch of Western Union and international and national phone cards for sale.

Newspapers Local dailies include *Diario de Cádiz,* with a relatively right-wing agenda, selling for .90€ ($1.10) each, and the more centrist Cádiz *Información,* also priced at .90€ ($1.10) per copy. For information on cultural and pop events in Andalusia, the tourist office distributes a free monthly tourist magazine, *¿Qué Hacer?*

Pharmacy Each of the many pharmacies scattered throughout the city prominently displays the name, address, and phone number of whatever pharmacy is scheduled to be open overnight. A particularly central pharmacy to the Old City is **Farmacia María T. Colorado,** Calle Cristóbal Colón y Cobos (© **95-628-26-03**).

Post Office The main branch is at Plaza de las Flores (aka Plaza Topete; © **90-219-71-97** or 95-621-05-12). It's open Monday to Friday 8:30am to 8:30pm, and every Saturday 9:30am to 2pm.

Restrooms A few public toilets are scattered throughout various neighborhoods of the New and Old Towns, most notably a cluster positioned on the Avenida Ramón de Carranza, and one at the Plaza de Mina. Each requires the deposit of a .20€ (25¢) coin before their doors will open. If we're far from either of those points, we usually duck into the nearest bar, often opting to buy something (coffee, mineral water, sherry) on the way out.

EXPLORING CADIZ

A stroll along Cádiz's **seaside promenades** 🏃🏃 is reason enough to visit. The port city's *paseo* runs around Old Town and along the sometimes-turbulent Atlantic Ocean. There is no better way to get an understanding of the city and its relationship to the sea than to walk these handsomely landscaped waterfront *paseos* that double as public gardens. The southern and western promenades look out over the ocean; the most scenic is **Parque Genovés 2** 🏃, with exotic trees and plants from all over the world, including a palm garden, just like the type enjoyed in the oases of North Africa across the sea. Chattering monkeys are always on hand. Summer concerts are presented here.

> **Fun Fact Inhabitants from 80 Million Years Ago**
>
> All of the historic buildings within Cádiz's medieval core are crafted from a sedimentary limestone known locally as "oyster rock." Within many of the stones you can see the shells of crustacea that were alive 80 million years ago, and whose petrified carcasses (in the form of this rock) were brought to the surface at the point where the tectonic plates of Europe and Africa collided in Cádiz.

From the Parque del Genovés, if you follow Avenida Duque de Nájera, it will lead you to **Playa de la Caleta,** one of the most popular beaches of Cádiz. At the northern end of this bay stands **Castillo de Santa Catalina** (© 95-622-63-33). It was built in 1598 and for many decades was the port's main citadel. Except for the views there isn't that much to see here, but it's open for guided visits, leaving every half-hour. In summer it's open daily 10:30am to 8pm. In winter it is open only Sunday and Monday 10:30am to 6pm. Admission is free.

Other parks along the promenade include **Alameda Marqués de Comillas** and **Alameda de Apodaca.** The promenade stretches all the way to the New Town, and can be entered at many places, especially Plaza Argüelles or Calle Fermín Salvochea, off Plaza de España. Along this promenade, some of the most beautiful places or squares in the city look across to the far shore of Bahía de Cádiz.

TAKING A GUIDED TOUR

If you've arrived in Cádiz without a car, there's a local company that, for a per-person rate of 10€ ($12), will take you around selected sections of both the new and the old city as part of a bus tour that lasts—if you opt to remain on the same bus and not get off—about an hour. You can begin your tour at any of the points at which the company stops, and then get back on again, catching the next tour by waiting at any of the officially designated stops. The most convenient and easy-to-find starting point lies directly opposite Cádiz's railway station (bus no. 2 or 7), near the cruise-ship facilities of the Old Town, at Plaza de Sevilla.

Tours begin every day of the year at 10am, and continue until at least 7pm, and—if business is good, till as late as 9pm every day. Note that the company's cream-and-green-painted double-decker buses, like most motorized vehicular traffic in Cádiz, stick to a predefined itinerary that encircles the city's perimeter, but they don't venture into the claustrophobically narrow inner neighborhoods of the Old Town. Included, however, in the price of the bus tour is a brief walking tour of some of the inner sections of the Old Town, which, with guided Spanish and, to a lesser extent, English-language commentary, lasts about 40 minutes. Beginning and ending at the Plaza San Juan de Dios, the walking tour includes a visit to the city's baroque cathedral. For more information, contact **City Tour (Tour por Cádiz;** © 95-626-01-72). Tours leave every hour on the hour.

Catedral de Cádiz   This gold-domed architectural baroque peacock by architect Vicente Acero has a neoclassical interior dominated by an outstanding apse. Construction began in 1720 but the cathedral wasn't completed until 1838. The tomb of Cádiz-born composer Manuel de Falla (1876–1946) lies in a splendid crypt. Haydn composed *Seven Last Words* for this cathedral, which was the last great cathedral erected in Spain financed by riches from the New World. It is still laden with a treasure trove that includes the Custodia del Millón, a monstrance set with a million precious stones. On-site is a museum filled with art and more treasures. Much of the gold, silver, and precious jewels on show here came from the New World. Note Enrique de Arfe's processional cross, which is carried through the streets in the annual Corpus Christi parades.

Next door is the church, **Iglesia de Santa Cruz,** Plaza Fray Félix (© **95-628-77-04**), which was the original cathedral, built in the 1200s. The invading British destroyed this *catedral vieja* in 1592 but it has been rebuilt. The cathedral is open Tuesday to Thursday and Saturday 10am to 1pm and 5:30 to 8:30pm, Friday 9am to 1:30pm and 5:30 to 8pm, and Sunday 10:30am to 1pm and 6:15 to 7:30pm. Admission is free.

In back of the cathedral, whose technical name is La Catedral de San Salvador, are found the unimpressive ruins of what was once a mammoth **Teatro Romano** (© **95-621-22-81**) entered at Campo del Sur. It is open Sunday and Monday from 10am to 4pm; admission is free.

Plaza Catedral. © **95-628-61-54**. Admission 4€ ($4.80). Tues–Fri 10am–1:30pm and 4:30–7pm; Sat 10am–1pm.

El Oratorio de la Santa Cueva ✺ *(Finds)*   Often neglected by visitors, this neoclassical oratory was constructed in 1780 and is attached to a church, Iglesia del Rosario. At the complex there is a Capilla Baja (lower chapel) and a rather lavish, oval Capilla Alta (upper chapel). The upper chamber is the most interesting. Here, three of the chapel's eight arches frame **Goya's paintings** ✺ *The Guest at the Wedding, The Last Supper,* and *The Miracle of the Loaves and the Fishes.* Although this art is reason enough to visit, if you also want to see the subterranean chapel, take the steps that lead downstairs. Here you'll find a *Crucifixion* sculpture, an 18th-century work believed to have inspired Joseph Haydn to write the score of *Seven Last Words* for the Catedral de Cádiz (see above).

Calle Rosario 10. © **95-622-22-62**. Admission 2€ ($2.40). Tues–Fri 10am–1pm and 4:30–7:30pm (summer 5–8pm); Sat–Sun 10am–1pm. Bus: L2.

Hospital de Mujeres   This is one of the most notable baroque buildings in the city. This women's hospital has a patio courtyard dating from 1740 and a chapel with El Greco's painting *Ecstasy of St. Francis.*

Hospital de Mujeres 26. © **95-622-36-47**. Admission .80€ (95¢). Mon–Sat 10am–1:30pm. Bus: L2 or L7.

Museo de Cádiz ✺   This museum is housed in two different buildings, one a former Franciscan convent, the other a contemporary structure. It has three sections, two devoted to archaeology and fine arts, plus an ethnological collection. Among the ancient relics, the most intriguing collection is a series of two 5th-century B.C. Phoenician **sarcophagi** ✺ carved into human likenesses. Depicting both a man and a woman, these tombs were copied by Greek artists

---

⟨Finds The Great Composer's Not at Home

The former home of **Manuel de Falla,** at Calle Ancha 19, lies in Old Town. It boasts a plaque identifying it as the home of the composer, and a pair of the most elaborate door knockers in Cádiz, plus a tiled entranceway laid out in mudéjar patterns. There's nothing else to see, since the rest of the building has locked up tight since its subdivision into private condominiums. Bus: 2 or 7.

Fun Fact Will the Real Havana Please Stand Up?

Cádiz's seafront Malecón closely resembles parts of Havana, Cuba, and is often used by filmmakers as a stand-in for that city. During the filming in 2002 of the James Bond movie *Die Another Day,* with Halle Berry and Pierce Brosnan, the crews used the Malecón for the crowd scenes. According to a local newspaper, "Cádiz's unemployment problem was solved for 15 days, during which everybody played extras in the film."

---

after Egyptian models. There is also an intriguing collection of rare Phoenician jewelry and (mostly) headless Roman statues. The Fine Arts Department is rich in 17th-century Spanish painting, and is known especially for its works by **Zurbarán.** Dating from the peak of his mastery between 1630 and 1640, these 21 magnificent **paintings** 🖈🖈 of angels, saints, and monks were brought here from a Carthusian monastery in Jerez de la Frontera and are today the pride of Cádiz. Zurbarán was at his best when painting his *Quartet of Evangelists.* Murillo and Ribera are among the other Spanish old masters represented. In the ethnological section, the folklore of the province lives again in the Tía Norica puppet theater, with its props and characters that have delighted young and old for years.

Plaza de Mina s/n. ✆ **95-621-22-81.** Admission 1.50€ ($1.80). Tues 2:30–8pm; Wed–Sat 9am–8pm; Sun 9:30am–2:30pm. Bus: L2.

Museo de Las Cortés de Cádiz   This is the city's history museum, its chief exhibit being a big, detailed model of Cádiz as it looked in the 1700s at the height of its glory. It was made in mahogany and marble for King Carlos III, and is so fascinating it makes the museum worth a visit even if you don't look at the other exhibitions. The museum also has exhibits relating to the declaration of the Spanish constitution in 1812, including the original documents and a mural of the declaration.

Calle Santa Inés 9. ✆ **95-622-17-88.** Free admission. June–Sept Tues–Fri 9am–1pm and 5–7pm, Sat–Sun 9am–1pm; Oct–May Tues–Sun 9am–1pm and 4–7pm. Bus: L1 or L7.

THE OLD TOWN 🖈🖈🖈

Even if you have to skip all the monuments, take a stroll through the Old Town. Start at **Plaza San Juan de Dios,** one of the busiest squares, lying directly south of the water-bordering Avenida del Puerto and the wide "green lung" of Paseo de Canalejas. This is an ideal place to sit at a sidewalk cafe and people-watch. You'll also be in the shadow of the neoclassical Isabelino **Ayuntamiento (Town Hall),** Plaza San Juan de Dios s/n (✆ **95-624-10-00**), which is open on Saturday only from 11am to 3pm; admission is free. Built in two sections, one in 1799 and the other in 1861, the town hall is dramatically illuminated at night. Inside there's not much to see except an impressive chapter house.

If you follow Rosario Mendizabal west from Plaza de San Juan de Dios you arrive at another bustling landmark square, **Plaza de San Francisco.** Enveloped by white and yellow town houses, the square is studded with orange trees and adorned with beautiful street lamps. It is one of the best places for an evening *paseo* (promenade).

To the immediate west of Plaza de San Francisco is Cádiz's third landmark square, **Plaza de Mina** 🖈, site of the Museo de Cádiz (see above). This is a big, leafy plaza studded with palm trees. There are plenty of benches about if you'd like to anchor here and watch the world go by. On the western side of the plaza, you can gaze on the stunning, heavily ornamented facade of the Colegio de Arquitectos (College of Architects).

Oratorio de San Felipe Neri   if you head up Calle San José from Plaza de la Mina, you come to one of the city's finest baroque churches where the country's first liberal constitution was declared in 1812. The Cortés (Parliament) met here to reform the government, which at the time was under the control of Joseph Bonaparte, stooge of his brother Napoleon. Inside the oval-shaped interior, the main work of art, an *Immaculate Conception* by Murillo, is displayed over the main altar. The church is crowned by a vast cupola.

Calle Santa Inés 38. Admission 1.20€ ($1.45). Daily 8:30–10am and 7:30–9:45pm. Closed July. Bus: L2 or L7.

Torre Tavira–Cámara Obscura   During the 18th- and early-19th-century heyday of Cádiz's monopoly of trade with the New World, wealthy merchants throughout Cádiz competed for the first views of their ships returning home. To facilitate this, many of the city's merchants added towers as observation platforms to their homes and businesses, sometimes stationing eagle-eyed employees who constantly scanned the surrounding seas for returning ships as well as for French or English invaders.

One of the tallest of these, Torre Tavira, has installed an industrial-style metal staircase that allows visitors, after a lung-wrenching journey, to reach the top of one of the original towers. You'll pay an admission fee at the base. Once on top, you'll be treated to an explanation in English of the Cámara Obscura, formed of a pipe, a magnifying lens, and a concave-shaped drum, about 1.5 to 1.8m (5–6 ft.) in diameter, that's covered in nonreflective white canvas. By manipulating the direction of the lens, the operator can give the audience a surprisingly clear view over the top of the city.

And then there's that horrific climb back down the steel staircase to the street.

After visiting Torre Tavira, head southeast for a couple of blocks to visit **Plaza de Topete** ✦ where caged birds sing and the flower stalls of the **Mercado Central (Central Market)** bloom flamboyantly. Locals call the square Plaza de las Flores (Plaza of the Flowers).

Marqués del Real Tesoro 10. ✆ **95-621-29-10**. Admission 3.50€ ($4.20) adults, 2.80€ ($3.35) students and children. June 15–Sept 15 daily 10am–8pm; off season daily 10am–6pm. Bus: L2 or L7.

(*Finds*   **Private Treasures, Hidden Corners**

Cádiz is loaded with hidden treasures, many of which appear unexpectedly as you walk through the Old Town. One such place is the lobby of a strictly private, members-only club, **Casino Gaditano,** which was established in 1844 in a pink-fronted building antique building set within a corner of the Plaza San Antonio. If the front door is open, and if you ask permission of the concierge, you can wander into the building's exquisitely crafted mudéjar-revival lobby, where a splashing octagon-shaped fountain, soaring columns, and a bar reserved for members only re-create an upscale venue from the mid–19th century. Admission is free, but you won't be encouraged to linger after your brief visit. In theory, the club is open daily from 9am to 6pm, but if there's a reception or function scheduled at the time of your arrival, it won't be very easy to get in. To find it, look for a sign reading **Fundación Centro de Estudios Constitucionales 1812,** in the Plaza San Antonio s/n. Bus: 2 or 7.

BEACHES

Most beachgoers, unless they come from Cádiz's Old Town, usually visit the wide-open and sunny sands of the **Playa Victoria** ✪, an intensely developed but still very appealing beach that's a household name for beach lovers throughout the region. In our opinion, this is one of the best beaches in Spain, with very wide and champagne-colored sands. This beachfront is constantly made wider by a government-sponsored campaign to keep pumping tons of sand here from points offshore. Arc lights illuminate the beach like a stage every night until around midnight. Dozens of different tapas bars, restaurants, and nightlife options are found adjacent to the edge of the beach. It's richly developed and commercial but not junky. On Playa Victoria's outer fringes there is an isolated and savage section where the waves pound more heavily and the sense of isolated nature increases. This savage beachfront is especially strong on the causeway linking modern Cádiz to its outlying suburbs and the rest of Spain.

Paseo Marítimo is the main drag along Playa Victoria and in summer has the most active *chiringuitos* (beach bars) in the province.

But for residents of the La Viña neighborhood in Old Cádiz, there's only one beach that matters: **Playa de la Caleta.** It's relatively narrow and is hemmed in by rocky shoals at low tide. There are no changing booths or public toilets. Known as a "natural beach," it's immediately adjacent to structures and fortifications whose foundations in some cases are more than 3,000 years old. Just behind the seawall, you'll see the two biggest trees (both of them ficus) in Cádiz province. Set on the lawn of a stone-fronted building that houses the administration for a local hospital, they're each about a century old, and are reputed to have been planted in honor of missionaries who left Cádiz for good works in the New World. Set near the extreme western edge of the Old Town, Playa de la Caleta is sometimes known as "Baño de la Viña" after the neighborhood (Barrio de la Viña) that abuts it. That same neighborhood—a crowded, churning, overcrowded cauldron of local color—is credited with originating the version of Carnival that's now fervently celebrated in Cádiz and in some of Spain's former colonies, notably Cuba. Access to this "City Beach" is free and possible at all hours of the day and night without restriction and without supervision.

SHOPPING

Belle Epoque, Antonio López 2 (✆ **95-622-68-10**), is the best place to go in town to purchase such Andalusian artisans' crafts as ceramics and locally made wicker, even antiques. The location is conveniently near the Museo de Cádiz and the tourist office. Hours are Monday to Friday 10:30am to 1:30pm and 5 to 9pm, Saturday 5 to 9pm.

Set within a tucked-away corner of Plaza Candelaría, within a storefront where food has been sold since the 1750s, **Hecho in Cádiz,** Plaza Candelaria 7 (✆ **95-628-31-97**), specializes in food products that are grown, processed, or distilled by small-scale purveyors in the region around Cádiz. You'll find caches of honey, wines (especially sherries, some fine vintages selling for only around 7€/$8.40 per bottle), cheeses, olive oils, and processed meats, especially sausages *(chorizos).* Open Monday to Saturday 10am to 2pm and Monday to Friday 6pm to 9:30pm.

WHERE TO STAY

Cádiz has a number of inexpensive accommodations, some of which are quite poor. However, for a moderate price you can afford some of the finest lodgings in the city. During the February carnival, rooms are booked months in advance, so reserve early. Be aware that at that time hoteliers charge whatever the market will bear.

EXPENSIVE

Hotel Playa Victoria ☆☆☆   This is the best, most dramatic, and most comfortable hotel in Cádiz, rivaled only by the government-run parador, which does not have so spectacular a beach. Playa Victoria's hypermodern design makes many of its more conventional and conservative-looking competitors look a bit old-fashioned and dowdy, and its location directly on the sands of one of the best beaches in Andalusia guarantees a high room occupancy. Bedrooms are the most comfortable and most appealing of any hotel in Cádiz. Each contains an intriguing mix of polished beige stone and very dark tropical hardwood imported from one of Spain's former colonies in the New World, richly tiled or stone-sheathed bathrooms with tub and shower, comfortable furnishings that include a writing table, and best of all, a wide, serpentine-shaped balcony, all but a few of which overlook the spectacular beachfront and the sea. The lobby is a postmodern study in dramatic lighting, multilevel tiers, and stone-sided minimalism, imaginatively laid out around a cozy, big-windowed bar. The in-house restaurant, **Isla de León,** offers a breakfast buffet that's absolutely spectacular.

Glorieta Ingeniero La Cierva 4, 11010 Cádiz. ☎ **95-620-51-00.** Fax 95-626-33-00. www.palafoshoteles.com. 188 units. 115€–155€ ($138–$186) double. AE, DC, MC, V. Parking 12€ ($14) per day. Bus: 1 or 7. **Amenities:** Restaurant; bar; outdoor swimming pool; car-rental desk; room service (7am–11:30pm); laundry service/dry cleaning; nonsmoking rooms; rooms for those w/limited mobility. *In room:* A/C, TV, dataport, minibar, safe.

MODERATE

Hospedería Las Cortes de Cádiz ☆ *Finds*   One of Cádiz's newest hotels opened in 2003 within a patrician merchant's house originally built in 1859 on profits generated from trade with Spanish colonies in the New World. The hotel's centerpiece is a graceful three-story courtyard lined with stone columns and capped with a skylight. Each of the bedrooms evokes late-19th-century Cádiz, with a variety of mostly monochromatic color schemes that includes a courageous use of vibrant pinks, blues, and buttercup yellow. Each of the other rooms is named for a historical event or person significant to the history of Cádiz. A favorite of ours is La Caleta, with a mirador-style glassed-in balcony overlooking the busy pedestrian traffic on the street below. All the units contain neatly tiled bathrooms with tub/shower combos. This was the Old Town's first hotel to combine a historic core with modern-day conveniences.

Calle San Francisco 9, 11004 Cádiz. ☎ **95-622-04-89.** www.hotellascortes.com. 36 units. 96€–120€ ($115–$144) double. Rates include breakfast. AE, MC, V. Parking 12€ ($14) per day. Bus: 2 or 7. **Amenities:** Restaurant; bar; exercise room; minispa; sauna; limited room service; rooftop sun terrace. *In room:* A/C, TV, dataport, minibar.

Hotel Puertatierra ☆ *Kids*   Opened in 1993, this city-center hotel is Tryp La Caleta's chief competition, the latter having a slight edge. Close to the financial and shopping section of town, it was last renovated in 2003. Midsize bedrooms are furnished with modern pieces, color-coordinated fabrics, and often painted provincial wooden furniture. Each unit comes with a well-equipped tiled bathroom with a tub/shower combo. This neoclassical hotel stands less than 100m (328 ft.) from Santa María del Mar beach. This hotel has more varied accommodations than almost any other in town: double or double with lounge, triple, king size, and family units. Both regional and national dishes are served in the on-site restaurant or the more affordable cafeteria.

Av. de Andalucía 34, 11006 Cádiz. © **95-627-21-11.** Fax 95-625-03-11. www.hotelesmonte.com. 98 units. 120€–145€ ($144–$174) double. DC, MC, V. Parking 9€ ($11). Bus: 1, 2, or 7. **Amenities:** Restaurant; cafeteria/bar; 24-hr. room service; babysitting; laundry service/dry cleaning; nonsmoking rooms; rooms for those w/limited mobility. *In room:* A/C, TV, dataport, minibar, hair dryer, safe.

Parador de Cádiz ✪✪   Actually a modern resort hotel, this national parador is on one of the loveliest beaches of the Bay of Cádiz at the western edge of the Old Town, and is one of the best places to stay in Cádiz. Don't be fooled by its very modern appearance. It was originally built in 1929 as a private hotel that received good numbers of visits from the VIPs of that era. In the 1940s, it merged with Spain's network of government-owned, bureaucratically managed paradors, and in 1982, it was radically renovated into the boxy-looking but airy *moderno* structure you'll see today. This is the most luxurious setting in Cádiz's Old Town. Public rooms are accented with acres of white and russet-colored marble, there's a marble patio, a salon decked in rattan and cane, and spacious rooms that feature balconies with tables and chairs for relaxed ocean viewing. More than half of the rooms were renovated in 1995. All have bathrooms with tub/shower combos. This parador attracts large numbers of foreign tourists, and—in our opinion— has a sense of bureaucratic and somewhat banal conservatism.

Duque de Nájera 9, 11002 Cádiz. © **95-622-69-05.** Fax 95-621-45-82. www.parador.es. 99€–115€ ($119–$138) double; 225€–244€ ($270–$293) suite. Rates include breakfast. AE, DC, MC, V. Parking 7€ ($8.40) for garage. Bus: 2 or 7. **Amenities:** Restaurant; bar; outdoor pool; health club; sauna; limited room service; babysitting; laundry service/dry cleaning; nonsmoking rooms; rooms for those w/limited mobility. *In room:* A/C, TV, dataport, minibar, hair dryer, safe.

Tryp La Caleta ✪ *(Kids)*   Set directly across the sea-fronting boulevard from one of the best and most crowded beaches in Andalusia, this hotel (ca. 1993) competes directly with the also-recommended Playa Victoria, which lies less than 2 blocks away. A large, nine-story hotel with a highly desirable four-star rating from the local authorities, it lacks the dramatic and innovative design of Playa Victoria. Nonetheless, it's extremely comfortable (albeit conservative and just a bit staid), well equipped and maintained, and centrally located in the heart of the bar, beach, and nightlife action of new Cádiz. Expect scads of families with children in summer, an ongoing round of conventioneers traipsing in and out, and a winning collection, facing the beach, of bars and cafes that cater to guests and non-guests alike.

Rooms tend to be outfitted in color schemes of pink and cream, many with windows (but alas, no balconies) facing the sea. Each room comes with a tiled bathroom with a tub/shower combo. There's no swimming pool here, something we find surprising for a hotel of this size and rating, but the beach is a few steps away. The dining facilities feature children's menus.

Av. Amilcar Barca 47, 11009 Cádiz. © **95-627-94-11.** Fax 95-625-93-22. www.solmelia.com. 143 units. 79€–150€ ($95–$180) double; 160€ ($192) suite. AE, DC, MC, V. Parking 12€ ($14) per day. Bus: 1 or 7. **Amenities:** Restaurant; bar; cafeteria; business services; car-rental desk; limited room service; babysitting; laundry service/dry cleaning service; rooms for those w/limited mobility. *In room:* A/C, TV, minibar, hair dryer, safe.

INEXPENSIVE

Hotel de Francia y París   If you want to be smack in the heart of Cádiz, safe and relatively comfortable, this is an unpretentious, viable choice. Originally built in 1902, and later garnished with hints of both Art Deco and 1950s-era overlays, this five-story white-fronted structure is the most interesting of the very limited number of midsize, cost-conscious hotels in Cádiz's Old Town. There's just a whiff of Franco-era Spain about this place, and a guest list that reads like a who's who of Spanish culture. (Writers and poets Ortega y Gasset and José María Peman both stayed here, along with scads of lesser lights throughout the post–World War II era.) Bedrooms are simple but clean, and filled with somewhat dowdy angular wooden furniture that reeks of the early 1970s. Each bedroom comes with a midsize private bathroom in tile and equipped with tub and shower. Many of the rooms have small balconies opening onto the square.

Plaza de San Francisco 2, 11004 Cádiz. ℂ **95-621-23-19.** 57 units. 66€–73€ ($79–$88) double. AE, DC, MC, V. Bus: 2 or 7. **Amenities:** Restaurant; bar. *In room:* A/C, TV.

Regio 1   Built in 1978, this aging hotel is about a block inland from the harbor and the Paseo Marítimo and just 50m (164 ft.) from Playa Victoria. The small rooms are simple but airy and comfortable and reasonably priced. Each unit comes with a small bathroom with a tub/shower combo. Breakfast is the only meal served. The overflow from this hotel is sometimes directed to the hotel's twin, the superior Regio 2 (see below).

Av. Ana de Viya 11, 11009 Cádiz. ℂ **95-627-93-31.** Fax 95-627-91-13. www.hotelregiocadiz.net. 43 units. 70€–90€ ($84–$108) double; 90€–115€ ($108–$138) triple. Rates include breakfast. AE, DC, MC, V. Parking in garage 6€ ($7.20). Bus: L7. **Amenities:** Breakfast room; bar; limited room service; babysitting; laundry service/dry cleaning. *In room:* A/C, TV, hair dryer, safe.

Regio 2   Business was successful enough to justify the construction of this Regio 1 sibling (see above). Run by the same management and sharing some of their staff and luxuries in common, it was built in 1981 about 183m (600 ft.) from its twin. It offers bathrooms with tub/shower combos in each of its simple but pleasant rooms, which are more comfortable and in better shape than those of Regio 1. Both hotels are a very short walk from the ocean.

Av. de Andalucía 79, 11008 Cádiz. ℂ **95-625-30-08.** Fax 95-625-30-09. www.hotelregio2.com. 40 units. 66€–77€ ($79–$92) double. MC, V. Parking 6€ ($7.20). Bus: L7. **Amenities:** Bar; lounge; limited room service; laundry service/dry cleaning; nonsmoking rooms. *In room:* A/C, TV.

WHERE TO DINE
EXPENSIVE

El Ventorillo del Chato *Finds* ANDALUSIAN   El Chato ("pug nose") is the nickname of the original founder of this inn launched in 1780 on the isthmus linking the port city to the mainland. Culturally evocative, it is loaded with history. While technically under house arrest, the Spanish king, Fernando VII, came here for food, drink, and sex with the local prostitutes. It is a low-slung, whitewashed, and boxy-looking building that's perched incongruously beside the roaring highway (CA-33) stretching from New Cádiz toward the suburb of San Fernando. The back is only a few steps from the low dunes and scrub grasses of an isolated extreme end of the Playa Victoria. Inside you'll find a thick-walled shelter of enormous charm, with a wood-burning stove, flowers, and a collection of 19th-century antiques. There are two floors, including the basement, where flamenco shows are sometimes performed on the original *tablao* (special flamenco dance floor). The food is excellent. Try the *arroz del señorito* (a paella of shellfish that has been taken from the shells and cleaned before cooking), *arroz negro con chocos* (squid with rice colored by its own ink), or *dorada en berenjena confitada al vino tinto* (gilthead sea bream with eggplant cooked with red-wine sauce). Desserts are tempting, especially ice cream with three types of chocolate or homemade cake with orange sauce.

Carretera de Cádiz a San Fernando Km 2. ℂ **95-625-00-25.** Reservations recommended. Main courses 11€–22€ ($13–$26); tasting menu 33€–70€ ($40–$84) (not offered Sept–Oct). AE, DC, MC, V. Mon–Sat 1–4pm and 9pm–midnight.

MODERATE

Achuri ⭐ BASQUE/ANDALUSIAN   Achuri, a block behind the Palace of Congress in the historic district, is one of the best-loved restaurants in this old port city. It's been in the same family for half a century, earning a fine reputation. The interior is in a typical Mediterranean port style, white stucco walls adorned with paintings interspersed with windows letting in plenty of sunshine. The menu includes fresh anchovies in virgin olive oil with a green leaf salad, *merluza al achuri* (hake casserole with green asparagus sauce), and *pardo al brandy* (red snapper in brandy sauce). Another excellent dish is *bacalao en rosa verde* (salt cod in tomato-and-vegetable sauce). Desserts include lemon mousse or *tocinillo de cielo* (a hearty regional pudding).

Calle Plocia 15. ✆ **95-625-36-13.** Reservations recommended. Main courses 10€–16€ ($12–$19). AE, MC, V. Sun–Wed 10:30am–4:30pm; Thurs–Sat 10am–4:30pm and 8pm–midnight. Closed Dec 24–Jan 7. Bus: L2.

El Aljibe ⭐ ANDALUSIAN   A local favorite, this place simultaneously manages to be rustic in decor yet urban in its hipness. Pablo Grosso is beloved by local foodies, some of whom frequent the place at least once a week. Near the train station, this restaurant has interior balconies, wooden ornaments, and antique furnishings, a cozy ambience for its first-class cuisine. The restaurant itself was built at the dawn of the 19th century, but restored many times since. The food gets better every time we visit. Highly recommended are the foie gras of duckling with pepper sauce, scallops au gratin with prawns, and the lamb ribs with honey sauce. A signature dish is the duck casserole with wine sauce. Desserts are delicious and made fresh daily.

Calle Plocia 25. ✆ **95-626-66-56.** Reservations recommended. Main courses 9€–15€ ($11–$18). DC, MC, V. Daily 1–5pm and 8pm–midnight. Bus: 1.

El Faro ⭐⭐ SEAFOOD/ANDALUSIAN   Since being founded in 1964, this has been one of Old Town's best and most respected restaurants, featuring a busy tapas bar near the mudéjar entrance. It is decorated with beautiful tilework and marble, making for a genuinely fine, fabulous, and formal restaurant. It enjoys links to the political and media-related communities of Cádiz. A collection of photos on the walls is a virtual who's who of Spanish entertainment, politics, and bullfighting. Tables are elaborately decorated and set with crisp napery, lots of cutlery, crystal, and flowers. The waitstaff is the best in Cádiz. Specialties include fresh fish and shellfish based on the catch of the day. We prefer ours baked in a salt crust that seals in the aroma and juices. Begin perhaps with the seafood soup and follow with, say, the roulades of sole with fresh spinach, hake with green sauce, or an especially delectable monkfish with strips of Serrano ham. For dessert, try the homemade ice cream drenched with a sweet red Andalusian wine, Pedro Ximénez.

Calle San Félix 15. ✆ **95-621-10-68.** Reservations recommended. Main courses 12€–16€ ($14–$19); fixed-price menu 26€ ($31). AE, DC, MC, V. Daily 1–4:30pm and 8:30pm–midnight. Bus: 2 or 7.

La Leyenda ⭐ *Finds* CONTINENTAL   Permeated with a sense of 1960s chic, this *moderno* restaurant is judged by many Spanish-language restaurant critics as an upscale, *haute-bourgeois* dining enclave. It's more fussily gastronomic, with more meticulous and formal service rituals, than what you'll find in many of the nearby taverns. We very much like the bar that prefaces the restaurant. To fully appreciate La Leyenda, it's best to reserve a table and to show up between 8:30 and 10pm to avoid the service-related languor that descends upon the place just before closing. The cuisine is innovative, meticulously prepared, and based on

---

Finds **Cádiz's Most Famous Ice-Cream Parlor**

On a hot August day the best place to be in Cádiz is ordering a cone at **Heladería-Café Salón Italiano,** Calle San José 11-13 (⑦ **95-622-18-97**). This ice-cream emporium serves velvety smooth concoctions, more than 30 flavors in all. Two specialties are made with Sevillana oranges or prickly pears grown in Cádiz province. This place has been a local favorite since the 1940s. The setting is large, sun-flooded, and a bit antiseptic, with a marble bartop where adults tend to order coffee as well as scoops of ice cream. Open daily 9am to 11pm; one scoop costs .75€ ($1).

---

market-fresh ingredients. Menu items include a *zarzuela* of fish and shellfish (available only at lunchtime); breast of chicken with cheese and cream sauce; breast of duckling whose accompanying sauce is made from an Andalusian sweet red dessert wine (Pedro Ximénez); veal with bacon, dates, and Módena (balsamic) vinegar; and a degustación of meats, grilled and served house-style, with a medley of sauces.

Paseo Marítimo 20. ⑦ **95-626-21-85.** Reservations recommended. Main courses 8.50€–13€ ($10–$16). AE, DC, MC, V. Tues–Sat 1–4:30pm and 8–11:30pm; Sun 1–4:15pm. Bus: 1 or 7.

Restaurant Arteserrano CONTINENTAL/TAPAS   This is one of the largest and most substantial of the tapas bars and restaurants that front the sands of New Town's Playa Victoria. It enjoys a reputation for abundance and a fast-moving kitchen that chugs out vast amounts of food, especially after 10pm when the place can get mobbed. A tapas bar near the front entrance is trimmed in russet-colored porphyry marble, with lots of exposed brick and wood paneling. Sidewalk tables are placed in front. One dining area is perched on a balcony overlooking the crowded bar. Menu items include long lists of both meat and fish. One of the signature dishes is baked baby lamb; veal cutlets and grilled *langostinos* are other specialties. From a deli-style display case in front, you can take away selections of cheese, sausage, cured meats, and smoked fish that are served within. If you think Cádiz is a sleepy and laid-back place, duck in here during peak hours (10pm–1am most summer evenings), when it's hard to find a place to even stand.

Paseo Marítimo 2. ⑦ **95-627-72-58.** Reservations recommended for dinner. Main courses 7.50€–15€ ($9–$18). AE, DC, MC, V. Daily 1–6pm and 8pm–1:30am. Bus: 1 or 7.

Restaurant 1800 ⑦ CONTINENTAL   Whenever someone compiles a list of "important" restaurants in Cádiz, this seafronting establishment is usually on it. Set on the waterfront promenade of Cádiz, very close to the Playa Victoria and the Tryp La Caleta hotel, it occupies a faux Beaux Arts dining room that's prefaced with a dignified and somewhat restrained tapas bar. Salvador Rodríguez and members of his family have run the place since 1986, welcoming stars who have included Anthony Quinn and various winners of Spain's prestigious literary prize, *La Planeta.* The best menu items include *bacalau al pil-pil* (spicy codfish); roast lamb with roast potatoes; a Cádiz-style mixed fish fry; snapper with garlic sauce; and hake with Iberian cured ham and tomato sauce. The shellfish soup *(sopa de mariscos)* here is excellent, as is the veal stroganoff with paprika.

Paseo Marítimo 3. ⑦ **95-626-02-03.** Reservations recommended. Main courses 10€–15€ ($12–$18). DC, MC, V. Tues–Sun 1–4:30pm and 9pm–midnight. Closed 2 weeks in Feb and 2 weeks in Nov. Bus: 1 or 7.

Restaurant San Antonio ⭐ *Finds* GADITANA Set behind a pale pink facade that overlooks Cádiz's biggest plaza, this is a stylish and appealing restaurant that specializes in local recipes, many of whose origins go back at least a century. Nothing about the place evokes the kind of woodsy-looking taverns that proliferate within the Old Town: In fact, you'll get the definite sense that you're in a somewhat ambitious restaurant here, with uniformed waiters, a small zinc-covered bar near the entrance, tables that are just a bit too close together, and cork-covered walls dotted with paintings and photos. A well-intentioned and hardworking staff will recommend dishes that include a *parrillada* (mixed grill) of fish; house-style codfish; octopus prepared any way you like it (we prefer it either stuffed or deep-fried); Cádiz-style fried fish; cauliflower or shellfish soup; rice with shellfish; *arroz a la marinera* (rice with lobster, prawns, and shellfish); braised oxtail in brown sauce; and a dish that was exported to Cuba and popularized almost incessantly, *ropa vieja*—that is, braised skirt steak in brown sauce.

Plaza San Antonio 9. © **95-621-22-39.** Reservations recommended. Main courses 8.50€–15€ ($10–$18). AE, DC, MC, V. Daily 1–4pm and 8:30pm–midnight. Bus: 2 or 7.

INEXPENSIVE

Bar Zapata *Value* TAPAS This is a clean, convivial, and charming tapas bar without sit-down tables of any kind, and a long, bartop where many local residents come for afternoon or evening meals. If you don't mind eating standing up, you can get some very flavorful food here at very reasonable prices. It is immediately adjacent to the Plaza Candelaría, which at dusk every night tends to be mobbed with Andalusian families enjoying the drop in temperature. Fresh ingredients are stored within glass-fronted refrigerated cases on the bar. Peppered veal cutlets served sizzling from a tiny kitchen that's visible to anyone at the bar are as good as anything we've had in Cádiz. Other terrific items include veal cutlets with Roquefort sauce, roast loin of Iberian pork, anchovies in olive oil, and fried or scrambled eggs served with fresh asparagus, filets of pork, or cured Iberian ham.

Plaza de Candelaria s/n. © **95-626-09-91.** Reservations not accepted. Tapas and platters 1.40€–9€ ($1.70–$11); glasses of wine 1.80€–2.30€ ($2.15–$2.75). Mon–Sat noon–4pm and 8pm–midnight. Bus: 2 or 7.

Comedor & Terrazo Joselito *Finds* SEAFOOD This is a neighborhood joint with a difference: It's recognized by some of the leading publications of Spain as a tavern rich with history and local color. Short-term business travelers from as far away as Barcelona drop into its rough-and-tumble interior for cost-conscious fish and shellfish. The restaurant occupies a stone-fronted building with two of its sides open to the narrow streets outside. Most of the interior is devoted to a rectangular bar, where many patrons remain standing as they consume their beer, wine, and fried fish. There's an almost aggressively simple *comedor* (dining room) with sit-down tables in back. In the early 2000s, the place expanded into the Terrazo Joselito, where relatively flimsy plastic armchairs provide sidewalk seating for a hole-in-the-wall kitchen just around the corner from the establishment's original venue. Menu items in both areas are limited mostly to shellfish and grilled fish. Specialties include mixed fish fry, small fried cuttlefish, fried oysters, prawns or filet of hake in puff pastry, fried clams, garlic prawns, many different preparations of cod, and fresh anchovies in vinaigrette. There's an extremely limited selection of meat dishes that include savory meatballs. Don't expect grandeur. The venue is loaded with plastic breadbaskets, paper tablecloths, and a gruff but in most cases, friendly staff.

San Francisco s/n (Comedor) and Paseo Canalejas s/n (Terrazo). ℭ **95-625-55-51**. Reservations not accepted. Main courses 4.50€–7.70€ ($5.40–$9.25). AE, DC, MC, V. Daily 11am–4pm; Mon–Sat 8pm–2am. Bus: 2 or 7.

La Marea Mesa SEAFOOD/TAPAS   Come here for beer, cheap seafood, tapas, lots of bustle and local color, but expect a slightly cynical, overworked staff. La Marea Mesa defines itself as a beer hall *(cervecería)* with a busy kitchen; indeed, the venue is unpretentious and fast-paced, with good, abundant food. The decor is modern, with touches of varnished pine, bright lighting, and lots of bubbling aquariums. It gets busier as the evening progresses (it's jammed after 10:30pm). Although there are scads of outdoor tables under a tent facing the beach, you'll get a closer view of the culinary and social rituals here if you place yourself at the back of the stand-up bar. In summer, the clientele tends to be beer-soaked and sometimes sunburned holidaymakers from other parts of Spain and Europe.

The menu lists at least eight different preparations of rice, including versions with crayfish, with capers and rondelles of octopus, with salsa verde, and with cod; a salad of fried shrimp, braised codfish, and *revueltos* (scrambled eggs) with shellfish and fresh asparagus.

Paseo Marítimo 1. ℭ **95-628-02-47**. Half *raciones* 3.50€–6€ ($4.20–$7.20); *raciones* 3.10€–11€ ($3.70–$13); some shellfish *raciones* 31€ ($37). AE, DC, MC, V. Daily 1–5pm and 8:30pm–1am. Bus: 1 or 7.

A Working-Class Restaurant Row in Old Cádiz

Thanks to its location on a peninsula jutting toward North Africa and the Americas, the geography of old Cádiz is strictly delineated by constraints of space. Visitors are sometimes surprised to discover that even within the narrow confines and limited space of the Old Town, several distinctly defined neighborhoods exist. The one that's closest to the Malecón, a panoramic, sea-fronting promenade, is the La Viña neighborhood, where everyone seems to know everyone and families go back for generations. Visit the dyed-in-the-wool local haunts here at around 8:30pm to experience them at their most convivial. At that time the **Calle Virgen de la Palma** throws off its daytime slumber and revs into action.

The best way to decide where to go is to walk up and down the cobblestone street where at least a dozen workaday, unpretentious restaurants are jammed together. Many of them are proud of a particular tapa or *ración* that they prepare a bit differently from their neighbors. A good choice is **Bar La Palma**, Calle Virgen de la Palma 7 (ℭ **95-622-85-87**), an aggressively unpretentious hole-in-the-wall whose clients either stand up inside at the rough-and-tumble bar, or sit at a table on the street outside. Choose a variety of tapas and *raciones*, perhaps adding a portion of *papas alinades* (vinegar-soaked potato salad) with grilled peppers and a platter of grilled fish as *herreros*, *sardinas*, or *zapatillas*. Platters cost from 3.50€ to 7€ ($4.20–$8.40) each. The specialty of the house is grilled Spanish mackerel, simply but flavorfully prepared, procured from the nearby fish market and caught off the coast of Mauretania.

Restaurant Arana ANDALUSIAN   Unlike the more rustic and woodsy-looking restaurants that surround it on both sides, Arana is positioned directly in front of the beach, midway between Tryp La Caleta and the Hotel Playa Victoria. This is a high-style, post-*movida* restaurant with seafronting tables that sit under a high-tech tent. The rather formal indoor dining venue is accented with polished granite and high-grade plastics. Menu items include broad beans with ham, platters of cured Iberian meats, diced tuna with roasted peppers, braised oxtail, sirloin steak with Roquefort sauce, minted loin of codfish, breast of duck, and a fine version of local anchovies marinated in (what else?) local olive oil. The cookery is precise and reflects the region's high culinary standards.

Paseo Marítimo 1. ✆ 95-620-50-90. Tapas 1.20€–2.25€ ($1.45–$2.70); main courses 8€–18€ ($9.60–$22); set-price menu 14€ ($17). AE, DC, MC, V. Daily 1–5pm and 8pm–1am. Bus: 1 or 7.

Restaurant Fogón Puntaparilla GRILLED/ANDALUSIAN   Set directly on the narrow one-way street that fronts the beach, at the end of the Paseo Marítmo that's closest to Cádiz's Old Town, this is a well-managed, well-staffed grill restaurant. The specialty is meat, and to a much lesser extent, fish. It's charming and cozy, with fair prices and generous portions. It's obvious that a team of hardworking butchers has labored long and hard to load the glass-fronted refrigerated display cases with all kinds of steaks, chops, and cutlets. There's grilled lamb or chicken cutlets; chicken, pork, veal, or beef steaks; a mixed grill that comes with fried potatoes and garlic sauce; and a delicious local roasted veal specialty. If, perchance, you happen to be a vegetarian who has haplessly stumbled into this place by accident, there's a main course platter of grilled vegetables. A small selection of fish includes the ubiquitous local staple: *bacalao* (codfish). Overall, the food is excellent and the staff likable.

Paseo Marítimo-Cortadura. ✆ 95-620-13-32. Main courses 4.80€–21€ ($5.75–$25). AE, DC, MC, V. Daily noon–6:30pm and 8pm–1:30am. Bus: 1 or 7.

CADIZ AFTER DARK

In Cádiz, the city's role as a beach resort deeply affects the way night owls party after dark. In winter, when cold winds blow in from the Atlantic across the Bahía de Cádiz, nightclubbers find shelter in the Old Town, especially in its northernmost quadrant, the neighborhood radiating outward from the **Plaza de San Francisco.** Here, within a labyrinth of impossibly narrow streets, cubbyhole tapas bars get going after around 10pm and roar till 4am. After that, beginning around 4am, locals all head to the same dance club, **El Hoyo,** Calle Manuel Rancés (no phone), a short walk north of the Plaza de San Francisco. There's a somewhat arbitrarily imposed cover charge of 5€ ($6) (which tends to be waived if you're attractive and female, or male and friendly with the doorkeepers, or if you look like a Spanish pop star.) Beer costs 2.25€ ($2.70) per bottle.

For an early tapas adventure, you can head for **Casa Manteca,** corralón de los Carros 66 (✆ **95-621-36-03**), the best known tavern in the Barrio La Viña. Over the years this was the preferred hangout for local bullfighters and flamenco singers and dancers. Its sherry comes from the vineyards of neighboring Sanlúcar de Barrameda. Dig into the fresh anchovies, regional sausages, caviar, and the best-tasting *chacina* (Iberian ham) in town. Most tapas range from 1.50€ to 2.50€ ($1.80–$3). Hours are Tuesday to Sunday noon to 4pm and 8pm to 1am.

In summer (late May to late Sept), nightlife beginning after 10pm and continuing till around 4am or later, moves to the beachfronts, especially the Playa Victoria. Beginning around 2:30am, there's a migration to nightclubs that include **Barabass,** Calle Muñoz Arenillas 4–6 (✆ **95-607-90-26**) very close to

Glorieta Ingeniero La Cierva and the Playa Victoria Hotel. It's known for theme parties that vary with the night of the week. These might revolve around Brazilian (Love in Ipanema) or Dominican (Merengue Madness) music, or Mol Cool house and garage music. At least twice per summer, long-running White Parties (to which all attendees must wear white) are presented. These seem to have originated in New York during the '80s.

Also on the beachfront is another fun address, **Deep Ocean,** Paseo Marítimo 28 (© **628-04-90-46**). No one under 20 is allowed inside. Patrons include the beefiest of male models and a battalion of gorgeous female models. The venue, which contains an outer bar and pub and an inner dance floor with a bar of its own, is designed to emulate the underwater world as viewed through the windows of a submarine. Expect lots of gray-blues, sea greens, steel doors, electrical panels, and portholes. It's open Sunday to Thursday from 4pm till 3am, and Friday and Saturday from 4pm till 4am. There's no cover charge. Beers cost 1.80€ ($2.15) each.

Another beachfront favorite is **Woodstock Bar,** in the Edificio Europlaya, Paseo Marítimo 14 (© **95-626-51-74;** daily 4pm–3am). Big yet intimate, this place oozes permissiveness. Woodsy and paneled, it has big windows overlooking the beach and attracts a good-looking crowd in their 20s and 30s. Beer costs from 1.80€ to 2.50€ ($2.15–$3).

Until a recent management change, **Café Levante,** Calle Rosarío 35 (© **95-622-02-27**), was known as Cádiz's most popular gay bar, a role it advertised with a depiction of a handsome and horny sailor, laid out in painted *azulejos* (tiles) on its facade. Today, the sailor remains in place, but the clientele is fervently and aggressively heterosexual (albeit gay-friendly), a post-*movida* crowd of hard-drinking students and recent divorcées who are alert and well informed about the fast-changing cultural fabric of southern Spain. Expect a cozy 1920s-era decor of wood paneling and zinc, and controversial graphics and artwork. Beer costs 1.20€ ($1.45). Open daily from 5pm to 4am.

If your heart is young and gay, you face a dicey, unpredictable scene. There's lots of gay life in Cádiz, but it's not well organized. Gay taverns open and close with the lifespan of sickly butterflies; unfortunately, they don't publish their phone numbers and hours are unpredictable. Most get going after midnight and remain closed on Sunday, Monday, and sometimes Tuesday night. None of the gay bars serves food. They tend to lie close to the seedy areas of the railway station or the cruise-ship terminals, or even at the Plaza de Sevilla or on one of the narrow streets of the Old Town. The current "hot" addresses (all subject to change by the time of your arrival) include **Bar Poniente,** Calle Rafael de la Viesca s/n; **Bar Averno,** Calle San Antonio Abad s/n; and **Bar La Luna,** Calle Doctor Zuirta s/n.

2 Tarifa & Costa de la Luz ⭐

23km (14 miles) W of Algeciras, 713km (443 miles) S of Madrid, 98km (61 miles) SE of Cádiz

West of Cádiz, near Huelva and the Portuguese frontier, is the rapidly developing **Costa de la Luz (Coast of Light),** which hopes to pick up the overflow from Costa del Sol. The Luz coast stretches from the mouth of the Guadiana River, forming the boundary with Portugal, to Tarifa Point on the Straits of Gibraltar. Dotting the coast are long stretches of sand, pine trees, fishing cottages, and lazy whitewashed villages. The Costa de la Luz has much more of a Spanish flavor than the Costa del Sol, which is overrun by international visitors, especially northern Europeans.

The **Huelva district** forms the northwestern half of the Costa de la Luz. The southern half stretches from **Tarifa** to **Sanlúcar de Barrameda,** the spot from which Magellan embarked in 1519 on his voyage around the globe. Columbus also made this the homeport for his third journey to the New World. (See chapter 8 for more information.) To travel between the northern and southern portions of the Costa de la Luz, you must go inland to Seville, since no roads go across the Cota Doñana and the marshland near the mouth of the Guadalquivir.

With a population of some 15,000 people, Tarifa is the southernmost city in continental Europe. It's so close to the North African coastline, it's practically in Morocco, to which it was once joined in prehistoric times. It lies directly across the Strait of Gibraltar from the Moroccan coastal city of Tangier. This is one of the few places in the world where you can view two different continents and two wide-open seas at once, the Mediterranean and the Atlantic Ocean.

The old Moorish town of Tarifa lies on the coast between Cádiz, in the west, and Algeciras, which for most motorists is the gateway to the Costa del Sol (see chapter 10). Tarifa, the far eastern extension of the Costa de la Luz, makes a good stopover before plunging into the attractions of the Costa del Sol. It is mainly an industrial and shipping center and of little interest to visitors. In the distance you'll see Gibraltar, the straits, and the green hills of Africa—in fact, you can sometimes get a glimpse of houses in Ceuta and Tangier on the Moroccan coastline. Alternatively you can also visit Tarifa from Cádiz along a coastal route, although it's a much longer run. For more details on this drive, see below.

Named for the Moorish military hero Tarik, Tarifa has retained more of its Arab character than any other town in Andalusia. Narrow cobblestone streets lead to charming patios filled with flowers. The main square is the Plaza San Mateo.

Two factors have inhibited the development of Tarifa's beautiful 5km (3-mile) white beach, the **Playa de Lances:** It's still a Spanish military zone, and the wind blows almost half the time. For windsurfers, though, the strong western breezes are unbeatable. Tarifa is filled with shops that rent windsurfing equipment and give advice about the best locales.

ESSENTIALS

GETTING THERE **Transportes Generales Comes,** Calle San Bernardo 1 (© **95-667-57-55**), has good **bus** links from nearby towns and key points in Andalusia. When its office is closed, you can purchase tickets directly from the driver. The most frequented bus route is from Algeciras, 23km (14 miles) to the west. Ten buses per day make the run into Tarifa in just 30 minutes, a one-way fare costing 1.50€ ($1.80). There are also seven buses a day from Cádiz, taking 2½ hours, costing 7€ ($8.40) for a one-way ticket. There's even a bus link from Seville. Three buses a day run here, costing 14€ ($17), the trip taking 3 hours.

FRS Ferries (© **95-668-18-30**) make the run between Tarifa and Tangier. Departures are daily at 11:30am and 7:30pm; the trip takes only 35 minutes. Returns from Morocco are at 8:30am and 4pm (Morocco time). A round-trip passage costs 45€ ($54) for adults and 23€ ($27) for children.

Tarifa is the southernmost point on the E-5 (also known as the N-340). From Cádiz it's a 114km (98-mile) drive southeast, from Algeciras a 23km (14-mile) drive southwest.

VISITOR INFORMATION The **Tarifa Tourist Office** is on Av. de Andalucía s/n (© **95-668-09-93**), open June to September Monday to Friday 10am to 9pm, Saturday and Sunday 10am to 2pm and 6 to 8pm. From October to May hours are Monday to Friday 10am to 2pm and 5 to 7pm, Saturday 10am to 2pm.

FAST FACTS   For currency exchange and ATMs, head for the **Banco Santander Central Hispano,** Calle Batalla del Salado 17 (✆ **90-224-24-24**), open Monday to Friday 8:30am to 2pm and Saturday 8:30am to 1pm. In an **emergency**, dial ✆ **112.** The police station is at Plaza Santa María 3 (✆ **95-668-41-86**). In a **medical emergency,** call **Hospital de Tarifa** at ✆ **95-668-15-15.** The **post office** is at Calle Coronel Moscardó 9 (✆ **95-668-42-37**), lying off Plaza San Mateo. Hours are Monday to Friday 8:30am to 2:30pm and Saturday 9:30am to 1pm. Internet access is available at **Tarifa Diving,** Avenida de la Constitución (no phone), open Tuesday to Saturday 10:30am to 2pm and 5:30 to 9pm, charging 2.50€ ($3) per hour.

EXPLORING TARIFA

In the Old Town, begin with a look at the mudéjar **Puerta de Jerez,** the gateway to Tarifa, which was constructed by the Catholic monarchs after the Reconquista. Spend an hour or so wandering the bustling **Mercado (central marketplace)** on Calle Colón.

The most interesting church in town is **Iglesia de San Mateo** at the end of Calle Sancho IV El Bravo. It's open daily 9am to 1pm and 5:30 to 9pm; admission is free. Behind a decaying baroque facade, the church's interior is late Gothic, with elegant rib vaulting in the nave and more modern stained-glass windows above. Reliefs of Christ and his apostles decorate the vaulting and there is an impressive depiction of the crucified Christ by noted sculptor Pedro de Mena, dating from the 18th century. It can be seen on the right aisle. The church also possesses a tombstone from the 7th century that proves the Christians had settled in Tarifa before the arrival of the conquering Muslims in 711.

Even more interesting is the maze of tiny streets to the immediate south of the church. Their layout has not varied since Muslims ruled the town.

West of the Old Town towers **Castillo de Guzmán,** built in 960 on orders of Abd ar-Rahman III, the caliph of Córdoba. The castle came under siege in 1292 from Catholic troops. The fortress was held by Guzmán El Bueno ("the Good"). When Christian soldiers captured his 9-year-old son and demanded surrender of the garrison, Guzmán tossed them his dagger. He proudly said, "It's better to have honor without a son than a son with dishonor." The Spanish executed the little boy then took the garrison from the Muslims. Until the mid-1990s this was a garrison for Spanish troops. Since then it has been turned into a minor museum, with mementos of the town. Once inside the precincts, stroll along the parapets and take in the panoramic view from the towers. It is open Tuesday to Sunday 10am to 2pm and 4 to 6pm, charging an admission of 1.80€ ($2.15).

Serious bird-watchers come here to visit the spectacular **Mirador del Estrecho** 🐦🐦, a lookout point that's great for watching bird migrations across the Strait of Gibraltar and incidentally offers panoramic views. The lookout point is 7km (4⅓ miles) east on the E-5.

Another attraction is the Roman ruins at **Baelo Claudia,** 10km (6 miles) to the north. These ruins were from a settlement here from the 2nd century B.C. The hamlet grew rich from a relish known as *garum,* a rotting mass of horror made of fish blood, heads, entrails, and soft roe from tuna and mackerel. Most of what you see today is from the 1st century A.D. when Emperor Claudius made the town a self-governing township. Discovered in 1917, the town was excavated, including ruins of its forum, three temples (Jupiter, Juno, and Minerva), and the remains of a basilica. The ruins of a theater have been restored, and the former main street can be traversed. The ruins of public baths can also be seen,

even the fish factory where the highly valued garum was produced. The ruins
(𝒞 **95-668-85-30**) can be visited July to mid-September Tuesday to Saturday
10am to 6pm, Sunday 10am to 2pm. In other months, hours are Tuesday to
Saturday 10am to 5pm, Sunday 10am to 2pm. Admission is free (subject to
change).

BEACHES & WINDSURFING

If you're traveling between Cádiz and Tarifa along the coast and are a beach buff,
you may want to stop several times. Expect grand vistas of the coast of Africa and
a rolling, treeless, and scrub-covered savage landscape. The terrain is determined
by the constant drying winds blowing northward from the Moroccan Sahara.

Tarifa and the villages flanking it form the windsurfing capital of Andalusia.
Especially noteworthy is **Playa Zahara** near the hamlet of **Zahara de los Atunes,**
immediately northwest of Tarifa, reached on E-5. Zahara emerges from the isolated and beautiful landscape like a white-walled, fortified, and very Arabic-
looking village. A hard-drinking, athletic crowd of 20-somethings from northern
Europe, especially Germany and Belgium, congregate here for windsurfing or
eating and drinking at the stands selling fried and grilled fish along the beach.

Another popular spot for windsurfing is **El Porro en Ensenada de Valdeva-
queros,** the bay formed by Punta Paloma to the immediate west of Tarifa.

To the immediate south of Tarifa begins **Playa de los Lances,** whose white
sands stretch 5km (3 miles) along the Atlantic. The drawbacks here are high
winds and a strong undertow.

For windsurfing rentals, visit **Tarifa Spin Out Surfbase** (𝒞 **95-623-63-52**),
lying 9km (5½ miles) west of Tarifa. Rentals cost 24€ ($29) per hour or 48€
($58) per day.

There is also an uninterrupted stretch of fine beach covering most of the
coastline between Tarifa and **Conil** to the northwest. In this isolated landscape,
there are some simple, government-rated one-star hostals where surfers crash for
the night, plus a lot of nondescript cafes in the villages serving wine and fish
platters. **Playa El Palmar,** near Conil, is nice and sandy, but windy and has no
protection from the fierce sun.

WHERE TO STAY

Hostal Alameda   Set in a scenic area on the outskirts of the Old Town, this
hotel occupies an enviable position at the end of the seafront promenade. Close
to the beach, it was turned into a hotel in 1996. For these prices, you get clean
and comfortable, but basic rooms. They're small but tidy, and furnished with
mostly pinewood pieces. Each comes with a small tiled bathroom with shower.
The hospitality is welcoming, and the staff will serve you a continental breakfast. The place has a certain charm and character.

Paseo Alameda 4, 11380 Tarifa. 𝒞 **95-668-11-81.** 11 units. 50€–60€ ($60–$72) double. No credit cards.
Parking 12€ ($14). Closed Nov. **Amenities:** Restaurant. *In room:* Ceiling fan, TV, no phone.

Hurricane Hotel   This hotel 7km (4⅓ miles) west of Tarifa has some drawbacks but basically a lot going for it. It's so popular with the windsurfing set that
rooms are sometimes booked months in advance. It is charming architecturally,
built in the Moorish style with arches, balconies, and ivy climbing the walls. Set
in subtropical gardens, leading down to miles of beaches, the Hurricane Hotel
opens onto views over the Straits of Gibraltar to Morocco and has more amenities than others in the area. Bedrooms are midsize to spacious, each with a first-
rate tiled bathroom with a tub/shower combo. The accommodations in front of

the building are a little too close to the road; the more tranquil rooms are near the pools. The breakfast is rather skimpy.

Carretera de Cádiz Km 77, 11380 Tarifa. © **95-668-49-19.** Fax 95-668-03-29. www.hurricanehotel.com. 33 units. 80€–140€ ($96–$168) double; 140€–260€ ($168–$312) suite. Rates include continental break-fast. AE, DC, MC, V. Parking 12€ ($14). **Amenities:** Restaurant; 2 outdoor pools; health club; laundry service. *In room:* A/C, TV, dataport, minibar, hair dryer, safe.

La Calzada *(Value)* This is one of the great bargains of Tarifa, attracting those who prefer to stay off the main square of town rather than at one of the surfer joints along the beach. A formerly private home, it was converted at the dawn of the millennium into this little inn. Bedrooms are small but well maintained and comfortably but basically furnished. Decor relies for the most part on col-orful Andalusian tiles. Each room contains a very small tiled bathroom with shower and not much room to spread out your stuff. You can easily walk to the restaurants, tapas bars, and attractions of town. Don't expect too much and you should be delighted here, at least when it comes time to pay the bill.

Justino Pertínez 7, 113080 Tarifa. © **95-668-03-66.** 58€–70€ ($75–$91) double. MC, V. **Amenities:** Break-fast lounge. *In room:* TV.

La Codorniz *(Finds)* One of the best hotels in the area lies outside of town on the road to Cádiz, within walking distance of the beach at La Peña. Built in the mid-1970s and last renovated in 2003, it is a typically graceful Andalusian structure of two stories, with whitewashed walls and colored tiles. Bedrooms are a bit small but have balconies, tiled floors, simple but comfortable furnishings (very tasteful wooden pieces), plus well-maintained tiled bathrooms with tub/shower combos. Instead of a regular double, you can live more privately in one of the bungalows set on the landscaped grounds. If you don't want to travel back into Tarifa at night, you'll find a very good restaurant on site, serving regional dishes.

Carretera Cádiz Km 79, 11380 Tarifa. © **95-668-47-44.** Fax 95-668-41-01. www.tarifa.net/spain/hotel/la_codorniz.html. 37 units. 58€–105€ ($70–$126) double; 95€–137€ ($114–$164) suite. AE, DC, MC, V. Free parking. **Amenities:** Restaurant; bar; outdoor pool. *In room:* AC, TV, minibar, hair dryer.

Mesón de Sancho Although the Punta Azul wins for its beautiful garden and situation, this hacienda is the second best in the area. It will house you in style and comfort at a point 16km (10 miles) southwest of Algeciras and 11km (6½ miles) northeast of Tarifa on the road to Cádiz. An informal inn with good beds and excellent regional food, it also offers a pool surrounded by olive trees and terraces. The hotel still evokes the era (1955) in which it was built, but it was last renovated in 1995. The small rooms are modest but streamlined, each with a small tiled bathroom with tub and shower. The provincial dining room overlooks the garden.

N-340 Km 94, 11380 Tarifa. © **95-668-49-00.** Fax 95-668-47-21. www.mesondesancho.com. 40 units. 45€–68€ ($54–$82) double. AE, DC, MC, V. Free parking. **Amenities:** Restaurant; bar/cafe; outdoor pool; limited room service; laundry service; garden terrace. *In room:* TV, minibar, hair dryer.

Pensión Correos This rather basic guesthouse lies in front of the post office in the center of town. A former private house converted in 1999, it attracts guests on a budget. Bedrooms are simply furnished but comfortable and well maintained. Some surfers pile in here, sleeping three to five a room. Each unit comes with a little tiled bathroom with shower. Bedrooms on the ground floor don't get enough daylight, but the upper accommodations open onto scenic vis-tas of the town. If your room doesn't have a view, you can always head to the roof terrace enclosed by low white walls. There are virtually no amenities, but many restaurants lie just a short walk from the doorstep.

Calle Coronel Moscardó 8, 11380 Tarifa. ☏ **95-668-02-60**. 8 units. 30€–70€ ($36–$84) double. No credit cards. Parking 12€ ($14) nearby. *In room:* Ceiling fan, no phone.

Punta Azul   The is the best place to stay and dine in the area. A surrounding park envelops the inn lying 8km (5 miles) north of Tarifa. The bedrooms are midsize and well kept with tidy bathrooms with tub and shower. Some guests prefer to stay in one of the equally comfortable outlying bungalows. The staff can arrange horseback riding from a stable nearby. The hotel also offers the best Andalusian cuisine around, even better than its leading rival, Mesón de Sancho. If you're traveling through the area by day, you can stop in here for lunch.

La Peña 2, Carretera Cádiz-Málaga Km 77, 11380 Tarifa. ☏ **95-668-43-26**. Fax 95-668-04-72. www. balcondespana.com. 34 units. 71€–125€ ($85–$150) double. Rates include breakfast. AE, MC, V. Free parking. Closed Oct 25 and Nov–Mar 1. **Amenities:** Restaurant; bar; outdoor pool; tennis court; limited room service; laundry. *In room:* TV.

WHERE TO DINE

You won't find Tarifa written up in gourmet books as town restaurants tend to be mediocre. The Punta Azul (reviewed above) is a good option.

Restaurante Villanueva ANDALUSIAN   This 1888 *fonda* is still going strong. In the town center, near Puerta de Jerez, it was built in the Moorish style with a terrace, plenty of tiles, and wrought-iron furniture. Its family-style settings conjure up a canteen for blue-collar workers coming in from a sweaty day outdoors. The warm hospitality covers up for the simple, austere decor. The best choice is the fresh fish purchased that day at the market and the best preparation is *a la plancha* (grilled). It could also be laden with garlic *(al ajillo)* or fried. We are especially fond of the fresh tuna caught off local waters. Sole with meunière sauce is another choice item. Pieces of white fish end up in a fish fry medley with mussels and shrimp, all of it served with a savory tomato sauce. Whitefish is oven baked and served au gratin. Fish is very expensive in Spain, but prices remain reasonable here.

Av. de Andalucía 11. ☏ **95-668-41-49**. Reservations recommended. Main courses 5€–15€ ($6–$18). DC, MC, V. Tues–Sun 1–4pm and 8–11pm. Closed Aug.

3 Huelva

92km (57 miles) W of Seville, 629km (390 miles) SW of Madrid

Huelva, capital of the beautiful province of the same name, is itself rather ugly and industrial. For those heading west into bordering Portugal, the area makes a good stopover for at least 2 nights. Many history buffs also come here, for it was from this region that the explorer gathered men to sail with him on his voyage to the New World. Columbus devotees can explore the monastery at La Rábida and also visit the bay from which the explorer set sail at Palos de la Frontera.

Huelva is the center of one of the largest concentrations of beaches in Spain, and is visited mainly by Spaniards who don't actually settle at the port itself, but at the swanky resorts along the coast. The city of Huelva, home to some 140,000, also has a number of attractive first-class hotels.

ESSENTIALS

GETTING THERE   The port city of Huelva has good rail links with the rest of Spain. RENFE **trains** arrive at Avenida de Italia (☏ **90-224-02-02**). There are three to four trains per day from Seville, taking 1½ hours and costing 6.35€ ($7.60), one-way.

Huelva also has **bus** links to Cádiz, a long 5 hours. One bus a day pulls into Huelva, costing 15€ ($19) for a one-way ticket. There are also buses from Seville, perhaps 9 to 20 per day, taking 1 hour and costing 6.10€ ($7.35) for a one-way ticket. The bus station is at Avenida Dr. Rubio (© **95-925-69-00**).

If you're driving, most motorists arrive from Seville. Follow E-1 (also called A-49) west from Seville. There is no coastal road linking Cádiz and Huelva. Motorists from Cádiz head north on an express highway, E-5 (also A-4), then cut west toward Huelva south of Seville.

VISITOR INFORMATION   The **tourist office** is near the bus station at Av. de Alemania 12 (© **95-925-74-03**), open Monday to Friday 9am to 7pm, Saturday and Sunday 10am to 2pm. Unfortunately they're not particularly helpful.

FAST FACTS   For currency exchange, the most central place with ATMs is **Banco Santander Central Hispano** at Calle Palacios 10 (© **90-224-24-24**), open Monday to Friday 8:30am to 2pm and Saturday 8:30am to 1pm. The **Huelva post office** is at Av. Tomás Domínguez de Ortiz 1 (© **95-924-91-84**). Hours are Monday to Friday 8:30am to 8:30pm and Saturday 9:30am to 2pm. The **Huelva police station** is at Av. Tomás Domínguez de Ortiz 2 (© **95-924-93-50**). For **Internet** access, go to the Cybercafe Interpool, Calle Vásquez Limón 9 (© **95-980-24-78**), open Monday to Friday 10am to 1am, Saturday and Sunday 6pm to 1am. The charge is 1€ ($1.20) per half-hour's use. **Cruz Roja (Red Cross)** is at Paseo Buenos Aires s/n (© **95-926-20-20**), fronting the cathedral. This is for emergency treatment only. For other ailments, go to the **Hospital General Juan Ramón Jiménez** on Carretera Huelva-Seville (© **95-920-10-00**).

EXPLORING HUELVA

When Columbus set out from across the Río Tinto to chart a new sea passage to India, he brought rugged Huelvan sailors with him. After the sailors stumbled on the Americas, Huelva entered into a grand period of prosperity based on trade with the New World. Eventually Huelva's supremacy was lost to Seville and later to Cádiz, which came to dominate the gold and silver routes from the New World. A final blow was the Lisbon earthquake of 1755 that flattened much of Huelva. The city entered a long period of decline, and only in the past 50 years has it begun to make a comeback.

A major event is the **Fiestas Colombinas** ⚘ beginning on August 3, a week-long riot of concerts, *corridas* (bullfights), food, processions, and competitive races.

A large statue on the west bank of the river at Punta del Sebo commemorates the departure of Columbus on his third voyage of discovery. About 7km (4½ miles) up on the east bank of the Tinto River, this monument marks the exact spot where Columbus' ships were anchored while being loaded with supplies before departure.

To see other sights of Huelva, begin in the center of town at **Plaza de las Monjas,** a palm-lined square. From here, you can branch out in several directions to take in the highlights.

To the immediate northwest, reached along Avenida Martín Alonso Pinzón, is the **Museo Provincial,** Alameda Sundheim 17 (© **95-925-93-00**), open Tuesday 2:30 to 8:30pm, Wednesday to Saturday 9am to 8:30pm, and Sunday 8:45am to 2:30pm. Admission is free. The archaeology department focuses on the port's illustrious past. Regrettably, this museum is in decline and some of its treasures are in storage with no set date for their return. Notably this includes its Bellas Artes collection of fine paintings. You'll have to make do with what's left,

Huelva

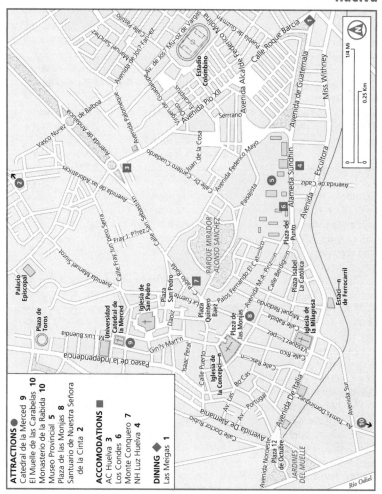

ATTRACTIONS ●
Catedral de la Merced **9**
El Muelle de las Carabelas **10**
Monasterio de la Rabida **10**
Museo Provincial **5**
Plaza de las Monjas **8**
Santuario de Nuestra Señora
de la Cinta **2**

ACCOMODATIONS ■
AC Huelva **3**
Los Condes **6**
Monte Conquero **7**
NH Luz Huelva **4**

DINING ◆
Las Meigas **1**

including artifacts that range from the Stone Age to the era of the Moorish takeover and an exhibition about the ancient city of Tartessus. Otherwise, a good dusting is in order.

After leaving the museum, you can visit **Barrio Reina Victoria,** east of the museum alongside Avenida de Guatemala. Constructed by the Río Tinto Mining Company in the early part of the 20th century, it was designed by British architects to evoke their homeland. Workers lived along the tree-lined streets in bungalows with rose gardens. Gables are in the mock Tudor style. This is a curiosity, not a major attraction.

Huelva's grandest church is **Catedral de la Merced,** entered on Plaza de la Merced s/n (no phone). Constructed in 1606, it was not damaged in the earthquake. Its facade is painted a vivid salmon pink with beautiful belfries. On the interior, a white baroque decor predominates. The church contains an image of the Virgen de la Cinta, patron saint of Huelva. The building is usually open during the day, though it occasionally closes unexpectedly.

For a church with links to Columbus, head for the restored 15th-century **Santuario de Nuestra Señora de la Cinta,** Plaza Conquero (© **95-925-11-22**), lying 3km (1¾ miles) from the center on the road heading to Portugal. This was one of the churches where Columbus came to pray for the success of his voyage. Attractions under its mudéjar ceiling include an impressive altar grille, a fresco of the Madonna dating from the Middle Ages, and a series of 1920s tiles depicting scenes from the life of Columbus, each by the artist Daniel Zuloaga. To reach this church from the center, head west along Avenida de Manuel Siurot. The chapel lies off this route. Once here you can take in views of the Odiel estuary. Opening hours of this church vary. Admission is free.

At the little town of La Rábida, 8km (5 miles) east of Huelva, you can visit the **Monasterio de la Rábida** ⭐, Av. de la América s/n (© **95-935-04-11**), in whose white chapel Columbus prayed for success on the eve of his voyage. Columbus stayed at the monastery with his son, Diego, and it was here he revealed his plans to friars Juan Pérez and Antonio de Marchena. They were so convinced of the brilliance of his scheme for a new route to India that they interceded on his behalf with Queen Isabella who agreed to finance the expedition. This monastery, which is also called Santa María de La Rabadía, is known as "the birthplace of America."

The church's chief treasure is the venerated *Virgen de los Milagros* **(Virgin of the Miracles),** dating from the 1300s. In the gatehouse are frescoes painted in 1930 by Daniel Vázquez Díaz, a noted artist from Huelva. Of particular charm is a mudéjar cloister from the 15th century, adjoining the monks' refectory where Columbus and his son dined.

Upstairs you can visit a gallery with an exhibition of all the known pictures of the explorer, including Chantal Goya's *Admiral of the Ocean.* Also upstairs is the Sala Capitular (Chapter House) where Columbus made his final plans before disembarking.

The monastery is reached via Calle Rábida, which is lined with ceramic tiles marking all the countries of the New World. The buildings at the complex had to be restored after the devastating Lisbon earthquake of 1755. Admission is 2.50€ ($3), 1.50€ ($1.80) for children under 12. Hours March to July and September to October are Tuesday to Sunday 10am to 1pm and 3 to 7pm; in August, Tuesday to Sunday 10am to 1pm and 5 to 8pm; November to February Tuesday to Sunday 10am to 1pm and 4 to 6pm.

While pursuing Columbus' trail, you can also visit **El Muelle de las Carabelas,** the wharf from which his ships set sail, at Paraje de la Rábida, Palos de la Frontera (© **95-953-05-97**), 4km (2½ miles) north along the Río Tinto estuary and 2km (1¼ miles) from the monastery just visited. From this now heavily-silted bay below Iglesia San Jorge, three caravels—the *Pinta,* the *Niña,* and the *Santa María*—set out to explore the Sea of Darkness. In those days Palos was a busy little port. In the complex stand replicas of the three caravels—shockingly small to house a crew of 90, plus 30 officers, for 2 months and 10 days. Look also for maps tracing Columbus's voyage, and a 20-minute film of the trip, which kids will enjoy. Admission is 3€ ($3.60) for adults, 1.25€ ($1.50) for children 12 and under. From April to September hours are Tuesday to Friday 10am to 2pm and 5 to 9pm, Saturday and Sunday 11am to 8pm; from October to March, Tuesday to Sunday 10am to 7pm.

WHERE TO STAY

AC Huelva ⭐   Just a bit downscale from NH Luz Huelva, this is also a commercial, first-class hotel popular with business clients but equally suited to summer vacationers using the port city as their base for the Costa de la Luz. Set on landscaped grounds, the seven-story hotel dates from 2002. For what it offers, its prices are very reasonable. Bedrooms, although in the standard chain format, are comfortably furnished, mainly with wooden pieces, and are midsize for the most part. Each comes with an attractively tiled bathroom with a tub/shower combo. In lieu of a restaurant, the hotel offers a cafeteria with affordable prices. The location is at the entrance to the city on the highway coming in from Seville. It is close to the university area and only a 10-minute drive to the beaches of the Costa de la Luz.

Av. de Andalucía s/n, 21005 Huelva. © **95-954-52-00.** Fax 95-954-52-01. www.ac-hotels.com/swf/ac-hotels. html. 65 units. 82€–112€ ($98–$134) double. AE, DC, MC, V. Parking 10€ ($12). **Amenities:** Cafeteria; bar; sauna; 24-hr. room service; laundry service; nonsmoking rooms; rooms for those w/limited mobility. *In room:* A/C, TV, dataport, minibar, hair dryer.

Los Condes   This modern urban hotel, rising five floors, has been going strong since 1993 when it became a permanent fixture on the local scene. In the center of town, it is well situated and comfortable, though lacking any particular charm. Furnished with wooden pieces resting on tiled floors, most bedrooms are small to midsize, each with a tiled bathroom with a tub/shower combo. The better rooms open onto balconies. We prefer one of the top-floor accommodations or else a bedroom overlooking the patio. A noisy club immediately opposite the hotel may disturb light sleepers in the front rooms. The on-site cafeteria is very affordable.

Alameda Sundheim 14, 21003 Huelva. © **95-928-24-00.** Fax 95-928-50-41. www.hotelloscondes.com. 54 units. 48€–63€ ($58–$76) double. Rates include continental breakfast. AE, DC, MC, V. Parking 13€ ($16). **Amenities:** Cafeteria; bar; 24-hr. room service; babysitting; laundry service. *In room:* A/C, TV, dataport, minibar, hair dryer.

Monte Conquero ✦   This hotel has some drawbacks but is a suitable choice if both the AC Huelva and NH Luz are full. Rooms range from single to double, from king-size to triple, even junior suites. Most are midsize, comfortable, furnished with wooden furniture, and have good lighting, especially over the beds. Each comes with a tiled bathroom with tub and shower. The service here is better than the rooms. As for decor, ivy hangs from red banisters and the elevator is a Hyatt-style bubble. Many students are out and about this area at night, so it can be a bit noisy.

Pablo Rada 10, 21004 Huelva. © **95-928-55-00.** Fax 95-928-39-12. www.hotel-monteconquero.com. 166 units. 100€ ($120) double; 250€ ($300) suite. AE, MC, V. **Amenities:** Cafeteria; bar; 24-hr. room service; laundry service/dry cleaning; rooms for those w/limited mobility. *In room:* A/C, TV, dataport, hair dryer, safe.

NH Luz Huelva ✦   This modern hotel is as good as it gets in Huelva. Lying in midtown, a short distance from the Congress Hall and the train station, it opened in 1992 and was last renovated in 1999. A seven-story building with balconies, it is a first-class—not deluxe—hotel. Bedrooms, including five suites, are furnished in a traditional rather sober style, with matching fabrics and light wooden furniture. Most of the rooms are midsize, each with a well-maintained tiled bathroom with a tub/shower combo. A member of a Spanish chain, the hotel fills up mainly with business clients in the cooler months, drawing vacationers in the summer. What we like about it most is the attention to detail—a choice of pillows (firm, soft, or duvet), a breakfast for early risers, even a toiletries kit. The outdoor cafe and bar are lovely in summer.

Alameda Sundheim 26, 21003 Huelva. © **95-925-00-11.** Fax 95-925-00-11. www.nh-hoteles.com. 107 units. 77€–90€ ($92–$108) double; 134€ ($161) suite. AE, DC, MC, V. Free parking. **Amenities:** Cafe; 2 bars; room service (8am–8pm); babysitting; laundry service/dry cleaning; nonsmoking rooms. *In room:* A/C, TV, dataport, minibar, hair dryer.

ON THE OUTSKIRTS

Parador de Mazagón ★★   One of the best accommodations in the area is 23km (14 miles) west of Huelva and 6km (3½ miles) from the center of Mazagón. The parador was constructed on a pine grove cliff overlooking a sandy beach. A rambling 1960s structure, it has comfortable, spacious rooms with balconies and terraces overlooking an expansive garden. All units have bathrooms with tub/shower combos. Pine groves slope down to the white sand beach at Mazagón, which is a small village with a number of restaurants. We prefer to stay in this village outside Huelva than at one of the more impersonal hotels within the city center. Even if you're just driving and exploring the area, consider a luncheon stopover here. The chef specializes in regional dishes, including stuffed baby squid.

Carretera de San Juan del Puerto a Matalascañas s/n, 21130 Mazagón. ⓒ **95-953-63-00.** Fax 95-953-62-28. 63 units. 107€–123€ ($128–$148) double; 142€–168€ ($170–$202) suite. AE, DC, MC, V. Free parking. Exit from Magazón's eastern sector, following the signs to the town of Matalascañas. Take the coast road (Hwy. 442) to the parador. **Amenities:** Restaurant; bar; lounge; outdoor pool; indoor pool; outdoor unlit tennis court; gym; Jacuzzi; sauna; limited room service; babysitting; laundry service/dry cleaning; nonsmoking rooms; rooms for those w/limited mobility. *In room:* A/C, TV, dataport, minibar, hair dryer, safe.

WHERE TO DINE

El Paraíso ★ (Finds ANDALUSIAN   This restaurant lies on the road from Huelva to El Portil, serves some of the finest meals in the area, and is well worth the search if you have wheels. When you arrive, El Paraíso's setting and ramshackle appearance may turn you off. However, once you're inside, seated at one of the rustic tables in a dining room that looks like a straw hut, the food is superb.

The fish dishes are the best and freshest in the area, especially *lubina a la sal,* sea bass cooked in a salt crust (removed before serving), to seal in the juices. Sea bass is also served with a bay leaf–flavored sauce. Several rice dishes are popular with local foodies, including our favorite, fresh crab with vegetables grown in the province. The catch of the day can be ordered grilled *(a la brasa)* or else with garlic *(al ajillo).* The meat eater will enjoy the juicy steaks, and the reliable dessert menu features a series of homemade sweets, including the chef's special pine nut and chocolate cheesecake.

Carretera de Huelva/El Portil, El Rompido. ⓒ **95-931-27-56.** Reservations recommended. Main courses 17€–20€ ($20–$24). DC, MC, V. Daily 12:30–5pm and 8:30pm–midnight. From Huelva follow the signs to Punta Umbría and cross the bridge over the Odiel River. Continue toward Punta Umbría, passing under 2 bridges. At the 2nd bridge, turn right for 1km (⅔ mile) until you come to the restaurant.

Las Meigas GALICIAN/BASQUE   This modern restaurant combines two of Spain's best northern cuisines in a far southern setting—a real change of pace from typical Andalusian fare. In front of Plaza América, it is decorated in a typical rustic-tavern style, with wooden furniture, candles, and glass. In a town not noted for first-class restaurants, Las Meigas's fine food and total lack of pretension stand out. Regardless of the cost of ingredients, the chef is determined to price all the dishes the same, even scampi, which is usually paralyzingly high in Andalusia. On a recent visit, we enjoyed fried sea bass flavored with lots of garlic and parsley, and scampi with local ham and a white sauce. One regional dish on the menu is a platter of small squids flavored with their own *tinta* (ink) and cooked with rice. A Basque classic is the hake *(merluza)* with potatoes, garlic, pepper, and olive oil. Desserts are made fresh daily.

Av. Guatemala 44. ℭ **95-927-19-58.** Reservations recommended. Main courses 13€–17€ ($16–$20). AE, DC, MC, V. Daily 1–4pm and 8pm–midnight.

HUELVA AFTER DARK

Most foreigners head for **Docklands,** Aragón 7 (ℭ **95-925-82-70**). In the center of Huelva, next to Iglesia San Pedro, it is an Irish-style pub with a fun crowd and flowing beer. With its smoked glass windows and yellowing walls, it's one of the best places to hang out in Huelva on a Friday or Saturday night. It shuts down in August, but otherwise is open Tuesday to Sunday 4pm to 1am.

While making a tapas crawl through the Old Town, stop in at **Taberna El Condado,** Sor Angela de la Cruz 3 (ℭ **95-926-11-23**), a rustic tavern beloved by locals. Here you can enjoy fried hake, succulent hams, salmon, and various meat dishes, including meatballs. Tapas and *ración* range from 2.50€ to 18€ ($3–$22). It is open Tuesday to Sunday 8pm to 1am, closing for 15 days in August (dates vary). Rustic **El Portichuelo,** Gran Vía 1 (ℭ **95-924-57-68**), near Plaza de Las Monjas, is a similar option. This wooden bar with a dancing area serves an array of tapas and *raciones* that changes seasonally, but always includes baby squid, savory meatballs in a tomato sauce, and regional hams and olives. Tapas cost from 2€ ($2.40). Open daily 10:30am to 5:30pm and Monday to Saturday 8:30pm to midnight. Closed all day Sunday from May 25 to September 15.

4 Side Trips from Huelva

The coastal areas east and west of Huelva are more intriguing than the industrialized city itself. You can head west toward the Portuguese border and the frontier town of Ayamonte or east to explore the Cota de Doñana National Park, Spain's largest wildlife reserve.

AYAMONTE

Built on the slopes of a hill on which a castle-fortress once stood, scruffy little Ayamonte is full of beach-fronting high-rises, which, for the most part, are studded with vacation apartments for the Spaniards who flock here in vast numbers in July and August. The town, which lies 37km (22 miles) east of Huelva, via the E-1 (also called N-430), has more of a Portuguese flavor than any other in Andalusia. That's perfectly understandable since Portugal, or more specifically the unremarkable town of Vila Real de Santo Antonio, lies only a short ferry ride away. Ferries leave hourly throughout the day until 9pm, charging 4€ ($4.80) for a one-way passage which takes only 10 minutes. Ferries depart from the riverside promenade, Muelle de Portugal, in Ayamonte. Motorists can drive over the International Bridge over the Guadiana.

If you don't drive from Huelva to Ayamonte, you can take one of the frequent buses connecting the two. Buses arrive in Ayamonte at the station at Avenida de Andalucía east of the town center. Don't expect much guidance from the **tourist office** at Calle Huelva 37 (ℭ **95-932-18-71**), open Monday to Friday 11am to 1pm and 6 to 9pm (at least in summer).

There's not much in the way of sightseeing in Ayamonte. In an hour or so, you can see the Old Town with its warren of narrow streets centered around **Paseo de la Ribera,** the principal square. Duck into the **Iglesia de San Francisco** on Calle San Francisco, to see its stunning mudéjar *artesonado* ceiling. The church dates from 1521 and was declared a landmark in 1935. Its chief artistic treasure is an altarpiece from the 16th century. Continue on the same street to **Iglesia de San Salvador,** dating from the 15th century. You can climb its tower (if it's open) for a panoramic view of the town, the river, and the Algarve coast of Portugal to the west.

Most visitors spend little time in Ayamonte and head instead to its major beach, **Playa Isla Canela** ⊛, 7km (4⅓ miles) to the south. Buses from Ayamonte run there, departing summers-only from the Paseo de la Ribera.

If Isla Canela is too crowded you can continue eastward to another good beach, **Playa Punta del Moral.** The beaches of Ayamonte open onto calm waters because of sandbars 50 to 100m (164–328 ft.) from the shore. These sandbars became virtual islands at low tide.

Most visitors eat at one of the tapas bars in the old fishing village of **Punta del Moral,** slightly to the north. Fresh fish is the way to go here. You'll also find plenty of places for lunch in Ayamonte, most clustered around Paseo de la Ribera in the heart of town. Go for the *raciones* of Jabugo ham and the fresh fish based on the catch of the day. The best seafood in town is served at **Casa Luciano,** Calle Palma 2 (℃ **95-947-01-71**), lying on the eastern side of the harbor. It features a daily menu for around 15€ ($18).

WHERE TO STAY & DINE

AC Quinta Canela Golf ⊛⊛⊛   This is the grandest resort along the Costa de la Luz, featuring a magnificent 18-hole golf course set against a backdrop of orange, olive, and eucalyptus trees with slopes made by sand dunes. Built near an estuary of the Río Guadiana, this stunningly modern hotel with traditional architectural designs was created specifically for golf tourism. The stately structure evokes an elegant Portuguese country house, with Andalusian motifs and even faux Arab stuccos. The course is carefully tended, and is more or less a flat terrain with furrowed pathways that wind around the dunelike contours. The lakes and water traps were not artificially created but are canals and marshes with the local flora and fauna left intact. Within an easy drive of the famous beach at Isla Canela, the resort is set on landscaped grounds.

Bedrooms are spacious and luxurious, each with a beautiful tiled bathroom filled with amenities including a tub/shower combo and elegant toiletries. The food here is even better than at the parador. From July 24 to August 29, a minimum stay of 5 nights is required.

Golf Norte, Carretera de Isla Canela s/n, 21409 Ayamonte. ℃ **95-947-78-30.** Fax 95-947-78-31. 58 units. 275€ ($330) double. AE, DC, MC, V. Closed Dec 15–Jan. **Amenities:** Restaurant; bar; coffee shop; outdoor pool; 18-hole golf course; fitness center; sauna; steam bath; car-rental desk; business services; salon; 24-hr. room service; nonsmoking rooms; laundry service. *In room:* A/C, TV, dataport, minibar, safe.

Hotel Riavela ⊛ *(Finds*   This is the oldest and most traditional favorite in the area and the only really good choice for visitors who want to stay in Ayamonte's Old Town. A rustic decoration and a big welcome greet you here. The best rooms open onto balconies with town views. Accommodations are midsize and furnished simply with handcrafted Andalusian wooden pieces; each contains a private bathroom with tub and shower. No meals, other than breakfast, are served but several restaurants lie within a 5-minute walk of the hotel's doorstep.

Calle Canto de la Villa 15, 21400 Ayamonte. ℃ **95-947-19-19.** Fax 95-947-19-29. www.hotellabarca.com/rv/engprincrv.html. 25 units. 75€ ($90) double. MC, V. **Amenities:** Breakfast lounge. *In room:* A/C, TV.

Parador de Ayamonte ⊛⊛ *(Value*   One of the leading accommodations in Ayamonte is this parador that opened in 1966. Commanding a sweeping view of the river and the surrounding towns along its banks—sunsets are memorable here—the parador stands about 30m (100 ft.) above sea level on the site of the old castle of Ayamonte. It was built in a severe modern style and boasts Nordic-inspired furnishings. Most rooms are medium-size and comfortably appointed, with bathrooms with tub/shower combos.

Av. de la Constitución s/n, 21400 Ayamonte. ☎ **95-932-07-00.** Fax 95-902-20-19. www.parador.es. 54 units. 89€–110€ ($107–$132) double; 137€–173€ ($164–$208) suite. Rates include breakfast. AE, DC, MC, V. Free parking. From the center of Ayamonte, signs for the parador lead you up a winding road to the hilltop, about 1km (½ mile) southeast of the center. **Amenities:** 2 restaurants; bar; outdoor pool; limited room service; babysitting; laundry service/dry cleaning; nonsmoking rooms; rooms for those w/limited mobility. *In room:* A/C, TV, minibar, hair dryer, safe.

ISLA CRISTINA

As the name suggests, this was once an island. Today, however, landfill has linked it to the mainland. It lies 8km (5 miles) east of Ayamonte and 55km (34 miles) west of Huelva. Enveloped by tidal estuaries, Isla Cristina is today a building block of holiday apartments, many owned by Sevillanos who flock here in July and August. The fishing port here, second most important in Huelva province, supplies fish to Córdoba and Seville, even Madrid. Stroll along **Carretera de la Playa,** with its mammoth eucalyptus trees, to the town's sandy beach. An even better beach, **Playa Central,** lies 2km (1¼ miles) east of the center. In the heart of the village itself, life centers on Plaza de las Flores.

To the southeast of this square is the **tourist office,** Av. de España 4 (☎ **95-933-26-94**), open Tuesday to Saturday 10am to 2pm and 6 to 8pm, Sunday 10am to 2pm. Frequent buses from Huelva arrive at the bus terminal along Avenida de Huelva, two blocks north of Plaza de las Flores.

The town, especially in summer, is filled with little fish eateries and tapas joints, some of which come and go with the seasons. For more substantial dining, you can patronize the restaurants of the two leading hotels (see below).

For tapas before dinner, head to the northwest point of town, a peninsula lying between the harbor and the already mentioned Plaza de las Flores. Walk the narrow, cobblestone streets flanked by whitewashed homes of Cristina's fishing colony. You'll find many bars serving freshly made tapas in this area, some with outdoor patios. Flamenco can be heard at some of these taverns in summer, when the visitors pile into town.

WHERE TO STAY & DINE

Los Geranios   Near the beach, this was the first hotel to open at Isla Cristina. It was renovated in 2002, and is now the resort's best hotel. The architecture evokes the late 1960s (no great compliment), but the midsize rooms are attractively and comfortably furnished, mostly with rustic wooden pieces and flowery fabrics. Each comes with an attractively tiled bathroom with tub and shower. The on-site restaurant turns out an array of good-tasting regional specialties costing from 18€ ($22).

Av. de la Playa, 21410 Isla Cristina. ☎ **95-933-18-00.** Fax 95-933-19-50. www.hotellosgeranioslaplata.com. 24 units. 144€ ($173) double. AE, DC, MC, V. **Amenities:** Restaurant; bar; outdoor pool; 24-hr. room service; babysitting; laundry service. *In room:* A/C, TV, dataport, hair dryer, safe.

Paraíso Playa *Value*   Opening onto the fishing port, this seaside, two-story house with yellow walls and a stone fence opened in 1972, two years after Los Geranios (see above) launched tourism on the island. Like its slightly nicer competitor, Paraíso has kept up with the times, each year experiencing minor renovations to keep it in top form. Well run and with a good staff, the hotel offers somewhat smallish bedrooms furnished with light wood pieces; each comes with a tiled bathroom with a tub/shower combo. Reserve early in July and August.

The restaurant serves very good and very fresh fish dishes, usually relying on the catch of the day. Meals begin at 15€ ($18).

Av. de la Playa, 21410 Isla Cristina. ℂ **95-933-02-35.** Fax 95-933-02-35. www.hotelparaisoplaya.com. 32 units. 95€ ($114) double. AE, DC, MC, V. Closed Dec 15–Jan 15. **Amenities:** Restaurant; bar; outdoor pool. *In room:* A/C, TV.

COTA DE DOÑANA NATIONAL PARK ★★★

Covering some 76,080 hectares (188,000 acres), Cota de Doñana National Park is Spain's largest wildlife reserve and one of the continent's last great wildernesses. At an estuary of the River Guadalquivir, it is also one of the world's greatest wetland sites for migrating birds. Birdwatchers by the thousands flock here in spring when hundreds of flocks of breeding birds fly in to nest in the wetlands. In all, there are 300 different species of rare birds, along with colonies of storks, buzzards, kites, kestrels, and egrets, plus 33 species of mammals, 12 species of fish, and 18 species of reptiles. There have even been sightings of the almost-extinct Spanish imperial eagle.

Mammals on the verge of extinction, including a rare lynx, also live here. Wild boar can be seen in the *marismas* (swamps).

The park is also the home of more than 10 separate kinds of orange, tangerine, and citrus trees, an estimated 300,000 trees in total, many of them cultivated within the park hotel's sprawling, 1,000-hectare (2,471-acre) farmlands. (The hotel is reviewed below). Thanks to the efforts of the local government, the park is also the site of an aggressive reforestation program.

The best bird-watching base is the village of **El Rocío** on the northwestern edge of the marshes. The enveloping marshes and pinewoods here teem with honking wild geese and white storks. The Doñana Visitor Center lies at **La Rocina** (ℂ **95-944-23-40**), less than 2km (1 mile) west of El Rocío. A footpath has been cut through the wetlands here, and you can walk its 3.5km (2 miles) daily from 9am to 2pm and 3pm to sunset. Free maps are provided. Along the way you might encounter such creatures as the red-crested pochard or the magnificent hoopoe, even flamingos and hundreds of singing nightingales.

There's another information center at **El Palacio de Acebrón,** 5km (3 miles) to the west and with the same hours. This former hunting lodge has an exhibition tracing the history of the park. Bring a picnic as this is an ideal spot for lunch.

From La Rocina a drive of 9km (5½ miles) will take you west to the **Centro Recepción del Acebuche** (ℂ **95-943-04-32**), the park's main interpretive center. It's open daily June to September 8am to 9pm; October to May daily 8:30 to 3pm. Jeep tours, which must be reserved in advance, depart from here hourly, cost 20€ ($24) per person, and last 4 hours. These tours take you through an area of the park stretching for 70km (43 miles) across scrubland, sand dunes, salt marshes, and beaches. Bring a pair of binoculars. In summer most of the birds disappear when the marshes dry up. In their place you'll see grazing horses and deer.

To reach Acebuche, drive 12km (7½ miles) south on the A-483 from El Rocío, then go for 1.6km (1 mile) west (it's signposted). At Acebuche there are footpaths to birdwatching sites overlooking the lagoon.

WHERE TO STAY & DINE

El Cortijo de Los Mimbrales ★ *Finds* Set 3km (1¾ miles) southwest of Rocío on 1,000 hectares (2,471 acres) of flatlands that are mostly devoted to farming and the cultivation of citrus crops, this is the best place to stay in the park. It's a sprawling, solidly constructed compound of white-walled, tile-roofed cottages along walkways lined with trees. The resort's centerpiece is a gracefully designed three-story tower with big windows overlooking the surrounding landscape. Decor focuses on rustic, earthy farm implements and terra cotta that farmers and hunters in the region have used for centuries. There is a kind of rustic yet modernized chic, with thick masonry walls and ample use of tiles and stone, plus occasional splashes of bright, vibrant color, especially ocher and blue. A few of the cottages and villas on-site are privately owned condos. Others are clean, functional, and even cozy, albeit a bit sunbaked and dusty during the hottest months of midsummer. All include bathrooms.

During the Rocío Feria, the area's biggest folkloric and religious event, the hacienda can be crowded and boisterous. Otherwise, it is quiet, restrained, and committed to exposing the natural beauty of the surrounding park to visitors who want to explore its botanic and zoological wealth. Come here to experience the park, to rest and relax, and to experience country life. Don't come expecting nightlight or entertainment other than walks and horseback riding, which can be arranged on the fringes of the park.

The in-house restaurant prepares a hearty mix of regional and international cuisine, specializing in duck prepared with local oranges; at least three kinds of local saltwater fish, either grilled or baked in salt crusts; freshwater crayfish with local wines; and roasted goat in the style of Segovia.

Carretera Rocío a Matalascañas, A-483 Km 20, 21750 Almonte. ✆ **95-944-22-37**. Fax 95-944-24-43. www. cortijomimbrales.com. 28 units. 125€–200€ ($150–$240) double; 250€ ($300) suite for 2; 350€ ($420) suite for 4. Rates include breakfast. Rates are higher during Christmas, Holy Week, and the Rocío Feria. AE, MC, V. **Amenities:** Restaurant; bar; outdoor pool; golfing at a site 11km (6¾ miles) away; horseback riding; mountain bike rentals. *In room:* A/C, TV, minibar, safe.

10

The Costa del Sol

The mild winter climate and almost-guaranteed summer sunshine make this stretch of Mediterranean shoreline known as the **Costa del Sol**—Coast of the Sun—a year-round destination. From the harbor city of Algeciras it stretches east to the port city of Almería. Sandwiched in between is a steep, rugged coastline set against the Sierra Nevada. You'll find poor to fair beaches, sandy coves, whitewashed houses, olive trees, lots of new apartment houses, fishing boats, golf courses, souvenir stands, fast-food outlets, and a wide variety of visitors.

This coastal strip, quite frankly, no longer enjoys the chic reputation it had in Franco's day. It's overbuilt and spoiled, though you can still find posh sections (including Puerto Banús, with its yacht-clogged harbor).

Today, frankly, the coast is better for **golf** than for beaches. The best resorts are **Los Monteros** (© 95-277-17-00), in Marbella, the leading course; **Parador Nacional del Golf** (© 95-238-12-55), between Málaga and Torremolinos; **Hotel Atalaya Park** in Estepona (© 95-288-90-00); and

Golf Hotel Guadalmina in Marbella (© 95-288-22-11). To learn more, pick up a copy of the monthly magazine *Costa Golf* at any newsstand. Many golfers prefer to play a different course at every hotel. Usually, if you notify your hotel reception desk a day in advance, a staff member will arrange a playing time.

Water-skiing and windsurfing are available in every resort, and all types of boats can be rented from various kiosks at all the main beaches. You don't have to search hard for these outfitters—chances are they'll find you.

From June to October the coast is mobbed, so make your hotel reservations in advance. And keep in mind that October 12 is a national holiday—visitors should make doubly sure of reservations at this time. At other times, innkeepers are likely to roll out the red carpet.

Many restaurants close around October 15 for a much-needed vacation. Remember, too, that many supermarkets and other facilities are closed on Sunday.

1 Algeciras

679km (422 miles) S of Madrid, 132km (82 miles) W of Málaga

Not really a destination in and of itself, Algeciras is a refueling stop on the way to **Tangier** in Morocco (3 hr. away by ferry) or to chic-er oases like **Marbella** to the east. Algeciras is also a base for day trips to **Gibraltar** (see below). If you don't have time to visit "the Rock," you can at least see it from Algeciras—it's only 10km (6 miles) away.

Despite an intriguing history, there is very little of interest here. Lying near the southern tip of Iberia, Algeciras was once the ancient Roman port of Portus Albo. In 713 it was refounded by the Moorish invaders. In 1344 Alfonso XI of

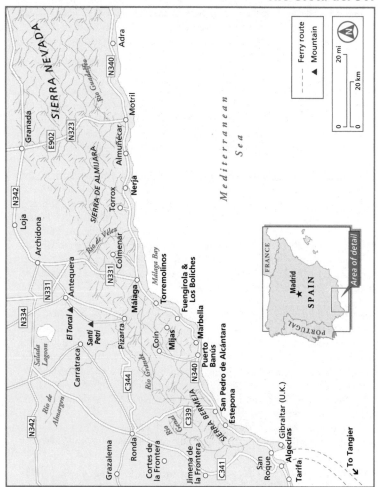

Castile recaptured it in the name of the Christians, but it was destroyed once again by Mohammed V of Granada in 1368.

Today, little remains from all these conquerors, and in fact, Algeciras's architecture is some of the most undistinguished of any port its size along the Costa del Sol. Franco's dream was to turn the dreary port into a commercial hub that would dwarf Gibraltar's success. (Of course, his ultimate goal was to force Her Majesty's Army out of Iberia.) He set about building ugly concrete bunker-type architecture and ill-conceived high-rises that remain to this day. And so do the British, who still house their troops on Gibraltar.

If you're waiting for a boat and have time to spare, head for **La Plaza Alta,** the palm tree studded square with a fountain in the center of town. Dating from 1807, the square boasts two churches, **Iglesia de Nuestra Señora de la Palma,** constructed in 1723, and the **Capilla de Nuestra Señora de Europa,** constructed some time in the 1700s as well.

Better yet, if you have even more time to spare, head for the nearest good beach. The best one is **Playa de Getares,** lying 5km (3 miles) south of the port. It's unattractively built up, but the sands are golden and stretch for some 3km (2 miles).

ESSENTIALS

GETTING THERE & DEPARTING   The local RENFE office is at Calle Juan de la Cierva (© **90-224-02-02**). From Madrid, two **trains** daily make the 6- to 10-hour trip; the fare is 35€ to 53€ ($42–$64). From Málaga, you have to transfer in Bobadillo; the fare is 14€ ($17). The trip takes 3 hours and 50 minutes and runs along most of the Costa del Sol, including Marbella and Torremolinos.

Various independent **bus companies** serve Algeciras. Empresa Portillo, Av. Virgen de Carmen 15 (© **95-665-10-55**), 1½ blocks to the right when you exit the port complex, runs nearly 20 buses a day along the Costa del Sol to Algeciras from Málaga. It also sends six buses a day to Córdoba (6 hr.) and two buses a day to Granada (5 hr.). To make connections to or from Seville, use Line Sur, Av. Virgen del Carmen 30 (© **95-666-76-49**). Eight buses a day go to Jerez de la Frontera, and eleven to Seville. **Transportes Generales Comes,** Hotel Octavio, Calle San Bernardo 1 (© **95-665-34-56**), sells tickets to **La Línea,** the border station for the approach to Gibraltar.

Most visitors in Algeciras plan to cross to Tangier, Morocco. **Ferries** leave every hour on the hour daily from 7am to 10pm. A ticket costs 25€ ($30) per person. To transport a **car** costs 79€ ($95), and vehicles cannot be transported in stormy weather. The trip takes 2½ hours. An express service that runs twice a day at 9am and 1:45pm costs 27€ ($32) and only takes 1¼ hours. Discounts are available: 20% for Eurailpass holders, 30% for InterRail pass holders, and 50% for children 4 to 12. For more information call © **395-666-60-61** or 90-219-50-14. There's an inexpensive baggage storage depot at the ferry terminal if you want to store your things.

Carretera de Cádiz (E-15/N-340) runs from Málaga west to Algeciras. If you're driving south from Seville (or Madrid), take highway N-IV to Cádiz, then connect with the N-340/E-5 southwest to Algeciras.

VISITOR INFORMATION   The **tourist office** at Juan de la Cierva (© **95-657-26-36;** www.andalusia.com) is open Monday to Friday 9am to 2pm.

WHERE TO STAY

Alborán 🔆 *(Finds)*   One of the best nearby hotels is 4km (2½ miles) outside Algeciras along the N-340. A good beach is only a 2-minute walk from the grounds. Dating from 1990 and last renovated in 2004, the hotel is attractive architecturally, built in the typical Andalusian style with patios and Mozarabic motifs. Rooms are flooded with sunlight and comfortably furnished, each with a modern tiled bathroom with tub and shower. Lots of plants and flowers make for an inviting ambience.

Alamo, 11205 Algeciras. © **95-663-28-70.** Fax 95-663-23-20. www.hotelesalboran.com. 79 units. 65€–100€ ($78–$120) double; 106€–122€ ($127–$146) suite. AE, DC, MC, V. **Amenities:** Restaurant; bar; 24-hr. room service; babysitting; laundry service/dry cleaning; nonsmoking rooms; solarium. *In room:* A/C, TV, hair dryer.

Don Manuel *(Value)*   Only slightly less desirable than the Alarde, this is more like a guesthouse or small inn. Because of its central location, it's ideal for quick getaways if you have to catch an early boat. Built in 1992, the little inn was last

Teeing Off: A Golden Triangle of Golf

Faced with more than 40 places to take a swing on the Costa del Sol, golfers are often overwhelmed by the choice of courses, many of which are championship venues. Here's a trio of courses that rank among the greatest in Europe—no apologies to Scotland.

- **San Roque Club,** Urbanización San Roque, Carretera A-7 Km 126.5, Sotogrande-San Roque (ℂ **95-661-30-30**), was created by two Englishmen, former Ryder Cup players Tony Jacklin and Dave Thomas, on the grounds of the summer palace of the Domecq sherry dynasty. The back 9 features two of the finest holes along the coast.

- **Club de Golf Valderrama,** Av. de los Cortijos s/n, Sotogrande-San Roque (ℂ **95-679-12-00**), is in our view *número uno* among the golf courses of continental Europe. *Golf World* called it "daring, dramatic, demanding" and we agree. The course was first designed by the grand old man himself, Robert Trent Jones, Sr. Steve Ballesteros (the "Arnold Palmer of Spain") designed the notorious 17th hole, which Ryder Cup players describe as "one of the most strategically challenging holes in the world." Pines and cork trees keep this par-72 course wickedly challenging.

- **Real Club de Golf Sotogrande,** Paseo del Parque, Sotogrande (ℂ **95-678-50-14**) is a par-72 course also laid out originally by Robert Trent Jones, Sr. Its 11th hole is buffeted by two prevailing winds blowing in different directions. Many of the fairways are 40 to 50 yards long, and the course is riddled with shimmering lakes evocative of Florida.

renovated in 2003. Its bedrooms are small but comfortably and tastefully furnished, with slightly cramped bathrooms that nonetheless have tub/shower combos. There's not much in the way of facilities or amenities, but at these prices, no one complains.

Segismundo Moret 4, 11201 Algeciras. ℂ **96-563-46-06.** 15 units. 50€ ($60) double. AE, DC, MC, V. **Amenities:** Laundry service. *In room:* A/C, TV, hair dryer (in some).

Hotel Alarde ⭐ 🄥ⁱ🅥ₐₗᵤₑ   If you want to get away from the tacky, noisy port area, consider staying at this hotel near the Parque María Cristina. It's a central location in a quiet commercial section of town. The small double rooms have balconies and Andalusian-style furnishings, including bathrooms with tub/shower combos. During our most recent stay we were impressed with both the staff and the inviting atmosphere.

Alfonso XI no. 4, 11201 Algeciras. ℂ **95-666-04-08.** Fax 95-665-49-01. 68 units. 70€–84€ ($84–$101) double. AE, DC, MC, V. Parking 9€ ($11). **Amenities:** Restaurant; bar; laundry service/dry cleaning. *In room:* A/C, TV, dataport, safe.

Hotel Al-Mar ⭐   The government-rated three-star Al-Mar is one of the best choices in town, with better rooms than the Alarde. It's near the port, where the ferries leave for Ceuta and Tangier. This large hotel boasts blue-and-white Sevillian and Moorish decor. The midsize guest rooms are well maintained, furnished

> ### *Tips* Beaches: The Good, the Bad & the Nude
>
> We'd like to report that the Costa del Sol is a paradise for swimmers
> and sunbathers. Surprisingly, it isn't, although it was the allure of
> beaches that originally put the "sol" in the Costa del Sol in the 1950s.
> The worst beaches—mainly pebbles and shingles—are at Nerja,
> Málaga, and Almuñécar. Moving westward, you encounter the gritty,
> grayish sands of Torremolinos. The best beaches here are at El
> Bajondillo and La Carihuela (which borders an old fishing village).
> Another good stretch of beach is along the meandering strip between
> Carvajal, Los Boliches, and Fuengirola. In addition, two good
> beaches—El Fuerte and La Fontanilla—lie on either side of Marbella.
> However, all these beaches tend to be overcrowded, especially in July
> and August. Crowding is worst on Sundays May to October when
> beaches are overrun with family picnickers and sunbathers.
> All public beaches in Spain are free, and you shouldn't expect
> changing facilities. There might be a cold shower on the major
> beaches—but that's it.
> Although it's not sanctioned or technically allowed by the govern-
> ment, many women go topless on the beaches. Nudity is common on
> some of the less frequented beaches, although it is against the law. If
> you take off your suit, you could be arrested by the civil guard. Many
> bathers flout the law and go nude anyway, but it's not advised. If you
> want to bare it all, head for the **Costa Natura,** about 3km (2 miles)
> west of Estepona. This is the site of the only official nudist colony
> along the Costa del Sol.

in an Andalusian style, with good beds and bathrooms with tub/shower combos.
A fourth-floor drawing room provides a panoramic view of the Rock.

Av. de la Marina 2–3, 11201 Algeciras. © **95-665-46-61.** Fax 95-665-45-01. www.eh.etursa.es/almar. 192
units. 74€–76€ ($89–$91) double; 77€–79€ ($92–$95) suite. Rates include buffet breakfast. AE, DC, MC,
V. Parking 7€ ($8.40). **Amenities:** Restaurant; bar; babysitting; laundry service/dry cleaning; rooms for those
w/limited mobility. *In room:* A/C, TV, dataport, hair dryer, safe.

Hotel Octavio   Conveniently located in the center of town near the railway
station, the Octavio is our second choice after the Reina Cristina (and slightly
more affordable). Last renovated in 2003, the good-size rooms are nicely furnished and well maintained, with excellent beds and bathrooms with
tub/shower combos.

San Bernardo 1, 11207 Algeciras. © **95-665-27-00.** Fax 95-665-28-02. 77 units. 90€–125€ ($108–$150)
double; 200€–250€ ($240–$300) suite. AE, DC, MC, V. Parking 10€ ($12). **Amenities:** Restaurant; bar; laun-
dry service/dry cleaning. *In room:* A/C, TV, dataport, minibar, hair dryer, safe.

Hotel Reina Cristina ⭐   In its own park on the southern outskirts of the city
(a 10-min. walk south of the rail and bus stations), this is the town's leading
hotel, having hosted over the years everyone from Sir Winston Churchill to
Franklin D. Roosevelt, along with a lot of World War II spies. A Victorian building accented with turrets, ornate railings, and a facade painted with pastels, the
Reina Cristina offers a view of the faraway Rock of Gibraltar. On the premises

are a small English-language library and a semitropical garden. The comfortable, high-ceilinged rooms have excellent furnishings, including comfortable beds and bathrooms with tub/shower combos.

Paseo de la Conferencia s/n, 11207 Algeciras. ℂ **95-660-26-22.** Fax 95-660-33-23. www.reinacristina.com. 188 units. 105€–132€ ($126–$158) double; 171€–178€ ($205–$214) suite. Rates include breakfast. AE, DC, MC, V. Free parking. **Amenities:** 2 restaurants; 2 bars; 2 pools; tennis courts; sauna; room service; babysitting; laundry service/dry cleaning. *In room:* A/C, TV, hair dryer (in some), safe.

WHERE TO DINE

Because Algeciras is not known for its restaurants, many visitors dine at their hotels instead of taking a chance at the dreary little spots along the waterfront.

Montes SPANISH/ANDALUSIAN   This is no more than a little port-side eatery, but it's the most popular and the most serviceable joint in town. Throughout the afternoon and deep into the night, the casual diner is filled with foreign travelers, most of whom are either returning or going to Morocco on one of the ferries. You can fill up on nearly 30 varieties of freshly made tapas, most of them fish or vegetable based. The fresh catch of the day is always featured on the menu, usually fried, although it can be stewed. One of the chef's specialties is a very filling paella studded with shellfish. Among the meat dishes, the baby beef roast is the perennial favorite.

Calle Juan Morrison 27. ℂ **95-665-42-07.** Main courses 9.65€–30€ ($12–$36). MC, V. Daily noon–5pm and 7:30pm–midnight.

2 Gibraltar

20km (12 miles) E of Algeciras, 77km (48 miles) SW of Marbella

Where else would you find a town that is also a country? Gibraltar is only 5.8 sq. km (2¼ sq. miles) in size, but it has its own airport, currency, postage stamps, naval and military garrisons, two cathedrals, its own newspapers, radio, and TV—and a casino. "The Rock" enjoys a pleasant climate and has a recorded history dating from A.D. 711 and traces of cave occupation 40,000 years ago.

The Rock of Gibraltar is a massive limestone rock rising out of the sea to a height of 425m (1,396 ft.), and is often referred to as the Gateway to the Mediterranean. It was originally a Phoenician trading post called Calpe. In Greek mythology it was the northern bastion of the Pillars of Hercules. Abyla (now Jebel Musa at Ceuta) was the southern bastion. Hercules is said to have stood with a foot on each "pillar," pushed them apart, and formed a bridge across the straits. During Phoenician domination of the Mediterranean, it was recorded that Calpe was the end of the world, the point beyond which no trader should venture.

In 711, a Berber called Tariq ibn-Ziyad landed and named the Rock Gibel Tarik (mountain of Tarik), from which the name of Gibraltar is derived. The Rock was captured from the Moors in 1309 by the marauding Guzman El Bueno, then recaptured by the Moors in 1333. In 1462 Spain seized and fortified the Rock against further attack but, in 1704, during the Spanish War of Succession, a joint Anglo-Dutch fleet, under the command of Prince George of Hesse Darnstadt, made a surprise attack, capturing the fortress with little opposition.

The Spanish and the French have since made attempts to conquer the Rock by siege, bombardment, tunneling, and, finally, with specially reinforced ships, upon which the British rained red-hot cannon balls which set the ships afire.

There have been three treaties confirming Gibraltar as a British possession—Utrecht, 1713; Seville, 1727; and Versailles, 1783. In two world wars, the Rock was invaluable in keeping the Mediterranean open in spite of aerial bombardment. Its only land frontier—referred to by many Gibraltarians as the Garlic Wall—was closed by the Spaniards in 1966, in an attempt to enforce Spanish sovereignty on the people. The Spanish finally banned all trade to Gibraltar in 1969 in an attempt to bring further pressure to bear. But the Gibraltarians, in a free vote, decided by 12,138 to 44 to remain under British rule.

The Franco government closed the gate to Gibraltar, creating a blockade and causing much hardship for people on both sides of the frontier. The closure lasted from 1969 to 1985. Under King Juan Carlos, the frontier was reopened to visitors entering from Spain. "Gib," its nickname, is today a major offshore financial center.

Two languages are spoken, English and Spanish. The community is made up of Gibraltarians, Britons, Spaniards, and a few Italians and Indians. More recently, Moroccans have taken over many of the jobs.

The town of Gibraltar lies on the west side of the Rock around the harbors. You can visit the top attractions in 3 to 4 hours. Most visitors, however, allot a full day.

ESSENTIALS

GETTING THERE If you're **driving** to Gibraltar, you arrive first in the Spanish town of La Línea. From the western part of the Costa del Sol, take the N-340 east toward La Línea, turning south at the signpost into town. If you are in the eastern Costa del Sol—say Estepona or Marbella—follow N-340 southwest to the turnoff for La Línea. Park your car and proceed through Customs, crossing the border into Gibraltar.

Warning: If you decide to take your rented car into Gibraltar, expect long delays at the border. Spain, as if by deliberate policy, doesn't make the border crossing into Gibraltar easy.

There are no **buses** that take you right into Gibraltar from the Costa del Sol. However, all the major towns on the coast are linked to La Línea, the Spanish border town. The most frequent run is from Algeciras and takes 40 minutes. Departures are daily every half-hour from 7:45am to 10:15pm; a one-way fare costs 1.55€ ($1.85).

You can also fly directly from London to Gibraltar (with no touchdown in Spain) on **British Airways** (© 350-793-00). The flight takes 2½ hours from London, and there are two planes per day. Flights cost from £170 to £235 ($281–$388) one-way. For more information, call the **Gibraltar Airport** at © 350-730-26.

Whether you arrive by car or bus, once you clear Spanish customs and then Gibraltar customs, bus no. 9 or 10 will take you into the center of town or to the base of the funicular station, where you'll be taken "upstairs" to see the major attractions of the "rock nation," all of which tower over Gibraltar (see below). For bus information and schedules, call **Empressa Portillo,** Av. Virgen del Carmen 15 (© **95-665-43-04**) in Algeciras. A one-way trip costs .70€ (85¢).

If you're walking, go left onto Avenue Winston Churchill when the road forks with Corral Lane.

GETTING AROUND Since driving is difficult, you can explore Gibraltar on foot, by cable car, by bus, or by inexpensive taxi tour. Bus nos. 9 and 10, which are caught at the border, are used mainly from getting from one point to another in Gibraltar. Once you've reached either the town or the top of the cable-car

Gibraltar

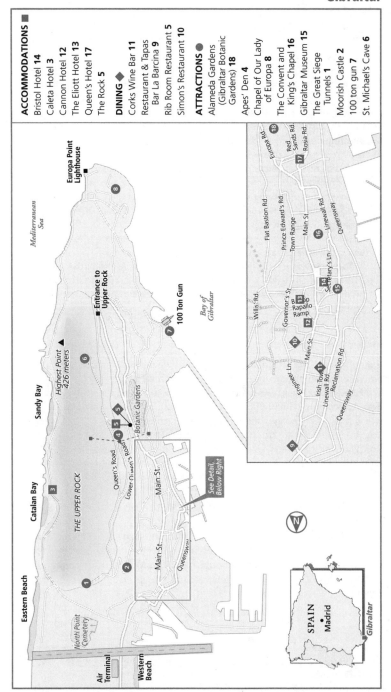

ACCOMMODATIONS ■
Bristol Hotel **14**
Caleta Hotel **3**
Cannon Hotel **12**
The Eliott Hotel **13**
Queen's Hotel **17**
The Rock **5**

DINING ◆
Corks Wine Bar **11**
Restaurant & Tapas Bar La Barcina **9**
Rib Room Restaurant **5**
Simon's Restaurant **10**

ATTRACTIONS ●
Alameda Gardens (Gibraltar Botanic Gardens) **18**
Apes' Den **4**
Chapel of Our Lady of Europa **8**
The Convent and King's Chapel **16**
Gibraltar Museum **15**
The Great Siege Tunnels **1**
Moorish Castle **2**
100 ton gun **7**
St. Michael's Cave **6**

Eastern Beach

Catalan Bay

Sandy Bay

Mediterranean Sea

Europa Point Lighthouse

Highest Point 426 meters ▲

THE UPPER ROCK

Entrance to Upper Rock

100 Ton Gun

Bay of Gibraltar

Queen's Road

Lower Queen's Road

Botanic Gardens

Main St.

Main St.

Queensway

See Detail, Below Right

North Point Cemetery

Air Terminal

Western Beach

Queensway

SPAIN
Madrid •
Gibraltar

Europa Rd.
Red Sands Rd.
Rosia Rd.
Flat Bastion Rd.
Prince Edward's Rd.
Town Range
Main St.
Linewall Rd.
Queensway
Willis' Rd.
Secretary's Ln.
Governor's St.
Bishop Rapallo Ramp
Main St.
Engineer Ln.
Irish Town
Linewall Rd.
Reclamation Rd.
Queensway

Cultural Conflicts in a British Colony

Gibraltar is a disconcerting and sometimes uncomfortable place. It's not quite British, but neither is it Spanish. Gibraltar is actually a self-governing British colony, even though Spain continues its relentless push to take over the country.

Cultural conflicts are an ongoing embarrassment, and the presence of such a strong British military presence is a direct and sometimes insulting reminder of humiliations endured by Napoleonic Spain in regimes past. References to Lord Nelson and British colonialism are evident almost everywhere you look, and somehow, the allure of Merrie Olde England rings hollow in the blazing south Iberian sun. And there's just a whiff of British-derived hooliganism in some of the earthier pubs.

If for some reason you're nostalgic for the heady days of Queen Victoria and the British Empire, rest assured that you'll find more fish and chips platters and more pints of bitter per capita than anywhere else along the Mediterranean.

To many visitors, Gibraltar is a tourist trap. One British expat who lives in Marbella told us, "I cross the border for the day just to stock up on duty-free tobacco and liquor. Then before the sun sets, I'm back in Spain."

station, you can explore on foot. If you plan to use the buses frequently, you can purchase an unlimited day pass right on the bus for 2€ ($2.40.)

The most convenient way to explore the Rock is in a taxi operated by **Gibraltar Taxi Association** (© **350-700-27** or 350-700-52). The drivers know the terrain well and can easily navigate the twisting, narrow streets. For only £7 ($12), they'll take you to all the major attractions. A minimum of four participates in these tours, which last about 1½ hours. Of course, if you want to see everything, more extensive tours can be arranged. Your group can either select the so-called "Official Rock Tour" or create your own tour based on our recommendations below.

You can catch a taxi at the stands at the Gibraltar/La Línea frontier or in the center of town at such points as Cathedral Square, Coach Park, Casemates, and Piazza–Town Centre.

VISITOR INFORMATION For tourist information go to the **Duke of Kent House,** Cathedral Square (© 350-749-50), where you'll encounter the most unhelpful staff on the Iberian peninsula. Hours are Monday to Friday 9am to 5:30pm. There's a small information booth at the Spanish border open daily 7am to 10pm.

FAST FACTS: Gibraltar

Area Code When calling Gibraltar from Spain, the area code is **9567**. But when calling from another country, such as the U.K., the code is **350**.

Bookshop & Newspaper The Gibraltar Bookshop, 300 Main St. (© **350-718-94**), is the biggest and best stocked in the colony, with many different

English newspapers and the most complete section of books about Gibraltar on display anywhere.

Currency Euros are accepted in most of the shops, but expect a bad exchange rate, however. In lieu of euros, you can use British pounds, or the Rock's own sterling government notes.

Dentists If you have a dental emergency, contact the **Dental Care Center,** 216 Main St. (✆ **350-788-44**).

Emergencies For an ambulance or in case of fire , dial ✆ **190;** for a police emergency, dial ✆ **112** or 199.

Internet Access **The PC Clinic,** 17 Convent Place (✆ **350-499-91;** www.pc-clinic-gib.com), about a block uphill from Main Street, charges £3 ($4.95) per hour.

Hospital For medical services, including emergencies, go to **St. Bernard's Hospital** on Hospital Hill (✆ **350-797-00**).

Pharmacy **Calpe Pharmacy,** 232 Main St. (✆ **350-772-31**), is one of the most visible in the colony. If you happen to have an emergency, the owner publishes his home phone (✆ **350-785-07**) for after-hours assistance, and also posts the address and phone of other pharmacies with different opening hours.

Post Office The **Gibraltar post office** lies at 104 Main St. (✆ **350-756-62**) and is open June to mid-September Monday to Friday 9am to 2:15pm, Saturday 10am to 1pm. Off-season hours are Monday to Friday 9am to 4:30pm and Saturday 10am to 1pm. All charges must be paid in British pounds sterling.

EXPLORING GIBRALTAR

If you're pressed for time, we suggest you bypass most of the attractions of Gibraltar and concentrate instead on **The Upper Rock Nature Preserve** ★★★, accessible from Jews' Gate, where you will find: St. Michael's Cave, the Apes Den, the Great Siege Tunnels, and the ruins of the old Moorish Castle. All of these attractions are open daily from 9:30am to 6:30pm. A combination ticket to the attractions costs £7.50 ($13) and includes the price of the one-way cable car to the Upper Rock. You can purchase a ticket for only the cable car if you wish, a round-trip ticket going for £6.50 ($11), £5 ($8.25) one-way, but individual tickets to the attractions. The cable-car departure point is signposted near the eastern end of Main Street in the center of Gibraltar. Cable cars (✆ **350-778-26**) depart every 10 minutes form 9:30am to 5:15pm, with the last return at 5:45 pm.

The cable car stops first at the **Apes Den** ★, along Old Queen's Road. Here you can see the famous Barbary apes cavorting on the sides of rocks. Despite their name, they aren't really apes but cinnamon-colored tail-less monkeys (macques). Legend has it that the first monkeys were either brought in by the Moors or that they found their way through a tunnel that linked St. Michael's Cave with Africa. Regular mealtimes—the monkeys are fed daily at 8am and 4pm by a member of the Gibraltar Regiment—have helped to stop their descending to the town for food. The monkeys are carefully tended and protected by the British, since they have a saying, "When the apes leave the Rock, so will the British."

The other two major attractions here are located in opposite directions from the Apes Den. To reach **St. Michael's Cave** 🛇, you have to walk east along Queen's Road. The caves are a natural grotto whose magnificent auditorium is used for concerts and live performances. The lower cave and lake, reached by guided tour, are connected to the Upper Cave (open to the public) by a passage spanning the 15 to 45m (50- to 150-ft.) difference in depth. A labyrinth of passages has formed naturally in the porous rock and it's possible for even an amateur to travel miles underground.

The final of the big three attractions, **The Great Siege Tunnels** 🛇 lie at the western end of the Nature Preserve, facing Spain. To reach them, you have to walk west along Queen's Road, bypassing the Apes Den.

There are fine observation points along the road with views over the harbor and toward Spain. At the end of the road you reach The Upper Galleries, now known as The Great Siege Tunnels. These are not picture galleries but large tunnels hewn in solid rock which are used mostly as vantage points for guns hauled up to the Rock to protect it from the Spanish mainland. The tunnels were carved out during the Great Siege of 1779 to 1782. Governor Lord Napier entertained Ulysses S. Grant, the former U.S. president, in 1878, with a banquet here in St. George's Hall.

Directly south of the tunnels lie the ruins of the **Moorish Castle,** which you can skip if you're short of time. It was constructed by the descendants of Tariq who captured the Rock in 711. The nearby **Tower of Homage** dates from 1333, dominating the only land entrance to Gibraltar. The tower and adjoining walls are floodlit at night, a dramatic sight for passengers on ships sailing through the Straits of Gibraltar. Little remains of the original castle, other than parts of its outer walls running between the castle, the harbor, and the ancient Moorish Pier.

Most day-trippers end their sightseeing of Gibraltar at this point. Those who want to make a full day of it return to the Apes Den and take the cable car back down into the center of Gibraltar, where they can explore some of the city attractions. A few hearty souls walk down the mountain, some of them spending as much as 2 hours doing so.

Once you reach the heart of town you can cover the attractions immediately below on foot.

The Gibraltar Museum, Bomb House Lane (© **350-742-89**), is installed in a 14th-century Muslim bathhouse. The museum lies close to the Roman Catholic cathedral, just off Main Street. To anyone intrigued with the history of the Rock, the exhibits are fascinating. There is a large-scale model of the Rock, showing every dwelling existing in 1865, plus the land reclamations since then. There is also a reproduction of the famous "Gibraltar woman," the ancient skull discovered in 1848 in Forbes's Quarry. Other exhibits depict the history, from prehistoric cave-dwelling days to the present. There is a mass of artifacts, cannon balls, weapons, and military uniforms. Charging £2 ($3.30) for admission, the museum is open Monday to Friday 10am to 6pm and on Saturday 10am to 2pm.

The **Convent and King's Chapel,** Main Street, is the official residence of the governor, Queen Elizabeth's representative on Gibraltar. The Changing of the Guard takes place every Monday at 10:30am—a ceremonial occasion with the full band and the governor and his family on the balcony to take the salute. The convent was named in 1531 when a wealthy Spaniard gave the Franciscan friars land, materials, and money to erect a convent and a chapel for the burial of himself and his family. There is no sign today of their graves. King's Chapel is open to view, but the convent, a private home, is not. There is a 1,000-year-old

Dragon Tree standing on the grounds that you can see if you look down the hill behind the Roman Catholic cathedral.

Main Street, which means what it says, runs from Casemates Square, the street proceeding between old buildings and modern stores past the Main Post Office and on to the Piazza, a colonnaded entrance to a paved square where people drink, children play, and desultory business is conducted.

A wander among the narrow lanes and streets leading into Main Street will give you a sense of the past. You come next to the square facing the impressive Roman Catholic **cathedral,** a converted mosque and one of the first buildings on the Rock. Then it's on to Cathedral Square where the Anglican Cathedral faces a green garden and the harbor.

Just outside the town gate, where there was once a drawbridge and a moat, is the **Trafalgar Cemetery,** a charming garden blazing with geraniums. Tombstones commemorate many who fell in the battles of Algeciras, Trafalgar, Cádiz, and Málaga in the early years of the 19th century.

For a final look at Gibraltar, many visitors like to head out to **Europa Point**, called by many visitors "the end of Europe." Europa Point can either be a stop on your taxi tour or you can reach it from the center of Gibraltar via bus no. 3 or 1B from Line Wall Road, lying just on Main Street. Departures are every 15 minutes during the day, costing 70p (90¢) one-way.

The most southerly point in Europe is actually **Tarifa** (p. 278), which is in Spain and can be viewed in the distance. Europa Point was one of the two ancient Pillars of Hercules. The other so-called pillar is 23km (14 miles) across the Straits of Gibraltar in North Africa. At Europa Point is the **lighthouse** built in 1841 by Trinity House, the general lighthouse and pilotage authority for Great Britain, incorporated in 1514 by Henry VIII.

Standing by the lighthouse, you can see across the straits to the west of Ceuta to Jebel Musa (formerly Mount Abyla), the other Pillar of Hercules. Here also is Lloyd's of London's only foreign spotting station, recording every merchant ship entering or leaving the Mediterranean.

On Europa Road, back toward the town and east of the Rock, stands the **Chapel of Our Lady of Europa.** This chapel is much venerated and often saluted by passing vessels. Before the lighthouse was built, the small chapel kept a light burning day and night to warn vessels of the treacherous passage. This small Catholic chapel, converted in 1462, was once a mosque. Today there is a small museum with a 1462 statue of the Madonna and some artifacts. Admission free, the chapel can be entered Monday to Friday 10am to 7pm.

SHOPPING

Golden Eagle Liquors Come here for a good selection of Spanish, French, Italian, and Australian wines, and an even better selection of the kinds of whiskeys that made the British Empire function. Like virtually everything else in Gibraltar, the venue is cross-cultural, and you'll almost certainly find the kinds of liquors you like. 286 Main St. © 350-759-13.

Marks & Spencer In a colony that's as English as Gibraltar obviously is, stumbling across a well-lit branch of Britain's most omnipresent department store chain doesn't exactly come as a surprise. This one is appropriately air-conditioned and appropriately loaded with an abbreviated but still very British collection of men's and women's clothing. Yes, you can buy an umbrella, a Burberry raincoat, and all manner of headgear, as well as porcelain from Wedgwood and English marmalade made with (guess what?) Spanish oranges. Be alert to the fact that this particular store appears in two separate branches along the same street, almost immediately adjacent to one another. 235 and 215 Main St. ℂ 350-758-57.

WHERE TO STAY

Accommodations in Gibraltar are limited and tend to be more expensive in general than those along the Costa del Sol. During the summer, advance reservations are strongly recommended.

Bristol Hotel   In the center of Gibraltar, this is a colonial-style hotel with a subtropical garden and a swimming pool. This bright, white-painted building lies on a pretty square opposite the Anglican church. From the rooms, panoramic views open onto the bay. For the most part, bedrooms are spacious and exceedingly comfortable. Prices of bedrooms depend on whether the accommodations face outward or to the interior. The majority of bedrooms have twin beds, though some family rooms (two adults and two children) are available.

10 Cathedral Sq., Gibraltar. ℂ **350-768-00.** Fax 350-776-13. www.gib.gi/bristolhotel/bedrooms.html. 60 units. £64–£69 ($106–$114) double; £74–£81 ($122–$134) suite. DC, MC, V. **Amenities:** Restaurant; bar; outdoor pool; laundry service; nonsmoking rooms; rooms for those w/limited mobility. *In room:* A/C, TV, dataport, hair dryer, iron/ironing board.

Caleta Hotel ⋆   This rather upmarket choice, Gibraltar's largest hotel, lies at the end of the bay on the eastern side of the Rock. A holiday hotel, it was built on the rocks over the sea with sun terraces and a swimming pool with steps down to the water. Most of the bedrooms have balconies overlooking the water. The bedrooms are attractively and comfortably furnished, each with a tiled bathroom with a tub or shower. The hotel enjoys private access to a small, sheltered sandy beach overlooking both the Spanish and North African coastlines. A grace note is the hotel's small and leafy English garden with nice views. Its Italian dining room is one of the best hotel restaurants on the Rock and the English bar here is a cozy retreat for a pint.

Sir Herbert Miles Rd., Catalan Bay, Gibraltar. ℂ **350-765-01.** Fax 350-710-50. www.caletahotel.com. 169 units. £110–£160 ($182–$264) double. Winter reductions. AE, DC, MC, V. **Amenities:** Restaurant; bar; outdoor pool; gym; 24-hr. room service; babysitting; laundry service; nonsmoking rooms. *In room:* TV, dataport, minibar, hair dryer, safe, beverage maker.

Cannon Hotel   Owned and operated by Joe Bossano, one of the former chief ministers of Gibraltar, this informal downtown hotel occupies an old-fashioned 19th-century house on a narrow lane a few steps north of Main Street. Don't expect grandeur, as everything is very English-pubby-style, with a reception desk a few steps from the bar top, a lobby-cum-drinking area where everyone sees and hears everything. The staff, though not technically English Cockney, evokes the style and speech patterns of some of the gang members of Fagin's 19th-century London. Rooms are very simple at this government-rated one-star hotel. The midsize units are light and airy with twin beds.

9 Cannon Lane, Gibraltar. ℂ **350-517-11.** Fax 350-517-89. www.cannonhotel.gl. 18 units. £37 ($60) double without bathroom; £45 ($74) double with bathroom. Rates include English breakfast. MC, V. **Amenities:** Restaurant; bar; nonsmoking rooms. *In room:* No phone.

The Eliott Hotel ⋆⋆   An old Holiday Inn has been converted into this winning choice on a delightful tree-lined square in the Old Town. Bedrooms are among Gibraltar's finest, each furnished with contemporary, comfortable pieces. Most of the rooms open onto the Straits of Gibraltar and beyond to North Africa. The Palm Court and the Victoria Garden restaurant are among the

Rock's better dining choices, with both international and Mediterranean specialties, backed up by a *carte* of regional wines. The tinkling sounds of a grand piano can be heard in the Veranda Bar at night. The highlight of the hotel is its rooftop pool and sun terrace, with panoramic views.

Governor's Parade, Gibraltar. © **350-705-00.** Fax 350-702-43. www.gib.gi/eliotthotel.com. 114 units. £175–£185 ($289–$305) double; £205–£310 ($338–$512) suite. AE, DC, MC, V. **Amenities:** 2 restaurants; 2 bars; outdoor pool; gym; sauna; 24-hr. room service; nonsmoking rooms; rooms for those w/limited mobility. *In room:* A/C, TV, dataport, hair dryer, safe, beverage maker, trouser press.

Queen's Hotel   This is hardly our favorite hotel in Gibraltar, but on the overcrowded Rock it might come in handy in a pinch. Queen's Hotel is close to the bottom station of the cable car that travels to the top of the Rock. It's a rather plain, tall building in an area that gets heavy traffic. The furnishings are very dark and Spanish, with regional artifacts scattered about. Bedrooms are midsize and comfortably, though not stylishly, furnished. The high-ceilinged lobby is genteel but a bit shabby. Public rooms include a spacious lounge, a bar, and a sun terrace. The major drawback here is the staff's attitude, among the worst we've encountered in Gibraltar. The main shopping center, Main Street, is a short walk away.

1 Boyd St., Gibraltar. © **350-740-00.** Fax 350-400-30. www.queenshotel.gi. 60 units. £40–£70 ($66–$116) double; £85 ($140) family room for 4; £95 ($157) suite. Rates include English breakfast. AE, DC, MC, V. Free parking. **Amenities:** Restaurant; bar; babysitting; laundry service. *In room:* A/C, TV, hair dryer.

The Rock ★★   This is one of the Mediterranean's most famous hotels and clearly the best in Gibraltar. This long-enduring favorite is set in a beautiful 3.6-hectare (9-acre) landscaped garden on the Rock's sunny western side with panoramic views of the Spanish coastline and North Africa. It's the place for the British traditionalist dreaming of lost colonial empires. There are nature walks through the geranium-bright gardens, as well as a wisteria-covered terrace for a sundowner. Built by the marquis of Bute in 1932, the hotel offers spacious and attractively refurbished bedrooms in the colonial style. From some balconies you can see the Rif Mountains in Morocco. Rooms have more amenities than any hotel on the Rock, including bathrobes and the like. The use of bamboo and ceiling fans add to the *Casablanca*-like atmosphere. Bathrooms are old-fashioned but work just fine, each with a large tub/shower combo.

3 Europa Rd., Gibraltar. © **350-730-00.** Fax 350-735-13. www.blandgroup.gi. 143 units. £180 ($297) double; £230 ($380) suite. AE, DC, MC, V. **Amenities:** Restaurant; bar; outdoor pool; 24-hr. room service; laundry service/dry cleaning; nonsmoking rooms; casino. *In room:* A/C, TV, hair dryer, beverage maker, trouser press.

WHERE TO DINE

Corks Wine Bar   This place long ago abandoned the practice of serving glasses of rare vintage wine. Today, it's a bustling, sometimes raucous, English-style pub, with a busy lunch business, and a bar list that includes beer and whiskeys, but not a lot of wine. The few wines that are served cost from £1 to £2.50 ($1.65–$4.15) per glass. It's one of the preferred venues for Gibraltar's business community, who appreciate the free tapas (the selection changes daily) served every day from 5 to 9pm. You'll find up to five kinds of beer on tap here, with pints selling for £2 ($3.30) each; Friday nights, a DJ spins danceable music to a clientele that includes sailors from a variety of ports, worldwide, but especially England.

79 Irish Town. © **350-755-66.** Lunch main courses £6.50–£7.25 ($11–$12). AE, MC, V. Mon–Sat 9am–2am. Hot food Mon–Sat noon–3:30pm.

Restaurant & Tapas Bar La Barcina   Pleasant and with a staff that usually copes gracefully with the crowds, this restaurant occupies a tucked-away corner of a pedestrian-only landmark square on Main Street. It combines an indoor tapas bar with lots of outdoor tables positioned on the gently sloping terrain of the square. The best menu items include a spicy Iberian fish stew, a house steak in a mustard-flavored cream sauce, a collection of grilled fish that includes Dover sole imported from English waters, and a savory array of tapas.

Casemates Sq. ℂ 350-411-00. Main courses £6–£12 ($9.90–$19). MC, V. Daily 10am–11pm. Closed Sun July–Aug.

Rib Room Restaurant ✰✰ INTERNATIONAL   In prestigious The Rock Hotel, this is the single finest dining room on Gibraltar. From your table, you can enjoy panoramic views across the bay to the Spanish coastline and Morocco. Chefs feature both an a la carte menu as well as a daily changing menu. The seafood is fresh, and other top-quality dishes include pan-roasted filet of lamb with a basil salsa, and a delectable seared filet of beef served with grilled baby leeks and a truffle foie gras. The starters are especially appealing and imaginative; we loved the pumpkin and pancetta risotto and the wok-seared black pepper beef with asparagus and a charred pineapple salad. For dessert, try chocolate soufflé pancakes with cold vanilla custard.

In The Rock Hotel, 3 Europa Rd. ℂ 350-730-00. Reservations required. Fixed-price menu £23 ($38); main courses £20–£25 ($33–$41). AE, DC, MC, V. Daily 7–10pm.

THE ROCK AFTER DARK

The bustle on Main Street, with "downtown" Gibraltar's densest concentration of shops, dies down when the shops close. After dark, the scene migrates 1 block south of Main Street's western end to a parallel street known formally as Irish Town, and informally as "Back Street."

Two of the best bars here are **The Clipper,** 78B Irish Town (ℂ **350-797-91**), and **The Royal Oak,** 59C Irish Town (ℂ **350-717-08**), both of which have decor dotted with engravings of clipper ships and memorabilia of the Royal Navy, foaming pints of beer, and shots of whiskey. Both serve English breakfasts throughout the day and evening, jacket potatoes stuffed in ways you'd expect from a local neighborhood pub in the Midlands, sandwiches, and such main courses—priced at £5 ($8.25) each—as steak and kidney pie or beef Stroganoff.

Other recommended pubs are **All's Well,** Grand Casemates Square (ℂ **350-729-87**), known for its Bass beers and steak and ale pie; **The Star Bar,** Parliament Lane (ℂ **350-759-24**), said to be the oldest bar in Gib; and **Lord Nelson Bar Brasserie,** 10 Casemates Sq. (ℂ **350-500-09**), done out to represent Nelson's ship with a cloud and sky ceiling crossed with beams, containing a spacious terrace.

Gamblers can check out **Ladbrokes Casino,** 7 Europa Rd. (ℂ **350-766-66**), which requires smart casual dress. Its cocktail bar is open daily from 7:30pm to 4am, and the gaming room is open from 9pm to 4am. Roulette, baccarat, craps, blackjack, boule, and chemin der fer are played here. There is a wide terrace overlooking the lights of the harbor.

3 Estepona

85km (53 miles) W of Málaga, 639km (397 miles) S of Madrid, 46km (29 miles) E of Algeciras

A town of Roman origin and the most westerly of the coast's burgeoning fishing villages, Estepona hasn't yet been completely taken over by high-rises. Less developed than either Marbella or Torremolinos and with a more Spanish feel than expat-heavy Marbella, it is more likable than either. It still has an old quarter of narrow cobblestone streets and dozens of tascas.

Traces of the past remain: a round tower constructed to protect the villagers from the raids of Barbary pirates, who took not only all valuables, including food, but the most beautiful women as well.

Today, Estepona's recreational port is an attraction, as are its beaches: Costa Natura Km 257 on the N-340, the first legal nude beach of its kind along the Costa del Sol; La Rada, 3km (2 miles) long; and El Cristo, only 550m (1,800 ft.) long. After the sun goes down, stroll along the Paseo Marítimo, a broad avenue with gardens on one side, beach on the other. Estepona also contains an interesting 15th-century parish church, with the ruins of an old aqueduct nearby (at Salduba).

ESSENTIALS

GETTING THERE   The nearest **rail** links are in Fuenginola. However, Estepona is on the **bus** route from Algeciras to Málaga. If you're driving, head east from Algeciras along the E-5/N-340.

VISITOR INFORMATION   The **tourist office,** Av. San Lorenzo 1 (© **95-280-20-02;** www.infoestepona.com), is open Monday to Friday 9am to 8pm, Saturday 10am to 1:30pm.

WHERE TO STAY

Estepona offers four of the top resorts along the Costa del Sol, the ultimate in (government-rated) five-star living. If you want the most idyllic, the most luxurious, and the grandest, stay at the Sofitel Las Dunas, although all of the top hotels are luxe all the way.

What's missing in Estepona are the cheap concrete block bunkers catering to package tours. If you're a frugal traveler who really wants "the beach on a budget," head for Torremolinos. It's not as grand but a lot easier on your wallet.

EXPENSIVE

Andalucia Princess ✿   Although we don't like this place quite as much as Las Dunas, Kempinski, and the Costa del Sol Princess, it's still well run, well groomed, and inviting. The Andalucía Princess burst onto the scene back in the early '80s and was upgraded in 2000. Convenient to the beach, it lies about 500m (1,640 ft.) from the sea and 8km (5 miles) from the heart of Estepona. The decor is traditional Mediterranean, with much use of sky-blue colors and gleaming white. Bedrooms are small to midsize, each comfortably furnished, with a tiled bathroom containing tub and shower. Prices reach their zenith in July and August but if you book in here during the off season, rates are more reasonable and can even be negotiated downward. The cuisine is first-rate, though never rising to moments of inspiration.

Noreste, 29689 Estepona. © **95-280-88-33.** Fax 95-280-26-52. www.princess-hotels.com. 383 units. 200€–270€ ($240–$324) double. AE, DC, MC, V. **Amenities:** 2 restaurants; bar; 3 pools (1 indoor); tennis court; gym; sauna; room service (8am–11pm); babysitting; laundry service/dry cleaning; rooms for those w/limited mobility. *In room:* A/C, TV, dataport, minibar, hair dryer, safe.

Atalaya Park Golf Hotel & Resort ✿✿ *Kids*   Midway between Estepona and Marbella, this modern resort complex attracts sports and nature lovers. Its tranquil beachside location sits amid 8 hectares (20 acres) of subtropical gardens. Spacious rooms furnished in elegant modern style are well maintained and inviting. All units have neatly kept bathrooms with tub/shower combos. Guests have complimentary use of the hotel's extensive sports facilities, including two magnificent golf courses. Many northern Europeans check in and almost never leave the grounds.

Carretera de Cádiz Km 168.5, 29688 Estepona. ✆ **95-288-90-00**. Fax 95-288-90-02. www.atalaya-park.es. 502 units. 166€–270€ ($199–$324) double; 226€–306€ ($271–$367) suite; 345€–580€ ($414–$696) bungalow. Rates include breakfast. AE, DC, MC, V. Free parking. **Amenities:** 6 restaurants; 2 bars; nightclub (summer only); 6 outdoor pools; 2 18-hole golf courses; 9 outdoor tennis courts, 6 lit; health club; nautical sports center; sauna; car-rental desk; kids club; babysitting; laundry service/dry cleaning, solarium. *In room:* A/C, TV, dataport, minibar, hair dryer, safe.

Costa del Sol Princess ★★ *Kids*

While comparable to the Andalucía Princess (see above), we'd give the Costa del Sol Princess a slight edge as far as cuisine, its bedrooms, and helpful staff go. We won't pretend that this is the best member of the Princess chain we've stayed at—not by a long shot. But it has a certain comfort and style, and on our latest rounds we noted a lot of happy visitors. This hotel, dating from 1985, was looking a bit tired before its wholesale renovation in 2000. Its bedrooms are midsize for the most part, furnished with contemporary furnishings and Mediterranean styling. Rooms are sunny and bright, and each comes with a tiled bathroom with tub and shower. A miniclub for children with qualified supervision makes this great for families. The location is 9km (5½ miles) from the center of town.

Noreste, 29689 Estepona. ✆ **95-279-30-00**. Fax 95-280-26-52. www.princess-hotels.com. 143 units. 240€–270€ ($288–$324) double. AE, DC, MC, V. Free parking. **Amenities:** 2 restaurants; bar; 2 pools (1 indoor); children's pool; tennis court; gym; sauna; room service (8am–11pm); laundry service/dry cleaning; rooms for those w/limited mobility. *In room:* A/C, TV, dataport, minibar, hair dryer, safe.

Kempinski Resort Hotel ★★★

One of the most luxurious retreats in this part of the Costa del Sol, this modern resort hotel allows you to enjoy a lush, elegant lifestyle. Between the main coastal route and the beach, the Kempinski borrowed heavily from nearby Morocco to create this oasis of charm and grace with hanging gardens adding a dramatic touch. A member of "The Leading Hotels of the World," the property opens onto beautifully landscaped and luxuriant palm-studded gardens fronting the ocean. Bedrooms are airy and spacious, with balconies or private terraces overlooking the sea. Each comes with a deluxe bathroom with tub and shower. Many expats who live in the area flock here for the Sunday afternoon jazz brunch, the most elaborate at the western part of the Costa del Sol. Top European chefs turn out carefully crafted regional specialties and well-executed international dishes.

Carretera de Cádiz Km 159, Playa el Padrón, 29680 Estepona. ✆ **95-280-95-00**. Fax 95-280-95-50. www.kempinski-spain.com. 148 units. 325€–515€ ($390–$618) double; 590€–705€ ($708–$846) junior suite; from 755€ ($906) suite. AE, DC, MC, V. Free parking outside; 13€ ($16) garage. **Amenities:** 3 restaurants; 2 bars; 4 pools (1 indoor); outdoor unlit tennis court; fitness center; gym; spa; sauna; salon; 24-hr. room service; babysitting; laundry service/dry cleaning; nonsmoking rooms. *In room:* A/C, TV, dataport, minibar, hair dryer, safe.

Sofitel Las Dunas ★★★

One of the Costa del Sol's great resorts and a member of the "Leading Hotels of the World," Las Dunas attracts fashionable Europeans looking to be pampered. Site of a world-class spa, this five-star government-rated hotel is constructed in a U-shape, evocative of a gigantic hacienda. It stands in the midst of gardens and fountains; regrettably, the beach nearby is mediocre. Suites outnumber standard doubles, and most units have balconies overlooking the Mediterranean. All are sumptuously comfortable and equipped with roomy bathrooms containing tub/shower combos.

Urbanización La Boladilla Baja-Noreste, Carretera de Cádiz Km 163.5, 29689 Estepona. ✆ **95-279-43-45**. Fax 95-279-48-25. www.las-dunas.com. 73 units. 260€–350€ ($312–$420) double; 410€–650€

($492–$780) junior suite; 780€–2,220€ ($936–$2,664) suite. Free parking. **Amenities:** 2 restaurants; bar; outdoor pool; health club; sauna; whirlpool; spa; 24-hr. room service; babysitting; laundry service/dry cleaning; library. *In room:* A/C, TV, minibar, hair dryer, safe, Jacuzzi (in some).

MODERATE
El Paraíso Costa del Sol ⭐   The impressive El Paraíso Costa del Sol is the leading moderately priced establishment in town, lying between Marbella and Estepona in front of Costalita Beach. This modern building, constructed in the 1980s and last renovated in 2004, lies 12km (7½ miles) from the center of Estepona. The most exciting element of the bedrooms is that they open onto balconies fronting the Mediterranean. Otherwise, expect midsize to fairly spacious accommodations, furnished in a typical resort style—comfortable but not special. Guests can indulge in many activities in the area, including golf nearby. The best feature here is the panoramic bar on the seventh floor with a nudist sunning terrace. The hotel also has a children's play area, although it's hardly a reason to check in if you have kids.

Urbanización El Paraiso, Noreste, Carretera de Cádiz Km 167. ℂ 800/465-9936 in the U.S., or 95-288-30-00. Fax 95-288-20-19. www.hotelparaisocostadelsol.com. 171 units. 128€–185€ ($154–$222) double; 240€–302€ ($288–$362) suite. AE, DC, MC, V. Free parking. **Amenities:** 2 restaurants; 4 bars; 2 pools (1 indoor); children's pool; sauna; 24-hr. room service; babysitting; laundry service/dry cleaning. *In room:* A/C, TV, dataport, minibar, hair dryer, safe (for a fee).

INEXPENSIVE
Buenavista   This comfortable if modest little *residencia* beside the coastal road opened in the 1970s. The tiny rooms are likely to be noisy in summer because of heavy traffic nearby. Beds are comfortable, and the little bathrooms have shower stalls. Buses from Marbella stop nearby.

Av. de España 180, 29680 Estepona. ℂ 95-280-01-37. Fax 95-280-55-93. 38 units. 45€–60€ ($54–$72) double. MC, V. **Amenities:** Restaurant. *In room:* TV.

WHERE TO DINE
In summer, the cheapest places to eat in Estepona are the ***chiringuitos,*** little dining areas set up by local fishermen and their families right on the beach. Naturally they feature seafood, including sole and sardine kabobs grilled over an open fire. You can usually order a fresh salad and fried potatoes; desserts are simple.

La Alcaría de Ramos ⭐ *Finds* SPANISH   Your best meal in Estepona awaits at this restaurant en route to San Pedro. This country retreat has been decorated in the style of an old summerhouse along the Spanish coast. There's a beautiful terrace garden where customers may dine as weather permits. The chef and owner, José Ramos, has won many national gastronomic competitions, and has been creating intriguing variations on traditional recipes since the early 1990s. He will regale you with such dishes as *tortas de patatas* (potato cakes—yes, potato cakes, and how good they are!). Try also his *crepes de aguacate con gambas* (avocado crepes with shrimp) and his *pato asado con puré de manzana y col roja* (grilled duck with apple purée and red cabbage). Also worth ordering is the *parrillada de pescado y mariscos* (assorted grilled fish and shellfish). For dessert order his clever *helado frito con frambuesa* (fried ice cream with raspberry sauce).

Urbanización El Paraíso Vista al Mar 1, N-340 Km 167. ℂ 95-288-61-78. Reservations recommended. Main courses 9€–18€ ($11–$22). MC, V. Mon–Sat 7:30pm–midnight.

Lido ⭐⭐⭐ INTERNATIONAL   In the deluxe Sofitel Las Dunas (see above), one of the grandest and most elegant restaurants along the Costa del Sol holds forth. Panoramic views, a mammoth crystal chandelier, and romantic piano tunes set the tone at this octagonal restaurant with floor-to-ceiling windows opening onto a sheltered terrace. Expect nothing but culinary delights on the ever-changing menu. Some of the dishes evoke the Pacific Rim, others draw upon inspiration from Europe. Only the finest products are used: duck from Nantes, lamb from Provence, beef and veal from Spain's Basque country, or tender and delectable chicken from Bresse (in our view, Europe's best). Picture it: sea bass carpaccio in a basil vinaigrette, fresh lobster in delicate saffron sauce, veal sweetbreads with *fines herbes*. Two irresistible desserts are crepes with a Grand Marnier froth filling and a sauce made from blood-red oranges, or chilled lemon grass crème brûlée with chilled mocha cream and fat, juicy raspberries.

Urbanización La Boladilla Baja-Noreste, Carretera de Cádiz Km 163.5. © **95-279-43-45.** Reservations required. Main courses 20€–39€ ($24–$47); set menus 58€ ($70) for 3 courses, 80€ ($96) for 5 courses. AE, DC, MC, V. Daily 8–11pm. Closed mid-Jan to mid-Feb.

Playa Bella ANDALUSIAN/INTERNATIONAL   Though nowhere near as fine as the previously recommended restaurants, this is a good choice for a shellfish dinner near the beach, 7km (4½ miles) from the center. Waiters dash about serving the freshly caught fish and shellfish, although there is also a good selection of well-prepared meat dishes. We particularly enjoy the *arroz a la marinera* (seafood-studded rice), and you can also look for daily specials. The decor is Andalusian regional, and mostly visitors form the clientele. A well-chosen list of Andalusian wines appears on the *carte*.

Urbanización Playa-Bella Noreste. © **95-280-16-45.** Reservations recommended. Main courses 19€–30€ ($23–$36). MC, V. Daily 1–11pm. Closed Jan 8–Feb 8.

ESTEPONA AFTER DARK

The hotels often bring in flamenco dancers and musicians to entertain in the summer months. Otherwise, after-dark diversions consist mostly of hitting the tapas bar. You'll find most of them—called *freidurías* (**fried-fish bars**)—at the corner of Calle de los Reyes and La Terraza. Tables spill onto the sidewalks in summer, and *gambas a la plancha* (**shrimp**) are the most popular (but not the cheapest) tapas to order. The two best ones are **Bodega Sabor Andaluz,** Caridad 4 (© **95-279-10-30**), which has especially good seafood, and also **La Escollera,** Puerto Pesquero (© **95-280-63-54**), whose tapas are mostly based on the fresh catch of the day.

4 Puerto Banús

8km (5 miles) E of Marbella, 782km (486 miles) S of Madrid

A favorite resort for international celebrities, the coastal village of **Puerto Banús** was created almost overnight just for tourists in the traditional Mediterranean style. It's a dreamy place, the very image of what a Costa del Sol fishing village should look like, but rarely does. Yachts can be moored nearly at your doorstep. Along the harbor front you'll find an array of expensive bars and restaurants. Wandering through the quiet back streets, you'll pass archways and patios with grilles. For accommodations, you can stay at one of the resorts at Marbella (see below).

To reach the town, you can take one of 15 **buses** that run daily from Marbella or drive east from Marbella along the E-15.

WHERE TO DINE

Antonio ✿ SEAFOOD/INTERNATIONAL   There's no better place to sit and watch Puerto Banús's chic port life than this long-time favorite. Opt for a table on the terrace if the weather's right and watch a parade of beautiful people who believe in traveling the world in style.

The first-class cuisine here lives up to the setting, which has lots of modern paintings on the wall, an abundance of greenery, and predominant colors of black and white. The chef, Juan Trujillo, knows how to balance colors, textures, and flavors, creating such tasty fare as the best filet mignon we've tasted in the area, well-flavored pork chops with fries and vegetables, and a tender, moist loin of veal. However, our all-time favorite here is sea bass baked in salt to retain its moisture and aroma. A lot depends on the catch of the day. Perhaps it'll be a delectable sea bream or else grilled kabobs of *rape* (monkfish).

Muella de Ribera. ✆ **95-281-35-36**. Reservations required. Main courses 16€–28€ ($19–$34). AE, DC, MC, V. Daily 1–4pm and 7:30–11pm (until 12:30am Aug–Sept).

Aquavit ✵ *(Finds)* THAI/INTERNATIONAL When you can't face another platter of paella or bowl of gazpacho, head to this fashionably modern house for a real change of pace. Many guests indulge in one (or more) of the 50 different vodkas. If you are still standing after that, you can order some of the best and freshest tasting sushi in the area. Lobster is also available, but can be very expensive. We like to begin with a small helping of a delightful Swedish caviar, moving on to the savory Thai fish cakes or the chef's specialty, potato and anchovy gratin served with a shot of chilled Aquavit. A fresh arugula salad accompanies most platters. The decor is a bit jazzy with handcrafted and illuminated tables among other touches.

Plaza del Puerto, Puerto Banús. ✆ **95-281-91-27**. Reservations recommended. Main courses 19€–30€ ($23–$36). AE, MC, V. Tues–Sun 6pm–midnight.

Cipriano ✵✵ SEAFOOD/MEDITERRANEAN Serving the finest food at the port, this deluxe restaurant is the number-one choice of the rich and sometimes famous who arrive in Puerto Banús on multimillion-dollar yachts. Near the beach, it's in a modern building, like everything else at this posh port. Cipriano is divided into several sections for maximum privacy. Each is luxuriously decorated in an Andalusian style, with lots of elegant fabrics and many colors. There is a casual, semiformal atmosphere among the well-heeled guests.

We recently dined here with a princess from some long-forgotten kingdom in Eastern Europe, who demanded that all the table order lobster with champagne and green peppers. Although that dish was terrific, we can also highly recommend the paella Cipriano and the medley of shellfish. You can also order a perfectly grilled, tender entrecote in a zesty pepper sauce, followed by one of the freshly made desserts of the day, such as baked apple with cinnamon ice cream.

Edificio de Sevilla, Av. Playas del Duque. ✆ **95-281-10-77**. Reservations required. Main courses 19€–35€ ($23–$42); fixed-price menus 42€–118€ ($50–$142). AE, DC, MC, V. June–Sept daily 1–4pm and 8pm–midnight; off season daily 1–4pm and 7:30pm–midnight. Closed Jan 6–Feb 6.

Dalli's Pasta Factory *(Value)* PASTA The meals here, consisting of pasta, pasta, and more pasta served with garlic bread and a carafe of house wine, are a great bargain in pricey Puerto Banús. In a setting that's a cross between high-tech and Art Deco, you can order nutmeg-flavored ravioli with spinach filling, *penne all'arrabbiata,* lasagna, and several kinds of spaghetti. More filling are the chicken cacciatore and scaloppine of chicken and veal. They are served with— guess what?—a side dish of pasta. The owners, incidentally, are a trio of Roman-born brothers who were reared in England and educated in California.

Muelle de Rivera. ✆ **95-281-86-23**. Pastas 9€–14€ ($11–$17); meat platters 14€–20€ ($17–$24). AE, MC, V. Daily 1:30–4pm and 7pm–midnight.

Don Leone INTERNATIONAL Many residents in villas around Marbella drive to this luxuriously decorated dockside restaurant for dinner, and it can get crowded at times. Begin with the house minestrone, then follow with pasta in clam sauce; lasagna is also a regular treat. Meat specialties include veal parmigiana and roast baby lamb, and the fish dishes are also worth a try, especially the *frita mixta de pescados* (mixed fish fry). The food is competently prepared with fresh ingredients, although at times it fails to capture authentic Spanish flavor. The wine list is one of the best along the coast.

Muelle de Rivera 44. (𝄌 **95-281-17-16.** Reservations recommended. Main courses 15€–22€ ($18–$26). AE, MC, V. Daily 1–4pm and 8pm–midnight (June 21–Sept 21 daily 7:30pm–1:30am). Closed Nov 21–Dec 21.

5 Marbella ⭐

60km (37 miles) W of Málaga, 45km (28 miles) W of Torremolinos, 80km (50 miles) E of Gibraltar, 76km (47 miles) E of Algeciras, 600km (373 miles) S of Madrid

Although packed with visitors and only slightly less popular than Torremolinos, **Marbella** is still the chicest resort along the Costa del Sol, with some of the region's best upscale resorts coexisting with more affordable hotels. An Andalusian port at the foot of the Sierra Blanca, traces of Marbella's past survive in its palatial town hall, medieval ruins, and ancient Moorish walls. The biggest attractions in Marbella, however, are **El Fuerte** and **La Fontanilla,** the two main beaches. There are other, more secluded beaches, but you need your own transportation to get there.

Marbella's chic reputation dates from the beginning of the Eisenhower era. The Marquis don Ricardo Soriano and his nephew, Prince Alfonso Hohenlohe, started spreading the word in 1953. Soon the Duke and Duchess of Windsor and lesser mortals began arriving to see what this sleepy coastal town was all about. The Rothschilds heard about it, as did Saudi emirs. Marbella was on its way; its discovery by jet-setters bringing long-overdue prosperity.

Many resorts have better beaches and more attractions than Marbella. Which raises the question, "Why do such chic people still flock here, people who could vacation anywhere?" A local resident, Rafael Trujillo, said, "Rich people come here because other rich people come here." Marbella's fans and detractors agree on only one thing: the prices are a joke.

One can only regret not having seen Marbella in the 1960s and 1970s, even though Franco was in power. Those were the days before ugly concrete tower blocks grew up around its old quarter and fishing port. Fortunately, old Marbella with its flower-filled balconies and whitewashed houses remains delightful. Make the **Patio de los Naranjos (Court of the Orange Trees)** ⭐⭐⭐ your focal point for a night wandering the cobblestone streets of the Old Town. Here you can enjoy the fountains and cafes with sidewalk tables where you can sit back and watch the world go by.

ESSENTIALS

GETTING THERE Twenty **buses** run between Málaga and Marbella daily. Three buses each come from Madrid and Barcelona. The bus station is located on the outskirts of Marbella on Avenida Trapiche, a 5-minute ride from the center of town.

If you're driving, Marbella is the first major resort as you head east on the N-340/E-15 from Algeciras.

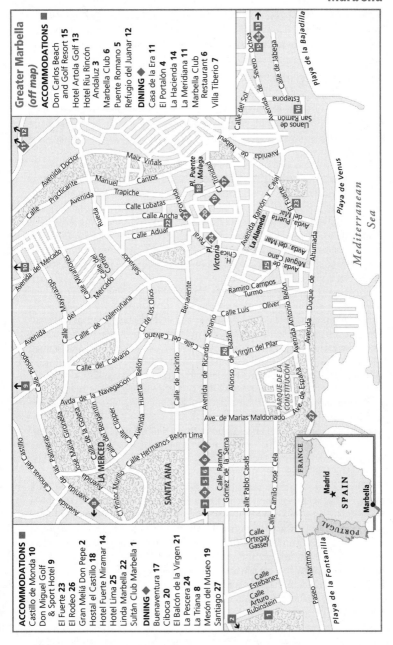

Marbella

Greater Marbella (off map)

ACCOMMODATIONS ■
Don Carlos Beach and Golf Resort **15**
Hotel Artola Golf **13**
Hotel Riu Rincón Andaluz **3**
Marbella Club **6**
Puente Romano **5**
Refugio del Juanar **12**

DINING ◆
Casa de la Era **11**
El Portalón **4**
La Hacienda **14**
La Meridiana **11**
Marbella Club Restaurant **6**
Villa Tiberio **7**

ACCOMMODATIONS ■
Castillo de Monda **10**
Don Miguel Golf & Sport Hotel **9**
El Fuerte **23**
El Rodeo **26**
Gran Meliá Don Pepe **2**
Hostal el Castillo **18**
Hotel Fuerte Miramar **14**
Hotel Lima **25**
Linda Marbella **22**
Sultán Club Marbella **1**

DINING ◆
Buenaventura **17**
Ciboca **20**
El Balcón de la Virgen **21**
La Pescera **24**
La Triana **8**
Mesón del Museo **19**
Santiago **27**

315

VISITOR INFORMATION   The **tourist office,** Glorieta de la Fontanilla s/n
(© **95-277-14-42;** www.marbella.es), is open Monday to Friday 9:30am to
9pm, Saturday 10am to 2pm. Another tourist office with the same hours is on
the Plaza de los Naranjos (© **95-282-35-50**).

ENJOYING THE BEACHES

From Guadlalamina to Cabopino, the Marbella coastline stretches for 26km (16
miles) of sunny, sandy beaches. In the post-millennium, Marbella's beaches have
been cleaned up and better landscaped with oases of palms. In some places traditional showers have been replaced with giant elephant statues spraying water
from their trunks.

Within the limits of Marbella and bordering it on either side are two equally
good beaches, **La Fontanilla** and **El Fuerte,** where the season extends from May
to October, since the shores are protected by the Sierra Blanca Mountains. These
beaches have fine golden sand and are flanked by a pedestrian promenade and
filled with hammocks, parasols, and a scattering of seaside taverns, bars, even
modest shops. Many kiosks rent sporting equipment such as sun beds and water
bikes. In summer there are lifeguards; showers and public toilets are installed.
Unfortunately, both are overcrowded in summer, because they are so convenient
to the city center.

Other good beaches include **Playa Puento Romano** lying between Hotel
Don Carlos and Hotel Puento Romano. This fine brown sand beach usually
attracts guests from the hotels. Hammocks and umbrellas are supplied and security guards from the hotels keep an eye on things. Next to Puente Romano is
Playa Nagueles, frequented by guests of the exclusive Marbella Club among
others. On the so-called "Golden Mile" of Marbella, this beach has mostly gray
sand and is flanked by a promenade. It is often very crowded, and its watersports
include windsurfing, kayaking, jet-skiing, and other activities. The beach is very
well maintained, with showers and public toilets, and it has hotel security guards
in summer.

Playa Casablanca lies between Puerto Banús and the western fringe of Marbella, connecting with La Fontanilla (see above). Jet skis, canoes, and other
equipment can be rented. There are public toilets and showers along with lifeguard towers in summer.

Playa El Baro is a small beach with brown sand that is protected by the dock
of Marbella's yachting port. From here you can easily walk to **Playa de la
Bajadilla,** which you reach before arriving at the fishing port of Marbella. Filled
with northern Europeans lying on sun beds, it is a beach with grayish sand and
calm waters. Here you will also find a trio of beach-fronting restaurants, along
with public toilets, showers, and summer lifeguards.

Bajadilla is actually a continuation of **Playa de Venus,** lying between Marbella's twin harbors. Sailing and other watersports are popular here, as the beach
is sheltered in a cove. Showers, public toilets, and summer lifeguard towers are
available.

Other beaches include **Playa El Cable,** a small city beach with gray sand
where football matches are played on weekends. It lies close to the fishing port,
and has showers and public toilets along with fish restaurants and summer lifeguard towers. Less crowded in summer is the adjoining **Playa El Pinillo,** which
extends for almost 3km (1¾ miles). It offers kiosks renting canoes for river sailing and has summer lifeguards.

Playa Los Monteros, near El Pinillo, is part of the urban development complex of Los Monteros. Its rock-free beach of gray sand is separated from the

development by sand dunes. Two beach restaurants are here along with a beach club, and there are showers, public toilets, and summer lifeguards.

The gray sands of **Playa Alicante** lie at Urbanización Sea and are filled with restaurants and bars. It contains showers, public toilets, and lifeguard stations in summer. **Playa Real de Zaragoza,** also connected with an urban development, has public toilets, showers, and summer lifeguards. **Playa Vivora** is linked to the Urbanización Elvia. This calm beach that's not well known is set against a back-drop of some ugly buildings and has showers, public toilets, and summer life-guards. Finally, there's **Playa Las Canas,** connected with the urban development of Artola. It possesses few services, but offers good snorkeling and diving (bring your own equipment).

SHOPPING

While other Andalusian villages may inspire you to buy handicrafts, Marbella's international glamour might just incite so much insecurity you'll want to rush out to accessorize. Should you feel underdressed, head for the Old Town, where the cornucopia of designers includes **Versace,** in the Centro Commercial Ben-abola 8, Puerto Banús (© **95-281-02-96**).

If art is your passion, tour the art galleries that pepper the town. You'll spot high-rolling investors picking up contemporary treasures as part of a holiday shopping spree. Two of Marbella's most appealing galleries lie in the Old Town: the **Galleria d'Arte Van Gestel,** Plaza de los Naranjos 11 (© **95-277-48-19**), and **Galleria H,** Calle 3D (© **95-281-12-66**). And if your search for fine art carries over to **Puerto Banús,** consider an overview of the contemporary artwork displayed at the **Sam-mer Gallery,** Av. de Julio Iglesias 3, Las Terrazas de Banús, Local 10–16 (© **95-281-29-95**). If you'd like to purchase some of Andalusia's regional ceramics, your best bet is **Cerámica San Nicolás,** Plaza de la Iglesia 1 (© **95-277-05-46**).

On Saturday morning, forget the shops and head with the locals to **Nueva Andalucía flea market.** You can find anything from Spanish leather goods to local pottery.

WHERE TO STAY

Because the setting is ideal, some of the best hotels along the Costa del Sol are in Marbella.

VERY EXPENSIVE

Marbella Club ★★★   This is the grande dame of all Costa del Sol resorts. Until a few equally chic hotels were built along the Costa del Sol, the snobbish Marbella Club reigned almost without equal as the exclusive hangout of aristo-crats and tycoons. Established in 1954, the resort sprawls over a landscaped property that slopes from its roadside reception area down to the private beach. Composed of small, ecologically conscious clusters of garden pavilions, bunga-lows, and small-scale annexes, the Marbella Club has some of the loveliest gar-dens along the coast. Hotel rooms along the Costa del Sol don't come much better than these varied and spacious choices, often with canopy beds. Most of the bathrooms are roomy, with dual basins and tub/shower combos. Rooms have private balconies or terraces. The clientele is discreet, international, elegant, and appreciative of the resort's small scale and superb service.

Bulevar Príncipe Alfonso von Hohenlohe s/n, 29600 Marbella. © **95-282-22-11.** Fax 95-282-98-84. www.marbellaclub.com. 137 units. 250€–645€ ($300–$774) double; 645€–1,825€ ($774–$2,190) suite; 990€–3,750€ ($1,188–$4,500) bungalow. AE, DC, MC, V. Free parking. **Amenities:** 2 restaurants (see "Where to Dine," below); 3 bars; 2 outdoor pools; 24-hr. room service; massage; babysitting; laundry serv-ice/dry cleaning; nonsmoking rooms. *In room:* A/C, TV, minibar, hair dryer, safe.

Puente Romano ★★ Devotees rank this resort right up there with the Marbella Club, but we'll give it the runner-up prize. This hotel was originally built as a cluster of vacation apartments, which influenced the attention to detail and the surrounding landscaping. In the early 1970s, a group of entrepreneurs transformed it into one of the most unusual hotels in the south of Spain. Although it sits close to the frenetic coastal highway midway between Marbella and Puerto Banús, and some critics have dismissed it as "more flash than class," it still enjoys a loyal following. Inside the complex, arbor-covered walkways pass cascading water, masses of vines, and a subtropical garden. The spacious Andalusian-Mediterranean-style accommodations have semisheltered balconies. Bathrooms have tub/shower combos.

Carretera de Cádiz Km 177, 29600 Marbella. ℂ 800/448-8355 in the U.S., or 95-282-09-00. Fax 95-277-57-66. www.puenteromano.com. 274 units. 237€–370€ ($284–$444) double; 278€–2,300€ ($334–$2,760) suite. AE, DC, MC, V. Free parking. By car, take the E-15 4km (2½ miles) west of Marbella. **Amenities:** 2 restaurants; bar; 3 outdoor pools; 4 tennis courts; health club; sauna; 24-hr. room service; babysitting; laundry service/dry cleaning; nonsmoking rooms; solarium; rooms for those w/limited mobility. *In room:* A/C, TV, dataport, minibar, hair dryer, safe.

EXPENSIVE

Don Carlos Beach and Golf Resort ★★★ One of the most dramatic hotels on the coast, the Don Carlos rises on a set of angled stilts above a pine forest. Between the hotel and its manicured beach, the best in Marbella, are 4 hectares (9¾ acres) of award-winning gardens. With cascades of water and thousands of subtropical plants, they require a full-time staff of 22 gardeners. The hotel's low-lying terraces attract high-powered conferences from throughout Europe. Each of the roomy accommodations has lacquered furniture, and a bathroom that boasts a tub/shower combo.

Carretera de Cádiz Km 192, 29600 Marbella. ℂ 95-283-11-40. Fax 95-283-34-29. www.hoteldoncarlos.com. 235 units. 138€–326€ ($166–$391) double; 238€–943€ ($286–$1,132) suite. AE, DC, MC, V. Free parking. **Amenities:** 2 restaurants; 2 bars; 2 outdoor pools; 12 tennis courts; health club; sauna; 24-hr. room service; babysitting; laundry service/dry cleaning; rooms for those w/limited mobility. *In room:* A/C, TV, dataport, minibar, hair dryer, safe.

Don Miguel Golf & Sport Hotel ★★ At the foot of the mountain overlooking Marbella, this deluxe hotel with an 18-hole golf course rises over a scenic location a 20-minute walk from Marbella's center. It's giving other government-rated four-star hotels serious competition. From the terrace of the rooms and suites, the views of either the ocean or mountains are panoramic. The subtropical gardens are among the most spectacular along the coast, and swimming pools and golf dominate the activity calendar. The tennis club is the best along the coast, as is a state-of-the-art sports center. Rooms are beautifully styled and spacious; bathrooms have tub/shower combos.

The restaurants serve first-class Andalusian and international food, with top-rated chefs in the kitchens.

Camino del Trapiche s/n, 29600 Marbella. ℂ 95-105-90-00. Fax 95-105-90-09. www.don-miguel.net. 502 units. 262€–362€ ($314–$434) double; 404€–544€ ($485–$653) suite. Rates include breakfast. AE, DC, MC, V. **Amenities:** 2 restaurants; 3 bars; nightclub/disco; 4 pools (1 indoor); 2 18-hole golf courses; 16 tennis courts; gym; sauna; watersports center; Jacuzzi; babysitting; laundry service/dry cleaning; rooms for those w/limited mobility. *In room:* A/C, TV, dataport, minibar, hair dryer, safe.

El Fuerte ★★ *Kids* We'd give the edge to Gran Meliá Don Pepe, but of the hotels within Marbella proper, this resort is in a neck-to-neck race with the Fuerte Miramar. Opening onto a good sandy beach, the hotel opened back in

Marbella's jet-setting heyday, but was completely overhauled in 2003. It is surrounded by some of the best-maintained and most beautiful hotel gardens along the coast. Decorators have been busy here, matching the draperies and adding splashes of color in the various wallpapers. There is lush carpeting, creamy tones, and much use of comfortable wooden furniture. Rooms for the most part are midsize, although some are spacious, and each comes with a tiled tub/shower combo. A beach restaurant specializes in grilled fish based on the catch of the day. The staff here is helpful, and the amenities are excellent.

Av. El Fuerte, 29600 Marbella. © **95-286-15-00.** Fax 95-282-44-11. www.fuertehoteles.com. 261 units. 171€–201€ ($205–$241) double; 285€–339€ ($342–$407) suite. Rates include continental breakfast. AE, DC, MC, V. Free parking outside; 6€ ($7.20) inside. **Amenities:** 2 restaurants; bar; nearby golf course; 2 pools (1 indoor); tennis court; gym; sauna; spa; children's playground; room service (8am–midnight); laundry service/dry cleaning. *In room:* A/C, TV, dataport, minibar, hair dryer, safe (for a fee).

Gran Meliá Don Pepe ★★★

Within the confines of Marbella itself, and right next to a good beach, this is a government-rated five-star hotel and a favorite of the rich and famous. Meliá is a popular upmarket chain in Spain, and this is one of its finest showcases. A short stroll from the city's historic core, the hotel is rated *gran deluxe,* the highest such accolade in Spain. All the midsize to spacious bedrooms were refurbished in 2004, and units open onto views of the Mediterranean and well-landscaped tropical gardens. Expect tasteful fabrics, creamy colors, rich classically styled decorations, and a vaguely Moorish motif in part. All accommodations come with luxurious tiled bathrooms with tub and shower. To stay here is to stay in style.

José Meliá, 29600 Marbella. © **95-277-03-00.** Fax 95-277-99-54. www.granmeliadonpepe.solmelia.com. 184 units. 208€–306€ ($250–$367) double; 403€–560€ ($484–$672) suite. Rates include continental breakfast. AE, DC, MC, V. **Amenities:** 2 restaurants; 2 bars; 2 outdoor pools; nearby golf; 2 tennis courts; gym; sauna; salon; 24-hr. room service; laundry service/dry cleaning; nonsmoking rooms; rooms for those w/limited mobility. *In room:* A/C, TV, dataport, minibar, hair dryer, safe.

Hotel Fuerte Miramar ★★

This hotel is more modern than its sibling, El Fuerte, having opened on the Marbella beachfront in 2001. Its main claim to fame is its complete hydrotherapy and spa center offering a wide range of treatments. The hotel is very comfortable; its midsize to spacious bedrooms have tiled bathrooms with tub/shower combos, along with balconies opening onto Mediterranean vistas. There is a bright, airy feeling to the rooms and lots of carpeting and minor decoration, but the net result is more functional than stylish. The heated outdoor pool stays in use early in the spring and late into the autumn. Many guests stay on the premises of this self-contained resort at night, taking advantage of such features as an Internet room, and the good Spanish/Andalusian food.

Plaza José Luque Manzano, 29600 Marbella. © **95-276-84-00.** Fax 95-276-84-14. www.fuertehoteles.com. 201 units. 171€–268€ ($205–$322) double; 246€–319€ ($295–$383) suite. Rates include continental breakfast. AE, DC, MC, V. Free parking outdoors; 6€ ($7.20) indoors. **Amenities:** Restaurant; 2 bars; outdoor pool; spa/hydrotherapy center; room service (8am–2am); laundry service/dry cleaning. *In room:* A/C, TV, dataport, minibar, hair dryer, safe (for a fee).

Sultán Club Marbella ★

On the outskirts of Marbella a 10-minute drive from the center, this apartment hotel is in the residential district of Milla de Oro, just a short walk to the beach. It opened in 1997 and is meant to evoke luxury living such as the sultans of old enjoyed. The interior brims with tropical plants and fountains. The apartments contain one or two bedrooms, each with a large balcony, a small dining room, and a fully equipped kitchen, along with such extras as spacious bathrooms with tub/shower combos.

Calle Arturo Rubinstein, 29600 Marbella. © **95-277-15-62.** Fax 95-277-55-58. www.monarquehoteles.es. 76 units. 100€–240€ ($120–$288) 1-bedroom apt; 130€–240€ ($156–$288) 2-bedroom apt. AE, DC, MC, V. Parking 8€ ($9.60). **Amenities:** Restaurant; bar; 2 pools (1 indoor); health club; spa; sauna; whirlpool; limited room service; massage; babysitting; laundry service/dry cleaning. *In room:* A/C, TV, hair dryer, safe.

MODERATE

El Rodeo *Value*   Even though this modern hotel is just off Marbella's main coastal road, within walking distance of the bus station, the beach, and the old quarter, it is quiet and secluded. The facilities include a newly renovated piano bar where many guests and locals gather. The midsize rooms are functional; all contain bathrooms with tub/shower combos. The hotel is open year-round; peak season rates run June through October.

Víctor de la Serna s/n, 29600 Marbella. © **95-277-51-00.** Fax 95-282-33-20. www.monarquehoteles.es. 100 units. 85€–140€ ($102–$168) double. AE, DC, MC, V. **Amenities:** Restaurant; outdoor pool. *In room:* A/C, TV, safe.

Hotel Riu Rincón Andaluz ⭐   In a stylish area of Marbella 1km (⅔ mile) from Puerto Banús, this government-rated four-star hotel is meant to evoke a *pueblo andaluz* (Andalusian village). The resort lies only 500m (1,640 ft.) from a good beach. Lying in a park, the low-level rustic-style buildings form an ideal retreat. The large rooms are tastefully decorated and fully equipped, and all units have at least a small living room (those in the suites are larger). Ground-floor rooms have direct access to the gardens; others open onto balconies.

Carretera de Cádiz Km 173, 29660 Marbella. © **95-281-15-17.** Fax 95-281-41-80. www.riu.com. 315 units. 100€–137€ ($120–$164) double; 150€–200€ ($180–$240) suite. Rates include breakfast. AE, DC, MC, V. Free parking. **Amenities:** Restaurant; 2 bars; 3 pools (1 indoor); 24-hr. room service; laundry service/dry cleaning; nonsmoking rooms; rooms for those w/limited mobility. *In room:* A/C, TV, minibar, hair dryer, safe.

INEXPENSIVE

Hostal El Castillo   At the foot of the castle in the narrow streets of the Old Town, this small hotel opens onto a minuscule triangular area used by the adjoining convent and school as a playground. There's a small, covered courtyard. The spartan rooms are scrubbed clean and have bathrooms with tub/shower combos. No breakfast is served, and the staff only speaks a little English.

Plaza San Bernabé 2, 29600 Marbella. © **95-277-17-39.** www.hotelelcastillo.com. 25 units. 35€–45€ ($42–$54) double. MC, V. Free parking. *In room:* TV, no phone.

Hotel Artola Golf ⭐   Between Fuengirola and Marbella, .8km (½ mile) from the beach, this charming place was originally an old staging post for travelers en route to Gibraltar. In the 1970s it was converted into an inn. The architecture is typically Andalusian, with a stucco and wood facade under a terra-cotta roof. A garden and patio surround the building. The interior decoration has retained some of its historical aura with colorful tiles plus decorative wooden wall panels and beams. The midsize rooms are comfortably furnished and tastefully decorated, often with Moorish details. All units have balconies and fully equipped bathrooms with tub/shower combos.

Carretera de Cádiz Km 194, 29600 Marbella. © **95-283-13-90.** Fax 95-283-04-50. www.hotelartola.com. 35 units. 82€–105€ ($98–$126) double; 128€–151€ ($154–$195) suite. AE, MC, V. Free parking. **Amenities:** Bar; outdoor pool; golf course; limited room service; babysitting. *In room:* A/C (in some), TV.

Hotel Lima *(Value)*   Tucked in a residential area right off the N-340/E-15 and near the beach, the Lima is more secluded than other hotels nearby. The modern structure features plain rooms last renovated in 2000 with Spanish provincial furnishings and private balconies. All rooms contain bathrooms with tub/shower combos.

Av. Antonio Belón, 29600 Marbella. © 95-277-05-00. Fax 95-286-30-91. www.hotellimamarbella.com. 64 units. 59€–99€ ($71–$119) double. Rates include continental breakfast. AE, DC, MC, V. Parking 12€ ($14). **Amenities:** Restaurant; room service (8am–11pm); babysitting; laundry service/dry cleaning. *In room:* A/C, TV, dataport, minibar, hair dryer, safe.

Linda Marbella *(Value)*   Bargains are hard to come by in the center of Marbella, but this is your best bet if you like more of a bed-and-breakfast style room. The little inn opened only in 2002 and became deservedly popular almost overnight. Don't expect grand living, however. Accommodations are small but exceedingly well maintained and comfortable, with mostly wooden furniture. Bathrooms are a bit cramped but serviceable, each containing a shower stall. Many good seafood restaurants lie only a short walk from the inn.

Ancha 21, 29600 Marbella. © 95-285-71-71. Fax 95-285-71-71. lindamarbellasl@terra.es. 14 units. 80€ ($96) double. MC, V. **Amenities:** Laundry service. *In room:* A/C, TV.

NEARBY PLACES TO STAY

Castillo de Monda *(Finds)*   In 1996, a group of entrepreneurs transformed the crumbling ruins of an 8th-century Moorish fortress into this showplace, which lies in a sleepy "white" village 12km (7½ miles) north of Marbella. El Castillo de Monda adds a soothing note of calm and quiet to a region that grows glitzier by the year. Rooms are beautifully maintained, generous in size, and traditionally furnished. Bathrooms have tub/shower combos.

Monda, 29110 Málaga. © 95-245-71-42. Fax 95-245-73-36. www.costadelsol.spa.es/hotel/monda. 26 units. 113€–136€ ($136–$163) double; 194€–224€ ($233–$269) suite. AE, MC, V. Free parking. **Amenities:** Restaurant; bar; outdoor pool; 24-hr. room service; babysitting; laundry service/dry cleaning; nonsmoking rooms; rooms for those w/limited mobility. *In room:* A/C, TV, hair dryer.

Golf Hotel Guadalmina *(Kids)*   In the residential area of Guadalmina, right outside Marbella, this resort hotel is surrounded by two scenic golf courses and the Mediterranean. The hotel has been a landmark on the coast since 1959 but recently underwent a wholesale renovation and expansion, reopening in 2002. All the accommodations, both in the original building and in a new 91-room wing, are midsize to spacious. Bedrooms are comfortable and well furnished, and the decor is typical Andalusian. Rooms open onto the sea (these are the most desirable), one the golf courses, or the hotel's gardens. Spanish and international cuisine is served at the first-class **La Terraza.** Golfers check in here in droves, and families with kids love the impressively large pool as well as the shallow kiddie pool.

Urbanización Guadalmina Baja, 29678 Marbella. © 95-288-22-11. Fax 95-288-22-91. www.hotelguadalmina. com. 180 units. 153€–248€ ($184–$298) double; 213€–353€ ($256–$424) junior suite; 368€–708€ ($442–$850) suite. Rates include breakfast. AE, DC, MC, V. **Amenities:** Restaurant; bar; 2 outdoor pools; spa; fitness center; 2 nearby golf courses; babysitting; laundry service/dry cleaning; limited room service; rooms for those w/limited mobility. *In room:* A/C, TV, minibar, hair dryer, safe.

Refugio del Juanar *(Finds)*   The former hunting lodge of King Alfonso XIII has been turned into this hotel and restaurant, an ideal retreat from Marbella. Over the years it has attracted both aristocrats and politicians, including Charles de Gaulle. The *refugio* lies 4km (2½ miles) from the town of Ojén, which is

10km (6 miles) north of Marbella. In the heart of the Sierra Blanca, the inn stands at the southern edge of a mountainous wilderness, Serranía de Ronda, which is inhabited by wild ibex. The forests surrounding the inn have well-marked paths for those who want to go trekking.

Bedrooms are rather standard but comfortable, each midsize, containing a private bathroom with tub or shower. An old-fashioned Spanish hacienda style prevails, with iron headboards and flowery fabrics. A log fire roars downstairs in winter and six of the accommodations have their own fireplaces. You can also drive up from Marbella for a lunch or dinner: The on-site restaurant serves an excellent Spanish cuisine and is decorated in a rustic style. In autumn game is a specialty. If you're just dropping by for lunch while touring the area, you'll find good-tasting meals costing from 25€ ($30).

Sierra Blanca s/n, 29610 Ojén. ℂ **95-288-10-00.** Fax 95-288-10-01. www.juanar.com. 23 units. 98€–112€ ($118–$134) double; 175€ ($210) suite. AE, DC, MC, V. **Amenities:** Restaurant; bar; outdoor pool; tennis court; room service (8am–midnight); laundry service. *In room:* TV, minibar, hair dryer.

WHERE TO DINE
EXPENSIVE

Buenaventura ✿ ANDALUSIAN/SPANISH   Other restaurants in Marbella, including La Hacienda, are more glamorous, but Buenaventura holds its own with solidly reliable food at reasonably affordable prices. Located in the oldest quarter of Marbella, it is full of charm and grace notes. The 1937 building was constructed in the typical Andalusian style with an internal patio, hanging flowerpots, and wooden columns. The restaurant has heavy wooden furniture. For many years, it's been known for excellent red wines, including the best vintages from the vineyards of the province. Chef Francisco Gálvez will dazzle with his savory creations. He is known for his roast pork, perfectly flavored with cumin. He also shops for the best and freshest of fish from the day's catch, which he then grills. If you wish, he'll serve the platter with a velvety smooth béchamel sauce.

Plaza de la Iglesia de la Encarnación 5. ℂ **95-285-80-69.** Reservations recommended. Main courses 18€–25€ ($22–$30); menú degustación 45€ ($54). MC, V. May–Oct daily 7pm–1am; Dec–Oct daily 11:30am–12:30am. Closed Nov.

El Portalón ✿ SPANISH/INTERNATIONAL   This is one of Marbella's most stylish dining enclaves. Its urbane staff serves patrons from throughout Europe with aplomb and obvious pride. Menu selections include some time-honored Iberian dishes, such as suckling lamb and pig slowly roasted in a wood-burning oven, grilled meats, and impeccably fresh fish imported daily. Low-fat dishes are like those you might expect to find at a California spa—lobster salad, grilled sea bass with a julienne of fresh vegetables, and entrecôte of beef with fresh vegetables and red-wine sauce. In an Art Deco–style pavilion called the "vinoteca," you can enjoy an excellent selection of wines from all over Spain. The restaurant is about a mile west of town beside the road leading to Puerto Banús, across from the beach and adjacent to the entrance to the Marbella Club.

Carretera de Cádiz Km 178. ℂ **95-282-78-80.** Reservations recommended. Main courses 22€–32€ ($26–$38). AE, DC, MC, V. Mon–Sat 1–4pm and 8–11:30pm.

La Hacienda ✿✿✿ INTERNATIONAL   La Hacienda, a tranquil choice 13km (8 miles) east of Marbella, serves some of the best food along the Costa del Sol. In cooler months you can dine in the rustic tavern before an open fireplace. In fair weather, meals are served on a patio partially encircled by open Romanesque arches. Appetizers often include foie gras with lentils and lobster croquettes. For a main dish, try roast guinea hen with cream, minced raisins, and port. The flavorful food is prepared with the freshest ingredients and presented with style. An iced soufflé finishes the meal nicely.

Urbanización Hacienda Las Chapas, Carretera de Cádiz Km 193. © **95-283-12-67.** Reservations recommended. Main courses 18€–24€ ($22–$29); fixed-price menu 50€ ($60). AE, DC, MC, V. Summer daily 8:30pm–midnight; winter Wed–Sun 1–3:30pm and 8:30–11:30pm. Closed Jan 3–Feb 8.

La Meridiana ★★★ ITALIAN/INTERNATIONAL   If not the most sophisticated restaurant along the Costa del Sol, La Meridiana certainly has the most romantic setting, with a garden terrace, and arguably serves the best cuisine as well. A sweep of a glass-enclosed porch has been added to the original restaurant. La Notte, a nightclub, has opened on a nearby terrace and has become the hot spot along the coast for late-night revelers. The menu of Italian and Andalusian specialties changes four times yearly. You don't just get the routine gazpacho here but such cold soups as curried pumpkin or chilled white almond and garlic with melon and grapes. Tiny boneless chicken comes stuffed with couscous, raisins, almonds, and spices, and there are many high-end favorites like foie gras, Beluga caviar, lobster, and fine Ibérico ham.

Camino de la Cruz s/n. © **95-277-61-90.** Reservations required. Main courses 16€–47€ ($19–$56); tasting menu 53€ ($64). AE, DC, MC, V. Daily 8:30pm–midnight. Closed Jan 9–Feb 10.

Marbella Club Restaurant ★★ INTERNATIONAL   Our favorite meals here have been on the terrace in good weather. Lunch is traditionally an overflowing buffet served in the beach club. Dinners are served amid blooming flowers, flickering candles, and the strains of live music—perhaps a Spanish classical guitarist, a small chamber orchestra playing 19th-century classics, or a South American vocalist. Menu items, inspired by European cuisines, change with the season. You might begin with beef carpaccio or lobster salad delicately flavored with olive oil. Specialties include one of the coast's most savory paellas, and tender veal cutlets from Avila.

In the Marbella Club, Bulevar Príncipe Alfonso von Hohenlohe s/n. © **95-282-22-11.** Reservations recommended. Lunch buffet 60€ ($72); dinner main courses 12€–34€ ($14–$41). AE, DC, MC, V. Summer daily 1:30–4pm and 9pm–12:30am; winter daily 1:30–4pm and 8:30–11:30pm.

Villa Tiberio ★ ITALIAN/INTERNATIONAL   Villa Tiberio's proximity to the upscale Marbella Club (a 5-min. walk away) ensures a flow of visitors from that elite hotel. In what was originally built as a private villa during the 1960s, it serves the most innovative Italian food in the region, and attracts the many north European expatriates living nearby. Appetizers include thinly sliced smoked beef with fresh avocados and oil-and-lemon dressing, and *fungi fantasia* (a large wild mushroom stuffed with seafood and lobster sauce). Especially tempting is the *pappardelle alla Sandro*—large flat noodles studded with chunks of lobster, tomato, and garlic. Other versions come with cream, caviar, and smoked salmon. Main dishes include sea bass with cherry tomatoes, basil, and black truffle oil; duck baked with orange and Curaçao liqueur; and *osso buco* (braised veal shanks).

Carretera de Cádiz Km 178.5. © **95-277-17-99.** Reservations recommended. Main courses 17€–24€ ($20–$29); fixed-price menus 42€–47€ ($50–$56). AE, DC, MC, V. Mon–Sat 7:30pm–12:30am.

MODERATE

Ciboca SPANISH   Set in the heart of Marbella's historic medieval core, the attractive Ciboca occupies a 500-year-old building ringed with vines and flowers. Tables are moved onto the historic square outside whenever the weather is balmy. A full roster of Spanish wines accompanies dishes that include virtually any kind of fish. We particularly like the sea bass baked in a salt crust. Also appealing is roasted lamb scented with Andalusian herbs, and tournedos served with a perfectly made béarnaise sauce. Staff is cooperative and hardworking.

Plaza de las Naranjos 6. ✆ **95-277-37-43**. Reservations recommended. Main courses 11€–25€ ($13–$30). MC, V. Daily noon–11pm.

El Balcón de la Virgen SPANISH/ANDALUSIAN   In an antique house in the historic core of old Marbella, this restaurant is named after a 200-year-old statue of the Virgin that adorns a wall niche surrounded by flowers and vines. A short walk from the Plaza de los Naranjos, it's popular for its good food, attentive service, and reasonable prices. The menu—derived mostly from Andalusia and, to a lesser degree, the rest of Spain—features Málaga-style meat stew, baked hake with olive oil and herbs, marinated swordfish, roasted pork, and grilled filets of beef.

Remedios 2. ✆ **95-277-60-92**. Reservations recommended. Main courses 12€–19€ ($14–$23). AE, DC, MC, V. Wed–Mon 1:30–4:30pm and 8:30pm–1:30am.

La Pescera ANDALUSIAN/INTERNATIONAL   Beside a historic square in the heart of old Marbella, this is a bustling, well-managed restaurant. It has loyal local clientele and a reputation for serving well-prepared fish and seafood. There's a worthwhile roster of meat dishes, such as grilled steaks and pork filets, but most diners opt for fish. Specialties range from working-class dishes such as *bacalao frito* (fried cod) to more esoteric versions of shellfish and crayfish—kept alive and healthy until the last moment in big on-site holding tanks.

Plaza de la Victoria s/n. ✆ **95-276-41-74**. Reservations recommended. Main courses 15€–30€ ($18–$36). AE, DC, MC, V. Daily 10:30am–12:30am.

La Tirana ⭐ ANDALUSIAN/SPANISH   In the center of Marbella, this charmer of a restaurant is in a 1940 Andalusian house with a Moorish-style garden. The decor is inviting, with much use of heavy wooden furniture, mirrors, and candles. In some ways, it evokes a country restaurant in North Africa. The skillful cooking is very up-to-date, with inventive flavor combinations. Most diners begin with a classic bowl of gazpacho, served here with slices of avocado. Another recommended soup is a Costa del Sol specialty, *ajo blanco a la malagueña* (almond soup). For main courses, try the savory oven-baked lamb with Moroccan-style couscous and mint sauce. Fish fanciers will love the fresh tuna sautéed with spices and served in a tangy tomato sauce. The restaurant opens onto a beautiful Andalusian courtyard.

Urbanización La Merced Chica–Huerta Márquez. ✆ **95-286-34-24**. Reservations recommended. Main courses 18€–21€ ($22–$25). AE, DC, MC, V. May–Oct Tues–Sat 8pm–midnight; Nov–Apr Sat–Sun 1–4pm. Closed Jan 15–Feb 15.

Mesón del Museo FRENCH   Mesón del Museo is on the upper floor of an 18th-century building containing one of the oldest art and antiques galleries in Marbella. The dining room is decorated with Iberian accessories and Andalusian antiques. Try the delicious fried Camembert, followed by filet of sole in a champagne and truffle sauce. A selection of French and Spanish wines complements the menu.

Plaza de los Naranjos 11 (1st floor). ✆ **95-282-56-23**. Reservations recommended. Main courses 15€–20€ ($18–$24). MC, V. Tues–Sun 7:30–11pm. Closed July.

Santiago ⭐ SEAFOOD/INTERNATIONAL   As soon as you enter Santiago, the bubbling lobster tanks give you an idea of what's in store. The decor, the tapas bar near the entrance, and the summertime patio together with fresh fish dishes make this one of the most popular places to eat in town. Savory fish soup is well prepared and well spiced. Follow with a generous serving of sole in champagne or grilled or sautéed turbot. On a hot day, the seafood salad, garnished with lobster, shrimp, and crabmeat and served with a spicy sauce, is especially recommended. In addition to seafood, the menu offers many meat dishes. For dessert, we suggest a serving of manchego cheese.

Duque de Ahumada 5. (C) 95-277-00-78. Reservations required. Main courses 12€–22€ ($14–$26). AE, DC, MC, V. Daily 1–5pm and 7pm–1am.

INEXPENSIVE

Casa de la Era (★) (Finds) ANDALUSIAN   This little discovery outside Marbella lies in a rustic house, very much in the style of an old hacienda with internal patios decorated with plants, trees, and flowers. Wooden furniture only adds to the old-fashioned look, along with hanging hams and ceramics used for decoration. In addition, the restaurant offers a beautiful terrace. On a full night the place is a whirl of color and activity. The charming waiters rather proudly bring out the chef's specialties.

Our party recently enjoyed the filet of turbot with fried garlic, and the squid *a la moruna* (with hot peppers). The flavor of a perfectly grilled and tender veal cutlet was enlivened with fresh rosemary, bay leaf, zesty pepper, garlic, and onion. Believe it or not, the taste didn't get lost under that overload. For beefeaters, the sirloin *a la ibérica* came with a sauce made of fresh bay leaf and cloves, creating a tangy and very appetizing flavor.

Finca El Chorraero-Noreste. (C) 95-277-06-25. Reservations recommended. Main courses 9€–19€ ($11–$23). AE, DC, MC, V. May–Oct Mon–Sat 1–4pm and 8pm–midnight; Nov–Apr Mon–Sat 1–4pm.

MARBELLA AFTER DARK

There's more international wealth hanging out in the watering holes of Marbella, and a wider choice of glam (or pseudoglam) discos than virtually anywhere else in the south of Spain. Foremost among these is the chic **Oliva Valer,** in the Carretera Istan, N-340 Km 177 ((C) **95-282-88-45**). Open Friday and Saturday from midnight to 7am with a cover of 30€ ($36). A fashionable place to rendezvous at night, **La Notte** (no cover), Camino de la Cruz s/n ((C) **95-286-69-96**), stands next to the swank La Meridiana Restaurant. Decorated in a Marrakesh style, it offers a terrace and an elegant atmosphere with rich decoration. Live music and shows are presented here during its nightly hours from 11pm until 7am. It is closed from November 1 to December 21.

If you're in the heart of historic Marbella, enjoy a night in the bodegas and taverns of the Old Town. One that's conveniently located adjacent to one of the town's widest thoroughfares is **Bodega La Venensia,** Plaza de los Olivos s/n ((C) **95-277-99-63**). Its wide choice of sherries, wines, and tapas draws lots of chattering patrons. One with a particularly large assortment of wines is **Vinacoteca,** Plaza Joaquín Gómez Agüera 2 ((C) **95-277-52-03**). Dedicated to offering as many Spanish wines as possible, it provides the opportunity to compare the vintages produced in the surrounding region.

The best flamenco club in town is **Ana María,** Plaza del Santo Cristo 4–5 ((C) **95-277-56-46**). We think it's the most authentic place for foreign visitors with a limited knowledge of Spanish. The long, often-crowded bar area sells tapas, wine, sherry, and a selection of more international libations. On the stage, singers, dancers, and musicians perform flamenco and popular songs. This is late-night entertainment—the doors don't open till 11pm, and the crowd really gets going between midnight and 4am. It's closed November through March. Drink prices start at 10€ ($12), including cover.

Moments A Marbella Tasca Crawl

To really rub shoulders with the locals and experience a taste of Spain, take your meals in the tapas bars. Marbella boasts more hole-in-the-wall tapas bars than virtually any other resort town in southern Spain. Even if you set out with a specific place in mind, you'll likely be distracted en route by a newer, older, bigger, smaller, brighter, or just plain old more interesting joint you want to try. That's half the fun.

Prices and hours are remarkably consistent: The coffeehouse that opens at 7am will switch to wine and tapas when the first patron asks for it (sometimes shortly after breakfast), then continue through the day dispensing wine, sherry, and, more recently, bottles of beer. On average, tapas cost 3€ to 8€ ($3.60–$9.60), but some foreign visitors configure them into *platos combinados.*

Tapas served along the Costa del Sol are principally Andalusian in origin, with an emphasis on seafood. The most famous plate, *fritura malagueña,* consists of fried fish based on the catch of the day. Sometimes *ajo blanco,* a garlicky local version of gazpacho made with almonds, is served, especially in summer. Fried squid or octopus is another favorite, as are little Spanish-style herb-flavored meatballs. *Tortilla* (an omelet, often with potatoes) is the most popular egg dish. Other well-known tapas include pungent tuna, grilled shrimp, *piquillos rellenos* (red peppers stuffed with fish), *bacalao* (salt cod), and mushrooms sautéed in olive oil and garlic.

Tapas bars line many of the narrow streets of Marbella's historic core, with rich pickings around Calle del Perral and, to a somewhat lesser extent, Calle Miguel Cana. In August especially, when you want to escape wall-to-wall people and the heat and noise of the Old Town, head for one of the shoreline restaurants and tapas bars called *chiringuitos.* All serve local specialties, and you can order a full meal, a snack, tapas, or a drink. One of our favorites is **Los Sardinales,** Playa de los Alicates (© **95-283-70-12**), which serves some of the best sangria in the area. Another favorite is **Chiringuito La Pesquera,** Playa Marbellamar (© **95-277-03-38**), where you can order a plate of fresh grilled sardines.

Ten kilometers (6 miles) west of Marbella, near Puerto Banús, **Casino Marbella,** Andalucía Plaza, Urbanización Nueva Andalucía (© **95-281-40-00**), is on the lobby level of the Andalucía Plaza resort complex at Urbanización Nueva. Unlike the region's competing casino, at the Hotel Torrequebrada, the Marbella does not offer cabaret or nightclub shows. The focus is on gambling, and mobs of visitors from northern Europe engage with abandon. Individual games include French and American roulette, blackjack, punto y banco, craps, and chemin de fer. Hours are daily noon to 5am for coin machines, daily 7pm to 5am for the main body of the casino. There is a 5€ ($6) admission.

You can dine before or after gambling in the **Casino Restaurant,** a few steps above the gaming floor. The tasting menu is about 30€ ($36) per person including wine. Jackets are not required for men, but shorts and T-shirts will be frowned on. The casino is open daily from 8pm to 4 or 6am. There's a cover charge of 5€ ($6). A passport is required for admission.

6 Fuengirola & Los Boliches

32km (20 miles) W of Málaga, 104km (64 miles) E of Algeciras, 574km (356 miles) S of Madrid

The fishing towns of **Fuengirola** and **Los Boliches** lie halfway between the more famous resorts of Marbella and Torremolinos. A promenade along the water stretches some 4km (2½ miles). Less developed Los Boliches is just .8km (½ mile) from Fuengirola.

These towns don't have the facilities or drama of Torremolinos and Marbella, but except for two major luxury hotels, Fuengirola and Los Boliches are cheaper. This has attracted hordes of budget-conscious European tourists.

Santa Amalja, Carvajal, and **Las Gaviotas,** the best beaches, are broad, clean, and sandy. Everybody goes to the big **flea market** at Fuengirola on Tuesday. It's the largest along the coast. Many British retirees who live in the holiday apartments nearby attend this sprawling market, later hitting one of the Irish or British pubs for a pint just as they did back in their home country.

ESSENTIALS

GETTING THERE   From Torremolinos, take the Metro at La Nogalera station (under the RENFE sign). **Trains** depart every 30 minutes. The fare is 1.15€ ($1.40). Fuengirola is on the main Costa del Sol **bus** route from either Algeciras in the west or Málaga in the east. Call **Alsina Graella Sur** (© **95-231-82-95**). If you're driving from Marbella, take the N-340/E-15 east from Marbella.

VISITOR INFORMATION   The **tourist office,** Paseo Jesús Santos Rein 6 (© **95-246-74-57;** www.fuengirola.org), is open Monday to Friday 9:30am to 2pm and 5 to 7pm, Saturday 10am to 1pm.

EXPLORING FUENGIROLA

Don't—repeat don't—come here for the attractions. There aren't many, and you can skip all of them without suffering cultural deprivation. Frankly, if you have a day for sightseeing, we'd recommend that you not spend it in Fuengirola but head for the hilltown of **Mijas,** one of the Pueblos Blancos (white villages) of Andalusia. For complete details, see chapter 8.

Fuengirola is known for its 8km (5 miles) of sandy beaches, set against high-rise hotels and residential blocks. Many Spanish nationals own these summer apartments. There is a promenade flanked by palm trees. **Playa Torreblanca** is one of the most popular beaches, a stretch of fine golden sand with tranquil waters that are safe for children. It offers watersports ranging from windsurfing to fishing and kayaking. The beginning of Torreblanca is actually **Playa de Los Olimpos,** a smaller beach with golden sand. Fishing is possible from an artificial dock, and the beach flanks a campground. Another beach with fine golden sand is **Playa Gaviotas,** lying between the Fuengirola and Torreblanca urban developments. It adjoins Playa Los Boliches (see below). Young people flock to this beach for windsurfing. Nearby **Playa Los Boliches** is the largest in the area and the best equipped, flanked by seafood restaurants, hotels, and shops.

Playa de Fuengirola lies between Los Boliches and Playa Santa Amalia, beside the port. This beach is usually filled with lots of pleasure craft, and many fishermen set off from here. **Playa Santa Amalia** is one of the best-equipped beaches in the area. It's very much a family beach and is flanked by seafood restaurants, shops, and hotels. Fishing, windsurfing, and sailing are popular pastimes.

Playa El Ejido is right before you cross the Fuengirola River on the N-340, adjoining Playa Santa Amalia. This small lake formed before the river joins the sea attracts families with children to its safe waters.

Highway of Death

The N-340—known variously as the **Carretera Nacional** or the **Carretera Cádiz** (the road to Cádiz)—is one of the most dangerous in all of Europe. More like a city street than a highway, it stretches for 100km (62 miles) right through the town centers, where there are a lot of drunken revelers even at midday, and divides *urbanizaciones* (overcrowded urban developments).

Even so, motorists—both Costa del Sol natives and visiting foreigners—treat it like a raceway. There are some 100 fatalities a year. A lot of the accidents are caused by Brits unfamiliar with driving on the left-hand side. Two particularly horrendous areas are the stretch of highway between the Málaga airport and the resort of Torremolinos to the west, and the stretch of road west from Marbella along the highway to the port of Algeciras.

Fortunately, the opening of **Autopista del Sol,** a four-lane motorway, has somewhat alleviated the dangers. This new toll expressway links Estepona in the west to Nerja (via Málaga) in the east.

WHERE TO STAY

Byblos Andaluz ★★★   This luxurious resort with excellent recreational facilities is in a golf club setting 5km (3 miles) from Fuengirola and 10km (6 miles) from the beach. The grounds contain a white minaret, Moorish arches, tile-adorned walls, and an orange-tree patio inspired by the Alhambra grounds. The large rooms and suites are elegantly and individually designed and furnished in Roman, Arabic, Andalusian, and rustic styles. Private sun terraces and lavish bathrooms with tub/shower combos add to the comfort. For many visitors, especially from Europe, the major attraction is the Thalassotherapy Centre, considered the most advanced in Europe. Nearby are two international class golf courses designed by Robert Trent Jones, Sr.

Urbanización Mijas Golf, 29650 Mijas Costa Málaga. ℭ **95-247-30-50.** Fax 95-247-67-83. www.byblos-andaluz.com. 144 units. 260€–420€ ($312–$504) double; from 455€–1,230€ ($546–$1,476) suite. Rates include breakfast. AE, DC, MC, V. Free parking. **Amenities:** 3 restaurants; 2 bars; 5 pools (3 indoor); 2 golf courses; 4 outdoor lit tennis courts; health spa; sauna; 24-hr. room service; babysitting; laundry service/dry cleaning; disco; solarium. *In room:* A/C, TV, dataport, minibar, hair dryer, safe.

Las Pirámides   This resort, a favorite of northern Europeans and tour groups, is a citylike compound about 46m (150 ft.) from the beach. The government-rated four-star resort consists of two buildings connected by a hall, each with 10 floors. All the rooms are good size and have slick modern styling as well as terraces. Bathrooms contain tub/shower combos. On the beach guests enjoy a wide range of watersports, including pedal boating, water-skiing, windsurfing, para-sailing, boating, and fishing. The reception desk at the hotel can also advise about the best golf courses in the area, and horseback riding is available near the hotel. You can also rent bikes nearby.

Calle Miguel Márquez 43, 29640 Fuengirola. ℭ **95-247-06-00.** Fax 95-258-32-97. www.hotellaspiramides.com. 316 units. 120€–165€ ($144–$198) double; 148€–181€ ($178–$217) suite. AE, MC, V. Parking 12€ ($14). **Amenities:** 2 restaurants; cafe; 3 bars; 2 pools (1 indoor); fitness center; car-rental desk; salon; 24-hr. room service; babysitting; laundry service/dry cleaning; nonsmoking rooms; rooms for those w/limited mobility. *In room:* A/C, TV, dataport, minibar, hair dryer, safe.

Villa de Laredo ⓡ *Finds*   With a panoramic site on the waterfront promenade, this good-value inn lies a block east of the main port. One of the more modern hotels in town, it benefits from a central location without even attempting to equal the luxury offered on the periphery by such resorts as Byblos Andaluz. Bedrooms are newly styled and comfortably furnished, containing small bathrooms with tub and shower. Try for one of the rooms with a small terrace opening onto the seafront promenade. The featured attraction of the villa is its rooftop pool, opening onto views of the Paseo Marítimo.

Paseo Marítimo Rey de España 42, 29640 Fuengirola. ⓒ 95-247-76-89. Fax 95-247-79-50. 74 units. 54€–123€ ($65–$148) double. Rates include half-board. AE, DC, MC, V. **Amenities:** Restaurant; bar; outdoor pool; room service; laundry service; nonsmoking rooms; rooms for those w/limited mobility. *In room:* A/C, TV, minibar, hair dryer, safe.

WHERE TO DINE

Don Pé CONTINENTAL   In hot weather, Don Pé patrons dine in a courtyard where the roof can be adjusted to allow in light and air. In cold weather, a fire on the hearth illuminates the heavy ceiling beams and rustic accessories. The menu features a selection of game dishes, including medallions of venison, roast filet of wild boar, and duck with orange sauce. The ingredients are imported from the forests and plains of Andalusia.

Calle de la Cruz 17 (off the Av. Ramón y Cajal), Fuengirola. ⓒ **95-247-83-51.** Reservations recommended. Main courses 7€–20€ ($8.40–$24). MC, V. Mon–Sat 7pm–midnight.

El Paso MEXICAN   Chefs here give you one of the few chances along the coast to enjoy the cuisine of another Spanish-speaking country. This 150-year-old building was originally the hamlet's largest plant for the canning of the local fleet's catch of sardines. You can order from a wide selection of Mexican beers and tequilas at the long and convivial bar area, or head into either of two dining rooms for such New World specialties as chimichangas, tortillas, burritos, fajitas, and guacamole. Any of the barbecued meats make a savory main course.

Calle Francisco Cano 39, Los Boliches. ⓒ **95-247-50-94.** Reservations recommended. Main courses 9€–21€ ($11–$25). MC, V. Daily 6:30–11:30pm.

La Langosta ⓡ INTERNATIONAL/SEAFOOD   Just a stone's throw from Fuengirola and 2 blocks from the beach, La Langosta is one of the best restaurants in the area. The stylish Art Deco dining room is a welcome relief from the ever-present Iberian rustic style of so many other restaurants. The menu features a variety of seafood, as well as Spanish dishes like *gazpacho andaluz* and prawns *al ajillo* (in olive oil and garlic). Lobster is prepared thermidor style or virtually any other way you want; among the beef offerings is an especially succulent version of chateaubriand. The staff is particularly well trained and helpful.

Calle Francisco Cano 1, Los Boliches. ⓒ **95-247-50-49.** Main courses 13€–29€ ($16–$35); tasting menu 30€ ($36). AE, DC, MC, V. Mon–Sat 7–11:30pm. Closed Dec–Jan.

Monopol ⓡⓡ *Kids* SEAFOOD   This popular dining spot is in a neck-and-neck race with Patrick Bousier for the title of best restaurant in Fuengirola. With its nautical decor and blue-and-white Mediterranean colors, it's popular with the boating (or yachting) set. A bright, cheery place with a friendly waitstaff, it hires chefs who prepare some of the best and freshest tasting seafood in the area. Lobster can be prepared several ways, and a kettle of well-flavored mussels is always a delight. Our party happily shared three tantalizing seafood dishes: crab au gratin, grilled prawns, and angelfish, the latter with a delicate saffron flavoring. A kid's menu is available on request.

Palangreros 7. (C) **95-247-44-48**. Reservations recommended. Main courses 21€–35€ ($25–$42). AE, DC, MC, V. Mon–Sat 8–11:30pm. Closed July 15–Aug 15.

Moochers Jazz Café & Restaurant INTERNATIONAL   You can view this popular spot near the beach as both your dining and entertainment option for the night. Live music is presented nightly in summer. You may not necessarily hear the sounds of New Orleans, but expect blues and perhaps some rock. London expats Yvonne and Andy have a menu different from any other in town— they specialize in huge crepes filled with seafood, chicken, vegetables and more. They also prepare delicious tasting vegetarian courses as well. If you arrive before 7:30pm, there's a 10% discount on the food.

Calle La Cruz 17. (C) **95-247-71-54**. Reservations required. Main courses 8€–20€ ($9.60–$24). AE, DC, V. Daily 6pm–1am.

Patrick Bousier ★★ *Finds* FRENCH   The chef, Patrick Bousier, once cooked for Paul Bocuse, the most famous chef in Paris. Today, Patrick has forged ahead, making his own culinary statement here. Ingredients are fresh, and every dish has a special twist, elevating it to the sublime. Recent favorites included a supreme of turbot sautéed in a sherry wine sauce, grilled sea bass with fresh tarragon, and sautéed sirloin steak with a mustard sauce and a side order of wild mushrooms. The staff is especially helpful in guiding you to what's best and fresh on any given day, and the well-chosen wine list features an array of Andalusian and international vintages.

Rotonda de la Luna, Pueblo López. (C) **95-258-51-20**. Reservations required. Main courses 12€–20€ ($14–$24); fixed-price menu 23€ ($28). DC, MC, V. Mon–Sat 7:30–10:30pm. Closed Jan and July.

Portofino ANDALUSIAN/INTERNATIONAL   In front of the Paseo Marítimo promenade, this popular eatery was constructed in 1996 in the tasca style, meaning a rustic-style tavern with lots of hanging plants and regional artifacts. A casual dining room, drawing an international crowd, its kitchen fashions fresh ingredients into several tasty concoctions, including pastas ranging from a creamy lasagna with meat to one with vegetables only. Meat fanciers will find the tender grilled pork served with port wine sauce and fresh herbs. Shredded deer meat is also a specialty. Most diners, however, order one of the fresh fish dishes of the day, like the filet of sole with fresh vegetables. A final specialty is an array of various types of potato salad. Desserts are fairly standard.

Rey de España 29, Paseo Marítimo. (C) **95-247-06-43**. Reservations recommended. Main courses 9€–21€ ($11–$25). AE, DC, MC, V. Tues–Sun 1:30–4:30pm and 8:30–11:30pm. Closed July 1–15 and Aug 1–15.

FUENGIROLA AFTER DARK

Plays, concerts, English-language musicals, and performances by amateur local troupes, are all regularly staged at the **Salón de Varie Variétés Theater,** Emancipación 30 ((C) **95-247-45-42**). The season runs from October to May. Most tickets cost 15€ ($18) for adults or half-price for children. The box office is open Monday to Friday 10:30am to 1:30pm and 7 to 8pm. Concerts are also presented at the **Palacio de la Paz,** Recinto Ferial, Avenida Jesús Santos Rein ((C) **95-258-93-49**). This modern theater lies between Los Boliches and the town center of Fuengirola.

Otherwise, an evening in Fuengirola means hopping from one tasca to another, indulging in tapas and wine. Much of the nightlife centers on **Plaza Constitución** and along the **Paseo Marítimo,** but we'll let you in on a secret.

The Costa: An Ode to Lost Virginity

Once the Costa del Sol was a paradise, a retreat of the rich and famous, and in the words of British author Laurie Lee, "beautiful but exhausting and seemingly forgotten by the world." The world has now discovered this Mediterranean coastline with a vengeance. A more recent description from leading critic Kenneth Tynan denounced it as "inbred and amoral, a land of Sodom and Gomorrah."

Some social historians claim that the Costa del Sol—no one knows when or how that touristy moniker debuted—had its roots in 1932 when Carlotta Alessandri arrived, buying property west of the village of Torremolinos and announcing that she was going to launch "a Spanish Riviera to equal the French Riviera." But before she could achieve her dream, the Spanish Civil War intervened.

The marquis of Najera arrived in Torremolinos after World War II, bringing his fellow bluebloods. In time, many Spanish noble families, along with a collection of more questionable royals and aristocrats, arrived to bask in the sun. Artists, writers like Ernest Hemingway and James Michener, even movie stars, followed suit.

In the 1960s, hippies arrived in Torremolinos, and brought their drugs with them. You would never have known a right-wing dictator was in power: Flower power and the wafting smell of pot filled the streets.

Turmoil in the Middle East and the 1973 oil crisis drove thousands of Arabs to the coast, seeking safer havens. The fall of the shah of Iran drove many other rich Iranians here. Their presence is still felt in large measure today.

In the 1970s, the London tabloids dubbed Costa the "Costa del Crime." A lack of extradition laws between Spain and Britain—a situation that's since been remedied—encouraged the arrival in Spain of dozens of "British jack-the-lad crooks." These embezzlers and con artists fled justice in England and headed for the coast where they partied extravagantly and uninhibitedly.

By the time the 1980s arrived, the reputation of the coast had largely shifted from caviar and champagne to burgers and beer. Despite that, many big names continued to visit. Sean Connery, for example, was an annual visitor until 1998, and Antonio Banderas and Melanie Griffith own a second home in Los Monteros on the outskirts of Marbella. Julio Iglesias has a villa near Coín, and Bruce Willis owns a retreat outside Estepona.

Today, Torremolinos, and to a lesser extent other parts of the coast, is a place where everyone and anyone can let loose. Lager louts from the industrial Midlands of England parade through the narrow streets at night pursuing wine, women, and drugs. Religious cultists, real-estate hawkers, Las Vegas–style showgirls, and male hustlers in well-filled bikinis all feel at home here. Even young Middle Eastern women, minus their burkas, can be seen on the beach in bikinis smoking dope (illegally).

As far as letting it all hang out and having a great time, there's nowhere quite like Torremolinos. Confession time: In spite of our negativity we always have a blast in this "City of Tourists," as the sign outside town reads.

We generally skip these and head for **Plaza Yates,** an enclosed square that's the most charming in town. On the square itself and on streets branching off it are several little tapas bars. Poke your nose in and check them out. If one appeals, head inside.

If you're looking for something a bit more upscale, head over to **El Tostón,** San Pancracio, Alfonso XII (© **95-247-56-32**), which is also a regular restaurant—and a good one at that. The *jamón ibérico,* costing 9€ ($11) per serving, is reason enough to trek over. It's air-conditioned inside with a terrace outside.

7 Torremolinos

15km (9 miles) W of Málaga, 122km (76 miles) E of Algeciras, 568km (353 miles) S of Madrid

This Mediterranean beach resort is Spain's biggest. It's known as a melting pot of visitors, most of them European and American. Many relax here after a whirlwind tour of Europe—the living is easy, the people are fun, and there are no historical monuments to visit. Once a sleepy fishing village, Torremolinos has been engulfed in a cluster of cement-walled resort hotels. Prices are on the rise, but it remains one of Europe's vacation bargains.

But just because Torremolinos is one of the oldest and most famous resorts along the Costa del Sol, that doesn't mean it's the best: Marbella is a classier act. Because of its ghastly concrete block architecture, filled with cheap rooms for package tours, Torremolinos has been called a holiday inferno.

It's fashionable for travel writers to mock it. One Spanish-language guide, written for nationals, recommends that visitors from other parts of Spain give Torremolinos "wide berth." Many Americans prefer to anchor in Seville, planning side trips to Granada and Córdoba. Yet for all its detractors, this resort is a kitschy hit, attracting crowds of northern Europeans who come here year after year for the sheer, offbeat fun of it.

ESSENTIALS

GETTING THERE   The nearby Málaga airport serves Torremolinos, and frequent **trains** also run from the terminal at Málaga. For train information, call © **90-224-02-02. Buses** run frequently between Málaga and Torremolinos; call © **95-235-00-61** for schedules.

If you're driving, take the N-340/E-15 west from Málaga or the N-340/E-15 east from Marbella.

VISITOR INFORMATION   The **tourist office** at the Plaza de la Independencia (© **95-237-42-31;** www.visitetorremolinos.com) is open daily from 9:30am to 2pm.

GETTING AROUND   Driving around Torremolinos in a car is no way to spend a relaxing holiday. However, if you're a daredevil in traffic, you might find a bike or scooter rental useful. Be extremely careful, however, as the road conditions along Carretera de Cádiz are extremely dangerous. The best outfitter is **Moto Mercado,** Plaza de las Comunidades Autónomas, along Paseo Marítimo (© **95-205-26-71**). A valid driver's license from your home country is required, and you must be 16 or older to rent scooters and motorcycles. Bikes require a 50€ ($60) deposit and are leased at a rate of 10€ ($12) daily, whereas scooters take a 100€ ($120) deposit, plus 24€ to 30€ ($29–$36) per-day rental. Motorcycles also require a credit card deposit (the price depends on the vehicle), and costs begin at 42€ ($50) per day, going up to 120€ ($144) for the more deluxe cycles. Hours are Monday to Saturday 9:30am to 7:30pm, Sunday 9am to 2pm.

Torremolinos

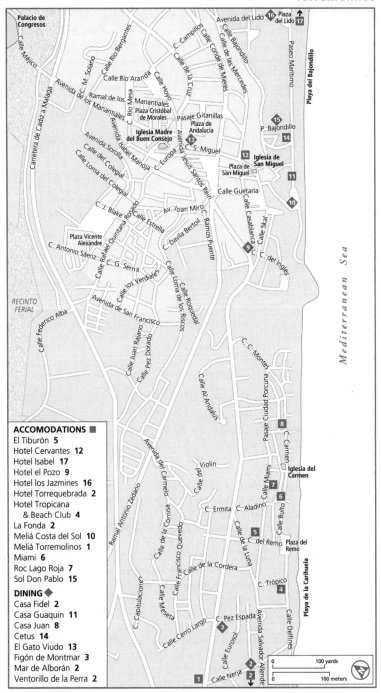

ACCOMODATIONS ■
El Tiburón **5**
Hotel Cervantes **12**
Hotel Isabel **17**
Hotel el Pozo **9**
Hotel los Jazmines **16**
Hotel Torrequebrada **2**
Hotel Tropicana
 & Beach Club **4**
La Fonda **2**
Meliá Costa del Sol **10**
Meliá Torremolinos **1**
Miami **6**
Roc Lago Roja **7**
Sol Don Pablo **15**

DINING ◆
Casa Fidel **2**
Casa Guaquin **11**
Casa Juan **8**
Cetus **14**
El Gato Viudo **13**
Figón de Montmar **3**
Mar de Alborán **2**
Ventorillo de la Perra **2**

EXPLORING TORREMOLINOS & BENALMADENA

The one thing you won't find here are the towers *(torres)* and windmills *(molinos)* that originally gave the little fishing village its name. They have been bulldozed under and replaced with soulless concrete bunkers. Today Torremolinos has been rechristened "Torrie" by its hordes of package tour devotees.

Most visitors are here for the beaches, not the mudéjar architecture. There are two: **El Bajondillo** (also known as Playa de Bajondill) and **La Carihuela,** the latter bordering the old fishing village that is now engulfed in development. The bad news is that the sands aren't golden but a gritty gray.

These beaches are packed in July and August, when you'll find yourself lying next to a dishwasher from Hamburg, a shoe salesman from Leicester, and a janitor in an office building in Stockholm. Let the rich and famous enjoy Marbella. Torremolinos is blue collar—and proud of it.

Unless Torremolinos is leveled to the ground and rebuilt, it will always be a tacky parody of a Spanish seaside resort. Even so, there have been signs of improvement, especially in the recently finished promenade along the seafront that runs all the way to the old fishing village of La Carihuela. It's quite panoramic for the most part. Some of the most offensive stores in the old quarter of Torremolinos—those hawking dildos, for example—are now largely gone, and it's amusing to wander the narrow streets and maze of old alleys. You certainly never have to worry about getting a drink, as the bar-per-block ratio is about three to one.

City officials try to amuse their summer visitors with free events, including music and dance festivals, even jazz concerts. There are sporting competitions as well. Ask at the tourist office about events being staged at the time of your visit.

TORRIE'S HEARTLAND & LA CARIHUELA

While visiting Torrie's overcrowded streets, keep a close grip on your purse or wallet. The resort is divided into two parts, the main town and the fishing village down below. Locals, especially British expats, call the main square **"Central T-town."** It centers on the traffic-clogged Plaza Costa del Sol where you are likely to see an international parade of passersby. The main shopping street is **Calle San Miguel,** hawking some of the junkiest souvenirs in Andalusia. But, surprise, some excellent Spanish goods will often appear in a shop selling otherwise tawdry crafts that aren't worth stuffing in your suitcase.

Brash, bold **Plaza Nogalera** in the heart of Torremolinos is active day and night. Expect sangria bars, gay hangouts, dance clubs, tascas (taverns)—and inflated prices. Pick and choose carefully here.

For strolling, we prefer nearby **Pueblo Blanco,** lying off Calle Casablanca. It doesn't assault you quite as vigorously as Nogalera.

La Carihuela ⚓ lies west of Torrie's center and is most often approached via Avenida Carlotta Alessandri. It has far more Spanish flavor than the town itself, and there are many old fishermen's cottages remaining, but none so compelling that you have to visit for that reason.

Most visit Carihuela for its excellent fish restaurants, many of which are quite naturally found along Paseo Marítimo. On a summer evening when the center of Torremolinos is blistering hot, a summer promenade in Carihuela, enjoying the fresh sea breezes, is the way to go. Andalusian families, who throng here by the thousands, seem to agree.

If you have children in tow, you can take them to **Aquapark,** lying off the bypass in the vicinity of the Palacio de Congresos (a convention center). This water park (✆ **95-238-88-88**) is filled with the usual attractions, including "water mountains," pools, artificial waves, and water chutes. Other attractions include "kamikaze," the highest water toboggan on the continent, and a "black hole," composed of tubes with sharp drops and turns. At least it's a great way to cool off in summer. Charging an admission of 15€ ($17) adults, 10€ ($12) kids, it is open May to June and in September daily from 10am to 6pm and in July and August daily 10am to 7pm.

MORE FUN IN BENALMADENA

Lying 9km (5½ miles) west of Torremolinos, Benalmádena (also called Benál-madena-Costa) is a virtual suburb of Torremolinos, although in the past decade it has been making a somewhat hopeless attempt to establish its own identity.

Package tour operators fill up most of the hotels here. It's not the kind of place you should expect to pay full price. **Puerto Marina Benalmádena,** its yachting haven, is its toniest part and is a popular rendezvous on a hot summer night, especially with the youth of the area. Also intriguing is the village proper, **Benalmádena-Pueblo,** the center of the Old Town or what's left of it. It sprawls across a *sierra* (mountain), lying 7km (4 miles) from the coast. Unlike the heart of old Torremolinos, this pueblo hasn't been completely spoiled. It'll give you a preview of what a small Andalusian town looks like, providing you decide to venture no farther inland. The area is bounded by shops, bars, and other services.

One of the best aquariums in Andalusia is **Sea Life Benalmádena,** at Puerto Marina Benalmádena (✆ **95-256-01-50**). In summer it is open daily from 10am to midnight (closes at 6pm in the off season), charging an admission of 8€ ($9.60). Most of the fish come from local waters, including some fierce sharks, sunfish, and rays swimming around the walk-through glass tunnel.

Tivoli World is the largest amusement park along the coast. Lying at Arroyo de la Miel (✆ **95-244-28-48**), its chief attraction is a 4,000-seat open-air auditorium. Sometimes world-class artists perform here; check at the time of your visit. Expect anything from Spanish ballet to flamenco to corny French cancans. There are at least three dozen restaurants here along with snack bars, plus a Ferris wheel and roller coasters. Naturally, there are also so-called Wild West shows of the Buffalo Bill and Calamity Jane variety. On Sunday a rather junky flea market is staged here from 11am to 2pm when entrance costs only 1€ ($1.20). Otherwise April to October hours are daily from 1pm to 1am (off season Sat–Sun noon–8pm). Regular admission is 4€ ($4.80).

To cap off your visit, board the *teléferico* (**cable bar**), close to Tivoli World. For 7.50€ ($9), you can ascend to the top of Monte Calamorro, for a panoramic sweep of the Costa del Sol. Also rewarding is a 12€ ($14) boat cruise linking Benalmádena with Fuengirola in the west or Málaga in the east. In the peak season, there are about four sailings per day depending on demand. Boats depart from **Costasol Cruceros** at the harbor at Benalmádena. For more information or reservations, call ✆ **95-244-48-81**.

WHERE TO STAY
MODERATE

Hotel Cervantes ✦   The government-rated four-star Cervantes lies in a shopping center, a 7-minute walk from the beach. It has a garden and is adjacent to a maze of patios and narrow streets of boutiques and open-air cafes. Rooms have modern furniture and spacious terraces; many have balconies with sea views. Bathrooms have tub/shower combos. In midsummer this hotel is likely to be booked with tour groups from northern Europe, many of whom can be seen sunning themselves on the hotel's rooftop terrace. A special feature in summer is the luncheon buffet and barbecue by the pool.

Calle las Mercedes s/n, 29620 Torremolinos. (℃) **95-238-40-33**. Fax 95-238-48-57. www.hotasa.es. 397 units. 97€–142€ ($116–$170) double; full board 161€–205€ ($193–$246) double. AE, DC, MC, V. **Amenities:** Restaurant/cafeteria; 2 bars; 2 pools (1 indoor); health club; sauna; limited room service; babysitting; laundry service/dry cleaning; rooms for those w/limited mobility. *In room:* A/C, TV, dataport, hair dryer, safe.

Hotel Isabel *(Value)* One of the best bargains within Torremolinos itself, as opposed to on the outskirts, is this hotel on the beach with a series of balconied terraces for those who demand a sea view. Fully refurbished in 2001, the hotel was built in the late '80s. Thirty-six of its accommodations offer sea-view rooms, and naturally they are rented first. Units for the most part are midsize and furnished comfortably, with matching spreads and curtains and bland art placed here and there. Tiled floors are soothing in the heat. Each unit comes with a tiled bathroom with a tub and shower. There is no restaurant, but literally dozens lie within a 5-minute walk from your door.

Paseo Marítimo 97, 29620 Torremolinos. (℃) **95-238-17-44**. Fax 95-238-11-98. www.hotelisabel.net. 91€–126€ ($109–$151) double. Rates include continental breakfast. MC, V. **Amenities:** 2 bars; outdoor pool; room service (8am–11pm); babysitting; laundry service; rooms for those w/limited mobility. *In room:* A/C, TV, safe (for a fee).

Hotel Tropicana & Beach Club *(★)* Completely renovated and redecorated in 2004, this government-rated four-star hotel stands right on a beach at the beginning of the La Carihuela coastal strip. Boasting its own beach club, Tropicana is desirable mainly because it's removed from the summer hysteria in the heart of Torremolinos. In honor of its namesake, a tropical motif dominates, causing you to feel that you're in a resort more typically found in the Caribbean. Exotic plants, bamboo furnishings, and raffia floor matting only add to that impression.

Some decorators tried to give a little flair to the comfortably furnished and midsize bedrooms, each with a combo tub/shower. Most of the rooms open onto private balconies with sea views. When not on the beach, most of the guests can be found sunning themselves around the kidney-shape pool. Many seafood restaurants lie only a 5-minute stroll from the hotel's door, or else you can patronize Restaurante Mango, with its terrace facing the sea. Most of the international dishes served here are built around fresh fish.

Trópico 6, 29620 Torremolinos. (℃) **95-238-66-00**. Fax 95-238-05-68. www.hotel-tropicana.net. 84 units. 96€–148€ ($115–$178) double. Rates include continental breakfast. AE, DC, MC, V. Free parking. **Amenities:** Restaurant; bar; outdoor pool; beach club; game room; 24-hr. room service; babysitting; laundry service. *In room:* A/C, TV, dataport, minibar, hair dryer, safe.

Meliá Costa del Sol *(★)* There are two Meliá-chain hotels in Torremolinos. The one listed directly below is more luxurious; this one is more centrally located, lying right on the seafront along Playa de Bajondillo, a 10-minute walk from the shopping area of Torremolinos. The midsize rooms are modern and well maintained, and each has a well-kept bathroom with a tub/shower combo. However, the hotel is popular with package tour groups, so you may not feel a part of things if you come alone.

Paseo Marítimo 11, 29620 Torremolinos. (℃) **800/336-3542** in the U.S., or 95-238-66-77. Fax 95-238-64-17. www.solmelia.es. 535 units. 75€–132€ ($90–$158) double; 236€–321€ ($283–$385) suite. AE, DC, MC, V. Free parking. **Amenities:** Restaurant; 2 bars; outdoor pool; salon; 24-hr. room service; babysitting; laundry service/dry cleaning; nonsmoking rooms; rooms for those w/limited mobility; disco. *In room:* A/C, TV, dataport, minibar, hair dryer, safe.

Meliá Torremolinos *(★★)* This is the more luxurious of the two Meliá hotels at the resort, but farther removed from the center, lying in a residential area about 300m (984 ft.) from the beach and 1km (⅔ mile) from the fishing village of Carihuela. Bedrooms are divided between two seven-story buildings. Both public and private rooms open onto panoramic views of the sea or the hotel's tropical gardens. This hotel has deliberately lowered its official government rank from five stars to four, which means you can enjoy the better service at lower prices. The hotel stands in its own gardens on the western outskirts of town on the road to Cádiz. Rooms range from small to spacious, and bathrooms are well furnished and contain tub/shower combos.

Carlota Alessandri 109, 29620 Torremolinos. (C) **800/336-3542** in the U.S., or 95-238-05-00. Fax 95-238-05-38. www.solmelia.com. 289 units. 76€–140€ ($91–$168) double; from 190€–280€ ($228–$336) suite. AE, DC, MC, V. Free parking. Closed Nov–Feb. **Amenities:** Restaurant; 2 bars; outdoor pool; 2 tennis courts; aerobics classes; 24-hr. room service; babysitting; laundry service/dry cleaning; non-smoking rooms; rooms for those w/limited mobility. *In room:* A/C, TV, minibar, hair dryer, safe.

Roc Lago Rojo ⭐ *Finds*   In the heart of the fishing village of La Carihuela, Roc Lago Rojo is the finest place to stay. It stands only 45m (150 ft.) from the beach and has its own gardens and sunbathing terraces. Built in the 1970s and reno-vated at least once since then, it offers tastefully decorated studio-style rooms. All rooms have terraces with views. Bathrooms have showers. In the late evening there is disco dancing.

Miami 5, 29620 Torremolinos. (C) **95-238-76-66.** Fax 95-238-08-91. www.roc-hotels.com. 144 units. 42€–128€ ($50–$154) double. Children 2–12 50% discount. Rates include breakfast. AE, DC, MC, V. **Amenities:** Restaurant; bar; outdoor pool; babysitting; laundry service/dry cleaning. *In room:* A/C, TV, safe.

Sol Don Pablo ⭐   One of the most desirable hotels in the center of Torre-molinos, Don Pablo is in a modern building a minute from Playa de Bajondillo, surrounded by its own garden and playground areas. The surprise is the glam-orous interior, which borrows heavily from Moorish palaces and medieval castle themes. Arched-tile arcades have splashing fountains, and the grand staircase features niches with life-size stone nudes. The comfortably furnished rooms have sea-view terraces, and bathrooms have tub/shower combos.

Calle Bajondillo 36, 29620 Torremolinos. (C) **95-238-38-88.** Fax 95-238-37-83. www.soldonpablo.solmelia. com. 443 units. 85€–144€ ($102–$173) double. Rates include buffet breakfast. AE, DC, MC, V. **Amenities:** Restaurant; 2 bars; lounge; 2 pools (1 indoor); limited room service; babysitting; laundry service/dry cleaning. *In room:* A/C, TV, minibar, hair dryer, safe.

INEXPENSIVE

El Tiburón *Value*   Constructed in 1963 and lying 60m (196 ft.) from La Car-ihuela beach, this medium-size hotel was last renovated in 2003. It is one of the most affordable hotels in the area to the immediate west of Torremolinos, and many of its devotees book rooms year after year. It looks like an inviting, over-grown Mediterranean seaside house, with a beautiful terrace overlooking the water and the shade of palm trees. Life revolves around a central patio in the classic Andalusian style. The small to midsize bedrooms are traditionally and comfortably furnished, each with a tub/shower combo. Things tend to be ster-ile, not lavish, but it's so affordable you don't expect too much. Some 32 of the bedrooms open onto their own private terraces, and some of the accommoda-tions are suitable for triple use. There is no restaurant, but some excellent seafood eateries lie only minutes from your doorstep.

Los Nidos 7, 29620 Torremolinos. (C) **95-238-13-11.** Fax 95-238-22-44. www.hoteltiburon.com. 40 units. 40€–70€ ($48–$84) double. AE, DC, MC, V. **Amenities:** Bar; outdoor pool; laundry service. *In room:* TV, safe (for a fee), fan.

Hotel El Pozo *Value*   This hotel isn't for light sleepers—it's in one of the liveli-est sections of town, a short walk from the train station. It's usually filled with budget travelers, including many students from northern Europe. The lobby level has professional French billiards, heavy Spanish furniture, and a view of a small courtyard. From your window or terrace you can view the promenades below. The small rooms, which contain tub/shower combos, are furnished in a simple, functional style—nothing special, but the price is right.

Casablanca 2, 29620 Torremolinos. ℂ **95-238-06-22.** Fax 95-238-71-17. 28 units. 40€–62€ ($48–$74) double. DC, MC, V. **Amenities:** Bar. *In room:* A/C, TV, safe.

Hotel Los Jazmines Located on one of the best beaches in Torremolinos, Los Jazmines faces a plaza at the foot of the shady Avenida del Lido. Sun-seekers will find it replete with terraces, lawns, and an irregularly shaped swimming pool. The small rooms (all doubles) seem a bit impersonal, but have their own little balconies and compact bathrooms with tub/shower combos. From here it's a good hike up the hill to the town center.

Av. de Lido 6, 29620 Torremolinos. ℂ **95-238-50-33.** Fax 95-237-27-02. 100 units. 50€–75€ ($60–$90) double. AE, DC, MC, V. **Amenities:** Bar; pool. *In room:* A/C, TV, safe.

Miami 𝒦 *Finds* The Miami, near the Carihuela section, might remind you of a 1920s Hollywood movie star's home. High walls and private gardens surround the property. Fuchsia and bougainvillea climb over the rear patio's arches, and a tile terrace is used for sunbathing and refreshments. The country-style living room contains a walk-in fireplace, and the compact rooms are furnished in a traditional, comfortable style and contain bathrooms with tub/shower combos. Each has a balcony. Breakfast is the only meal served.

Calle Aladino 14, 29620 Torremolinos. ℂ **95-238-52-55.** www.residencia-miami.com. 26 units. 35€–57€ ($42–$68) double. No credit cards. Free parking. **Amenities:** Bar; outdoor pool; laundry service. *In room:* A/C, safe.

NEARBY PLACES TO STAY

Where Torremolinos ends and Benalmádena-Costa to the west begins is hard to say. Benalmádena is packed with hotels, restaurants, and tourist facilities.

Hotel Torrequebrada 𝒦𝒦 In the late 1980s this became one of the largest government-rated five-star luxury hotels along the Costa del Sol, and it is without a doubt the most luxurious place to stay in the greater Torremolinos area. Five kilometers (3 miles) west of Torremolinos, it opens onto its own beach and offers a wide range of facilities and attractions. Because of its casino, it is the favorite hotel for gamblers. The spacious, handsomely furnished rooms have large terraces with sea views, and bathrooms have tub/shower combos.

Av. del Sol s/n, 29630 Benalmádena. ℂ **95-244-60-00.** Fax 95-244-27-46. www.torrequebrada.com. 350 units. 249€–292€ ($299–$350) double; 311€–358€ ($373–$430) suite. Rates include breakfast. AE, DC, MC, V. Parking 10€ ($12). **Amenities:** 2 restaurants; 2 bars; 3 pools (1 indoor); tennis court; health club; 2 saunas; salon; 24-hr. room service; babysitting; laundry service/dry cleaning; casino; nonsmoking rooms; rooms for those w/limited mobility. *In room:* A/C, TV, dataport, minibar, hair dryer, safe.

La Fonda 𝒦 *Finds* What is sorely missing in most hotels in Benalmádena and Torremolinos is an inn with true Andalusian flavor. La Fonda succeeds in filling in that gap, lying in an attractive building on one of the more charming streets in a village without many other grace notes. The hotel bills itself as an oasis of tranquillity, and so it is.

The main building itself is filled with plants, regional artifacts, and local furnishings, and is built in the typically Mediterranean villa style, whitewashed and studded with little balconies. The hotel also rents studios and apartments, which are distributed throughout four small buildings 50 to 180m (164–590 ft.) from the main inn itself. These are more impersonal and furnished in a comfortable though somewhat generic international style. In all, there are 11 studios, 20 one-bedroom apartments, and eight two-bedroom apartments, each with a private bathroom with a tub/shower combination. Each unit comes with marble floors, flowery fabrics, and whitewashed walls. Many open onto views of the sea while others front an interior and typically Andalusian courtyard. The on-site pool is heated in winter.

Under different management but in the same building is a restaurant that's the training ground for the official hotel and catering school based in Málaga. You can check it out for lunch only, Monday to Friday.

Santo Domingo 7, in the Sierra de los Castillejos. ✆ 95-256-82-73. 39 units. 60€–70€ ($72–$84) studio; 75€–90€ ($90–$108) apt for 2–3 persons; 87€–105€ ($104–$126) apt for 4–5 persons. AE, DC, MC, V. **Amenities:** Restaurant; bar; outdoor pool. *In room:* TV, minibar.

WHERE TO DINE

The cuisine in Torremolinos is more American and Continental than Andalusian. The hotels often serve elaborate four-course meals, but you might want to sample more casual local offerings. A good spot to try is the food court **La Nogalera** (✆ **95-238-15-00**), the major gathering place between the coast road and the beach. Head down Calle del Cauce to this compound of modern whitewashed Andalusian buildings. Open to pedestrian traffic only, it's a maze of passageways, courtyards, and patios for eating and drinking. You can find anything from sandwiches and pizza to Belgian waffles and scrambled eggs.

AT THE TORREMOLINOS SEAFRONT

Cetus ✿ INTERNATIONAL   Spanish gourmet guides—and we concur—generally concede that this seafront-bordering restaurant is the finest choice within the bustling heart of Torremolinos proper. For other good restaurants, you have to head down to the fishing village of La Carihuela or else fan out to those establishments at Benalmádena to the west. This elegant 1977 house has been decorated with wooden furnishings and creamy colors, providing an inviting spot for dining. Try to reserve a table on the terrace overlooking the sea. We recently enjoyed a creamy red lobster dish served with rice. The kitchen also offers a number of delightful meat dishes. Particularly recommended are the lamb ribs sweetened with honey and flavored with fresh spices and the tender sirloin cooked with port wine sauce and served with fresh vegetables, many from the fields of Andalusia.

Paseo Marítimo. ✆ 95-237-41-18. Reservations recommended. Main courses 16€–28€ ($19–$34). AE, DC, MC, V. Mon–Sat 1–4pm and 7–11pm.

AT LA NOGALERA

El Gato Viudo SPANISH   El Gato Viudo has been a local dining tradition for almost 40 years. Simple and amiable, this old-fashioned tavern occupies the street level and cellar of a building off Calle San Miguel and offers sidewalk seating. The menu includes such good dishes as grilled fish; marinated hake; roasted pork, steak, and veal; calamari with spicy tomato sauce; grilled shrimp; and shellfish or fish soup. The atmosphere is informal, and the staff is accustomed to coping with diners from virtually everywhere.

La Nogalera 11. ✆ 95-238-51-29. Main courses 9€–20€ ($11–$24). AE, DC, MC, V. Daily noon–4pm and 6pm–midnight.

AT LA CARIHUELA

If you want to get away from the high-rises and honky-tonks, head to nearby La Carihuela. In the old fishing village on the western outskirts of Torremolinos you'll find some of the best bargain restaurants. Walk down the hill toward the sea to reach the village.

Casa Guaquín _Finds_ SEAFOOD   On every visit to Torremolinos, we always head for this little charmer of a restaurant, lying in the fishing village of La Carihuela and opening onto a water-bordering terrace, the most desirable tables in summer. A modern building, Guaquín is decorated in a typical nautical style—nothing special—with wooden furnishings. Waiters are often overworked but reasonably efficient. Whatever you order always seems to taste better with the fine and affordable selection of Andalusian wines. We always begin with an order of _coquinas,_ wedge-shaped clams that are a succulent delight. If you think anchovies are just something to put on pizza, order _boguerones fritos,_ sautéed fresh anchovies. Although an acquired taste for some, they are a delight. Some of the main courses are market fresh, including fried cod filet in garlic sauce (our favorite) and some are imported, such as a perfectly roasted salmon. The chef's specialty is fish baked in salt crust to seal in the juices and flavor. Both salt and skin are peeled off before the fish is served to you. Desserts are typical Spanish fare, with the inevitable flan.

Paseo Marítimo 63. ✆ **95-238-45-30.** Reservations recommended. Main courses 20€–31€ ($24–$37). AE, MC, V. Tues–Sun 1–3:30pm and 8–11:30pm. Closed Dec 15–Jan 15.

Casa Juan _ SEAFOOD   In a modern-looking building in La Carihuela, this seafood restaurant is about 1.6km (1 mile) west of Torremolinos's center. Menu items include selections from a lavish display of fish and shellfish prominently positioned near the entrance. You might try _mariscada de mariscos_ (shellfish), a fried platter of mixed fish, cod, kabobs of meat or fish, or paella. Of special note is _lubina a la sal_—sea bass packed in layers of roughly textured salt, broken open at your table, and deboned in front of you. When the restaurant gets busy, as it often does, the staff is likely to rush around hysterically—something many local fans think adds to its charm.

Calle San Gines 18–20, La Carihuela. ✆ **95-237-35-12.** Reservations recommended. Main courses 10€–22€ ($12–$26). AE, DC, MC, V. Tues–Sun 12:30–4:30pm and 7:30–11:30pm. Closed Dec.

Figón de Montemar _ SPANISH/ANDALUSIAN   One of the better restaurants of Torremolinos, Figón de Montemar lies near the beach and like so many others is decorated with glass, tiles, and various nautical paraphernalia. Its chefs call its cuisine _cocina de mercado,_ which means its menus are based on what was good and fresh at the market that day, including the daily seafood catch. From the mountains in the distance comes lamb that is perfectly roasted and seasoned with garlic and spices and served with a mint sauce. _Merluza_ (hake) is baked with fresh spices, and fresh codfish is prepared in a delightful red sauce. Want something more adventurous? You can also order oxtail, a local specialty. Desserts are typical selections, hardly worth saving room for.

Av. Espada 101. ✆ **95-237-26-88.** Reservations recommended. Main courses 26€–32€ ($31–$38). AE, DC, MC, V. Sun–Mon noon–1:30pm; Tues–Sat noon–1:30pm and 5:30–8pm. Closed Jan 15–Feb 15.

AT BENALMADENA

Casa Fidel SPANISH/ANDALUSIAN   During the afternoon you put aside to wander on foot in Benalmádena-Pueblo (the Old Town section of Benalmádena-Costa), perhaps on a shopping spree, consider this rustic restaurant for a lunch stopover. If you're staying in the area, you can also visit for dinner. In the cooler months, a big roaring fireplace greets you, but in summer the shaded courtyard is more alluring. Large wooden beams and dark furnishings evoke Andalusia of yesterday.

Unlike Ventorillo de la Perra (see below), the menu here is quite up-to-date. Chefs, using market-fresh ingredients, lure you with inventive recipes. Among the two signature appetizers on the menu are zucchini tantalizingly stuffed with goat cheese, a perfect combination, or red pepper soup laced with fresh cream and given added flavor with spring onions. If you're visiting in the windy off sea-son the big T-bone steak for two is a perfect choice. It is well flavored with lots of garlic and grilled to your specifications. For lighter fare, try the succulent king prawns flavored with tangy shallots fresh from the garden and garbanzo beans. Desserts are standard, although the cooks make a perfect flan. Regrettably, the employees' attitude seems to be modeled on the restaurant's namesake.

Maestra Ayala 1. ⓒ **95-244-91-65.** Reservations recommended. Main courses 12€–28€ ($14–$34). Thurs–Mon 1–3:30pm; Wed–Mon 7–10pm. Closed Aug.

Mar de Alborán ✦✦ BASQUE/ANDALUSIAN This restaurant's elegantly airy decor is appropriate for its location near the sea, just a short walk from the resort's Puerto Marina. It serves the specialties of both Andalusia and the Basque region of northern Spain. Menu items might include cold terrine of leeks; *kokotxas,* the Basque national dish of hake cheeks in green sauce with clams; anglerfish with prawns; or foie gras served with sweet Málaga wine and raisins. The restaurant's game dishes (available in season) are renowned. Dessert might be a frothy peach mousse with purée of fruit and dark-chocolate sauce.

Alay 5. ⓒ **95-244-64-27.** Reservations recommended. Main courses 12€–20€ ($14–$24); tasting menu 40€ ($48). AE, DC, MC, V. Sun 1:30–4pm; Tues–Fri 1:30–4pm and 8:30pm–midnight; Sat 8:30pm–midnight. Closed Dec 22–Jan 22.

Ventorillo de la Perra ✦ *Finds* ANDALUSIAN/SPANISH If you'd like to eat at a good restaurant while visiting Tivoli World, try this old inn from 1785, one of the oldest restaurants we've found along the Costa del Sol. In this theme park where everything looks as if it were built in 1972 out of concrete, this is a nostalgic journey back to Andalusia of the 1800s. It's the way the Costa del Sol used to be before the invading hordes conquered it.

You can eat on a shaded patio, ideal on a summer day, or head for the inti-mate dining room with its cozy bar. Andalusian cured hams hang from the ceil-ing. You may think you know what gazpacho is until you order *gazpacuelo malagueño,* which is actually served warm. It's a combination of both rice and potatoes, enlivened with fresh shrimp. Another typical soup specialty is *ajo blanco,* a cold almond soup, heavy on the garlic. Almonds appear again in a sauce with your order of rabbit *(conejo).* Lamb appears frequently on the menu as does fresh fish based on the day's catch. What's the catch here? The food is good but the staff seems to go out of their way to be unhelpful.

Av. Constitución 115 Km 13, Arroyo de la Miel. ⓒ **95-244-19-66.** Reservations recommended. Main courses 10€–22€ ($12–$26). AE, DC, MC, V. Tues–Sun 1–3pm and 7–10pm. Closed Nov.

TORREMOLINOS AFTER DARK

Torremolinos has more nightlife than any other spot along the Costa del Sol. The earliest action is always at the bars, which stay lively most of the night, serv-ing drinks and tapas. Sometimes it seems that in Torremolinos there are more bars than people, so you shouldn't have trouble finding one you like. Note that some bars are open during the day as well.

We like the **Bar Central,** Plaza Andalucía, Bloque 1 (ⓒ **95-238-27-60**), for cof-fee, brandy, beer, cocktails, limited sandwiches, and pastries, served indoors or on a large, French-style covered terrace. It's a good spot to meet people. Prices begin at 1.10€ to 1.35€ ($1.30–$1.60) for a beer, 3€ to 3.60€ ($3.60–$4.30) for cock-tails. Open Monday through Saturday from 8am to 1am (later in summer).

La Bodega, San Miguel 40 (© **95-238-73-37**), relies on its colorful clientele and the quality of its tapas to draw customers, who seem to rank this place above the dozens of other tascas in this popular tourist zone. Many guests come here for lunch or dinner, making a satisfying meal from the plentiful bar food. You'll be lucky if you find space at one of the small tables, but once you begin to order—platters of fried squid, pungent tuna, grilled shrimp, tiny brochettes of sole—you might not be able to stop. Most tapas cost 1.75€ ($2.10). A beer costs 1.30€ to 1.60€ ($1.55–$1.90), a hard drink at least 2.70€ to 3€ ($3.25–$3.60). Open daily from 12:30pm to 11:30pm (closes at 7pm on Sun).

Ready to dance off all those tapas? **El Palladium,** Palma de Mallorca (© **95-238-42-89**), a well-designed nightclub in the town center, is one of the most convivial in Torremolinos. Strobes, spotlights, and a loud sound system set the scene. There's even a swimming pool. Expect to pay 3€ ($3.60) or more for a drink; cover is 6€ ($7.20), including one drink after 11pm. Open from 11pm to 6am in summer months only.

For flamenco, albeit it of a touristy kind, head for **Taberna Flamenca Pepe López,** Plaza de la Gamba Alegre (© **95-238-12-84**), in the center of Torremolinos. In an old house (at least old in the Torremolinos sense), this is a tavern-style joint with darkened wooden furnishings. Many of the artists come from the *boîtes* of Seville and Granada, and they perform nightly at 10pm April to October. Shows are substantially reduced during the cooler months, and confined mainly to the weekends—call to confirm first. A 23€ ($28) cover includes your first drink and the show.

Gay men and women from throughout northern Europe are almost always in residence in Torremolinos; if you want to meet some of them, consider a drink or two at **Isadora,** La Nogalera 714 (no phone), open daily 6pm to dawn. Other options, all around La Nogalera, include **Anfora,** La Nogalera 521 (no phone, same hours as Isadora), which does not get busy till well after 10pm, and **Morbos,** La Nogalera 113 (no phone), which is open 6pm till 5am. The most popular gay disco in town is the **Passion,** Av. Palma de Mallorca (no phone), which plays popular dance music for a very cruisy crowd 10pm to 6am.

One of the Costa del Sol's major casinos, **Casino Torrequebrada,** Avenida del Sol, Benalmádena-Costa (© **95-244-60-00**), is on the lobby level of the Hotel Torrequebrada (see "Where to Stay," earlier in this chapter). It has tables devoted to blackjack, chemin de fer, punto y banco, and two kinds of roulette. The casino is open daily from 9am to 5am. The nightclub offers a flamenco show year-round, at 10:30pm Tuesday to Saturday nights; in midsummer, there might be more glitz and more frequent shows (ask when you get there or call). Nightclub acts begin at 10:30pm (Las Vegas revue) and 11:30pm (Spanish revue). The restaurant is open nightly from 9 to 11pm. Casino admission is 4€ ($4.80); with one drink, both shows, casino and cabaret/nightclub admission, it's 32€ ($38), with dinner, 65€ ($78). Bring your passport to be admitted.

8 Málaga ⟨★⟩

548km (340 miles) S of Madrid, 132km (82 miles) E of Algeciras

Málaga is a bustling commercial and residential center with an economy that does not depend exclusively on tourism. With a population of 550,000, Málaga is not only the capital of the Costa del Sol but also Andalusia's largest coastal city. It was the birthplace of Pablo Picasso, and a museum devoted to the artist is its chief attraction today.

Málaga

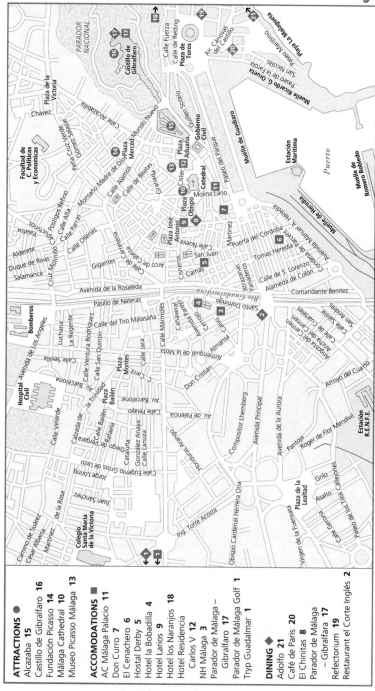

ATTRACTIONS ●
Alcazaba **15**
Castillo de Gibralfaro **16**
Fundación Picasso **14**
Málaga Cathedral **10**
Museo Picasso Málaga **13**

ACCOMODATIONS ■
AC Málaga Palacio **11**
Don Curro **7**
El Cenachero **6**
Hostal Derby **5**
Hotel la Bobadilla **4**
Hotel Larios **9**
Hotel los Naranjos **18**
Hotel Residencia
  Carlos V **12**
NH Málaga **3**
Parador de Málaga –
  Gibralfaro **17**
Parador de Málaga Golf **1**
Tryp Guadalmar **1**

DINING ◆
Adolfo **21**
Café de París **20**
El Chinitas **8**
Parador de Málaga
  – Gibralfara **17**
Refectorium **19**
Restaurant el Corte Inglés **2**

343

In spite of its crime, noise, pollution, and traffic, it is also the cultural capital of the coast, with more museums and historic monuments than any other resort in this chapter. For most rail and air passengers, Málaga is the gateway to the Costa del Sol, but most visitors move on to other resorts in the east or west before nightfall.

However, those who linger in Málaga find much to reward them, including the city's *casco antiguo,* the cultural heart of the Old Town. Linger at least long enough to taste the sweet Málaga wine, famous since antiquity and served from 500-liter barrels in little tascas and bodegas.

Paseo del Parque is the center of town. It begins at Plaza de la Marina (you'll find underground parking here), and curves to the east. This is a palm-lined pedestrian promenade filled with banana trees and fountains, even duck-filled ponds.

The beaches, for the most part, are popular for their bars, not their gritty, grayish sands. Paseo Marítimo runs along La Malagueta Beach, but even better are the beaches lying to the east of Baños de Carmen and El Palo.

ESSENTIALS

GETTING THERE Travelers from North America must transfer for Málaga in Madrid or Barcelona. From within Europe, some airlines (including British Airways from London) offer nonstop flights to Málaga. **Iberia** has frequent service, and even more flights offered through its affiliate airline, **Binter.** Flights can be booked through Iberia's reservations line (© **800/772-4642** in the U.S., or 90-240-05-00 in Spain).

At least five **trains** a day arrive in Málaga from Madrid (trip time: 4 hr.). Three trains a day connect Seville and Málaga (3 hr.). For ticket prices and rail information in Málaga, call RENFE (© **90-224-02-02**).

Buses from all over Spain arrive at the terminal on the Paseo de los Tilos, behind the RENFE offices. Buses run to all the major Spanish cities, including eight buses per day from Madrid (trip time: 7 hr.), five per day from Córdoba, and 10 per day from Seville. Call © **95-235-00-61** in Málaga for bus information.

From resorts in the west (such as Torremolinos and Marbella), you can drive east along the N-340/E-15 to Málaga. If you're in the east at the end of the Costa del Sol (Almería), take the N-340/E-15 west to Málaga, with a stopover at Nerja.

VISITOR INFORMATION The **tourist office** at Pasaje de Chinitas 4 (© **95-221-34-45**; www.andalusia.org) is open Monday to Friday 8:30am to 8:30pm, Saturday 10am to 5pm, Sunday 10am to 2pm.

SPECIAL EVENTS The most festive time in Málaga is the first week in August, when the city celebrates its reconquest by Ferdinand and Isabella in 1487. The big *feria* (**fair**) is an occasion for parades and bullfights. A major tree-shaded boulevard, the Paseo del Parque, is transformed into a fairground featuring amusements and restaurants.

EXPLORING MALAGA

Unlike the rest of the Costa del Sol, Málaga has several historical sites of interest.

Alcazaba ☆ The remains of this ancient Moorish palace are within easy walking distance of the city center, off the Paseo del Parque. Plenty of signs point the way up the hill. The fortress was erected in the 9th or 10th century, although there have been later additions and reconstructions. Ferdinand and Isabella stayed here when they reconquered the city. With orange trees and purple bougainvillea making the grounds even more beautiful, the view overlooking the city and the bay is among the most panoramic on the Costa del Sol.

Plaza de la Aduana, Alcazabilla. (℃ **95-221-60-05.** Admission 1.80€ ($2.15). Museum Tues–Sun 8:30am–7pm. Bus: 4, 18, 19, 24, or 135.

Castillo de Gibralfaro

On a hill overlooking Málaga and the Mediterranean are the ruins of an ancient Moorish castle-fortress of unknown origin. It is near the government-run parador, and might easily be tied in with a luncheon visit.

Warning: Do not walk to Gibralfaro Castle from town. Readers have reported muggings along the way, and the area around the castle is dangerous. Take the bus from the cathedral.

Cerro de Gibralfaro. Admission 1.80€ ($2.15). Daylight hours. Microbus: 35, leaving hourly from cathedral.

Fundación Picasso

A well-told tale concerns the birth of Picasso: In October 1891, when the artist was born, he was unable to draw breath until his uncle blew cigar smoke into his lungs. Whether this rather harsh entry into the world had any effect on his work is mere speculation. What cannot be denied is the effect he was to have on the world. He was born in a five-story building in the heart of Málaga's historic quarter; this is where he spent the first 17 months of his life. Today, the house is both headquarters of the Picasso Foundation and a library for art historians. The Picasso family lived on the second floor, called Casa Natal. Regrettably, the original furnishings are long gone. What you'll see today is a permanent exhibit of Picasso ceramics, sculpture, and engravings. The museum mounts temporary exhibitions featuring avant-garde works from Picasso's time.

Plaza de la Merced 15. (℃ **95-206-02-15.** Free admission (Casa Natal 1€/$1.20). Mon–Sat 10am–8pm; Sun 10am–2pm.

Málaga Cathedral

This 16th-century Renaissance cathedral in Málaga's center, built on the site of a great mosque, suffered damage during the Spanish Civil War. However, it remains vast and impressive, reflecting changing styles of interior architecture. Its most notable attributes are the richly ornamented choir stalls by Ortiz, Mena, and Michael. The cathedral has been declared a national monument.

Plaza Obispo. (℃ **95-221-59-17.** Admission 2€ ($2.40). Mon–Sat 10am–6:30pm. Closed holidays. Bus: 14, 18, 19, or 24.

Museo Picasso Málaga ✮✮✮

In the old quarter of the city, a short walk from the Picasso's birthplace, a museum has opened displaying some of his important works. The new museum combines a restored 16th-century mudéjar palace, Palacio de Buenvista, with a series of modernist buildings that evoke the Pueblos Blancos in the hills above Málaga. The Spanish dictator Franco detested Picasso, his politics, and his "degenerate art," and refused the artist's offer to send paintings from France to Málaga in the 1950s. Ultimately, the collection here was made possible by two of Picasso's heirs: his son Paulo's wife, Christine Ruiz-Picasso, and Bernard, Christine and Paulo's son. Many of the artworks are virtual family heirlooms, including paintings depicting one of the artist's wives, such as *Olga Kokhlova with Mantilla*, or one of his lovers, *Jacqueline Seated*. Basically this is the art Picasso gave to his family or else the art he wanted to keep for himself—in all, more than 200 paintings, drawings, sculpture, ceramics, and graphics. Some other notable works on display—many of them never on public view before—include *Bust of a Woman with Arms Crossed Behind Her Head*,

Woman in an Armchair, and *The Eyes of the Artist.* There is also a memorable painting of Picasso's son, done in 1923.

San Agustín 8. ℂ **95-260-27-31.** www.museopicassomalaga.org. Combined permanent collection and exhibitions 8€ ($9.60); half-price for seniors, students, and children 10–16; free for children under 10. Tues–Sun 10am–8pm; Fri–Sat 10am–9pm.

SHOPPING

The region around Málaga produces artfully rustic pottery, which makes a nice gift or souvenir. A handful of appealing outlets are scattered throughout the city's historic core. One of the best is **Los Artesanos,** Cister 13 (ℂ **95-260-45-44**). Outside the town limits, the most comprehensive collection of ceramics and pottery can be found at **La Vistillas,** Carretera Mijas Km 2 (ℂ **95-245-13-63**), about 2km (1¼ miles) from Málaga's center.

WHERE TO STAY

For such a large city in a resort area, Málaga has surprisingly few hotels. Book well in advance, especially if you want to stay in a parador.

EXPENSIVE

AC Málaga Palacio ⭐ The leading hotel in the town center, the Palacio opens onto a tree-lined esplanade near the cathedral and the harbor. Most balconies offer views of the port, and below you can see horses pulling century-old carriages. The midsize rooms are traditionally furnished and have firm beds and bathrooms with tub/shower combos. The street-floor lounges mix antiques with more modern furnishings. One Toronto couple writes that the breakfast buffet is excellent but you "can't get a hot cup of coffee here no matter how you try."

Cortina del Muelle 1, 29015 Málaga. ℂ **95-221-51-85.** Fax 95-222-51-00. www.ac-hoteles.com. 214 units. 123€–180€ ($148–$216) double; 147€–324€ ($176–$389) suite. AE, DC, MC, V. Parking 16€ ($19) nearby. Bus: 4, 18, 19, or 24. **Amenities:** Restaurant; bar; outdoor pool; fitness center; sauna; 24-hr. room service; babysitting; laundry service/dry cleaning; nonsmoking rooms; rooms for those w/limited mobility. *In room:* A/C, TV, minibar, hair dryer.

Hotel Larios ⭐ On the main street of the Old Town, a 5-minute walk from the Picasso Museum, this hotel ranks just behind the parador as the most desirable place to stay in town. The interior is contemporary and stylish, with a terrace opening onto a panoramic view of the city. The midsize rooms are decorated in a minimalist but stylish way. All have comfortable furnishings, including bathrooms with tub/shower combos, and the suites come with whirlpool tubs. Because of the hotel's popularity you should book well in advance.

Calle Marqués de Larios 2, 29005 Málaga. ℂ **95-222-22-00.** Fax 95-222-24-07. www.hotel-larios.com. 40 units. 115€–153€ ($138–$184) double; 134€–186€ ($161–$223) suite. AE, DC, MC, V. **Amenities:** Restaurant; bar; 24-hr. room service; babysitting; laundry service/dry cleaning. *In room:* A/C, TV, minibar, hair dryer, safe.

Parador de Málaga-Gibralfaro ⭐⭐ Restored in 1994, this is one of Spain's oldest, most tradition-heavy paradors. It enjoys a scenic location high on a plateau near an old fortified castle. Overlooking the city and the Mediterranean, it has views of the bullring, mountains, and beaches. Rooms have private entrances, living-room areas, and wide glass doors opening onto private sun terraces. Bathrooms have tub/shower combos.

Castillo de Gibralfaro s/n, 29016 Málaga. ℂ **95-222-19-02.** Fax 952-22-19-04. www.parador.es. 38 units. 122€–123€ ($146–$148) double. AE, DC, MC, V. Free parking. Take the coastal road, Paseo de Reding, which becomes Av. de Pries and then Paseo de Sancha. Turn left onto Camino Nuevo and follow the small signs. **Amenities:** Restaurant (see "Where to Dine," below); bar; outdoor pool; limited room service; laundry service/dry cleaning; currency exchange; rooms for those w/limited mobility. *In room:* A/C, TV, dataport, minibar, hair dryer, safe.

Tryp Guadalmar ☆ (Kids)   Drenched in sunlight, this nine-story modern hotel sits across from a private beach 3km (2 miles) west of the center of Málaga. It benefited from a radical renovation in 1996 and a takeover by the well-respected Tryp chain. Accommodations are spacious, airy, and simply furnished; each room has a private sea-view balcony and a bathroom with tub/shower combo. Families check in here to use the beach in front, one of the safest in the area. The staff plans activities for children from June to September, including swimming lessons. An air of anonymity prevails as the staff struggles with constant exposure to the comings and goings of large numbers of vacationers.

Calle Mobydick 2, Urbanización Guadalmar, 29004 Málaga. ℂ 95-223-17-03. Fax 95-224-03-85. www.solmelia.com. 194 units. 168€ ($202) double; 303€ ($364) junior suite; 415€ ($498) suite. Children under 12 stay half-price in parent's room. AE, DC, MC, V. Free parking. **Amenities:** 2 restaurants; bar; 2 pools (1 indoor); health club; Jacuzzi; sauna; limited room service; babysitting; laundry service/dry cleaning; non-smoking rooms; rooms for those w/limited mobility. *In room:* A/C, TV, dataport, minibar, hair dryer, safe.

MODERATE

Don Curro   Right in the center of Málaga, just around the corner from the cathedral, this is a typical government-rated three-star hotel 100m (328 ft.) from Malagueta Beach. Traditional in style, it is half a century old, although it was last renovated in 2004. Most of the rooms are midsize, a mix of classical and modern decor, with lots of wooden furniture. The most desirable rooms are those in the more modern wing at the rear of the building. Each room comes with a tiled bathroom with tub/shower combo. The hotel is family run and extends a welcoming atmosphere. Public rooms are paneled in wood, and there is a cozy fireplace lounge.

Sancha de Lara 7, 29015 Málaga. ℂ 25-222-72-00. Fax 95-221-59-46. www.hoteldoncurro.com. 112 units. 81€–102€ ($97–$122) double; 94€–118€ ($113–$142) suite. Children under 12 stay free in parent's room. AE, DC, MC, V. Parking 13€ ($16). **Amenities:** Restaurant; bar; room service (8am–2am); laundry service/dry cleaning. *In room:* A/C, TV, dataport, minibar, hair dryer (in some), safe.

Hotel los Naranjos (Value)   The well-maintained Hotel los Naranjos is one of the more reasonably priced choices in the city. It's 1.6km (1 mile) from the heart of town on the eastern side of Málaga, past the Plaza de Toros (bullring), near the best beach in Málaga, the Baños del Carmen. The hotel offers midsize, contemporary rooms. Some bathrooms have only showers. Breakfast (which costs extra) is the only meal served.

Paseo de Sancha 35, 29016 Málaga. ℂ 95-222-43-19. Fax 95-222-59-75. www.hotel-losnaranjos.com. 41 units. 98€–110€ ($118–$132) double; 126€–140€ ($151–$168) suite. AE, DC, MC, V. Parking 11€ ($13). Bus: 11. **Amenities:** Restaurant; bar; limited room service; laundry service/dry cleaning. *In room:* A/C, TV, dataport, minibar, hair dryer, safe.

NH Málaga   Lying in the commercial and historic center, this 1999 hotel is not near a beach but convenient for sightseeing and shopping. Next to the Puente (bridge) de la Esperanza, it is a functional and well-managed choice with soundproof windows cutting down on the traffic noise. Its bedrooms, furnished with wooden floors and mainly dark furnishings, are a bit small. The adjoining bathrooms with tub/shower combos are also small. There is a wide variation in the price of rooms. Only four are in the expensive category, and they are virtually junior suites, the best in the house. Otherwise, accommodations here are quite affordable. For such a standard chain format, there are surprising extras such as a choice of pillows (firm, soft, duvet), and deluxe toiletries.

Av. Río Guadalmedina s/n, 29007 Málaga. ℂ 95-207-13-23. Fax 95-239-38-62. www.nh-hoteles.com. 133 units. 76€–249€ ($91–$299) double. Rates include continental breakfast. AE, DC, MC, V. Free parking. **Amenities:** Restaurant; 2 bars; gym; sauna; car rental; 24-hr. room service; babysitting; laundry service/dry cleaning; rooms for those w/limited mobility. *In room:* A/C, TV, dataport, minibar, hair dryer.

Parador de Málaga Golf ☆☆ A tasteful resort hotel created by the Spanish government, this hacienda-style parador is flanked by a golf course on one side and the Mediterranean on another. It's less than 3km (2 miles) from the airport, 11km (6½ miles) from Málaga, and 4km (2½ miles) from Torremolinos. Rooms have private balconies with water views. Some units have whirlpool tubs, others just tiled showers. The furnishings are attractive, and the beds excellent.

This restaurant has an indoor/outdoor dining room and a refined country-club atmosphere. The Spanish dishes range from 12€ to 24€ ($14–$29).

Carretera de Málaga, Apartado de Correos 324, 29080 Torremolinos, Málaga. ℂ **95-238-12-55.** Fax 95-238-89-63. www.parador.es. 60 units. 114€–181€ ($137–$217) double. AE, DC, MC, V. Free parking. **Amenities:** Restaurant; bar; lounge; outdoor pool; golf course; tennis courts; limited room service; babysitting; laundry service/dry cleaning; nonsmoking rooms; rooms for those w/limited mobility. *In room:* A/C, TV, dataport, minibar, hair dryer, safe.

INEXPENSIVE

El Cenachero Opened in 1969, this modest little hotel is 5 blocks from the park near the harbor. The nicely carpeted rooms are simply and functionally furnished; half have showers, the rest full bathrooms. No meals are served.

Barroso 5, 29001 Málaga. ℂ **95-222-40-88.** 14 units. 43€–50€ ($52–$60) double. No credit cards. Bus: 4 or 14. **Amenities:** Lounge. *In room:* TV.

Hostal Derby ☆ *Value* This is an amazing discovery not because it's an exceptional place to stay—it's not—but because it charges prices the town hasn't seen since the Franco era. A fourth-floor boardinghouse, it's in the heart of town, on a main square directly north of the train station. Some of the rather basic, cramped rooms have excellent views of the Mediterranean and the port of Málaga. Most units have a shower only. No breakfast is served, and the hotel is very light on extras.

San Juan de Dios 1, 29015 Málaga. ℂ **95-222-13-01.** 16 units, 12 with bathroom. 33€ ($40) double with sink; 36€–45€ ($43–$54) double with bathroom. No credit cards. Bus: 7, 9, 12, 14, 15, 16, or 17. **Amenities:** Lounge.

Hotel Residencia Carlos V This hotel is in a central location near the cathedral, with an interesting facade decorated with wrought-iron balconies and *miradores* (viewing stations). It's a reliable, conservative choice. The small rooms are furnished in a no-frills style, but are well maintained and equipped with bathrooms containing tub/shower combos.

Cister 10, 29015 Málaga. ℂ **95-221-51-20.** Fax 95-221-51-29. carlosv@spa.es. 50 units. 55€–62€ ($66–$74) double. AE, DC, MC, V. Parking 10€ ($12). Bus: 3 from the rail station. **Amenities:** Breakfast room. *In room:* A/C, TV.

A LUXURIOUS PLACE TO STAY NEARBY

Hotel La Bobadilla ☆☆☆ An hour's drive northeast of Málaga, La Bobadilla is the most luxurious retreat in southern Spain. It is a secluded oasis in the foothills of the Sierra Nevada near the town of Loja, which is 71km (44 miles) north of Málaga. La Bobadilla is a 21km (13-mile) drive from Loja.

The hotel complex is built like an Andalusian village, a cluster of whitewashed *casas* constructed around a tower and a white church. Every *casa* has a roof terrace and a balcony overlooking the olive grove–studded district. Each is sumptuous and individually designed, from the least expensive doubles to the most expensive King's Suite (which has plenty of room for bodyguards). All rooms have extravagant bathrooms containing tub/shower combos. The hotel caters to a pampered coterie of international guests, and the service is perhaps the finest in Spain.

The hotel village stands on a hillside, on 404 hectares (1,000 acres) of private, unspoiled grounds. If you get bored in this lap of luxury, you can always drive to Granada, an hour away. Should you decide to marry your companion at the resort, there's a chapel with a 9m-high (30-ft.) organ and 1,595 pipes.

An haute cuisine is prepared in the formal dining room, La Finca, which specializes in fresh shellfish and paellas, but also includes some local specialties such as marinated partridge. The other restaurant, El Cotijo, serves local favorites such as gazpacho, seafood rice, small codfish cakes, and fresh sardines roasted on bamboo sticks.

Finca La Bobadilla, Apartado 144E, 18300 Loja (Granada). ✆ **95-832-18-61.** Fax 95-832-18-10. 62 units. 264€–303€ ($317–$364) double; 342€–391€ ($410–$469) suite. Rates include breakfast. AE, DC, MC, V. Free parking. From the Málaga airport, follow signs toward Granada, but at Km 175 continue through the village of Salinas. Take road marked SALINAS/RUTE; after 3km (2 miles), follow signposts for hotel to the entrance. **Amenities:** 2 restaurants; bar; 2 pools (1 indoor); 2 outdoor unlit tennis courts; fitness center; sauna; whirlpool; salon; 24-hr. room service; babysitting; laundry service/dry cleaning; rooms for those w/limited mobility; horseback riding. *In room:* A/C, TV, dataport, minibar, hair dryer, safe.

WHERE TO DINE
EXPENSIVE
Café de París 🎔🎔 FRENCH/SPANISH   Café de París, Málaga's best restaurant, is in La Malagueta, the district surrounding the Plaza de Toros (bullring). Proprietor José García Cortés worked at many important dining rooms before carving out his own niche. His son, José Carlos García, is the chef. Much of Cortés's cuisine has been adapted from classic French dishes to please the Andalusian palate. You might be served crepes gratinées filled with baby eels or local whitefish baked in a salt crust. Stroganoff is given a Spanish twist with the use of ox meat. Save room for the creative desserts, such as citrus-flavored sorbet made with champagne or custard-apple mousse.

Vélez Málaga 8. ✆ **95-222-50-43.** Reservations required. Main courses 18€–26€ ($22–$31); *menú del día* 35€ ($42); tasting menu 70€ ($84). AE, DC, MC, V. Mon 1:30–3:30pm; Tues–Sat 1:30–3:30pm and 8:30–11pm. Closed July 1–15. Bus: 13.

Escuela de Hostelería 🎔 *Finds* MEDITERRANEAN   We were surprised and pleased to discover this restaurant that's part of a hotel and catering school housed in a villa from the 1800s. It's 8km (5 miles) outside Málaga and 3km (1¾ miles) from the international airport. In business since the early 1990s, this place is mainly patronized by discerning locals with a taste for good food. The menu is changed monthly. Dishes are no mere student experiments, but carefully crafted dishes. Freshly caught *merluza* (hake) is perfectly prepared with zesty mussels and mushrooms in a parsley-laced sauce. In autumn, loin of deer might appear on the menu with a chestnut purée. An excellent dish we recently sampled was loin of beef broiled and served with a red-wine sauce. Another specialty that frequently appears is ham-covered filet of pork served with a Málaga wine sauce. The desserts are made fresh daily and are sumptuous. The villa is old but the dining room adjoining it is modern, opening onto a garden.

Finca La Cónsula, Churriana. ✆ **95-262-25-62.** Reservations required. Main courses 18€–22€ ($22–$26); fixed-price lunch 27€ ($32). AE, DC, MC, V. Mon–Fri 1–4pm. Closed Aug.

MODERATE
Adolfo 🎔 INTERNATIONAL/ANDALUSIAN   Along the ocean-bordering Paseo Marítimo, this restaurant has been one of the best and most reliable in Málaga ever since opening to instant success in the mid-1990s. The decor is regional, with hardwood floors and exposed brick walls. Backed up by an excellent

wine list strong on Andalusian vintages, the restaurant has a friendly, helpful staff. Well worth ordering are such daily specials as hake in a green sauce and duck glazed with a sweet wine. The big favorite here, often ordered on festive occasions, is roast suckling pig flavored with garden herbs. Two other delicious choices are stewed anglerfish with prawns and wild mushrooms and roast baby kid in a rosemary-flavored honey sauce.

Paseo Marítimo Pablo Ruiz Picasso 12. 📞 **95-260-19-14**. Reservations recommended. Main courses 12€–20€ ($14–$24). AE, DC, MC, V. Mon–Sat 1:30–4pm and 8:30–11pm. Closed June.

El Chinitas ✦ SPANISH/MEDITERRANEAN In the heart of Málaga, a short walk from the tourist office, is this well-established restaurant. Many regular patrons consume a round of tapas and drinks at the associated Bar Orellana next door (which maintains the same hours, minus the midafternoon closing), then head to Chinitas for a meal. The place is often filled with locals, always a good sign. The menu changes but might include a mixed fish fry, grilled red mullet, shrimp cocktail, grilled sirloin, or shellfish soup. The service manages to be both fast and attentive.

Moreno Monroy 4. 📞 **95-221-09-72**. Reservations recommended. Main courses 8€–20€ ($9.60–$24). DC, MC, V. Daily 1–4pm and 8pm–midnight.

Parador de Málaga-Gibralfara SPANISH This government-owned restaurant, on a mountainside high above the city, is especially notable for its view. You can look down into the heart of the Málaga bullring, among other sights. Meals are served in the attractive dining room or under the arches of two wide terraces with views of the coast. Featured dishes include *hors d'oeuvres parador*—your entire table will covered with tiny dishes full of tasty tidbits. Two other specialties are an omelet of *chanquetes,* tiny whitefish popular in this part of the country, and chicken Villaroi. Otherwise, the quality of the food varies greatly.

Monte Gibralfara. 📞 **95-222-19-02**. Main courses 11€–23€ ($13–$28); fixed-price menu 25€ ($30). AE, DC, MC, V. Daily 1–4pm and 8:30–11pm. Microbus: 35.

INEXPENSIVE

For more inexpensive dining options, see "Málaga After Dark," below.

Refectorium SPANISH Located behind the Málaga bullring, this place becomes hectic during any bullfight, filling up with fans and often, after the fight, with the matadors too. The cuisine has an old-fashioned flair, and the servings are generous. Try a typical Málaga soup, *ajo blanco con uvas* (cold almond soup flavored with garlic and garnished with big muscatel grapes). Another classic opener is garlicky mushrooms with bits of ham. The fresh seafood is a delight, including *rape* (monkfish) and angler; lamb might be served with a saffron-flavored tomato sauce. Desserts are like Mama made, including rice pudding.

Calle Cervantes 8. 📞 **95-221-89-90**. Reservations recommended on weekends and at bullfights. Main courses 6€–18€ ($7.20–$22). AE, DC, MC, V. Mon–Sat 1:30–5pm and 8pm–midnight.

Restaurante El Corte Inglés SPANISH Although it originated to lure shoppers into Málaga's best department store, this restaurant quickly developed a clientele of its own, and today enjoys a stream of steady customers who come here to eat, not just to shop. On the sixth floor of El Corte Inglés, it offers an array of salads, hot and cold meats, and fish. The setting is dignified and comfortable, and the staff well trained. You might try green peppers stuffed with shellfish, filet of pork in pepper-cream sauce, or sirloin steak with spices. There's a long wine list.

In El Corte Inglés department store, Av. de Andalucía 4–6. 📞 **96-207-65-00**. Main courses 8€–19€ ($9.60–$23). AE, DC, MC, V. Mon–Sat 10am–9:30pm. Bus: 15.

MALAGA AFTER DARK

The fun of nightlife in Málaga is just wandering, although there are a few stand-out destinations. More than just about any other city in the region, Málaga offers night owls the chance to stroll a labyrinth of inner-city streets, drinking wine at any convenient tasca and talking with friends and new acquaintances.

Start out along the town's main thoroughfare, **Calle Larios,** adjacent to the city's port. Off Calle Larios, you can gravitate to any of the tascas, discos, and pubs lining the edges of the **Calle Granada.** Particularly fun and atmospheric is **La Posada,** Calle Granada 33 (no phone).

If you want to eat well and cheaply, do as the locals do and head for the taverns below. Don't expect a refined experience, but the food is some of the most enjoyable and least expensive in Málaga. You can easily fill up on two or three orders of tapas because portions are extremely generous.

The entrance to **Bar Logüeno,** Marín García 9 (© **95-222-30-48**), is behind a wrought-iron-and-glass door. It leads into a stucco-lined room decorated in a local tavern style—enough hams, bouquets of garlic, beer kegs, and sausages to feed a village for a week. However, there's hardly enough room to stand, and you'll invariably be jostled by a busy waiter shouting "Calamari!" to the cooks.

Nearby, an all-pedestrian street, **Calle Compagnía,** and a square, the **Plaza Uncibaj,** are home to simpler tascas. Completely unpretentious (and in some cases without any discernable name), they serve glasses of wine and tapas similar to those available from their neighbors.

A popular dance bar is **Saloma,** Calle Luis de Velázquez 5 (© **95-222-05-03**), and **Cosa Nuestra,** Calle Las Lazcano 5. Don't even think of heading there before 11pm, but the music will probably continue till at least 4am.

The main theater in the province is **Teatro Cervantes,** Ramos Marin s/n (© **95-222-41-09**), which opened its doors in the second half of the 19th century. Reopened in 1987 after a long closure by Queen Sofia, this is an elegant yet austere building. Its programs include plays in Spanish, but also a number of concerts and flamenco entertainment of interest to all. The major performances of the Málaga Symphony Orchestra are staged here in winter. The theater is open from mid-September until the end of June; its box office is open Monday to Saturday 9am to 3pm.

9 Nerja 🖈🖈

52km (32 miles) E of Málaga, 168km (104 miles) W of Almería, 548km (340 miles) S of Madrid

Nerja is known for its good beaches and small coves, its seclusion, its narrow streets and courtyards, and its whitewashed flat-roofed houses. Nearby is one of Spain's greatest attractions, the **Cave of Nerja.**

At the mouth of the Chillar River, Nerja gets its name from the Arabic word *narixa,* meaning "bountiful spring." Its most dramatic spot is the **Balcón de Europa (Balcony of Europe)** 🖈🖈, a palm-shaded promenade jutting out into the Mediterranean. The walkway was built in 1885 in honor of a visit from the Spanish king Alfonso XIII in the wake of an earthquake that had shattered part of nearby Málaga. To reach the best beaches, head west from the Balcón and follow the shoreline.

ESSENTIALS

GETTING THERE   At least 18 **buses** per day make the 1½-hour trip from Málaga. From Almería, eight buses a day take 3½ to 4 hours. Call the bus station, Av. Pescia s/n (© **95-252-15-04**), for information and schedules.

If you're driving, head along the N-340/E-15 east from Málaga or take the N-340/E-15 west from Almería.

VISITOR INFORMATION   The **tourist office** at Puerta del Mar 2 (*C* **95-252-15-31;** www.nerja.org) is open Monday to Friday 10am to 2pm and 4:30 to 7pm, Saturday 10am to 1pm.

SPECIAL EVENTS   A **cultural festival** takes place here in July. In the past it has drawn leading artists, musicians, and dancers from around the world.

EXPLORING THE CUEVA DE NERJA

The most popular outing from Málaga and Nerja is to the **Cueva de Nerja (Cave of Nerja)** ★★, Carretera de Maro s/n (*C* **95-252-96-35**). Scientists believe this prehistoric stalactite and stalagmite cave was inhabited from 25,000 to 2000 B.C. It was undiscovered until 1959, when a handful of boys found it by chance. When fully opened, it revealed a wealth of treasures left from the days of the cave dwellers, including Paleolithic paintings. They depict horses and deer, but as of this writing the room with cave paintings is not open to the public. The archaeological museum here contains a number of prehistoric artifacts. You can walk through stupendous galleries where ceilings soar to a height of 60m (200 ft.).

The cave is in the hills near Nerja. From here you get panoramic views of the countryside and sea. Open daily 10am to 2pm and 4 to 6:30pm. Admission is 5€ ($6) adults, 2.50€ ($3) children 6 to 12, free for children under 6. Buses to the cave leave from Muelle de Heredia in Málaga hourly from 7am to 8:15pm. Return buses run every two hours until 8:15pm. The journey takes about 1 hour.

WHERE TO STAY
EXPENSIVE

Hotel Riu Mónica ★ *Kids*   This government-rated four-star hotel is an isolated beachfront location about a 10-minute walk from the Balcón de Europa. In a seven-story building, the comfortable, good-size rooms were recently renovated and have private balconies and midsize bathrooms with tub/shower combos.

Playa de la Torrecilla s/n, 29780 Nerja. *C* **95-252-11-00.** Fax 95-252-11-62. www.riu.com. 257 units. 80€–190€ ($96–$228) double. AE, DC, MC, V. Free parking. **Amenities:** Restaurant; bar; outdoor pool; kids' pool; outdoor unlit tennis court; children's playground; limited room service; babysitting; laundry service/dry cleaning; nonsmoking rooms; rooms for those w/limited mobility; entertainment. *In room:* A/C, TV, minibar, hair dryer, safe.

Parador de Nerja ★★   This government-owned and -rated four-star hotel is on the outskirts of town, a 5-minute walk from the center. On the edge of a cliff, next to the sea, the hotel centers on a flower-filled courtyard with splashing fountain. The spacious rooms are furnished in understated but tasteful style, and midsize bathrooms have tub/shower combos.

Calle Almuñécar 8, 29780 Nerja. *C* **95-252-00-50.** Fax 95-252-19-97. www.parador.es. 98 units. 89€–175€ ($107–$210) double. AE, DC, MC, V. Free parking. **Amenities:** Restaurant; bar; outdoor pool; tennis courts; limited room service; babysitting; laundry service/dry cleaning; nonsmoking rooms; rooms for those w/limited mobility. *In room:* A/C, TV, dataport, minibar, hair dryer, safe.

MODERATE

Carabeo ★ *Finds*   There is no more tranquil oasis in Nerja than this little inn, one of our favorite stopovers along the coast—and it's very affordable as well. A boutique hotel of charm and sophistication, Carabeo lies in the old sector of town in a typical Andalusian house, but is also within an easy walk of the center and a 5-minute walk to a good beach. Taste and care have gone into the comfortable furnishings, and the place is filled with antiques and original art. The bedrooms are generally spacious, each with a small bathroom with a tub/shower combo. Each is individually furnished, with well-chosen fabrics—in all, the British owners have created a rather homelike feel. The five nicest rooms open onto views of the sea. These sea-view bedrooms also contain a terrace large enough to shelter sun beds and a small table for breakfast. There's even a good restaurant on-site, with a contemporary Mediterranean cuisine that uses regional products, especially the fresh catch of the day. Children under 12 not accepted at the hotel.

Hernando de Carabeo 34, 29780 Nerja. ℂ **95-252-54-44.** Fax 95-252-26-77. www.hotelcarabeo.com. 12 units. 66€–185€ ($79–$222). Rates include continental breakfast. AE, DC, MC, V. **Amenities:** Restaurant; bar; exercise room; sauna; outdoor pool; 24-hr. room service; laundry service/dry cleaning. *In room:* A/C, TV, minibar, hair dryer, safe.

Hotel Balcón de Europa   Occupying the best position in town, at the edge of the Balcón de Europa, this 1970s hotel offers guest rooms with private balconies overlooking the water and the rocks. At a private beach nearby, parasol-shielded tables are a peaceful place to enjoy the vista. The comfortable, midsize rooms have modern furniture and firm beds. Bathrooms have tub/shower combos. There's a private garage a few steps away.

Paseo Balcón de Europa 1, 29780 Nerja. ℂ **95-252-08-00.** Fax 95-252-44-90. www.hotel-balconeuropa.com. 110 units. 83€–131€ ($100–$157) double; 131€–171€ ($157–$205) suite. AE, DC, MC, V. Parking 8€ ($9.60). **Amenities:** 2 restaurants; bar; outdoor pool; sauna; limited room service; babysitting; laundry service. *In room:* A/C, TV, minibar, hair dryer, safe.

Hotel Perla Marina   Next to a good beach, Torrenueve, and within walking distance from the center of town, this well-run 1990 hotel was last renovated in 2004. With its whitewashed walls and balconies for some bedrooms, it is a light, airy choice, very Mediterranean in style. The hotel's most attractive feature is a landscaped area looking out to the sea. During the season, guests are entertained by flamenco shows and live music. Bedrooms are on the small side, but well furnished, often with dark wood pieces, and each unit comes with a tiled bathroom with tub and shower.

Mérida 7, 29780 Nerja. ℂ **95-252-33-50.** Fax 95-252-40-83. www.hotelperlamarina.com. 106 units. 114€ ($137) double. Rates include continental breakfast. AE, DC, MC, V. **Amenities:** Restaurant; bar; outdoor pool; rooms for those w/limited mobility. *In room:* A/C, TV, minibar upon request, hair dryer.

Plaza Cavana 🜨 *Finds*   In the center of town, just behind El Balcón de Europa and a short walk from the beach, this two-story hotel is imbued with old-fashioned Andalusian charm. It lies behind a typical white facade with wooden balconies. The lobby has a classic decor with marble floors, and there is a garden patio where guests can relax. Rooms are elegant, spacious, and comfortable, and open onto balconies with either sea or mountain views. The neatly kept bathrooms have tub/shower combos.

Plaza Cavana 10, 29780 Nerja. ℂ **95-252-40-00.** Fax 95-252-40-08. 39 units. 70€–120€ ($84–$144) double. AE, DC, MC, V. Parking 9€ ($11). **Amenities:** Restaurant; bar; 2 pools (1 indoor); Jacuzzi; sauna; laundry service/dry cleaning. *In room:* A/C, TV, minibar, hair dryer, safe.

INEXPENSIVE

Hostal Miguel   The family-run Miguel is a pleasant, unpretentious inn on a quiet back street about a 3-minute walk from the Balcón de Europa, across from the well-known Pepe Rico Restaurant. The simply furnished, somewhat small rooms have been renovated to add more Andalusian flavor. Bathrooms have shower stalls. Breakfast is the only meal served, usually on a lovely roof terrace with a view of the mountains and sea.

Almirante Ferrándiz 31, 29780 Nerja. © **95-252-15-23**. Fax 95-252-65-35. 9 units. 28€–45€ ($34–$54) double. MC, V. **Amenities:** Breakfast room. *In room:* Fridge, no phone.

Paraíso del Mar ★ *Finds*　Next door to the more upmarket Parador de Nerja, this little hacienda also offers a panoramic view of the coastline. The former home of a wealthy expatriate has been turned into this comfortable villa lying near the edge of a cliff opening onto the fabled Balcón de Europa. Bedrooms are tastefully furnished but not luxurious, and four of them come with tub baths, the others have showers. Most people request a sea-view room; the rooms in the rear that lack views make up for it by being larger or including a Jacuzzi. You can absorb that view from one of the hotel's public terraces.

Prolongación del Carabeo 22, 29780 Nerja. © **95-252-16-21**. Fax 95-252-23-09. www.jpmoser.com/paraisodelmar.html. 17 units. 60€–104€ ($72–$125) double; 105€–140€ ($126–$168) suite. Rates include breakfast. DC, MC, V. Parking 10€ ($12). **Amenities:** Breakfast room; bar; outdoor pool; laundry service/dry cleaning. *In room:* A/C, TV, minibar, hair dryer, safe.

WHERE TO DINE

Casa Luque *Value* INTERNATIONAL　With its impressive canopied and balconied facade near the heart of town, Casa Luque looks like a dignified private villa. The interior has an Andalusian courtyard, and in summer there's a sea-view terrace. Dishes are tasty and portions are generous. Meals change according to the season and might include Andalusian gazpacho, pork filet, or grilled meats. The limited selection of fish includes grilled Mediterranean grouper.

Plaza Cavana 2. © **95-252-10-04**. Reservations required. Main courses 9€–20€ ($11–$24). DC, MC, V. Daily 1:30–3:30pm and 7:30–11pm.

El Colono *Kids* ANDALUSIAN　El Colono is a family place just made for a night of Spanish fun. Near the Balcón de Europa, it's a 3-minute walk from the main bus stop in Nerja. Guitar music and flamenco dancing are the entertainment highlights in this 2-century-old tavern where the set menus include local specialties like duck with ginger, paella, and a *zarzuela* (seafood with cognac sauce). If you just want a glass of wine, you can still enjoy the shows (three per evening, from 8pm until "the wee hours").

Granada 6. © **95-252-18-26**. Reservations required. Wed and Fri flamenco shows with fixed-price menus 25€–35€ ($30–$42); Thurs main courses 10€–18€ ($12–$22). No credit cards. Wed–Fri 7:30–11:30pm. Closed Nov–Jan.

Pepe Rico Restaurant ★ INTERNATIONAL　Opened in 1966, Pepe Rico is one of Nerja's finest restaurants. Dine in a tavern room or alfresco on the patio. The specialty of the day, which might be a Spanish, German, Swedish, or French dish, ranges from almond-and-garlic soup to duck in wine. The impressive list of hors d'oeuvres includes smoked swordfish, salmon mousse, and prawns pil-pil (with hot chile peppers). Main dishes include filet of sole, roast leg of lamb, prawns Café de Paris, and steak dishes. Considering the quality of the food, the prices are reasonable.

Almirante Ferrándiz 28. © **95-252-02-47**. Reservations recommended. Main courses 12€–18€ ($14–$22); fixed-price menu 10€ ($12) at lunch, 24€ ($29) at dinner. MC, V. Mon–Sat 12:30–3pm and 7–11pm. Closed 2 weeks in Dec and 1 week in Jan.

Restaurante Rey Alfonso ★ SPANISH/INTERNATIONAL　Few visitors to the Balcón de Europa realize they're standing directly above one of the most unusual restaurants in town. The restaurant's menu and decor don't hold many surprises, but the close-up view of the crashing waves makes dining here worth-while. Have a drink at the bar if you don't want a full meal. Specialties include a well-prepared *paella valenciana*, Cuban-style rice, five preparations of sole (from grilled to meunière), several versions of tournedos and entrecôte, crayfish in whisky sauce, and crêpes suzettes for dessert. You enter from the bottom of a flight of stairs that skirts the rocky base of a late-19th-century *mirador* (viewing station), which juts seaward as an extension of the town's main square.

Paseo Balcón de Europa s/n. ℂ **95-252-09-58.** Reservations recommended. Main courses 7€–15€ ($8.40–$18). DC, MC, V. Mon–Sat noon–3pm and 7–11pm. Closed Nov 15–Dec 15.

Udo Heimer ⚜ SPANISH/PORTUGUESE A German, who named the restaurant after himself, welcomes you to his friendly precincts, a stylish Art Deco villa in a modern development east of the center. This restaurant serves top-quality food. If it goes with your food, we recommend you request a delectable and hard-to-find white wine called Gran Caus. We are especially drawn to his signature dishes such as young pigeon in a port wine sauce, served with fresh vegetables. You might also opt for *tartar de lubina*, raw sea bass cut into thin slices and seasoned with bay leaf. From the hills comes a tender lamb, roasted perfectly and seasoned with rosemary and thyme. The dessert specialty is memorable, a mango ravioli with a mousselike texture.

Pueblo Andaluz 27. ℂ **95-252-00-32.** Reservations recommended. Main courses 18€–30€ ($22–$36). AE, DC, MC, V. Daily 7pm–midnight. Closed Jan.

Verano Azul INTERNATIONAL Near the Balcón de Europa, this Andalusian-style restaurant is small and simple, on the second floor of a modest modern building. But it's known by the locals and discerning visitors for its good fresh food. Dishes are marked by intense but refined flavors. We generally gravitate to the catch of the day, which can be grilled to your specifications. A little garlic, some fresh herbs, and lemon are fine with most diners. We also like the chef's paella Andalusia, made with fresh shellfish. For non-fish eaters, the chef offers a grilled sirloin steak with garlic. For some real Costa del Sol flavor, opt for the chef's clam soup as a starter. Desserts usually aren't impressive.

Almirante Ferrándiz 31. ℂ **95-252-69-62.** Reservations recommended. Main courses 19€–26€ ($23–$31). MC, V. Daily 7:30pm–midnight. Closed Nov 15–Dec 15.

Appendix:
Southern Spain in Depth

The sea brought the cultures of the east to Andalusia long before civilization had come to other parts of Spain. Empires from the east came and went, none more notable than the Moors who arrived from North Africa. The continents of Europe and Africa come very close together at Europe's southernmost point. Africa is only 14km (9 miles) to the south.

In a strange reversal of fortune in the centuries to come, after having faced so many conquerors from the East, Spain itself was an eastern empire when it set out to forge a western empire with the discovery of the Americas.

History 101

IN THE BEGINNING

The Bronze Age Kingdom of Tartessus was founded sometime in the 1st millennium B.C. Establishing itself at the mouth of the Río Guadalquivir, bordering Seville and Huelva provinces, Tartessos (its Greek name) flourished for centuries. By siding and trading with the Greeks, it encouraged the wrath of Carthage. That African kingdom sent its fleets across the Mediterranean to destroy the centuries-old Tartessus civilization. In Andalusian archaeological museums, particularly those in Seville, you can still see artifacts of Tartessus.

After bloody battles with the Carthaginian forces of Hannibal and other of his generals, Romans reigned over Andalusia. Rome sent General Publius Cornelius Scipio to Spain in 209 B.C., where he seized Carthaginian bases and either killed the opposition or forced it back to Africa.

After internal battling, particularly among the forces of Julius Caesar and Pompey, Rome occupied southern Spain, a domination that would last for some seven centuries. Julius Caesar himself governed Andalusia from 61 to 60 B.C. The major Roman base was

Dateline

- 9th to 4th century B.C. Bronze Age Kingdom of Tartessus flourishes in Andalusia.
- 5th century B.C. Carthage destroys Tartessus and colonizes Andalusia.
- 209 B.C. Romans conquer Andalusia and begin colonization.
- 5th century A.D. Vandals, then Visigoths, invade Andalusia.
- 8th century A.D. Moors conquer Andalusia.
- 1212 Reconquista begins.
- 1492 Last Moorish stronghold at Granada falls to Catholic monarchs; Columbus sails to the New World.
- 1556 Philip II comes to the throne and launches the Counter-Reformation.
- 1588 England defeats Spanish Armada.
- 1700 Felipe V becomes king. War of Spanish Succession follows.
- 1713 War ended by Treaty of Utrecht, with loss of Spanish colonies.
- 1808 French occupy Spain.
- 1812 Cádiz drafts liberal constitution.
- 1936–39 Spanish Civil War; Franco dictatorship begins.
- 1975 Death of Franco; restoration of democracy.
- 1980 Andalusia votes to become an autonomous region of Spain.
- 1985 Andalusia along with Spain joins the European Community.

at **Itálica,** whose ruins you can visit outside Seville (p. 120).

Under the Romans, the colony of Andalusia became one of the richest in the Roman Empire. A golden age was proclaimed and the economy relied on such products as wine, grain, olive oil, and a foul-smelling fish sauce called *garum.*

- **2002** Spain adopts the Euro as its national currency.
- **2003** New Picasso Museum opens in Málaga (p. 345).
- **2004** Al Qa'ida strikes Spanish trains in deadliest terrorist attack in Europe since WWII.

THE COMING OF THE BARBARIANS

In time, Rome's control over Andalusia began to decline. Sweeping across the Pyrenees in the 4th century B.C. came the first of the barbarian invasions from the north of Europe. They were not an immediate menace to the south but by A.D. 409 the vandals had made inroads. Their rule over Andalusia was a bit weak; their reign was marked by much infighting and forced conversions to Christianity, especially among the downtrodden Jews.

Eleven Visigoth kings between 414 and 711 were assassinated. When the invading African Muslims arrived in southern Spain, the Visigothic monarchy was totally unprepared.

With extraordinary speed, Tariq ibn-Ziyad, the governor of Tangier, a far western outpost of the Caliphate of Damascus, crossed the Straits of Gibraltar in A.D. 711 with only 7,000 Berber warriors. The Moorish conquest of Andalusia had begun in earnest and Tariq ibn-Ziyad established himself at Gibraltar.

The last of the Visigothic kings, Roderick, pulled together an army to confront these African invaders. He disappeared, and his fate was lost to history, his armies either killed or fled.

In three decades, Muslim rulers established control of what they called **al-Andalús.** The capital of Islamic Spain became Córdoba, which went on to become the leading center of learning and culture in the west.

THE LEGACY OF AL-ANDALUS

The Moors (Muslims who were an ethnic mixture of Berbers, Hispano-Romans, and Arabs) occupied southern Spain for nearly 8 centuries, leaving behind an intellectual and cultural legacy that influences modern life to this day. This was a time of soaring achievement in philosophy, medicine, and music.

Moorish rule brought the importation of the eggplant and the almond, as well as the Arabian steed. It brought astronomy (including charting the positions of the planets), a new and different view of Aristotle, Arab numerals, and algebra. Ibn Muadh of Jaén wrote the first European treatise on trigonometry.

Intellectual giants like the Córdoba-born Jewish philosopher Maimónides emerged. It is said that Columbus evolved his theories about a new route to the East after hours and hours of studying the charts of Idrisi, an Arabian geographer who drew up a world map as early as 1154. Arabs relied upon the compass as a navigational aid long before its use among Portuguese explorers.

Córdoba wished to shine more brightly than Baghdad as a center of science and the arts. In time it attracted Abd ar-Rahman II, who introduced the fifth string to the Arab lute, leading to the development of the six-string guitar. He also ordained the way food should be eaten at mealtimes, a legacy that lives to this day. Before, everybody just helped him- or herself randomly to whatever had been prepared; but he devised a method where courses were served in a regimented order, ending with dessert, fruit, and nuts.

Flamenco claims significant Middle Eastern influences, and Arab poetry may have inspired the first ballads sung by European troubadours, which had an enormous impact on later Western literature. Many Spanish words have their origins in the Arabic language, including *alcázar* (fortress), *arroz* (rice), *naranja* (orange), and *limón* (lemon).

The Moors brought an irrigation system to Andalusia, which increased crop production; many of today's systems follow those 1,000-year-old channels. And paper first arrived in Europe through Córdoba.

However, the Moors were not to rule forever. In the 10th century Abd ar-Rahman III, the Muslim king, proclaimed himself an independent Western Islamic Empire, breaking with the eastern Caliphate of Baghdad. (Visitors can explore his ruined pleasure palace, **Madinat Al-Zahra,** outside Córdoba.) In time, the Muslims began to war among themselves as the Romans had before them. A new invasion arrived from Africa in 1086, the fanatically Islamic **Almoravids,** followed in 1147 by the **Almohads,** the latter left as their legacy the Giralda at Seville.

By 1212, the Reconquista had begun. A turning point in Spanish history, Alfonso VIII in 1212 defeated the Muslim armies at the battle of Las Navas de Tolosa in Jaén. It was the beginning of the end of al-Andalus, but many more decades would pass before the complete reconquest had been carried out.

THE RECONQUISTA

By 1236 Córdoba had been conquered by King Ferdinand III. But the sultans must not have thought they would ever lose Andalusia because 2 years later construction began on the monumental Alhambra in Granada. In all, it would take a final 156 years before the conquest was complete.

In the 13th century, Christian soldiers began to knock down Moorish fortresses and take over their cities. Such rulers as James the Conqueror of Aragón and Fernando III of Castile attacked Baeza and Úbeda in 1233, Córdoba in 1236, Jaén in 1245, and, finally, Seville in 1248.

As the 13th century came to a close, only the Nasrid Kingdom of Granada remained under Muslim rule. One of the reasons that it was to survive for such a long time was that it made payments to the monarchs of Castile.

Granada's fate was sealed with the marriage of Los Reyes Católicos (the Catholic monarchs) Isabella I of Castile and Ferdinand V of Aragón. Uniting the kingdoms of Aragón and Castile in 1469, they also fired up religious bigotry and in the following year ushered in the dreaded Spanish Inquisition. By 1492 some 400,000 Jews had been forced to flee the country.

That previous year they had set out to reclaim Granada. Boabdil, the last of the Caliphs of Granada, watched in sorrow as his armies fell to 50,000 Christian foot soldiers and calvary men.

In the same year of the completion of the Reconquista, 1492, a Genoese sailor, Christopher Columbus, sailed from Huelva. Instead of the riches of the East, he discovered the West Indies. He laid the foundations for a far-flung empire that brought wealth and power to Spain during the 16th and 17th centuries. Many of those riches from the New World were funneled through Andalusian cities like Cádiz and Seville.

THE HAPSBURGS & THE BOURBONS

The province as a whole did not benefit from the exploitation of the New World. The crown in Castile grabbed the treasures to fuel foreign wars and other horrors. Except for such ports as Cádiz and Seville, most of Granada languished.

The glory days of the Muslims long gone, the people were mired in poverty. Many emigrated to the New World.

Unlike Andalusia, Spain itself had entered its golden age, with an empire that extended eventually to the Philippines. But the country squandered much of its wealth and human resources in religious and secular conflicts. At a great loss to Andalusia, the Jews, then the Muslims, and finally the Catholicized Moors were driven out—and with them much of the country's prosperity.

When a Hapsburg, Carlos I (who 5 years later ruled the Holy Roman Empire as Charles V) came to the throne in 1516, little attention was paid to Andalusia. He was more interested in propping up his empire with gold and silver from the New World than in the needs of the people on his southern tier.

When Philip II ascended to the throne in 1556, Spain was at the epicenter of a great empire, not only the New World colonies but the Netherlands, Sicily, and Naples, and even parts of Austria and Germany. But the seeds of destruction had already been planted.

A fanatical Catholic, Philip became the standard bearer for the Counter-Reformation. He also zealously renewed the Inquisition. He wanted a "final solution" (sound familiar?) to the problems of the Moriscos (Moors) in Las Alpujarras (p. 211), who still clung to their Moorish traditions. He forcibly deported them to other parts of the country. He was followed by Felipe III, who was even harsher in his persecution of the Moriscos of Andalusia.

In April of 1587 the forces of Sir Francis Drake attacked the port of Cádiz, which was filled with some 60 vessels. Within 24 hours, the English forces had destroyed or captured almost half of these vessels. A year later Spain, aided by vessels from Andalusia, launched the Armada against England. The Spaniards were ignominiously defeated, their loss symbolizing the decline of Spanish power. The Armada was commanded by Andalusia's premier nobleman, the Duke of Medina Sidonia.

In 1700 Felipe V became king, bringing with him the War of Spanish Succession. His right to the throne was challenged by the Hapsburg archduke, Charles of Austria, who was assisted by the British. When the Treaty of Utrecht ended the war in 1713, Spain lost most of its colonies. The British had landed in Gibraltar, conquering it and holding it to this day like a thorn in Spain's side.

A historic moment occurred at the Battle of Trafalgar off the coast of Cádiz in 1805. The Spanish fleet was defeated. As a result of these Napoleonic Wars, King Carlos IV abdicated in 1808, and Napoleon installed his brother, Joseph, on the throne. Most of the artistic heritage of Andalusia was ransacked during this period of French domination. The War of Independence (also called the Peninsular War) saw the arrival of the troops of the duke of Wellington onto the shores of Andalusia. Joseph fled back to France. On another front, the American colonies had begun to assert their independence.

The rest of the century didn't bring much relief to either Spain or Andalusia. The country was at war with itself, as a right-wing monarchy clashed with the aspirations of liberal reformers.

In 1812, the Cortés (the Spanish name for parliament) met in Cádiz and daringly drafted a liberal constitution. When the despotic Fernando VII returned to the throne, he abolished their constitution. It was this constitution, which introduced the word "liberal" to describe a political movement.

The loss of Spain's colonies brought a deathblow to Andalusia's economy, and in the 1870s a phylloxera plague wiped out its vineyards. Despite all these woes, this period in Andalusian history became known as the Romantic Age, as depicted in such operas as *The Barber of Seville* and *Carmen*.

THE 19TH CENTURY TO THE PRESENT

In 1876, Spain became a constitutional monarchy. But labor unrest, disputes with the Catholic Church, and war in Morocco combined to create political chaos. Conditions eventually became so bad that the Cortés was dissolved in 1923, and General Miguel Primo de Rivera formed a military directorate. Early in 1930, Primo de Rivera resigned, but unrest continued.

On April 14, 1931, a revolution occurred, a republic was proclaimed, and King Alfonso XIII and his family were forced to flee. Initially, the liberal constitutionalists ruled, but soon they were pushed aside by the socialists and anarchists, who adopted a constitution separating church and state, secularizing education, and containing several other radical provisions (for example, agrarian reform and the expulsion of the Jesuits).

The extreme nature of these reforms fostered the growth of the conservative Falange party (*Falange española,* or Spanish Phalanx), modeled after Italy's and Germany's fascist parties. By the 1936 elections, the country was divided equally between left and right, and political violence was common. On July 18, 1936, the army, supported by Mussolini and Hitler, tried to seize power, igniting the Spanish Civil War. General Francisco Franco, coming from Morocco to Spain via Andalusia, led the Nationalist (rightist) forces in the 3 years of fighting that ravaged the country. Towns were bombed and atrocities were committed in abundance. Early in 1939, Franco entered Barcelona and went on to Madrid; thousands of republicans were executed. Franco became chief of state, remaining so until his death in 1975.

Although Franco adopted a neutral position during World War II, his sympathies obviously lay with Germany and Italy. Spain, as a nonbelligerent, assisted the Axis powers. This intensified the diplomatic isolation into which the country was forced after the war's end—in fact, it was excluded from the United Nations until 1955.

Before his death, General Franco selected as his successor Juan Carlos de Borbón y Borbón, son of the pretender to the Spanish throne. After the 1977 elections, a new constitution was approved by the electorate and the king; it guaranteed human and civil rights, as well as free enterprise, and canceled the status of the Roman Catholic church as the church of Spain. In 1980 Andalusia voted to become an autonomous region of Spain. With a regional government based in Seville, Andalusia assumed control of a large part of its destiny for the first time in its history.

In 1981, a group of ring-wing military officers seized the Cortés and called upon Juan Carlos to establish a Francoist state. When the king refused and the conspirators were arrested, the fledgling democracy had overcome its first trial. Its second major accomplishment—under the Socialist rule of Prime Minister Felipe González, the country's first leftist government since 1939—was to gain Spain's entry into the European Union.

This event occurred in 1986. Spain, and by extension, Andalusia, had at long last become part of the modern world.

Index

See also Accommodations and Restaurant indexes, below.

FROMMER'S® COMPLETE TRAVEL GUIDES

Alaska
Alaska Cruises & Ports of Call
American Southwest
Amsterdam
Argentina & Chile
Arizona
Atlanta
Australia
Austria
Bahamas
Barcelona, Madrid & Seville
Beijing
Belgium, Holland & Luxembourg
Bermuda
Boston
Brazil
British Columbia & the Canadian
   Rockies
Brussels & Bruges
Budapest & the Best of Hungary
Calgary
California
Canada
Cancún, Cozumel & the Yucatán
Cape Cod, Nantucket & Martha's
   Vineyard
Caribbean
Caribbean Ports of Call
Carolinas & Georgia
Chicago
China
Colorado
Costa Rica
Cruises & Ports of Call
Cuba
Denmark
Denver, Boulder & Colorado
   Springs
England
Europe
Europe by Rail
European Cruises & Ports of Call

Florence, Tuscany & Umbria
Florida
France
Germany
Great Britain
Greece
Greek Islands
Halifax
Hawaii
Hong Kong
Honolulu, Waikiki & Oahu
India
Ireland
Italy
Jamaica
Japan
Kauai
Las Vegas
London
Los Angeles
Maryland & Delaware
Maui
Mexico
Montana & Wyoming
Montréal & Québec City
Munich & the Bavarian Alps
Nashville & Memphis
New England
Newfoundland & Labrador
New Mexico
New Orleans
New York City
New York State
New Zealand
Northern Italy
Norway
Nova Scotia, New Brunswick &
   Prince Edward Island
Oregon
Ottawa
Paris
Peru

Philadelphia & the Amish
   Country
Portugal
Prague & the Best of the Czech
   Republic
Provence & the Riviera
Puerto Rico
Rome
San Antonio & Austin
San Diego
San Francisco
Santa Fe, Taos & Albuquerque
Scandinavia
Scotland
Seattle
Shanghai
Sicily
Singapore & Malaysia
South Africa
South America
South Florida
South Pacific
Southeast Asia
Spain
Sweden
Switzerland
Texas
Thailand
Tokyo
Toronto
Turkey
USA
Utah
Vancouver & Victoria
Vermont, New Hampshire &
   Maine
Vienna & the Danube Valley
Virgin Islands
Virginia
Walt Disney World® & Orlando
Washington, D.C.
Washington State

FROMMER'S® DOLLAR-A-DAY GUIDES

Australia from $50 a Day
California from $70 a Day
England from $75 a Day
Europe from $85 a Day
Florida from $70 a Day
Hawaii from $80 a Day

Ireland from $80 a Day
Italy from $70 a Day
London from $90 a Day
New York City from $90 a Day
Paris from $90 a Day
San Francisco from $70 a Day

Washington, D.C. from $80 a
   Day
Portable London from $90 a Day
Portable New York City from $90
   a Day
Portable Paris from $90 a Day

FROMMER'S® PORTABLE GUIDES

Acapulco, Ixtapa & Zihuatanejo
Amsterdam
Aruba
Australia's Great Barrier Reef
Bahamas
Berlin
Big Island of Hawaii
Boston
California Wine Country
Cancún
Cayman Islands
Charleston
Chicago
Disneyland®
Dominican Republic
Dublin

Florence
Frankfurt
Hong Kong
Las Vegas
Las Vegas for Non-Gamblers
London
Los Angeles
Los Cabos & Baja
Maine Coast
Maui
Miami
Nantucket & Martha's Vineyard
New Orleans
New York City
Paris

Phoenix & Scottsdale
Portland
Puerto Rico
Puerto Vallarta, Manzanillo &
   Guadalajara
Rio de Janeiro
San Diego
San Francisco
Savannah
Vancouver
Vancouver Island
Venice
Virgin Islands
Washington, D.C.
Whistler

FROMMER'S® NATIONAL PARK GUIDES

Algonquin Provincial Park
Banff & Jasper
Family Vacations in the National
  Parks

Grand Canyon
National Parks of the American
  West
Rocky Mountain

Yellowstone & Grand Teton
Yosemite & Sequoia/Kings
  Canyon
Zion & Bryce Canyon

FROMMER'S® MEMORABLE WALKS

Chicago
London

New York
Paris

San Francisco

FROMMER'S® WITH KIDS GUIDES

Chicago
Las Vegas
New York City

Ottawa
San Francisco
Toronto

Vancouver
Walt Disney World® & Orlando
Washington, D.C.

SUZY GERSHMAN'S BORN TO SHOP GUIDES

Born to Shop: France
Born to Shop: Hong Kong,
  Shanghai & Beijing

Born to Shop: Italy
Born to Shop: London

Born to Shop: New York
Born to Shop: Paris

FROMMER'S® IRREVERENT GUIDES

Amsterdam
Boston
Chicago
Las Vegas
London

Los Angeles
Manhattan
New Orleans
Paris
Rome

San Francisco
Seattle & Portland
Vancouver
Walt Disney World®
Washington, D.C.

FROMMER'S® BEST-LOVED DRIVING TOURS

Austria
Britain
California
France

Germany
Ireland
Italy
New England

Northern Italy
Scotland
Spain
Tuscany & Umbria

THE UNOFFICIAL GUIDES®

Beyond Disney
California with Kids
Central Italy
Chicago
Cruises
Disneyland®
England
Florida
Florida with Kids
Inside Disney

Hawaii
Las Vegas
London
Maui
Mexico's Best Beach Resorts
Mini Las Vegas
Mini Mickey
New Orleans
New York City
Paris

San Francisco
Skiing & Snowboarding in the
  West
South Florida including Miami &
  the Keys
Walt Disney World®
Walt Disney World® for
  Grown-ups
Walt Disney World® with Kids
Washington, D.C.

SPECIAL-INTEREST TITLES

Athens Past & Present
Cities Ranked & Rated
Frommer's Best Day Trips from London
Frommer's Best RV & Tent Campgrounds
  in the U.S.A.
Frommer's Caribbean Hideaways
Frommer's China: The 50 Most Memorable Trips
Frommer's Exploring America by RV
Frommer's Gay & Lesbian Europe
Frommer's NYC Free & Dirt Cheap

Frommer's Road Atlas Europe
Frommer's Road Atlas France
Frommer's Road Atlas Ireland
Frommer's Wonderful Weekends from
  New York City
The New York Times' Guide to Unforgettable
  Weekends
Retirement Places Rated
Rome Past & Present

Travel Tip: He who finds the best hotel deal
has more to spend on facials involving
knobbly vegetables.

Hello, the Roaming Gnome here. I've been nabbed from the garden and taken round the world. The people who took me are so terribly clever. They find the best offerings on Travelocity. For very little cha-ching. And that means I get to be pampered and exfoliated till I'm pink as a bunny's doodah.

travelocity®

1-888-TRAVELOCITY / travelocity.com / America Online Keyword: Travel

Travel Tip: Make sure there's customer service for any change of plans — involving friendly natives, for example.

One can plan and plan, but if you don't book with the right people you can't seize le moment and canoodle with the poodle named Pansy. I, for one, am all for fraternizing with the locals. Better yet, if I need to extend my stay and my gnome nappers are willing, it can all be arranged through the 800 number at, oh look, how convenient, the lovely company coat of arms.

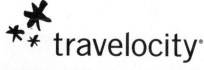